In a most attractive, readable and scholarly way this rich volume presents historic Christianity as Baptists have absorbed it and been confessing it for the last 333 years in this grand statement of our best Confession of Faith. This book is a tremendous achievement and destined never to go out of print.

GEOFF THOMAS
Former pastor for over fifty years of Alfred Place Baptist Church (Independent), Aberystwyth, Wales

This commentary on the 1689 contains all the riches needed in this peculiarly relevant undertaking. It is set in its rich historical context without destroying its ongoing contemporary relevance. The authors are committed to the confession's theological position in the context of rigorous biblical exposition. Both the content of the confession and the outlay of its exposition contains all the strengths of doctrinal catholicity, orthodoxy, evangelicalism, and Baptist thought. Each author has a deep grasp of the rich heritage of historical theology and the issues involved in canonical biblical interpretation and brings these to bear on the specific article under discussion. This volume will add richness to the weekly study of a pastor and give an invaluable book for church groups for enriching their biblical knowledge and the contextual consistency and doctrinal coherence of the inspired Scriptures.

TOM J. NETTLES
Senior Professor of Historical Theology,
The Southern Baptist Theological Seminary, Louisville, Kentucky

This volume fulfils admirably the contemporary need for a thorough, detailed exposition of the 1689 Baptist Confession of Faith. Biblically rooted, theologically careful and engagingly written, this work is also consistently warm in its tone and practical in its application, authored as it is by pastors who are committed to the biblical truths that the Confession teaches. Anyone wanting a clearer understanding and firmer grasp of those truths will benefit greatly from this book.

ROBERT STRIVENS
Pastor, Bradford on Avon Baptist Church, Wiltshire
(Former Principal, London Seminary)

In this volume you will find men who have wrestled with the cardinal doctrines of Christianity and produced a commentary that sheds a warm light on the 1689 Confession. Difficult passages have been explained. Instructive detail has been provided. Here is a tool for every follower of Christ who desires to see Jesus, our altogether lovely One, more clearly, understand His redemptive labors more fully, and walk more nearly to Him in applied truth. May God give us all such unifying, reviving sights of Himself and His work as we make diligent use of this helpful volume.

JOHN SNYDER
Pastor, Christ Church, New Albany, Mississippi
Director of Media Gratiae

I am grateful that there is a growing interest in doctrinal Christianity here in Africa and all over the world. Whereas there are many books dealing with one or two aspects of theology, it is good to have one book that gives those coming to Reformed Baptist convictions a comprehensive view of what we believe. The New exposition of the London Baptist Confession of Faith of 1689, written by proven men in ministry, is such a resource. Let us make it available to many. The fruit will be evident for all to see for generations to come!

CONRAD MBEWE
Pastor, Kabwata Baptist Church
Founding Chancellor, African Christian University, Lusaka, Zambia

This is an important resource for Baptists to understand their historic doctrines that were rooted in the Reformation. While I would disagree with some of the comments that argue for credobaptism, many of the chapters are superb in their biblical, theological, and experiential understanding and application of the great truths of Scripture.

JOEL R. BEEKE
President, Puritan Reformed Theological Seminary,
Grand Rapids, Michigan

The 1689 London Baptist Confession, apart from a few issues relating to baptism and polity, is a mirror of the 1646 Westminster Confession of Faith (to which I subscribe). Both endorse Calvinism with its robust doctrines of divine sovereignty in creation, redemption, regeneration and final judgement. In an age of relativism and unregulated piety, a return to the doctrines of grace espoused by this confession is urgently needed. The exposition of these truths given in this volume is masterful. May its publication and use aid in the reformation of the church in our time.

DEREK W. H. THOMAS
Senior Minister, First Presbyterian Church,
Columbia, South Carolina
Chancellor's Professor, Reformed Theological Seminary
Teaching Fellow, Ligonier Ministries

It may seem odd that a convinced Presbyterian should write a warm commendation to this volume expounding the 1689 Baptist Confession. However, I do so with pleasure and seriousness. Throughout church history, confessions of faith have served the church admirably, helping to guard the church's biblical identity and gospel calling. You do not need to agree with every sentence in this 1689 Confession to benefit greatly from its exposition by men of theological orthodoxy and pastoral integrity. Martin Bucer's maxim, 'True theology is not theoretical but pastoral; the end of it is to live a godly life', is richly expounded throughout this fine volume. Read and sink your mind and heart into the rich truths as expressed in this new work.

IAN HAMILTON
Principal, Westminster Presbyterian Theological Seminary,
Newcastle

In second Timothy, the apostle Paul, nearing the end of his mortal life, was earnestly concerned that Timothy would hold fast the heritage of truth passed on to him. Many of the contributing expositors of the chapters in this new exposition of the 1689 are veteran pastors in the latter years of their longstanding pastorates. Central to their ministries has been a competent public proclamation of the Word of God and a holding to this great historic document. May the following generations be faithful stewards as they have been, in profession and practice, of the "sound words" they have set forth in this new work. Herein is a legacy of truth to be bought and not sold (Prov. 23:23).

GEORGE McDEARMON
Pastor, Ballston Lake Baptist Church, Ballston Lake, New York

A New Exposition of The London Baptist Confession of Faith of 1689

Rob Ventura, General Editor

MENTOR
Encouraging Christians to Think

Copyright © Rob Ventura 2022

Hardback ISBN 978-1-5271-0890-5
Ebook ISBN 978-1-5271-0980-3

10 9 8 7 6 5 4 3 2 1

Published in 2022
in the
Mentor Imprint
by
Christian Focus Publications Ltd.,
Geanies House, Fearn, Ross-shire,
IV20 1TW, Scotland, Great Britain

www.christianfocus.com

Cover design by James Amour
Printed by Bell & Bain, Glasgow

CONTENTS

EDITOR'S PREFACE

It has been correctly said that true Christianity "is confessional Christianity," and that a church with "a little creed is a church with a little life."[1] The true church has always confessed her faith openly for there is a "faith which is once for all delivered to the saints" (Jude 3). As Christians, we should never be ashamed of this fact. Sadly, there is a motto which is proclaimed by some professed believers which says, "No creed but the Bible." The problem with such a slogan is that it completely cuts people off from the body of instruction that God has so wonderfully given to the churches by means of gospel teachers throughout the centuries (cf. Eph. 4:11, 12). Such a notion, if embraced, leaves an individual with only what one particular group believes and teaches. This is dangerous and has resulted in many being misled.

B. H. Carroll (1843-1914), who was a pastor, theologian, and first president of Southwestern Baptist Theological Seminary, put it this way: "The modern cry: 'Less creed and more liberty,' is a degeneration from the vertebrate to the jellyfish, and means less unity and less morality, and it means more heresy. Definitive truth does not create heresy—it only exposes and corrects. Shut off the creed and the Christian world would fill up with heresy unsuspected and uncorrected, but none the less deadly."[2]

Historically, Baptists have set forth what they believe in Confessions of Faith. Of all their Confessions, the London Baptist Confession of Faith of 1689[3] became the most popular Confession among the Reformed Baptist churches. This Confession has been in greater or lesser use among the churches at various stages of history. But whenever it was heartily embraced and faithfully applied, the churches were the strongest and purest doctrinally and morally.

---

1. Tom Ascol article: B. H. Carroll and Robust Confessionalism: www.founders. org/2017/02/23/b-h-carroll-and-robust-confessionalism/accessed June 27, 2020.

2. B. H., Carroll An Interpretation of the English Bible, Vol. 11, Colossians, Ephesians, Hebrews (Nashville: Broadman, 1948; reprint, Grand Rapids: Baker, 1973) 140.

3. Although this confession is commonly called the "1689," it was originally published unsigned in 1677.

It is encouraging to see in our day a revival of interest in this Confession among our churches. I say this because this theologically robust document plainly puts forth those things "most surely believed among us" (Luke 1:1, KJV). As congregations, it is vital that we don't merely say, "We believe the Bible." Rather, we must show people exactly what it is from the Bible that we believe. For example, if we say, "We believe in Christ," could not the cults say the same? Sadly, they could (2 Cor. 11:4). But who is Christ? What is His nature? And why did He come and what did He accomplish, etc.? Here is where a good Confession of Faith is wonderfully useful. This resource lets people know exactly what we believe about major subjects in Scripture, things which are foundational to our faith. Additionally, being a confessional church lets people know that we are not "new kids on the block." Rather, it proves that we are part of a stream of theology and practice that our Baptist predecessors have held for centuries. For these reasons, it is my hope that this new exposition of this historical text will serve the churches well for decades to come.[4]

I have selected the authors for this work carefully. They are longtime friends and faithful pastors who, although they may not agree with each other's every "jot and tittle" that he has written, are nonetheless in substantial agreement. Further, there is great love and gospel goodwill among them, for which I praise the Lord.

I want to thank each author for his diligent labors. All have worked hard to finish their chapters amid many pressing duties. Brothers, I trust that our combined efforts will be that which we can look back on in the years ahead and praise our great God for His wonderful assistance. May the Lord Jesus Christ be pleased to use this work to promote the glorious biblical faith we hold. And may He use this book to encourage His followers to get into "His book," the Bible, which alone is our final authority for all things.

I close with words from the preface to the 1689 London Baptist Confession of Faith which Charles Haddon Spurgeon republished for his congregation in 1865. He said:

> This little volume is not issued as an authoritative rule, or code of faith, whereby you are to be fettered, but as an assistance to you in controversy, a confirmation in faith, and a means of edification in righteousness. Here the younger members of our church will have a body of divinity in small compass, and by means of Scriptural proofs, will be ready to give an account for the hope that is in them. Be not ashamed of your faith; remember it is the ancient gospel of martyrs, confessors, reformers and saints. Above all, it is "the truth of God," against which the gates of Hell cannot prevail. Let your lives adorn your faith, let your example adorn your creed. Above all live in Christ Jesus, and walk in Him, giving credence to no teaching but

---

4. Over thirty years ago, Dr. Sam Waldron wrote a helpful exposition of The London Baptist Confession of Faith of 1689 that now appears in its fifth edition on Evangelical Press. While I continue to highly commend that work, I hope that this present volume will be welcomed for many reasons, including its being the expression of many voices concerning our confessional standard for a new generation of believers.

that which is manifestly approved of Him, and owned by the Holy Spirit. Cleave fast to the Word of God which is here mapped out for you.[5]

Editor's Acknowledgments

There are several others who, along with some contributors to this book, have been a tremendous help in seeing this volume come to completion. These individuals made useful edits and suggestions throughout, and for this I thank them. They are Jack Buckley, Robert Gemma, Phil Dziuba, Mark Chanski, Mark Raines, D. Scott Meadows, Mark Womack, Bart Carlson, Alan Dunn, Paul Smalley, Libby Koziarski, Rexford Semrad, Blake Cassell, Dr. Robert J. Burrelli Jr., Tim Weiner, Christopher Sheffield, Jeff Johnson, Carissa Feathers, and Daniel Scheiderer. I am thankful as well to Melvin Vargas for his administrative help, and *The Five Solas Foundation* for their financial contribution to this project.[6] Lastly, I would like to thank Christian Focus Publications for publishing this work in their Mentor Imprint. Specifically, I am thankful for Willie Mackenzie, Rosanna Burton, Margaret Roberts, and Malcolm Maclean. It has been a joy working with you all.

I dedicate this volume to every follower of Christ who is unequivocally committed to Scripture and unashamed to apply its truth wherever it takes them. May God help you to be faithful and courageous in this regard. And may you find assistance from those who have gone before you who were not afraid to write down the truths of God's Word in historic Confessions of Faith even as is expounded in this work.

—Rob Ventura 2022

---

5. Cited on the copy of the 1689 published by Chapel Library.
6. www.thefivesolasfoundation.org.

CONTRIBUTORS

Earl M. Blackburn retired after forty-five years of pastoral ministry and had conferred on him the honorary title of *pastor emeritus*. He is the author of several books including *Jesus Loves the Church and So Should You*, *50 World-Changing Events in Christian History*, and is the general editor of *Covenant Theology: A Baptist Distinctive*, plus a number of booklets including *How Can I Honor Christ in Fighting Cancer?* He and his wife Debby now reside in the mountains of North Carolina where he is engaged in a vigorous writing ministry.

Brian Borgman is the founding pastor of Grace Community Church in Minden, NV. He is the author of numerous books, including *Feelings and Faith* (Crossway). He and his wife Ariel have three grown children and three grandchildren.

Dave Chanski is a pastor of Trinity Baptist Church, Montville, New Jersey.

David Charles is one of the pastors of the Reformed Baptist Church in Toledo, Ohio. He is co-author of *A Workman Not Ashamed*: *Essays in Honor of Albert N. Martin* and is one of the administrators and contributors at the Reformed Baptist fellowship blogsite.

Jason Ching pastors at Dayspring Church in Reno, NV. Dayspring is a church plant of Grace Community Church in Minden, NV. Jason and his wife Naomi have three sons.

Victor Claudio is a member of Grace Community Baptist Church, North Providence, Rhode Island. He is currently a student at Reformed Baptist Seminary pursuing his M.Div.

Jim Domm has served as one of the pastors of Englewood Baptist Church in Englewood, NJ since 1995. He and his wife Brenda have been married since 1979. They have one married daughter and three grandchildren.

Gary Hendrix was one of the pastors of Grace Reformed Baptist Church of Mebane, NC, from 1970–2020. He retired at the beginning of 2020 to write. He went to glory in October 2020 and is survived by his wife Sherry, three children, and nine grandchildren.[1]

Steven Hofmaier graduated from Trinity Ministerial Academy in 1981. He labored as a missionary in the Philippines for thirty-four years before returning to the USA because of family responsibilities. He joined the eldership of Trinity Baptist Church in 2018. He and his wife Carol have two adult children, one living in the USA and one in the Philippines.

Jeff Johnson has been serving as one of the pastors of the Grace Immanuel Reformed Baptist Church of Grand Rapids, Michigan since 2008. He is a board member and part of the faculty for the Reformed Baptist Seminary. He is married to Lisa and they have two children.

Mitch Lush grew up on a dairy farm in Nebraska and was educated at Grace College and Trinity Ministerial Academy. Since 1981 he has pastored Grace Church, Downingtown, Pennsylvania and worked alongside friends internationally in pastoral training. He is married to Nancy, and they have two daughters and eight grandchildren.

Lee McKinnon is one of the pastors of Covenant Reformed Baptist Church in Bluefield, WV. Lee was sent there in 1996 to be part of a church-planting effort, which constituted in 1998. Lee and his wife, Wanda, were high school sweethearts and married in 1971. They have one daughter.

John Price has been the pastor of Grace Baptist Church in Rochester, NY since its founding in 1995.

Mike Renihan is former pastor at Heritage Baptist Church in his hometown of Worcester, MA. He is also visiting professor emeritus in the History and Political Science department at Worcester State University, one of his alma maters. He earned a PhD, studying under Alister McGrath at Wycliffe Hall, from Oxford University. He also holds several additional honors and degrees. He is married with six believing adult children.

John Reuther is the pastor of Covenant Baptist Church in Lumberton, NJ. He is also the author of *The Gift of the Holy Spirit*.

Mark Sarver has been one of the pastors of Albany Baptist Church, Albany, NY, since 1989. In the 1990s he taught the four historical theology courses offered by Trinity Ministerial Academy, and since then he has taught a course on the theology of the Reformers for Reformed Baptist

---

1. I am thankful to God that in His good providence, Gary was able to contribute to this book before he went home to be with the Lord. Gary was a beloved pastor and friend to many around the world. He will be greatly missed—the editor.

Seminary. His research and writing concentration is on late medieval thought and on the theology of the Reformers.

Jim Savastio has been one of the pastors of The Reformed Baptist Church of Louisville, KY, since 1991. He is also the President of the Board of Directors at Practical Shepherding. He is married to Becky and they have four children.

Jeffery Smith has been in pastoral ministry since 1990, and since 2009 has been serving at Emmanuel Baptist Church, Coconut Creek, FL. In addition to his regular pastoral and preaching responsibilities, Jeff serves on the governing board and as a lecturer for Reformed Baptist Seminary. He is the author of *The Plain Truth About Life After Death* (Evangelical Press, 2019) and *Preaching for Conversions* (Free Grace Press, 2019).

Rob Ventura is one of the pastors of Grace Community Baptist Church of North Providence, Rhode Island. He is the author of *Expository Outlines and Observations on Romans* (Mentor Books, 2023); a co-author of *A Portrait of Paul and Spiritual Warfare;* and he is the general editor of *Going Beyond the Five Points, Covenant Theology, and Lectures in Systematic Theology.* He has also contributed articles to journals, periodicals, and the Reformation Heritage KJV Study Bible. He and his wife, Vanessa, and family live in Rhode Island.

Calvin Walden has been the pastor of Reformed Baptist Church of Lenawee in Adrian, Michigan since the church was first constituted in 1986. He also has the privilege to serve as a Chaplain for the Pro Medical Hospital in Adrian as well as a Chaplain for the Michigan State Police. He and his wife Tricia have three children and six grandchildren.

Sam Waldron is the president of Covenant Baptist Theological Seminary and a pastor of Grace Reformed Baptist Church in Owensboro, Kentucky. He is the author of numerous books, including *The End Times Made Simple* and *MacArthur's Millennial Manifesto: A Friendly Response.*

Austin Walker recently retired after serving for over forty years as a pastor of Maidenbower Baptist Church, Crawley, UK. He is married to Mai and they have four children and ten grandchildren. He is the author of *The Excellent Benjamin Keach and God's Care for the Widow.*

Jeremy Walker serves as a pastor of Maidenbower Baptist Church, Crawley, and is married to Alissa, with whom he enjoys the blessing of three children. He has authored several books and is grateful to preach and to write as opportunity provides.

INTRODUCTION

DAVE CHANSKI

I love Confessions of Faith—good ones, anyway. I love them because they are so useful, and I love them because they are so delightful. They are delightful because they express and summarize the teaching of the Bible, and the Bible is the very Word of God. A good Confession is not the very Word of God, but if it is faithful to the Word of God, it is saying what God's Word says, similar to the way that a faithful preacher says what God's Word says (Isa. 52:7). Someone who truly loves God's Word should truly love a good Confession. He shouldn't love it as much as he loves Scripture itself, but he should love it for the way it speaks, expounds, and illuminates the Word of God.[1]

Good Confessions should also be loved because they are useful to the Christian and to the Christian church. Excellent works have been written on this subject. Robert Paul Martin, for example, presents a few of the important uses of Confessions in "The Legitimacy and Use of Confessions," which is his introduction to Sam Waldron's volume, *A Modern Exposition of the 1689 Baptist Confession of Faith*. He mentions four specific uses of a good Confession:

1) It aids in the public affirmation and defense of truth.
2) It provides standards of church fellowship and discipline.
3) It outlines concise standards by which to evaluate ministers of the Word.
4) It contributes to our sense of historical continuity.[2]

These are all good things; and they are all things that Satan opposes. As Spurgeon said, "Weapons which are offensive to our enemies should never be allowed to rust."[3] Our Baptist Confession of Faith is one of these weapons. I am very happy to see the publication of this present volume

---

1. cf. 1 Thessalonians 5:12, 13.

2. Robert Paul Martin, "The Legitimacy and Use of Confessions," in Samuel E. Waldron, *A Modern Exposition of the 1689 Baptist Confession of Faith* (Durham: Evangelical Press, 1989), 9-23; Samuel Miller, *The Utility and Importance of Creeds and Confessions* (Philadelphia: Presbyterian Board of Publication, 1839).

3. Cited in Martin, "The Legitimacy and Use of Confessions," 20-21.

because, as Spurgeon says, there is a perennial danger that we will allow the "weapon" of a good Confession to rust. I am concerned about this danger in our present generation for a couple of reasons.

First, many present-generation Christians who hold to the Second London Baptist Confession have had the Reformed and baptistic doctrine it affirms handed to them on a platter, so to speak, so that they did not have to work hard to come to their own personal convictions about the matters contained in it.

Over forty years ago, I studied in a theological academy that held to the 1689 Confession. The pastors and teachers who taught us were part of a generation which had come to hold to that Confession as a result of their own personal, theological, ecclesiastical, and spiritual struggles. In these struggles, they were guided by the Word and Spirit of God, and they were assisted by the writings of theological giants of the past, Confessions of Faith included. By the time that I was studying in seminary, the men who taught me had reached settled conclusions in their own hearts and minds regarding the most important truths of Scripture. Those conclusions accurately reflected the teaching of Scripture. The same men, as well as others of their generation, also found those scriptural truths accurately summarized in the Second London Confession.

I am grateful that I was taught how to study, understand, and expound the Scriptures by hard "labor" (1 Tim. 5:17). But I must also admit that men who had endured many more "dangers, toils, and snares" than I, in the form of theological battles, delivered well-prepared theological meals to me and my fellow students in their lectures. That meant that the onus was on me and my fellow students to spend the rest of our days not simply heating and re-heating the same meals for the people we teach, but also to engage in the difficult labor of searching out for ourselves the truth from the Scriptures, aided by the study of church history and the writings of our theological forefathers. The same responsibility falls, to some degree, upon Christ's people who are not pastors and scholars by calling. We should all take care, consistent with our God-given abilities and opportunities, to see that we imitate the Bereans and search the Scriptures daily (Acts 17:11), taking pains to discover, discern, and hold fast their rich treasures (Prov. 2:1-5). Confessions of Faith that accurately reflect the Bible's teaching are an immense help in such an endeavor.

Confessions also help remind us that our job is not to discover new doctrines. The faith we are called to contend for is the faith which was "once for all delivered to the saints" (Jude 3). We are to understand that faith, to preserve it, and to pass it on, unabridged and unimpaired, to the next generation. We must give attention to Jude's words, and also to Paul's: "O Timothy! Guard what was committed to your trust, avoiding the profane and idle babblings and contradictions of what is falsely called knowledge—by professing it some have strayed concerning the faith" (1 Tim. 6:20-21). We need more than simply the love of truth and the diligence to drill down deep to mine that truth from the Word of God. We also need the awareness and the humility to acknowledge that that truth is already faithfully expressed in Confessions of Faith that have been handed down to us. This is not to say that the faith is *faultlessly* expressed in those Confessions; but it is *faithfully* expressed.

A second reason for my concern regarding the danger of allowing our Confession of Faith to "rust" is that, just as in past generations, we face pressures to abandon faithful Confessions, to one degree or another. There is a belief, even among Christians who hold to good Confessions of Faith, that we ought to make the truth more "accessible" to people, and that one of the ways to do that is to streamline our Confessions of Faith. Some recommend that we either find or create a simpler (that is, briefer) Confession of Faith for believers of Reformed and baptistic persuasion. I, however, am personally convinced that we should not aim to make the truth more accessible by trimming or scaling down our Confession. I believe that we need to make the truth accessible to people by teaching it faithfully, simply, clearly, and tirelessly. I believe it is fair to say that when you trim or pare a Confession, you inevitably lose. That has been true historically and it will always be true. Read church history, and you will see that, where people have abandoned good Confessions, the cause of God and truth has suffered greatly.[4] There are very good commentaries already available on various reformed Confessions of Faith. Among them is Sam Waldron's on the 1689 Confession. But since he wrote that volume, my wife and I have had children born into the world, who in turn have had their own children. It is time for another good commentary on our Confession; one that will serve the needs of Christ's church today. Years ago, I read an article by R. L. Dabney in which he made the point that every generation of God's people needs to wrestle with the great matters addressed in the Bible and come to their own settled convictions regarding the truths it teaches. I believe this volume can assist our generation in fulfilling that sacred obligation.

---

4. See Robert W. Oliver, *History of the English Calvinistic Baptists,* 1771-1892 (Edinburgh: The Banner of Truth Trust, 2006).

THE 1677/1689 CONFESSION OF FAITH:
A HISTORICAL OVERVIEW

AUSTIN WALKER

A General Assembly of baptized churches from England and Wales met in London in the early autumn of 1689. It was an historic occasion; the first time any such assembly had been convened. A narrative of the proceedings of that Assembly was published in the same year. One hundred and eight churches were represented at the Assembly. There were thirty-three pastors and messengers who formally signed a Confession of Faith in the name and on behalf of the churches represented at the Assembly. They declared that it was a full statement "containing the Doctrine of our Faith and Practice." This document became known as the Second London Baptist of Faith and has been popularly referred to as "the 1689" (hereafter referred to as The Confession). The Assembly called on other Christians who differed from them over the matter of baptism to carefully consider The Confession. In addition, they recommended it to the members of the baptized churches they represented.

> We the Ministers and Messengers of, and concerned for, upwards of one hundred Baptized Congregations in *England* and *Wales* (denying *Arminianism*) being met together in *London* from the 3*d* of the 7*th* Month to the 11*th* of the same, 1689, to consider of some things that might be for the Glory of God, and the good of these Congregations; have thought meet (for the satisfaction of all other Christians that differ from us in the point of Baptism) to recommend to their perusal the Confession of our Faith, Printed for, and sold by, Mr. *John Harris* at the *Harrow* in the *Poultrey*; Which Confession we own, as containing the Doctrine of our Faith and Practice; and do desire that the Members of our Churches respectively do furnish themselves therewith.[1]

It is clear from the narrative that declaring their adherence to the statements in The Confession was no mere formality. It was a "Confession we own." It reflected their strong convictions about the Christian religion

---

1. A Narrative of the Proceedings of the General Assembly Of divers Pastors, Messengers and Ministering Brethren of the Baptized Churches, met together in London, from September 3 to 12 1689, from divers parts of England and Wales: Owning the Doctrine of Personal Election, and final Perseverance (London: 1689), 18.

that they sincerely professed. Other Christians could read the document for themselves and see that these Baptist churches were orthodox in their beliefs and practices and were part of mainline Protestantism and English Nonconformity.

The Assembly was seeking to establish the credibility of this group of Baptists. They were persuaded of their legitimate place in what had taken place in the sixteenth and seventeenth centuries in England. However, they had to fight for that credibility. In their own minds they knew their place in those events. This can be demonstrated in the preface to a book by Philip Cary published the year after the Assembly had met.[2] Five names are attached to the preface—William Allen, John Harris, Richard Adams, Robert Steed and Benjamin Keach. It is a reasonable guess to suggest that Keach was the author. These six men were all London Baptists who had been present at the General Assembly the previous year. Philip Cary was from Devon but together they shared a common conviction, what I have termed elsewhere as "a Particular Baptist consciousness."[3] They were very aware that their roots were to be found in Reformation theology.

This "consciousness" is plainly evident from what they said in the preface. Keach and his fellow Baptists saw themselves as a "third wave"—following on from the Reformers and earlier Puritans. They traced out the trajectory of the Reformation in the following way. The first wave was associated with Luther and Calvin, exposing the corruption of antichrist and bringing to light such important biblical truths as justification by faith. The second wave they closely associated with the Puritans, and the Congregationalists (Independents) in particular. They mentioned William Ames, Henry Ainsworth, and John Owen. These men had identified what they were persuaded was the true visible gospel church. Rejecting the idea of a national church in which everyone became a member by infant baptism they had insisted that the true church was comprised of those who were saints by profession. These saints had given themselves up to the Lord and to one another by solemn agreement to practice the ordinances of Christ. Baptists such as the signatories of Cary's preface had taken a step further and rejected infant baptism as practiced not only by the Congregationalists (with whom they had much in common) but also by the Anglican Church, the Presbyterians, and the Roman Catholics. This perspective was reflected in the statements made by the actual authors of The Confession as will be seen later in this introduction.

While The Confession has become known as the 1689 Confession of Faith, there is no evidence that it was published in 1689.[4] It was already

---

2. Philip Cary, *A Solemn Call unto all that would be owned as Christ's Faithful Witnesses, speedily and seriously, to attend unto the Primitive Purity of the Gospel Doctrine and Worship: or, a Discourse concerning Baptism* (London: 1690).

3. Austin Walker, *The Excellent Benjamin Keach*, 2nd revised edition (Ontario: Joshua Press, 2015), 39.

4. See Donald Wing, *Short-Title Catalogue of Books Printed in England, Scotland, Ireland, Wales, and British America and of English Books Printed in Other Countries 1641-1700*, 2d ed., (New York: The Index Committee of the Modern Language Association of America, 1972), 1:369.

in existence. It had been published in 1677, again in 1688, and a further edition appeared in 1699. That is why *The Narrative* told its readers where The Confession could already be obtained, from "Mr. *John Harris* at the *Harrow* in the *Poultrey*."

The Rationale for Confessions of Faith

Those who drew up The Confession had a very specific purpose as we shall discover. Some of the reasons may have changed, but Confessions are still to be valued nearly 350 years later. It is a sad reflection on the state of the church today that many have little or no appreciation of Creeds and Confessions of Faith. Some suggest that such Confessions and Creeds curb individual freedoms, others that they are divisive and even schismatic, and still others who say theology has moved on and to adopt something that is so old is a backward step. Others rest content with minimal statements of faith, which by their very nature are theologically open-ended. A question remains, however. If what our Baptist forefathers were confessing is biblical truth, why should the church of the twenty-first century confess less truth? That is surely a backward step.

The Sources of the 1677 Confession of Faith

It is almost certain that the Second London Baptist Confession of Faith originated in the Petty France Church in London. The church minute book for August 26, 1677 states: "It was agreed that a Confession of faith, with the Appendix thereto having been read & considered by the Bre[thren]: should be published."[5] William Collins and Nehemiah Coxe were co-pastors of that congregation. They had been ordained the same day in 1675. They appear to be the men responsible for editing The Confession.

They were certainly equipped for the task. Nehemiah Coxe was the son of an earlier leader Benjamin Coxe, who had signed the First London Confession of Faith in 1644. Besides being a qualified physician, he was also proficient in Latin, Greek, and Hebrew, and a judicious theologian. William Collins received a thorough education and was also a capable theologian.[6] The need for a Confession of Faith became more pressing when the West Country evangelist, church planter, and author, Thomas Collier, rejected the orthodoxy of the Calvinistic Baptist churches. In 1674, Collier had published *The Body of Divinity*. It also had an alternate title: *A Confession of Faith*. Some London and Bristol elders requested Coxe to reply in print to Collier's views. In 1677, Coxe published *Vindiciae Veritatis, or a Confutation of the Heresies and Gross Errours Asserted by Thomas Collier*. His book was a capable, biblically-based refutation of Collier's views. In it he asserted that "There can be no Gospel Peace without truth, nor Communion of Saints, without an agreement in *fundamental principles of the Christian religion*." Later in the same book he claimed that he could

---

5. Samuel D. Renihan, *The Petty France Church (Part 1)*, Centre for Baptist Studies, Resourcing Baptist History: Seventeenth Century Series, Volume 9 (Oxford: Regents Park College, 2019), 104.

6. For more details of Coxe and Collins, see Renihan, *The Petty France Church*, 57-96, 133-70.

defend Reformed doctrine, "any time, if called to it… from the confessions of Faith of all the reformed Churches, and from the Writings of all the worthy Reformers."[7]

The 1677 Confession of Faith was not a document produced privately by Coxe and Collins and the church in Petty France. It arose out of much wider concerns and initially involved churches in Bristol as well as London. It was a public declaration of agreement with the fundamental truths of the Reformed faith, over against those of Thomas Collier. The title page of the publication indicated that it contained the views of "many congregations of Christians… in London and the Country."

The Confession was put to good use. In 1681, both Hanserd Knollys and Nehemiah Coxe quoted from Chapter 26 on "The Church." In the following year Thomas Whinnell, formerly a member of a General Baptist church, sought to join the Broadmead Church in Bristol.[8] In order to test his convictions and to ensure he was in agreement with the church, they used the 1677 Confession for that purpose.[9] Whinnell subsequently became pastor of the Taunton Particular Baptist Church in Somerset. His name appeared as one of the thirty-three signatories of The Confession at the 1689 General Assembly.

This Confession quickly became the standard of orthodoxy in the churches. It is not possible to determine the number, or even the identity, of all the "many congregations… in London and the Country" in 1677 willing to confess their faith by means of this document. However, when the General Assembly was convened in 1689, many of the churches who were represented by their pastors and messengers would be among them.

The Identity of these "Baptized Congregations in *England* and *Wales* (Denying *Arminianism*)"

An earlier Confession of Faith has already been mentioned, first published over thirty years before. In fact, there were two editions, 1644 and 1646. The title page to the 1644 reads "The Confession of Faith, of those Churches which are commonly (though falsely) called Anabaptists." It was published by seven London congregations. It has been commonplace to identify these churches as Particular Baptists (as opposed to General Baptists), yet there is no evidence to suggest that this term was used by them or by anyone else. It was not even used in the 1689 General Assembly. It was a label that began to appear at the

---

7. Quoted by Renihan, *The Petty France Church*, 105. (Italics are original.)

8. The term "General Baptist" needs to be clarified. The usual division between General and Particular Baptist can be easily misunderstood. They were not labels used by either group during the seventeenth century. Those termed "General Baptists" can be traced back to John Smyth and Thomas Helwys in the first decades of the seventeenth century. They were essentially Arminian baptistic congregations, and the evidence suggests that there was little meaningful interaction between them and the Calvinistic baptistic congregations. See Matthew C. Bingham, *Orthodox Radicals: Baptist Identity in the English Revolution* (Oxford: OUP, 2019), 17-18.

9. James M. Renihan, *Edification and Beauty: The Practical Ecclesiology of the English Particular Baptists, 1675-1705*, Studies in Baptist History and Thought, Vol.17 (Milton Keynes: Paternoster, 2008), 27.

end of the seventeenth century and became accepted and widespread in the eighteenth century. This matter has been thoroughly examined in a recent publication by Matthew C. Bingham in *Orthodox Radicals: Baptist Identity in the English Revolution*.[10]

There is a clear thread linking the men responsible for the 1644 and 1646 Confessions, those responsible for the 1677 Confession, and the men who convened the 1689 Assembly. For example, Benjamin Coxe, the father of Nehemiah Coxe, William Kiffen, and Hanserd Knollys were among the names associated with both Confessions. In 1645 Kiffen published *A Brief Remonstrance of the Reasons and Grounds of Those People Commonly Called Anabaptists*. Bingham observes,

> Throughout that discourse, Kiffen refers to himself and the churches with whom he associated variously as "our Congregations," "our separated Congregations," and "gatherings of the Saints together," but he is never able to settle on a consistent, positive self-identifier.[11]

The seven churches that emerged from the Southwark congregation in London are often referred to as the Jacob-Lothropp-Jessey church after the first three pastors. This church was a Congregational church having its roots in English Separatism. It was firmly Calvinistic in its doctrine. In the late 1630s and early 1640s a number of members of the church became persuaded that infant baptism was not a biblical practice and left, usually in an amicable manner, to form new congregations and practice the baptism of believers. It is for this reason that Bingham refers to these churches as "baptistic congregationalists."[12] It was these men who were responsible for drawing up the 1644 and the 1646 Confessions of Faith.

Hostility, often born of hatred, or fear, prejudice, and misunderstanding, confronted these new congregations practicing believer's baptism. At this point England was enmeshed in a civil war (1642-1651) between Parliamentarians and Royalists. The Westminster Assembly of divines had been convened to draw up a new Confession of Faith to modify the Thirty-Nine Articles of the national church. That Assembly was principally comprised of Presbyterians and Congregationalists.

These newer baptistic congregations, almost certainly aided by their Congregationalist friends in the Assembly, wanted to promote their credentials as churches and pastors who espoused and defended Calvinistic orthodoxy. They made it clear that they disassociated themselves from Arminianism. One of the Scottish Presbyterian commissioners at the Assembly, Robert Baillie, was honest enough to admit that the Confession of the seven churches reflected the affirmations of the Synod of Dort by rejecting all five of the Arminian Articles.[13] The

---

10. Matthew C. Bingham, *Orthodox Radicals: Baptist Identity in the English Revolution* (Oxford: OUP, 2019).

11. Ibid., 43.

12. Bingham defends and explains his use of "baptistic congregationalists," admitting that none of them used that term either! See Ibid., 43-44.

13. Ibid., 36.

1646 Confession was an attempt to clarify further and emphasize their commitment to established Calvinistic orthodoxy. However, their efforts to persuade Parliament and the Assembly were in vain despite their insistence that they held firmly to original sin, and rejected both free will, and the possibility of falling away from grace.

The ghost of Anabaptism re-emerged. Presbyterian hardliners and heresy hunters targeted these new churches. Men like Daniel Featley employed cynical and contemptuous language to dismiss them: "They cover a little rats-bane in a great quantity of sugar, that is that they may not be discerned."[14]

Despite being rejected by Parliament and by the Westminster Assembly, the documents these seven London churches produced and the doctrines they espoused did not go away. Men like William Kiffen, Hanserd Knollys and Benjamin Coxe continued to champion the cause of "baptistic congregationalists." The number of congregations grew during the Civil War and during the Commonwealth period under Oliver Cromwell. Men like Knollys were actively involved in evangelistic work outside of London. New churches grew up in London and in the country. In many cases they formed themselves into regional associations to strengthen and encourage one another.[15]

There was a dramatic turn of events in 1660 when Charles II was restored to the monarchy. Bishops were re-introduced and Anglican Church principles and practices were imposed on the nation by the 1662 Act of Uniformity. Presbyterians, Congregationalists and Baptists (together with Quakers) all stood their ground. There were fines and imprisonments and some, like the Baptist Thomas DeLaune, died in prison for asserting and defending liberty of conscience. In 1685 the Monmouth Rebellion failed. Opposed to the appointment of James II as the new king, those who had taken part were subjected to severe punishment by the civil authorities. William Kiffen's two grandsons were among the victims.

The 1677 Confession was conceived in the Petty France church during this long period of persecution from 1660 until toleration was granted in 1689. That opposition continued until the removal of the openly-Catholic James II and the recognition of the Protestant king William of Orange (William III). A new day dawned for Nonconformity that brought joy to the hearts of these men.

The Second Confession of Faith
By 1677, the first generation of men who had left the London Congregational Church of Henry Jessey and adopted believer's baptism had died. Two notable exceptions were Kiffen and Knollys. Nehemiah Coxe became a pastor in the Petty France church in 1675, but he died the May before the General Assembly gathered in London in 1689. There was one other man who was to play a prominent role in the Assembly. He was Benjamin

14. Ibid., 12. (Rats-bane is rat poison.)
15. For details of the associations see Renihan, *Edification and Beauty*, 154-83.

Keach, but as far as we know he played no part in the drawing up of the 1677 Confession. Keach was a relative newcomer to London, who at one point admitted he had never heard of the 1644 Confession until it was mentioned at the Assembly. That is not surprising as he was only four years old in 1644 and was brought up in Buckinghamshire. He was converted to Christ and ministered among Arminian Baptists before persecution drove him to London in 1668 where he came in contact with Knollys, and subsequently abandoned his Arminian sympathies.

Men like Kiffen and Knollys would have remembered the hostility they had initially encountered when the first Confession of Faith was published in the 1640s. This opposition was alluded to by the publishers of the 1677 Confession:

> There were those who did not thoroughly understand what our principles were, or had entertained prejudices against our Profession, by reason of the strange representation of them, by some men of note, who had taken very wrong measures, and accordingly led others into misapprehensions, of us, and them.[16]

They went on to acknowledge that subsequently there were other men who cleared them of the charges of heresy and error that had been unjustly laid at their door. Nevertheless, over forty years had passed since the publication of the first Confession. It was time for a restatement of their principles and practices. Although much water had gone under the bridge since the 1640s, they were still facing persecution and being misunderstood, and Thomas Collier could not be allowed to be heard as if he were the authentic voice of these Baptists.

We have already noted Keach's appreciation of the identity of the churches with whom he was associated. They had developed a self-awareness of being the "third wave" of the Reformation. That is reflected very clearly in The Confession. The quaint phrase, we have "no itch to clogge religion with new words" is taken from the first edition from a preliminary statement entitled "To the Judicious and Impartial Reader" that precedes the Confession. Here is the fundamental reason why the 1677 Confession follows closely both the Presbyterian Westminster Confession of Faith of 1646 and the Congregationalist document, the Savoy Declaration of 1658. The publishers of the Confession set out their rationale in the following manner:

> finding no defect...in that fixed on by the assembly, and after them by those of the Congregational way, we did readily conclude it best to retain the same *order* in our present confession: and also, when we observed that those last mentioned, did in their confession (for reasons which seemed of weight both to themselves and others) choose not only to express their mind in words concurrent with the former in sense, concerning all those articles wherein they were agreed, but also for the most part without any

---

16. "To The Judicious and Impartial Reader" in *A Confession of Faith. Put Forth by the Elders and Brethren Of many Congregations of Christians (Baptized upon Profession of their Faith) in London and the Country* (London: n.p., 1677).

variation of the terms we did in like manner conclude it best to follow their example in making use of the very same words with them both, in these articles (which are very many) wherein our faith and doctrine is the same with theirs, and this we did, the more abundantly, to manifest our consent with both, in all the fundamental articles of the Christian Religion, as also with many others, whose orthodox confessions have been published to the world; on behalf of the Protestants in divers Nations and Cities: and also to convince all, that we have no itch to clogge Religion with new words, but do readily acquiesce in that form of sound words, which hath been, in consent with the holy Scriptures, used by others before us; hereby declaring before God, Angels, & Men, our hearty agreement with them, in that wholesome Protestant Doctrine, which with so clear evidence of Scriptures they have asserted.[17]

This is a very important statement. It makes clear that they were affirming their agreement with both Presbyterians and Congregationalists in the fundamental doctrines of the Christian faith. They deliberately chose to depart from the pattern set out in the first Confession and instead used existing orthodox Confessions to show their agreement with their brethren. They were declaring that they belonged to the tradition established by the Reformation. Their Calvinism also reflected the theology stated in the Canons of Dort. They desired to be recognized by others as belonging to English Reformed and confessional Christianity. They did not regard their different ecclesiology, and in particular their adoption of believer's baptism, as a barrier to being recognized in that way.

In an appendix to the Confession they set out in more detail their understanding of the practice of believer's baptism. They were at pains to avoid contention and unnecessary division.

> And although we do differ from our brethren who are Paedobaptists; in the subject and administration of Baptisme, and such other circumstances as have a necessary dependence on our observance of that Ordinance, and do frequent our own assemblies for our mutual edification, and discharge of those duties, and services which we owe unto God, and in his fear to each other: yet we would not be from hence misconstrued, as if the discharge of our own consciences herein, did any wayes disoblige or alienate our affections, or conversation from any others that fear the Lord; but that we may and do as we have opportunity participate of the labors of those, whom God hath indued with abilities above our selves, and qualified, and called to the Ministry of the *Word*, earnestly desiring to approve our selves to be such, as follow after peace with holyness, and therefore we alwaies keep that blessed *Irenicum*, or healing *Word* of the Apostle before our eyes; if in any thing ye be otherwise minded, God shall reveal even this unto you; nevertheless whereto we have already attained; let us walk by the same rule, let us mind the same thing, *Phil* 3. *v.* 15, 16.[18]

17. Ibid.

18. "An Appendix," in *A Confession of Faith. Put Forth by the Elders and Brethren Of many Congregations of Christians (Baptized upon Profession of their Faith) in London and the Country,* (London: n.p., 1677).

It was their doctrine of the church that made them distinctive. They had rejected the notion of a comprehensive national church in which everyone was a member having been baptised as an infant. With the Congregationalists they were persuaded that individual congregations were the only New Testament expression of the visible church, and that its members were to be visible saints. The Congregationalists retained infant baptism for the children of believing parents. Taking a step further, the Baptists were convinced that the New Testament did not sanction the baptism of infants, even if they had believing parents. They had concluded that baptism was for believers and the visible church should be comprised of baptised believers.

The distinctive elements of their teaching on the church are to be found in article XXXIII of the 1644 Confession and Chapter 26 of the 1677 Confession of Faith. These sections mark them out from their Nonconformist brethren in the Presbyterian and Congregational churches. We concur with James Renihan that "ecclesiology was the driving force behind the Baptist movement, and is the head of theology that gives the two Confessions their distinct emphases."[19]

The Confession after the Seventeenth Century

The Confession has had a chequered history during the last three centuries but has risen to global prominence in the latter part of the twentieth and the first decades of this century. We can only trace out the broad picture in this introduction.

There had been close ties between Baptists in England and America from the middle of the seventeenth century. For example, when the First Baptist Church of Boston was founded in 1655, three of the original nine members "had walked in that order in old England" (including a member of William Kiffen's church, Richard Goodall). John Myles and many of his church members moved from Wales to Swansea, Massachusetts in 1663. After emigrating, William Screven, a member of one of the West Country churches, founded a new assembly in Maine in 1682. When the First Baptist Church of Boston published an apology, that is an explanation, for its existence in 1680, the book included a preface signed by William Kiffen, Hanserd Knollys, William Collins, Nehemiah Coxe, and two others. They said: "The authors of this apology have declared their perfect agreement with us both in matters of Faith and Worship, as set down in our late Confession."[20]

The Keach family played a significant role in the introduction of the 1677 Confession into American churches. Elias Keach, a son of Benjamin Keach, had come to America in 1684. After his conversion he became associated with the Pennepek Church, Pennsylvania. Several churches came into existence through his labors in eastern Pennsylvania and southern New Jersey. Though he returned to England in 1692 he had

---

19. Renihan, http://www.reformedreader.org/ctf.htm, 1999.

20. For this information about the seventeenth century I have drawn from Renihan, http://www.reformedreader.org/ctf.htm, 1999.

brought with him to America his father's strong doctrinal convictions and urged the churches to use The Confession. From these churches the Philadelphia Baptist Association was formed in 1707. Subsequently, The Confession became the approved Confession of that Association of churches and The Confession was reprinted in 1742 and again in 1765. They were using it to answer issues facing the churches in the 1720s two decades before the reprinting.[21]

The Philadelphia Association set the pattern for other Associations. In 1766 the Ketockton, Virginia Association adopted The Confession as did the Charleston, South Carolina Association, and the Warren, Rhode Island Association the following year. Through these Associations, and others, and the constituent churches, the doctrine and practices of The Confession molded much of the early thinking among Baptists in America.[22]

In England, The Confession thrived best in the West Country Association through the leadership of Bernard Foskett and the Broadmead Church in Bristol. Foskett maintained the doctrinal integrity of the Association by insisting on making The Confession the doctrinal standard of the Association. He became the principal of Bristol Academy and carried those strong Calvinistic convictions with him. However, after his death in 1758 the influence of The Confession began to wane, though the Academy continued to hold fast to the Calvinism represented in The Confession, mainly by using Beddome's *A Scriptural Exposition of the Baptist Catechism*.[23]

Churches in London, by comparison, did not consistently or vigorously maintain those convictions. Once the generation of Keach, Knollys and Kiffen had died, some of the churches drifted into hyper-Calvinism. Others simply did not promote the distinctive Calvinism of their forefathers. In the eighteenth century, distaste for Creeds and Confessions became widespread. The Particular Baptist, Abraham Booth, proved to be a notable exception. His book *The Reign of Grace*, published in 1768, stated and defended the fundamental articles of the gospel and the sovereignty of divine grace in salvation. He was aware of The Confession and his doctrine certainly reflected that document. The generation associated with Andrew Fuller and William Carey tended to make the "Five Points of Calvinism" their identity marker rather than The Confession, though they were aware of it. However, there were already some among the Particular Baptists, for example Robert Hall Jr., who rejected particular redemption.

Sadly, in the early nineteenth century, The Confession drifted almost into oblivion as the Baptists forsook their heritage. One clear example of this is demonstrated by the differences between the Calvinistic

21. For further details about Elias Keach, see Walker, *The Excellent Benjamin Keach*, 242-47.

22. Renihan, http://www.reformedreader.org/ctf.htm, 1999.

23. Benjamin Beddome, *A Scriptural Exposition of the Baptist Catechism* (Birmingham, AL: Solid Ground Christian Books, 2006).

doctrinal basis of the 1813 Baptist Union and that of 1832. The latter gave no creedal basis at all but was founded on "those sentiments generally denominated evangelical."[24] Those sentiments were never defined. Quite a few Particular Baptist churches joined the new union in 1832.

The decline of Calvinism was a predominant characteristic of Nonconformity in the British Isles during the nineteenth century. There was a shift away from Calvinism that reflected the "whole ethos of the times."[25] Arminianism was deemed to be more in tune with the age of Romanticism than the apparent rigors of Calvinism. Richard Muller has observed that "the 1830s marked the end of the era of Reformed confessionalism and could be called the era of deconfessionalisation."[26] Some more discerning men among the Particular Baptists were aware of the trend. Caleb Evans, of the Broadmead Church in Bristol and a successor of Bernard Foskett in the Bristol Academy, was bemoaning the anti-creedal spirit among the churches as early as 1767. Andrew Fuller had died in 1815, and John Ryland in 1825. These men had far more in common with The Second London Baptist Confession of Faith. They, and their colleagues in the Northamptonshire Baptist Association, were not responsible for the shift away from the Calvinism of the seventeenth-century Particular Baptists.

The need to maintain the doctrinal standards of the church of Christ by upholding a full confession of faith became very evident in the nineteenth and first part of the twentieth century. Spurgeon, wanting to testify plainly to the leading doctrines of the gospel, republished The Confession in October 1855. It was only the second year of his ministry at the New Park Street Chapel, Southwark. He told his congregation it was published "not as an authoritative rule or code of faith, whereby you may be fettered, but as a means of edification in righteousness. It is an excellent, though not inspired, expression of the teaching of those Holy Scriptures by which all confessions are to be measured."[27] The "Downgrade" that he resisted closer to the end of his life, and which led him to leave the Baptist Union, not only marked the loss of Calvinism among those Baptists, but also a rejection of some of the fundamental articles of the faith.

It was among Strict Baptists in England that Calvinism was largely upheld in the first part of the twentieth century. In 1959 three Strict Baptists —John Doggett, Leslie Mills and a Mr. Haddow—were responsible for republishing Spurgeon's 1855 version of *Things Most Surely Believed Among*

---

24. Ernest E. Payne, *The Baptist Union: A Short History* (London: The Baptist Union of Great Britain and Ireland, 1959), 61.

25. Kenneth Dix, *Strict and Particular: English Strict and Particular Baptists in the nineteenth century* (Didcot, Oxon: Baptist Historical Society, 2001), 270.

26. Richard A. Muller, *Calvin and the Reformed Tradition: On the Work of Christ and the Order of Salvation* (Grand Rapids, MI: Baker Academic, 2012), 549.

27. C. H. Spurgeon, *Things Most Surely Believed Among Us: The Baptist Confession of Faith 1689* (London: Alabaster and Passmore, 1855), preface.

Us.[28] John Doggett was a London barrister who often preached in Strict Baptist churches, and he was primarily responsible for the publication. He owned a copy of Spurgeon's 1855 version. The republication (which is still in print) led to a revival of interest in Calvinism among some Baptists and also in Confessions of Faith. This was happening at the same time as the distinctive Reformed ministry of Dr. Martyn Lloyd Jones at Westminster Chapel in London was impacting British evangelicalism. Furthermore, the Banner of Truth Trust had begun to republish Puritan books. During the rest of the twentieth century, a number of editions of The Confession were published both in England and America by Reformed Baptists. Churches adopted The Confession as a summary of what they believed. Sometimes editions were published in which the language was updated but the essence of The Confession had not been changed.

In the period since 1959, Reformed Baptist churches have been established in many nations and The Confession has become an international confession and has been translated into other languages. There are now churches scattered across the United Kingdom, Western and Eastern Europe, together with churches in America and Canada who have adopted The Second London Baptist Confession of Faith. In Latin America, including the Caribbean, in Australia, New Zealand, in the Philippines and south-east Asia, and the Indian subcontinent the pattern has been repeated. The same is true in Africa, notably in South Africa, Kenya, and Zambia, but also in other African nations. These are but samples of the widespread use of The Confession today.[29]

As we reflect today on the global significance of The Confession nearly three hundred and fifty years after its first publication the editors of the 1677 Confession, Nehemiah Coxe and William Collins, would probably be amazed. That overriding sense of historical continuity alluded to earlier by Dr. Bob Martin is plainly demonstrated. Sadly, Baptists have not been consistent in confessing the truths of Scripture summarized in the thirty-two chapters of The 1677/1689 Confession of Faith during those three centuries. The fortunes of The Confession have waxed and waned during that time. Some have been too quick to proclaim "Calvinism" as dead and buried. They have proved to be clearly mistaken. God's truth, the whole counsel of God, revealed by Him in the inspired and infallible Scriptures, can never be silenced and will always have people who believe and defend it all their days.

---

28. I am indebted to Dr. Robert Oliver for information about these men and the republication. That information is contained in private email correspondence stretching back over several years.

29. This is not to say that all these churches subscribe to The Confession and "own" it in the way the churches at the General Assembly did in 1689. Some use it as a teaching tool, others require their office holders to subscribe to it, but it is not the confession of the entire church membership.

LETTER TO THE READER

TO THE JUDICIOUS AND IMPARTIAL READER (FROM THE ORIGINAL WRITERS OF THE CONFESSION)

Courteous Reader,

It is now many years since divers of us (with other sober Christians then living and walking in the way of the Lord that we professe) did conceive our selves to be under a necessity of Publishing a *Confession of our Faith*, for the information, and satisfaction of those, that did not throughly understand what our principles were, or had entertained prejudices against our Profession, by reason of the strange representation of them, by some men of note, who had taken very wrong measures, and accordingly led others into misapprehensions, of us, and them: and this was first put forth about the year, 1643 in the name of seven Congregations then gathered in *London*; since which time, diverse impressions thereof have been dispersed abroad, and our end proposed, in good measure answered, inasmuch as many (and some of those men eminent, both for piety and learning) were thereby satisfied, that we were no way guilty of those Heterodoxies and fundamental errors, which had too frequently been charged upon us without ground, or occasion given on our part. And forasmuch, as that *Confession* is not now commonly to be had; and also that many others have since embraced the same truth which is owned therein; it was judged necessary by us to joyn together in giving a testimony to the world; of our firm adhering to those wholesome Principles, by the publication of this which is now in your hand.

And forasmuch as our method, and manner of expressing our sentiments, in this, doth vary from the former (although the substance of the matter is the same) we shall freely impart to you the reason and occasion thereof. One thing that greatly prevailed with us to undertake this work, was (not only to give a full account of our selves, to those Christians that differ from us about the subject of Baptism, but also) the profit that might from thence arise, unto those that have any account of our labors, in their instruction, and establishment in the great truths of the Gospel; in the clear understanding, and steady belief of which, our comfortable walking with God, and fruitfulness before him, in all our ways, is most neerly concerned; and therefore we did conclude it necessary to expresse our selves the more fully, and distinctly; and also to fix on such a method as might be most comprehensive of those things which we designed to explain our sense, and belief of; and finding no defect, in this regard, in that fixed on by the assembly, and after them by those of the Congregational way, we did readily conclude it best to retain the same *order* in our present confession: and also, when we observed that those last mentioned, did in their confession (for reasons which seemed of weight both to themselves and others) choose not only to express their mind in words concurrent with the former in sense, concerning all those articles wherein they were agreed, but also for the most part without any variation of the terms we did in like manner conclude it best to follow their example in making use of the very same words with them both, in these articles (which are very many) wherein our faith and doctrine is the same with theirs, and this we did, the more abundantly, to manifest our consent with both, in all the fundamental articles of the Christian Religion, as also with many others, whose orthodox confessions have been published to the world; on behalf of the Protestants in divers Nations and Cities: and also to convince all, that we have no itch to clogge Religion with new words, but do readily acquiesce in that form of sound words, which hath been, in consent with the holy Scriptures, used by others before us; hereby declaring before God, Angels, & Men, our hearty agreement with them, in that wholesome Protestant Doctrine, which with so clear evidence of Scriptures they have asserted: some things indeed, are in some places added, some terms omitted, and some few changed, but these alterations are of that nature, as that we need not doubt, any charge or suspition of unsoundness in the faith, from any of our brethren upon the account of them.

In those things wherein we differ from others, we have exprest our selves with all candor and plainness that none might entertain jealousie of ought secretly lodged in our breasts, that we would not the world should be acquainted with; yet we hope we have also observed those rules of modesty, and humility, as will render our freedom in this respect inoffensive, even to those whose sentiments are different from ours.

We have also taken care to affix texts of Scripture, in the margin for the confirmation of each article in our confession; in which work we have studiously indeavoured to select such as are most clear and pertinent, for the proof of what is asserted by us: and our earnest desire is, that all into whose hands this may come, would follow that (never enough commended) example of the noble *Bereans,* who searched the Scriptures daily, that they might find out whether the things preached to them were so or not.

There is one thing more which we sincerely professe, and earnestly desire credence in, *viz.* That contention is most remote from our design in all that we have done in this matter: and we hope the liberty of an ingenuous unfolding our principles, and opening our hearts unto our Brethren, with the Scripture grounds on which our faith and practise leanes, will by none of them be either denied to us, or taken ill from us. Our whole design is accomplished, if we may obtain that Justice, as to be measured in our principles, and practise, and the judgement of both by others, according to what we have now published; which the Lord (whose eyes are as a flame of fire) knoweth to be the doctrine, which with our hearts we must firmly believe, and sincerely endeavor to conform our lives to. And oh that other contentions being laid asleep, the only care and contention of all upon whom the name of our blessed Redeemer is called, might for the future be, to walk humbly with their God, and in the exercise of all Love and Meekness towards each other, to perfect holiness in the fear of the Lord, each one endeavouring to have his conversation such as becometh the Gospel; and also suitable to his place and capacity vigorously to promote in others the practice of true Religion and undefiled in the sight of God and our Father. And that in this backsliding day, we might not spend our breath in fruitless complaints of the evils of others; but may every one begin at home, to reform in the first place our own hearts, and wayes; and then to quicken all that we may have influence upon, to the same work; that if the will of God were so, none might deceive themselves, by resting in, and trusting to, a form of Godliness, without the power of it, and inward experience of the efficacy of those truths that are professed by them.

And verily there is one spring and cause of the decay of Religion in our day, which we cannot but touch upon, and earnestly urge a redresse of; and that is the neglect of the worship of God in Families, by those to whom the charge and conduct of them is committed. May not the grosse ignorance, and instability of many; with the prophaneness of others, be justly charged upon their Parents and Masters; who have not trained them up in the way wherein they ought to walk when they were young? but have neglected those frequent and solemn commands which the Lord hath laid upon them so to catechize, and instruct them, that their tender years might be seasoned with the knowledge of the truth of God as revealed in the Scriptures; and also by their own omission of Prayer, and other duties of Religion in their families, together with the ill example of their loose conversation, have inured them first to a neglect, and then contempt of all Piety and Religion? we know this will not excuse the blindness, or wickedness of any; but certainly it will fall heavy upon those that have thus been the occasion thereof; they indeed dye in their sins; but will not their blood be required of those under whose care they were, who yet permitted them to go on without *warning*, yea led them into the paths of destruction? and will not the diligence of Christians with respect to the discharge of these duties, in ages past, rise up in judgment against, and condemn many of those who would be esteemed such now?

We shall conclude with our earnest prayer, that the God of all grace, will pour out those measures of his holy Spirit upon us, that the profession of truth may be accompanyed with the sound belief, and diligent practise of it by us; that his name may in all things be glorified, through Jesus Christ our Lord, *Amen.*

CHAPTER 1
OF THE HOLY SCRIPTURES

JOHN REUTHER

1. The Holy Scripture is the only sufficient, certain, and infallible rule of all saving knowledge, faith, and obedience,[1] although the light of nature, and the works of creation and providence do so far manifest the goodness, wisdom, and power of God, as to leave men inexcusable; yet are they not sufficient to give that knowledge of God and his will which is necessary unto salvation.[2] Therefore it pleased the Lord at sundry times and in divers manners to reveal himself, and to declare that his will unto his church;[3] and afterward for the better preserving and propagating of the truth, and for the more sure establishment and comfort of the church against the corruption of the flesh, and the malice of Satan, and of the world, to commit the same wholly unto writing; which maketh the Holy Scriptures to be most necessary, those former ways of God's revealing his will unto his people being now ceased.[4]

2. Under the name of Holy Scripture, or the Word of God written, are now contained all the books of the Old and New Testaments, which are these,
Of the Old Testament.
Genesis, Exodus, Leviticus, Numbers, Deuteronomy, Joshua, Judges, Ruth, I Samuel, II Samuel, I Kings, II Kings, I Chronicles, II Chronicles, Ezra, Nehemiah, Esther, Job, Psalms, Proverbs, Ecclesiastes, The Song of Solomon, Isaiah, Jeremiah, Lamentations, Ezekiel, Daniel, Hosea, Joel, Amos, Obadiah, Jonah, Micah, Nahum, Habakkuk, Zephaniah, Haggai, Zechariah, Malachi
Of the New Testament.
Matthew, Mark, Luke, John, The Acts of the Apostles, Paul's Epistle to the Romans, I Corinthians, II Corinthians, Galatians, Ephesians, Philippians, Colossians, I Thessalonians, II Thessalonians, I Timothy, II Timothy, To Titus, To Philemon, The Epistle to the Hebrews, Epistle of

---

1. 2 Timothy 3:15-17; Isaiah 8:20; Luke 16:29, 31; Ephesians 2:20
2. Romans 1:19-21; Romans 2:14, 15; Psalms 19:1-3
3. Hebrews 1:1
4. Proverbs 22:19-21; Romans 15:4; 2 Peter 1:19, 20

James, The first and second Epistles of Peter, The first, second, and third Epistles of John, The Epistle of Jude, The Revelation. All of which are given by the inspiration of God, to be the rule of faith and life.[5]

3. The books commonly called Apocrypha, not being of divine inspiration, are no part of the canon (or rule) of the Scripture, and, therefore, are of no authority to the church of God, nor to be any otherwise approved or made use of than other human writings.[6]

4. The authority of the Holy Scripture, for which it ought to be believed, dependeth not upon the testimony of any man or church, but wholly upon God who is truth itself, the author thereof; therefore it is to be received because it is the Word of God.[7]

5. We may be moved and induced by the testimony of the church of God to an high and reverent esteem of the Holy Scriptures; and the heavenliness of the matter, the efficacy of the doctrine, and the majesty of the style, the consent of all the parts, the scope of the whole which is to give all glory to God, the full discovery it makes of the only way of man's salvation, and many other incomparable excellencies, and entire perfections thereof, are arguments whereby it doth abundantly evidence itself to be the Word of God; yet not withstanding, our full persuasion and assurance of the infallible truth, and divine authority thereof, is from the inward work of the Holy Spirit bearing witness by and with the Word in our hearts.[8]

6. The whole counsel of God concerning all things necessary for his own glory, man's salvation, faith and life, is either expressly set down or necessarily contained in the *Holy Scripture*; unto which nothing at any time is to be added, whether by new revelation of the *Spirit*, or traditions of men.[9] Nevertheless, we acknowledge the inward illumination of the Spirit of God to be necessary for the saving understanding of such things as are revealed in the Word,[10] and that there are some circumstances concerning the worship of God, and government of the church, common to human actions and societies, which are to be ordered by the light of nature and Christian prudence, according to the general rules of the Word, which are always to be observed.[11]

7. All things in Scripture are not alike plain in themselves, nor alike clear

---

5. 2 Timothy 3:16
6. Luke 24:27, 44; Romans 3:2
7. 2 Peter 1:19-21; 2 Timothy 3:16; 2 Thessalonians 2:13; 1 John 5:9
8. John 16:13, 14; 1 Corinthians 2:10-12; 1 John 2:20, 27
9. 2 Timothy 3:15-17; Galatians 1:8, 9
10. John 6:45; 1 Corinthians 2:9-12
11. 1 Corinthians 11:13, 14; 1 Corinthians 14:26, 40

unto all;[12] yet those things which are necessary to be known, believed and observed for salvation, are so clearly propounded and opened in some place of Scripture or other, that not only the learned, but the unlearned, in a due use of ordinary means, may attain to a sufficient understanding of them.[13]

8. The Old Testament in *Hebrew* which was the native language of the people of God of old,[14] and the New Testament in *Greek* which at the time of the writing of it was most generally known to the nations, being immediately inspired by God, and by his singular care and providence kept pure in all ages, are therefore authentic; so as in all controversies of religion, the church is finally to appeal to them.[15] But because these original tongues are not known to all the people of God, who have a right unto, and interest in the Scriptures, and are commanded in the fear of God to read[16] and search them,[17] therefore they are to be translated into the vulgar language of every nation unto which they come,[18] that the Word of God dwelling plentifully in all, they may worship him in an acceptable manner, and through patience and comfort of the Scriptures may have hope.[19]

9. The infallible rule of interpretation of Scripture is the Scripture itself; and therefore when there is a question about the true and full sense of any Scripture which is not manifold, but one, it must be searched by other places that speak more clearly.[20]

10. The supreme judge, by which all controversies of religion are to be determined, and all decrees of councils, opinions of ancient writers, doctrines of men, and private spirits, are to be examined, and in whose sentence we are to rest, can be no other but the Holy Scripture delivered by the Spirit, into which Scripture so delivered, our faith is finally resolved.[21]

Introduction

There are many good books on the doctrine of the Word of God, but The Confession of Faith of 1689 gives us a splendid summary of the most important matters. In these ten paragraphs of the first chapter of the Confession we survey the subjects which every believer should

12. 2 Peter 3:16
13. Psalms 19:7; Psalms 119:130
14. Romans 3:2
15. Isaiah 8:20
16. Acts 15:15
17. John 5:39
18. 1 Corinthians 14:6, 9, 11, 12, 24, 28
19. Colossians 3:16
20. 2 Peter 1:20, 21; Acts 15:15, 16
21. Matthew 22:29, 31, 32; Ephesians 2:20; Acts 28:23

understand in order to build his life securely on the Word of God. Naturally, the Confession does not cover every subject in the doctrine of the Word, thus making further study particularly important. But it offers the simple understanding we need, explaining the essential parts of the doctrine of the Word. We will learn how great Scripture revelation is and place a higher value on the treasure of the Word of God which we have.

There are ten subjects in the ten paragraphs of *Chapter 1* A grasp of these matters will enrich your love for God's Word so that you will be able to say with enthusiasm, "Oh, how I love Your law! It *is* my meditation all the day" (Ps. 119:97).

Paragraph 1: The Bible as Rule and Revelation
Two words call for our attention: *rule* and *revelation*. We need a rule, a guide, an authority, for our lives. We need a rule from God so that we may entrust our souls to His truth. Revelation is this rule because it is a *rule* that *reveals* the true God. In reverse, the true God *reveals* a *rule* by which we must guide our lives. We have this in God's great gift of the Bible.

Think about the Bible as the *rule* given by God. Rule refers to an accurate guide (like a ruler or guidelines). But the Confession also mentions His *will*, making the rule of Scripture His will: the "knowledge of God and his will which is necessary unto salvation," "to be his will," and "revealing his will." So, the rule that reveals God is His will, that which He commands and shows us to do, which is for our salvation and temporal and eternal good. The rule which God has given us in Scripture reflects His sovereign rule over this world as well. He is sovereign over all: "For the LORD Most High is awesome; *He is* a great King over all the earth" (Ps. 47:2). In the beautiful acrostic tribute to the Law of God (the Bible) in Psalm 119, the law of the Lord is His *Word*, which is His *will*, His *way*, and His *wisdom* for life. The sovereign God has revealed Himself and His will in His rule, the Bible.

We read that the "Holy Scripture is the only sufficient, certain, and infallible *rule* of all saving knowledge, faith, and obedience." This statement speaks to the nature of the rule of Scripture and its purpose. It is *sufficient*. This is a truth that is repeated throughout the chapter. *Sufficient* means adequate for the purpose. In order to be *sufficient*, it must be sure or *certain*, unquestionable, and therefore satisfying for the purpose envisioned. And it is *infallible*. This means that it is exempt from the liability of error. Challenges from false teachers, Bible critics, and compromisers in our generation have of necessity moved the church to be more specific and employ the word *inerrant* along with *infallible*. Inerrancy means that the Scripture is without error on every subject which it touches, such as matters of faith, history, science, etc. Infallibility means it will never lead us astray.

This means that Scripture is trustworthy. How could it be a rule if it is anything less? How could it not be trustworthy if it is a divine revelation? And it is a rule for "all saving knowledge, faith, and obedience." There can be no margin of error when it comes to salvation from sin and the judgment of God! Faith is not an elusive thing about which people may have their own ideas. Faith is based on accurate knowledge (truth), requires personal acknowledgement to revealed truth (assent), and leads to trust. Faith is living by revealed truth to which one can safely entrust his or her entire life, death, and eternal safety.

This rule is *revealed*. We believe, and the Confession teaches, that truth is revealed by God; man does not figure out truth about God. He cannot, just as the philosophers could not and cannot. We respond to what God reveals about Himself and about us. In this paragraph we have a helpful exposition of the two forms of revelation by which God communicates to us. The first is the *general* revelation in the works of creation and providence, and the second is described, using the words of Hebrews 1:1, as God revealing Himself "at sundry times and in diverse manners" ("at various times and in various ways"), and then preserving and committing those revelations "wholly unto writing." This is *special* revelation.

The universal mode of revelation is *general* revelation, the revelation of God in the creation. We also call this *creation* revelation. God's providence is essential to creation because God created and controls the world; He provides for His creation. God brought the worlds into existence by speaking His Word. He brought the world into existence "out of nothing" (Heb. 11:3). But He provides for the world He created. His work of providing for the ongoing care and control of His creation is God's *providence*.[22] He did not create and abandon, get tired of what He had made, go off somewhere and do something else—just the opposite. He is intimately involved in providing for His creation. This speaks of His *immanence*. Psalm 104, a creation psalm, shows us some of the practical ways in which creation and providence concur. And creation and providence "manifest the goodness, wisdom, and power of God." How encouraging to see these realities every day as we move about in the world. We have food, provisions, fire, energy, sunshine, rain, gentle breezes, mountains, valleys, trees, flowers, birds, art, music, and other delights. The world is an ordered system which reveals the Designer and Sovereign. Yet, as wonderful as these blessings are, they do not "give that knowledge of God and his will which is necessary unto salvation." Neither creation, beauty, provision, supplies, comforts, nor any other thing found in the creation, can make us right with the God against whom we have sinned and before whose righteousness we stand condemned.

"Therefore it pleased the Lord" to reveal Himself in *special revelation* (in contrast to *general* revelation). This revelation is "the only sufficient, certain, and infallible rule of all saving knowledge, faith, and obedience." This pleasure of the Lord points us to His grace. Special revelation comes by the grace, which means the favor of God. Favor is a free bestowal, not an earned benefit. And not only for salvation, faith, and obedience,

---

22. Herman Bavinck, *In the Beginning* (Grand Rapids: Baker, 1999), 234, calls it *pro-vidence*.

but the Lord revealed Himself in this way for other reasons which the *Confession* mentions. He did it for His church, the body of Christ in this world. He committed this special revelation to writing for "the better preserving and propagating" of the truth. He did it "for the more sure establishment and comfort of the church against the corruption of the flesh and the malice of Satan, and of the world." This is an impressive list of reasons why God committed His Word to writing, thus making "the Holy Scriptures to be most necessary." There are three major reasons given here. First, He did it for the believers in Christ who form the church. Second, He did it to preserve and propagate His Word, meaning that He intended it to be with us until the end of time. Third, He did it to empower us in our spiritual warfare with the world, the flesh, and the devil.

In the Scripture verses listed under this paragraph, we will note the main passages and the supporting passages.

Psalm 19 is the prominent passage which teaches both *general (creation)* (Ps. 19:1-6) and *special (Scripture)* revelation (Ps. 19:7-14). There is no transition from verse six to seven between David's presentation of the two forms of revelation. He simply places one atop the other, and by this indicates that we should carefully compare the two forms. Both sections praise the work of God in revealing Himself in the respective forms. "The heavens declare the glory of God" (Ps. 19:1). "The law of the LORD is perfect" (Ps. 19:7). And there is a definite sense in this transition that what the revelation in the heavens cannot do is accomplished by the revelation in the law of the Lord (Scripture).

Warfield shows the relationship:

> They constitute together a unitary whole, and each is incomplete without the other. In its most general idea, revelation is rooted in creation and the relations with His intelligent creatures into which God has brought Himself by giving them being. Its object is to realize the end of man's creation, to be attained only through knowledge of God and perfect and unbroken communion with Him. On the entrance of sin into the world, destroying this communion with God and obscuring the knowledge of Him derived from Nature, another mode of revelation was necessitated, having also another content, adapted to the new relation to God and the new conditions of intellect, heart and will brought about by sin.[23]

The major passage in the New Testament on general (creation) revelation is Romans 1:19-23. Paul explains here that man has known about God from the beginning of the creation, "for God has shown *it* to them" (Rom. 1:19), "by the things that are made" (Rom. 1:20). Paul explains the sinful, rebellious response to what is revealed in creation where "His invisible *attributes* are clearly seen…. His eternal power and Godhead" (Rom. 1:20). "Although they knew God, they did not glorify *him* as God, nor were

23. Benjamin B. Warfield, *The Works of Benjamin B. Warfield, Vol. 1, Revelation and Inspiration* (Grand Rapids: Baker, 2003), 7.

thankful, but became futile in their thoughts, and their foolish hearts were darkened" (Rom. 1:21).

The two foremost passages on special revelation are listed as 2 Timothy 3:16 and 2 Peter 1:19-21. These passages present the clearest teaching which explains the doctrine of verbal, plenary inspiration. These are two important terms that explain what we mean by inspiration. Verbal means that the words of the Bible are God's Word, and plenary means that every word of Scripture is from His mouth. These words are part of the vocabulary of the doctrine of the Word: verbal, plenary inspiration of the infallible, inerrant, authoritative, self-authenticating Bible. The rest of Chapter 1 develops these concepts.

"All Scripture *is* given by inspiration of God" (2 Tim. 3:16). Literally, "All Scripture is God-breathed." This statement reminds us of man's creation in God's image, "And the LORD God formed man *of* the dust of the ground, and breathed into his nostrils the breath of life; and man became a living being" (Gen. 2:7). All Scripture has been *breathed out of God*. It has the life of God. We refer to this as "inspiration," but it should be viewed as "expiration" (*breathed out* of, not *breathed into*). Just as man is the product of God's Spirit and has his life from God, so the Bible is breathed out of God and is, as Jesus said, "spirit, and *they* are life" (John 6:63). Peter, in 2 Peter 1:19-21, explains the relationship between God who spoke (breathed) His Word and the human authors. In 2 Timothy 3:16, Paul only refers to the divine source of Scripture and its resulting quality; it is *God-breathed* Scripture. Peter refers to the product *and* the process. It possesses divine authority, infallibility, and inerrancy. And because every Scripture (every word, every portion, every book) is God-breathed, it is "profitable for doctrine, for reproof, for correction, for instruction in righteousness" (2 Tim. 3:16).

Peter explains how the divine and the human elements concur.

> And so we have the prophetic word confirmed, which you do well to heed as a light that shines in a dark place, until the day dawns and the morning star rises in your hearts; knowing this first, that no prophecy of Scripture is of any private interpretation, for prophecy never came by the will of man, but holy men of God spoke *as they were* moved by the Holy Spirit (2 Pet. 1:19–21).

Warfield is helpful:

> Here is as direct an assertion of the Divine origin of Scripture as that of 2 Tim. 3:16. But there is more here than a simple assertion of the Divine origin of Scripture. We are advanced somewhat in our understanding of how God has produced the Scriptures. It was through the instrumentality of men who "spake from him." More specifically, it was through an operation of the Holy Ghost on these men which is described as "bearing" them. The term here used is a very specific one. It is not to be confounded with guiding, or directing, or controlling, or even leading in the full sense of that word. It goes beyond all such terms, in assigning the effect produced specifically to the active agent. What is "borne" is taken up by the "bearer," and conveyed by the "bearer's" power, not its own, to the "bearer's" goal,

not its own. The men who spoke from God are here declared, therefore, to have been taken up by the Holy Spirit and brought by His power to the goal of His choosing. The things which they spoke under this operation of the Spirit were therefore His things, not theirs. And that is the reason which is assigned why "the prophetic word" is so sure. Though spoken through the instrumentality of men, it is, by virtue of the fact that these men spoke "as borne by the Holy Spirit," an immediately Divine word.[24]

The Greek word translated "interpretation" means loosing, and releasing, and is saying that the prophets did not originate the prophecies. They spoke, but the origination was from God's Spirit as He bore them in His providence.

The Bible tells us how it was written, where it originated, and how the divine and human elements worked together to produce Scripture that in the final product is *God-breathed*. The Bible is one of God's great works. It is a majestic creation like the rivers, oceans, valleys, forests, mountains, and constellations of nature.[25]

Supporting texts are given in the first paragraph of the Confession. There are five: "To the law and to the testimony! If they do not speak according to this Word, *it is* because *there is* no light in them" (Isa. 8:20). "So that your trust may be in the LORD; I have instructed you today, even you. Have I not written to you excellent things of counsels and knowledge, that I may make you know the certainty of the words of truth, That you may answer words of truth To those who send to you?" (Prov. 22:19-21). "Having been built on the foundation of the apostles and prophets, Jesus Christ Himself being the chief *cornerstone*" (Eph. 2:20). "For whatever things were written before were written for our learning, that we through the patience and comfort of the Scriptures might have hope" (Rom. 15:4). "For when Gentiles, who do not have the law, by nature do the things in the law, these, although not having the law, are a law to themselves, who show the work of the law written in their hearts, their conscience also bearing witness, and between themselves *their* thoughts accusing or else excusing *them*" (Rom. 2:14-15).

Paragraph 2: Canonicity
It is necessary to identify the books which God inspired, and which consequently comprise the canon of Scripture. Since there are other books that some also believe are part of the canon, we must identify them and explain why they are not. The *Confession* does this in Paragraphs 2 and 3.

Although Paragraph 2 merely lists the books of the Bible, it reminds us that God has given us not a book, but a library. Warfield wrote:

---

24. Benjamin B. Warfield, *The Works of Benjamin B. Warfield*, Vol. 1, Revelation and Inspiration (Grand Rapids: Baker, 2003), 82, 83.

25. I once wrote a concise evangelistic booklet called, "The Seven Wonders of God" (like "The Seven Wonders of the World"). I describe those wonders as creation, providence, Scripture, Christ, the cross, the church, and the greatest of all, God's love.

No less than sixty-six separate books, one of which consists itself of one hundred and fifty separate compositions, immediately stare us in the face. These treatises come from the hands of at least thirty distinct writers, scattered over a period of some fifteen hundred years, and embrace specimens of nearly every kind of writing known among men. Histories, codes of law, ethical maxims, philosophical treatises, discourses, dramas, songs, hymns, epics, biographies, letters both official and personal, [prophecies],—every kind of composition known beneath heaven seems gathered here in one volume.[26]

Hopefully, you know how it feels to be in a real library (in contrast to searching the internet). You sense that a wealth of knowledge is there for you, and you may spend hours there pursuing the resources in quiet. That is how we should feel about the Bible. We should come to it always ready to dig in! And there is so much rich material in which to dig and discover. Searching the divine library is knowing the joy of discovery. Leland Ryken wrote about the "value in the artistry that is everywhere evident in the Bible. [Seeing] the individual works in the Bible as achievements that evoke delight and admiration. [Enhancing] our enjoyment in reading the Bible not only because of what the Bible says, but also because of the perfection of technique with which it says it."[27]

Paragraph 3: Apocryphal Books
This paragraph refers to the inclusion of those books called the *Apocrypha* into the canon of Scripture by the Roman Catholic Church. *Apocrypha* means *spurious*. These are books that are outside of the recognized canon of Scripture revelation. The Apocrypha contains some important history, such as is found in the books of Maccabees. These books give us important historical background of the Jews during the four hundred "silent" years between Malachi and Matthew. F. F. Bruce explains:

The Authorized (King James) Version of 1611 was formally a revision of the last (1602) edition of the Bishops," Bible; it included a version of the Apocrypha as a matter of course. Four years later, the Archbishop of Canterbury, George Abbot, a firm Calvinist in theology, forbade the binding or selling of Bibles without the Apocrypha on penalty of a year's imprisonment. This measure seemed to be necessary because of the increasingly vocal Puritan objection to the inclusion of the Apocrypha among the canonical books. In 1589 an attack on their inclusion by John Penry ("Martin Marprelate") had called forth a spirited reply from an earlier Archbishop, John Whitgift. Now, despite the penalty enacted by Archbishop Abbot, copies of the AV/KJV without the Apocrypha began to be produced in the years from 1626 onward.

The tide was running in the Puritan favour in those years: in 1644 the Long Parliament ordained that the Apocrypha should cease to be read in services of the Church of England. Three years later the Assembly of Divines

26. Warfield, *The Works.*, 436.
27. Leland Ryken, *Words of Delight: A Literary Introduction to the Bible* (Grand Rapids: Baker Academic, 1992), 22.

at Westminster introduced their historic Confession of Faith with a chapter "Of the Holy Scripture." In order to make it plain precisely which books were comprised in the holy scripture the second paragraph [of Chapter One of the WCF/LBC was composed which included the names of the sixty-six books in the canon].[28]

The Jews rejected the Old Testament Apocrypha as non-canonical. The manuscripts of the Greek version of the Hebrew Old Testament, the Septuagint, included them as an addendum to the canonical books. As the Latin Bible was translated from the Greek Bible, so they made their way into Jerome's Latin Vulgate translation. At the Council of Carthage (A.D. 397) they were recognized as suitable for reading. In 1548, the Council of Trent recognized the majority of the Apocryphal books as having unqualified canonical status. The Reformers rejected the Apocrypha as unworthy and contradictory to the true canon of Scripture. Our Confession aligns with the Reformers, the early church, and the Jews of old in rejecting these books as non-canonical.

Paragraph 4: The Authority of Scripture
Here our two major texts are again noted, 2 Peter 1:19-21 and 2 Timothy 3:16. The subject of authority connects to the earlier subject of rule and revelation. If Scripture is our *rule*, then it stands in a position of *authority* in our lives. This brief statement of Scripture authority is speaking about the duty of exercising faith in the Word of God (Scripture). And it states, first, that faith does not depend on the testimony of any man or church, and second, that faith is rooted in the authority of God Himself.

This paragraph and the next are important historically because the Church of Rome teaches that the authority of the Bible depends on the testimony of the Catholic Church. The way of life issuing from such a belief is that a person trusts the Bible because it trusts the Church of Rome. But the Confession teaches, and we believe, that the authority of the Bible depends on the testimony of God alone. No church need approve the Bible to be a person's authority.

Neither does any person need to approve the authority of the Bible for himself or others. We said earlier that the Bible is self-authenticating, it "speaks for itself." "The modern position amounts to this, that it is man's reason that decides. You and I come to the Bible and we have to make our own decisions on this basis of certain standards which are obviously in our own minds."[29] Paul said, "For this reason we also thank God without ceasing, because when you received the word of God which you heard from us, you welcomed *it* not *as* the word of men, but as it is in truth, the word of God, which also effectively works in you who believe" (1 Thess. 2:13).

How does a person believe that the Bible is the Word of God? "God from the beginning chose you for salvation through sanctification by the

28. F. F. Bruce, *The Canon of Scripture* (Downers Grove, IL: IVP, 1988), 108-09.
29. D. Martyn Lloyd-Jones, *Authority* (Edinburgh: Banner of Truth, 1997), 35.

Spirit and belief in the truth" (2 Thess. 2:13). We believe the Bible because God chooses and draws us for salvation and grants us faith to believe. No one comes to faith in God and obedience to the Bible apart from God's electing, predestinating, choice. "Blessed are you, Simon Bar-Jonah, for flesh and blood has not revealed *this* to you, but My Father who is in heaven" (Matt.16:17). The Lord said, "It is written in the prophets, 'And they shall all be taught by God.' Therefore everyone who has heard and learned from the Father comes to Me" (John 6:45). "But you do not believe, because you are not of My sheep" (John 10:26). But men do believe in it and receive it as such because God has chosen them to receive it (1 Cor. 2:10-12).

Unbelief and rejection do not detract from the authority of Scripture. The gospel commands men to believe and submit to its authority. Jesus said, "This is the work of God, that you believe in Him whom He sent" (John 6:29). The authority of the spoken and written Word is found in God who is truth Himself. The next paragraph explains this further.

Paragraph 5: Our Persuasion and Assurance
The testimony of the church to the divine origin of Scripture is acknowledged here. Though the Bible bears witness to itself, the church testifies that it is the Word of God. This testimony is encouraging and strengthens our assurance. The last sentence in this excellent paragraph is the most important because in it we learn that being persuaded and assured about the divine origin and authority of the Word of God is the work of the inner (indwelling) witness of the Holy Spirit.

The key word here is *evidences* that the Bible is the Word of God. The church bears witness that Scripture is the Word of God. The church encourages a reverent esteem for the Word of God in order to strengthen the believers, but the full persuasion and assurance of the believer comes from the witness of the Spirit. Lloyd-Jones writes about the ministry of the Spirit, "He takes His own Word, He illumines it, and takes our minds and enlightens them, and we are thus made receptive to the Word."[30] Since the Holy Spirit carried the writers along so that what they wrote was and is the Word of God, then we would expect the Holy Spirit to work in us to understand, believe, and receive the Word.

But the Confession expresses in the most beautiful way that the Bible has many evidences that help us. These *commend* the Scripture to the support of our faith. They are also compelling, and the Spirit uses these (because He is using His Word) to aid in persuading and assuring us that the Bible is the Word of God. Faith and submission to the Word of God is an unqualified duty. We believe the Bible because it comes to us with the full and persuasive authority of the Word of God (1 Thess. 2:13). Yet our faith is still aided by the evidences which commend it to us as the Word of God. There should be no tension between faith and evidences

---

30. Ibid., 63.

in this matter. The Confession speaks about the harmony and balance which exists between the two.

"The heavenliness of the matter." Jesus said to Nicodemus, "If I have told you earthly things and you do not believe, how will you believe if I tell you heavenly things?" (John 3:12). The Bible testifies about heavenly things. We have been speaking about its divine *origin*. Here we are speaking about its heavenly subject *matter*. Warfield wrote:

> The conception of God which is here presented—how unutterably divine is it! Apart from the Bible, man has never reached to such a conception. This element of it, and that element of it, has, indeed, through the voice of nature, separately dawned upon his soul; but the complete ideal is conveyed to him only by this book. Infinite and eternal spirit—pure and ineffable— unlimited by matter, or space or time, infinite, eternal and unchangeable in essence and attributes! And what a circle of attributes! Infinite power, infinite wisdom, infinite justice, infinite holiness, infinite goodness, infinite mercy, infinite pity, infinite love! Verily, if this conception be not a true image of a really existent God, the human heart must say it ought to be. And this is the conception of God which the Bible holds up before us—more than that, which it dramatizes through an infinite series of infinitely varied actions through a period of millenniums of years in perfect consistency of character. Everywhere in its pages God appears as the all-powerful, all-wise, necessarily just and holy One; everywhere as the all-good, all-merciful, necessarily pitiful and loving One. Never is a single one of these ineffable perfections lost or hidden or veiled.[31]

"The efficacy of its doctrines." Efficacy means power and purpose. The gospel is the power of God unto salvation to everyone who believes (Rom. 1:16). "For the Word of God *is* living and powerful, and sharper than any two-edged sword" (Heb. 4:12). "Oh, taste and see that the LORD *is* good; Blessed *is* the man *who* trusts in Him!" (Ps. 34:8). "But without faith *it is* impossible to please *Him*, for he who comes to God must believe that He is, and *that* He is a rewarder of those who diligently seek Him" (Heb. 11:6). The Bible is our support and strength, for through it we draw near to God through Jesus Christ. The Word of God is living and so conveys life to our souls.

Warfield said:

> Their writers, too, were of like diverse kinds. The time of their labors stretches from the hoary past of Egypt to and beyond the bright splendor of Rome under Augustus. They appear to have been of every sort of temperament, of every degree of endowment, of every time of life, of every grade of attainment, of every condition in the social scale... One half is a mass of Hebrew writings held sacred by a race which cannot look with patience on the other half, which is a mass of Greek writings claiming to set aside the legislation of a large part of its fellow. Yet it is this [collection] of [writings] which has had, and still has, this immense influence. The Hebrew half never conquered the world until the Greek half was added to it; the Greek half did not conquer save by the aid of the Hebrew half. The

31. Warfield, *The Works.*, 441.

whole mass, in all its divinity, has attained the kingship.

Where does this book, seemingly thus cast together by some whirlpool of time, get its influence? If influence is not *natural* to such a volume, must it not point to something *supernatural* in it?[32]

"The majesty of the style." Although the Bible is written for the common man, and the unlearned as well as the learned can understand it (paragraph 7), it does have a majestic style. Consider the simple majesty of the creation account in Genesis 1, the pre-incarnate Christ in John 1, the preaching of God's love by Moses in Deuteronomy 1–11, the Torah Psalms 1, 19, and 119, the creation Psalms 8, 19, and 104, the shepherd Psalm 23, the penitential Psalms 32 and 51, the majestic utterances of Job, the glorious preaching of Isaiah and Jesus, the theological treatises of Paul in Romans, Ephesians, and Galatians, the majestic presentation of Christ the high priest in Hebrews, and the spectacular visionary drama of the book of Revelation.

"The consent of all the parts." This is one of the great evidences of the divine origin of the Bible. The Bible is the record of redemptive history from the creation of the world to the establishment of the Christian church through the labors of the apostles. When you consider the number of authors, the variety of personalities and callings of those authors, the time span, and the kinds of genre in the Bible (history, law, poetry, prophecy, wisdom, apocalyptic, gospel, epistle), it is a work of divine orchestration that the Bible has internal harmony throughout all its books and with all of its authors. It is consistent, rational, progressive, and possesses integrity and consent in all its parts.

Warfield spoke about this:

> Observe the internal character of the volume, and a most striking unity is found to pervade the whole; so that, in spite of having been thus made up of such diverse parts, it forms but one organic whole. The parts are so linked together that the absence of any one book would introduce confusion and disorder. The same doctrine is taught from beginning to end, running like a golden thread through the whole and stringing book after book upon itself like so many pearls. Each book, indeed, adds something in clearness, definition, or even increment, to what the others proclaim; but the development is orderly and constantly progressive. One step leads naturally to the next; the pearls are certainly chosen in the order of stringing.
>
> An unbroken historical continuity pervades the whole book. It is even astonishing how accurately the parts historically dovetail together, jag to jag, into one connected and consistent whole. Malachi ends with a finger-post pointing through the silent ages to a path clearly seen in the Gospels. The New Testament fits on to the Old silently and noiselessly, but exactly, just as one stone of the Jewish temple fitted its fellow prepared for it by exact measurement in the quarries; so that, on any careful consideration of the two coexisting phenomena—utter diversity in origin of these books, and yet utter nicety of combination of one with all—it is as impossible to doubt that they were meant each for the other, were consciously framed each for

---

32. Warfield, Ibid., 436, 437.

its place, as it is to doubt that the various parts of a complicated machine, when brought from the factory and set up in its place of future usefulness, were all carefully framed for one another.[33]

"The scope of the whole, which is to give all glory to God." When we study the Bible, we look at one part at a time, and this is good. But step back and look at the whole volume and realize that in it God is glorified, man exposed, and the love of God displayed to our sinful race. He receives all the glory because He is the infinite, and we are the finite. He is the Righteous One, and we stand in need of His righteousness. He is all wise and powerful, and we are fools and weak. He is gracious and compassionate, and we are depraved and stand in need of salvation.

Many verses of Scripture do this for us. "And blessed *be* His glorious name forever! And let the whole earth be filled *with* His glory. Amen and Amen" (Ps. 72:19). "And one cried to another and said: 'Holy, holy, holy *is* the LORD of hosts; The whole earth *is* full of His glory!'" (Isa. 6:3). "For of Him and through Him and to Him *are* all things, to whom *be* glory forever. Amen" (Rom. 11:36). "To God, alone wise, *be* glory through Jesus Christ forever. Amen" (Rom. 16:27). "Now to the King eternal, immortal, invisible, to God who alone is wise, *be* honor and glory forever and ever. Amen" (1 Tim. 1:17). "To God our Savior, Who alone is wise, *Be* glory and majesty, Dominion and power, Both now and forever. Amen" (Jude 25).

"The full discovery of the only way of man's salvation." The Bible is ultimately about "the portraiture of one person... On its first page he comes for a moment before our astonished eyes; on the last he lingers still before their adoring gaze."[34] The Bible truly reveals the way of salvation to man. It is a lamp to our feet and a light to our path. Not only does it reveal the way, it guides us on the path to glory. It has guided multitudes upon multitudes to final salvation and deliverance from God's wrath, and it will guide us if we obey it.

"Many other incomparable excellencies and entire perfections." The authors of the Confession believed that the Bible is an inexhaustible treasure of good things and that it possesses a great variety of evidences (here called *excellencies* or *perfections*) that encourage the believer in his or her faith. We ought to read, study, and memorize our Bibles, and listen to sermons, with the expectancy that God will show us wonderful things out of His law (Ps. 119:18). This is one of the points which the composer of Psalm 119 was making in his tribute to the Torah.

As great and persuasive as these evidences are to the believer, the Confession says, "our full persuasion and assurance of the infallible truth, and divine authority thereof, is from the inward work of the Holy Spirit bearing witness by and with the Word in our hearts."

This witness of the Spirit is personal and internal. It is in the heart of the Christian. It is the moving of the Spirit in us through His indwelling. But notice that it is not from one's own experience; nor from one's own

33. Ibid., 437.
34. Ibid., 448.

mind. It is specifically "by and with the Word." It is only by reading, study, and meditation upon the Word of God that the Holy Spirit bears witness in our hearts. The passages cited in the Confession are John 16:13, 14; 1 Corinthians 2:10-12; and 1 John 2:20, 27.

Warfield spoke of the personal element in the Bible's witness to us:

> We must, however, turn to note another general characteristic of Scripture—the remarkable simplicity of its manner and the transparent honesty of its tone; so that its words, even when describing the most utter marvels, possess that calm, quiet ring which stamps them with indubitable truthfulness. If we are asked why we trust a friend in whom we have every confidence, and credit his every statement, we may be somewhat at a loss for a definite answer. "We know him," we say. This same evidence is good also for a book. We may judge of the truthfulness of men's writings by all those little intangible characteristics which when united go toward making a very strong impression of actual proof, but which one by one are almost too small to adduce or even notice, just as we may judge of the trustiness of men's characters by all the innumerable looks, gestures, chance expressions, little circumstances which make their due impression on us. Combined, they are convincing, though each by itself might seem ambiguous or valueless. The conclusion in each case is, however, valid and rational, and the evidence is unmistakably good evidence. Now, for the Bible, this evidence is unusually strong.[35]

In John 16:13-14, the Spirit is called the "Spirit of Truth." The truth is the Word of God. Jesus said, "Sanctify them by Your truth, Your word is truth" (John 17:17). As the Spirit of truth, He guides us into all the truth of inscripturated revelation. He sovereignly aids us by opening our eyes to the truth (Ps. 119:130).

In 1 Corinthians 2:12-13, the Spirit, whom we have freely received, is from God, so that we might know the things freely given to us by God. And what are those things? They are words taught by the Spirit, the Spirit-inspired truths of Scripture. In this chapter of 1 Corinthians, we see the process of special revelation in action. The Spirit *searches* the depths of God, for He is the Spirit of God (1 Cor. 2:10). No one could know God any other way (1 Cor. 2:11). But the Spirit who searches the depths of the being and character and will of God is in every true believer, and also *reveals* those things that He Himself has searched out (1 Cor. 2:12).

In 1 John 2:20, 27, the work of the Spirit is called an anointing. Anointing was a sign in the Old Testament that prophets, priests, and kings were called and equipped by Jehovah for their special work. Here we find an amazing thing in comparison. Each believer has an anointing from the Spirit of God for the purpose of knowing the truth of God. Apart from the Gnostic heresy that John is trying to deal with—a teaching about "secret knowledge" that can be attained only by initiation into the cult of the Gnostic teachers—John is saying that the Holy Spirit is their direct teacher. John is not denying that God has appointed teachers in the

---

35. Warfield, Ibid., 443.

church. He is only denying errors of contemporaries who sought to lock the Scriptures up as secrets for a select group to discover. No. John has already stated that the fruits of Scripture are for all, "And these things we write to you that your joy may be full" (1 John 1:4).

We must believe and act on the Word of God (1) because God possesses all authority; (2) because the Word of God proves itself to be from God, commending itself to our consciences with remarkable evidences; and (3) because there is a living internal, personal witness in our own hearts as we prayerfully commune with God through written Scripture. That witness is given by the Holy Spirit.

Paragraph 6: The Sufficiency of Scripture

Scripture contains the whole counsel of God which provides all things necessary for man's salvation, faith, and life. Some truths are expressly stated in commands and doctrines, while others are necessarily contained in principles, implications, and applications derived from them. Since this is the whole counsel of God, nothing need be added by new revelations of the Spirit or by the traditions of men, nor is it the will of God to add to Scripture. This paragraph qualifies the matter of adding to the Word of God by teaching that certain circumstances of the worship of God are common to human actions and societies and are ordered by the light of nature, Christian prudence, and the general rules of the Word of God.

God has given us a complete revelation. It is called the "whole counsel of God" in Acts 20:27. The Bible is sufficient to save us and nourish the life of faith in us. Nothing therefore need be added. Yet there are many things in which God wants us to use wisdom and discernment, applying the general principles of the Word to practical situations that the Word of God may not explicitly address.

Express teachings (which the Confession describes as "expressly set down") are God's Law: the Ten Commandments, all commands, testimonies, precepts, and wisdom found in the Proverbs, and Christian duties and other forms of direct teaching that are found in the gospels and epistles. Derived teachings (which the Confession calls "necessarily contained in the Holy Scripture") are principles, implications, and applications that derive from Scripture biography, the types and symbols of worship, parables, and other implications of gospel revelation and Christian doctrine. Together, these make up the whole counsel of God, which reminds us that "His divine power has given to us all things that *pertain* to life and godliness, through the knowledge of Him who called us by glory and virtue" (2 Pet. 1:3).

Notice that the two great issues mentioned are the glory of God and the salvation of man. God's glory is far more important than the needs of man. Yet God has shown mercy to man through saving grace.

When we speak of the sufficiency of the Bible, we mean that it is sufficient to accomplish God's purposes in the world, in the church, and in our lives. The Bible was not given to help people build bridges and buildings, to do lab experiments, or to sell real estate. It is certainly applicable in working out these and any other occupations. It is not a manual for biology, physics, history, or economics. But it is accurate and infallible whenever it touches on any of these areas, and applicable to any one of these disciplines. It will build a foundation for any discipline within which that area of study can and ought to move. From its teachings we have ethical principles for medicine, running a business, marital and sexual ethics, legal ethics, etc.

It is sufficient to direct sinners to Christ for salvation. It is sufficient to equip believers to live by faith: "The just shall live by faith" (Rom. 1:17). This is a benefit and a warning. Since the Bible contains everything that sinners and saints need for salvation, they must not add to the revelation that provides for them. The Confession speaks of two tendencies in history where additions to the Word of God are most prevalent.

The first is new revelations of the Spirit. We see how Paul dealt with this problem in 1 Corinthians 12–14. Church history evidences this tendency early in the second century through a teacher named Montanus, after whom the movement known as Montanism was named. This movement was directed against the coldness and spiritual apathy of the professing church. It championed the charismatic gifts and the continuing direct revelation of the Spirit through gifted men. It resisted systematic study of the Bible and emphasized experience more than knowledge. Tertullian was a defender of this position. It was the precursor of both the pietistic and Pentecostal movements in modern times.

Today we see some evangelicals emphasizing that there is continuing revelation of the Spirit. This, modern advocates assert, is through the still functional gift of prophecy (1 Cor. 12, 14). It is believed that someone may stand up in a church service and deliver a message from the Spirit of God. It may contain direction to the church or to an individual in the church. It may contain direct information relating to God's specific will and guidance for individuals or the church.[36]

This position undermines the authority of the Bible and denies its sufficiency. Do we need a prophet to speak to us "through the Spirit" to tell us when and where we should move our family, or what job to take? Do we need "a revelation of the Spirit" to indicate to us that we should go and talk to a person about an important matter? If the completed canon of Scripture is sufficient, then we do not. But how then does the Bible act as sufficient for faith and life? The answer is that as we search the Scriptures to discover its teachings and learn its principles, and as we live in the Spirit, we have God's guidance leading us to face every decision with *wisdom*. The Holy Spirit leads us through the written Word, sovereignly helping us to discern truth and wisdom and apply the truth to specific issues in life. As we prayerfully seek to be filled with the Spirit and the Word of God, we can live confidently in the guidance of God through the Word.

---

36. For a refutation, see O. Palmer Robertson, *The Final Word* (Edinburgh: Banner of Truth, 1993).

While the Spirit does not add new revelation, He does shed light on the written revelation. This is the doctrine of *illumination*. The main passage cited in the Confession reference is 1 Corinthians 2:9-12.

The illumination of the Word by the Spirit of God is "necessary for the saving understanding of such things as are revealed in His Word." This was one of the critical emphases of the Reformers who drew attention to the vital connection of the Word and the Spirit. The Holy Spirit illumines the Word of God. He speaks in and through the Word, and not apart from the Word. The Word can only be understood and obeyed with the aid of the Spirit. This aid comes in the form of enlightenment to the eyes of faith so that we can see the wonderful truths of God's Word. Paul prayed for this blessing to be the portion of the Ephesian Christians in Ephesians 1:15-19 and 3:14-21.

The Holy Spirit illuminates and applies the work of Christ to the believer. In John 7:38-39, Jesus compared the work of the Spirit to rivers of living water flowing from a person's innermost being. But this is only experienced by drinking of Christ. We drink of Christ and we are filled with the Spirit of Christ. We drink of Christ by beholding the Son and believing in Him (John 6:40).

In John 16:14, Jesus taught His disciples that the Holy Spirit would take the things of Christ and show those things to them. This means that the Spirit draws our attention to Christ. He shines the light of understanding upon Jesus. He has no work of His own detached from Christ.

When you study the Upper Room Discourse in John 14-16, you are reading the most important teaching on the Holy Spirit found in the New Testament. All other revelation in the New Testament is rooted in what Jesus said about the Spirit there. His main emphasis there was on the ministry of the Spirit in relation to the truth (the Bible), and to Himself (Jesus). In both of these ministries we see the Holy Spirit's work of illumination.

The mandate for the believer then is to "abide in Him" (1 John 2:27-28). John remembers the words of the Lord Jesus in the upper room (John 14-16) where Jesus emphasized that abiding in Him meant having His Word abide in us (John 15:7). The Spirit does this teaching through the Word.

We have already considered Paul's teaching in 1 Corinthians 2. But it is also applicable here. The inward illumination of the Spirit is not a mystical, personal (secret), ephemeral, communication of the Spirit. It is rational, using words (1 Cor. 2:13), and pervasively biblical, utilizing the completed canon of Scripture.

The second tendency is the addition of the traditions of men. Rome has added the doctrines of its councils, and the allegedly infallible decisions of the Pope to the pure teachings of the Word of God.

Reformation teachings, from which our Confession arose, combatted both of these tendencies, and so must we. We must be led by the Spirit (Rom. 8:14), be filled with the Spirit (Eph. 5:18), and walk in the Spirit (Gal. 5:16, 25). We must not grieve the Spirit (Eph. 4:30), nor quench the Spirit

(1 Thess. 5:19). But all these elements of the Spirit's working are, as the Confession says, "by and with the Word in our hearts" (Paragraph 5). We are forbidden to add to Scripture. And we are not to add to it in subtle ways, or by carelessly interpreting it or inappropriately applying it. We may also do this by being stricter than God and requiring things that He does not require in the Bible. The Pharisees are the clearest warning to us about adding to Scripture, as Jesus said in Matthew 15:1-14 and 23:1-36. They invalidated the Word of God by their traditions (Mark 7:5-13).

Finally, the Confession points out that there is a commonality in the church to human actions and societies in the area of the worship of the church. The passages cited are 1 Corinthians 11:13-14 and 1 Corinthians 14:26, 40. All things are to be done decently and in an orderly manner: "For God is not *the author* of confusion but of peace, as in all the churches of the saints" (1 Cor. 14:33). While the Bible gives us broad outlines and sufficiently describes the activities of the New Testament Church, it also leaves many things to the light of nature, Christian prudence or common Christian sense, and the general rules of the Word of God.

How do we distinguish between these two? First, we look at the central passages of the New Testament to find the regulative principles that govern our worship. We see how our worship is regulated by Acts 2:42 (teaching, which would include preaching, fellowship, the Lord's Supper, and corporate prayer), the pastoral epistles with their emphasis on sound doctrine and teaching, Ephesians 5:19 and Colossians 3:16 (singing), and evangelism. The New Testament reveals that the church exists for the proclamation and application of the Word of God in preaching, teaching, and counseling. Also, for public corporate worship of the gathered saints to hear the Word, shepherding the souls of God's people, corporate prayers, disciple baptism and the observance of the Lord's Supper, singing, and Christian fellowship.

The Confession says that there are many factors in the structuring of these requirements for worship that we must work out as God's people under appointed leadership. And what might those things be? They include times and frequency of public meetings, length of meetings, teaching sessions such as Sunday schools, nurseries, conducting of church business, structuring Christian fellowship, administration of church affairs and aspects of church polity necessitated by individual needs of a local church, follow-up of the people of God, details of evangelistic outreach, etc.

The Confession is not opening the door to the addition of elements in Christian worship that would usurp or detract from the New Testament elements. Churches must safeguard the elements that are revealed.

Paragraph 7: The Clarity of Scripture
This paragraph states that all Scripture is not equally plain and clear, while the things necessary for salvation are clear. The Bible clearly reveals those things that are necessary for salvation. The educated and the uneducated can attain to a sufficient understanding of those things in a

due use of ordinary means. They must, of course, receive the illuminating ministry of the Holy Spirit: "For it is the God who commanded light to shine out of darkness, who has shone in our hearts to *give* the light of the knowledge of the glory of God in the face of Jesus Christ" (2 Cor. 4:6).

In Paragraph 6 we learned that the inward illumination of the Spirit of God is necessary for the saving understanding of the things that are revealed in the Word. This paragraph is emphasizing human responsibility in Bible study. This is what it means to "seek the Lord." If we want to know God, we must seek for Him. And we seek him by "ordinary means," reading the Bible, interpreting its plain language, praying for light from the Holy Spirit, etc. When we do these things, the Bible will become clearer to us. You do not need to be a scholar to understand the Bible. Yet, scholars and teachers and pastors do help us by giving us the background of passages, and other relevant aids to help us understand and apply the truths of Scripture accurately. Men of God are commanded, "Be diligent to present yourself approved to God, a worker who does not need to be ashamed, rightly dividing the word of truth" (2 Tim. 2:15).

"The law of the LORD *is* perfect, converting the soul; The testimony of the LORD *is* sure, making wise the simple; The statutes of the LORD *are* right, rejoicing the heart; The commandment of the LORD *is* pure, enlightening the eyes; The fear of the LORD *is* clean, enduring forever; The judgments of the LORD *are* true *and* righteous altogether" (Ps. 19:7-9). "The entrance of Your words gives light; It gives understanding to the simple" (Ps. 119:130).

We cannot deny that there are many things in the Bible that are difficult to understand. The first indication comes from Peter as he speaks about Paul, "as also in all his epistles, speaking in them of these things, in which are some things hard to understand, which untaught and unstable *people* twist to their own destruction, as *they do* also the rest of the Scriptures" (2 Pet. 3:16). A second indication comes from Paul: "For the time will come when they will not endure sound doctrine, but according to their own desires, *because* they have itching ears, they will heap up for themselves teachers" (2 Tim. 4:3). Paul is speaking of people who cannot bear the teachings of the Word of God. Jesus encountered this kind of person – "This is a hard saying; who can understand it?" (John 6:60). The reason they cannot bear up under the teachings of the Word of God is because of their spiritual inability to work through the issues of Bible truth, history, and doctrine. And this is one of the reasons why the Bible is not equally plain in every place. One must study diligently, search, compare Scripture with Scripture, pray, listen, and learn.

Other indications that the Scriptures are not equally plain are found in some "hard sayings" of the Bible such as parables and difficult church issues with which the apostles dealt. It is evident that we need teachers who can help us to understand the historical background, the theology, and the practical implications of such passages.

God has provided for us the gift of pastors–teachers in the church to help us understand the Bible. God does reveal Himself to His children through His Word even without teachers. John says that in 1 John 2:20, 27. But this is only one side of the coin of learning revealed in the Bible. We need teachers. Ephesians 4:1-16 is an important passage for Christians to understand in this connection. It shows us how we are brought to strength, maturity, and conformity to Christ in the church. Verse 11 is the key. It says that God has given apostles, prophets, evangelists, and pastors and teachers to equip us in this way. Notice that each of these offices relates to the Word of God. Each one declares the Word of God to the people.

Paragraph 8: The Preservation of Scripture
The Bible is the product of divine inspiration. It has been providentially preserved by God through history. The Scriptures are therefore authentic. The Scriptures must therefore be translated into the languages of all the nations.

This paragraph explains how the Bible was written and preserved. It was written in the Hebrew and Greek language (and portions in Aramaic). It was wonderfully preserved by God's "singular care and providence," and "kept pure in all ages." This is a reference to the providence of God in the copying of manuscripts from the originals as they came from Him through His servants. This is a vast field of study and is there to emphasize the importance of translating the copies of the original Hebrew and Greek manuscripts into all the languages of man. The reason is that not all are able to read the original languages. They need Scripture in their own tongues.

Paragraph 9: The Interpretation of Scripture
The Bible is its own final interpreter. The statement found in the last two paragraphs are further applications of the section on the sufficiency of the Bible, which is found in Paragraph 6, and the clarity of the Bible in Paragraph 7. Since Scripture is sufficient and clear, it is the final authority. It speaks the final word in all controversies. And because of these things our faith is always "finally resolved."

The Bible is its own interpreter. This refers to a rule of interpretation that we must always apply in our reading and understanding of Scripture. How does the reader ultimately come to understand the precise meaning of a passage of Scripture? He applies rules of hermeneutics (the science of studying the Bible to find its meaning). But in the end, the only infallible rule of interpretation is Scripture itself. The Bible student must always search out and confirm his interpretation by the authority of other passages of Scripture and the overall teaching of Scripture.

Acts 15:15-16 is offered as proof of this. This passage reads: "With this the words of the prophets agree, just as it is written." And this is what Paragraph 9 is asserting. These words were written against the background of the Roman Catholic dogma that the church is the only infallible interpreter of Scripture and the final judge of the meaning of Scripture. This is heretical teaching. The Bible is the final interpreter and believers who possess the Holy Spirit can attain to the true meaning of the Scriptures. The Church of Rome, and any other religious body that asserts its indispensability for the interpretation of Scripture, is in error.

There is a difference between recognizing our need to be taught by good and faithful teachers and saying that the Scriptures cannot be understood apart from teaching. Interpreting Scripture is a serious work. We are entrusted with the Word of God, and we have a stewardship to interpret it correctly. We must not interpret it carelessly or incorrectly. We must take pains to understand the Bible. And this basic rule should always be the first tool that we use. Let Scripture be its own interpreter! Prove all interpretations by Scripture itself. Search the Scripture. Look to the clearer passages in the interpretation of the more difficult passages.

The Confession also states that the true and full sense of any Scripture is not manifold, but one. In the history of interpretation of the Bible the church developed allegorical interpretation where the Bible had a literal meaning and a spiritual or a hidden meaning. Farrar cites instances of the allegorical interpretations of the otherwise sound man of God, Augustine:

> In the narrative of the Fall the fig-leaves become hypocrisy, and the coats of skins mortality, and the four rivers of Eden the four cardinal virtues. In the story of the Deluge the Ark is pitched within and without with pitch to show the safety of the Church from inward and outward heresies.[37]

Snodgrass relates Augustine's interpretation of the parable of the Good Samaritan:

> A frequently cited and most revealing example of allegorizing is Augustine's interpretation of the parable of the Good Samaritan, in which virtually every item is given theological significance: the man is Adam; Jerusalem is the heavenly city; Jericho is the moon, which stands for our mortality; the robbers are the devil and his angels who stripped the man of his immortality and beat him by persuading him to sin; the priests and Levites are the priesthood and the ministry of the OT; the good Samaritan is Christ; the binding of the wounds is the restraint of sin; the oil and wine are the comfort of hope and the encouragement to work; the donkey is the incarnation; the Inn is the church; the next day is after the resurrection of Christ; the innkeeper is the apostle Paul; and the two denarii are the two commandments of love or the promise of this life and that which is to come.[38]

This is that to which the Confession is referring when it states that the true and full sense of any Scripture is not manifold, but one. We find the meaning of Scripture using the Reformation guidelines which brought

---

37. Frederic W. Farrar, *History of Interpretation* (New York: E. P. Dutton, 1886), 238.
38. Klyne R. Snodgrass, *Stories with Intent* (Grand Rapids: Eerdmans, 2008), 4.

such needed clarity to hermeneutics: the *historical, grammatical,* and *theological* interpretation of Scripture.[39]

Paragraph 10: The Supremacy of Scripture in Controversy
The Bible is the supreme judge of all controversies and final resolution of our faith. The second line of thought relates to controversies of religion, opinions, and decrees of councils and private men. This paragraph asserts that in all such cases, the Bible has final authority.

This does not mean that opinions and decrees, statements, and creeds are wrong in themselves. There is a legitimate place for decrees of councils, opinions of ancient writers, doctrines of men, and individuals. But these decrees and expressions of faith must be tested, supported, and approved by the final authority, the Bible.

The council at Jerusalem, recorded in Acts 15, is a perfect example of what this final paragraph is dealing with. There was a controversy regarding the faith, so a meeting of the elders was called. The controversy was explained and dealt with. Men spoke and gave their opinions. But the final resolution to the problem came as the Scriptures were brought to bear on the question.

The Confession itself is a good example of this. In this exposition of Chapter 1, and the expositions which follow, we are examining and explaining the Confession to show that the Confession represents the teachings of Scripture. Specific passages have been considered in a fuller way, others in a passing reference. But in each case, we have seen that the statements of the Confession represent the teaching of the Word of God. Our Confession is a means of Bible study, interpretation, personal confession of faith, and a standard by which to judge truth from error. It is a necessary means for us to use in the building of the church of Jesus Christ. But always and only as it faithfully declares what the final authority of our faith, the Bible, declares.

---

39. See Bernard Ramm, *Protestant Biblical Interpretation,* 3rd ed. (Grand Rapids: Baker, 1970).

CHAPTER 2

OF GOD AND THE HOLY TRINITY

SAM WALDRON

1. The Lord our God is but one only living and true God;[1] whose subsistence is in and of himself,[2] infinite in being and perfection; whose essence cannot be comprehended by any but himself;[3] a most pure spirit,[4] invisible, without body, parts, or passions, who only hath immortality, dwelling in the light which no man can approach unto;[5] who is immutable,[6] immense,[7] eternal,[8] incomprehensible, almighty,[9] every way infinite, most holy,[10] most wise, most free, most absolute; working all things according to the counsel of his own immutable and most righteous will[11] for his own glory;[12] most loving, gracious, merciful, long-suffering, abundant in goodness and truth, forgiving iniquity, transgression, and sin; the rewarder of them that diligently seek him,[13] and withal most just and terrible in his judgments,[14] hating all sin,[15] and who will by no means clear the guilty.[16]

---

1. 1 Corinthians 8:4, 6; Deuteronomy 6:4
2. Jeremiah 10:10; Isaiah 48:12
3. Exodus 3:14
4. John 4:24
5. 1 Timothy 1:17; Deuteronomy 4:15, 16
6. Malachi 3:6
7. 1 Kings 8:27; Jeremiah 23:23
8. Psalms 90:2
9. Genesis 17:1
10. Isaiah 6:3
11. Psalms 115:3; Isaiah 46:10
12. Proverbs 16:4; Romans 11:36
13. Exodus 34:6, 7; Hebrews 11:6
14. Nehemiah 9:32, 33
15. Psalms 5:5, 6
16. Exodus 34:7; Nahum 1:2, 3

2. God, having all life,[17] glory,[18] goodness,[19] blessedness, in and of himself, is alone in and unto himself all-sufficient, not standing in need of any creature which he hath made, nor deriving any glory from them,[20] but only manifesting his own glory in, by, unto, and upon them; he is the alone fountain of all being, of whom, through whom, and to whom are all things,[21] and he hath most sovereign dominion over all creatures, to do by them, for them, or upon them, whatsoever himself pleaseth;[22] in his sight all things are open and manifest,[23] his knowledge is infinite, infallible, and independent upon the creature, so as nothing is to him contingent or uncertain;[24] he is most holy in all his counsels, in all his works,[25] and in all his commands; to him is due from angels and men, whatsoever worship,[26] service, or obedience, as creatures they owe unto the Creator, and whatever he is further pleased to require of them.

3. In this divine and infinite Being there are three subsistences, the Father, the Word or Son, and Holy Spirit,[27] of one substance, power, and eternity, each having the whole divine essence, yet the essence undivided:[28] the Father is of none, neither begotten nor proceeding; the Son is eternally begotten of the Father;[29] the Holy Spirit proceeding from the Father and the Son;[30] all infinite, without beginning, therefore but one God, who is not to be divided in nature and being, but distinguished by several peculiar relative properties and personal relations; which doctrine of the Trinity is the foundation of all our communion with God, and comfortable dependence on him.

Introduction

Nothing is more challenging in all of theology than theology proper—or, the doctrine of God. Here we come as finite beings face to face with the Infinite. What could be more intellectually challenging? In no other area of theology are we forced to grapple so continually with the Infinite. In the doctrines of the Word, Man, or Church we are at least dealing with matters that are related to humanity, but in this it is the infinite God about whom we attempt to speak and confess our faith. The doctrine of

---

17. John 5:26
18. Psalms 148:13
19. Psalms 119:68
20. Job 22:2, 3
21. Romans 11:34-36
22. Daniel 4:25, 34, 35
23. Hebrews 4:13
24. Ezekiel 11:5; Acts 15:18
25. Psalms 145:17
26. Revelation 5:12-14
27. 1 John 5:7; Matthew 28:19; 2 Corinthians 13:14
28. Exodus 3:14; John 14:11; 1 Corinthians 8:6
29. John 1:14, 18
30. John 15:26; Galatians 4:6

God above all is a call to a deep sense of our intellectual and spiritual insufficiency. As we study this chapter, our souls should humbly cry out again and again, "Who is sufficient for these things?" (2 Cor. 2:16).

Certainly, the only safe course is to stay very close to the Word of God. Our only sure knowledge of God is gained from what the inscrutable and mysterious God has told us about Himself. God is too great for us to trust our own hearts to devise the truth about Him (Rom. 11:33-36). We must not indulge in rational speculation or personal opinion. A sense of our insufficiency must turn our souls to the Word of God in humble reverence as the only safe guide for our understanding of God.

The Classical Connections of the Chapter
This chapter states the orthodox doctrine of God and the Holy Trinity. It asserts, in other words, classical Christian theism. It identifies itself with the historic doctrine of the church on the subject of God and the Holy Trinity, as formulated in the Nicene Creed. It distances itself from every form of anti-trinitarianism. On the other hand, it so describes the attributes of God and His relations to the creatures as to anticipate the Reformed emphasis on the sovereignty of God in Chapter 3.

There are minor deviations from the Westminster Confession in each of the three paragraphs, but none bring the 1689 into any doctrinal conflict with the teaching of Westminster. The most significant alterations are found in Paragraph 3 on the Trinity. When we come to that paragraph, we will see that those alterations have the character of expansion and clarification and never of disagreement. Again, the 1689 Baptist Confession is in fundamental and pervasive agreement with the Westminster Confession and Savoy Declaration. All three teach classical Christian theism in unison.

In these paragraphs there is a wonderful, balanced, and practical presentation of the character or attributes of God. The religion of our day needs more of contemplating God and living with the conscious reality that this is the God with whom we have to do.

1. The attributes of God
An examination of Paragraph 1 shows that no effort has been made to classify the attributes of God into communicable and incommunicable attributes.[31] Still, while no particular method of classification is given

---

31. Frequently, theologians divide the attributes into those that are communicable and those which are incommunicable. Communicable attributes are those in some degree communicated to creatures. This refers to attributes like love, goodness, wisdom, and justice. Incommunicable attributes are those which are not communicated in any way to creatures. This refers to attributes like simplicity, eternity, or aseity. Though this classification is common in Reformed treatments of theology proper, it is by no means universal. Richard Muller contradicts the popular notion that it is the dominant or classic way of classifying the divine attributes. Muller comments on the distinction between communicable and incommunicable attributes. He resists the notion that this distinction is dominant in Reformed theology: "There is, of course, the well-known distinction, somewhat mistakenly viewed by Heppe and others as the dominant model from early on in the development of Reformed orthodoxy" [Richard Muller, *Post-Reformation Reformed*

confessional status, it is true that similar characteristics are dealt with together in this paragraph.

This last thought suggests the importance of an analysis of paragraph 1. At first, indeed, the attributes appear to be simply listed in no particular order. On closer inspection, however, the listing of attributes divides itself into eight sections.[32] This division brings some help in analyzing the seemingly random listing of attributes. I have taken the liberty to label each section as seemed most appropriate to me.

- **Singularity**: *The Lord our God is but one only living and true God;*
- **Aseity**: *whose subsistence is in and of himself, infinite in being and perfection;*
- **Incomprehensibility**: *whose essence cannot be comprehended by any but himself;*
- **Simplicity**: *a most pure spirit, invisible, without body, parts, or passions, who only hath immortality, dwelling in the light which no man can approach unto;*
- **Infinity**: *who is immutable, immense, eternal, incomprehensible, almighty, every way infinite, most holy, most wise, most free, most absolute;*
- **Sovereignty**: *working all things according to the counsel of his own immutable and most righteous will for his own glory;*
- **Love**: *most loving, gracious, merciful, long-suffering, abundant in goodness and truth, forgiving iniquity, transgression, and sin;*
- **Justice**: *the rewarder of them that diligently seek him, and withal most just and terrible in his judgments, hating all sin, and who will by no means clear the guilty.*

Space does not permit the exposition of each of these attributes. Thankfully, biblically faithful treatments of each of them are available.[33] In this chapter, I will simply provide brief explanations of the first four attributes in my outline: singularity, aseity, incomprehensibility, and simplicity.

The unit which I have attempted to summarize as treating *simplicity* also includes impassibility. The way in which the Confession connects these attributes is instructive, suggesting a close relationship between

---

Dogmatics (Grand Rapids: Baker Academic, 2003), 3:216]. Muller's perspective and the confessional approach allows freedom in the method used for the classification of the attributes.

32. Long ago someone suggested to me that paying attention to the punctuation of the Confession may provide insight into its construction. I think this observation is of help here and especially if we pay attention to the semicolons found in Paragraph 1. It must be noted, however, that the punctuation in the facsimile of the 1677 which I possess [published by B&R Press, Auburn MA] in 2000 does not contain the same exact punctuation as the version of the 1689 which I am using [*The Baptist Confession of Faith & The Baptist Catechism* with a foreword by James Renihan published jointly by Solid Ground Christian Books (Birmingham, AL) and Reformed Baptist Publications (Carlisle, PA)] in 2010].

33. Stephen Charnock's *Existence and Attributes of God* comes immediately to mind (Grand Rapids: Baker Book House, 1979).

them. Interestingly, it is these attributes which are most discussed with regard to classical Christian theism today. I will, therefore, focus the attention of my exposition of this paragraph on these closely related attributes.

Singularity: *The Lord our God is but one only living and true God;*

Strictly speaking, the confessional assertion that God is "one" asserts the unity of singularity. The later assertion that God is "without parts" asserts the unity of simplicity. The unity of singularity and unity of simplicity are distinguished by Bavinck.[34] The two kinds of oneness, of course, imply one another. They point, however, to different aspects of the divine glory. The unity of singularity or oneness refers to the fact that there is only one God, a frequent assertion of both the Old and New Testaments. The confessional prooftexts are 1 Corinthians 8:4, 6 and Deuteronomy 6:4.

The singularity of God is practically valuable in manifold respects. It means that the one God is to be worshiped only and that He is to be loved supremely. Furthermore, it means that in constructing the doctrine of the Trinity this oneness of God must not be compromised. The attributes must not be sub-divided between the different persons. Each of the attributes of God as well as the whole, divine essence must be affirmed of each of the divine persons. The singularity of God practically controls our daily living, religious worshiping, and our doctrinal thinking.

Aseity: *whose subsistence is in and of himself, infinite in being and perfection;*

Aseity literally means that God is *a se*. The Latin means "from Himself." Synonyms are self-existence or absolute independence. Other synonyms might be self-sufficiency, self-containment, and absolute-ness. Aseity might lead one to think that God is self-caused. This, however, is not implied. It is misleading to speak of God as self-caused because, strictly speaking, God has no cause at all. He simply "is" in splendor and glory from all eternity.

The foundation for the divine aseity is laid in the personal name of God, Yahweh (Exod. 3:14). In that name ("I am that I am") the unchanging faithfulness and constancy of God in His covenant commitments is implied. He is "from-within-determined"[35] and, therefore, self-existent or independent. If God is absolutely immutable in His being, the implication must be that He was never brought into existence by another. Thus, He is self-existent and independent. Key passages which assert the divine self-existence are:

Isaiah 48:12: "Listen to Me, O Jacob, And Israel, My called: I am He, I am the First, I am also the Last."

---

34. Bavinck, *Reformed Dogmatics*, 2:173, remarks: "The oneness of God does not only consist in a unity of singularity, however, but also in a unity of simplicity."

35. This is the terminology of Geerhardus Vos, *Biblical Theology* (Grand Rapids: Wm. B. Eerdmans, 1948), 134.

Jeremiah 10:10: "But the LORD is the true God; He is the living God and the everlasting King. At His wrath the earth will tremble, And the nations will not be able to endure His indignation."

John 5:26: "For as the Father has life in Himself, so He has granted the Son to have life in Himself."

Acts 17:25: "Nor is He served by human hands, as though He needed anything, since He Himself gives to all people life and breath and all things."

Rich, indeed, are the practical implications of the divine aseity. We must never sully the divine glory by assuming in our preaching, practice, or thinking that God is in need of us. We need everything from Him. He needs nothing from us. Thus, we must never doubt the resources of God to help us. No situation is beyond the reach or resources of the self-sufficient God. The glory of such a self-existent God should entrance us, summon us to worship, and encourage us to seek life from Him in the most deadly of circumstances.

Incomprehensibility: *whose essence cannot be comprehended by any but himself;*

The scriptural evidence for divine incomprehensibility is vast and comes to us in several, distinct categories. The name of God is incomprehensible (Gen. 32:29; Judg. 13:18; Prov. 30:4; Exod. 3:13, 14). The nature of God is incomprehensible (Job 11:7; 36:26; Pss. 139:6; 145:3; Isa. 40:12). The works of God are incomprehensible in creation (Job 5:9; 26:14; 37:5); in judgment (Ps. 90:11); and in redemption (Rom. 11:33; Eph. 3:8, 19-21; Phil. 4:7). Finally, the invisibility of God (1 Tim. 6:16), the holiness of God (Ex. 15:11), and the incomparability of God (Isa. 40:18, 25; 46:5) each require His incomprehensibility.

Divine revelation even in the Son, while providing us a personal, true, accurate, and comforting sense of God and who God is and what His purposes are, does not serve to remove completely our awe and ignorance of the divine majesty. Divine incomprehensibility means that, though we have a personal, true, accurate, and comforting knowledge of God as Christians, we do not and cannot have an exhaustive knowledge of Him that removes an awesome sense of vast and eternal mystery. Have you lost your sense of the divine incomprehensibility? If you think you have a God that you fully can understand or predict beyond what He promises in His Word, your God is not the biblical God! We must stand in awe of the incomprehensible God and never doubt His promises no matter how mysterious His ways.

Simplicity: *a most pure spirit, invisible, without body, parts, or passions, who only hath immortality, dwelling in the light which no man can approach unto;*

Though the 1689 Baptist Confession does not use the words "simple" or "simplicity," it does articulate the doctrine of simplicity when it asserts that God is "one" and "without parts."[36]

From one standpoint simplicity is an implication of aseity. If God is self-existent, immutable, and eternal, then He is not "composed." This is the fundamental meaning of simplicity in classical theology. It asserts that God is not the product of composition.[37] God is not composed of pre-existing things, nor the product of the combination of these entities. He is self-existent. His divine being is not the result of the combination of any pre-existing factors. Were this so, then those pre-existing factors would be more ultimate than God! The idea is unthinkable. Everything in God is God. Nothing that is God can be subtracted from God, and God still be God.

However, as understood in classical Christian theism, the divine simplicity does not mean that God is without distinctions. The assertion that God is not composed is not, and never has been, in this tradition a denial of the doctrine of the Trinity. God is not *composed* of the persons of the Trinity. The persons of the Godhead may (and must!) be distinguished, but they cannot be separated. The assertion that God is not composed also is not opposed to the distinctions between the different attributes of God that this entire discussion presupposes.[38]

On the whole issue of the relation between the attributes and the essence of God and the relation between the different attributes, two extreme positions have been taken that must be avoided. On the one extreme, there is the view that sees the attributes of God as different things which together compose God. This is a direct denial of the simplicity of God. On the other extreme, there is the view that the attributes are simply different names for the same thing. This is a mistaken understanding of the doctrine of divine simplicity. Charles Hodge remarks:

> In attempting to explain the relation in which the attributes of God stand to his essence and to each other, there are two extremes to be avoided. First, we must not represent God as a composite being, composed of different elements; and secondly, we must not confound the attributes, making them all mean the same thing, which is equivalent to denying them all together.[39]

The easiest way to present this point is to look at the biblical passages which are most often brought forward on this matter and consider them: "God is spirit" (John 4:24); "God is light" (1 John 1:5); "God is love" (1 John

---

36. *The Belgic Confession*, Article 1, does assert divine simplicity explicitly.

37. John Frame, *The Doctrine of God* (Phillipsburg: P&R Publishing, 2002), 225, remarks: "To say that God is simple, in scholastic philosophy, is to say that there is no composition in his being." Richard Muller, *Post-Reformation Reformed Dogmatics*, makes this same point again and again as over against modern writers who have misinterpreted its purport and understood to imply that God is without distinctions, 3:38-45.

38. John Frame, *The Doctrine of God*, 228, sees the attributes of God as different perspectives on His essence.

39. Charles Hodge, *Systematic Theology*, 1:369. cf. Bavinck, *Reformed Dogmatics*, 2:118, 224.

4:8, 16). In the first place, it is clear that we have here three descriptions of the divine essence—"God *is*..." Thus, we learn that the attributes of God are ways of describing the essence of God and inseparable from that essence. Hence, it follows that we know the essence of God and not merely the attributes of God. A distinction between attributes and essence is not biblical. In the second place, it is clear that we have here three distinct qualities or attributes of God: spirit, light, and love. We must maintain that spirit, light, and love do not all mean the same thing. The Bible intends to attribute different qualities to God in each of these contexts. Thus, though all these describe one and the same essence of God, and though these attributes do not *combine* and together *compose* the divine essence, yet these attributes are not mere names for the same thing, but they describe different qualities of the divine essence.

In a sense, of course, this does not solve the mystery of the relation of the essence and the attributes. It simply describes the problem and the boundaries that must be maintained in any solution of the problem. The attributes are all descriptions of the simple essence of God. Yet these attributes and descriptions are distinct and do not all mean the same thing.

It is vitally important in the discussion of simplicity to keep in mind that this attribute is not contrary to the assertion of distinctions in God. Too often those who suppose themselves advocates of this doctrine have drawn facile deductions from it which Scripture does not support. Below we will discuss one such unnecessary deduction with regard to the distinction between the persons of the Trinity. Here we may also mention that divine simplicity is not contrary to the clear and vital biblical distinction between the decretive (secret) and preceptive (revealed) will of God. We must maintain that God's will is simple, but this does not mean that vital distinctions in this simple will must not be made. It is wrong to conclude from divine simplicity that there are no such distinctions. It is also wrong to turn divine simplicity against the free offer of the gospel which is also taught in the 1689 Baptist Confession (cf. Chapter 7, paragraph 2).

Closely related to simplicity is the attribute of the impassibility of God.[40] Impassibility is not commonly, specifically, or formally treated as a divine attribute in the Reformed tradition. Muller remarks: "It is worth noting here that the Reformed orthodox theologians do not typically argue 'impassibility' as an attribute."[41] Muller follows this with an impressive list of Reformed theologians whose treatment of the issue supports his assertion and makes clear that the pivotal issue was immutability—not impassibility. He admits, however, that these theologians "are quite adamant in stating that God has no *passiones*," but argues that their predilection for ascribing the attribute of immutability rather than an attribute of impassibility shows their distance from a Stoic notion of

---

40. For a helpful treatment of this subject, the Editor points you to *Reformed Systematic Theology: Revelation and God, Vol. 1*, Beeke and Smalley, Crossway, 829-51.

41. Muller, *Post-Reformation Reformed Dogmatics*, 3:309.

divine *apatheia*.[42] He says: "Impassibility when attributed to God in the Christian tradition and, specifically, in medieval and Protestant scholastic thought, indicates, not a Stoic notion of *apatheia*, but an absence of mutation, distress, or any other sort of negative *passiones*."[43] Also, relevant in this connection are the wise words of Herman Bavinck: "Immutability…should not be confused with monotonous sameness or rigid immobility."[44]

The doctrine of impassibility finds its classic, confessional affirmation in the statement of the Second London Baptist Confession (which echoes the Irish Articles, the Thirty-Nine Articles of the Church of England, the Westminster Confession, and the Savoy Declaration) that God is without "body, parts, or *passions*." The assertion is clear enough. What is not so clear to many is exactly what the Confession means to imply when it says that God is *without passions*. The word, passions, in both its older and more recent English usages, has a variety of meanings.

Several comments will clarify its meaning here. First, we must not forget that the English word derives from a Latin word that means suffering. Most basically it means that God does not suffer. Second, this statement is associated with the assertion that God is without body and parts. This relates the assertion to the doctrine of the divine simplicity. Third, in classical Christian theology the assertion of impassibility meant that God was not subject to created influences. He acted, but He was never acted upon. Thus, Muller argues that Reformed Scholasticism accepted the idea of divine affections, while at the same time rejecting the concept of divine passions. The distinction between the two words, affection and passion, was important.

Since a passion has its foundation or origin *ad extra* and its terminus *ad intra*, it cannot be predicated of God and, in fact, fails to correspond in its dynamic with the way God knows. An affection or virtue, by way of contrast, has its foundation or source *ad intra* and terminates *ad extra*, corresponding with the pattern of operation of the divine communicable attributes and, in particular, with the manner of the divine knowing. This understanding of affections and passions corresponds, moreover, with the etymology of the terms: an *af-* or *ad-fectio*, to exert an influence on something—in other words, an influence directed toward, not a result from, something; whereas *passio*, from *patior*, is a suffering or enduring of something—it can refer to an occurrence or a phenomenon and even to a disease.[45]

---

42. Ibid., 3:309-10.

43. Ibid., 3:310.

44. Bavinck, *Reformed Dogmatics*, 2:158.

45. Muller, *Post-Reformation Reformed Dogmatics,* 3:554. It needs to be said that there is disagreement among Reformed theologians about whether God may be said properly to have affections. If the word is defined carefully as Muller does here, I believe that it is helpful to use the term, affections, to describes the moral or relational perfections of God. Some prefer simply to call these "affections" perfections, but I do not think that this adequately communicates the divine attributes of love, goodness, and justice to our generation. Aseity, simplicity, and infinity are also divine perfections, but love is a different

What is Muller saying? He is saying that passions and affections may be contrasted in a way that allows us to say that God has affections but does not have passions. Passions arise outside of us from an outside influence (*ad extra*) but affect us on the inside. Affections are different. They arise from the inside of us (*ad intra*) and have effects on the outside. Distinguished in this way, it is appropriate to say that God has affections but does not have passions.

Muller, therefore, concludes that modern writers have misrepresented classical Reformed dogmatics when they assert that it was so caught up with the idea of God as unmoved mover that they did not pay sufficient attention to God's relation to the world.[46] Muller shows that the Reformed dogmaticians certainly paid a great deal of attention to the subject of God's relation to the world.

I will argue that we must affirm the doctrine of divine impassibility as defined above. To do so, however, we must also affirm a clear doctrine of divine relationality. As noted above, divine impassibility does not mean that God sustains no relation to or action in the world. Though God does not experience emotional changes because of the world, He does have unchanging affections with regard to things in the world and acts in the world on the basis of those unchanging affections.

Where biblical statements ascribe affections or passions to God inconsistent with such immutability, those statements must be qualified in terms of the clear biblical statements regarding divine immutability and interpreted anthropopathically. Nevertheless, such virtues, perfections, or *affections* as goodness, righteousness, and love really do exist in God when properly defined, and thus also may be used to describe the *ad extra* works of God in the world.

Jurgen Moltmann and others today have made suffering essential to God and the idea of a crucified God essential to their doctrine of God.[47] This view forgets the anthropopathic and anthropomorphic character of all of Scripture. It also confuses the divine and human natures of the Christ. True, the Son of God in His human nature suffers, is influenced by the actions of others, and even is wracked by overwhelming emotions like fear (though never to the point of sinning). This human nature is, however, different from His divine nature in regard to suffering and passions.

---

kind of divine perfection for which, I think, we need a name like affections.

46. Muller, *Post-Reformation Reformed Dogmatics*, 3:560: "This understanding of the divine affections as movements or attractions in some sense defined by their external object is a significant element of the Reformed orthodox system, both in terms of the implications of the concept for the orthodox theology as a whole and in view of the frequently heard claim that the older theology was so caught up in the Aristotelian conceptuality of God as Unmoved Mover that it paid scant attention to the biblical language of God in relation to his world. Quite to the contrary, the orthodox doctrine of the divine essence presses out into the rest of the theological system with the assumption of attributes requiring external objects and capable of being understood only insofar as they are relations ad extra."

47. Frame, *The Doctrine of God*, 611-15.

The apparent, biblical evidence for the divine passibility can be presented in a way that seems very impressive. It is necessary, therefore, to offer clear, scriptural proof for the impassibility of God. Thankfully, the considerations which require the doctrine of divine impassibility are clear and persuasive.

The first such consideration is this. Impassibility is a necessary inference from the related and commonly acknowledged attributes of God. I refer to the attributes of divine immutability, eternity, and simplicity.

The second such consideration is the direct, scriptural assertions of divine impassibility. This is probably the more important or compelling argument for most Christians. I want to focus attention here on Elihu's words to Job found in Job 35:4-8:

> I will answer you, And your companions with you. Look to the heavens and see; And behold the clouds—They are higher than you. If you sin, what do you accomplish against Him? Or, if your transgressions are multiplied, what do you do to Him? If you are righteous, what do you give Him? Or what does He receive from your hand? Your wickedness affects a man such as you, And your righteousness a son of man.

What shall we think of Elihu's words to Job? This question must be answered before we can decide how we should apply his words to ourselves. Why? Job's three other friends are the reason. Though there are elements of truth in their speeches, God condemned them for not speaking what was right about him (Job 42:7). Why, then, should we think of Elihu as divinely inspired in what he says? There are many reasons:

- The difference between Elihu and Job's three friends is emphasized (Job 32:1). Thus, very significantly, he is not rebuked by or included in the displeasure of God mentioned in Job 42:7-9.
- The motivation of Elihu's speech (his anger) was righteous. It was motivated by a jealous anger for the glory of God (Job 32:2-3). It was restrained by a sense of what was fitting and proper (Job 32:4).
- The timing of Elihu's speech was humble and discreet (Job 32:4, 6).
- The placement of Elihu's speech is significant and suggestive. His speech precedes the appearance of God and leads into it (Job 37:21-38:1). Elihu is the forerunner of God in Job, as John the Baptist was the forerunner of the Son of God in the New Testament.
- The content of Elihu's speech is distinct both from that of Job and that of Job's three friends and God-glorifying.
- Elihu claims arguably to be inspired (Job 32:8; 33:2-4). If he is not, then Elihu is not just a little wrong, he is a false prophet.
- The substance of Elihu's speech is not allowed to be answered (Job 33:5; 38:1). No response is made to him by Job or his three friends, and no criticism is offered by God. What follows is the appearance and speech of God Himself.

For all these reasons we must take Elihu's words as true and inspired.

What does Elihu say? He says that God is not and cannot be moved by self-interest to pervert justice. God has no needs which could be used to tempt Him to do evil. In making this point Elihu teaches that God is perfectly impervious to human influences. Just as the clouds are unchanged by human sin or righteousness, so God is unchanged and above being hurt or helped by our worst sins or our best deeds. This means that, as defined above, He is impassible. Job 35:4-8 teaches that God does not have passions in the sense that He is influenced by creation. He is not hurt or helped, harmed or strengthened, by anything men do. God is eternally blessed and happy in the Trinity of His persons. He does not need men. He has never needed men.

Does the Bible confirm Elihu's assertions? Yes, the Bible is full of texts that speak of God's infinite greatness as compared to creation. Psalm 90:1-2 reflects on the infinite difference between God and men: "Lord, You have been our dwelling place in all generations. Before the mountains were brought forth, Or ever You had formed the earth and the world, Even from everlasting to everlasting, You *are* God." Though Psalm 90 reflects on God's anger against the sins of men, it is clear that this anger is not aroused by any danger in which man's sin places God. Other texts explicitly reflect on the insignificance of men in relation to God's greatness and directly imply the divine impassibility:

Isaiah 40:15: "Behold, the nations are as a drop in a bucket, And are counted as the small dust on the scales; Look, He lifts up the isles as a very little thing."

Job 37:23: "As for the Almighty, we cannot find Him; He is excellent in power, In judgment and abundant justice; He does not oppress."

Job 40:4: "Behold, I am vile; What shall I answer You?"

For these reasons we must affirm the classical doctrine of divine impassibility. Several practical results of this doctrine must here be underscored.

There is instruction. Often when we speak of passions, we mean passions in the sense of uncontrollable emotions. Those emotions are so strong, violent, and uncontrollable because men have needs for which they need others to satisfy them. Think about it. God has no such needs! He is never tempted to become wrongly emotional out of a sense of personal need.

There is qualification. Does impassibility mean that God is apathetic and unconcerned about human affairs? No, the Bible is clear that God is very concerned about human affairs. It teaches that God has strong feelings about human affairs. But these strong feelings do not arise out of personal need. He can be neither hurt nor helped, harmed nor benefitted, by the world He has freely chosen to create. He did not need to create that world. He has freely chosen to care and intervene in human affairs.

He moves into the world in wrath and grace out of His own will and not because He is forced to by His creatures.

There is distinction. When Job 35:4-8 is compared with passages that speak of God's strong emotions and reactions to human events, some distinction is required. Some contemporary theologians believe that God's divine attributes must be supplemented by covenantal properties which He takes to Himself in order to have dealings with His creatures. Such distinctions create enormous theological problems with regard to divine simplicity. The Reformed tradition has addressed these difficulties with a hermeneutical distinction between more literal statements about God like we have in Job 35 and anthropopathic assertions about God in other places.

There is consolation. There is something wonderfully consoling in the fact that our great God who loves us so much has always been eternally blessed in the heavens and not in need of human praise or help or righteousness. It is wonderful to know that His electing love cannot change and is not affected by anything in us or about us.

There is communication. How are we to speak of God with regard to this subject?

- Some have wished to go no further than ascribing *perfections* to God. But this falls short of Scripture. Our contemporaries want to know more than if God has *perfections*. They want to know if God is personal and relational—if He has "feelings."
- The common ascription of *virtues* to God comes closer to expressing the teaching of the Bible, but still falls short of answering the question of our contemporaries. They want to know if God is such a one as I can relate to. They want to know if God cares. This is why simply denying that God has passions or emotions is liable to misrepresent God and ourselves to them.
- Perhaps the best word to use to communicate the truth to our contemporaries is *affections*. Affections when applied to God must be understood as originating *ad intra* (in God) and being expressed *ad extra*. The word, affection, asserts something about God's personal and relational character that is important to convey to our culture. We must not speak of God as having *passions*. The theological meaning of this word forbids it. Should we say that God has *emotions*? To be emotional suggests being subject to mood swings or emotional changes. God is certainly not emotional in this sense. The key issue is not to deny divine affections or something about God that may suggest to us emotion. It is rather to deny that God is subject to *emotional changes*.

2. The Relations of God (To His Creatures)

In the outline of this second chapter I have described this paragraph as speaking of the relations of God to His creatures. A word of explanation seems necessary with regard to the relation of the first and second paragraphs. When they are compared, paragraph 1 focuses on the attributes of God in Himself. The second paragraph focuses on the relations of God to His creatures in light of those attributes. The distinction is not perfect. It is not as if the first paragraph says nothing about His relations to the creature. This is why I have spoken of the *focus* of the two paragraphs.

The focus of paragraph 2 serves to clarify and crystallize the meaning and significance of the attributes listed in paragraph 1. Our generation needs to have our relations to the God described in paragraph 1 emphasized and specified. A brief word is necessary about each of the five sections of this paragraph which I divide as follows:

A. His Self-Sufficient Independence from Them
2. God, having all life, glory, goodness, blessedness, in and of himself, is alone in and unto himself all-sufficient, not standing in need of any creature which he hath made, nor deriving any glory from them, but only manifesting his own glory in, by, unto, and upon them;

As we have seen, God is simple and impassible. He needs nothing from us. He fears nothing from us. He is in no way dependent upon us. He may choose to manifest His glory in us, but not because He needs our love, fellowship, or support.

B. His Sovereign Dominion over Them
he is the alone fountain of all being, of whom, through whom, and to whom are all things, and he hath most sovereign dominion over all creatures, to do by them, for them, or upon them, whatsoever himself pleaseth;

Since God is the Creator, He is the "Lord, God Most High, the Possessor of heaven and earth" (Gen. 14:19, 22). All of creation absolutely belongs to Him. He has the right to dispose of His own possessions as He sees fit.

C. His Absolute Knowledge of Them
in his sight all things are open and manifest, his knowledge is infinite, infallible, and independent upon the creature, so as nothing is to him contingent or uncertain;

As opposed to the opinions of Open Theism, God knows absolutely everything. This includes complete knowledge of the future. As the Confession affirms, His knowledge is not dependent on the creature. It does not depend on what man chooses to do in the future. Nor is it in any way contingent or uncertain. His eternal decree determines the future. Thus, knowing Himself and His decree, His knowledge is infinite.

D. His Utter Sanctity before Them
he is most holy in all his counsels, in all his works, and in all his commands;

Modern man presumes to stand in judgment of God. He even assumes the right to be angry with Him for His deeds. What blasphemy! Yahweh is utterly separate and above all such presumption on the part of the creature to stand in judgment of His counsels, works, and commands. We are to stand in reverential fear of Him even when His ways mystify our minds and disappoint our desires.

E. His Intrinsic Claims upon Them
to him is due from angels and men, whatsoever worship, service, or obedience, as creatures they owe unto the Creator, and whatever he is further pleased to require of them.

Thus, finally, God is absolutely due anything He may choose to ask of us by way of service, suffering, or devotion. His essential right to the submission of men and angels is absolute.

3. The Tri-unity of God
Paragraph 3 is interesting because it combines statements from the First London Baptist Confession and the Westminster Confession. It thus provides a more detailed and emphatic (though not a doctrinally different) statement of the Trinity than any of them. Perhaps the tendency of the General Baptists and others in England during the seventeenth century (so-called because of their Arminianism and specifically because of their belief in a general atonement) was to fall into the heresy of Unitarianism that such detail seemed important to the authors.

This doctrine of the Trinity is a divine mystery. It is a misconception of the creeds of the church generally and of the Nicene Creed specifically (which is summarized in this paragraph of the Confession) to think that they were intended to explain this mystery. Historically, the opposite was really the case. In the Modalist (also known as the Sabellian or Monarchian) heresy, the church was offered the option of explaining the mystery by saying that God was ultimately only one person in three successive modes of existence. In the Arian heresy the church was offered the option of explaining the mystery by saying that Jesus Christ and the Spirit were not God in the full sense of the word. Both options would have resolved the logical tension in the doctrine of the Trinity, yet the church refused to adopt either viewpoint. It maintained the mystery by maintaining that God was in one sense one and in another sense three. It asserted that God was ultimately both one and three: one essence or substance and three persons or subsistences. The creeds of the church fence this mystery. They do not explain it. The incomprehensibility of God means that the doctrines of the faith will involve holy mysteries which transcend human reason and contradict fleshly wisdom. (Note, for instance, Chapter 3: "Of God's Decree," and Chapter 8: "Of Christ the Mediator.") Such mysteries must be accepted with humility and reverence by an intellect weaned from the arrogant and foolish notion of rationalism that finite and fallen human reason can comprehend the divine being (Ps. 131).

There are three basic parts in the historic and biblical doctrine of the Trinity.[48] The three questions dealing with the Trinity in a well-known children's catechism identify them quite adequately. "Are there more gods than one? No, there is only one God. In how many persons does this one God exist? In three persons. Who are they? The Father, the Son and the Holy Spirit." There is one God, who exists in three persons, each with distinguishing personal properties. We will take up these three, simple questions in order.

Are there more Gods than one? No, there is only one God. The Bible everywhere teaches that there is only one true God. The witness of the Old Testament to this truth is indisputable and central to its message and religion. Deuteronomy 6:4 reads: "Hear, O Israel! The LORD our God, the LORD is one!" The clear witness of the New Testament to the doctrine of the Trinity does not dim its testimony to the oneness of the true God (Mark 12:29; Luke 18:19; John 8:41; Acts 3:13; 4:24; 17:24; Rom. 3:30; 1 Cor. 8:4; 8:6; Gal. 3:20; Eph. 4:6; 1 Tim. 2:5; James 2:19).

In how many persons does this one God exist? In three persons. If we are to rightly assess the evidence which supports the idea of three divine persons, we must keep in mind the jealous monotheism of the New Testament and its emphasis on the oneness of God. In such a context the fact that two other persons are mentioned repeatedly in close conjunction with God the Father is of great significance. God will not give His glory to another. He stands alone and high above all created reality. Yet God the Father is joined by God the Son and God the Holy Spirit in many key passages in the New Testament. Nothing can explain this except that God exists in three persons. The key passages are Matthew 3:16-17; Matthew 28:18-20; and 2 Corinthians 13:14. These key passages are supported by the many texts which speak in close conjunction of the persons of the Father and the Son (Matt. 11:27; John 3:35; 5:19) and the many others that mention together the three persons (John 3:34; 14:16; 14:26; Acts 2:33; Rom. 8:9; 15:30).

But what does the confessional tradition mean by speaking of three *persons*? Much of the contemporary discussion of the Trinity tends to obscure and over-qualify the real and distinct personhood of the three persons. In this connection it is important to notice the addition of the word *subsistence*[49] to the word *person* in the 1689 Baptist Confession.

---

48. Of course, a thoughtful and detailed analysis of the historic doctrine of the Trinity as expressed in the ancient creeds reveals that there are perhaps ten truths that must be supported from Scripture in order to prove the historic doctrine. They are (1) the oneness of God; (2-4) the deity of Father, Son, and Holy Spirit; (5-7) the distinct personality of the Father, Son, and Holy Spirit; (8-10) the monarchy of the Father, the eternal generation of the Son, and the eternal procession of the Holy Spirit. Several of these truths are exegetically non-controversial (like the deity and personality of the Father) and need not be the subject of specific comment here.

49. The word has a different connotation here than it does in paragraph 1 of this chapter where the Confession uses the word, subsistence, to speak of the single substance or essence of God. Here it emphasizes that these persons are distinct entities. Muller in his *Dictionary of Latin and Greek Theological Terms* (Grand Rapids: Baker Academic, 1985), 290, provides this definition: "...indicating a particular being or existent, an individual instance

Whatever else this word means, it certainly points to the fact that there are three real, personal entities in God. The words for person in both Greek and Latin could mean something like a role or a mask used in a play in which one person played several parts. Subsistence is added to emphasize precisely the point that person, as used with reference to the persons of the Trinity, refers to real, distinct persons.

This is a point at which the current emphasis on the simplicity of God requires qualification. As was said earlier, simplicity has never been understood in classical Christian theism as contradicting the doctrine of the Trinity. Though God's mind and will are one and simple, it must be added that each of the three persons distinctly appropriate this one mind and will according to their different personalities. As John Owen remarks:

> It is true, the will of God the Father, Son, and Holy Ghost, is but one. It is a natural property, and where there is but one nature there is but one will: but in respect of their distinct personal actings, this will is appropriated to them respectively, so that the will of the Father and the will of the Son may be considered [distinctly] in this business; which though essentially one and the same, yet in their distinct personality it is distinctly considered, as the will of the Father and the will of the Son. Notwithstanding the unity of essence that is between the Father and the Son, yet is the work distinctly carried on by them; so that the same God judges and becomes surety, satisfieth and is satisfied, in these distinct persons.[50]

Such a qualification of the simplicity of God's mind and will is necessary. Only with it can we make sense of the distinct love of the Father for the Son and the Son for the Father (Matt. 3:16-17; John 14:31; 15:9; 17:26); the fact that the Father speaks to the Son and the Son speaks to the Father (Matt. 3:16-17; John 17:26); and the eternal, covenant of redemption in which God the Father made promises to God the Son and the Son undertook distinct obligations from the Father (Titus 1:2; 2 Tim. 1:9). It is not, then, Social Trinitarianism[51] to acknowledge genuine, interpersonal relationships in the Holy Trinity. The use of the word *subsistence* in the Confession to describe what is meant by person requires such fellowship among the three persons of the Trinity. Only if we assert that the unity of the Godhead consists merely in such fellowship do we adopt the error of Social Trinitarianism.

Who are they? The Father, the Son and the Holy Spirit. This is the third question in the children's catechism. It is doctrinally rich with significance

---

of a given essence. In this latter sense, the Latin equivalent of *hypostasis*, a more technical and philosophically adequate term than *persona...*"

50. John Owen, *The Works of John Owen* (Edinburgh: Banner of Truth Trust, 1976), 12:497. This is found in "Vindication of the Gospel," Chapter 27.

51. Social Trinitarianism is the view that the oneness of the Godhead consists in their perfect fellowship or agreement as three persons. Historic Trinitarianism, in contrast, has traced this oneness to their sharing one and the same divine nature through the communication of that nature from the Father to the Son and Spirit.

and rife with consequences. This consequential significance is also quite controversial in our day.

The Nicene Creed[52] articulated the Trinitarian orthodoxy formulated in the early church period. The key assertions of the Nicene Creed on this subject are these:

> We believe in one God, the Father Almighty, Maker of all things visible and invisible. And in one Lord Jesus Christ, the Son of God, begotten of the Father [the only-begotten; that is, of the essence of the Father, God of God,] Light of Light, very God of very God, begotten, not made, consubstantial with the Father; By whom all things were made [both in heaven and on earth];[53]

Nicene orthodoxy found in the names of the persons of the Trinity indications of their distinct, personal properties or identities. This viewpoint was substantially unchallenged among orthodox Christians until the Enlightenment when some who were in other respects orthodox Trinitarians began to reject the doctrines of the eternal generation of the Son, and the eternal procession of the Holy Spirit as irrational.[54] This has led to widespread doubt with regard to these doctrines among well-known evangelicals in the last century.

The heart of the biblical evidence supporting the idea that the names of the different persons of the Trinity reveal their distinct, personal identities is found in its teaching regarding the eternal generation of the Son. On the one hand, this evidence directly implies the monarchy of the Father. On the other hand, it provides a clear and crucial precedent for the doctrine of the eternal procession of the Spirit. The evidence for eternal generation may be summarized as follows.

- The economy of redemption is that of creation (John 1:1-3; Heb. 1:2; 1 Cor. 8:6). In both creation and redemption, the external works of the Trinity are from the Father, through the Son, and in the Holy

---

52. The Nicene Creed underwent later expansion in 381 in what is known as the Niceno-Constantinopolitan Creed. In this version of the Creed the consubstantial deity of the Holy Spirit is made explicit by the addition after the words, "And in the Holy Ghost," of the words, "the Lord and Giver of life, who proceedeth from the Father, who with the Father and the Son together is worshiped and glorified, who spake by the prophets." These words reflect the strong assertion of the deity of the Holy Spirit by the Cappadocian Fathers. Later still, of course, the East objected to the West's addition of the word, *filioque*, which specified that the Holy Spirit proceeds from both the Father and the Son.

53. These are the words of the Nicene Creed as adopted in 325. The later revisions do not alter them materially.

54. Samuel Miller, *Letters on the Eternal Sonship of Christ: addressed to the Rev. Professor Stuart, of Andover* (Philadelphia, W.W. Woodward, 1823), 25, 35: "The celebrated Herman Alexander Roell, of Holland, before alluded to, was, if I mistake not, the first Trinitarian who ever distinguished himself by embracing and publishing the doctrine on that subject which you now hold." Moses Stuart and Nathaniel Emmons (apparently with most of the New England theologians) also rejected the eternal generation of the Son. Thus, the above letters of Miller to Stuart. Robert L. Dabney, *Lectures in Systematic Theology*, (Grand Rapids: Zondervan, 1972), 202-211, argues for the eternal generation of the Son and rejects the denial of eternal sonship by Roell, Ridgeley, Emmons, Stuart, and "the notorious Alexander Campbell" (206).

Spirit. Surely it is strange that both in the economy of creation and the economy of redemption the same order is maintained, if this economic subordination does not reflect a certain order in the Trinity itself. Thus, the eternal generation of the Son is implied by this order. The Nicene Creed reflects on this order when it confesses, on the one hand, its faith in God the Father Almighty as Maker of heaven and earth and, on the other hand, that all things were made through the Son..[55]

- The Bible teaches explicitly that the Son is begotten (John 1:14, 18; 3:16, 18; 1 John 4:9). The translation of "only begotten" was disputed by recent scholarship. Some translate it in the traditional way "only begotten," while others prefer the translation, "unique." Evidence has emerged in recent years that the traditional meaning of "only begotten" of the Greek word is correct.[56]

- Proverbs 8:22-25 also contains explicit teaching to this effect, if applied to the Son of God: "The LORD possessed me at the beginning of His way, Before His works of old. I have been established from everlasting, From the beginning, before there was ever an earth. When there were no depths I was brought forth, When there were no fountains abounding with water. Before the mountains were settled, Before the hills, I was brought forth." The New Testament seems to apply this passage to the Son of God (Col. 2:3; 1 Cor. 1:24, 30; Luke 11:49). Note also Micah 5:2.

- It has sometimes been argued that the designation "Son" is never used of the pre-incarnate Christ. Allowing for the sake of argument this interpretation, it does not explain the use of the

---

55. The Greek of the Nicene Creed uses the instrumental preposition, *dia*, at this point.

56. In support of the arguments I will cite here that the meaning of *monogeneis* is only begotten, let me cite the excellent work of Lee Irons ["Let's Go Back to Only Begotten," https://www.thegospelcoalition.org/article/lets-go-back-to-only-begotten/] and Denny Burk ["Deep in the Weeds on MONOGENES and Eternal Generation," http://www.dennyburk.com/deep-in-the-weeds-on-monogenes-and-eternal-generation/] on its meaning. In support of the meaning "only begotten" for *monogeneis* these arguments must be considered. First, the Nicene Creed and the Greek Fathers used the word in a way that assumed this meaning. Who knows better the meaning of the word than the fourth century Greek Fathers? Second, every literal use of the word shows that it means not merely unique, but uniquely begotten (cf. Judg. 11:34; Luke 7:12; 8:42; 9:38; Heb. 11:17). The word, used literally, is exclusively used of only children and never to mean merely only or unique. Third, there is a reason why the word is used of one uniquely begotten. *Monogenes* is made up of two words: one meaning "one" or "only" and the other meaning either "begotten" (from *gennao*) or "kind" (from *ginomai*). There is debate about the origin of the second component. In either etymology the idea of derivation could be present. Burk says: "Moody is correct that the Greek suffix –GENES derives from the word GENOS. But Moody is wrong about the semantic range of GENOS and the suffix derived from it. In some contexts, GENOS means 'kind,' but in other contexts it means 'offspring.' In fact, in John's one use of the term GENOS, it clearly refers to 'offspring' or 'one that is begotten from another' (Rev. 22:16). 'Offspring' is the only attested meaning for this term in John's writings! Moody is also wrong about the semantic range of the –GENES suffix. There are many examples of this suffix that indicate 'begottenness.' For example, OIKOGENES means 'home-born' (Gen. 15:3 LXX). Paul uses the term EUGENES to mean 'well-born' (1 Cor. 1:26). Again, Moody has misconstrued both the meaning of GENOS and the suffix derived from it."

term, Father, of the first person of the Trinity where it describes His relationship to the second before the incarnation (John 10:36; 16:28; 1 John 4:14). It is impossible to disassociate this term from the idea of One who is the source, or begetter. The Father is the Father, specifically to the Son (John 5:18; Col. 1:3; Eph. 1:3; 2 Cor. 1:3; 1 Cor. 8:6).

- The argument that the term Son is never used of the pre-incarnate Christ is completely unconvincing and seems to contradict multiple scriptural assertions (John 3:16, 17; 10:36; 11:27; Rom. 8:3; Gal. 4:4; Col. 1:13-17; Heb. 1:2; 7:3; 1 John 3:8; 4:9, 10, 14; 5:20).
- The argument that the term "Son" means nothing but equality simply does not carry conviction. I do not deny that it does denote equality of essence. To say, however, that it denotes only this contradicts everything we know not only about the word, father, but also the word, son. "Son" conveys not only equality of essence, but also a personal (father-son) relationship. The Nicene Creed clearly assumes that sonship implies not only equality of essence but derivation or generation of the person.
- Further evidence for the doctrine of eternal generation is gained from what we may call the doctrine of eternal utterance. The other designation of the Son is the Word. Surely this designation intimates a relationship of generation or derivation from the person designated as the God and the person designated as the Word in John 1:1. As to their essence both are unqualified deity. "The Word was God." As to their persons, however, one is called "the God" (*ho theos*) and the other is called "the Word" (*ho logos*) of God. As such the Word is generated by or derived from the Father.
- Without the eternal generation of the Son and the eternal procession of the Spirit it is impossible to distinguish the different persons of the Trinity. There are no revealed personal relations or properties. Even terminology like the First, Second, or Third Person of the Trinity becomes illegitimate. We are left with three colorless, unvarying, indistinguishable persons in the Trinity (a triplet trinity). This result smells of the barrenness of human philosophy, not the richness of biblical revelation.
- Throughout the New Testament the personal name given to God the Father is "the God" (*ho theos*); (cf. among many such places: John 1:1; 2 Cor. 13:14; and Gal. 4:6). This description of the Father implies that He is the eternal originating principle of the Trinity.
- Finally, the suppression of a real eternal fatherhood and a real eternal sonship lessens the glory of redemptive love and the gospel. Is not the glory of the Father giving His Son for our redemption lessened if we limit the idea of sonship in this sentence to mere equality? The result is that one neutered divine person gives another colorless divine person. On this idea, where is the glory of the Father's sacrifice? Where is the glory of the Son's filial obedience?

What are the modern objections to the doctrine of the eternal generation of the Son? The modern suspicion of eternal generation is based on certain objections. A brief response to these objections is necessary.

The first objection may be put this way. Eternal generation is eternal nonsense (as Nathaniel Emmons said).[57] The objection is that to combine eternal with the concept of generation is contradictory. In response it must be said that the Bible simply does not agree with such logic. Furthermore, the Nicene Creed certainly did not agree with it. The Son was God and eternally begotten. The essence of its response to Arianism is that the Son was eternally begotten, but not created.

The second objection derives from the Reformed commitment to the self-existence of the Son as taught by Calvin. How can the Son be self-existent and eternally generated? Once more in response it must be said that neither Calvin nor the Reformed Confessions saw these two ideas as contradictory. Calvin affirmed both clearly.[58] The doctrine of the Trinity is built on the distinction between (one) essence and (three) persons. The essence of the Son is self-existent. The person of the Son is eternally generated.

The third objection and perhaps most weighty is that the doctrine of eternal generation involves the notion that the Son is in some way eternally subordinate to the Father. This is perhaps the main reason why Warfield and other well-known Reformed theologians have taken exception to the doctrine.[59] In response to this objection it must be affirmed that neither in the Nicene Creed nor elsewhere is the orthodox doctrine of eternal generation equivalent to the early and serious error of *Subordinationism* regarding the Trinity. Here is why. This early error grew out of the Greek idea of the hierarchy of being and the Logos Christology derived from it. It asserted that the deity of Christ was a diluted form of deity. Thus, it affirmed that the deity of the Son was essentially subordinate to that of the Father. Clearly, the Nicene Creed does not regard eternal generation as involving this implication. It affirms rather that the Son is "very God" and "consubstantial with the Father." Once more a clear distinction is necessary between the divine essence and the divine persons. The essence is underived and self-existent. The person of the Son is derived by way of eternal generation from the Father.

---

57. Bruce Stephens, "Horace Bushnell and New England Theology," *Dialog 14* (Autumn, 1975) 271-72.

58. For Calvin's assertion of the self-existence of the Son, see *Institutes of the Christian Religion,* 1:13:23-25. For typical assertions of the eternal generation and an order of first, second, and third in the Trinity, see also 1:13:23-25 and 1:13:19-20.

59. B. B. Warfield, "The Biblical Doctrine of the Trinity," in *The Works of Benjamin B. Warfield,* (Grand Rapids: Baker, 1981), 2: 133-174. Warfield accepts eternal Sonship, but only in the sense that this means that the Son is equal to the Father. He doubts if it means either subordination or derivation. He adds that there is no evidence for subordination even in modes of subsistence, but only in modes of operation. He describes the doctrines of eternal generation and procession as remnant suggestions of subordination and derivation that are pushed further and further into the background in the Western Trinitarian tradition. He does not think that the terminology of Father, Son, and Spirit is intended to tell us of eternal relations in the Trinity.

All of this brings up the current controversy over the issue of eternal functional subordination of the Son to the Father. Well-known evangelical theologians have taught that the Son is eternally and functionally subordinate to the Father. Oddly, these theologians at the same time as teaching this also rejected the eternal generation of the Son.[60] This is odd because the very reason many Reformed theologians accepted and others rejected subordination in modes of subsistence was precisely because they saw such subordination as required by the doctrine of eternal generation.

If this issue is to be understood, three kinds of subordination must be distinguished. There is subordination in the modes of operation. This has reference to the subordination of the Son and the Spirit to the Father in both the economy of creation and the economy of redemption. This may be called economic subordination. Secondly, there is subordination in the modes of subsistence. This has reference to an order and relationship of derivation among the persons (or hypostases) of the Trinity itself. The Son is begotten of the Father. The Spirit proceeds from both. This may also be called hypostatic (or personal) subordination. Thirdly, there is subordination in essence. This has reference to the idea that the deity of the Son and Spirit is a qualified form of the deity of the Father. This may be called essential subordination. It is this third idea which has been historically and properly known as Subordinationism.

Carefully defined in this way, what should we think of subordination in modes of subsistence or personal subordination?

- First, it is certainly not Subordinationism properly so called. Subordination in modes of subsistence teaches that as to their essence the Son and Spirit are equal in power and glory to the Father, but as to their persons they are eternally generated and eternally proceed from the Father. Thus, as to their essence, they are self-existent, while as to their persons, they are eternally derived from the Father. This is not Subordinationism. That term is properly reserved for the teaching that the Son and the Spirit are as to their essence less God than the Father and essentially less transcendent.

- Second, there is a relational order among the persons of the eternal Trinity. This order of Father, then Son, and then Spirit is reflected everywhere in the Scripture, as we have seen. Where there is an order, there is a first, second, and third. The Confession speaks of the Son as the "second" person of the Trinity (Chapter 8, paragraph 2). Where there is a first and a second, there is a kind of subordination.

- Third, it cannot be denied that the order found in the eternal Trinity is reflected in the subordination of the Son and Spirit and the primacy of the Father in the economies of creation and

60. I speak, of course, of Wayne Grudem and Bruce Ware. I am thankful that both men have now accepted the eternal generation of the Son.

redemption. This certainly suggests that we speak of a kind of subordination in modes of subsistence among the persons of the eternal Trinity.[61]

- Fourth, the eternal covenant of redemption reflects this order. The Father takes the lead by making a promise to the Son which the Son reciprocates in filial submission to the Father's plan (Titus 1:2, 2 Tim. 1:9). The Father elects, thus authoring redemption; the Son redeems, thus accomplishing redemption; and the Spirit regenerates, thus applying redemption (2 Cor. 13:14; Eph. 1:3-14).

- Fifth, the fact that the preincarnate Son is sent and sanctified by the Father points to His personal subordination to His Father. Such subordination cannot be attributed to His human nature (John 3:17; 10:36; Rom. 8:3; 1 John 4:9, 10, 14).

- Sixth, many important, orthodox theologians of the church have seen in the order of the persons subordination in modes of subsistence. I will place in the footnote many references to such theologians,[62] but several important theologians must be quoted here:

Hilary of Poitier, the early church father and ally of Augustine, comments:

> That the Son is not on a level with the Father and is not equal to Him is chiefly shown in the fact that He was subjected to Him to render obedience… in that He submits in all things to the will of Him who sent Him. But the subordination of filial love is not a diminution of essence, nor does pious duty cause a degeneration of nature, since in spite of the fact that both the Unborn Father is God and the Only-begotten Son of God is God, God is nevertheless One, and the subjection and dignity of the Son are both taught in that by being called Son He is made subject to that name which because it implies that God is His Father is yet a name which denotes His nature. Having a name which belongs to Him whose Son He is, He is subject to the Father both in service and name; yet in such a way that the subordination of His name bears witness to the true character of His natural and exactly

---

61. John Owen on Hebrews 1:1-2 remarks: "But yet the rise and spring of this mystery was in the Father; for the order of acting in the blessed Trinity follows the order of subsistence. As the Father, therefore, is the fountain of the Trinity as to subsistence, so also as to operation. He 'hath life in himself;' and 'he giveth to the Son to have life in himself,' John 5:26. And he doth it by communicating unto him his subsistence by eternal generation. And thence saith the Son, 'As my Father worketh, so I work,' John 5:17. And what he seeth the Father do, that doeth the Son likewise, John 5:19; not by imitation, or repetition of the like works, but in the same works in order of nature the will and Wisdom of the Father doth proceed. So also is it in respect of the Holy Ghost, whose order of subsistence denotes that of his operation" [*An Exposition of the Epistle to the Hebrews* (Grand Rapids: Baker Book House, 1980), 3:34-35.]

62. The failure to explicitly refer to the idea of subordination in modes of subsistence does not mean that a theologian did not hold it, but the following is a list of well-known theologians beside those of Hilary, Owen, and Vos cited above that explicitly affirm subordination in modes of subsistence: John Calvin according to Richard Muller, *Post-Reformation Reformed Dogmatics*, 4:80, 324; Jonathan Edwards Miscellanies 1062.1 Economy of the Trinity and Covenant of Redemption. http://edwards.yale. eduarchive?path=aHR0cDovL2Vkd2FyZHMueWFsZS5lZHUvY2dpLWJpbi9uZXdwa Glsby9nZXRvYmplY3QucGw/cC4xOTo0NDQud2plbw==; Augustus H. Strong, *Systematic*

similar essence.[63]

John Owen remarks: "... the joint working of Father and Son doth not infer any other subordination but that of subsistence and order ... "[64]

Geerhardus Vos says:

> Although these three persons possess one and the same divine substance, Scripture nevertheless teaches us that, concerning their personal existence, the Father is the first, the Son the second, and the Holy Spirit the third, that the Son is of the Father, the Spirit of the Father and the Son. Further, their workings outwardly reflect this order of personal existence, since the Father works through the Son, and the Father and the Son work through the Spirit. There is, therefore, subordination as to personal manner of existence and manner of working, but no subordination regarding possession of the one divine substance.[65]

Perhaps the most important objection lodged against personal subordination is that it is a violation of the simplicity of the divine will. Submission, so the argument goes, requires the submission of one will to another will, but in God there is only one will.[66] The will of God, though one, is distinctly appropriated by each of the divine persons. Therefore, we may and must (given the biblical evidence) conceive of these distinct appropriations of the divine will as subordinately arranged from the Father.

The lengthy treatment of eternal generation may seem unnecessary, but much of the practical application of the doctrine of the Trinity depends on a clear understanding of the distinctions between the persons of the Trinity. The Confession points to the important, practical application of the doctrine of the Trinity by describing it in the closing words of this chapter as "the foundation of all our communion with God, and comfortable dependence on him."

Applications
The first and most important of the practical applications of the Trinity is that it vastly enriches our understanding and experience of salvation. Second Corinthians 13:14, the great Trinitarian benediction of the New Testament, calls us to hold communion with each of the three persons

Theology, Volume I, The Doctrine of God (Philadelphia: Judson Press, 1907), 275-76; James Petigru Boyce, *Abstract of Systematic Theology* (Hanford, CA: Den Dulk Christian Foundation, 1887), 143-44; Charles Hodge, *Systematic Theology* (New York: Scriber and Company, 1871) 1:462f.; Louis Berkhof, *Systematic Theology* (Eerdmans: Grand Rapids, 1996), 88.

63. *De Synodis*, 51.

64. John Owen, *An Exposition of the Epistle to the Hebrews* (Grand Rapids: Baker Book House, 1980), 3:75.

65. Geerhardus Vos, *Reformed Dogmatics: Volume One: Theology Proper* (Bellington, WA: Lexham Press, 2012-2014), 43.

66. Perhaps the best-known statement of this argument is by D. Glenn Butner Jr., "Eternal Functional Subordination and the Problem of the Divine Will," JETS 58/1 (2015), 131-49.

of the Trinity in their distinct works in redemption. We are distinctly to enjoy communion with the grace of the Lord Jesus Christ as the accomplisher of redemption; the love of God the Father as the author of redemption; and the fellowship of the Holy Spirit as the applier of redemption. John Owen's wonderful treatment of this subject should be read and savored.[67]

A second practical application of the doctrine of the Trinity is that it manifests how virulently anti-Christian is the foundational claim of modern feminism and egalitarianism. That foundational claim is that genuine equality between men and women (and anyone else) requires role-interchangeability. This is the claim of Letha Scanzoni and Nancy Hardesty in their seminal book, *All We're Meant to Be*. For these "Christian feminists" equality means role-interchangeability—a maximum of equality of every kind.[68] For feminism there is no equality where persons have different roles and especially different roles that entail a kind of subordination. As we have seen, however, the persons of the eternal Trinity have distinct personal properties and identities which entail a clear order among them, a kind of personal subordination of the Son and Spirit to the Father, and distinct and appropriate roles in the external works of the Trinity. Essential equality and personal subordination are consistent in the eternal Trinity and thus also in God's creation. They are not impossibly contradictory as egalitarianism claims.[69]

---

67. John Owen, *Communion with God, Works* (Edinburgh: Banner of Truth Trust, 1965), 2:5-274.

68. Letha Scanzoni and Nancy Hardesty, *All We're Meant to Be* (Waco: Word, 1974), 110. cf. Susan T. Foh's discussion of this claim in *Women and the Word of God* (Grand Rapids: Baker Book House, 1980), 38-45. In these pages Foh shows that there are indications in their writings that this definition of equality has a frankly secular origin.

69. The doctrine of the Trinity also has, I think, interesting implications for the problem of the one and many because it shows that the one and the many (the universal and particular) are co-ultimate. This may be important to vindicate the possibility of knowledge. The doctrine of the Trinity also shows how fundamental interpersonal relationships are. In the Trinity the interpersonal relationships of the three (as well as their essential oneness) are ultimate realities in the universe. We cannot underestimate, then, the importance and influence for good or evil of the personal relationships into which we enter in human society. Reflection on the interpersonal relations of the Trinity also sheds an interesting light on attributes of God like His love, simplicity, impassibility, and serenity. It is also interesting that eternal life itself involves essentially a personal relationship with the Holy Trinity (John 17:3).

CHAPTER 3

OF GOD'S DECREE

DAVID CHARLES

1. God hath decreed in himself, from all eternity, by the most wise and holy counsel of his own will, freely and unchangeably, all things, whatsoever comes to pass;[1] yet so as thereby is God neither the author of sin nor hath fellowship with any therein;[2] nor is violence offered to the will of the creature, nor yet is the liberty or contingency of second causes taken away, but rather established;[3] in which appears his wisdom in disposing all things, and power and faithfulness in accomplishing his decree.[4]

2. Although God knoweth whatsoever may or can come to pass, upon all supposed conditions,[5] yet hath he not decreed anything, because he foresaw it as future, or as that which would come to pass upon such conditions.[6]

3. By the decree of God, for the manifestation of his glory, some men and angels are predestinated, or foreordained to eternal life through Jesus Christ,[7] to the praise of his glorious grace;[8] others being left to act in their sin to their just condemnation, to the praise of his glorious justice.[9]

---

1. Isaiah 46:10; Ephesians 1:11; Hebrews 6:17; Romans 9:15, 18
2. James 1:13; 1 John 1:5
3. Acts 4:27, 28; John 19:11
4. Numbers 23:19; Ephesians 1:3-5
5. Acts 15:18
6. Romans 9:11, 13, 16, 18
7. 1 Timothy 5:21; Matthew 25:34
8. Ephesians 1:5, 6
9. Romans 9:22, 23; Jude 4

4. These angels and men thus predestinated and foreordained, are particularly and unchangeably designed, and their number so certain and definite, that it cannot be either increased or diminished.[10]

5. Those of mankind that are predestinated to life, God, before the foundation of the world was laid, according to his eternal and immutable purpose, and the secret counsel and good pleasure of his will, hath chosen in Christ unto everlasting glory, out of his mere free grace and love,[11] without any other thing in the creature as a condition or cause moving him thereunto.[12]

We live in a world which appears at times to be a contradiction of chaos and order, freedom and restraint, joy and tears, hope and despair, vanity and purpose. The thoughtful soul needs only a short time of reflection to beg the question, "Is there a reason, a purpose, or a plan to all of this?" Honest consideration reveals two possible answers to this question: Life, with all its opportunities and disappointments, is either (1) all darkness with only an illusion of significance, or (2) it is a kaleidoscope of a masterful display of an immense and infinite mind. The impossible philosophy of Nihilism[13] chooses the first answer: There is no mind or meaning behind life. At bottom, everything is nothing. The Christian religion, however, maintains that all of creation is the creative work of a gracious and powerful Creator. Every nursing baby, every beast of land and sea, the silent glow of a starry sky shouts that there is a God, and, further, He is majestic. All creatures and events serve part of a grand plan. No event is meaningless in or devoid of playing a part in the outworking of a larger, even glorious goal. Even mankind's most urgent need, his redemption, is the result of God's own plan, or, His decree. Here we are confronted with a choice: embrace the darkness and despair of Nihilism or enjoy life with all its promises and challenges as we await the great day of consummation.

The third chapter of The 1689 London Baptist Confession of Faith on God's decree—situated as it is between the main source of theological knowledge (Chapter 1), the object of theological knowledge (Chapter 2) and creation (Chapter 4)—states one overarching theological principle: All that was, is, or will be is well-grounded in the eternal purpose of the Triune God.

---

10. 2 Timothy 2:19; John 13:18

11. Ephesians 1:4, 9, 11; Romans 8:30; 2 Timothy 1:9; 1 Thessalonians 5:9

12. Romans 9:13, 16; Ephesians 2:5, 12

13. This view is summarized well by atheist Alex Rosenberg: "Is *there a God*? No. *What is the nature of reality*? What physics says it is. *What is the purpose of the universe*? There is none. *What is the meaning of life*? Ditto. *Why am I here*? Just dumb luck. *Does prayer work*? Of course not... *Does history have any meaning or purpose*? It's full of sound and fury, but signifies nothing" (Alex Rosenberg, *The Atheist's Guide to Reality: Enjoying Life without Illusions* [New York, N.Y. W.W. Norton & Company], 2, 3).

What we encounter in this chapter is a challenge even to the most earnest and well-informed students of divinity. Readers unfamiliar with this document may be confused with a first or even second reading of this chapter. There are two reasons that account for this: the language and the theological concepts behind the language. The former reason is best explained by Derek Thomas as he observed that the Westminster divines[14] were men who "loved truth so much that they dared to express it in ways so 'precise' that we still find ourselves endeavoring to interpret it today. Truth mattered to them."[15] The seventeenth-century men wrote to be understood rightly and labored to avoid any unnecessary misunderstanding.[16]

Regarding the latter reason, all theological reflection will involve limited and incomplete knowledge. As the saints have often sung, God dwells "in light inaccessible, hid from our eyes." This is referred to as the *incomprehensibility of God*. We must humbly admit that "finite creatures can never completely understand their infinite God."[17] Recognizing that our knowledge of God is not exhaustive is not to say that we have no true theological knowledge, but that our knowledge of God is not the same as God's knowledge of Himself.[18] With respect to the divine decree in particular, "These are deep waters, and we admit that we only splash in the shallows of theology."[19]

The Second London Baptist Confession of Faith's chapter on God's decree is plain that all events, and every detail of those events, are the outworking in time of God's eternal plan: *God hath decreed in himself, from all eternity, by the most wise and holy counsel of his own will, freely and unchangeably, all things, whatsoever comes to pass…*

This decree displays both divine wisdom and holiness. There is also divine liberty in the decrees: "God is not under any necessity bound to act as he has. He decrees out of his own freedom."[20] The decree of God has a goal, which is "to the praise of the glory of his wisdom, power, justice, infinite goodness, and mercy…" (5.1) Scripture, likewise, is plain

---

14. The London Baptist Confession of Faith (1677/89) is based largely on the Westminster Confession of Faith (1646). See James Renihan, *A Toolkit for Confessions* (Palmdale, Ca.: RBAP, 2017), 41-51.

15. Ligon Duncan III, editor, *The Westminster Confession into the 21st Century* (Fearn, Ross-shire, Scotland: Christian Focus Publications, Mentor imprint 2009), 287.

16. See also James Renihan, *A Toolkit For Confessions,* 38.

17. Greg Nichols, *Lectures in Systematic Theology, volume 1* (2019): "No man, or group of men can ever exhaustively explain who and what he is (his nature), or what he does (his works), or why he decided to do it (his decree)" 149.

18. See the entry "Theologia" in Richard A. Muller, *Dictionary of Latin and Greek Theological Terms: Drawn Principally from Protestant Scholastic Theology* (Grand Rapids: Baker Book House, 1985), 298.

19. Chad Van Dixhoorn, *Confessing the Faith* (The Banner of truth Trust, 2014), 45.

20. Morton H. Smith, *Systematic Theology, Volume One: Prolegomena, Theology, Anthropology, Christology,* electronic ed. (Escondido, CA: Ephesians Four Group, 1999), 155. "There can be nothing higher than God and nothing below God that can impede or determine his will" (Richard A. Muller, Post-Reformation Reformed Dogmatics, Volume 3 [Grand Rapids, Mi. Baker Academic], 447).

on this score. God has an eternal purpose and plan: "In Him [Christ] also we have obtained an inheritance, being predestined according to the purpose of Him who works all things according to the counsel of His will" (Eph. 1:11). From this text we may be certain that "everything is included in God's universe-embracing plan."[21]

Isaiah the prophet faithfully recorded the command of God: "Remember the former things of old; for I am God, and there is no other; I am God, and there is none like Me, declaring the end from the beginning, and from ancient times things that are not yet done, saying, 'My counsel shall stand, and I will do all My pleasure'" (Isa. 46:9-10). Commenting on this passage, the eighteenth-century Baptist John Gill wrote: "The purposes and decrees of God, which are within himself, wisely formed by him, eternal and unfrustratable; and which shall stand, or be accomplished, being the counsels of him who is all-wise, all-knowing, all-powerful, unchangeable, true, and faithful; whether they respect the providence of God in relation to the world in general, and the government of it, or to particular persons, and their affairs, from the time of their birth to their death."[22]

Every muscle of every squirrel moves according to God's eternal decree—every leap, bounce, and climb are exactly as God had planned. Same, too, with the child whose body is sick and weak with toxins. Whatever the source of the deadly agent, it did not act independently of God Himself.[23] Such a notion is difficult to reconcile with all that we know of God.

It raises questions of both God's relationship to evil and the freedom of creatures. However we understand these concerns, at this point the reader should pause and reflect on his or her life. Every aspect and detail of life is part of God's wise and holy plan. Louis Berkhof explains: "God causes everything in nature to work and to move in the direction of a predetermined end."[24] The joys and the tears of all your days are in God's keeping (Pss. 56:8; 63:6-8). Psalm 139:16 says: "Your eyes saw my substance, being yet unformed. And in Your book they all were written, the days fashioned for me, when as yet there were none of them." Not even a single hair on your head is independent of the blessed Trinity (Luke 12:7)!

There is much that is mysterious and strange here. And yet we know, despite it all, that wonderful and familiar passage from Romans 8:28 —"All things work together for good to those who love God, to those

21. William Hendriksen, *Exposition of Ephesians*, volume 7, New Testament Commentary (Grand Rapids: Baker Book House, 1953–2001), 88-89.

22. John Gill, *An Exposition of the Old Testament*, volume 5, The Baptist Commentary Series (London: Mathews and Leigh, 1810), 272.

23. "God's internal and immanent acts are the same as His essence: such an act is the Divine decree: and, therefore, as God's essence is eternal, so His decree must also be eternal. Now the decree is God's decreeing, because whatever is in God is God; it is God Himself by one eternal act, decreeing and determining whatever should come to pass to the praise of His own glory" (Christopher Ness, *Antidote against Arminianism* [London 1700], 10).

24. L. Berkhof, *Systematic Theology* (Grand Rapids: Wm. B. Eerdmans, 1938), 173.

who are the called according to His purpose"—is ever true. History is
the unfolding of God's decree, which includes all that comes to pass in
the world, both the good and the evil. Yet, our Confession is careful to
note that God [is] neither the author of sin nor hath fellowship with any
therein.

God's decree is strange and foreign to us creatures who are limited
by space and time. God and creation are in their very essence different
from each other. God is an eternal, infinite, and independent being of a
simple nature, while we are temporal, finite, and dependent beings with
a complex nature. Our dependence on God fills every moment of our
existence: "For in him we live and move and have our being" (Acts 17:28).
This relationship involves us in a mystery that is difficult to reconcile
with our usual manner of thinking.

In the created order, we see a relationship of cause and effect. We
can normally trace any event back to a cause or set of causes. Scripture,
however, instructs us to think that all the causes we witness are not the
first cause, but a second cause with God as the first cause. Consequently,
we witness a world of "caused causes."[25] As Proverbs 16:33 says: "The
lot is cast into the lap, but its every decision is from the LORD." "Come
now, you who say, 'Today or tomorrow we will go to such and such a
city, spend a year there, buy and sell, and make a profit;' whereas you do
not know what will happen tomorrow. For what is your life? It is even a
vapor that appears for a little time and then vanishes away. Instead you
ought to say, 'If the Lord wills, we shall live and do this or that'" (James
4:13-15). Likewise, our Lord Jesus taught us that God "makes His sun
rise on the evil and on the good, and sends rain on the just and on the
unjust" (Matt. 5:45).

God in His decree is the first cause of all that will take place in
history; yet, all that happens in history occurs by *secondary causes* all
acting according to their particular creaturely nature. Part of this nature
is *contingency*, or, acting freely—yet always according to that nature. Sin
and evil arise from the creature and not from God who has no fellowship
with it, even though God does work in and through it. The theological
term for the relationship between God as the first cause and secondary
causes is *concurrence*. While there is debate about how to best understand
this term,[26] R. C. Sproul explains it well when he writes: "Concurrence
refers to the actions of two or more parties taking place at the same
time."[27] While it appears strange to us, in all events there are two causes:
one temporal and dependent, the other eternal and independent.

As a biblical example, consider first, Joseph who was mistreated and
abused by his brothers and then later by those in Egypt (Genesis 37;

25. James E. Dolezal, "Agency, Concurrence, and Evil: A Study in Divine Providence,"
Journal of IRBS Theological Seminary (Palmdale, CA: RBAP, 2019): 61-89. Here is one of the
best contemporary treatments addressing issues related to God and the problem of evil.

26. See L. Berkhof, *Systematic Theology*, 171-75.

27. R. C. Sproul, *Does God Control Everything?*, First edition, vol. 14, The Crucial
Questions Series (Orlando, FL: Reformation Trust, 2012), 56.

39-40). Those who mistreated him did so both willfully and sinfully. They could have chosen differently and treated Joseph with love and respect. His brothers, in particular, were cruel and uncaring, and they were guilty for doing so. Yet, we encounter those words by Joseph to his bewildered brothers that have been a thunderclap since they were first spoken: "But as for you, you meant evil against me; but God meant it for good, in order to bring it about as it is this day, to save many people alive." Second, and most importantly, recall that in the Bible, we see that though evil men engaged in the greatest evil in the terrible crucifixion of the Lord Jesus, it was all according to God's plan and purpose (Acts 4:27-28) and unto our greatest good (Rom. 8:29-31) and for God's own glory and praise (Rom. 9:23; 2 Cor. 4:15; Eph. 1:6).

Both accounts illustrate a simple fact: all of history, since the fall, is the record of human sin, sorrow, and suffering with each actor at every moment doing as each desires. And still, God is also at work in those same events doing good, and oftentimes doing good even to those who produce the evil![28] Many have attempted to moderate the doctrine of God's providence so that the creature is free of God as the first cause. One such attempt is addressed with these words: *Although God knoweth whatsoever may or can come to pass, upon all supposed conditions, yet hath he not decreed anything, because he foresaw it as future, or as that which would come to pass upon such conditions.*

God certainly does know all possibilities in all possible worlds with all the contingencies and conditions of those possibilities. However, He did not decree anything because of such knowledge. Rather, His knowledge of the future is due to His decree of the future.

Ultimately, God's eternal purposes are centered on the Lord Jesus Christ: *...some men and angels[29]are predestinated, or foreordained to eternal life through Jesus Christ,"* while others are *"left to act in their sin to their just condemnation."* Those predestined to life are for *"the praise of God's glorious grace"* while the others are *"to the praise of his glorious justice."*

---

28. "We must assert that God has permitted sin for the purpose of overruling it in the interests of righteousness and benevolence, for His own glory and our highest good" (A. A. Hodge and Charles Hodge, *The Confession of Faith: With Questions for Theological Students and Bible Classes* [Simpsonville, SC: Christian Classics Foundation, 1996], 68).

29. The inclusion of angels as ordained "to eternal life through Jesus Christ" reflects a growing consensus of seventeenth-century thought. For example, in a sermon by the Particular Baptist Benjamin Keach titled, "And ye are compleat in him, who is the Head of Principalities and Powers," he says: "Christ is God, and he is the preserver of the Elect Angels; they are committed to him, and under his Power, and he upholds them, though he never died for them; and shall we think he will not preserve his Elect Saints, or that their Election should not as absolutely secure them, for whom he as their blessed Lord and Head died, and to whom he is a Redeemer, as the Elect Angels to whom he is only a Confirmer?" (Benjamin Keach, "Sermon VIII: And ye are compleat in him, who is the Head of Principalities and Powers" in *A Golden Mine Opened: Or, The Glory of God's Rich Grace Displayed in the Mediator to Believers: and His Direful Wrath against Impenitent Sinners Containing the Substance of near Forty Sermons Upon Several Subjects* [London: Printed, and sold by the Author at his house in Horse-lie-down, and William Marshall at the Bible in Newgate-street, 1694], Kindle Edition, 181). This reference was suggested to me in an unpublished paper by Richard C. Barcellos, "Some Men and Angels, are predestinated, or fore-ordained to Eternal Life, through Jesus Christ."

Two pressing observations must be made at this point. First, note that God will be praised because of His glory known either in grace through Jesus Christ or experienced in justice. The eternal God who made all animate and inanimate creation had divine praise as His goal. Here is the inescapable fact of every particle of your existence. In this life, if there is no praise from your lips to God who sent the Lord Jesus Christ for the salvation of all who believe, you may be certain that, in the next life, the entire cosmos will praise God in your just condemnation.

Second, there is a difference between *predestination to life* and being *left to act in their sin*. Though God's decree determines the one as well as the other, they differ at a fundamental level. Robert Letham's comments on the Westminster Confession are deeply insightful: "We should note the disparity between election and reprobation. Election is by grace and is rooted in Christ; reprobation, or preterition (passing by) is in connection with sin and God's justice. There is asymmetry, not a parallel. Ultimately, both depend on the unchangeable, wise, holy, eternal will of God, but in themselves they differ considerably."[30] God's active grace in Jesus Christ unto redemption is not the same as His *passing by* those who are left in their sin and rebellion.[31]

Few topics produce as much emotional heat and discomfort as that of God's predestination of sinners to eternal life. For some, this makes God into a fiendish monster of cosmic proportions. Others respond with adoring praise and thanksgiving (Rom. 11:33-36). The churches arising out of the sixteenth-century Reformation were on this point decidedly "Augustinian." Augustine wrote on matters related to the grace of God in the fourth century after his own conversion from a life of debauchery and unbelief. He went on to serve as one of the greatest theologians of all time, championing the doctrine of grace against several forms of heresy. This defense of the gospel was an articulation of God's exclusive work of grace in the entire scope of redeeming lost sinners to Himself. This is not only the grace that is seen in history when Christ went to the cross, or the grace experienced at the time of conversion in the Spirit's work of applying Christ's work of redemption, but also the grace before creation in the eternal determination by the Blessed Trinity of who would believe in Christ unto salvation.

Not understanding God's eternal decree both diminishes our knowledge of His free grace and hinders us from giving Him glory. "According to the mature Augustinian position, empirical human beings had so fallen from the intention of God that they were incapable to turning to him, unless their wills were completely reorientated by the

---

30. Robert Letham, *The Westminster Assembly* (Phillipsburg, NJ: P&R Publishing Company, 2009), 183.

31. On the question of Supralapsarianism and Infralapsarianism, see Derek Thomas, "The Westminster Confession into the 21st Century," 267-89. Bavinck can be so bold as to write: "The churches, however, consistently opposed this supralapsarian scenario. As a result there is not a single Reformed confession that contains it" (Herman Bavinck, John Bolt, and John Vriend, *Reformed Dogmatics: God and Creation,* vol. 2 [Grand Rapids, MI: Baker Academic, 2004], 366).

work of God's grace, freely bestowed according to his determination. So the reason why some sinners are saved and others lost is to be found ultimately in God. It is according to God's sovereign purpose, his eternal decree, that some sinners are rescued whilst others are left in their sin; so in the last resort salvation depends upon the sovereign divine decision in regard to the individual."[32] It must always be remembered that the decree is unto "the praise of God's glorious grace" (Eph. 1:6).

To assure the church of the gracious and absolutely independent nature of God's decree, the Confession once again underscores God's exclusive prerogative: *Those of mankind that are predestinated to life, God, before the foundation of the world was laid, according to his eternal and immutable purpose, and the secret counsel and good pleasure of his will, hath chosen in Christ unto everlasting glory, out of his mere free grace and love, without any other thing in the creature as a condition or cause moving him thereunto.*

This is commonly referred to as *unconditional election*. As a biblical word, election (Matt. 24:22; Luke 18:7; Rom. 8:33; Col. 3:12; 1 Pet; 1:2) is not rejected by most students of the Bible. However, that this election of some to life rests entirely upon God's own *purposes* and *free grace and love* are often met with hostility, resistance, denunciation, and misrepresentation.[33] The Baptist Confession concurs with other Reformed Confessions that tenaciously maintain that God's election is entirely of His own sovereign choice and free grace, and thus independent of any foreseen behavior in those elected, either by faith or any good works.[34]

God saves sinners. This statement is simple enough for a young child to understand and is deep enough to astonish and occupy great theological minds for a lifetime. Salvation that was decreed in eternity by God is accomplished and experienced in time. Election is a most marvelous truth of revealed religion, yet it is not election that saves sinners. Rather, election only determines the sinners which God will save. Restoring man who has *fallen in Adam* to one of happy sonship with God as his Father involves some necessary means: *As God hath appointed the elect unto glory, so he hath, by the eternal and most free purpose of his will, foreordained all the means thereunto...*

These means are *Christ's redemption* (see 8.4); *effectual calling* (*vocation*) where the sinner is regenerated and enabled to respond with faith; *justification* where the sinner is declared righteous by faith; *adoption*

---

32. *New Dictionary of Theology, Historical and Systematic,* edited by Martin Davie, Tim Grass, Stephen R. Holmes, John McDowell, and T.A. Noble (Downers Grove, IL: InterVarsity Press, 2016), 700.

33. "Decretum horribile" terrifying decree; a much-abused term from Calvin. It does not translate into "horrible decree" and in no way implies that the eternal decree is somehow unjust or horrifying, but only that the decree is awesome and terrifying, particularly to those who are not in Christ. Richard A. Muller, *Dictionary of Latin and Greek Theological Terms: Drawn Principally from Protestant Scholastic* Theology (Grand Rapids, Mich.: Baker Book House, 1985), 88.

34. B. B. Warfield said, "We observe then the fact of Absolute Predestination is the common presupposition of the whole body of Reformed creeds" (*Predestination in the Reformed Confessions, in The Works of Benjamin B. Warfield* [Grand Rapids, MI: Baker, 1991], 9:219).

where the sinner is brought into the family of God; *sanctification* that separates the sinner from the power of sin; and then being preserved or *kept* by God for final salvation.[35] Like beautiful facets of a diamond, these are all the work of God who alone saves His elect people from their sins.

Dogmatic and systematic theologians have often distinguished between Christ's work of redemption accomplished in His life and death and that work applied by the Spirit. Both are the necessary, God-appointed means in saving the elect. The application of redemption is referred to as the *ordo salutis*, or *order of salvation*.[36] All the means of redemption find their origin in God's eternal decree.

Understanding that God works alone[37] in salvation is not an invitation to indifference, passivity, or sloth, a "let go and let God"[38] attitude. The Confession instructs readers ...*that the high mystery of predestination is to be handled with special prudence and care, that men attending the will of God revealed in his Word, and yielding obedience thereunto...*

With a close reading of this chapter, one discovers that God's will is taught in two different ways. The eternal will of God is most wise, holy, free and *secret*. God's predestination of some to life and others to just condemnation is a *high mystery* that does not invite speculation into these matters. Rather, we are to submit to God's will *revealed* in Holy Scripture. That revealed will is simply that all people to whom the gospel comes must "yield obedience," which is to repent, believe, and be saved. Here and here alone may any "be assured of their eternal election." It

---

35. Each of these, along with faith, repentance, and good works, are treated in separate chapters in the Confession.

36. "Thus, theologians have matched the historia salutis with an ordo salutis ('order of salvation'), whereby the accomplished work of Christ is applied to particular persons in their own life stories. The order of salvation basically sketches the contours of the Christian life, describing the activities of God for and within the believer and then locating the believer's actions in this theological context. As Reformed churches have sought to organize their faith and practice according to the Word of God, they have seen fit to fashion a fairly distinctive order of salvation. Indeed, the way in which the Christian life unfolds marks a key difference between the Reformed churches and the Roman Catholic Church, from which they emerged in the sixteenth century" (R. Michael Allen, *Reformed Theology, Doing Theology* [New York; London: T&T Clark, 2010], 76).

37. Reformed theologians express this by the term "monergism." Particularly in all matters related to regeneration or the effectual call: "Regeneration is monergistic: that is, entirely the work of God the Holy Spirit. It raises the elect among the spiritually dead to new life in Christ (Eph. 2:1-10). Regeneration is a transition from spiritual death to spiritual life, and conscious, intentional, active faith in Christ is its immediate fruit, not its immediate cause. Regeneration is the work of what Augustine called 'prevenient' grace, the grace that precedes our outgoings of heart toward God" (J. I. Packer, *Concise Theology: A Guide to Historic Christian Beliefs* [Wheaton, IL: Tyndale House, 1993], 158). The Canons of Dort likewise reject those "Who teach: That grace and free will are partial causes which together work the beginning of conversion, and that grace, in order of working, does not precede the working of the will; that is, that God does not efficiently help the will of man unto conversion until the will of man moves and determines to do this" (*Historic Creeds and Confessions*, electronic ed. [Oak Harbor: Lexham Press, 1997]).

38. Commenting on Philippians 2:13, G. Walter Hansen observes that "[s]uch slogans [let go and let God] for the Christian life express a passivism not consonant with Paul's call to the persistent obedience of working out salvation in the life of the church" (G. Walter Hansen, *The Letter to the Philippians*, The Pillar New Testament Commentary [Grand Rapids, MI; William B. Eerdmans Publishing Company, 2009], 177).

may appear overly simple, but the first question to be asked is not, "Did God decree my salvation;" but "Have I believed on the Lord Jesus unto salvation?" The second question, when answered, assures us regarding the first question, even as the knowing of the first question will *afford matter of praise, reverence, and admiration of God, and of humility, diligence, and abundant consolation to all that sincerely obey the gospel.*

Returning to where we began this chapter, we are invited to stand in thankful adoration of *"the manifestation of the glory of [God's] eternal power, wisdom, and goodness"*[39] as we marvel at all the various forms and features of that grand display. Indeed! We do see the splendor of the Creator in the creature. He is always at work, bringing about what He wisely decreed would be.

Additionally, in the mystery of His eternal decree, the body of the child sickened by unknown toxins now shows the hopeful signs of recovery. Doctors played their role, mindful parents did what they could do, and the people of God prayed. All of these were the means that God used in the realization of what was determined to be. Though it may seem paradoxical to most, at the little church prayer meeting there were words of thanksgiving and praise to God who hears prayers[40] even as He "works all things according to the counsel of His will" (Eph. 1:11).

---

39. See Chapter 4 of the Confession.

40. "Prayer is not appointed for the furnishing of God with the knowledge of what we need, but is designed as a confession to Him of our sense of need. In this, as in everything, God's thoughts are not as ours. God requires that His gifts should be sought for. He designs to be honoured by our asking, just as He is to be thanked by us after He has bestowed His blessing" (Arthur W. Pink *The Sovereignty of God,* [Grand Rapids, Mi: Baker, 1984] 171).

CHAPTER 4

OF CREATION

EARL M. BLACKBURN

1. In the beginning it pleased God the Father, Son, and Holy Spirit,[1] for the manifestation of the glory of his eternal power,[2] wisdom, and goodness, to create or make the world, and all things therein, whether visible or invisible, in the space of six days, and all very good.[3]

2. After God had made all other creatures, he created man, male and female,[4] with reasonable and immortal souls,[5] rendering them fit unto that life to God for which they were created; being made after the image of God, in knowledge, righteousness, and true holiness;[6] having the law of God written in their hearts,[7] and power to fulfil it, and yet under a possibility of transgressing, being left to the liberty of their own will, which was subject to change.[8]

3. Besides the law written in their hearts, they received a command not to eat of the tree of knowledge of good and evil,[9] which whilst they kept, they were happy in their communion with God, and had dominion over the creatures.[10]

Perhaps no time in human history has the doctrine of creation been so important and needed as now. The advancements of modern science, the rejection of the once prominent Christian worldview in western civilization, and the militant anti-Christian atheism, pluralism,

---

1. John 1:2, 3; Hebrews 1:2; Job 26:13
2. Romans 1:20
3. Colossians 1:16; Genesis 1:31
4. Genesis 1:27
5. Genesis 2:7
6. Ecclesiastes 7:29; Genesis 1:26
7. Romans 2:14, 15
8. Genesis 3:6
9. Genesis 2:17
10. Genesis 1:26, 28

relativism, and skepticism of twenty-first century culture combine to war against the biblical teaching of the origins of the earth and universe. Science fiction writings and computer-generated television programs and movies have become the *de facto* gurus and usurpers of the authority of the Holy Scriptures. Seeds have been so cleverly and insidiously sown into the modern mind via technology attempting to overthrow what Almighty God has authoritatively declared and clearly revealed. Many have been duped by these wily schemes, thinking these stratagems are harmless and innocent.

Not so with our seventeenth-century forefathers! They understood clearly the Bible's teaching on the origin of material and life. Understanding it, they boldly and unashamedly confessed it before a watching and perishing humanity. They believed in *true* science (as opposed to atheistic, unproven hypotheses and theories) and saw no contradiction between science and Scripture. In three short paragraphs, strategically placed immediately after: "Of the Holy Scriptures," "Of God and the Holy Trinity," and "Of God's Decree," this chapter lays the foundation of all that is to follow. Why is this chapter "Of Creation" put here rather than at the end of the Confession, or simply omitted altogether? The framers of the Confession knew that God, as Creator and originator of His creation, put into place human responsibility and accountability to Himself. If God is not the Creator and men and women are not His creation, then there is no responsibility and accountability to anyone or anything divine. Further, such questions needed to be answered as: How did it all get here? And what about the sun, moon, stars, and planets, the vast expanse of the universe, the galaxies? And what about the most amazing of all creatures called man? How did all these come to be?

These are the most foundational of all questions in human existence which need to be answered according to God's inspired revelation, the Bible. Many conjectures and beliefs exist that seek to answer these questions. Modern science and the unbelieving mind have concocted elaborate theories to bypass the plain and simple teaching of Holy Scripture. Among them are the "Big Bang Theory" (BBT), Charles Darwin's theory of evolution, and theistic evolution. These attempt to answer how nothing became something.

The BBT is often explained as this:

> Today, the consensus among scientists, astronomers and cosmologists is that the Universe as we know it was created in a massive explosion that not only created the majority of matter, but the physical laws that govern our ever-expanding cosmos. This is known as The Big Bang Theory... The basics of the Big Bang theory are fairly simple. In short, the Big Bang hypothesis states that all of current and past matter in the universe came into existence at the same time, roughly 13.8 billion years ago. At this time, all matter was compacted into a very small ball with infinite density and intense heat called a Singularity. Suddenly, the Singularity began expanding, and the

universe as we know it began.[11]

While the BBT seeks to explain the origin of the universe, the theory of evolution seeks to discover the origin of earth's species. Billions of years ago on the edges of the sea, there were pools of transparent jelly; "here and there on the surface a little scum of slime."[12] Out of these pools of slime, amoebas suddenly and spontaneously, on their own power, came to life and eventually evolved through the process of other creatures into humans.

Coupled with Darwinian evolution is the erroneous belief of theistic evolution (TE) or sometimes referred to as progressive creationism. This belief wants to marry God and modern science. It does not deny that God created, but claims that He used evolution to create. It denies that each day in Genesis 1 is a literal 24-hour day. Each day represents "ages" (long periods of time), with each day-age possibly being billions or trillions of years. TE is little more than humanistic Deism, which embraces the theories of modern science over the teaching of Holy Scripture.

These three theories, *and theories they are* without any proof of observable evidence, demand two questions. *One*, how did this singularity, this compact ball of infinite density and intense heat come into existence? Where and how did it originate? Atheistic scientists have no answer. *Two*, how can dead pools of slime suddenly produce life? Deadness cannot and does not produce life. This is contrary to every law of science.

Of course, the Bible has the answers to all of creation and life (see Genesis 1 and 2). Following the lead of the early church Fathers, the Protestant Reformers[13] and the Westminster and Savoy divines, the seventeenth-century Particular Baptists confessed their biblical beliefs in Chapter 4 — Of Creation.

The Origin of Creation

The Time — the Confession begins where the Bible begins, in Genesis 1:1, *"In the beginning…"* What beginning? It certainly was not the beginning of God because as you learned in the previous chapters, God is "infinite in being…immutable, immense, eternal." God the Lord had no beginning, nor will He ever cease to be. So, the beginning spoken of here is the beginning of time, as we know it. God constructed time. He does not exist in time but outside of it, and yet He works in and through time. Furthermore, what must be understood is that He is neither bound or controlled by time, nor restricted or hindered by any event within time. He is absolutely sovereign over all time and creation, not vice versa! At

11. https://www.universetoday.com/84147/singularity/: accessed 02/20/2020. Some even speculate this could have happened seventeen plus trillion years ago.

12. https://books.google.com/books?id=CioDAAAAMBAJ&pg=PA27&lpg=PA27&dq=man+evolved+from+a+pool+of+slime&source: accessed 02/20/2020.

13. *What did the Reformers Believe about the Age of the Earth?* Dr. Joel R. Beeke (Petersburg, Kentucky: Answers in Genesis, 2014).

the beginning of time, God did something. As you shall see later, this was Day One.

The Creator — the One that did something in the beginning (on Day One) is specifically identified as God – "in the beginning God..."[14] This truth destroys *atheism* (i.e., there is no God), *materialism* (i.e., matter has always existed), and *pantheism* (i.e., God *is* all things and, *in* all things, everything is God). Before considering the specifics of this God, you need to understand His nature and essence. There are several things about Him. Everything on earth and in the heavens depends upon something else. We recognize this when we speak of the law of cause and effect. In Himself, God is the ultimate cause of all things and is Himself uncaused. He is self-existent, which means that God had no origins and is not dependent on anyone or anything.

In Himself, God is unknowable to His creatures (only He knows Himself perfectly). Everything we see, smell, hear, taste, or touch has origins. As a result, we hardly ever think of anything except in these categories. Since God is the cause beyond everything, then He cannot be explained or known like other objects. (Note: He can be known generally in creation, and specifically and savingly in the Holy Bible, dealt with in the first chapter of the Confession.)

In Himself, God is answerable to no one. This is why philosophy and science have, for the most part, been unfriendly towards God. Boice gives an explanation:

> These disciplines [of philosophy and science] are dedicated to the task of accounting for things and are impatient with anything that refuses to give an account of itself. The scientist will admit that there is much he or she does not know. But it is quite another thing to admit that there is something that we can never know and which, in fact, we do not have a technique for discovering. To avoid this the scientist may attempt to bring God down to his level, defining him as "natural law," "evolution," or some such principle. But God eludes them.[15]

Again, God's self-existence means that He is not dependent, or answerable to anyone. Unbelievers do not like this because they want God to give an account of Himself to them, as if He owes them something. While God sometimes explains things to us, He does not have to and often does not. God does not have to explain Himself to anyone! And, God is independently self-sufficient (*aseity*, Latin *a se – from self*). This means that God has no needs and depends on no one. We constantly depend on other things (e.g. oxygen, water, food, etc.). Not so with God. If God possessed none of the elements which we so desperately need, it would not affect Him, and He would continue to exist. Self-sufficiency runs contrary to popular ideas about God today:

---

14. God is the most important word in this chapter! This why so much attention will be given to it here.

15. James Montgomery Boice, *Genesis*, vol. 1 (Grand Rapids: Baker Books, 2006), 27.

- That God cannot do anything unless we co-operate with Him.
- That God lacked glory and created us to supply it.
- That God needed love and created us to love Him.
- That God was lonely and created us to keep Him company.
- That God has an ego problem and needs worshipers.
- That God cannot do everything and needs helpers. So, He made us to serve Him.
- That God is limited and needs others to defend Him.

Though we glorify Him, love Him, fellowship and have communion with Him, worship Him, serve Him, and defend His truth, these things do not add to God! They do not make Him larger or assist Him in His existence and sufficiency! These things help us, not God.

Furthermore, the God who created is eternal and everlasting. He has always existed. He never had a time in which He was born and came into existence nor shall there ever be a time when He shall die and cease to be (Ps. 90:1-2; Isa. 6:3, cf. Rev. 4:8, 21:6). He can be trusted to remain as He has revealed Himself to be. God is unchangeable in all His perfections/attributes, essence, being, counsel, will, truth, and promises. Furthermore, God is inescapable. Jonah the prophet realized this too late (Jonah 1:3-17). He is not a man that He should lie, nor a son of a man that He should repent (Num. 23:19). No matter where we turn, God makes Himself and His presence known. His eternality demonstrates that He cannot be avoided in this life, or on the final Day.

Finally, God is absolutely all-powerful. This means that God *alone* holds all power over every part of His creation. No part of His creation stands outside the scope of His dominion and His sovereign control. As R. C. Sproul so often reminded us, if there is one molecule in all the universe that is not under His control, then that molecule is more powerful than God! God is able to do anything He wishes; He does *all* His holy will. There is nothing too hard for the Lord! As the ancient prophet Jeremiah said to his great Redeemer: "Ah Lord GOD! behold, You have made the heavens and the earth by Your great power and stretched out arm. There is nothing too hard for You" (Jer. 32:17). In truth and in practice, God the Creator has the power to do everything that His rational and moral perfection wills to do.

This does not mean that God can do literally everything: He cannot sin, lie, change His nature, or deny the demands of His holy character (Num. 23:19; 1 Sam. 15:29; 2 Tim. 2:13; Heb. 6:18; James 1:13); nor can He make a square circle, for the notion of a square circle is self-contradictory; nor can He cease to be God. But all that He wills and promises He can and will do.[16]

Although these truths were discussed in Chapter 2, creation cannot be fully grasped unless they are kept fresh in our minds.

---

16. J.I. Packer, *Concise Theology, A Guide to Historic Christian Beliefs* (Wheaton, Illinois: Tyndale House Publishers, Inc., 1993) 36.

Now the Confession turns to the unique reality of the only true and living God: *"God the Father, Son, and Holy Spirit."* Described here is not some nebulous concept of God, as people often imagine Him in modern culture. The name "God" is often so vaguely used that it can mean anything to anyone. This was not the case with the framers of the Confession. They spoke of a certain God, the Trinitarian God of Holy Scripture, who is one God made known in three Persons. The scriptural references given in the Confession reveal that each Person of the holy Trinity was actively involved in creation. The triune God is the only God and Creator! (See again Chapter 2.)

The Why—contrary to popular belief, God was not lonely and wanted someone with whom He could fellowship and share life. Nor was He bored and wanted something to do. Quite clearly, you are instructed that God did these things with intent and design *"for the manifestation of his eternal power, wisdom, and goodness."* He conceived and wanted His creatures to see the immensity of His glory and worship Him (see Isa. 43:7ff.). The making known of Himself to His creatures was His chief reason for all His actions and works.

The What—God acted by divine fiat (Latin – *let it be done*), out of nothing *"to create or make the world, and all things therein, whether visible or invisible."*[17] This is vividly seen in Genesis 1:3 where it is declared: "And God said, Let there be light: and *light there was*" (lit. *Hebrew*).[18] God worked, when there was absolutely nothing but God Himself, and spoke everything into existence with the word of His power. *All things therein* include everything; things seen and unseen! The universe, the sun, moon, and stars (Gen. 1:16), which can be seen. Yet, it goes even deeper to the atoms, quarks, molecules, amoebas, plants, animals, and creatures, seen and unseen. All were made and fashioned by Him, the Creator. Additionally, every breath you take, every beat of your heart, every step you take is sustained and held together by Christ (Col. 1:16-17). This is why Paul the apostle declared to the Greek philosophers on Mars Hill in Athens: "For in Him we live, and move, and have our being" (Acts 17:28).

The How—Are we to believe this magnificent work of creation took billions of years (and some even think trillions) to come into its present shape and condition? Are people to read Genesis 1 and 2 and conceive of the word *day* (Heb. *yom*) as extending into prolonged periods of time/ ages of millions or trillions of years? Is there some type of mystical gap between Genesis 1:1 and 1:2 that would account for such protracted ages (e.g., the Gap Theory)? Must these same chapters be read as a poetic literary device that is *not* literal, thus allowing for a type of theistic, progressive evolution to accommodate modern science (e.g., Framework Hypothesis)? Our forefathers, standing on the solid ground of Holy

---

17. *The Westminster Confession of Faith* (WCF) and *The Savoy Declaration (SD)* add (between the words *create* and *world*) the phrase "or make of nothing" (Latin – ex nihilo).

18. Eight times it is announced in Genesis 1 that God spoke and said (vv. 3, 6, 9, 14, 20, 24, 26, 29) and six times it is declared *"and it was so"* (vv. 7, 9, 11, 15, 24, 30).

Scripture, stated "NO!" Without equivocation they inserted a small, yet powerful, little clause: *"in the space of six days."*[19]

EXCURSUS on the Six Days of Creation:

What happened during the first six days of the universe and the world's existence? Herbert Spence (1820–1903), an English philosopher and biologist, was famous for applying scientific discoveries to philosophy. Throughout his writings, especially in his book *First Principles*, he came up with an interesting discovery for which he is still heralded. He stated everything that can be known in the natural world fits into five categories: time-force-action-space-matter.[20] What took unbelieving man nineteen centuries to discover is found in the first chapter of Genesis.

Time	→	In the beginning
Force	→	God
Action	→	created
Space	→	the heavens
Matter	→	and the earth

In Genesis 1, an orderly correlation is found in the six days between form and fullness.

Form	*Fullness*
1st Day – Light & Dark	4th Day – Lights of Day & Night
2nd Day – Sea & Sky	5th Day – Creatures of Water & Air
3rd Day – Fertile Earth	6th Day – Creatures of the Land

Consider each day of creation.

Day One (Gen. 1:1-5). The first day has a special designation in the Hebrew different from the other five days. It is known as Day One. A spherical ball covered with water called the earth was created and was set spinning on its axis. Three descriptions are given of the earth: it was without form and was void, it was covered in darkness, and the Spirit of God moved (hovered) over the face of the deep (vv. 1-2). Then God created Light, which was before and preceded the creation of the sun. Interestingly, in the final vision of Revelation 22:5, the light outlasts the sun. Why is this? To show that all light emanates from God, that light is the gift of God (not the sun), and that God alone is to be worshiped, not the sun! (After the fall, "The ancient world was a sun-worshiping world.")[21]

Then, God divided the light from the darkness. The light He called Day and the darkness He called Night. Note two things about Day One: if you had been present, you would have observed a beautifully-illumined blue ball sitting in the vast expanse of nothingness; and, even though

---

19. See also WCF (1646) 4:1 and SD (1658) 4:1.

20. http://www.Britannica.com/HerbertSpencer/. Accessed 06/09/2020.

21. E.J. Young, *In The Beginning: Studies in Genesis One* (Edinburgh: Banner of Truth Trust, 1964), 40.

the sun had not been created, there was still an evening and morning because the earth rotated on its axis while the light God created remained stationary. Explanation is given by Burgess:

> Even though the exacts events of Day One are a mystery, we can be certain that the Earth possessed its spherical shape.... At the end of Day One, the Earth had all its foundations in place... [and] had a covering of water because the water was ready to be separated on Day Two [the second day].[22]

The Second Day (Gen. 1:6-8). God created the firmament, which most Bible scholars conclude refers to the Earth's atmosphere, and the *"waters above the firmament"* refers to a water vapor in the upper levels of the atmosphere, which was "in the form of an invisible water canopy that probably existed until the time of Noah's flood."[23] The purpose of the second day was to separate the waters on the earth from the waters in the atmosphere, which would come into play in Genesis 6:1ff, with its collapse and deluge upon the earth at the judgment of the Flood.[24]

The Third Day (Gen. 1:9-13). God then separated the water *"under the heavens"* and formed dry ground. The dry land/ground God called the earth and the water He called the Seas (v. 10). Then, upon the dry land, God formed all types of vegetation "according to its own kind" (vv. 11-12), which denotes every plant and herb. Furthermore, it expresses maturity. God did *not* create the seeds, plant them, and then wait years for growth and fruit. Instead, He created all flora fully grown. At the end of the third day, the earth would have looked very beautiful from space with its blue seas, blue atmosphere, brown land, and green vegetation. Everything was now ready for the earth to be filled.

The Fourth Day (Gen. 1:14-19). Transition is now made from form to fullness, as God fills the vast expanse of the universe and the earth. He creates the "lights" that are different from the Light on Day One, and separates light from darkness, day from night, so seasons, days, and years could be established. The two great lights He created are the greater light (the sun) to rule the day and the lesser light (the moon) to rule the night. Although humor is not looked for in the Holy Scriptures, sometimes it is found (see v. 16c). Moses adds (humorously, I think) the sentence: "[And by the way], *He made the stars also*," as if it was a small thing. Scientists have been puzzled by the stars for millennia and still cannot fathom their depths. Yet, what is mystifying and far-reaching for the most educated human minds is a small matter with our omnipotent Creator! At the end of the fourth day, the heavens were brilliant with radiance. The sun was set in place, along with the moon and stars. The

---

22. Stuart Burgess, *He made the stars also* (Epsom, Surry, England: Day One Publications, 2002), 12, 50-51.

23. Burgess, 13.

24. Also, this water vapor canopy explains the longevity of human life in Genesis 5. The canopy shielded Earth's inhabitants from the destructive ultraviolet rays of the Sun and caused them to live longer.

constellations (Orion, Ursa Major and Minor, etc.) were positioned and the North Star was fixed. Light shined even in darkness![25]

The Fifth Day (Gen. 1:20-23). With divine power, God created animal life to fill the waters and air. The seas and rivers became teeming with aquatic creatures. There were fishes, whales, sharks, dolphins, "leviathan" (possibly crocodiles), and lesser colorful creatures, many of which were unknown until the twentieth century. Winged creatures of every imaginable sort populated the air, from giant condors to tiny hummingbirds to bats and bugs. At the end of the fifth day, the waters were dynamic with swimming creatures and the skies were active with winged inhabitants.

The Sixth Day (Gen. 1:24-31). Finally, God created the cattle, creeping things, and every beast of the earth (vv. 24-25). Hughes' explanation is correct: "The categories are generic and are meant to encompass every terrestrial beast."[26] Then, beginning with verse 26, an entire section is given over to the creation of man, made in God's image and the crown of His creation. At the end of the sixth day, the land was stirring with two and four-legged beasts and sounds of every imaginable pitch and tenor formed a symphony to God's glory. Unique to all of them was a two-legged creature called *man* (Heb. אָדָם – *adam*). He was fully mature, extremely intelligent (he specifically named all the creatures—Gen. 2:19-20), and was articulate in speech. He was given a divine commission and authority to rule over all that was in the seas, in the skies, and on the land. All of this transpired in six literal 24-hour days because there was an evening and morning. Or, as our forefathers stated it—*in the space of six days*.[27]

The End Result—*"and all very good."* We are told several times that God saw that the different days were good. Each day was brought into existence with order and purpose and everything was assigned place and meaning. The Scriptures are making the point that it is God the Creator who gives meaning to all things, not man. This includes not only creation, but life, death, and eternity. In creation, absolutely nothing was done haphazardly. All was initiated and brought to fruition with divine design and intent. Finally, a grand crescendo is given at the completion of all His creation work: "Then God saw everything that He had made, and indeed it was *very good*. So the evening and the morning were the sixth day" (Gen. 1:31).

What is meant by the word good? It is often used in a relative manner (e.g. "This apple pie is good," or "She's a good little girl"). However, in the Genesis 1 sense, the word is not relative or comparative, but absolute; it was perfectly good because there was nothing with which to compare. The psalmist teaches us that God is "good and does good" (Ps. 119:68).

---

25. Paul refers to this event in 2 Corinthians 4:6.

26. R. Kent Hughes, *Genesis: Beginning and Blessing* (Wheaton: Crossway, 2012) 35.

27. See James M. Renihan, "In the Space of Six Days," a paper delivered at the Southern California Reformed Baptist Pastors Conference, 2017.

God is not only good; He is ultimately the *only* good. Furthermore, He *alone* determines what is good. Thus, everything God does is good, and this is exhibited so wisely and wonderfully clear in creation.

The Uniqueness of Man in Creation

The sixth day of creation is divided into two parts; 1:24-25 and 1:26-31; the second part deals with the creation of man. The Confession follows in the same pattern as it starts paragraph 2. The Scriptures and the Confession separate man from all the other creatures. God is showing the uniqueness of man, which is the crown of all His creation. Contrary to modern scientific thought, man is not an animal. No other creature is like him. Man has specific qualities and features that no animal possesses. It is true that many creatures are endowed with instinctual abilities that man does not have.

Man cannot fly like falcons, swim submerged across oceans like sharks, or run in excess of seventy miles per hour like cheetahs, but lacking these capabilities does not make him inferior. Man is superior to all in the zoological kingdom. This will become evident as the Confession progresses.

The next clause unveils an irrevocable distinction in humanity; God made them *"male and female."* The male/man was created first, and when God saw that it was *not* good for man to be alone, He took a rib from Adam's side and made the first female/woman, Eve. All children born to this first couple would be either male or female, and nothing in between. Men and women are equal before God, without ontological superiority of one over the other. However, they are not indistinguishable. God made man to be a man and woman to be a woman.

Their unmistakable features and biological functions are self-evident (e.g., the prostate gland that produces semen, breasts that produce milk, and menstruation to list a few). This male and female distinction cannot be ignored, eradicated, or replaced, because it is inextricably wired into the human DNA. A baby's gender is determined at conception by its sex chromosome makeup: XY (one X and one Y chromosome) is a male and a child born XX (two X chromosomes) is a female. This DNA reality cannot be altered by blood transfusions, sex-change operations, hormonal mutating medicines, or the way a person *feels* or dresses.

The implications of this DNA determination are far reaching, especially in our day of cultural insanity. This excludes and condemns homosexuality, lesbianism, transvestitism, transgenderism, polyamory, non-binarism, effeminacy in men and androgyny in women! God, the infinitely wise Creator, made them *male and female* with distinction and purpose. Thus, the Holy Scripture teaches, and our Confession confesses.

What, then, are the qualities that differentiate men and women from animals? Herein lies the confessional, spiritual makeup of humans. *First*, they possess *"reasonable and immortal souls."* Rather than living solely by instinct, like the animals, they can reason through matters and reach a viable conclusion. And, unlike animals they are born with a soul, which has a capacity for a God-consciousness; they know there is a God. You will never see a lion in the wilderness worshiping or bowing his head and thanking God for the food he is about to eat! The immortal soul *fits* humans to live presently unto God and ensures them that we will live forever in eternity, even after physical death.

Second, humans are made in the *"image of God."* What does this mean? Negatively, it does not mean a physical image because God is Spirit and does not have a body of flesh and bones (John 4:24). Also, it does not mean that humans are part God or constituted with a divine nature. Nor does it mean that we are endowed with the incommunicable perfections and attributes of God such as omniscience, omnipotence, omnipresence, immutability, and infinity. Positively (as mentioned above), it means that all humans have built within them a God conscientiousness. This awareness is stamped into the human essence; thus Atheism is irrational. Imbedded in God's image within man is personality, the range of which cannot even be distinguished in the animal kingdom. Plus, it reveals morality. Man was created with *knowledge*, and *in righteousness and true holiness*. Humans are moral beings with an innate knowledge of right and wrong. That is because *having the law of God written their hearts*, they knew how to live life pleasing unto God. Hence, no human is amoral; neither moral nor immoral. Everyone has a morality, either good or evil! Originally, God gave the first man and woman *"the power to fulfill it"* (i.e., His law).

Notwithstanding the above, God initially created the first man with a liberty of the will with the potential of *"subject to change."* He could choose to love God and live righteously by obeying His law or choose to go against God's law and sin. Here portends a precursor to what will happen in Genesis 3 and will be developed further in the next paragraph and more fully explicated in Chapters 6 and 9.

The Blessedness of Creation
The Law Engraved Again, the framers of our Confession remind the readers of God's *law written in their hearts*. This point is restated to instruct that the law did not intend to bring bondage and gloom. Instead, it was designed to inspire love and generate liberty and joy. Love to God and fellow man, as Jesus taught, is the great purpose of the law (Matt. 22:37-40). Obedience to God's law shows love, produces joy, and delivers people from the wayward commandments of men. Blessedness and bounty surrounded man in his first hours on earth (the sixth day). Adam and Eve knew who made them, how they came into being, and what they were to do and not do.

A Prohibition Imposed—Added to the above, Adam and Eve received a prohibition. They must never *eat of the tree of the knowledge of good and evil*. They had the freedom to do whatsoever they desired, as often and abundantly as they wished in accord with the dictates of their unsoiled nature in fulfillment of the purposes God had ordained for them. But there was this one prohibition that must be perpetually *kept*.

A Bliss Enjoyed — The first created man and woman enjoyed the bliss and bounty of creation in the Garden of Eden because God's law instructed them how to love, live, and think. He and his wife were genuinely happy and enjoyed direct *communion with God* their Creator frequently, every day. This was indeed a paradise that cannot be matched by anything in today's world!

A Dominion Empowered — Responsibility was laid upon man and a commission was imparted. He was to rule and have *dominion* over all the earth and all its creatures. Man was designated God's vice-regent and caretaker of all that the Lord God made. Like God Himself, there was to be no idleness or laziness, but work, creativity, and magisterial ruling; the exercising of sovereignty in the Earth.

Conclusion

Much more could be said about creation, but the framers of the Confession said all that needed to be said and confessed to the world.[28] Creation is the foundation of human society, and when properly understood and believed, imparts harmony and comfort to the human heart. It gives reason to and for our existence and trains us to look beyond ourselves to Him, the Creator of all things. However, in its false notion of autonomy, the bulk of humanity has rejected the biblical and confessional records of creation (Rom. 1:20, 22). The chief antagonist is the atheistic community of modern science. Not liking to retain God in their thinking and knowledge, unbelieving scientists take speculative hypotheses and formulate unproven theories.

These, in turn, become scientific doctrine that has infiltrated most institutions of higher learning around the world. Unscientific propaganda has become the *de facto* belief of myriads. These ungodly indoctrinations militate against biblical and Christian beliefs. Without realizing it, atheistic scientists have fabricated their own religion—the religion of modern science. Humble apostolic and orthodox Christianity finds itself often at odds, and at times even at war, with the intelligentsia of the scientific community. Many Christians are easily intimidated as they are mocked by the highly educated high priests of the scientific parish for their humble belief in the Genesis account of creation. Believers often question if there will ever be a recovery of the biblical and confessional truth of creation. Each Christian should be assured of two unchanging certainties: *one*, the rejection and unbelief toward the doctrine of creation does not nullify its unchangeable truthfulness; and *two*, there is absolutely no need to question or worry because there will be a definitive recovery!

In the end, God will be proven to be true and every man a liar (cf. Rom. 3:4). Ponder the words of Robert Jastrow, a former Director of NASA's Goddard Institute and well known for previously writing two books

---

28. See *Creation and Change: Genesis 1:1-2:4 in the Light of Changing Scientific Paradigms*, Douglas F. Kelly (Ross-shire, Scotland: Christian Focus Publications, 1997, revised & updated 2017); and, *Did God Create in Six Days?* Editors Joseph A. Pipa, Jr. and David W. Hall (Taylors, SC: Southern Presbyterian Press, 1999).

entitled *Red Giants and White Dwarfs* and *Until the Sun Dies*. In a book entitled *God and the Astronomers*, he describes the dismay and frustration of scientists who are drawn back by their own method to a point beyond which it will not allow them honestly to go forward. Jastrow says in it:

> There is a kind of a religion in science; it is the religion of a person who believes there is order and harmony in the Universe. Every event can be explained in a rational way as the product of some previous event.... This religious faith of the scientist is violated by the discovery that the world has a beginning under conditions in which the known laws of physics are not valid, and as a product of forces or circumstances we cannot discover.... At this moment it seems as though science will never be able to raise the curtain on the mystery of creation. For the scientist who has lived by his faith in the power of reason, the story ends like a bad dream. He has scaled the mountains of ignorance; he is about to conquer the highest peak; as he pulls himself over the final rock, he is greeted by a band of theologians who have been sitting there for centuries.[29]

In the end, Christians will be able to tell the atheistic scientists, "We told you so!" There is a God who created everything, visible and invisible, and the world and universe as we know it, in the range of six normal 24-hour days (as normal language dictates). Furthermore, by His own sovereign will and power all things consist and are held together (Col. 1:16-17). This will be proven beyond all argument and resistance on the Last Day. Until then, may we worship, believe, confess, and serve this great and glorious triune God!

"You are worthy, O Lord, to receive glory and honor and power; for You created all things, and by Your will they exist and were created" (Rev. 4:11).

---

29. Robert Jastrow, *God and the Astronomers* (New York: London: W.W. Norton & Company, Inc., 1978), 113, 114, 116. Referred to by James M. Boice.

CHAPTER 5

OF DIVINE PROVIDENCE

JIM DOMM

1. God the good Creator of all things, in his infinite power and wisdom doth uphold, direct, dispose, and govern all creatures and things,[1] from the greatest even to the least,[2] by his most wise and holy providence, to the end for which they were created, according unto his infallible foreknowledge, and the free and immutable counsel of his own will; to the praise of the glory of his wisdom, power, justice, infinite goodness, and mercy.[3]

2. Although in relation to the foreknowledge and decree of God, the first cause, all things come to pass immutably and infallibly;[4] so that there is not anything befalls any by chance, or without his providence;[5] yet by the same providence he ordereth them to fall out according to the nature of second causes, either necessarily, freely, or contingently.[6]

3. God, in his ordinary providence maketh use of means,[7] yet is free to work without,[8] above,[9] and against them[10] at his pleasure.

4. The almighty power, unsearchable wisdom, and infinite goodness of God, so far manifest themselves in his providence, that his determinate counsel extendeth itself even to the first fall, and all other sinful actions both of angels and men;[11] and that not by a bare permission, which also

---

1. Hebrews 1:3; Job 38:11; Isaiah 46:10, 11; Psalms 135:6
2. Matthew 10:29-31
3. Ephesians 1:11
4. Acts 2:23
5. Proverbs 16:33
6. Genesis 8:22
7. Acts 27:31, 44; Isaiah 55:10, 11
8. Hosea 1:7
9. Romans 4:19-21
10. Daniel 3:27
11. Romans 11:32-34; 2 Samuel 24:1, 1 Chronicles 21:1

he most wisely and powerfully boundeth, and otherwise ordereth and governeth,[12] in a manifold dispensation to his most holy ends;[13] yet so, as the sinfulness of their acts proceedeth only from the creatures, and not from God, who, being most holy and righteous, neither is nor can be the author or approver of sin.[14]

5. The most wise, righteous, and gracious God doth oftentimes leave for a season his own children to manifold temptations and the corruptions of their own hearts, to chastise them for their former sins, or to discover unto them the hidden strength of corruption and deceitfulness of their hearts, that they may be humbled; and to raise them to a more close and constant dependence for their support upon himself; and to make them more watchful against all future occasions of sin, and for other just and holy ends.[15] So that whatsoever befalls any of his elect is by his appointment, for his glory, and their good.[16]

6. As for those wicked and ungodly men whom God, as the righteous judge, for former sin doth blind and harden;[17] from them he not only withholdeth his grace, whereby they might have been enlightened in their understanding, and wrought upon their hearts;[18] but sometimes also withdraweth the gifts which they had,[19] and exposeth them to such objects as their corruption makes occasion of sin;[20] and withal, gives them over to their own lusts, the temptations of the world, and the power of Satan,[21] whereby it comes to pass that they harden themselves, under those means which God useth for the softening of others.[22]

7. As the providence of God doth in general reach to all creatures, so after a more special manner it taketh care of his church, and disposeth of all things to the good thereof.[23]

The opening chapters of the Confession are concerned with the foundations of the Christian faith. Among these foundational concerns are truths pertaining to the original creation. This is where we find the chapter on divine providence—right in the midst of three chapters

12. 2 Kings 19:28; Psalms 76:10
13. Genesis 1:20; Isaiah 10:6, 7, 12
14. Psalms 1:21; 1 John 2:16
15. 2 Chronicles 32:25, 26, 31; 2 Corinthians 12:7-9
16. Romans 8:28
17. Romans 1:24-26, 28; Romans 11:7, 8
18. Deuteronomy 29:4
19. Matthew 13:12
20. Deuteronomy 2:30; 2 Kings 8:12, 13
21. Psalms 81:11, 12; 2 Thessalonians 2:10-12
22. Exodus 8:15, 32; Isaiah 6:9, 10; 1 Peter 2:7, 8
23. 1 Timothy 4:10; Amos 9:8, 9; Isaiah 43:3-5

that are concerned with the original creation.[24] This underscores the foundational importance and abiding relevance of the doctrine of divine providence.

There is an important connection between this chapter on divine providence and Chapter 3 on the decree of God. We may think of God's decree as His plan drawn up in eternity, and God's providence as His execution of that plan in history. Whatever God has planned in eternity will come to pass in history. All that comes to pass in history was planned in eternity. The orderly progression of thought in the opening chapters of the Confession are clear to see. God plans (Chapter 3), creates (Chapter 4), and directs (Chapter 5).

1. Overview of the Doctrine of Divine Providence (Paragraph 1)

Eight things about the doctrine of divine providence are touched upon in this paragraph.

1. Its Author

According to Paragraph 1, the Author of divine providence is "God the good Creator of all things." We read in Genesis 1:31, "And God saw all that He had made, and behold, it was very good." The divine Author of creation is also the divine Author of providence. The Baptist Confession refers to God as "the good Creator," while the Westminster Confession describes Him as "the great Creator." It appears that the writers of the Baptist Confession were concerned to emphasize the goodness of divine providence.

2. Its Foundation

The foundation of divine providence is described in Paragraph 1 as "His infinite power and wisdom." The framework of both creation and providence is God's infinite power and wisdom. "He has made the earth by His power, He has established the world by His wisdom..." (Jer. 10:12a). Christ, the wisdom of God, through whom all things were created, upholds all things by the word of His power (Heb. 1:3).

3. Its Essence

The essence of divine providence is described in Paragraph 1. God "doth uphold, direct, dispose, and govern." These are the four essential activities of God in His providence. He upholds, directs, disposes, and governs all that He has created. He "works all things according to the counsel of His will" (Eph. 1:11). God actively works upon, in, and through what He has created.[25]

---

24. Chapter 4 (Creation) is concerned with the establishment of the original creation, Chapter 5 (Providence) with the government of the original creation, and Chapter 6 (Sin and the Fall) with the defilement of the original creation.

25. See also Psalm 135:6; Isaiah 46:10, 11; Daniel 4:35; Acts 17:25-28; Romans 8:28.

4. Its Extent

Divine providence extends to "all creatures and things, from the greatest even to the least." In Matthew 10:29-31 Jesus said, "Are not two sparrows sold for a copper coin? And not one of them falls to the ground apart from your Father's will. But the very hairs of your head are all numbered. Do not fear therefore; you are of more value than many sparrows." Jesus argues from the lesser to the greater. If even the sparrows are kept by God, how much more are you? In the context, the practical application of all this is that we should put away sinful anxiety, especially in the face of opposition and persecution.

5. Its Nature

God directs and governs all things "by His most wise and holy providence." The psalmist declares, "The LORD *is* righteous in all His ways, Gracious in all His works" (Ps. 145:17). The Confession uses two words to describe the nature of divine providence: wise (meaning that there are no errors), and holy (meaning that there is no evil).

6. Its Design

God directs and governs all things "to the end for the which they were created." The apostle Paul writes: "For by Him all things were created that are in heaven and that are on earth, visible and invisible, whether thrones or dominions or principalities or powers. All things were created through Him and for Him. And He is before all things, and in Him all things consist" (Col. 1:16, 17). All things were created for a purpose, and they are upheld and directed for the realization of that purpose. God's *control* of creation is compatible with His *purpose* in creation. Providence is the direction of all creation to its intended purposes, not the least of which are redemptive. Creation is the stage upon which redemption is played out.

7. Its Causes

God directs and governs all things "according unto His infallible foreknowledge, and the free and immutable counsel of His own will" (Eph. 1:11). God's perfect foreknowledge and unchangeable will are the exclusive determining causes of divine providence. While "foreknowledge" in the Bible often refers to God's special, previous knowledge of *persons*, it certainly includes His special, previous knowledge of *events*. God knows beforehand what will happen because He has determined beforehand that it will happen.

8. Its Goals

God directs and governs all things "to the praise of the glory of His wisdom, power, justice, infinite goodness, and mercy." Three times in Ephesians 1, where the apostle Paul highlights the sovereignty of God, he asserts that its ultimate goal is the praise of God's glory (Eph. 1:6, 12, 14).

From this overview, it is evident that the biblical doctrine of divine providence exposes at least two common errors:

The Idea that Things Happen by Chance. The word "chance" is found in our English Bibles.[26] When it occurs, it simply refers to a happening or event, without specifying the agency by which it came about. The idea that events occur that are unknown to God or outside of His control is foreign to the Bible (cf. Prov. 16:33; Matt. 10:29). The concept of things randomly occurring without any connection to God is essentially a pagan idea.

The Idea that Things Happen by Fate. The doctrine of fate says that events will inevitably and unalterably occur due to blind, mechanical forces. This is the philosophy that says, "Whatever will be will be." Like the word "chance", the word "fate" also appears in our English Bibles,[27] but it never refers to events inevitably or unchangeably occurring apart from God's previous determination and present control. Like the doctrine of fate, the doctrine of divine providence asserts that events will certainly and inevitably occur. Unlike the doctrine of fate, however, the doctrine of divine providence asserts that their occurrence isn't due to blind, mechanical forces, but the sovereign predetermination of God. Fate is a meaningless, merciless, hopeless doctrine. Sometimes you're dealt a good hand. Sometimes you're dealt a bad hand. Whatever you're dealt, there is no purpose or design behind it. In sharp contrast, the doctrine of divine providence is full of meaning, mercy, and hope. All of God's dispensations have meaning and purpose, for they come from the hand of a wise, loving, and holy God who is working all things for His own glory and His people's good.

If we had to choose three adjectives to describe God's providence, they would have to be "sovereign," "wise," and "good." The Bible requires us to believe that all the events in our lives are under God's sovereign control, and that everything in His providence is wise and good. This belief will help to protect God's people against five things that hinder spiritual growth and maturity:

1. Sinful Anxiety. This includes worry about money, work, health, relationships, an uncertain future, and a host of other things. Anxiety, in itself, is not necessarily sinful.[28] It can actually sharpen courage and preserve one from recklessness. Anxiety becomes sinful, however, when it leads to disobedience to God. Without a doubt, Jesus was anxious in the Garden of Gethsemane, but His anxiety never brought Him to disobey His Father. The doctrine of divine providence stimulates courage and safeguards against sinful anxiety.

2. Blame-shifting. It's one thing to place responsibility where it belongs. It's quite another to use other people as an excuse for one's own failings, or to hold them ultimately responsible for providential occurrences that cause inconvenience or pain. Carnal blame-shifting feeds bitterness,

---

26. See 1 Samuel 6:9; 2 Samuel 1:6; Ecclesiastes 9:11; Luke 10:31.

27. See Numbers 16:29; Psalm 81:15.

28. cf. 2 Corinthians 11:28.

resentment, and division. The doctrine of divine providence enables faith to see beyond secondary agencies.

3. Discontentment. Dissatisfaction can be good if it motivates to right actions, but discontentment that springs from lust and greed is wrong. Such discontentment is aimed directly at God. The refusal to accept the station in life that God has allotted is to argue with Him, and to question His wisdom, goodness, and love. The doctrine of divine providence helps to neutralize an attitude of carnal discontentment.

4. Complaining. The frequent verbalizing of dissatisfaction with circumstances or other people is a sure indicator that one has not practically embraced the doctrine of divine providence. Again, carnal complaining is directly aimed at God. The doctrine of divine providence is a powerful antidote to complaining.

5. Ingratitude. The root of all discontentment and complaining is an unthankful spirit. We must remember that, as believers, God has not dealt with us according to our sins. We're not in hell, but we deserve to be. Whatever our station or condition, we have much to be thankful for. The doctrine of divine providence is an incentive to gratitude to God.

The biblical doctrine of divine providence is very practical. It affects the way one responds to people and circumstances. Do you really see all things as coming from the hand of a wise, holy, and loving God? How you respond to trials, afflictions, persecution, setbacks, and disappointments is telling you how big your God really is. The doctrine of divine providence also does away with carnal boasting and presumption, for if there is anything good about what we are or what we have, it is God who has done it. He must receive all the praise and glory.

2. The Salient Features of the Doctrine of Divine Providence (Paragraphs 2–7)

Granting that God upholds, directs, disposes, and governs all creatures and things by His wise and holy providence to the praise of His own glory, some questions immediately come to mind.

- Does it make any difference what I do? Should I try to get a better job? Do I need to see a doctor? Should I pray for the unconverted? Should I evangelize?
- How can God blame me for my sins? If God is in control of all things, how can He hold me responsible for my sin?
- What possible good can come from my sin? How can something that is evil be a part of His holy plan?
- How can a loving God harden people in their sin? Doesn't this make God a minister of sin?

These are some of the perplexing questions that are taken up in the remainder of this chapter. At least three salient features of divine providence are addressed in these paragraphs: The Place of Means (Paragraphs 2, 3), The Problem of Sin (Paragraphs 4-6), and the Preservation of the Church (Paragraph 7).

The Place of Means (Paragraphs 2, 3)
What are "means"? Very simply, "means" are things useful to achieve
an intended end. For example, a car is a means of transportation to bring
you to some desired location. A hammer is a means of driving nails to
construct a building. Means are tools or instruments that are used to
achieve some desired end. Paragraphs 2 and 3 address the matter of the
use of means. Since God providentially orders all things and sovereignly
brings to pass every end and result, and since no one can thwart God's
sovereign purposes, then does what I do really matter? Does what I do
in the use of means really make any difference?

1. A Concession (Paragraph 2a). *Although in relation to the foreknowledge
and decree of God, the first cause, all things come to pass immutably and infallibly;
so that there is not anything befalls any by chance, or without His providence;*

The writers of the Confession here reiterate the teaching of paragraph
1 in shorter form. However, they express it in the form of a concession. The
idea is that although what has been asserted is certainly true, something
else is equally true—something unexpected, something that may even
appear to be utterly contradictory. Yet it is still true.

2. An Assertion (Paragraph 2b). *yet by the same providence He ordereth
them to fall out according to the nature of second causes, either necessarily,
freely, or contingently.* This is the same truth that was asserted back in
Chapter 3, Paragraph 1, on the Decrees of God: *God hath decreed...all
things, whatsoever comes to pass; yet [not] so [that]...the liberty or contingency
of second causes [is] taken away, but rather established.* "Second causes" are
means. The Confession clearly asserts that all of God's determinations
are providentially ordered and fall out according to means (secondary
agencies).

Three adverbs in Paragraph 2 describe how this occurs. It occurs
necessarily. That is, certainly and inevitably, according to God's
predetermination. It occurs *freely.* That is, not by coercion, especially in
matters involving human choice. People freely choose what they want.
Their choices aren't forced upon them. Finally, it occurs *contingently.* That
is, in dependence upon both the means and the ends ordained by God.

From the divine perspective, all things are predetermined, even the
means. From the human perspective, all things take place through a
series of events, and through the use of means, some planned, and some
"random." To us, the outcome is uncertain, and depends in large measure
upon our choices and actions, as well as the apparent effectiveness
of the means. In other words, the sovereign providence of God in no
way suspends or negates the necessity and use of means. What we do
or don't do does indeed make a difference in the outcome of things.
The Bible confronts us with a tension between divine sovereignty and
human responsibility—a tension between divine sovereignty and free,
contingent events. This tension appears to contradict logic and human
reason. Sam Waldron expresses this tension in the following way: "A
course of events consisting of a series of free and contingent events is

said to produce a predetermined result."[29] God is accomplishing fixed, predetermined purposes through free, responsible, and contingent agencies. As illogical or contradictory as this may seem,[30] it is nevertheless true, as the following passages clearly demonstrate:

Genesis 50:20: "But as for you, you meant evil against me; but God meant it for good, in order to bring it about as it is this day, to save many people alive." The free, contingent events in this case were, amazingly, acts of sin which were intended by Joseph's brothers for his destruction. Yet God used these very acts for the realization of His plan for His people.

Or, consider 1 Kings 12:15, 24a: "So the king did not listen to the people; for the turn of events was from the LORD, that He might fulfill His word, which the LORD had spoken by Ahijah the Shilonite to Jeroboam the son of Nebat... Thus says the LORD, 'You shall not go up nor fight against your brethren the children of Israel. Let every man return to his house, for this thing is from Me.'"

Or again, the division of the nation was ordered by God, yet it came about through human sin.[31] 1 Kings 22:30, 34: "And the king of Israel said to Jehoshaphat, 'I will disguise myself and go into battle; but you put on your robes.' So the king of Israel disguised himself and went into battle... Now a *certain* man drew a bow at random, and struck the king of Israel between the joints of his armor. So he said to the driver of his chariot, 'Turn around and take me out of the battle, for I am wounded.'"

In this chapter, Ahab and Jehoshaphat consider attacking the Arameans. Micaiah the prophet declares that Ahab will not return from the battle alive. Ahab took steps to ensure his own safety. In spite of his efforts to preserve his life, he was killed in battle just as the Lord had announced through the prophet. The "random" shot of the Syrian bowman was the means of bringing about the predetermined death of Ahab.

Proverbs 20:18: "Plans are established by counsel; by wise counsel wage war." Proverbs 21:31: "The horse is prepared for the day of battle, but deliverance is of the LORD." Taken together, the two texts above teach that no military commander may expect his campaigns to succeed without careful planning. Yet victory or defeat are predetermined by God.

Luke 13:3, (5): "I tell you, no; but unless you repent you will all likewise perish." John 8:24: "Therefore I said to you that you will die in your sins; for if you do not believe that I am He, you will die in your sins." Salvation or condemnation are predetermined by God. Yet, no one will be saved apart from repentance and faith.

---

29. Samuel E. Waldron, *A Modern Exposition of the 1689 Baptist Confession of Faith* (Welwyn Garden City: Evangelical Press, 1989, 2016), 106.

30. It isn't actually illogical or contradictory. Our inability to explain something doesn't necessarily involve a contradiction. For example, we may be unable to explain how God can be one and three at the same time. But this doesn't demand the conclusion that the doctrine of the Trinity is illogical or contradictory.

31. See 1 Kings 11:11, 31; 12:1-15

Philippians 1:19: "For I know that this will turn out for my deliverance through your prayer and the supply of the Spirit of Jesus Christ." Paul was delivered. His deliverance was from God, but it came about through the prayers of God's people.

These and many, many other passages in Scripture demonstrate that free, contingent events produce divinely predetermined results.

3. A Qualification (Paragraph 3). *God, in His ordinary providence maketh use of means, yet is free to work without, above, and against them at His pleasure.*

God ordinarily uses means for the realization of His sovereign purposes, but He is not bound to them. He is certainly able to suspend the laws of nature and perform miracles (Acts 7:36). He is certainly able to work *without* means (1 Sam. 5:1-4; Luke 1:31-35), *above* means (Gen. 21:1, 2; 1 Sam. 23:15-29), and *against* means (Dan. 3:26, 27; Matt. 27:62-66, 28:11-15).

In all our decisions and actions, we must determine the best ends, in accordance with the teaching of Scripture, the best means to achieve those ends, again in accordance with the teaching of Scripture, and then leave the results with God. Consider how this applies in the following ten areas:

- Obeying Traffic Laws: wearing seat belts, observing speed limits, driving carefully.
- Health Care: eating properly, taking care of our bodies, seeing a doctor when necessary.
- Education: studying and preparing for one's vocation.
- Work: pray that God will give you your daily bread, then go to work.
- Financial Planning: savings, investments, insurance, retirement.
- Procreative Stewardship: plan and prepare as you are being fruitful and multiplying.
- Parenting: bring your children up in the discipline and instruction of the Lord. God must save them. At the same time, under the blessing of God, the rod and reproof give wisdom (Prov. 29:15).
- The Means of Grace: use prayer, Bible reading, corporate worship, and fellowship for the spiritual nurture of your soul.
- Evangelism: faith comes by hearing, and hearing by the Word of God. How will sinners hear without a preacher? (Rom. 10:13-17)
- Conversion/Salvation: faith in Christ and repentance from sin are the appointed means of salvation. No one is saved without them (Acts 20:21).

3. The Problem of Sin (Paragraphs 4-6)

Three questions about the problem of sin and its connection to divine providence are addressed in Paragraphs 4–6.

Question 1: If God is in control of all things, then how can God hold me responsible for my sins?

The sinful human heart will look for anything, even divine sovereignty, to excuse itself from its responsibility for its sins. But the Word of God will not allow this, as Paragraph 4 makes clear:

> The almighty power, unsearchable wisdom, and infinite goodness of God so far manifest themselves in His providence, that His determinate counsel extendeth itself even to the first fall, and all other sinful actions both of angels and men; and that not by a bare permission, which also He most wisely and powerfully boundeth, and otherwise ordereth and governeth, in a manifold dispensation to His most holy ends; yet so, as the sinfulness of their acts proceedeth only from the creatures, and not from God, who, being most holy and righteous, neither is nor can be the author or approver of sin.

This is the same truth that is asserted in Chapter 3, Paragraph 1 on the Decrees of God. Be it God's decree in eternity, or God's providence in time, God sovereignly determines and controls all things. God's providence extends even to the sinful actions of His creatures. Yet He is not the Author of sin. Human reason stumbles at such an assertion because it doesn't seem logical. We may not completely understand this or be able to explain it, but the Word of God brings all debate to an end. The Bible clearly asserts that divine providence extends even to the sinful actions of people. At the same time, the Bible is equally clear when it asserts that God is not the Author of sin. Consider the following passages:

Genesis 50:20: "But as for you, you meant evil against me; but God meant it for good, in order to bring it about as it is this day, to save many people alive." As we saw earlier, Joseph's brothers committed acts of sin which were intended for his destruction, and for which they were responsible. Yet God used these very acts for the realization of His plan for His people.

2 Samuel 24:1: "Again the anger of the LORD was aroused against Israel, and He moved David against them to say, 'Go, number Israel and Judah.'" 1 Chronicles 21:1: "Now Satan stood up against Israel, and moved David to number Israel." At first glance these statements appear to contradict one another. However, there is no contradiction. Satan was the agent by which God's anger stirred David up to number the people, an act which displeased God, an act for which God held David responsible, and which eventually brought God's judgment upon Israel.

1 Samuel 16:14: "But the Spirit of the LORD departed from Saul, and a distressing spirit from the LORD troubled him." Scripture describes several instances where God sends an evil spirit to people in order to trouble them and to lead them astray.[32] Yet God holds them accountable for their actions.

Acts 4:27, 28: "For truly against Your holy Servant Jesus, whom You anointed, both Herod and Pontius Pilate, with the Gentiles and the people of Israel, were gathered together to do whatever Your hand and Your purpose determined before to be done." No one would deny that Herod,

---

32. See Judges 9:23; 1 Samuel 16:14-16, 23; 18:10; 19:9; 1 Kings 22:19-23; 2 Chronicles 18:18-22; 2 Thessalonians 2:11, 12.

Pontius Pilate, the Gentiles, and the peoples of Israel were responsible for their actions in crucifying the Lord of glory. Yet everything they did was predetermined by God.

Let no one deny that divine providence extends even to the sinful actions of people. And let no one blame God for his sin. As James says, "Let no one say when he is tempted, 'I am tempted by God'; for God cannot be tempted by evil, nor does He Himself tempt anyone. But each one is tempted when he is drawn away by his own desires and enticed, (James 1:13, 14). It is no less mysterious than it is true that God is in sovereign control over all the actions of people, including sinful ones, yet so that He is never the Author of sin.[33]

Question 2: What possible good can come from my sin?
Anyone who is acquainted with both the holiness of God and the exceeding sinfulness of sin, and whose deep desire is to obey and please God will ask this question sometime during his or her life. Paragraph 5 addresses this important question. This paragraph could be entitled, "Divine Desertion." It can be divided into four parts.

1. The Indisputable Fact of Divine Desertion: *The most wise, righteous, and gracious God doth oftentimes leave for a season His own children to manifold temptations and the corruptions of their own hearts.* The fact of divine desertion as the occasional experience of the true Christian cannot be disputed.[34]

2. The Wise Purposes of Divine Desertion: *to chastise them for their former sins, or to discover unto them the hidden strength of corruption and deceitfulness of their hearts.* Two of the wise purposes of divine desertion mentioned in this paragraph are chastisement and self-discovery.

3. The Practical Effects of Divine Desertion: *that they may be humbled; and to raise them to a more close and constant dependence for their support upon Himself; and to make them more watchful against all future occasions of sin, and for other just and holy ends.* The experience of divine desertion serves to further develop humility, dependence, and watchfulness in the children of God. Other just and holy ends are achieved in addition to these.[35]

4. The Encouraging Attributes of Divine Desertion: *So that whatsoever befalls any of His elect is by His appointment, for His glory, and their good.* This statement is taken directly from Paragraph 5 of the First London Baptist Confession of Faith of 1646. Three encouraging attributes of divine desertion are mentioned. First, divine desertion comes about by divine appointment. It does not occur by accident. It is not outside of God's control. Second, it is for God's glory. Third, it is for the good of God's people.

The classic New Testament statement that demonstrates the truth of Paragraph 5 is Romans 8:28. "And we know that all things work together for good to those who love God, to those who are the called according to

---

33. See also 1 Kings 22:30, 34; Isaiah 45:7; Amos 3:6; Habakkuk 1:12, 13.

34. 2 Samuel 24:1; Isaiah 50:10.

35. Romans 5:3, 4; James 1:2-4; 1 Peter 1:6, 7.

His purpose." In addition, several examples in the Bible may be appealed to. God used illness to humble the pride of Hezekiah's heart (2 Chron. 32:24-26, 31). Peter, for a time, was left vulnerable to the influence of Satan so that his faith would be strengthened (Luke 22:31-34 with Matthew 26:69-75 and John 21:15-17). Paul received the thorn in the flesh to keep him from exalting himself (2 Cor. 12:7-9).

The truth of Paragraph 5 should help us to avoid two sinful extremes as we grapple with temptation and remaining sin. The first is *sinful presumption*. We must give no place to carelessness or rationalizing about our sins. Since God orders all things, we must not "sin that grace may abound" (Rom. 6:1). The second extreme is *sinful despair*. God is able to take the most severe and grievous sins, whether our own or others, and overrule them for His own glory and for our good.

Question 3: Can a loving God actually harden people in their sin?
Paragraph 6 addresses this question: *As for those wicked and ungodly men whom God, as a righteous judge, for former sin, doth blind and harden; from them He not only withholdeth His grace, whereby they might have been enlightened in their understanding, and wrought upon in their hearts; but sometimes also withdraweth the gifts which they had, and exposeth them to such objects as their corruption makes occasion of sin; and withal, gives them over to their own lusts, the temptations of the world, and the power of Satan, whereby it comes to pass that they harden themselves even under those means which God useth for the softening of others.*

According to Paragraph 6, God does three things with wicked and ungodly people. He withholds from them both grace and gifts, exposes them to temptation, and gives them over to sin. He does this because of their former sin, and it results in their being further hardened in their sin. This idea is highly offensive to human pride. Its offensiveness, however, doesn't make it any less true. The key passage in this regard is Romans 1 which describes the progressive divine abandonment of the wicked to their sins. This abandonment occurs in three stages.

First, they are abandoned to *sexual uncleanness*. Romans 1:24: "Therefore God also gave them up to uncleanness, in the lusts of their hearts, to dishonor their bodies among themselves."

The second stage in the progression is abandonment to *sexual perversion*. Romans 1:26, 27: "For this reason God gave them up to vile passions. For even their women exchanged the natural use for what is against nature. Likewise also the men, leaving the natural use of the woman, burned in their lust for one another, men with men committing what is shameful, and receiving in themselves the penalty of their error which was due."

The third stage in the progression is abandonment to a *calloused heart*. Romans 1:28: "And even as they did not like to retain God in *their* knowledge, God gave them over to a debased mind, to do those things which are not fitting."

Paul asserts that this three-stage progressive abandonment to sin is the present manifestation of divine wrath (Rom. 1:18). In the future God will punish impenitent sinners eternally in hell (Rom. 2:5-10). Now, in this life, however, His wrath is manifested by His giving them over to the power and bondage of their sins.

Other texts also teach the truth of divine hardening in sin.

Psalm 81:11, 12: "But My people would not heed My voice, And Israel would *have* none of Me. So I gave them over to their own stubborn heart, To walk in their own counsels."

Matthew 13:12: "For whoever has, to him more will be given, and he will have abundance; but whoever does not have, even what he has will be taken away from him."[36]

Romans 9:18: "Therefore He has mercy on whom He wills, and whom He wills He hardens."

Romans 11:7, 8: "What then? Israel has not obtained what it seeks; but the elect have obtained it, and the rest were blinded. Just as it is written: 'God has given them a spirit of stupor, eyes that they should not see And ears that they should not hear, To this very day.'"

2 Thessalonians 2:10-12: "…and with all unrighteous deception among those who perish, because they did not receive the love of the truth, that they might be saved. And for this reason God will send them strong delusion, that they should believe the lie, that they all may be condemned who did not believe the truth but had pleasure in unrighteousness."

This is the God with whom we have to do! He is not indifferent to human sin, especially sins against religious light and privileges. Furthermore, in divine abandonment God doesn't passively leave people to the power of their sins. He actively exposes them to sin and hardens them in it. This has repeatedly taken place in nations and societies in the past and present. Thankfully, the truth of Paragraph 7 is also found in the Bible.

4. The Preservation of the Church (Paragraph 7)

This paragraph presents the third salient feature of divine providence: the preservation of the church. *As the providence of God doth in general reach to all creatures, so after a most special manner it taketh care of His church, and disposeth of all things to the good thereof.*

The paragraph sets forth the biblical doctrine of the special providence of God. Divine providence extends to all creatures *generally*. At the same time it extends *specially* to the people of God. The Scriptures as well as the Confession teach that the special focus of God's providential care and attention is His people, the church.

Isaiah 43:3-5: "For I am the LORD your God, The Holy One of Israel, your Savior; I gave Egypt for your ransom, Ethiopia and Seba in your place. Since you were precious in My sight, You have been honored, And I have loved you; Therefore I will give men for you, And people for your

---

36. See also Matthew 25:29; Luke 19:26.

life. Fear not, for I *am* with you; I will bring your descendants from the east, And gather you from the west;"

Amos 9:8, 9: "'Behold, the eyes of the Lord GOD *are* on the sinful kingdom, And I will destroy it from the face of the earth; Yet I will not utterly destroy the house of Jacob,' says the LORD. 'For surely I will command, and will sift the house of Israel among all nations, As grain is sifted in a sieve; Yet not the smallest grain shall fall to the ground.'"

Ephesians 3:10, 21: "...to the intent that now the manifold wisdom of God might be made known by the church to the principalities and powers in the heavenly *places*... to Him *be* glory in the church by Christ Jesus to all generations, forever and ever. Amen."

Thanks be to God that the church is the object of God's special care! God is a shield to those who walk uprightly. He preserves the way of His saints (Prov. 2:7, 8). This is our great hope. Christ has accomplished a sure salvation for His people. We have been, are being, and shall be rescued from sin. Sin will not destroy the church because the church is the special object of God's preserving providence.

Sam Waldron's comments are a fitting summary of the teaching of this paragraph:

> Who, if anyone, enjoys God's special care? Is it the famous, the great, the political leaders, the Jews? No! It is the church. This is an often veiled, but very comforting fact. Where is the focal point of God's providence in the world? Is it Jerusalem, where the temple was? Is it Rome, at the Vatican? Is it Mecca? No, it is where we, the church, are. Do not imbibe a secular mentality as to what is important in life. It is for the sake of the church that everything in life happens.[37]

The biblical truth of divine providence should practically affect us in at least five ways. It should call us, first of all, to recognize *the greatness of God*. Nothing lies outside of His control. Secondly, it should call us to recognize *the goodness of God*. Even when we are suffering, we must remember that all that God does is good and right. Thirdly, it should call us to *repentance*. We have no idea where our sin might take us. We must therefore repent of it quickly. Fourthly, it should call us to *joyful confidence*. We are always in the hand of God. No matter what happens to us, we can be confident that the Lord will never leave us or forsake us. Fifthly, it should call us to *worship*. A God so great and so good should be worshiped and adored.

---

37. Samuel E. Waldron, *A Modern Exposition of the 1689 Baptist Confession of Faith* (Welwyn Garden City: Evangelical Press, 1989, 2016), 107.

CHAPTER 6

OF THE FALL OF MAN, OF SIN, AND OF THE PUNISHMENT THEREOF

BRIAN BORGMAN AND JASON CHING

1. Although God created man upright and perfect, and gave him a righteous law, which had been unto life had he kept it, and threatened death upon the breach thereof,[1] yet he did not long abide in this honour; Satan using the subtlety of the serpent to subdue Eve, then by her seducing Adam, who, without any compulsion, did willfully transgress the law of their creation, and the command given unto them, in eating the forbidden fruit,[2] which God was pleased, according to his wise and holy counsel to permit, having purposed to order it to his own glory.

2. Our first parents, by this sin, fell from their original righteousness and communion with God, and we in them whereby death came upon all:[3] all becoming dead in sin,[4] and wholly defiled in all the faculties and parts of soul and body.[5]

3. They being the root, and by God's appointment, standing in the room and stead of all mankind, the guilt of the sin was imputed, and corrupted nature conveyed, to all their posterity descending from them by ordinary generation,[6] being now conceived in sin,[7] and by nature children of wrath,[8] the servants of sin, the subjects of death,[9] and all other miseries, spiritual, temporal, and eternal, unless the Lord Jesus set them free.[10]

---

1. Genesis 2:16, 17
2. Genesis 3:12, 13; 2 Corinthians 11:3
3. Romans 3:23
4. Romans 5:12, etc.
5. Titus 1:15; Genesis 6:5; Jeremiah 17:9; Romans 3:10-19
6. Romans 5:12-19; 1 Corinthians 15:21, 22, 45, 49
7. Psalms 51:5; Job 14:4
8. Ephesians 2:3
9. Romans 6:20; Romans 5:12
10. Hebrews 2:14, 15; 1 Thessalonians 1:10

4. From this original corruption, whereby we are utterly indisposed, disabled, and made opposite to all good, and wholly inclined to all evil,[11] do proceed all actual transgressions.[12]

5. The corruption of nature, during this life, doth remain in those that are regenerated;[13] and although it be through Christ pardoned and mortified, yet both itself, and the first motions thereof, are truly and properly sin.[14]

The Confession proceeds to weave together its chapters on God's decree, creation and divine providence into the framework by which we understand the fall of man and the sobering consequences which proceeded from that fall.

The Beginning of Sin (6:1)

When considering the beginning of sin,[15] the Confession acknowledges humanity's privileged beginning. God created humanity "upright and perfect."[16] There was no fault in Adam—no sin or stain. Man stood righteous under the perfect Law of God and was indeed "very good."[17] Inherent in this perfection, man was able to not sin (*posse non peccare*) and able to not die (*posse non mori*). All of his faculties, mind, will, and affections, were working in perfect harmony. Thomas Boston noted: "There was light in his understanding, sanctity in his will, and rectitude in his affections; there was such an harmony among all his faculties, that his members yielded to his affections, his affections to his will, his will obeyed his reason, and his reason was subject to the law of God."[18]

God then entered into relationship with His perfect creation. Much debate surrounds the nature of this relationship, specifically whether this relationship was a covenant.[19] It is our position that this relationship was indeed a covenant relationship—a covenant of works. The authors of the Confession do not use the term "covenant," but they explain humanity's relationship with God in covenantal categories of stipulation, promise and threat.

The Confession identifies the stipulation that flowed from God's "righteous law" as "the command given unto them" regarding the eating

---

11. Romans 8:7; Colossians 1:21

12. James 1:14, 15; Matthew 15:19

13. Romans 7:18, 23; Ecclesiastes 7:20; 1 John 1:8

14. Romans 7:23-25; Galatians 5:17

15. The phrase is borrowed from Herman Bavinck: "Sin defies explanation; it is a folly that does not have an origin in the true sense of the word, only a beginning." Herman Bavinck, John Bolt, and John Vriend, *Reformed Dogmatics: Sin and Salvation in Christ*, vol. 3 (Grand Rapids, MI: Baker Academic, 2006), 28.

16. Ecclesiastes 7:29.

17. Genesis 1:31.

18. Thomas Boston, *The Complete Works of the Late Rev. Thomas Boston, Ettrick*. Edited by The Rev. Samuel M'Millan, Volume (Published in 1843. Reprinted, Wheaton, IL: Richard Owen Roberts, Publishers, 1980), Vol. 1, 232.

19. The Savoy Declaration of Faith states, "God having made a covenant of works and life..."

of "the forbidden fruit." By which, the Confession points us to Genesis 2:16-17: "And the LORD God commanded the man, saying, 'Of every tree of the garden you may freely eat; but of the tree of the knowledge of good and evil you shall not eat, for in the day that you eat of it you shall surely die.'" In order to keep the "law of their creation," Adam and Eve were prohibited from eating the forbidden fruit.

The Confession then identifies God's warning: "death upon the breach" of God's righteous law. Herein, the Confession appeals to the same Scripture as that of the stipulation, Genesis 2:17: "...for in the day that you eat of it you shall surely die."

Lastly, had Adam kept the stipulation, the Confession identifies the promised reward of life. The promise of life is not so explicitly identified in the text of Scripture as the threat of death, but the truth of the promise of life is implied throughout. The promise of life is recognized first in a basic question: If disobedience would bring death, what do we expect obedience to bring? The answer is clearly "life." Moreover, the very presence of the tree of life in the garden[20] further implies the promise of life. Life is held out as the reward of law-keeping[21] and the glorious hope of redeemed humanity.[22] Or, as Herman Bavinck aptly wrote, "Both in the covenant of works and that of grace, Scripture knows but one ideal for a human being, and that is eternal life."[23]

Putting these elements together, we find then that the relationship between God and Adam was defined by a stipulation, a promise and a threat. With such prominent covenantal categories employed by the Scripture and the Confession alike, one stands on solid ground to call this relationship a covenant. Man, in his righteous state lived in covenant relationship with his Creator. Adam uniquely stood as the federal head of the entire human race,[24] fully equipped to render to God perfect, perpetual, and personal obedience—unlike any of his descendants since.

But man "did not long abide in this honor." The Confession turns from humanity's perfect beginnings to humanity's fall. Satan is described as having "subdued" Eve, that is to say, Satan conquered and brought Eve into subjection.[25] Thus having overcome Eve, Satan proceeded to use Eve to seduce[26] Adam into Adam's transgression. It should be noted that, despite Eve's role, the primary responsibility for the fall is placed

---

20. Genesis 2:9.

21. E.g. Leviticus 18:5, Ezekiel 20:11, Matthew 19:17.

22. Revelation 22:2; cf. 2:7.

23. Herman Bavinck, John Bolt, and John Vriend, *Reformed Dogmatics: God and Creation*, vol. 2 (Grand Rapids, MI: Baker Academic, 2004), 565.

24. Romans 5:12-21; 1 Corinthians 15:22, 45-49.

25. Perhaps reflecting the "Anglo-French *soduire, subdure* to lead astray, overcome, arrest (influenced in form and meaning by Latin *subdere* to subject)..." Inc Merriam-Webster, *Merriam-Webster's Collegiate Dictionary*. (Springfield, MA: Merriam-Webster, Inc., 2003). Cf. 2 Corinthians 11:3

26. [Late Latin *seducere*, from Latin, to lead away, from se- apart + *ducere* to lead—more at tow] 15th century "to persuade to disobedience or disloyalty," Inc Merriam-Webster, *Merriam-Webster's Collegiate Dictionary*. (Springfield, MA: Merriam-Webster, Inc., 2003).

on Adam. The Confession makes clear that Adam was not compelled, Eve's seduction was not irresistible. Adam chose to break the law of their creation. Adam knew the command and could have kept it; thus, the responsibility falls squarely on his shoulders. *Adam did willfully transgress the law of their creation.* The Confession then reiterates its conclusion on divine providence from Chapter 5: Even this gross act of rebellion by humanity's head was purposed for the glory of God. Has God included evil in His sovereign plans?

Here, in arguably the greatest sin ever committed, the Confession states clearly that yes, indeed, God has ordained even evil. The Confession does not see conflict in claiming that this violation of God's command and the subsequent fall of humanity was both, "according to his wise and holy counsel" *permitted* and *purposed*. That which God permits, He decrees. Every death and disease, every betrayal and calamity submit to God's perfect plan for His own glory.[27] God's surpassing wisdom and unstained holiness are not contradicted by this evil, rather they are and will be vindicated by it. The child of God bows before matters "too profound" [28] for mere man.

The Implications of the Fall for Humanity (6:2-3)

The implications of the fall are now addressed in terms of the effects of the fall on Adam and Eve and then its effect on humanity ever after.

First, Adam and Eve were no longer righteous. Instead of being able to not sin and able to not die, now they are not able not to sin (non posse non peccare), and not able not to die. Rebels and lawbreakers cannot be said to be righteous before the Law of God. In such an alienated state, these rebels also lost the intimate fellowship they once knew with God. The Christian's heart aches for the loss. The fall involved more than the loss of humanity's righteous state. It was the violent disruption of the cosmic order, beginning with Adam and Eve's broken communion with God. The magnitude of the loss is incalculable. The sweetness and blessedness of that communion with God was what made Eden paradise. Now through one act of disobedience original righteousness was lost and that vital life with God was lost. Death became a reality. Man died spiritually that day. Man opened the gate to physical death that day. The penalty for disobedience was death. First, the threatened death was legal death, "dead in law, being a condemned man, laid under the curse, or sentence of the law, binding him over to the wrath of God, and to revenging justice."[29] Following legal death is real death, that is the execution of the sentence. Real death is spiritual, natural, and eternal. The threat of death initiated the process of physical death, it is "the stinged death of the body."[30] Spiritual death happened at the moment of disobedience. This spiritual death, if not remedied, would lead to eternal death in hell.

---

27. Romans 11:36.
28. Psalm 131:1.
29. Boston, Vol. 11, 208.
30. Ibid., 210.

Thomas Boston says, "The crown of immortality, which he held of his Creator, by virtue of the covenant made with him, fell from his head, and he became subject of the king of terrors."[31]

In this state of misery and death Adam and his posterity became wholly defiled in all his faculties. No longer would he have a pure mind to perceive truth, a free will to follow God fully, or holy affections to love what he ought to love and hate what he ought to hate. Pascal put it like this, "What a chimera[32] then, is man! What a novelty! What a monster, what a chaos, what a contradiction, what a prodigy! Judge of all things, imbecile worm of the earth; depository of truth, a sink of uncertainty and error; the glory and scum of the universe!"[33]

We who know such unrelenting battle with our ever-present sin reflect on the time when man walked in perfect relationship with his maker— and then threw it all away. The fall is no mere theological construct, it is the grievous truth that humanity forsook its highest purpose and greatest need: fellowship with its maker. The loss is indescribable.

Second, the devastation of the fall was not limited to Adam and Eve. These were our parents. The death into which they entered fell upon all of humanity.[34] Adam's sin was imputed to his posterity and his corruption was passed down to their nature. In Adam, all of his children inherited "a bad record and a bad heart."[35] Has the Confession overstated our plight when it says that humanity has become "wholly defiled in all the faculties and parts of soul and body?" No, indeed. The Confession has summarized with reserve the biblical description of a fallen humanity whose "mind and conscience are defiled,"[36] whose "heart is deceitful above all things, and desperately wicked."[37] Humanity's corruption knows no bounds except that of God's restraining grace.

The third paragraph of the Confession fleshes out this connection between humanity and its parents. As the tree is fed from what its roots provide, so humanity feeds upon the bitter poison provided by our parents. The individualist understandably rages against being represented in such fashion, but this representation is by God's own appointment. God decreed that Adam would stand in our "room,"[38] that is "place," and stead. This act of representation is the overwhelming testimony of Scripture.[39] Thus, their sin and fall from such privileged position is imputed to humanity. Their plight is our plight. Each

---

31. Ibid., 210.

32. A monster made up of incongruous parts.

33. Blaise Pascal, *Pascal's Pensées* (New York, E.P. Dutton and Co. 1958), 121 (section 434).

34. Romans 5:12 and following.

35. A reference to a sermon from Albert N. Martin, which was subsequently published (Simpson Publishing Company, 1989).

36. Titus 1:15.

37. Jeremiah 17:9; cf. Romans 3:10-19.

38. "Room"—"an appropriate or designated position, post, or station" or "Place, Stead," *Merriam-Webster's Collegiate Dictionary* (Springfield, MA: Merriam-Webster, Inc., 2003).

39. Romans 5:12-21; 1 Corinthians 15:21-22; Psalm 51:5.

generation that has proceeded by ordinary generation inherits that original sin, is enslaved to sin and by nature stands under the righteous wrath of God.[40] The Confession drives home the depth and breadth of this comprehensive disaster by describing these miseries as "spiritual, temporal and eternal." Lest this misery should overwhelm those sensitive to their dark circumstances, the Confession alludes to the hope that is greater than our despair, the light that is greater than our darkness: This condition can be overcome by the Lord Jesus who can set them free!

The English poet John Donne (1572–1631) captured the magnitude of Adam's fall:

> Adam sinned and I suffer,
> I forfeited before I had any possession or could claim any interest.
> I had a punishment before I had a being,
> And God was displeased with me before I was I.
> I was built up scarce fifty years ago in my mother's womb
> and I was cast down almost 6,000 years ago in Adam's loins
> I was born in the last age of the world, and died in the first
> How and How justly do we cry out against a man
> who has sold a town or sold an army,
> and Adam sold the world.

Humanity's Experience of the Fall (6:4)

With high-definition clarity, the Confession explains what our experience is on a daily basis. As a result of the fall, humanity is utterly averse to good, unable to do good and opposed to all good as God defines it.[41] Or, in other words, "wholly inclined to all evil." The Confession describes a totally depraved humanity.[42]

From this corrupt nature proceeds all sin. Humanity does not accidentally commit sin; humanity lives out their sinful nature.[43] The sinful tree bears sinful fruit. In this sobering assessment, we see how a biblical view of humanity radically shifts one's worldview. For example, how do we view a society composed of such a depraved humanity? If we are all model citizens, selfless and pure, then we will legislate and structure our society in one way. If this be the case, by all means, let's disband law enforcement and leave our doors unlocked. If, however, we are a society filled with those who are wholly inclined to all evil, we will structure our society in a very different manner. Those who hold a biblical anthropology will be reserved in their stance toward society. Take another example, that of religion. If we are good people who just make mistakes, then what kind of salvation do we need? Just a little help will do. The truth, however, is that all of Adam's posterity has become

---

40. Ephesians 2:3; Romans 6:20.

41. Romans 8:7; Colossians 1:21.

42. Romans 3:10-12; More on humanity's inability and propensity toward evil is found in Chapter 9, Of Free Will.

43. Matthew 15:19; James 1:14-15.

an unclean thing.[44] In our sin we are indisposed, we have no natural favorable disposition to our Creator.[45] We are wholly disabled, both morally and spiritually.[46] We are opposed to good and inclined to evil.[47] If we are wretched sinners standing under the wrath of God, what kind of salvation do we need? Only an almighty Savior will do.

Moreover, a Biblical view of humanity exalts the salvation of the Gospel. If we are merely prone to mistakes, then the freedom purchased by Christ means little. If we are slaves of sin, a sin that is dragging us inevitably to eternity in hell, then our hearts rightly soar to hear of a Savior who sets the captives free! Though the fall and its implications are dark indeed, this darkness is the contrast against which the Gospel truly shines.

The Effects of the Fall on the Regenerate (6:5)

Naturally, a question emerges from the previous paragraph: How are the regenerate affected by the fall? The Confession answers that the regenerate Christian still endures remaining corruption and sin. The Scriptures make clear that sin is the expected reality for Christians.[48] Christians confess sin,[49] and Christians battle against sin.[50] Sinless perfection is reserved for glory and no Christian should expect it until then.

Christians thus live in a great tension. Though their sin has been truly and totally pardoned in Christ's once for all time sacrifice, and though Christians have crucified the flesh,[51] yet they still commit and wrestle with acts that are truly sinful.[52] Even though a believing person is both redeemed and regenerated, the state of regeneration does not eradicate the remaining corruption of a fallen human nature. Indeed, it painfully and sadly "doth remain in those that are regenerated." Christians can truly rejoice that Christ has pardoned their sins,[53] yet the Christian with a new heart hates his sin and seeks to mortify it through Christ and His Spirit.[54] The Christ who pardons is the same Christ who empowers us to put sin to death. Both the pardon of sin and the mortification of sin anticipates Chapter 13 of the Confession, "Of Sanctification." The Christian is truly saved from both sin's guilt and power.

The Confession then says, "yet both itself, and the first motions thereof, are truly and properly sin." This is perhaps a corrective to the

---

44. Isaiah 64:6.
45. John 3:19.
46. John 6:44.
47. Jeremiah 13:23.
48. 1 John 1:8.
49. Matthew 6:12; 1 John 1:9.
50. Colossians 3:5; Ephesians 4:22.
51. Galatians 5:24.
52. Romans 7:23–25; Galatians 5:17.
53. Ephesians 1:7.
54. Romans 8:13.

idea that Christians no longer truly sin. The very first motions of sin in the believing heart are truly and properly sin. When the flesh wages war against the Spirit, it is sin.[55] That which is "truly and properly sin" is a transgression of the law,[56] and must be "truly and properly" confessed and forsaken.[57] Indeed, this remaining sin, which is truly and properly sin, is all the more grievous to the child of God since he sins against the knowledge of the love and grace of God in Christ.

Christians desperately need this understanding of their walk with the Lord. If a Christian is struggling in sin, the last thing they need on top of that struggle is to think that if they were truly saved they would be living in sinless perfection. They need the sober hope of the Scriptures: Yes, their sin is grievous and vile, yet their Savior had always planned on such sins and struggles. Though they sin, they are not outside the experience of the true believer.

In addition to many such sensitive souls, the distracted or apathetic believer also needs this understanding of remaining sin. There is no point in this life when we get to rest from mortification and sanctification. There is always rebellious and destructive sin at work in our life and thus we always have work to do. Our redemption is accomplished and yet a great, enduring battle lies before us. May every Christian be found faithful to this warfare!

Conclusion

So concludes the Confession's teaching on humanity's perfect beginning, tragic fall and wretched state ever since. The fall is the tragedy of tragedies in all human history. The fall is what has brought sin and death and untold misery into the world. The glorious beginning in the Garden, marked by the beauty of a harmonious covenantal relationship with God and the beautiful harmony of the relationship between Adam and Eve, was most certainly the way things ought to be. But that was obliterated by the deceit of Satan and the willful transgression of Adam. The suffering and loss produced by the fall would indeed be enough to drive humanity to despair—if not for the glorious hope of the Gospel. The life that the first Adam lost, the last Adam found. The death that Adam incurred, our conquering King has overcome. Where Adam brought condemnation, Christ brings justification. Where Adam corrupted our perfect nature, our gracious Savior not only restores what was lost but also crowns humanity with immutable glory. The bitter corruption that yet remains, that causes us such grief, is coming soon to an end. Jesus Christ will deliver us from this body of death and "the ransomed church of God will be saved to sin no more."

---

55. Galatians 5:17.

56. 1 John 3:4.

57. Proverbs 28:13.

Application

1. This world was made by God. It was made good. It reflected God's glory. But God had a purpose that went beyond the glory of this original creation, and so He purposed the fall for His own greater glory.

2. It is hard to imagine how sin fits into God's perfect plan, but we know by faith that it does. The fall of Adam and the sin of the human race exalts and glorifies the Son in His redeeming work. Without the fall there would be no glory in redemption.

3. But sin brings death and misery; it destroys lives. Our own inclinations to sin and our bondage to sin reveal that we cannot save ourselves or even help ourselves. We need the grace of God in Jesus Christ. God in Christ redeems our ruined lives for His glory.

4. As believers in Jesus, we still sin. But sin grieves the heart of the child of God. In this life we experience pardon through the blood of Jesus. In this life we experience warfare against remaining sin.

5. One area of theological weakness today among Christians is the doctrine of sin. The doctrine of original sin, imputed sin, and inherited sin doesn't get much attention. The doctrine of indwelling sin in the believer is also minimized. It is vitally important that we contemplate the fall and all its tragic consequences. We should reflect on how sin has ruined our lives. We should know what sins still cause us to stumble. A thorough doctrine of sin helps us to magnify the grace of God in Jesus Christ and it also compels us to conscientiously rely on Jesus Christ. It is only as we know that we are great sinners that we see Jesus Christ as a great Savior.

CHAPTER 7

OF GOD'S COVENANT

MITCH LUSH

1. The distance between God and the creature is so great, that although reasonable creatures do owe obedience unto him as their creator, yet they could never have attained the reward of life but by some voluntary condescension on God's part, which he hath been pleased to express by way of covenant.[1]

2. Moreover, man having brought himself under the curse of the law by his fall, it pleased the Lord to make a covenant of grace,[2] wherein he freely offereth unto sinners life and salvation by Jesus Christ, requiring of them faith in him, that they may be saved;[3] and promising to give unto all those that are ordained unto eternal life, his Holy Spirit, to make them willing and able to believe.[4]

3. This covenant is revealed in the gospel; first of all to Adam in the promise of salvation by the seed of the woman,[5] and afterwards by farther steps, until the full discovery thereof was completed in the New Testament[6]; and it is founded in that eternal covenant transaction that was between the Father and the Son about the redemption of the elect;[7] and it is alone by the grace of this covenant that all of the posterity of fallen Adam that ever were saved did obtain life and blessed immortality, man being now utterly incapable of acceptance with God upon those terms on which Adam stood in his state of innocency.[8]

---

1. Luke 17:10; Job 35:7-8
2. Genesis 2:17; Galatians 3:10; Romans 3:20-21
3. Romans 8:3; Mark 16:15-16; John 3:16
4. Ezekiel 36:26-27; John 6:44-45; Psalm 110:3
5. Genesis 3:15
6. Hebrews 1:16
7. 2 Timothy 1:9; Titus 1:2
8. Hebrews 11:6,13; Romans 4:1-2; Acts 4:12; John 8:56

Introduction

"For this is My blood of the new covenant, which is shed for many for the remission of sins" (Matt. 26:28).

The language of covenant is at the heart of biblical Christianity. In the verse above, Jesus connects His blood, the New Covenant, and the forgiveness of sins. As sinners saved by grace, we surely want to understand the meaning and relationship of shed blood, forgiveness, and covenant. In many of our churches, we regularly employ Paul's repetition of Jesus' words in our celebration of the Lord's Supper. We frequently hear "this cup is the new covenant in My blood. This do, as often as you drink it, in remembrance of Me" (1 Cor. 11:25). The word *covenant* is scattered from Genesis to Revelation in its three hundred and eighteen uses in the Bible. Additionally, God's historic covenants made with men are foundational to the very structure of Scripture. Our Lord's linkage of blood, covenant, and forgiveness; the Apostle's reference to covenant in the Lord's Supper; its frequent usage; and its structural characteristics all mandate that we understand the meaning of covenant. So what is God's covenant?

This chapter's title, "Of God's Covenant," and the key designation of "the covenant of grace" in paragraph two of the *London Baptist Confession of Faith* may lead the reader to think that there is one explicit, historic, biblical covenant represented by these terms. However, that is not the case. The Bible does not explicitly use the term *covenant of grace*. Nor does "Of God's Covenant" or the *covenant of grace* refer to one, specific, historic covenant that God made with Himself or with humanity.

It is important to understand that these three paragraphs of the London Baptist Confession of Faith actually refer to three different covenants. Paragraph three speaks of the "eternal covenant transaction" involving the Father and Son before time and is the first covenant in chronological order. This pre-time Trinitarian arrangement is often referred to as the "covenant of redemption"[9] or the "counsel of redemption."[10] Secondly, paragraph one refers to the provisions between God and sinless Adam as a covenant. Most often this is called the *covenant of works* or the *covenant of creation*.[11] Finally, in order of time, paragraph two explicitly mentions "the covenant of grace."[12] With over three-hundred references to the word *covenant* in the Bible, it is a prevalent biblical theme. Yet, there is no explicit and exact recording of *the covenant of grace*. Paul does write of several historic "covenants of promise" (Eph. 2:12), which plainly attest God's covenantal grace in the salvation of sinners. Throughout Biblical history, God has solemnly promised to graciously save based on Jesus' sacrificial death. There are different historic covenants between God and

9. Louis Berkof, *Systematic Theology* (Grand Rapids, MI: Wm. B. Eerdmans Publishing Co.,1977), 265.

10. Herman Bavinck, *Our Reasonable Faith: A Survey of Christian Doctrine* (Grand Rapids: Baker, 1977), 270.

11. O. Palmer Robertson, *The Christ of the Covenants* (Grand Rapids: Baker Book House, 1980), 67.

12. John Murray, *The Covenant of Grace* (Presbyterian and Reformed Publishing, 1988).

man, but they are unified by the same promise. So *the covenant of grace* is a theological concept like the Trinity, which is derived, not from a specific text in the Bible, but from the Bible's overall message. By using "covenant of grace," the Confession refers to God's oath-sworn promises to redeem sinful man, which progressively unfold in time and are founded on God's eternal plan to save a people for Himself. The *covenant of grace* "is called this because it issues from the grace of God, has grace as its content, and has its final purpose in the glorification of God's grace."[13]

BEFORE TIME	**IN TIME**
God's Eternal Plan to Save	God's Dealing with Man in Time
	God's Eternal Plan in History
Covenant of Redemption	
Covenant of Peace	***Covenant of Grace***
Covenant of Life	
Counsel of Peace	
Counsel of Redemption	

BEFORE TIME	**IN TIME**	**AFTER TIME**
God's All Embracive Decree and Its Outworking in Time and Eternity		
Trinitarian Economy of Salvation		

Our London Baptist Confession of Faith wants us to see the Lord Jesus as the great descendant of Eve who conquered the devil. Chapter 6 lays out the sad reality of Adam's sin and the ensuing punishment on our race. Chapter 8 speaks of Jesus as our redemptive Mediator "according to the covenant made between" the Father and the Son (LCF, 8.1). Therefore, this chapter on God's Covenant is the bridge from humankind's desperate plight in sin to the bright hope of salvation through the Mediator of the New Covenant (Heb. 8:6; 9:15; 12:24).

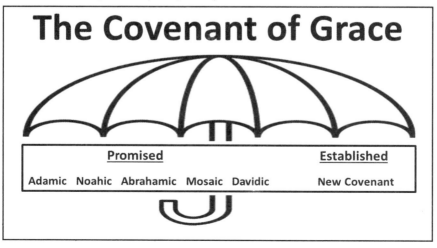

The Covenant of Grace

Promised	Established
Adamic Noahic Abrahamic Mosaic Davidic	New Covenant

Our Baptist Confession's chapter on God's Covenant differs significantly from the Westminster Confession or Savoy Declaration. Our 1689 Confession is much briefer, for we have only three paragraphs, while the Westminster has six and the Savoy has five.[14] Paragraph one in each is very similar. Our paragraph two is only slightly different from paragraph three in the Westminster and Savoy. However, our paragraph three is altogether different from the Westminster and Savoy. Our forefathers obviously wanted to retain the covenantal model as witnessed in our paragraphs one and two. However, they judged that biblical faithfulness required a departure from the Presbyterian and Independent models. "The 2LCF statement is briefer but, at the same time, is far more comprehensive than either of the paedobaptist statements. Its paragraph 3 is a wonderful redemptive-historical overview of the covenantal purpose of God in the gospel."[15]

Paragraph 1: The General Necessity of a Divine Covenant

The need for this divine covenant is found in the Creator/creature distinction. It is important to note that sin is not the reason for God making a covenant. The reason rather is because of "the distance between God and the creature. This need for voluntary condescension on God's part transcends the exigencies (demanding circumstances) of redemption."[16]

Robertson observes, "By the very act of creating man in his own likeness and image, God established a unique relationship between himself and creation. In addition to this sovereign creation-act, God spoke to man, thus determining precisely the role of man in creation."[17] God must condescend to man in order to tell Adam that there exists a probation with a tree of the knowledge of good and evil and the possibility of a confirmed righteousness with the tree of life. "Adam acted in a public capacity; not only his destiny but that of the whole race was bound up with his conduct, for good or for evil (Rom. 5:12-19; 1 Cor. 15:22, 45, 46)."[18] The terms for Adam acting as a sinless but mutable federal head of humanity are graciously spelled out by God. Later in the Bible, there is a direct comparison made between Adam and Christ. Murray says, "They stand in unique relations to mankind. There is none before Adam – he is the first man. There is none between – he is the second man.

---

14. Don Lowe, "A Tabular Comparison of the 1646 Westminster Confession of Faith, the 1658 Savoy Declaration of Faith, the 1677/1689 London Baptist Confession of Faith and the 1742 Philadelphia Confession of Faith," *Analogical Thoughts, The Virtual Home of James N. Anderson*, 2007, https://www.proginosko.com/docs/wcf_sdfo_lbcf.html. (accessed February 6, 2020).

15. Richard C. Barcellos, *Recovering a Covenantal Heritage: Essays in Baptist Covenant Theology* (Palmdale, Calif.: RBAP,2014), 66.

16. Greg Nichols, *Covenant Theology: A Reformed and Baptistic Perspective on God's Covenants* (Birmingham, Ala.: Solid Ground Christian Books, 2011), 6.

17. Robertson, *Christ of the Covenants*, 67.

18. John Murray, *Collected Writings of John Murray: Volume Two – Select Lectures in Systematic Theology* (Edinburgh: Banner of Truth Trust, 1977), 2:49.

There is none after Christ – he is the last Adam (1 Cor. 15:44-49)."[19] Jesus
is identified as the Mediator of the New Covenant, and similarly, the
terms of sinless Adam's acting for humanity must be and were graciously
spelled out by God. Nichols notes:

> This great reality forms the foundation and introduction of the presentation
> of divine covenant. This informs us that above all else, God's covenantal
> actions express his voluntary, loving condescension. In a covenant, God
> voluntarily condescends to bless man, who is an unprofitable servant, who
> has not merited it, even when he has walked in the path of obedience. At
> its very root, divine covenant displays voluntary condescension in which
> God blesses and rewards men in the pathway of obedience.[20]

Paragraph 2: The Focus and Implementation of the Covenant
This second paragraph is largely dependent on the wording of the third
paragraph of the Westminster and Savoy. Fundamentally, it describes
how God brings men out of wrath and into grace. First mentioned is
the universal offer of the gospel to sinners, which requires faith in Jesus
Christ. Then follows *the particular promise of regeneration* by the Holy Spirit
for the elect. Salvation is freely offered to sinners universally. However,
salvation actually comes to those who were chosen to receive the Holy
Spirit. These are important truths regarding how God implements His
gracious covenant. However, we need to recognize that this paragraph
does not provide us with a careful, biblical definition[21] of the *covenant
of grace*.[22] In this paragraph, the Particular Baptists underscored their
theological unity with the Westminster and Savoy divines,[23] for "both
sides, the covenant of grace is the covenant through which the elect
obtain salvation."[24]

Paragraph 3: Three Significant Features of the Covenant of Grace
While the second paragraph highlights unity, the third paragraph
shows advancement. This covenant is *progressively revealed* in the Bible,
beginning with Adam after the fall. This revelation begins with Genesis
3:15 and then progresses with the development of biblical revelation,
culminating in the New Testament (Heb. 1:1-2). Renihan remarks:

> In their Confession, the Particular Baptists directly tied the covenant of
> grace to the gospel. Where the gospel is found, there is the covenant of
> grace. As the gospel was progressively made known throughout history,
> the covenant of grace was progressively made known throughout history.
> The covenant of grace should not be flattened into two administrations,

19. Murray, *Collected Writings,* 2:49.

20. Nichols, *Covenant Theology,* 7.

21. Nichols, Ibid., 13.

22. Samuel E. Waldron, *A Modern Exposition of the 1689 Baptist Confession of Faith* (Darlington, England: Evangelical Press, 1989), 113.

23. Samuel D. Renihan, *From Shadow to Substance – The Federal Theology of the English Particular Baptists* (1642-1704) (Oxford, England: Regent's Park College, 2018), 185.

24. Ibid. 185.

oversimplifying its progressive revelation and complex relationship to the old covenant. Rather, the covenant of grace should be seen through "farther steps."[25]

Particular Baptists underscored that the covenant of grace was realized only in the New Covenant. "If Westminster federalism can be summarized as 'one covenant under two administrations,' that of the 1689 would be, 'one covenant revealed progressively and concluded formally under the new covenant.'"[26] In this, our Baptist forbears followed John Owen who argued that the *covenant of grace* was definitively established with the New Covenant at the death of Jesus (Heb. 8:6).[27] This progressive revelation, in time, is *based on an eternal Trinitarian plan* established prior to the creation of the world. In this explicit appeal, our Confession advances beyond its parent documents. It "closely connected the historical application of salvation, the covenant of grace, to the decree of salvation, the covenant of redemption."[28] Finally, God's grace in this covenant is *the only way of salvation* for all the sinful descendants of Adam.

These three paragraphs suggest a wide spectrum and a rich depth of biblical teaching. However, more can be said of the historic, divine covenants as revealed in the Bible. We will note a method of studying the divine covenants, an overview of the divine covenants, the relationship of the divine covenants, and the practical importance of the divine covenants.

1. Definition and Biblical Basis of Biblical Theology
In paragraph three, The London Confession of Faith speaks of the progressive revelation of the covenant of grace, thereby suggesting a particular discipline called Biblical Theology. Biblical Theology is the study of the history of God's revelation to man. It is one of the four major theological disciplines; the remaining three being Systematic Theology, Pastoral Theology, and Historical Theology.[29] Biblical Theology looks on the Bible not as one immediate word from God that dropped out of heaven but considers the historical process of revelation. It considers that God revealed Himself through different means in different eras of biblical history. It considers that the culmination of God's revelation came

---

25. Ibid., 188.

26. Pascal Denault, *The Distinctiveness of Baptist Covenant Theology: A Comparison Between Seventeenth-Century Particular Baptist and Paedobaptist Federalism* (Birmingham, Ala.: Solid Ground Christian Books, 2013), 63.

27. *Denault, The Distinctiveness of Baptist Covenant Theology*, 65. "All the obedience required in it, all the worship appointed by it, all the privileges exhibited in it, and the grace administered with them, are all given for a statute, law, and ordinance to the church. That which before lay hid in promises, in many things obscure, [...] was now brought to light; and that covenant which had invisibly, in the way of promise, put forth its efficacy under types and shadows, was now solemnly sealed, ratified, and confirmed, in the death and resurrection of Christ."

28. Renihan, *From Shadow to Substance*, 192.

29. Geerhardus Vos, *Biblical Theology: Old and New Testaments* (Grand Rapids: Wm. B. Eerdmans Publishing, 1975), 4.

to us in His Son, Jesus Christ. This approach of studying the Bible as a progressive unfolding was found in seed form in the early church.[30]

The biblical basis of this approach to Scripture is found most plainly in Hebrews 1:1-2. This text speaks, firstly, of a process. The Bible was not given all at once. God revealed His mind over thousands of years as He spoke "at various times." Next, the passage highlights the variation in the process of God's communication. God revealed Himself by "various ways" or different means including angels, dreams, audible voices, and a voice within the prophets. Thirdly, verse 2 tells how God's revelation came to its fulfillment in the Son because God "has in these last days spoken to us by His Son."

Biblical Theology traces the covenants down through biblical history. The covenants are very important to this study because they manifest a fundamental organizing principle of the Bible (2 Cor. 3:6; Heb. 8:13; 12:24). Further, God's redemptive dealings with man come in terms of these solemnized gospel promises. How does God save men? He makes covenants with leading biblical figures such as Noah, Abraham, Moses, and David. Jesus speaks of His shed blood as the blood of the New Covenant (Heb. 9:18-20; Luke 22:20). These covenants are foundational to our salvation. To be separated from God is to be excluded from the covenants of promise (Eph. 2:11-12). The covenants are at the heart of the Gospel, and therefore, we need to understand them. To what is Paul referring when he mentions these covenants of promise?

2. An Overview of the Historic Divine Covenants

1. The Introductory Usage of Covenant in the Bible
The Bible records covenants made between men such as Abimelech and Abraham (Gen. 21:22-34), Abimelech and Isaac (Gen. 26:28), and Laban and Jacob (Gen 31:44). The marriage relationship is founded on the marital vow known as a covenant between husband and wife before God (Mal 2:13-35) and between the married individual and God (Prov. 2:17). These covenants are solemn promises that are broken only at great personal peril. Then there are covenants made between men and God (Jer. 34:1-19). Of particular interest here is the human participants walking between split animals in a manner found among ancient treaties. It appears that, by walking between the divided animals, they acknowledge that a similar fate should come to those who break their solemn "covenanted" promise. Finally, Scripture speaks of covenants between God and man (Luke 1:72-73).

2. A Definition of Covenant
God's redemptive covenants to man may be defined as "a bond in blood sovereignly administered"[31] or a life or death bond sovereignly

---

30. J. Barton Payne, *The Theology of the Older Testament* (Grand Rapids: Zondervan Publishing House, 1980), 25.

31. Robertson, *Christ of the Covenants*, 4.

administered. The redemptive covenants create a bond that binds the parties together. The recurring covenantal theme is "I will be their God and they shall be my people" (Gen. 17:8; Jer. 31:33; 2 Cor. 6:16; Rev. 21:7). "In blood" is drawn from the oft-repeated graphic language in Hebrew of "cutting a covenant" (Gen. 15:18), Moses' sprinkling blood in the covenant ceremony (Ex. 24:8; Heb. 9:19-20), and the fact that the New Covenant is established by the shedding of our Savior's blood (Matt. 26:28; Heb. 13:20). The "in blood" or "life or death" speaks of the consequences of ignoring and despising God's covenant (Gen. 2:16; Jer. 34:18-20; Heb. 10:29). "Sovereignly administered" highlights the fact that God unilaterally initiates His covenants (Gen. 15:17-18) and they do not involve negotiation like human contracts. These covenants are gracious, which underscores the unmerited favor of God in His saving of sinners. If we think of sin as causing a great chasm between God and man, then the covenants make up the great bridge that spans the chasm. Or, to change the figure to the medical realm, the covenants are like the syringe by which the medicine of salvation is brought to man.

3. Identification of the Seven Historic Divine Covenants

3.1. The Pre-Fall Covenant of Creation

The pre-fall covenant of creation[32] or the *covenant of works* is not a redemptive covenant in the sense of the later post-fall covenants. Prior to the fall, there was no sin from which humans had to be redeemed. Yet, God did have an arrangement with Adam which proved instructive for the later redemptive covenants. In early Genesis, prior to the fall into sin, God told Adam that he would die if he disobeyed, implying that Adam would continue in perfection as long as he worked obedience (Gen. 2:16-17). Theologians have often called this pre-fall arrangement the *covenant of works*. After man's rebellion, there was need of redemptive grace, and so theologians spoke of the *covenant of grace* to highlight this need.

John Murray recommends the terminology of *Adamic Administration* over the *covenant of works* for the pre-fall arrangement to avoid unnecessary confusion.[33] Greg Nichols recommends naming this arrangement the *Adamic Covenant*.[34] Nichols points out that the London Confession of Faith does not follow the Westminster Confession or the Savoy Declaration in using the term *covenant of works* here in this chapter on God's Covenant. Our Baptist Confession is comfortable using the term *covenant of works* in 19.6 and 20.1. Without using the designation in 6.1, it still spells out the key features. Sam Renihan demonstrates that "A careful search for the covenant of works in the Particular Baptists' writings yields plentiful but

---

32. The Particular Baptist, Nehemiah Coxe, refers to this arrangement as "the covenant of creation, covenant of works, covenant of friendship and a covenant of rich bounty and goodness" (Barcellos, *Covenantal Heritage*, 29).

33. Murray, *Collected Writings*, 2:49.

34. Nichols, *Covenant Theology:* Appendix 2: The Adamic Covenant, 321.

scattered fruit."[35] Nehemiah Coxe, a likely editor of this chapter for the Particular Baptists, said, "Although it be not in Scripture expressly called a Covenant, yet it has the express Nature of a Covenant."[36] Whatever the name, this arrangement God made with His son, Adam, as a sinless creature was a filial relationship with household rules (Gen. 1:26; Luke 3:38) including the horrible consequence of death for disobedience and a strongly implied promise of eternal reward.

3.2. The Adamic Covenant

Very early on in history, we find a need for this redemptive covenant as God's redeeming grace first intrudes into man's rebellion (Gen. 3:15). Here is the initial promise of a human redeemer who will vanquish the devil. Already in Genesis 4, Cain and Abel knew of animal sacrifices, which of course all point to Christ. God initiates the Adamic Covenant since He promises to sever the sinful alliance between our first parents and the devil. The major salvific thrust of this promise, to crush the head of the serpent, is fulfilled at the cross and bears its fruits for all eternity.

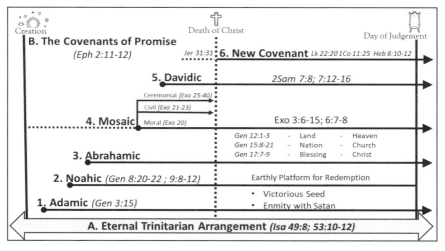

3.3. The Noahic Covenant

In Genesis 6:18, we find the first actual usage of the Hebrew word for covenant: *berith*. Here, God establishes His covenant with Noah. We learn that though man was deserving of wrath, Noah's family receives mercy. This Noahic Covenant is unusually broad. The earthly recipients of this covenant include all flesh, and it is not strictly a redemptive covenant (Gen. 9:12, 15). However, in this covenant, God guarantees to man that He will preserve the earth as the framework for His redemptive work. The world will continue with order so that God has a place to erect the cross on which redemption would be accomplished. Again, God is the initiator of this covenant, and it is obnoxious and foolish to think of man

---

35. Renihan, *From Shadow to Substance*, 181.

36. Ibid., 235.

introducing or even negotiating the terms of this gracious covenant (Gen. 6:18). Different from many of the other covenants, the duration of this covenant is not eternal. Rather, it is tied to the continuance of the earth (Gen. 8:20-22), guaranteeing the physical realm both for Christ's work on the cross and for individual believers coming to faith until the end of time.

3.4. The Abrahamic Covenant

Here, it is once again obvious that God is the initiator. God came to the idolaters of Abraham's family (Josh. 24:2; Gen. 12:1-3; 15:7-21). A striking feature of the Abrahamic Covenant is God's self-maledictory oath (Gen. 15:7ff) where it appears that God pledges to become like one of the split animals if He does not keep His word. The emphasis of the Abrahamic Covenant is God's faithfulness. Both parties, i.e., God and Abraham, do not walk between the split animals; not even Abraham by himself (Jer. 34:18-19). Jehovah alone, represented in the torch which passes between the pieces of the divided animals, walks through the slain animals. This covenant is chiefly a promise (Gen. 12:1-3) with the strong affirmation of God's faithfulness (Gen. 15:7ff). Abraham is still obligated to obey in this covenantal arrangement (Gen 17:1, 9, 14). There is a corresponding New-Covenant requirement of obedience (John 14:15; 15:6-10). Though this covenant is made with Abraham of old, it has very strong universal implications since, in Abraham's seed all the families of the earth will be blessed (Gen. 12:3). This blessing is ultimately fulfilled in the eternal life won for believers through the Lord Jesus. Surely, the core blessings of eternal salvation for believers among the nations make the Abrahamic Covenant an everlasting covenant (Gen. 17:7; Heb. 13:20). In the Abrahamic Covenant, God deals with both Abraham's physical and spiritual children. God promises Abraham a physical land, a physical people, and a largely temporal blessing. The benefits to Abraham's physical descendants fall away with the coming of Christ. Hebrews 11:9ff teaches that Abraham saw the Promised Land ultimately as heaven. Galatians 3:25ff shows that the true sons of Abraham are those who have faith in and belong to Christ. Galatians 3:12ff reveals that the blessing of Abraham comes by means of the sacrificial death of Jesus. Renihan shows how Nehemiah Coxe viewed these two levels in God's dealings with Abraham, "both as the Father of all true Believers, and the Father and Root of the Israelitish Nation."[37]

3.5. The Mosaic Covenant

God's covenant with Moses is, perhaps, the most misunderstood covenant in our day. It is instructive to again notice that God is the initiator (Gen.

---

37. Renihan, *From Shadow to Substance,* 242. "Coxe was setting out to articulate and defend... that Abraham had a twofold seed and that these seeds belonged to two distinct covenants.... Coxe's method for the remainder of the book was to distinguish and relate these two seeds and their respective covenants. He dedicated a section to the covenant of grace as revealed to Abraham, another to the covenant of circumcision given to Abraham, and a final section to the relationship between the two."

19:3-5). Can a covenant that comes from God be so defective as to include works-righteousness as some wrongly suggest? Does God really replace the justification-by-faith message to Abraham with a justification-by-works message to Moses? It is important to note that the Mosaic Covenant does not sweep away and annul the previous covenants but is specifically based on the Abrahamic Covenant. It is the God of Abraham who deals with Moses and the Israelites (Ex. 3:6-7; 3:13-16; 6:3-8). The vast amount of people Moses led out of Egypt was the nation that God had promised to Abraham (Gen. 12:2; 15:5; Deut. 10:22). The Promised Land to which Moses led Israel was the land promised to Abraham (Gen. 12:1; Deut. 1:8; 9:5; 34:4). The descendant of Abraham who would bless the nations (Gen. 12:3) comes from the nation of Israel (Gen. 12:3; 49:10). The substitutionary sacrifice that is essential to justification by faith is more plainly revealed in the detailed sacrificial system under Moses. Remember that sacrifices, whether in Abraham's day or Moses' day, are ultimately fulfilled in Christ's death on the cross. God revealed to Abraham that He would provide a sacrifice as dear as Abraham's only son. God gave Moses many more prophetical details about the coming, vicarious sacrifice who would die on behalf of others. Two examples, among many, are the Passover lamb (Ex. 12:3-13) and the two goats of the Day of Atonement (Lev. 16:21). It would indeed be odd and contradictory for God to give clearer teaching and pictures concerning the substitutionary death of Jesus Christ under Moses while at the same time supposedly introducing works-righteousness. The Mosaic Covenant with its emphasis on a transfer of guilt in the sacrifice continues the justification by faith explicitly revealed to Abraham.

On the other hand, it is plain from the book of Hebrews that there are significant aspects of the old covenant or Mosaic Covenant (Heb. 8:9) which are of a temporary nature. These temporary aspects of the Mosaic Covenant fall away with the work of Jesus on the cross (Heb. 8:6-13). Historically, some have viewed this old Mosaic Covenant as a return to the *covenant of works*.[38]

The Mosaic Covenant comprised chiefly of law—though there are rich prophetic portrayals of the coming work of Christ. There was the *moral law* (Ex. 20) or God's abiding standard of right and wrong, the *civil law* (Ex. 21-23) which governed Israel as a distinct and separate nation until the Christ would come, and the *ceremonial law* (Ex. 25–30) which specifies the method of worship and typifies the coming Lamb of God. In the New Testament, the civil laws for Israel as a distinct nation fall away (Eph. 2:13-16). Similarly, in the New Testament, the ceremonial laws with their prefiguring of Christ are no longer needed and fall away with the rending of the veil (Matt. 27:51; Col. 2:13-17). On the other hand, the moral

38. Renihan, *From Shadow to Substance*, 246-8. Nehemiah Coxe viewed the Mosaic Covenant with its spiritual and physical levels as a continuation of the Abrahamic Covenant. Alongside God's heavenly promises of the covenant of grace, God gave an earthly promise to Abraham regarding the multiplying of his physical offspring. Coxe argued that a covenant that disinherits its members for disobedience is a formal covenant of works.

law as God's summary of right and wrong abides because worshiping God supremely and telling the truth, etc. are always right (Rom. 13:8-10; Eph. 6:1; James 2:8-13).

3.6. The Davidic Covenant

God initiates this covenant since He is the one who took David from tending sheep (2 Sam. 7:8). David certainly did not start out hoping to have God make a covenant with him nor did he negotiate the amazing terms of God's promises to him. At the heart of the Davidic Covenant is the reality that this Son of David, who was greater than David, would have an eternal throne (2 Sam. 7:13, 16). Accordingly, there are graphic, prophetic pictures of the ministry of the Lord Jesus (Luke 1:32; Acts 2:29-36; 3:22-23; Rom. 1:3; 2 Tim. 2:8).

3.7. The New Covenant

The later Old Testament prophets by inspiration looked ahead to a new age and a new covenant associated with the coming of the Messiah (Jer. 31:31-33; Ezek. 37:24-28). They recognized that there would be a future and significant advancement associated with the Messiah. These Old Testament prophecies of the New Covenant speak of greater blessing and greater organizational clarity for the New Covenant people. In contradistinction to the mixture of believers and unbelievers among the Mosaic people of God, the New Covenant advances to the goal of an exclusively regenerate membership for the New-Covenant church (Heb. 8:6-13).

Jeremiah prophesies of this New Covenant advance, "No more shall every man teach his neighbor, and every man his brother, saying, 'Know the LORD,' for they all shall know Me, from the least of them to the greatest of them, says the LORD" (Jer. 31:34). In the Old-Covenant economy, physical birth was the basis of covenant participation. In the New Covenant, there is the explicit requirement of spiritual birth (John 1:12-13).

The New Covenant is not altogether new in the sense of being separate from or annulling all the previous covenants. Jesus Christ is the fulfillment of the Adamic (Gen. 3:15), Abrahamic (Gen. 12:3; Luke 1:72; Acts 3:25; Gal. 3:26), Mosaic (Acts 3:22; Heb. 3:1-6), and Davidic covenants (Luke 1:32; Acts 2:29-30). The New Testament makes it plain that the New Covenant is instituted with the Lord Jesus Christ's work on the cross (Luke 22:20) and does not wait for its institution in heaven. Of course, it will only be perfectly realized in heaven. The New Covenant made in conjunction with the sacrificial death of Jesus is explicitly an everlasting covenant (Heb. 13:20).

3. The Relationship of the Historic Divine Covenants

1. Historical Progress in the Divine Covenants

There are different recipients of the various covenants. In the first covenant, Adam stood for all men. Adam and Eve stood for all believers

(Gen. 3:15). Noah and all land animals are parties with God in the Noahic Covenant (Gen. 9:12-17). In the Abrahamic Covenant, God is dealing at one level with Abraham's physical children (Gen. 15, 17; John 8:39ff) and at another level with Abraham's spiritual offspring who have faith in Christ (Gal. 3:29). Again, in the Mosaic Covenant, the two levels of the physical and the spiritual exist alternately in view of a nation born of the flesh and a nation born of the Spirit (Gal. 6:16). However, the recipients of the New Covenant are believers alone. To be a member of the New-Covenant community, one must be born of the Spirit of God (Jer. 31:31-34, John 1:12-13; 3:7, 8:33, 37, 44).

There is distinct revelation with each covenant. The promises and regulations are new and varied along the way. Yet, the later revelation builds on the earlier content that God has given. There are different signs for the various covenants. One may have a rainbow, another circumcision, another the Sabbath, and the New Covenant has the token[39] of the cup of the Lord's Supper (Luke 22:20).

The Scriptures also emphasize a significant change from the Old Covenant (Mosaic—Jer. 31:32) to the New Covenant (Heb. 8). Paedobaptists tend to minimize this significant change. Dispensationalists disconnect each leading figure into a separate era which undermines the overall unity of God's covenants of "promise." The Bible, however, is marked by both *continuity and discontinuity*. It lays out a basic and fundamental unity while underscoring a significant progression and advancement in the New Covenant.

2. Theological Unity in the Divine Covenants

The Abrahamic Covenant's emphasis on "seed" (Gen. 22:18) is based on Genesis 3:15. The seed of Abraham and His redemptive blessing are not new concepts first found in Abraham. Further, the Mosaic is built on the Abrahamic Covenant (Ex. 3:6-8; 3:13-16). The Abrahamic is concerned with a land, a nation, and a blessing. As noted earlier, Moses leaves Egypt for a land promised to Abraham with a people promised to Abraham, with fuller revelation of the blessed descendant promised to Abraham. The Davidic is based upon the Mosaic, Abrahamic, and Adamic. David rules as king over the people promised to Abraham in the land promised to Abraham (and later Moses) and acquired by Moses' assistant, Joshua. King David implements the *civil law* given to Moses for Israel. Each historic covenant is not the displacement of an earlier covenant. Rather, the Davidic builds on the Mosaic, Abrahamic, Noahic, and Adamic, so that these several covenants are concurrent and in force at the same time. Finally, the New Covenant is not something altogether new that is first revealed in the New Testament. Instead, the New Covenant is built on all the previous covenants. Jesus Christ is the fulfillment of the Adamic (Gen. 3:15), Abrahamic (Gen. 12:3; Luke 1:72; Acts 3:25; Gal. 3:26), Mosaic (Acts 3:22; Heb. 3:1-6), and Davidic covenants (Luke 1:32; Acts 2:29,

---

39. Nichols, *Covenant Theology*: Appendix 2: The Adamic Covenant, 151, 268 and 288.

30). These are various historic covenants, but their share in the gospel promise unites them as "covenants of promise."

3. Eternal Foundation of the Historic Covenants

These various historic, divine covenants are unified as manifestations of the gospel promise in time. However, what unfolds in this world is reflective of God's plan prior to time. Accordingly, the various historic covenants are further unified by their common origin in the eternal, covenant transaction between the Father and the Son. The Bible teaches that God's redemption in time is governed by His eternal purpose (Isa. 46:10; Eph. 1:3-6; 3:10-11; 2 Tim. 1:9). Jesus made statements while on earth that indicate His redemptive work was planned before time (John 10:18; 14:23; 14:31; 17:2-4; along with Acts 2:23; 4:27). Several hundred years before the incarnation, it is obvious that there is a redemptive reward promised to the Messiah (Isa. 49:8; 53:10-12). Once again, this pre-temporal arrangement of the Godhead has been often called the *covenant of redemption* or the *counsel of redemption*. The covenant of grace, however, refers to God's historic manifestations in time of God's gospel promises and requirements for the salvation of sinners. These various covenants made in time with historical men are so united by their common origin in God's eternal purpose that they are referred to as a group as *the covenant of grace*.

4. The Practical Importance of the Divine Covenants

It ought to be obvious from this study that the divine covenants are indispensable to the salvation of sinners. From Adam and Eve cast out of the garden, to Abraham, to Moses, to David, and to our present era, believing in God's gospel promise is the sinner's only hope of forgiveness. When Paul wants to prove justification by faith in Christ for the New Covenant church, he appeals to the justification of Abraham and David (Rom. 4:1-6). There is one way of salvation. This message of the gospel begins in the bedrock of eternity-past and spans through time reaching eternity-future by means of God's redemptive covenants. Understanding the unity and similarity of the various covenants of promise ought to bolster our appreciation of and confidence in such a great salvation. The good news that comes by way of the covenants has been used to save multitudes down through the centuries. We ought, with clarity and confidence, to share this gospel with sinners in our own day. It is God's only means of saving sinners.

Secondly, some professing Christians so chop and divide the Bible that they think only the epistles are applicable to us today. Least of all, do such Bible-chopping Christians want to recognize that the moral law of God is a relevant ethical guide today. The covenants of promise emphasize a profound unity in the Bible. A right understanding of the historic covenants will help us appreciate the abiding place of God's moral law. This moral law was written on Adam's heart at creation (Rom. 2:15). At the fall, our innate understanding of God's law was marred.

Accordingly, at Sinai, God re-published His moral law by etching it on tablets of stone. With the advent of the Messiah and His New Covenant, this law is written on the hearts of believers (Jer. 31:31-34; Matt. 5:17-37; Rom. 13:8-10). There is a significant progression and development through the various covenants, but never forget that the moral law is written on our hearts as New Covenant believers! What can this mean, but that we value and seek to obey God's law from the heart (Rom. 3:31)?

Thirdly, scoffers of the Bible ought to notice the tremendous unity of this Scriptural library of sixty-six separate books written by some forty different human authors over the span of fifteen hundred years. Despite the diversity of the human authors, their cultures, and their times; this amazing book stands as an organic unit centering on this covenantal grace. To be outside of Christ is to be a stranger to the covenants of promise (Eph. 2:12). There is development and progression in the Bible reaching to the climactic revelation of God's Son. There is an amazing inter-relatedness amid the distinctive features of each redemptive covenant. As you study the divine covenants, note that God has gone to great pains to make Himself and His gospel of grace known to you. Be sure that you do not neglect this treasure of gospel grace. Rather, embrace the promised salvation by repentance and faith, and you will experience the blessings of God's covenant for all eternity.

CHAPTER 8

OF CHRIST THE MEDIATOR

JOHN REUTHER

1. It pleased God, in his eternal purpose, to choose and ordain the Lord Jesus, his only begotten Son, according to the covenant made between them both, to be the mediator between God and man;[1] the prophet,[2] priest,[3] and king;[4] head and Savior of the church,[5] the heir of all things,[6] and judge of the world; unto whom he did from all eternity give a people to be his seed and to be by him in time redeemed, called, justified, sanctified, and glorified.[7]

2. The Son of God, the second person in the Holy Trinity, being very and eternal God, the brightness of the Father's glory, of one substance and equal with him who made the world, who upholdeth and governeth all things he hath made, did, when the fullness of time was come, take upon him man's nature, with all the essential properties and common infirmities thereof,[8] yet without sin;[9] being conceived by the Holy Spirit in the womb of the Virgin Mary, the Holy Spirit coming down upon her: and the power of the Most High overshadowing her; and so was made of a woman of the tribe of Judah, of the seed of Abraham and David according to the Scriptures;[10] so that two whole, perfect, and distinct natures were inseparably joined together in one person, without conversion, composition, or confusion; which person is very God and very man, yet one Christ, the only mediator between God and man.[11]

---

1. Isaiah 42:1; 1 Peter 1:19, 20; Acts 3:22
2. Hebrews 5:5, 6
3. Psalms 2:6; Luke 1:33
4. Ephesians 1:22, 23
5. Hebrews 1:2
6. Acts 17:31
7. Isaiah 53:10; John 17:6; Romans 8:30
8. John 1:14; Galatians 4; 4
9. Romans 8:3; Hebrews 2:14, 16, 17; Hebrews 4:15
10. Matthew 1:22, 23
11. Luke 1:27, 31, 35; Romans 9:5; 1 Timothy 2:5

3. The Lord Jesus, in his human nature thus united to the divine, in the person of the Son, was sanctified and anointed with the Holy Spirit above measure,[12] having in him all the treasures of wisdom and knowledge;[13] in whom it pleased the Father that all fullness should dwell,[14] to the end that being holy, harmless, undefiled,[15] and full of grace and truth,[16] he might be thoroughly furnished to execute the office of mediator and surety;[17] which office he took not upon himself, but was thereunto called by his Father;[18] who also put all power and judgment in his hand, and gave him commandment to execute the same.[19]

4. This office the Lord Jesus did most willingly undertake,[20] which that he might discharge he was made under the law,[21] and did perfectly fulfill it, and underwent the punishment due to us, which we should have borne and suffered,[22] being made sin and a curse for us;[23] enduring most grievous sorrows in his soul, and most painful sufferings in his body;[24] was crucified, and died, and remained in the state of the dead, yet saw no corruption:[25] on the third day he arose from the dead[26] with the same body in which he suffered,[27] with which he also ascended into heaven,[28] and there sitteth at the right hand of his Father making intercession,[29] and shall return to judge men and angels at the end of the world.[30]

5. The Lord Jesus, by his perfect obedience and sacrifice of himself, which he through the eternal Spirit once offered up unto God, hath fully satisfied the justice of God,[31] procured reconciliation, and purchased an

---

12. Psalms 45:7; Acts 10:38; John 3:34
13. Colossians 2:3
14. Colossians 1:19
15. Hebrews 7:26
16. John 1:14
17. Hebrews 7:22
18. Hebrews 5:5
19. John 5:22, 27; Matthew 28:18; Acts 2:36
20. Psalms 40:7, 8; Hebrews 10:5-10; John 10:18
21. Galatians 4:4; Matthew 3:15
22. Galatians 3:13; Isaiah 53:6; 1 Peter 3:18
23. 2 Corinthians 5:21
24. Matthew 26:37, 38; Luke 22:44; Matthew 27:46
25. Acts 13:37
26. 1 Corinthians 15:3, 4
27. John 20:25, 27
28. Mark 16:19; Acts 1:9-11
29. Romans 8:34; Hebrews 9:24
30. Acts 10:42; Romans 14:9, 10; Acts 1:11; 2 Peter 2:4
31. Hebrews 9:14; Hebrews 10:14; Romans 3:25, 26

everlasting inheritance in the kingdom of heaven, for all those whom the Father hath given unto Him.[32]

6. Although the price of redemption was not actually paid by Christ till after his incarnation, yet the virtue, efficacy, and benefit thereof were communicated to the elect in all ages, successively from the beginning of the world, in and by those promises, types, and sacrifices wherein he was revealed, and signified to be the seed which should bruise the serpent's head;[33] and the Lamb slain from the foundation of the world,[34] being the same yesterday, and today and for ever.[35]

7. Christ, in the work of mediation, acteth according to both natures, by each nature doing that which is proper to itself; yet by reason of the unity of the person, that which is proper to one nature is sometimes in Scripture, attributed to the person denominated by the other nature.[36]

8. To all those for whom Christ hath obtained eternal redemption, he doth certainly and effectually apply and communicate the same, making intercession for them;[37] uniting them to himself by his Spirit, revealing unto them, in and by his Word, the mystery of salvation, persuading them to believe and obey,[38] governing their hearts by his Word and Spirit,[39] and overcoming all their enemies by his almighty power and wisdom,[40] in such manner and ways as are most consonant to his wonderful and unsearchable dispensation; and all of free and absolute grace, without any condition foreseen in them to procure it.[41]

9. This office of mediator between God and man is proper only to Christ, who is the prophet, priest, and king of the church of God; and may not be either in whole, or any part thereof, transferred from him to any other.[42]

10. This number and order of offices is necessary; for in respect of our ignorance, we stand in need of his prophetical office;[43] and in respect of our alienation from God, and imperfection of the best of our services,

---

32. John 17:2; Hebrews 9:15
33. 1 Corinthians 4:10; Hebrews 4:2; 1 Peter 1:10, 11
34. Revelation 13:8
35. Hebrews 13:8
36. John 3:13; Acts 20:28
37. John 6:37; John 10:15, 16; John 17:9; Romans 5:10
38. John 17:6; Ephesians 1:9; 1 John 5:20
39. Romans 8:9, 14
40. Psalms 110:1; 1 Corinthians 15:25, 26
41. John 3:8; Ephesians 1:8
42. 1 Timothy 2:5
43. John 1:18

we need his priestly office to reconcile us and present us acceptable unto God;[44] and in respect to our averseness and utter inability to return to God, and for our rescue and security from our spiritual adversaries, we need his kingly office to convince, subdue, draw, uphold, deliver, and preserve us to his heavenly kingdom.[45]

This chapter gives us a high and handy Christology, one that helps us grasp the essential truths of Christ's person and work as our Mediator. The title of this chapter points to the work of mediation, a central function to which Paul referred: "For *there is* one God and one Mediator between God and men, *the* Man Christ Jesus" (1 Tim. 2:5). The Greek word *mesitēs* refers to one who comes between two parties to arbitrate and remove the enmity. Paul said, "Now all things are of God, who has reconciled us to Himself through Jesus Christ, and has given us the ministry of reconciliation" (2 Cor. 5:18). The Confession presents the person and work of Christ under the rubric of Christ the Mediator.

Christ's mediation is mentioned in this chapter throughout most of the paragraphs. We will survey those portions now. "It pleased God, in His eternal purpose, to choose and ordain the Lord Jesus, His only begotten Son, according to the covenant made between them both, to be the mediator between God and man; the prophet, priest, and king; head and Savior of His church" (Para. 1). "The only mediator between God and man" (Para. 2). "Thoroughly furnished to execute the office of a mediator and surety" (Para. 3). "This office the Lord Jesus did most willingly undertake" (Para. 4). "Christ, in the work of mediation, acteth according to both natures" (Para. 7). "The office of mediator between God and man is proper only to Christ" (Para. 9).

Christ as Mediator is mentioned in four New Testament passages. "For *there is* one God and one Mediator between God and men, *the* Man Christ Jesus" (1 Tim. 2:5). This passage is listed under paragraphs 2 and 9 in the Confession. "But now He has obtained a more excellent ministry, inasmuch as He is also Mediator of a better covenant, which was established on better promises" (Heb. 8:6). "And for this reason He is the Mediator of the new covenant" (Heb. 9:15). This passage is listed under paragraph 5 of the Confession. "To Jesus the Mediator of the new covenant, and to the blood of sprinkling that speaks better things than *that of* Abel" (Heb. 12:24).

G. C. Berkouwer wrote:

> When we call the confession concerning the Mediator essential, this does not mean that we find this terminology everywhere in Scripture. Here, too, we realize that Scripture does not offer us a system of orderly dogmatic ideas but rather, because of the multiplicity of authors and varying situations, presents the person and work of Christ now in one way and now in another way. But when, in various instances, the idea of the Mediator is explicitly

---

44. Colossians 1:21; Galatians 5:17
45. John 16:8; Psalms 110:3; Luke 1:74, 75

mentioned, we observe how essential this idea is to the message concerning Jesus Christ.[46]

In addition to these passages where Jesus is named the Mediator, we have many others where the work of mediation, reconciliation, and intercession are found, and which are explained in the paragraphs of this chapter. Before we study the paragraphs individually, let us see the logical progression of thought in this wonderful presentation of Christ's mediatorial work on behalf of sinners.

Surveying the Picture of Christ the Mediator

Paragraphs 1 and 2 are a complete unit. The paragraphs contain only one long sentence each. Paragraph 1 presents the eternal plan or *purpose* of God "to choose and ordain the Lord Jesus... to be the mediator between God and man." Paragraph 2 explains the coming of the Son of God into the world to fulfill this plan, "The Son of God... did, when the fullness of time was come, take upon him man's nature... so that two whole, perfect, and distinct natures were inseparably joined together in one person, without conversion, composition, or confusion; which person is very God and very man, yet one Christ, the only mediator between God and man." These two paragraphs are bookended by the truth that Christ is Mediator. His work as Mediator was planned from eternity and fulfilled in the fullness of time.

Paragraph 3 presents His *life and ministry*. This paragraph is also one long sentence. The key thought here is that He was "thoroughly furnished to execute the office of a mediator and surety." Robert Peterson writes, "The Mediator had unique qualifications. He had to be both God and man to save us sinners. He had to be God because only God could save us. He had to become man because the work of salvation had to be performed by a human being for human beings."[47] He later writes: "This peace must be brought about by God but also by a human being. The reconciler must be God because only God can restore the rebels (Col. 1:19-20). The reconciler must be a man because death is necessary and God in heaven cannot die. The reconciler is Christ, God incarnate."[48]

Paragraphs 4 and 5 represent another unit, one long sentence each, and the theme of these paragraphs is *accomplishment* or *fulfillment*. He accomplished, in His life and ministry, the work and office to which He was called. Paragraph 4 speaks of how He "did most willingly undertake... that he might discharge" the office of Mediator. It speaks of how He "did perfectly fulfill it." Paragraph 5 also contains an emphasis on fulfillment when it says that He "hath fully satisfied the justice of God, procured reconciliation, and purchased an everlasting inheritance in the kingdom of heaven for all those whom the Father hath given unto him."

---

46. G. C. Berkouwer, *The Work of Christ* (Grand Rapids: Eerdmans, 1965), 284–85.

47. Robert A. Peterson, *Salvation Accomplished by the Son* (Wheaton, IL: Crossway, 2012), 27.

48. Peterson, Ibid., 89.

Paragraphs 6, 7, and 8 all speak of the *application* of His accomplishments. Paragraph 6 is a helpful explanation as to how the accomplishments of Christ in his life and work are applied to the *Old Testament* saints. "Although the price of redemption was not actually paid by Christ till after His incarnation, yet the virtue, efficacy, and benefit thereof were communicated to the elect in all ages successively from the beginning of the world." Paragraph 7 is a brief explanation that relates to the *two natures of Christ* presented in Paragraph 2. It explains how the application of His work of mediation is through both natures concurrently. Paragraph 8 explains the application of the accomplishments of Christ *in the Christian life* so that believers are enabled to persevere in their faith which is essential to their ultimate salvation.

Paragraph 9 can be called "Christ Only," the Reformation "Solus Christus." "This office or mediator between God and man is proper only to Christ... and may not be... transferred from him to any other."

Paragraph 10 can be called "Christ Sufficient."

Concluding our sweep over the whole chapter, the presentation of Christ the Mediator proceeds from the eternal *plan* [1] to the conception of Christ in the *incarnation* as one whole Person with two distinct natures [2]. His *life and ministry* are then presented [3] and the *accomplishment* of God's purpose in His incarnation fulfilled [4, 5]. His saving accomplishment applies to the *Old Testament* through the types and shadows of the promised coming Messiah [6] and in His incarnation *through both natures* [7]. Believers in this age from the cross to the second coming are blessed with His *intercession* on their behalf as our Prophet, Priest, and King [8]. Christ is the *only* Mediator between God and man [9] and *sufficient* for everything that we need as sinners [10]. We need Him; He is perfectly suited to our needs!

The Confession identifies the core concept of Christ's Person and work in the office of the Mediator. The particulars of Christ's Person and work are overlaid around this core. We confess Christ as our Mediator.

This chapter of the Confession will enrich our understanding and appreciation of the work of the Mediator. We sometimes need and value the role of an earthly mediator when we are in trouble with others. We want peace so we can prosper. Infinitely more important for us is our alienation from God for which we need Christ the Mediator.

Berkouwer explained the uniqueness of Christ's mediation:

> The word "mediator" already implies this, because it indicates a person who stands between two parties in order to reconcile them. Christ's mediatorship implies a complete reconciliation. The idea of a mediator presupposes the annihilation of the distance caused by sin and enmity. Christ's mediatorship is not primarily a cosmic bridge over the tremendous distance between God transcendent and our universe, but rather a soteriological solution to the condition of enmity. For that reason Scripture emphasizes the absoluteness and uniqueness of Christ's mediatorship.[49]

---

49. G. C. Berkouwer, *The Work of Christ* (Grand Rapids: Eerdmans, 1965), 285.

Looking Closely at the Picture of Christ the Mediator

Paragraph 1: Covenant Purpose

The opening paragraph begins with the eternal *purpose* of God. The fact of an eternal purpose in God shows that He is in control of human history and destiny. This is what it means to be God. It means to be sovereign, the Ruler and Lord of creation, providence, history, and destiny. This eternal purpose issued in a *plan* to *accomplish* His eternal purpose. For this He ordained the Mediator, the agent through whom He would *accomplish* the work which He would effectually *apply* to "a people to be his seed and to be by him in time redeemed, called, justified, sanctified, and glorified."

This election, according to God's eternal purpose, and for His own good pleasure, is referred to in Isaiah 42:1: "My Elect one;" in Psalm 2:6: "I have set My King On My holy hill of Zion;" in Isaiah 53:10: "and the pleasure of the Lord shall prosper in His hand;" in Hebrews 10:5: "When He came into the world, He said... a body You have prepared for Me;" and in John 17:4: "I have finished the work which You have given Me to do." These references describe a covenant which Reformed theologians call the Covenant of Redemption. This is an eternal covenant made between the Father and the Son in the Spirit. Robert Reymond explains:

> Reformed dogmaticians for the most part (e.g., Louis Berkhof) have come to designate this eternal order of the decrees as the *pactum salutis* or "covenant of redemption" to distinguish it from the concrete, tangible execution in history of the specifically redemptive aspects of the same eternal decree, which they designate the "covenant of grace." There seems to be some justification for this designation (1) in the fact that the persons of the Godhead determined before the foundation of the world what role each would fulfill in the redemption of the elect, and (2) in the words of Hebrews 13:20 where the writer speaks of "the blood of the *eternal covenant*" [διαθήκης αἰωνίου, *diathēkēs aiōniou*].

Some Reformed scholars, it is true, have preferred other designations for the order of the decrees. For example, J. Cocceius spoke of it as the "counsel of peace." Warfield was satisfied to refer to it as "the plan of salvation." Murray preferred the designation, "the inter-trinitarian economy of salvation." The Westminster Confession of Faith speaks of it simply as "God's eternal decree" (see the title of Chapter 3).[50]

Paragraph 1 first emphasizes the main features of Christ's mediatorial role and function, which are the offices of *Prophet*, *Priest*, and *King*. Each of the paragraphs in this chapter either alludes to them or describes them in detail. These are the primary offices which God instituted in the nation of Israel and by which He revealed His will to the people to redeem them for Himself. In addition, Christ is the Head and Savior of the Church, the new nation (though there is organic continuity). As *Head* He nurtures the church. As *Savior* He delivers the church. Christ is also

---

50. Robert L. Reymond, *A New Systematic Theology of the Christian Faith*, second ed. (Nashville: Thomas Nelson, 1998), 502.

the *heir* of all things, a reference to Hebrews 1:2, and the *judge* of all men, a reference to Acts 17:31. All things will be given to Him and all men will stand before Him for judgement.

The second emphasis is upon the benefits of Christ's mediation to "his seed." Five blessings of His mediation are listed. These are from the chain of salvation in Romans 8:30, "Moreover whom He predestined, these He also called; whom He called, these He also justified; and whom He justified, these He also glorified." The terms "redeemed" and "sanctified" are added to make a complete chain: redeemed, called, justified, sanctified, glorified. Verses in the epistles connect the parts of our salvation in different combinations, thus calling on us to systematize the elements into a complete whole. First Corinthians 1:30 tells us, "But of Him you are in Christ Jesus, who became for us wisdom from God—and righteousness and sanctification and redemption."

Paragraph 2: Two Natures in One Person

This is the longest paragraph in Chapter 8 and deals with the miraculous element of the divine and sinless natures of Christ. The paragraph speaks of His pre-incarnate glory and His incarnate humiliation. Yet, even in His humiliation (becoming a man), He is the God-man.

We learn in Scripture that different functions are carried out by each Person of the Trinity, usually called their *modes of operation*.[51] The Father plans and decrees. His eternal purpose stands unmoved through time and eternity. The Son accomplishes the work to which He was commissioned. The Holy Spirit applies the work accomplished by the Son.[52] Paragraph 1 introduces us to the decree of election that Christ is the Mediator between God and man. Yet, the Trinity acts as one since each Person of the Godhead is eternal and co-equal as the Trinity is one undivided essence in three hypostases (Persons).

We learn of His pre-existence in eternity. Hebrews 1:3 describes Christ as "the brightness of *His* glory." The Confession uses the expression "of one substance and equal with him." He is the Creator, "All things were made through Him, and without Him nothing was made that was made" (John 1:3). Referring to Jesus, "You, Lord, in the beginning laid the foundation of the earth, And the heavens are the work of Your hands" (Heb. 1:10). He is the Governor and Sustainer of all things, "who being the brightness of *His* glory and the express image of His person, and upholding all things by the word of His power" (Heb. 1:3). "And He is before all things, and in Him all things consist" (Col. 1:17).

The eternal Son of God "left heaven" to enter into our existence of mortal corruption, "I came forth from the Father and have come into the world. Again, I leave the world and go to the Father" (John 16:28).

---

51. Trinity studies distinguish between the *modes of subsistence* (the ontological Trinity in essence), and the *modes of operation* (the economic Trinity in saving sinners).

52. See two helpful books by Robert A. Peterson, *Salvation Accomplished by the Son: The Work of Christ* (Wheaton, IL: Crossway, 2012), and *Salvation Applied by the Spirit: Union with Christ* (Wheaton, IL: Crossway, 2014).

Yet the Confession emphasizes not the change of *realm* from heavenly to human, but the addition of *nature*, from eternal and divine to eternal, divine, and human (Phil. 2:6, 7). It is implied that He left heaven to come to the earth. The virgin birth was the means in this incarnation. It was the humiliation of the divine to enter the temporal world by becoming a man. Luke 1:35 is employed. Here the language of creation found in Genesis 1:2 is applied to the conception of Jesus. The Spirit of God was hovering over the waters of the newly created world. The Spirit of God hovered over Mary's womb and wrought conception without the agency or the seed of man, so that Jesus would be born of a woman (fulfilling the first gospel promise of Genesis 3:15), of the tribe of Judah, of the seed of Abraham and David, according to promise.

The emphasis of this paragraph is upon the incarnation, accomplished in "the fullness of time" (Gal. 4:4). This child was God yet possessed all the characteristics of a baby and a growing child: "And Jesus increased in wisdom and stature, and in favor with God and men" (Luke 2:52). He did not recite the commandments in the manger. But in this child were two whole perfect and distinct natures. In order to be the Mediator, really uniting a holy God and sinful men, He had to unite God and man in His own Person. He is Mediator in His Person *and* His work.

The paragraph declares the virgin conception (virgin birth) of Jesus, an essential doctrine of the Christian faith. Because He was born of *Mary*, He is the seed of Abraham and David, according to the Scriptures. In the virgin conception and birth, He maintains His divine nature and assumes His human nature, and rightful position as the Son of David and heir to His throne. "He will be great, and will be called the Son of the Highest; and the Lord God will give Him the throne of His father David" (Luke 1:32).

The paragraph marks the distinctness of these two natures while proclaiming the unity of the person. Why does it do that? The union of the divine and the human in Jesus Christ was not the creation of a third sort of being, in whom divine attributes altered human attributes and human attributes altered divine attributes. This comes from the words, "without conversion, composition, or confusion." The union of the two natures has been distorted by those who say that a divine spirit took the place of the human spirit in Jesus, or that in Christ neither pure divinity nor pure humanity existed, but a new sort of person resulting from the mixture of the two.

Archibald A. Hodge explained:

> Although but one Person, the divine and human natures in Christ are not mixed or confused in one, but remain two pure and distinct natures, divine and human, constituting one person for ever.
>
> It is impossible for us to explain philosophically how two self-conscious intelligences, how two self-determined free agents, can constitute one person. Yet this is the precise character of the phenomenon revealed in the history of Jesus. In order to simplify the matter, some errorists have supposed that in the person of Christ there was no human soul, but that his divine

Spirit took the place of the human soul in his human body. Others have so far separated the two natures as to make him two persons—a God and a man intimately united. Others have so pressed the natures together that neither pure divinity nor pure humanity is left, but a new nature resulting from the mixing of both. In opposition to this, we have proved above (a) that Christ had a true human soul as well as a human body, and (b) that he, although both a God and a Man, is only one single Person. The third point, viz., that Christ's two natures remain separate and unconfused, is self-evident. The very point proved in Scripture is that Christ always continued a true God and a true Man—not something else between the two. Now, the essential properties of divinity cannot be communicated to humanity; that is, humanity cannot be made to be infinite, self-existent, eternal and absolutely perfect. Because, if it possessed these, it would cease to be human and because even God himself cannot create divinity, and therefore cannot make humanity divine. The same is true with respect to Christ's divinity. If that should take on the limitations of humanity, it would cease to be divine, and even God is not able to destroy divinity. Hence, since Christ is both God and man, it follows that he cannot be a mixture of both, which is neither. Hence, while the Scriptures constantly affirm (as we have seen) of the one Person whatsoever is true, without exception, of either nature, they never affirm of either nature that which belongs to the other.[53]

Two natures in Christ does not mean that the human nature became endowed with divine attributes. It did not become omniscient and almighty, nor did the divine nature become endowed with human characteristics. The divine nature remained unaffected by His human nature, and His human nature did not become divine. The Confession stresses that the two natures are distinct, though joined in the one person of Jesus. The truth that the Confession is underscoring is that this Person is very God *and* very man, yet without sin. "For we do not have a High Priest who cannot sympathize with our weaknesses, but was in all points tempted as we are, yet without sin" (Heb. 4:15).

While the first paragraph supports our *faith* in the Mediator, this paragraph leads us to *worship* the Mediator. The power, majesty, and mystery of the physical creation leave us spellbound as we live in God's world. But in the union of the divine and the human in the Mediator our worship is heightened. We are overcome with wonder and worship when we think about being *in* Christ and saved by His grace. We should also be overcome with wonder and worship by meditating *on* Christ and the miracle of His incarnate Person. Peter indicated that the prophets of the Old Covenant "inquired and searched carefully" when "the Spirit of Christ who was in them was indicating when He testified beforehand the sufferings of Christ and the glories that would follow" (1 Pet. 1:10-11). Make it one of your life's ambitions to focus on the miracle of the Mediator's two natures in one glorious person.

53. Archibald A. Hodge, *Commentary on the Westminster Confession of Faith* (Logos Bible Software), 196.

Paragraph 3: Spirit-Filled Life and Ministry

We noted in the opening survey of the chapter that this paragraph contains the words, "[that] he might be thoroughly furnished to execute the office of mediator and surety; which office he took not upon himself, but was thereunto called by his Father." Berkouwer expands on the meaning of the word "office:"

> Let us now consider the meaning of the word "office." It obviously expresses the fact that one does not act on his own initiative but fulfills a given *commission*, as the Old Testament already stresses. Anointing was the symbol of this commissioning. The office is always superpersonal, not in the sense that it floats, like an abstract idea, above the living person, but it does come from above and can never be explained in the person, no matter how talented he may be. "Superpersonal" implies that human life itself lacks this authority and can receive it only indirectly in the calling to the fulfillment of a commission. One does not call himself to an office, but he *is* called to a task. The office is always a creaturely function and always presupposes a higher, i.e., a divine authority, which gives it a solid foundation. This is clearly illustrated in the Old Testament anointing. Another person intervenes in God's name and according to his commission. Everything is dependent, even the institution of the office and the act of anointing.[54]

Having expressed that He is thoroughly furnished to execute this office, we can now consider the ways in which He was so equipped. First, He possessed the Spirit of God "above measure." This is how His filling with the Spirit is described. Just as Christians are commanded to be filled with the Spirit (Eph. 5:18), Scripture reveals that Jesus was filled with the Spirit. "The fullness" dwelt in Him (Col. 1:19). The three texts referred to under this point are John 3:34: "for God does not give the Spirit by measure"; Colossians 2:3: "in whom are hidden all the treasures of wisdom and knowledge"; and Colossians 1:19: "For it pleased *the Father that* in Him all the fullness should dwell." The statement in John 3:34 means that Christ possesses the Spirit without any limitations or disharmony in His soul. This is why the Confession and Colossians 1:19 speak of "the fullness" of deity being in Him: "For in Him dwells all the fullness of the Godhead bodily" (Col. 2:9).

Two things are stated about His possession of the Spirit of God. First, He was sanctified or set apart for a unique purpose. Second, He was anointed. This language recalls the anointing of prophets, priests, and kings in Israel. These men were commissioned to fulfill their offices not in their own strength, but in the power and anointing of the Holy Spirit. Jesus was anointed and set apart with the fullness of the Godhead bodily and goes forth to accomplish all the work that a God-sent Mediator must accomplish to save men from the curse and corruption of sin.

The second is that Jesus possessed absolute holiness by the Spirit. In texts of Scripture, the Hebrew form of the Holy Spirit can be understood as "the Spirit of His holiness" (Isa. 63:10; Rom. 1:4). God is holy, therefore His

---

54. G. C. Berkouwer, *The Work of Christ* (Grand Rapids: Eerdmans, 1965), 63-64.

Spirit is holy, and holiness is the central feature of His power working in men, perfectly in Christ "to the end that being holy, harmless, undefiled, and full of grace and truth, He might be thoroughly furnished."

Seven things are mentioned here in relation to His possession of the holiness of the Spirit, ranging from the ethical and moral, to the official and mediatorial. He is holy in the moral sense, pure, innocent, not defiled by sin. He is blameless (the Confession says harmless). He is undefiled, not stained by sin in any way. "For such a High Priest was fitting for us, *who is* holy, harmless, undefiled, separate from sinners, and has become higher than the heavens" (Heb. 7:26). He is full of grace and truth, "And the Word became flesh and dwelt among us, and we beheld His glory, the glory as of the only begotten of the Father, full of grace and truth" (John 1:14). John adds, "And of His fullness we have all received, and grace for grace" (John 1:16). Glory and fullness are similar ideas.

He also possesses treasures of wisdom and knowledge. The filling of the Spirit in Jesus was a filling of His mind as a treasure-chest of good things to convey to man. Even Isaiah spoke of this blessing of the Spirit upon the Servant of the Lord: "The Spirit of the LORD shall rest upon Him, The Spirit of wisdom and understanding, The Spirit of counsel and might, The Spirit of knowledge and of the fear of the LORD" (Isa. 11:2). Here are six attributes of the Spirit, but notice wisdom, understanding, and knowledge. Colossians 2:3 says, "in whom are hidden all the treasures of wisdom and knowledge." This is His "furniture" for accomplishing His work as Mediator. In these seven things Christ was full of the Holy Spirit. He was thus endowed so that, "he might be thoroughly furnished to execute the office of a mediator and surety, which office he took not upon himself."

Robert Peterson illustrates:

> Imagine that in the first-century Jerusalem Gazette a listing appears in its "Help Wanted" section for the job of Redeemer of the world. There are three requirements for the job. First, the applicant must be God; no others need apply. That would narrow the job pool to three. Second, the applicant must also have become man. That would exclude all but one.
>
> The point of the passages in Hebrews that teach that the incarnate Son was made perfect is found in the third qualification in the job description for Redeemer. Not only must the applicant be God incarnate; he must also have on-the-job experience. Although Jesus's humanity was never sinful, in God's plan it must be tried and found true. God did not send his Son to earth as a thirty-three-year-old to die and be raised. He sent him as an infant in order for him to experience human life, with all of its trials and temptations, triumphantly. It is critical to note the purpose for the Son's being made perfect, that is, experientially qualified to be Savior by learning obedience through suffering.[55]

---

55. Robert A. Peterson, *Salvation Accomplished by the Son* (Wheaton, IL: Crossway, 2012), 49.

His fullness is something for which we give thanks, but it is also something to be "feared" because the Father put all power and judgement into His hand and gave Him commandment to execute that power in judgment against all who disobey and do not receive Him. God did not ordain the Mediator and give men the option of rejecting Him. He demands (yet with loving appeals) that men submit to His mediation. In submitting to His mediation, sinners submit to a complete, sufficient, and bountiful Savior.

If you belong to Christ, you also partake of the bountiful provisions of His life. He not only delivers from wrath and restores us to God, He also blesses us with the fullness of His own Spirit and the accompanying treasures of wisdom and knowledge. Imagine having the best education in the world without ever pursuing formal education. Imagine being wiser than the best philosophers of the world. But greater than these scenarios is to have the Spirit of God and Christ His Son in a Trinitarian fullness.

2 Peter 1:4 describes a great provision, "that through these you may be partakers of the divine nature, having escaped the corruption *that is* in the world through lust." Though there are some profound differences between the Christian and Christ Himself, there is a pattern that we share. We also partake of the divine nature through the regenerating Spirit of Christ. Do you see the divine nature at work in your life? You not only have the promise of eternal life. You also partake of a new nature. Though different than the God-man Jesus, you are still a uniquely new creation in Christ (2 Cor. 5:17; Gal. 6:15). This is something in which to rejoice, as well as something to safeguard and protect. We will seek to live honorably and with gospel dignity. We will seek to live in the Spirit and purge ourselves of all sin and impurity. Are you doing these things every day?

Paragraph 4: Sacrificial Death, Resurrection, Ascension, Session and Return

Paragraphs 4 and 5 are a presentation of the *accomplishment* of the plan and purpose for furnishing the Mediator first set forth in Paragraph 1 of this chapter. Here is the fulfillment (the application of His accomplishment comes in Paragraphs 6 through 8).

We are confronted at the outset with the horrifying description of the sufferings of the Mediator and His willingness to undertake this work. This is a sobering thought. His will was the will of the Father, and this involved unspeakable and unimaginable suffering, pain, and shaming by wicked men (though He of course was unashamed!). The paragraph surveys seven of the "nine saving events" (Peterson)[56] accomplished by

---

56. Robert A. Peterson, *Salvation Accomplished by the Son* (Wheaton, IL: Crossway, 2012) is a masterful presentation of the salvation accomplished by the Son. Peterson exegetes Christ's nine saving events: incarnation, sinless life, death, resurrection, ascension, session, Pentecost, intercession (associated with His work as Mediator of course), and second coming. In the second part of this book he develops the six major pictures in which the work of Christ is presented, which, he explains, come from six spheres of life: Christ

Christ: incarnation, sinless life, death, resurrection, ascension, session, and second coming.

In order to fulfill the work of Mediator, Christ must be born of a woman, under the demand and curse of the law. He must take the punishment measured out by that law, just as would be required of us because we are guilty of transgressing that law. This was the punishment of His death. Finally, the curse, the punishment, the shame, and the pain, were all turned to the vindication of His innocence and were the grounds for the victory of His mission. This overturned the shame and suffering of His death. Christ was vindicated because He was declared "not guilty" by God. The purpose of His death was to render a substitutionary sacrifice, and when He accomplished that, to move on to glory again.

The main passages that present this teaching are Galatians 3:13, "Christ has redeemed us from the curse of the law, having become a curse for us (for it is written, 'Cursed *is* everyone who hangs on a tree')." Galatians 4:4 says, "But when the fullness of the time had come, God sent forth His Son, born of a woman, born under the law." Psalm 40:8 is a beautiful reference to Jesus having the law in His heart when He came into the world: "I delight to do Your will, O my God, And Your law *is* within my heart."

The passages that refer to the substitutionary nature of His sacrifice are Isaiah 53:6: "All we like sheep have gone astray; We have turned, every one, to his own way; And the LORD has laid on Him the iniquity of us all;" Matthew 3:15: "But Jesus answered and said to him, 'Permit *it to be so* now, for thus it is fitting for us to fulfill all righteousness.' Then he allowed Him." Even in His baptism He identified with our sins and that is a pre-cross substitution. John 10:18 says: "No one takes it from Me, but I lay it down of Myself. I have power to lay it down, and I have power to take it again. This command I have received from My Father." 1 Peter 3:18 says: "For Christ also suffered once for sins, the just for the unjust, that He might bring us to God, being put to death in the flesh but made alive by the Spirit." 1 Peter 2:24 says: "who Himself bore our sins in His own body on the tree, that we, having died to sins, might live for righteousness—by whose stripes you were healed." Matthew 26:37 says: "And He took with Him Peter and the two sons of Zebedee, and He began to be sorrowful and deeply distressed."

The passages that refer to His ascension, exaltation, present session, intercession, and coming again as Judge are Acts 1:9-11; 10:42; 13:37; Romans 8:34; 14:9-10; 1 Corinthians 15:3-4; 2 Corinthians 5:21; and Hebrews 9:24.

Christ takes upon Himself a mountain of sin and bears it away so that it is remembered no more (Ps. 103:12; Isa. 43:25). He experiences the deepest grief and anguish known to man. But the scope also extends to Christ's movements. He comes all the way down to dwell with man and

---

our reconciler (human relationships), Redeemer (institution of slavery), legal substitute (the court of law), Victor (the battlefield), second Adam (creation), and sacrifice (worship). See p. 274.

die for the sins of man, but He rises as high as the highest heaven where God dwells, from whence He came.

Once the sinner turns to Christ to enjoy the benefits of His sacrificial death, he is filled with gratitude and devotion. Paul said, "For scarcely for a righteous man will one die; yet perhaps for a good man someone would even dare to die. But God demonstrates His own love toward us, in that while we were still sinners, Christ died for us" (Rom. 5:7-8). Here is reason for the deepest gratitude. If Jesus suffered the deepest anguish for us in His death, should we not offer the highest praise and thanks for our new life in Him?

Serve Him with the same willingness and devotion with which He served us by giving His life for us. Think daily through this simple pattern. He died for us. He died to sin. We die with Him. We die to sin. He loved us with a great love. We love Him by uniting ourselves to Him and fulfilling the purpose of His death on our behalf. If Christ died this agonizing and shameful death to take our eternal punishment, then why would we not willingly die daily to ourselves and our sin? Why do we continue to sin with no sorrow for our sins since He died for us?

Paragraph 5: Victorious Accomplishment
There are three parts to this statement. First, the *means* of the accomplishment, which is Christ's perfect obedience and sacrifice of Himself which He offered to God through the eternal Spirit. Second, the *ends* secured by the accomplishment, which are satisfaction of divine justice, reconciliation, and an everlasting inheritance in the Kingdom of Heaven. Third, the *recipients* of the benefits of the accomplishment, who are those whom the Father has given to Christ the Mediator.

Hebrews 9:14 says, "how much more shall the blood of Christ, who through the eternal Spirit offered Himself without spot to God, cleanse your conscience from dead works to serve the living God?" This asserts the union and unity of Father and Son in Christ's death. He committed His spirit to the Father: "And when Jesus had cried out with a loud voice, He said, 'Father, into Your hands I commit My spirit.' Having said this, He breathed His last" (Luke 23:46). The Father anointed Him with the Spirit. Christ, through the Spirit, offered Himself to the Father at His death. Though the Son experienced the Father forsaking Him as He bore the sin of His people, He, through the Spirit, brought the offering of the sacrifice of Himself, thus continuing the fellowship of the Godhead in an unbroken way.

The recipients of Christ's accomplishments are those whom the Father gave to Jesus. This is yet another reference to the doctrine of particular atonement. Christ's death was particular in that He died in the place of those whom the Father had given to Him, and to the end that they would certainly be saved. He did not die to make salvation possible, but actual and effectual. In this sense the atonement is *limited*, but it is precise to say it is *particular* because the plan to save is definite and effectual. In the Arminian view which teaches that the atonement is "unlimited," it *is* limited by man's unbelief and rejection. And worse yet, God could not save in that view "even if He desired" because, in this view, salvation is dependent on man's willingness (and human ability) to be saved! The Confession clearly teaches the doctrine of particular redemption. But although redemption is particular, there is still a sense of *universality* in that the offer goes out to all men, and it is a genuine and free offer of the gospel without any restrictions in the proclamation of the message.

The three blessings or benefits stated here all relate to the condition of enmity that exists between God and man. Man is at enmity with God and needs to be reconciled to God. God is angry with the sinner and His wrath hangs over man's head. The Mediator turns that wrath away (*propitiation*), appeases God's anger, reconciles man to Himself through the blood of His cross, and welcomes redeemed man into His Kingdom. We become His loyal subjects, sons and daughters, and friends. Romans 3:25-26, John 17:2, and Hebrews 9:15 are cited in support of these statements, and they are quoted below.

> Whom God set forth *as* a propitiation by His blood, through faith, to demonstrate His righteousness, because in His forbearance God had passed over the sins that were previously committed, to demonstrate at the present time His righteousness, that He might be just and the justifier of the one who has faith in Jesus (Rom. 3:25-26).

> As You have given Him authority over all flesh, that He should give eternal life to as many as You have given Him (John 17:2).

> And for this reason He is the Mediator of the new covenant, by means of death, for the redemption of the transgressions under the first covenant, that those who are called may receive the promise of the eternal inheritance (Heb. 9:15).

There are many other relevant Scripture passages under each benefit.

This section highlights the blessings of the reconciled relationship that we now have with God. Through faith we experience a great peace. We are now right with God and heirs of the Kingdom of Heaven. Jesus said, "Blessed *are* the poor in spirit, For theirs is the kingdom of heaven" (Matt. 5:3). We can seek God's Kingdom in this life knowing that we will have the fruit of it now and the fullness of it in eternity. This causes us unspeakable happiness in our earthly pilgrimages. Are you not richly blessed by the reconciliation you have in Christ? You may be poor here and now, but you are rich and someday your riches will be presented to you at the entrance of the Kingdom of Heaven. You may never receive an earthly inheritance of houses and lands, but you will most certainly receive an eternal inheritance in the life to come.

Paragraph 6: Christ's Accomplishment Applied to Old Testament Saints
Paragraphs 6 through 8 present the *application* section of Christ's accomplishments in this chapter of the Confession, as we noted at the beginning.

This paragraph states that believers under the Old Covenant were saved in the same way as believers under the New Covenant. The difference is that the Mediator had not yet come and accomplished the work that has been described thus far. Several passages are cited under this paragraph. Hebrews 4:2 says that "indeed the gospel was preached to us as well as to them." Galatians 3:8 is even more to the point: "And the Scripture, foreseeing that God would justify the Gentiles by faith, preached the gospel beforehand to Abraham, *saying*, 'In you all the nations shall be blessed.'" 1 Peter 1:10-11 describes the work of the Old Covenant prophets who prophesied of the grace that was to come to the nation through the sufferings of Christ and the glories that would follow. Revelation 13:8 also states the unity of the saving work of God through Christ both before and after His coming. It speaks of names being written before the foundation of the world in the book of life of the Lamb who has been slain. Finally, Hebrews 13:8 declares, "Jesus Christ *is* the same yesterday, today, and forever."

The Mediator does not appear unannounced or without preparation. The significance of the kind of death that Christ had to die needed to be systematically established before it took place, and God prepared the Israelites (and the world) for this in their everyday life and worship as God's chosen people.

The principle of sacrifice needed to be established. The people had to understand that blood offerings were required. Identification with the substitute was the only way to find acceptance with God. Pictures of the work of the Mediator, the ones we have been considering, had to be developed in the nation's life and worship. They were to understand the functional and essential roles of the prophets, priests, and kings in order to relate to the Mediator who would take all three offices into one Person. This is true of all the pictures of the Messiah that are found in the Old Covenant life and worship: atonement, forgiveness, cleansing, washing, temple, altar, animals, etc.

The certainty of the promise, the truthfulness of God who makes the promises, and the unchangeableness of the covenant, made faith in God's promised Mediator/Messiah as effective as our faith in the finished work of the Messiah. Justification, the imputation of righteousness to our account, has always been by faith (Gen. 15:6; Gal. 3:8; Rom. 3:21–4:25).

God's purpose does not change. The Father laid plans for the sacrifice of His Son and the redemption of a people for Himself before the foundation of the world. Christ is promised to return, but we are still waiting for this to happen, so take courage as you grip the sure and certain promises of God today. His promises always come to pass. Fulfilled prophecy bears witness to this truth. 2 Peter 3:8 says: "With the Lord one day is as a thousand years, and a thousand years as one day."

We do not relegate the authority or application of major aspects of the Old Testament to Israel alone. The whole Bible is ours because there is one great plan of salvation spanning the Old Testament and the New, in which God's eternal purpose to save a people for Himself is worked out. Rejoice in every picture and promise of the coming Mediator and marvel at the fulfillment in the Person and work of Jesus.

Paragraph 7: The Unity of Christ's Natures Applied to His Work as Mediator
This paragraph develops the teaching found in paragraph 2 on the natures of Christ. The human and divine natures of Christ act concurrently in the one person of Christ in ways proper to each nature. This explains why Jesus grew and developed just as any man develops. It explains why He did not know certain aspects of the Father's plan: "But of that day and hour no one knows, not even the angels of heaven, but My Father only" (Matt. 24:36). Jesus enjoyed unbroken fellowship with God in heaven while He was on the earth (John 5:19, 30; 14:16-23). The Father withheld the knowledge of the day and hour of the passing of heaven and earth from His Son while He was on the earth. This does not deny His Godhead, diminish His deity, or contradict His claims. It merely acknowledges a feature of His humanity that He shared with us. Consider that Jesus knew from the beginning who they were who did not believe in Him, and who it was that would betray Him (John 6:64).

Archibald A Hodge comments:

> That all Christ's mediatorial actions involve the concurrent activities of both natures, each nature contributing that which is proper to itself.
>
> Thus the divine nature of Christ is that fountain from which his revelation as prophet is derived. Other prophets reflect his light, or transmit what they receive from him. He is the original source of all divine knowledge. At the same time his humanity is the form through which his Godhead is revealed, his flesh the veil through which its glory is transmitted. His person as incarnate God is the focus of all revelations—the subject as well as the organ of all prophetical teaching.
>
> Thus, also, the human nature of Christ was necessary in order that his person should be "made under the law"; and it is the subject of his vicarious sufferings, and the organ of his vicarious obedience and intercession as our representative Priest and Intercessor. At the same time, it is only the supreme dignity of his divine person which renders his obedience supererogatory and therefore vicarious, and the temporary and finite sufferings of his humanity a full equivalent in justice-satisfying efficacy for the eternal sufferings of all the elect. Thus, also, the activities of his divinity and humanity are constantly and beautifully blended in all his administrative acts as King. The last Adam, the second man, the Head of a redeemed and glorified race, the Firstborn among many brethren, he has dominion over all creatures; and, with a human heart acting out through the energies of divine wisdom and power, he makes all things work together for the accomplishment of his purposes of love.
>
> All mediatorial acts are therefore to be attributed to the entire person of the Theanthropos—God-man. And in the whole of his glorious Person

is he to be obeyed and worshiped by angels and men.[57]

Sometimes in the gospel accounts we see the man Jesus performing divine works of power. John 3:13 is cited: "No one has ascended to heaven but He who came down from heaven, *that is*, the Son of Man who is in heaven." The Son of Man descended from heaven. Jesus turned the water into wine. He healed the sick and raised the dead. In these cases we are seeing the acts of the divine nature attributed to the human nature.

Paragraph 8: Christ's Accomplishments Applied to Christian Perseverance
This paragraph describes the manner in which Christ the Mediator saves His chosen people. He did it decisively, certainly, and absolutely. Six aspects are mentioned.

First, He does this by making intercession for us. Based on the references cited (John 6:37; 10:15-16; 17:9 and Romans 5:10), the authors are referring to His death as the basis of His prayers for the salvation of His elect. John 17:9 is the prayer in which He asks the Father for the safety and ultimate salvation of His elect. Hebrews 7:25 and Romans 8:34 are the two New Testament passages that refer to His present work of intercession at the right hand of God. This is His *priestly* work.

Second, He does this by uniting us to Himself by giving us His Spirit. We are in union with Christ because we have the Spirit of Christ, the Spirit of the risen Christ. Paul explained this relationship of Christ to the Spirit: "The first man Adam became a living soul. The last Adam became a life-giving Spirit" (1 Cor. 15:45). The work of mediation is personal and intimate, and that is why the Confession calls it wonderful and unsearchable. This also is a feature of His *priestly* work, a fruit of His intercession (John 14:16).

Third, He reveals the mystery of salvation to us. Paul develops this theme in Ephesians 1. First John 5:20 speaks of Him giving us an understanding such that we may know Him, the true God and eternal life. This is no small accomplishment. This is a component of His *prophetic* work.

Fourth, He persuades us to believe and obey. This is the doctrine of irresistible grace joined to the doctrine of the effectual call. His prophetic work teams up with His priestly work and we are drawn to faith in Him. This is His *kingly* work.

Fifth, He governs our hearts by His Word and Spirit. The same Spirit that unites us to Him personally, fosters obedience to His Word as disciples and subjects. This too is His *kingly* work.

Sixth, He overcomes all our enemies by His almighty power and wisdom. These last two are components of His *kingly* work. He rules in our hearts, indwelling there by the Word of God. He rules over our

---

57. Archibald A. Hodge, *Commentary on the Westminster Confession of Faith* (Logos Bible Software), 209-210.

lives, externally, by His government and providence, even over His and our enemies.

As the Confession goes deeper into the official work of the Mediator, joining in His Person the work of Prophet, Priest, and King, we see that He is perfectly suited to our need. This is all by the free, unmerited, and unconditional grace of God. The doctrine of unconditional election and particular redemption join together in the work of the Mediator. He did not do this for us because He foresaw faith in us. Our faith is the result of His choice, and His work in us (Eph. 2:8).

Paragraph 9: Christ Only

This paragraph expresses the truth stated in 1 Timothy 2:5: "For *there is* one God and one Mediator between God and men, *the* Man Christ Jesus." We use human mediators to help us with troubled relationships. Christ is appointed as the only Mediator between man and God. No other person can perform this work for us. Parents intercede for their children in prayer but cannot save them. Pastors preach the Word and shepherd in the household of God but cannot make a sinner right with God. Christ has His exclusive place as the sole object of faith, trust, and hope. We are "as servants of Christ and stewards of the mysteries of God" (1 Cor. 4:1). This is a great privilege, but the only Mediator between God and man is Jesus Christ the Lord.

Robert Peterson writes:

> After his death, resurrection, and ascension, Jesus sat down at the right hand of God the Father, the place of highest honor and authority in the universe. He did not walk, as in his earthly ministry; stretch out his arms, as on the cross; or lift his hands in priestly blessing, as he was carried to heaven in his ascension (Luke 24:50-51). Instead, he sat down to complete his exaltation begun in his resurrection and ascension. He sat down as prophet, priest, and king.[58]

Paragraph 10: Christ Sufficient and Satisfying

Ignorance of God, alienation from God, and rebellion against God is the true condition of every person born into this world. The curse of sin that entered into the world through our first parents Adam and Eve plunged mankind and human history into an existence marked by sin and trouble: "Behold, I was brought forth in iniquity, And in sin my mother conceived me" (Ps. 51:5); "Yet man is born to trouble, As the sparks fly upward" (Job 5:7). Yet here we see just how much trouble we are in with reference to our relationship to the God who created us, sustains our lives, and "who gives us richly all things to enjoy" (1 Tim. 6:17). We do not know Him. We are estranged from Him. We are rebels against Him. What wretchedness, and what an awful plight mankind is in apart from the mediatorship of Christ.

---

58. Robert A. Peterson, *Salvation Accomplished by the Son* (Wheaton, IL: Crossway, 2012), 203. See the helpful development of the three offices on pages 203-05.

Without Christ we are in a state of disintegration. In Christ the Mediator, who is furnished to execute the offices of *Prophet*, *Priest*, and *King*, we come to know God in truth, have peace with Him, and submit to His rule. Only then, through regeneration, do we begin the stage of reintegration and renewal, "according to His mercy He saved us, through the washing of regeneration and renewing of the Holy Spirit" (Titus 3:5).

This is the good news of the gospel, and the message that has been entrusted to us. Let us proclaim it with boldness and confidence. Let us be thoroughly furnished, as our Mediator is, with the accurate understanding which the Confession sets forth in this chapter. "For *there is* one God and one Mediator between God and men, *the* Man Christ Jesus" (1 Tim. 2:5). "Thanks *be* to God for His indescribable gift!" (2 Cor. 9:15).

CHAPTER 9

OF FREE WILL

BRIAN BORGMAN AND JASON CHING

1. God hath endued the will of man with that natural liberty and power of acting upon choice, that it is neither forced, nor by any necessity of nature determined to do good or evil.[1]

2. Man, in his state of innocency, had freedom and power to will and to do that which was good and well-pleasing to God,[2] but yet was mutable, so that he might fall from it.[3]

3. Man, by his fall into a state of sin, hath wholly lost all ability of will to any spiritual good accompanying salvation;[4] so as a natural man, being altogether averse from that good, and dead in sin,[5] is not able by his own strength to convert himself, or to prepare himself thereunto.[6]

4. When God converts a sinner, and translates him into the state of grace, he freeth him from his natural bondage under sin,[7] and by his grace alone enables him freely to will and to do that which is spiritually good;[8] yet so as that by reason of his remaining corruptions, he doth not perfectly, nor only will, that which is good, but doth also will that which is evil.[9]

5. This will of man is made perfectly and immutably free to good alone in the state of glory only.[10]

---

1. Matthew 17:12; James 1:14; Deuteronomy 30:19
2. Ecclesiastes 7:29
3. Genesis 3:6
4. Romans 5:6; Romans 8:7
5. Ephesians 2:1, 5
6. Titus 3:3-5; John 6:44
7. Colossians 1:13; John 8:36
8. Philippians 2:13
9. Romans 7:15, 18-19, 21, 23
10. Ephesians 4:13

Few concepts are as contentious as the topic of free will. This contention flows in no small part from the lack of clarity over what exactly one means by the term "free will." The answer, as one might imagine, requires substantial explaining.

Free Will Defined (9:1)

This chapter closely follows the Westminster Confession of Faith and the Savoy Declaration of Faith, reflecting the unity of the Reformed position on the will.

At the time of the Reformation, the great humanist scholar Desiderius Erasmus of Rotterdam was encouraged many times to write against Martin Luther. Erasmus was reluctant, but when he finally gave in, he decided to write "a little book on the freedom of the will" in 1524. In December of 1525, Martin Luther responded to Erasmus with what would become one of the most important books in the Reformation and beyond. Luther at one point says to Erasmus what our generation also needs to hear, "Your thoughts about God are all too human." Luther asserted that the phrase "free will" was problematic because man's will is actually not free in any meaningful way, and so the phrase "free will" really was an "empty phrase."

John Calvin also found the phrase "free will" so fraught that, he advised: "If anyone, then, can use this word without understanding it in a bad sense, I shall not trouble him on this account. But I hold that because it cannot be retained without great peril, it will, on the contrary, be a great boon for the church if it be abolished. I prefer not to use it myself, and I should like others, if they seek my advice, to avoid it."[11]

No doubt every proponent of the doctrines of grace has experienced at least part of the peril Calvin described. Many Christians today accept some vague notion of "free will" and this concept, often undefined, is used as a blanket refutation of divine election or even divine sovereignty. The notion of free will is held with such uncritical bias, that one would think that God is bound by man's so-called freedom. We hear it in clichés like, "God is always a gentleman, He always knocks, asks permission, etc." As if God was tethered to the choices of men and restricted in His actions to merely responding to man. All too often, many Christians talk about "free will" as if the truths of Chapter 6 on sin did not factor into the conversation. The most common notion of the will is that somehow it remains untouched by human sin and is neutral. Others reason that the Bible gives commands, and those commands could not be legitimate if man did not inherently have the ability to obey them. In other words, "ought" implies "can." To the contrary, "you must" does not presuppose "you can." God often commands what we cannot do in order to accomplish some purpose other than our achievement. Retaining the phrase "free-will" is most certainly fraught with peril. With this peril

---

11. John Calvin, *Institutes of the Christian Religion Vol. 2*, ed. John T. McNeill, trans. Ford Lewis Battles, vol. 1, The Library of Christian Classics (Louisville, KY: Westminster John Knox Press, 2011), 266.

most certainly in mind, the Confession sets out to clearly define what it means by "free will."

The Confession begins by explaining that God "endued the will of man with that natural liberty and power of acting upon choice." This freedom and power to choose means that human choice is not externally determined or compelled and men can be described as "free." But this freedom must be qualified. First, it should be reiterated that Adam in his original state of righteousness did possess a freedom of will that was unique to him in his unfallen state, which the Confession will address in 9.2. In 9.1, the language of the Confession deals with humanity in general, and the expression "endued man with that natural liberty and power of acting upon choice" is simply affirming what we all know by nature, that we have the power to choose. We can choose to eat lunch; we can choose to skip it. We can choose sourdough or we can choose rye. Human experience tells us that we are faced with thousands of choices every day and we have the faculty to make choices. We are not free in the libertarian sense, but neither are we automatons. The Confession goes even farther when it notes that not only are our choices unforced, but they are not "by any necessity of nature determined to do good or evil." This last phrase of the first paragraph may seem puzzling in light of "the bondage of the will," but the Confession is observing:

> There is not an action or decision of ours that can be reduced to some natural law, some kind of inevitable system of causation, some force of the universe, some biological inheritance from our parents. Thus, to consider one sort of influence, if a boy always wills very bad things, it cannot all be blamed on the father; if a woman grows up to will the best things, her mother cannot claim all the credit. We are not determined by these factors.[12]

There is no room in the Confession for biological determinism or psychological syndromes; rather, when a person chooses evil or chooses relative good, it is a real choice that is not determined in such a way as to undermine the validity and culpability of their choice.

As Calvin further explained: "But how few men are there, I ask, who when they hear free will attributed to man do not immediately conceive him to be master of both his own mind and will, able of his own power to turn himself toward either good or evil?"[13] Wayne Grudem continues the thought: "Thus, when we ask whether we have 'free will,' it is important to be clear as to what is meant by the phrase. Scripture nowhere says that we are 'free' in the sense of being outside of God's control or of being able to make decisions that are not caused by anything.... Nor does it

---

12. Chad Van Dixhoorn, *Confessing the Faith: A reader's guide to the Westminster Confession of Faith* (Edinburgh: Banner of Truth, 2014), 136.

13. John Calvin, *Institutes of the Christian Religion Vol. 2*, ed. John T. McNeill, trans. Ford Lewis Battles, vol. 1, The Library of Christian Classics (Louisville, KY: Westminster John Knox Press, 2011), 264.

say we are 'free' in the sense of being able to do right on our own apart from God's power."[14]

The Scriptures reject this type of libertarian free will. John Frame writes: "No biblical passage can be construed to mean that the human will is independent of God's plan and of the rest of human personality."[15] R.K. McGregor Wright notes: "It is not the *reality* of the will that is in question, but its *independence* from the rest of our fallen nature and its *capacity* to choose autonomously against God's eternal purposes."[16]

What kind of freedom does the Scripture describe? The Scriptures portray man as freely choosing according to his nature and desires. Real choice does take place,[17] yet that choice must be placed in the context of the state in which humanity exists. Each of the following paragraphs of the Confession will now address how free will exists in each respective state of humanity. As A.A. Hodge aptly summarized: "In all these estates man is unchangeably a free, responsible agent, and in all cases choosing or refusing as, upon the whole, he prefers to do."[18] To say it another way, humanity freely chooses according to who they are at heart.[19] God created man with the ability to choose. This freedom resists external compulsion and is not predetermined to good or evil.

Free Will in the State of Innocence (9:2)

The Confession turns first to the state of innocence in which man was created. Adam was free to will and do what God required. Adam could have perfectly kept God's law. Adam was able not to sin (*posse peccare, posse non peccare*). In this description, we see that Adam's state is radically different from both the world and even the regenerate. As described in Chapter 6, sin is evil, yet, in our lives, sin is expected and inevitable. Sin was not inevitable with respect to Adam's nature and will. In his innocence, Adam could have chosen to always do good.

But the Confession explains that Adam was "mutable" in this state of innocence "so that he might fall from it." The Confession is affirming that Adam was changeable in his original righteousness.[20] His unstained will was capable of being exercised but it was also capable of being lost. This perspective on Adam's original state and the power of his will echoes Chapter 6 where we dealt with the covenant of works and the stipulations placed on Adam. It is important to remember that Adam was the most

14. Wayne A. Grudem, *Systematic Theology: An Introduction to Biblical Doctrine* (Leicester, England; Grand Rapids, MI: Inter-Varsity Press; Zondervan Pub. House, 2004), 331.

15. John M. Frame, *Systematic Theology: An Introduction to Christian Belief* (Phillipsburg, NJ: P&R Publishing, 2013), 826.

16. R.K. McGregor Wright, *No Place for Sovereignty: What's Wrong with Freewill Theism* (Downers Grove, IL: 1996), 112. Italics are his.

17. e.g. Deuteronomy 30:19.

18. A. A. Hodge and Charles Hodge, *The Confession of Faith: With Questions for Theological Students and Bible Classes* (Simpsonville, SC: Christian Classics Foundation, 1996), 161-162.

19. Matthew 7:18.

20. "Mutable" is the word that both the WCF and the SDF use instead of our Confession's use of "unstable."

suitable human being to be put in that position. Adam had sufficient power of mind and will to obey God's command.

Free Will in the State of Sin (9:3)

The fall dramatically and tragically changed man's ability to choose. The Confession states that because of the fall, man has "wholly lost all ability of will to any spiritual good accompanying salvation." Again, we must clarify our meaning. Does man ever do worldly good or acts that might be described as civic righteousness? Man does indeed do such things.[21] Has man lost all ability to choose? No, man still chooses—but according to his fallen nature. This nature is now "altogether averse from" spiritual good. Herman Bavinck explains: "What humans have lost is the free inclination of the will toward the good. They now no longer want to do good; they now voluntarily, by a natural inclination, do evil. The inclination, the direction, of the will has changed. 'The will in us is always free but it is not always good.'"[22]

Scripture agrees with this picture of total inability. Fallen humanity is described as slaves of sin,[23] dead in sin,[24] and blind toward the Gospel.[25] Fallen man is not able not to sin (*non posse non peccare*). Fallen man still freely chooses but fallen man will never choose any good thing toward salvation. A. A. Hodge concurs with this description: "A man always wills as upon the whole he pleases, but he cannot will himself to please differently from what he does please. The moral condition of the heart determines the act of the will, but the act of the will cannot change the moral condition of the heart."[26] Man is fallen in sin, corrupted by sin, transformed by sin, pervaded by sin. Thus, all that natural, fallen man wants to choose is sin.

This understanding must shape our understanding of the lost. The natural man is dead in trespasses and sins.[27] In that state of spiritual death, he is separated from God, hates God, and is opposed to the good that God requires. Natural man has no innate ability to move in the right spiritual direction in order to "prepare himself," let alone, convert himself. The lost sinner is not in need of a new decision nor of new circumstances; the lost sinner is in need of a new nature! Who is sufficient for these things? When we do justice to the depravity of fallen man, we realize that only the power of God can accomplish this work! Unless the Lord empowers the sermon, they labor in vain who preach! Unless the Lord empowers the evangelist, they labor in vain who evangelize. Who

---

21. 2 Kings 10:29-30, 12:2; Romans 2:14.

22. Herman Bavinck, John Bolt, and John Vriend, *Reformed Dogmatics: Sin and Salvation in Christ*, vol. 3 (Grand Rapids, MI: Baker Academic, 2006), 121.

23. Romans 6:6, 17; John 8:34.

24. Ephesians 2:1.

25. 2 Corinthians 3:14.

26. A. A. Hodge and Charles Hodge, *The Confession of Faith: With Questions for Theological Students and Bible Classes* (Simpsonville, SC: Christian Classics Foundation, 1996), 164.

27. Ephesians 2:1.

is capable of raising the dead to new spiritual life? It is not us. But thanks be to God that we know the one who is capable of such things. May our every labor rest on His shoulders.

In short, fallen men continue to choose, but according to their fallen nature. If we are going to speak of "free will," we should be specific about our terms. Man's choices are governed by his nature.[28] Man's choices are not coerced or forced to go against his own nature. But man's choices are also controlled by internal influences, such as what his mind perceives or what his affections incline or disincline him to. Man's choices are also influenced by God sovereignly controlling man's circumstances and even his own heart.[29] Therefore, the biblical perspective on man's free will and God's sovereignty would be one of compatibilism, that is, man is free (in the terms described), he is a moral agent responsible for his choices, and such freedom operates within the sovereign control of God.

Free Will in the State of Grace (9:4)

The Confession proceeds to the new state ushered in by the Gospel. The one who trusts in Jesus Christ for salvation is set free from his "natural bondage under sin." God's work of regeneration accomplishes a radical change in fallen man. Regenerate man is able not to sin (*posse non peccare*). This truth undergirds every step of obedience in the Christian walk. The Lord calls His children to live, not as the slaves of sin they once were, but as the slaves of righteousness which they now are.[30] Regenerate man can choose the good things of the Lord. The Christian, with a renewed nature, including a renewed will, and with the indwelling Holy Spirit, can choose that which is pleasing in God's sight.

However, the Christian needs to understand that because of remaining sin, he cannot just live a life of choosing the right, the holy, and the good without conflict. Yes, the Christian is free from his natural bondage.[31] But the Christian needs the grace of God and the Holy Spirit to be working in him "both to will and do God's good pleasure."[32] Remaining sin will wage war against everything which has been made new.[33] The tension is real.

This war will seem overwhelming, especially as the Christian realizes what God has done in him in regeneration.[34] Every Christian battling for sanctification needs to know this. Though our sins be powerful, Christians are not enslaved to their sins anymore. That means resisting, escaping and killing sin are all possible because of the great work of God in the Gospel. We short-circuit the battle of faith when we deem our sins irresistible or unbeatable. God is not outmatched by our sin. The Creator

---

28. Matthew 7:15-20.

29. Proverbs 16:9; 19:21; 20:24; 21:1; Genesis 45:4-8; 50:20; Acts 2:23; 4:27-28.

30. Romans 6:16-19.

31. This is the glorious truth of Romans 6.

32. Philippians 2:12-13.

33. Galatians 5:17.

34. We believe this is the struggle described in Romans 7:14-25.

of heaven and earth is not overpowered by our weakness. Sometimes the battle is overwhelmingly difficult, but the Christian is a new creation in Christ, empowered for new warfare and new living.

The reason regenerate man still chooses evil is because of his remaining corruption.[35] This remnant of the old man means that a conflict exists in Christians such that they do not "perfectly nor only will that which is good" but they also "will that which is evil." Thus, the Confession again prepares the believer for the real Christian life, filled with ongoing sin, repentance and need for forgiveness.[36] And yet this battle must be seasoned by good news: "sin shall not have dominion over you!"[37] The old man is dead, and the Lord will have the victory.

So then, man in the state of grace gains new ability to choose what is good but continues to choose sin and imperfection because of his remaining corruption. The Christian lives in the profound tension of the already and the not yet. He has already experienced pardon and regeneration and is right now a new creation. But he also knows that he is not yet all that he shall be.[38]

Free Will in the State of Glory (9:5)
This state of conflict will not last forever, and the Confession points to the day when God completes the work He began. In the state of glory, man is "made perfectly and immutably free to good alone." There comes a day when glorified man will be unable to sin (*non posse peccare*)! There comes a day when man is conflicted no more and only wants what is good. Glorified man's nature will be good and his will, likewise, will be good. It is this final transformation that makes possible the glorious hope of the book of Revelation: "…there shall be no more death, nor sorrow, nor crying. There shall be no more pain, for the former things have passed away."[39]

Humanity will be free agents who are good, perfect and holy. "Humanity as God intended for it to be."[40] In the great scope of redemptive history, "Adam was holy and unstable… Glorified men are holy and stable.[41] We will want good and we will be good and all our actions will flow out of that perfected nature! We will be forever confirmed in that glorified state. There will be no probationary period. There will be no possibility of falling again. We will be perfectly conformed to the image of the last Adam."[42]

---

35. Colossians 3:5.

36. cf. 1 John 1:9.

37. cf. Romans 6:14.

38. 1 John 3:2.

39. Revelation 21:4.

40. John M. Frame, *Salvation Belongs to the Lord: An Introduction to Systematic Theology* (Phillipsburg, NJ: P&R Publishing, 2006), 231.

41. A. A. Hodge and Charles Hodge, *The Confession of Faith: With Questions for Theological Students and Bible Classes* (Simpsonville, SC: Christian Classics Foundation, 1996), 166.

42. Romans 8:29; Philippians 3:20-21.

The state of glory will be glorious because we shall see our Savior in glory. Faith will be turned to sight. All the misery caused by sin will be gone. All our sin will be gone. "The ransomed church of God will be saved to sin no more." This world, which laid so many snares to entangle our affections and allure our wills, will have passed away. This flesh, which so often pulled with such force on our choices, will be eradicated truly and forever. The devil, who plied his craft and drew us away, will be cast forever into the lake of fire. We will be saved from the presence of sin in the state of glory. We will have resurrected and glorified bodies, with wholly sanctified affections and a wholly sanctified will. Our wills will delight in all that is good and holy, and we will only choose what is good and holy. The work which He began, will be completed in the day of Christ Jesus.[43]

This great hope must be enjoyed often. Our sin plagues us so that we can hardly pass a single moment without engaging in some unholy thought or committing some loveless deed. Our course of life at times feels like a ceaseless string of drifting and weakness. It would be natural to draw the worldly conclusion that things will never change. What a bleak conclusion that would be. But the Lord has promised His people that everything will change—including our will. To accept the world's diagnosis will steal our joy and eclipse God's promises. When the world buffets believers with its torrent of despair, believers must know that our hope lies ahead. It honors God when His promises burn bright in our esteem. Likewise, it warms our souls to draw near to that gladdening fire. In our dark and challenging day, let us often look forward to what is to come.

Conclusion

Man's free will indeed exists but not as many often define it. Man's free will is always subject to his nature and the changes in that nature change dramatically across the scope of redemptive history. Free will is subject to the milestones of redemption: creation, fall, grace and glory.

Application

1. The choices we make are truly our own choices. We are responsible to God for every act of the will. However, unlike our first father before the fall, our choices are bent and broken. When Adam fell, he radically transformed human nature so that my mind, my affections, and my will now function from a fallen, sinful nature. I am free in one sense, but all I do is freely sin. I may do relative good or civic good, but even my motives in those choices are tainted with self-glory and pride. Charles Spurgeon once preached a sermon that sums up the problem, "Free will: A Slave."[44] Have I come to grips with my inclinations, which are not bent towards God, but away from Him? Have I seen myself as not only bound, but

---

43. Philippians 1:6.

44. Charles Haddon Spurgeon, "Free-will: A Slave," Dec. 2, 1855, Sermon No. 52, New Park Street Pulpit, Vol. 1.

helpless? If so, I can no longer look to myself, but I need to look outside of myself to Jesus Christ, my only hope, my only liberator. When I begin to do that, that is the Holy Spirit working on this corrupted will.

2. Isaac Watts beautifully captured this translation from the state of bondage and death to the state of life and true freedom:

> Why was I made to hear your voice,
> and enter while there's room,
> when thousands make a wretched choice,
> and rather starve than come?
>
> 'Twas the same love that spread the feast
> that sweetly drew us in;
> else we had still refused to taste,
> and perished in our sin.

Child of God, do you thank God that the Holy Spirit fixed your "chooser" so that you were empowered to trust Christ?

3. In this life, with the indwelling Spirit and a renewed will, I can fight remaining sin. My desires and inclinations have been transformed. I can fight the flesh and temptation with confidence in God's Word, by God's Spirit, through my risen Savior. I can look with great hope to the coming state where there will be no more conflict within, no more struggle, no more tension. That future state will be better than Eden! Child of God, do you look forward to the future state when you will be free from the very presence of sin? If so, then fight the power of sin today in the Holy Spirit, who will bring life to your mortal body.

CHAPTER 10

OF EFFECTUAL CALLING

JIM DOMM

1. Those whom God hath predestinated unto life, he is pleased in his appointed, and accepted time, effectually to call,[1] by his Word and Spirit, out of that state of sin and death in which they are by nature, to grace and salvation by Jesus Christ;[2] enlightening their minds spiritually and savingly to understand the things of God;[3] taking away their heart of stone, and giving unto them a heart of flesh;[4] renewing their wills, and by his almighty power determining them to that which is good, and effectually drawing them to Jesus Christ;[5] yet so as they come most freely, being made willing by his grace.[6]

2. This effectual call is of God's free and special grace alone, not from anything at all foreseen in man, nor from any power or agency in the creature,[7] being wholly passive therein, being dead in sins and trespasses, until being quickened and renewed by the Holy Spirit;[8] he is thereby enabled to answer this call, and to embrace the grace offered and conveyed in it, and that by no less power than that which raised up Christ from the dead.[9]

3. Elect infants dying in infancy are regenerated and saved by Christ through the Spirit;[10] who worketh when, and where, and how he pleases;[11] so also are all elect persons, who are incapable of being outwardly called by the ministry of the Word.

---

1. Romans 8:30; Romans 11:7; Ephesians 1:10-11; 2 Thessalonians 2:13-14
2. Ephesians 2:1-6
3. Acts 26:18; Ephesians 1:17-18
4. Ezekiel 36:26
5. Deuteronomy 30:6; Ezekiel 36:27; Ephesians 1:19
6. Psalm 110:3; Song of Solomon 1:4
7. 2 Timothy 1:9; Ephesians 2:8
8. 1 Corinthians 2:14; Ephesians 2:5; John 5:25
9. Ephesians 1:19-20
10. John 3:3, 5-6
11. John 3:8

4. Others not elected, although they may be called by the ministry of the Word, and may have some common operations of the Spirit,[12] yet not being effectually drawn by the Father, they neither will nor can truly come to Christ, and therefore cannot be saved: much less can men that receive not the Christian religion be saved;[13] be they never so diligent to frame their lives according to the light of nature and the law of that religion they do profess.[14]

Before studying this chapter, take a moment to notice where it is in the Confession, and how this matter "Of Effectual Calling" fits into the overall structure of the Confession.[15] Division 1 of the Confession is concerned with The Foundations of Christian Thought (chs. 1–8). Division 2 includes Chapters 9–20 and is concerned with Experimental Religion (Salvation Applied).[16] This section of the Confession includes three items. Chapter 9 presents The Setting of Salvation Applied ("Man's Will"). This is followed by The Blessings and Graces of Salvation Applied. This portion of the Confession examines the blessings that God bestows (chs. 10–13) and the graces that man exercises (chs. 14–18). The third and final concern in Division 2 is The Means of Salvation Applied (the Law and the Gospel, chs. 19 and 20). Effectual Calling, then, is one of the blessings that God bestows upon the elect when He applies to them, in their lifetimes, the salvation that was purchased for them in history by the Lord Jesus Christ through His sufferings and death.

1. A General Overview of Effectual Calling (Para. 1)
Seven things about the effectual call of God are featured in Paragraph 1:

1. The Recipients of the Effectual Call
The recipients of the effectual call are described in the Confession as "those whom God hath predestinated unto life." This is explicit in Romans 8:30: "Moreover whom He predestined, these He also called."

2. The Author of the Effectual Call
Paragraph 1 states: "Those whom God hath predestinated unto life he is pleased... effectually to call." We might want to think of the Holy Spirit as the divine Author of the effectual call. But the Bible depicts the Holy Spirit as the divine Agent of the effectual call, not its Author.[17] The Author of the effectual call is God—in particular, God the Father. According to Romans 8:29, 30, God predestines and calls those whom He foreknew

---

12. Matthew 22:14; Matthew 13:20-21; Hebrews 6:4-5

13. John 6:44-45, 65; 1 John 2:24-25

14. Acts 4:12; John 4:22; John 17:3

15. I am using Greg Nichols' outline found in earlier editions of Samuel E. Waldron's *A Modern Exposition of the 1689 Baptist Confession of Faith* (England: Evangelical Press, 1989), 433, 434. See also the analytical outline in the 5th edition of Waldron's *Exposition*, 503-507.

16. The application of salvation is the realized experience of gospel salvation in the individual life histories of the elect.

17. Titus 3:5.

to be conformed to the image of His Son. Similarly, in 1 Corinthians 1:9: "God *is* faithful, by whom you were called into the fellowship of His Son, Jesus Christ our Lord." The juxtaposition of "God" and "His Son" in these verses shows that the divine Person of the Trinity particularly referred to is God the Father. God the Father is the Author of the effectual call, not God the Son, and not God the Holy Spirit. This is important to note as it serves as a safeguard against an improper emphasis upon the Holy Spirit in the application of salvation. It shows that God the Father is directly involved in the application of salvation, not just the Holy Spirit. Recognizing this should provide a check against robbing God the Father of the glory that is due Him. It should also assist believers in properly directing their prayers to God the Father with respect to the application of salvation.

3. The Occasion of the Effectual Call

The Confession describes the occasion of the effectual call in Paragraph 1: "Those whom God hath predestinated unto life, He is pleased, in His appointed and accepted time, effectually to call." When does God effectually call His elect to salvation? In His appointed and accepted time. Jesus said in John 3:8, "The wind blows where it wishes, and you hear the sound of it, but cannot tell where it comes from and where it goes. So is everyone who is born of the Spirit." This in no way eliminates the necessary use of means (prayer, Bible reading, preaching, and evangelism). It doesn't mean that either the use or the neglect of means is unimportant or inconsequential. But it does remind us that regardless of means, God effectually calls sinners to Christ in His way and His time. Salvation does not ultimately depend upon the person who wills or runs, but upon God who shows mercy (Rom. 9:16).

4. The Efficacy of the Effectual Call

The Confession asserts in Paragraph 1, "He (God) is pleased, in His appointed and accepted time, effectually to call." God's call is an effectual one. It is not powerless or vain. It never fails or falls short of its object. The golden chain (as it has been called) of Romans 8:30 runs unbroken from predestination to calling to justification to glorification. The call of God in view here is not the outward general call of the gospel in the preaching of the Word, but the inward effectual call of God to salvation in Jesus Christ (Matt. 22:14; 1 Thess. 1:5).

5. The Means of the Effectual Call

Paragraph 1 states, "He is pleased… effectually to call, by His Word and Spirit." According to the Confession, the effectual call occurs by means of two things. The first is the Word of God. Paul tells the Thessalonians, "He called you by our gospel" (2 Thess. 2:14). Likewise, James asserts, "Of His own will He brought us forth by the word of truth" (James 1:18). In addition to the means (instrumentality) of the Word of God, the effectual call also comes through the means (agency) of the Holy Spirit. John 3:3,

6: "Jesus answered and said to him, 'Most assuredly I say to you, unless one is born again, he cannot see the kingdom of God. That which is born of the flesh is flesh, and that which is born of the Spirit is spirit.'" Both the Word and the Spirit constitute the means of the effectual call, not just one or the other. The Word and the Spirit must never be separated in the experience of the application of salvation. Religion that emphasizes the Word over the Spirit tends to dead orthodoxy.[18] Religion that emphasizes the Spirit over the Word tends to mysticism.[19] Both are dangerous errors. The Bible teaches that God doesn't call sinners effectually to Christ by the Word apart from the Spirit. Neither does He call sinners effectually to Christ by the Spirit apart from the Word. The fact that He is able to do either one isn't the issue. The concern is with what God is normally pleased to do. The Bible gives no one any reason to expect the effectual call of God to occur apart from either the Word or the Spirit.

6. The Transition Involved in the Effectual Call
The Confession asserts in Paragraph 1: "Those whom God hath predestinated unto life, he is pleased…effectually to call, by His Word and Spirit, out of that state of sin and death in which they are by nature, to grace and salvation by Jesus Christ." What change is involved in the effectual call? What is the "before" and the "after" in connection with the effectual call? Very simply, the effectual call involves a transition from death to life. Paul says in Ephesians 2:1, 4, 5: "And you *He made alive*, who were dead in trespasses and sins…. But God, who is rich in mercy, because of His great love with which He loved us, even when we were dead in trespasses, made us alive together with Christ…"

7. The Operations Involved in the Effectual Call
The remainder of Paragraph 1 describes the operations involved in God's effectual call: "enlightening their minds spiritually and savingly to understand the things of God; taking away their heart of stone, and giving unto them a heart of flesh: renewing their wills, and by his almighty power determining them to that which is good, and effectually drawing them to Jesus Christ; yet so as they come most freely, being made willing by his grace."

In the effectual call of God, the mind is enlightened (Eph. 1:18), the heart of stone is removed and replaced with a heart of flesh (Ezek. 36:26, 27), and the will is renewed (Phil. 2:13). God works upon the whole person—mind, emotions, conscience, and will—to bring about a profound transformation. By this transformation those who are effectually called by God are made willing to come to Him in the day of His power (Ps. 110:3). Though they are drawn to Christ by the power of God (John 6:44, 45), they come to Him freely and because they want to (Phil. 2:13). These, then, are the operations that are involved in the effectual call

---

18. Dead orthodoxy is the holding of correct doctrine without a transformed heart and life.

19. Mysticism is the attempt to have dealings with God apart from the Bible.

(enlightenment, removal, replacement, renewal, realignment, attraction). We must not think of these as disconnected processes. They all occur simultaneously. They are all part of the great transformation that God brings about in those whom He effectually calls.

Before proceeding to the final three paragraphs, there is an important observation to be made. If you've been paying careful attention, you may have noticed that Bible verses have been cited without distinguishing between the effectual call and the new birth (regeneration). That's because they are essentially the same thing. In effectual calling, the effective summons to Christ occurs simultaneously in conjunction with an inward transformation. The Bible speaks of these two things differently. But they are basically the same thing looked at in different ways. The following diagram helps to illustrate this.[20]

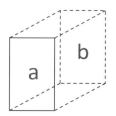

In the diagram, face "a" of the block is drawn with a solid line, and face "b" with a dotted line. Which face is nearer? Which face is farther away? It is impossible to tell. It all depends upon how you look at the diagram. In the same way, it is impossible to distinguish between the effectual call of God and the new birth. They are both the same thing only seen from different viewpoints. One is a calling or a summons (John 6:44). The other is a birth (John 1:13), a new creation (2 Cor. 5:17), an emancipation (Col. 1:13), a circumcision (Col. 2:11-13), a resurrection with Christ (Eph. 2:4-6). All these Bible expressions are referring to the same thing. They are all referring to effectual calling and regeneration.[21]

2. The Nature of Effectual Calling (Paras. 2-4)

1. God's Effectual Call is Monergistic (Para. 2)

"This effectual call is of God's free and special grace alone, not from anything at all foreseen in man, nor from any power or agency in the creature, being wholly passive therein, being dead in sins and trespasses, until being quickened and renewed by the Holy Spirit; he is thereby enabled to answer this call, and to embrace the grace offered and

---

20. I am indebted to Greg Nichols for this illustration.

21. Theologians debate whether effectual calling precedes or follows regeneration. While arguments are made for both views, neither is logically or temporally prior to the other. They occur at precisely the same moment. In the Westminster and Second London Confessions, the Savoy Declaration, and the Larger Catechism (Q. 67) effectual calling includes regeneration.

conveyed in it, and that by no less power than that which raised up Christ from the dead."

Monergism means "working one way," as opposed to synergism ("working two ways"). Synergism is two parties working together and cooperating with one another. The Bible describes gospel salvation in monergistic, not synergistic, terms. If we wonder why this is, the reason isn't difficult to discover. Sinners are spiritually dead in trespasses and sins (Eph. 2:1). Dead people can't call themselves. Dead people can't birth themselves. They can't create themselves, emancipate themselves, circumcise themselves, or resurrect themselves. Only God can do these things. Only God can create and give life. God's grace is the only efficient cause in the application of gospel salvation. Paul writes in 2 Timothy 1:9: "...who has saved us and called *us* with a holy calling, not according to our works, but according to His own purpose and grace which was given to us in Christ Jesus before time began."

Again, the apostle writes in 1 Corinthians 1:26-30:

> For you see your calling, brethren, that not many wise according to the flesh, not many mighty, not many noble, are *called*. But God has chosen the foolish things of the world to put to shame the wise, and God has chosen the weak things of the world to put to shame the things which are mighty; and the base things of the world and the things which are despised God has chosen, and the things which are not, to bring to nothing the things that are, that no flesh should glory in His presence. But of Him you are in Christ Jesus, who became for us wisdom from God—and righteousness and sanctification and redemption.

We read in Titus 3:5: "...not by works of righteousness which we have done, but according to His mercy He saved us, through the washing of regeneration and renewing of the Holy Spirit."

2. God's Effectual Call is Inscrutable (Para. 3).

"Elect infants dying in infancy are regenerated and saved by Christ through the Spirit; who worketh when, and where, and how he pleases; so also are all elect persons, who are incapable of being outwardly called by the ministry of the Word."

The Confession affirms that God's effectual call sometimes operates in surprising ways. This is described in Paragraph 3 which is carried over verbatim from the Westminster Confession.[22] This paragraph deals with supposed exceptions to Paragraph 1. Paragraph 1 teaches that God's effectual call normally comes about through the ministry of the Word ("by His Word and Spirit"). This raises an important question. What about persons who are incapable of being outwardly called by the ministry of the Word such as infants or mentally handicapped persons?[23] Paragraph 3 addresses these cases.

---

22. Paragraph 3 of the Savoy Declaration is identical to the Westminster and London Confessions except for the phrase "through the Spirit" which is omitted from the Savoy.

23. The case of people who never hear the gospel is addressed in Chapter 1, paragraph

The expression "elect infants" raises some questions. Are any or all infants elect? At what age is an infant no longer an infant? Considerable debate has surrounded these questions. The great Baptist preacher, C.H. Spurgeon, believed that all children dying in infancy were regenerated and saved.[24] In his edition of the Second London Confession, the word "elect" doesn't appear in paragraph 3. It simply reads, "Infants dying in infancy are regenerated and saved."[25]

A passage that is often used to "prove" that infants dying in infancy are saved is 2 Samuel 12:23 where David speaks of the child that resulted from his adulterous union with Bathsheba. God said that this child would die (2 Sam. 12:14). After the child died, David said in verse 23: "But now he is dead; why should I fast? Can I bring him back again? I shall go to him, but he shall not return to me." It is assumed from these words that this child was in heaven, which is why David said that he would go to the child, but the child would not return to him. So does this passage *prove* that any or all infants dying in infancy are saved? No, it does not. It allows this interpretation, but it doesn't prove it. Do any other passages prove this? There are none.[26] Appeal is made in the Confession to John 3:8: "The wind blows where it wishes, and you hear the sound of it, but cannot tell where it comes from and where it goes. So is everyone who is born of the Spirit." But again, this verse doesn't *prove* that any infants are elect, or that all infants dying in infancy are saved. It merely speaks of the inscrutable nature of the new birth. The cases of Jeremiah the prophet (Jer. 1:5) and John the Baptist (Luke 1:41, 44) are also cited, but they do not speak at all to the question of elect infants. As Samuel E. Waldron insightfully observes: "Even leaving aside the serious questions as to the significance of these passages, the problem remains that neither John nor Jeremiah died in infancy."[27]

Others see all infants dying in infancy and all mentally handicapped individuals (along with those who never hear the gospel) as in the class of reprobate persons. None of them are elect. They are all lost since they are incapable of being outwardly called by the ministry of the Word. This may well be an extreme position in the opposite direction. We can't be certain because the Bible isn't explicit about this either.[28]

The fact is that we don't know with certainty what happens in every case to infants who die in infancy. We may hope that they are saved, but we can't be sure because God hasn't told us in His Word. We do know

---

1 and in Chapter 20 of the Confession.

24. See Chapter 5: "Of Such is the Kingdom of Heaven" in his book *Come Ye Children*. Spurgeon believed that heaven will be filled with children.

25. The word "elect," however, was present in the original 1677 edition of the Second London Confession.

26. Luke 18:15-17 and the parallels are not conclusive.

27. Samuel E. Waldron, *A Modern Exposition of the 1689 Baptist Confession of Faith* (Welwyn Garden City: Evangelical Press, 1989, 2016), 176.

28. It must be remembered that all people are guilty of Representative Sin (Rom. 5:12-14) and Original Sin (Ps. 51:5) before they ever commit any Actual Sin.

that God has told us all that we need to know in the Bible. And we do know that the Judge of all the earth will do right (Gen. 18:25). We may safely leave the matter with Him. Whether an infant dying in infancy or a mentally handicapped person, God is certainly able to operate directly upon the soul and regenerate it apart from any outward means. But that is not the way God normally saves people.

Paragraph 3 reminds us that the effectual call of God is inscrutable. It is shrouded in mystery. This was asserted in Paragraph 1 where the Confession states that God is pleased to call His elect in His appointed and accepted time.

3. God's Effectual Call is Indispensable (Para. 4).
"Others not elected, although they may be called by the ministry of the Word, and may have some common operations of the Spirit, yet not being effectually drawn by the Father, they neither will nor can truly come to Christ, and therefore cannot be saved: much less can men that receive not the Christian religion be saved; be they never so diligent to frame their lives according to the light of nature and the law of that religion they do profess."

The effectual call of God is absolutely necessary if one hopes to be saved. God is not the Father of all people, not in the redemptive sense. There is no one world religion. There is no universal salvation (Matt. 25:46). There is no salvation apart from the Word of Christ and faith in Christ (Rom. 10:14). Apart from the gospel, there is no salvation (2 Thess. 2:14; 1 Peter 1:23). Apart from God's effectual call, there is no salvation (John 6:44). Many hear the outward call of God in the preaching of the gospel. But unless sinners are inwardly and effectually called of God, the outward call will be ineffective for salvation.

1 Thessalonians 1:5: "For our gospel did not come to you in word only, but also in power, and in the Holy Spirit and in much assurance."

Matthew 22:14: "For many are called, but few *are* chosen."
Scripture forces us to conclude that no one is normally saved apart from the outward and the inward call of the gospel.

Lessons to Think About
1. The biblical truth of effectual calling confronts us, in a pointed way, with the absolute sovereignty of God in salvation. The biblical truth of effectual calling is a sobering, awe-inspiring truth. It shows us the absolute necessity of the new birth in order to be saved. Sinners can do nothing to save themselves. God must act. God must effectually call them. He must give them new life, or they will forever remain apart from Christ. The privilege of gospel preaching alone will not save them. They must be effectually called by God. Jesus said, "You must be born again" (John 3:7).

The story is told of the famous evangelist of the First Great Awakening, George Whitefield. He would go about from place to place preaching and saying to the people, "You must be born again! You must be born again!"

A woman approached him and said, "Mr. Whitefield, why do you keep telling us that we must be born again?" He replied, "Because, dear lady, you must be born again!"

How many there are who rest satisfied with a mere nominal Christianity. Many are content with a form of godliness that has no power (2 Tim. 3:5). How many there are who have not been effectually called by God, yet presume they will see the face of God in peace after they die? Jesus was clear, however that if one is not born of the Spirit, he cannot enter the kingdom of God (John 3:5). It is a sad fact that many churches are filled with people who are trusting in sacraments, morality, orthodoxy, and a host of other things. But they are strangers to Christ and the new birth. If that doesn't change, they will hear Christ say to them, "Depart from Me. I never knew you" (Matt. 7:21-23).

Someone might ask, "How can I be sure if I've been effectually called? How can I know if I've been born again?" There is one simple way to know. Are you trusting in Christ alone to save you from your sins? Are you looking to Christ's sufferings and death on the cross as your only hope of forgiveness and acceptance with God? Are you looking to His shed blood alone to cover your sins? Jesus said, "All that the Father gives Me will come to Me" (John 6:37). All God's elect believe upon Christ, and no one believes upon Christ unless the Father first calls him. "No one can come to Me, unless the Father who sent Me draws him" (John 6:44). Faith in Christ is the single greatest evidence that one has been effectually called. It is not the *cause* of the new birth, but the *evidence* of it.

If we are persuaded of the sovereignty of God in salvation and the absolute necessity of His effectual call for salvation, it will have a significant impact on the methodology of our evangelism. Care will be taken to accurately present the biblical gospel to sinners. It is not reasonable to expect the Spirit of truth to empower a false, defective gospel. Further, our evangelistic activities will be accompanied by fervent, believing prayer. The very best efforts at evangelism do not work automatically. It is not reasonable to expect our evangelistic activities to be effective for anyone's salvation apart from prayer for the saving power of God to attend those activities. If God wasn't sovereign in saving sinners, there would be no point in praying. But since He is sovereign, we may confidently use the means He has given us (the ministry of the Word), ask Him to bless those means by effectually calling sinners to Himself, and leave the results with Him.

2. If you are a believer, marvel at the amazing mercy and goodness of God to you in choosing and effectually calling someone like you to Himself. In the third stanza of the hymn *How Sweet and Aweful is the Place*,[29] the question is raised:

---

29. Isaac Watts, "How Sweet and Aweful is the Place," 1707.

Why was I made to hear Thy voice,
and enter while there's room
When thousands make a wretched choice,
and rather starve than come?

The answer follows in stanza four:

'Twas the same love that spread the feast
that sweetly drew us in;
Else we had still refused to taste
and perished in our sin.

If you are a believer, marvel at God's love for you! Blessed are those who have heard the divine summons to faith in Christ. Salvation is not a matter of ancestry, intelligence, wealth, education, position, or any number of other advantages. It is purely a matter of the grace and mercy of God in Christ. If God was not pleased to be merciful to sinners, none would be saved. Here is fuel for praise, gratitude, and worship!

CHAPTER 11

OF JUSTIFICATION

MARK SARVER

1. Those whom God effectually calleth, he also freely justifieth,[1] not by infusing righteousness into them, but by pardoning their sins, and by accounting and accepting their persons as righteous;[2] not for anything wrought in them, or done by them, but for Christ's sake alone;[3] not by imputing faith itself, the act of believing, or any other evangelical obedience to them, as their righteousness; but by imputing Christ's active obedience unto the whole law, and passive obedience in his death for their whole and sole righteousness by faith,[4] which faith they have not of themselves; it is the gift of God.[5]

2. Faith thus receiving and resting on Christ and his righteousness, is the alone instrument of justification;[6] yet it is not alone in the person justified, but is ever accompanied with all other saving graces, and is no dead faith, but worketh by love.[7]

3. Christ, by his obedience and death, did fully discharge the debt of all those that are justified; and did, by the sacrifice of himself in the blood of his cross, undergoing in their stead the penalty due unto them, make a proper, real, and full satisfaction to God's justice in their behalf;[8] yet, inasmuch as he was given by the Father for them, and his obedience and satisfaction accepted in their stead, and both freely, not for anything in

---

1. Romans 3:24; Romans 8:30
2. Romans 4:5-8; Ephesians 1:7
3. 1 Corinthians 1:30, 31; Romans 5:17-19
4. Philippians 3:8, 9; Ephesians 2:8-10
5. John 1:12; Romans 5:17
6. Romans 3:28
7. Galatians 5:6; James 2:17, 22, 26
8. Hebrews 10:14; 1 Peter 1:18-19; Isaiah 53:5-6

them,[9] their justification is only of free grace, that both the exact justice and rich grace of God might be glorified in the justification of sinners.[10]

4. God did from all eternity decree to justify all the elect,[11] and Christ did in the fullness of time die for their sins, and rise again for their justification;[12] nevertheless, they are not justified personally, until the Holy Spirit doth in time due actually apply Christ unto them.[13]

5. God doth continue to forgive the sins of those that are justified,[14] and although they can never fall from the state of justification,[15] yet they may, by their sins, fall under God's fatherly displeasure;[16] and in that condition they have not usually the light of his countenance restored unto them, until they humble themselves, confess their sins, beg pardon, and renew their faith and repentance.[17]

6. The justification of believers under the Old Testament was, in all these respects, one and the same with the justification of believers under the New Testament.[18]

As Protestants we must not forget that Protestantism was born out of an agonizing struggle over the doctrine of justification by faith alone.[19] For Luther this doctrine was not merely one among many but, as the famous formula of Reformation theology reads, "the article by which the church stands or falls"[20] and on which its entire doctrine depends. This

9. Romans 8: 32; 2 Corinthians 5:21

10. Romans 3:26; Ephesians 1:6, 7; Ephesians 2:7

11. Galatians 3:8; 1 Peter 1:2; 1 Timothy 2:6

12. Romans 4:25

13. Colossians 1:21-22; Titus 3:4-7

14. Matthew 6:12; 1 John 1:7, 9

15. John 10:28

16. Psalms 89:31-33

17. Psalms 32:5; Psalms 51; Matthew 26:75

18. Galatians 3:9; Romans 4:22-24

19. This material was originally delivered in expanded form in the late 90s at Albany Baptist Church. In that setting it would have been tedious to mention every non-verbatim source, especially when expressing concepts common to various authors. Now, some twenty years later, it is impossible to retrace the research behind these lectures. Hence, if I have used phrases that are similar to those used by others without giving due credit, this was unintentional.

20. In his 1532/1533 lectures on the Psalms, Luther declared, "So you have heard... that this verse [Ps. 130:4] is the principle matter [*Summa*] of Christian doctrine and that sun which illuminates the Holy Church of God; for when this article stands, the church stands [*quia isto articulo stante stat Ecclesia*]; when this article falls, the church falls [ruente ruit Ecclesia]" (*D. Martin Luthers Werke. Kritische Gesamtausgabe* [Weimar, 1883-], 403:352, lines 1-3). Hereafter the Latin and German Weimarer Ausgabe (German for "Weimar Edition") of Luther's works, currently 121 volumes, will be abbreviated WA.

truth, he declares, "distinguishes our religion from all others."[21] With this assessment Calvin agreed, calling it "the main hinge on which religion turns."[22] Lose this doctrine, and Christ, the church and Christianity itself are lost. Therefore, in the Smalcald Articles (1537),[23] with the solemnity of one under oath, Luther stresses the momentous nature of this doctrine:

> Nothing in this article can be given up or compromised, even if heaven and earth and things temporal should be destroyed... On this article rests all that we teach and practice against the pope, the devil, and the world. Therefore we must be quite certain and have no doubts about it. Otherwise all is lost, and the pope, the devil, and all our adversaries will gain the victory.[24]

Another reason why we must diligently study and zealously defend this doctrine is found in the opposition that it continues to receive from its enemies. The doctrine of justification by faith alone as laid out in the 1689 Confession is still anathema to the Vatican. By insisting that justification has to do with an infusion of God's grace into the hearts of the faithful, Rome continues to confuse justification with sanctification. Moreover, by continuing to insist that all who would be released from the burden of their sins must continue to receive new infusions of God's grace by means of the sacraments, Rome still teaches its adherents that something else besides the imputed righteousness of Christ received by faith is necessary to a right standing before God.

Having looked at some of the reasons why we must give ourselves whole-heartedly to the study of this doctrine, we now come to what the Confession has to say concerning it.

1. The Distinct Nature of Justification (Para. 1)

A. The Subjects of Justification: Those Effectually Called

Those whom God effectually calleth, he also freely justifieth,

These words enunciate the truth that God justifies all those and only those whom He has effectually called by His grace. This is proven, first, by the express teaching of Scripture: "Whom he predestined, these He also called; whom He called, these He also justified" (Rom. 8:30). Second, this is established by the fact that only those who truly come to Christ by faith are justified (Rom. 3:21-22, 28; 5:1; Gal. 2:16), and only those who have been effectually called or regenerated can truly believe (1 Cor. 1:9; John 1:12-13; Acts 18:27; 26:18; Eph. 2:8).

---

21. Quoted in Paul Althaus, *The Theology of Martin Luther,* trans. Robert C. Schultz (Philadelphia: Fortress Press, 1966), 224.

22. *Institutes of the Christian Religion,* 3.11.1, trans. Ford Lewis Battles, The Library of Christian Classics (Philadelphia: Westminster Press, 1960), 20:726.

23. A summary of Luther's teachings written by Luther.

24. Smalcald Articles, 2.1.5, in *The Book of Concord: The Confessions of the Evangelical Lutheran Church,* trans. and ed. Theodore G. Tappert (Philadelphia: Fortress Press, 1959), 292 = WA 50:199.

B. The Essence of Justification: Pardon and Acceptance

not by infusing righteousness into them, but by pardoning their sins, and by accounting and accepting their persons as righteous;

1. Negatively: It Is Not Ethical Infusion

One of the most common ways this doctrine has been and still is perverted is by redefining the term. Justification does not mean that one is to *be, become* or *be made* inherently good or upright. Justification does not involve a change of nature but a change of the sinner's legal standing before God's law. God "justifies the ungodly" (Rom. 4:5). At that very moment—when he is declared just by God—the believer remains inherently sinful. This does not mean that at the moment of conversion God does nothing to make His people holy. But justification and sanctification are not the same. While sanctification has to do with one's internal conformity to the character of God, justification has to do with one's legal standing before the law of God.

It is one of the primary errors of Rome that it regards justification as the gracious infusion of a principle of holiness into our hearts and as a sanctifying process by which we are made holy. The Council of Trent (1545–1563), Rome's answer to the Reformation, explicitly anathematizes those who assert that men are justified solely by the "imputation of the justice of Christ" to the exclusion of the love poured forth in their hearts by the Holy Spirit.[25] By this justification the graces of faith, hope and love are "infused" into the hearts of those who co-operate with God's grace.[26] Against this teaching the 1689 Confession unambiguously denies that justification takes place "by infusing righteousness into them."

2. Positively: It Is a Judicial Transaction

God justifies those whom He effectually calls, the Confession states, "by pardoning their sins, and by accounting and accepting their persons as righteous." These are forensic terms, that is, terms having to do with one's legal standing before God.[27] Justification changes the sinner's legal status, not his inner nature. Martin Luther's rediscovery of the biblical doctrine of justification as a judicial declaration involved a radical break with the teaching of the Catholic scholastic theologians of the medieval church. In the thinking of these theologians one is *declared righteous* only when he has been *made righteous* by a supernatural infusion of divine grace. Hence, according to the medieval theologians, the verdict of justification is not the Judge's pronouncement of innocence but the Physician's attestation

---

25. The Canons and Dogmatic Decrees of the Council of Trent, session 6, canon 11, in Philip Schaff, ed., *The Creeds of Christendom*, 6th ed. (Harper and Row, 1931; reprint ed., Grand Rapids: Baker Book House, 1983), 2:112-13.

26. Ibid., session 6, Chapters 5 & 7, in Schaff, *Creeds of Christendom*, 2:92, 95-96.

27. As L. Berkhof defines it, "Justification is a judicial act of God, in which He declares, on the basis of the righteousness of Jesus Christ, that all the claims of the law are satisfied with respect to the sinner" (*Systematic Theology* [Grand Rapids: Wm. B. Eerdmans, 1939], 513).

of recovery, a "clean bill of health." But when Luther rediscovered the biblical doctrine of justification, he abandoned the *medical* imagery of infusion for the *forensic* concept of judicial declaration. Justification was returned from its medieval setting of a hospital bed to the biblical setting of a courtroom.[28] The medieval idea confused regeneration with justification. In regeneration God does the work of a divine physician, surgically removing the cancer of our sin and supernaturally imparting a new principle of life and holiness. All of this He does *within* us. But as the Judge who "justifies the ungodly" (Rom. 4:5), He renders a favorable judicial verdict. This He does *without* us: in the courtroom of heaven.

Even common usage of the word "justify" shows that justification does not mean to *make holy* but to *pronounce upright*. When a judge justifies the accused, he doesn't make that person upright. Rather, he simply declares that the man is not guilty of the crime of which he is accused. For the following reasons we believe that the Bible uses "justify" and related terms in the same way:

1) The Scriptures repeatedly set forth justification as the opposite of condemnation. In several places this contrast is used with reference to judicial pronouncements made by men. Judges must "justify the righteous and condemn the wicked" (Deut. 25:1; cf. Prov. 17:15; Isa. 5:23). What is it to condemn the wicked? It is certainly not making someone wicked by infusing wickedness into him. Rather, it is to judicially declare or pronounce him guilty because of his transgression of the law. Turning from the proceedings of human judges to those of God, we again observe that the terms "condemnation" and "justification" denote contrasting judicial pronouncements (Rom. 8:33-34; 5:16, 18; Isa. 50:8-9; Matt. 12:37). In each of these passages the justification and condemnation in view are equally forensic in nature.

2) In many places "justify" cannot mean anything other than to declare righteous; to substitute sanctification (making holy) for justification (declaring legally upright) would produce nonsense. According to Deuteronomy 25:1, judges must "justify the righteous and condemn the wicked." If "justify" means "to actually make righteous," why does the Lord insist that judges condemn the wicked? Why would He not rather require that judges make the wicked righteous? The answer is because judges have no ability to effect this change. They can do no more than make a declaration regarding the guilt or innocence of the one charged. Again we read, "He who justifies the wicked, and he who condemns the just, both of them alike are an abomination to the LORD" (Prov. 17:15). Would it be an abomination to the Lord to transform a criminal into a righteous man? Surely not! That which is condemned by this text is declaring the wicked to be righteous when he is not (cf. Isa. 5:23; Luke 7:29; 16:15).

3) A third proof of the judicial sense of the phrase "to justify" is found in the fact that the terms with which it is associated consistently

---

28. cf. Timothy George, *Theology of the Reformers* (Nashville: Broadman Press, 1988), 69-70.

designate one or another aspect of the process of judgment. The context of the doctrine is always judicial. In the book of Romans, where this doctrine is most thoroughly expounded, we have the following: a Judge (2:2), a judgement (2:16; 3:19), a tribunal (14:10), an indictment (3:9-10), an accuser (8:33), a witness (2:15), a conviction (3:19-20), an Advocate (8:34) and a pardon (4:7-8). If God makes the context of justification the courtroom, it is wrong for us to make it the hospital room.

4) That justification is a judicial declaration rather than an ethical infusion is confirmed by the way the Scriptures consistently represent the justification of those who are already believers as an instantaneous act in the past, not as an ongoing process in the present (Rom. 4:3, 9; 5:1, 9; Luke 18:14).

For these four reasons we are convinced that justification is not an infusion of holiness into one's heart, but a judicial declaration concerning the believer's standing before God. The 1689 Confession informs us that this judicial declaration includes two aspects: pardon and acceptance.

a. Pardon

Among men pardon is simply the prerogative of a merciful ruler who relaxes the claims of the law in a given case. But divine pardon is never an arbitrary absolution that dispenses with the claims of God's law. It is always based on the premise that the penalties due for every violation must be endured by either the sinner or a substitute (Rom. 3:23-26; 5:8-9; 2 Cor. 5:18-21; Gal. 3:10-13).

The pardon granted in justification is *full* and *free* (Isa. 55:7; 44:22; Eph. 1:7). It *extends to all sins*—no matter how great, aggravated and numerous (Ps. 103:3; cf. 130:3-4; Jer. 33:8; Isa. 1:18). It is *irrevocable* (Isa. 43:25; cf. Ps. 103:12; Jer. 31:34; Mic. 7:18-19). And it applies to all sins, *past, present and future* (Rom. 8:1, 32-34; Heb. 10:10-18; Ps. 32:1-2).

b. Acceptance

The Confession declares that God justifies those He has called, not only by pardoning their sins but also "by accounting and accepting their persons as righteous." By means of the former our sins are not reckoned unto us. By means of the latter we are treated as if we had fully performed all that the law requires. Suppose the owner of a large estate, before leaving for a trip, gave his servants ten prohibitions and assigned them ten tasks, threatening certain punishments for the violation of the prohibitions and promising rich rewards for the accomplishment of the assigned tasks. When the master returned, the faithful servant both avoided the threatened punishments and received the promised rewards. But the other servant had both violated the prohibitions and failed to perform his duties. Because he pled with tears for clemency, the master pardoned all his offences. But the servant could not be rewarded as if he had faithfully carried out all of his appointed duties. God does better than this. Not only does He treat us as if we had never violated His law, but He also accepts and rewards us as if we had perfectly accomplished every one of our assigned tasks. That justification not only includes pardon but also acceptance is shown by the following evidence:

1) The Bible repeatedly declares that our justification rests, not only on Christ's satisfaction of the justice of God (by which we are pardoned), but also on the ground of Christ's perfect obedience to the law of God (by which we are accepted). In order that we might be pardoned, our sins were put to His account (and no longer reckoned to ours). In order that we might be accepted as righteous, His righteousness has been put to our account (Rom. 4:6-8; 5:19; 10:3-9; 2 Cor. 5:21; 1 Cor. 1:30).

2) The effects of justification are greater than the release from punishment that comes with pardon. As J.I. Packer puts it: "[Justification] means the bestowal of a righteous man's status and a title to all the blessings promised to the just."[29] These blessings include peace with God, access to God, communion with Him, adoption, being joint-heirs with Christ, the sealing of the Holy Spirit, eternal life, and the hope of the glory of God (Rom. 5:1-2, 17-18, 21; 8:14-23, 30; Gal. 4:4-7; Eph. 1:13-14).

C. The Basis of Justification: Christ Alone

not for anything wrought in them, or done by them, but for Christ's sake alone;

1. Negatively: It Is Not Based on Us
The Church of Rome sets forth that which Christ merited, not as an objective righteousness worked out on behalf of the believer, but as an infused righteousness that must be improved upon by the cooperative efforts of the believer before he is meritoriously entitled to eternal life.[30] The teaching of Rome boils down to this: we are not justified by grace, pure and simple, but by the works that come from it. Over against this teaching our Confession asserts that believers are justified, "not for anything wrought in them, or done by them."

a. Its Basis Not Anything Wrought in Us
The Bible clearly rejects the notion that our justification is based on an inner transformation:

1) We can only be justified on the basis of a perfect righteousness, and the inherent sanctity of even the best of us is imperfect (Prov. 20:9; Job 9:20; 14:4; 15:14-15; 25:4-6; Eccl. 7:20; Isa. 6:5; 64:6; Rom. 3:10, 23; 1 John 1:8).

2) A righteousness wrought in us, even if it were absolutely perfect, and even if it guaranteed perseverance in sinless perfection forever, could not measure up to the righteousness demanded by the law. Why? It would do nothing to obliterate our many past transgressions. We need a righteousness that will remedy past as well as future sins (Ps. 130:3-4; Mic. 6:6-7).

---

29. *Baker's Dictionary of Theology*, 1978 ed., s.v. "Just, Justify, Justification," by James I. Packer, 305.

30. Council of Trent, Session 6, Chapters 5 and 16, and Canons 4 and 9, in Schaff, *Creeds of Christendom*, 2:92, 107-10, 111, 112.

3) If the righteousness by which men are justified is an inherent righteousness wrought in them, it could not be said that God "justifies the *ungodly*" (Rom. 4:5; cf. 5:6-9).

4) Our justification cannot be based on anything wrought in us, because the Bible explicitly declares that the righteousness by which we are justified is not our own (Phil. 3:3-9; Rom. 10:3).

When God reckons the righteousness of Christ to the sinner's account, He also inscribes the likeness of Christ on his soul. But the object of saving faith is Christ Himself, not the image of Christ within. "The bride doth well highly to esteem her husband's picture,... but it were ridiculous if she should dote on that so far as to slight her husband, and, when she wants money, clothes or the like, to go, not to her husband, but to the picture he gave her for all."[31] As long as you trust in Christ's image within more than Christ Himself, you will be plagued with subjectivism and doubt. The basis of our justification is not *anything* wrought in us, even the likeness of Christ Himself.

b. Its Basis Not Anything Done by Us

Whereas Trent mixed grace and works in justification, our Confession denies that sinners are justified for "anything done by them." Biblical support for this denial includes the following:

1) Even the obedience rendered by the holiest saint falls far short of the perfection required by God (cf. 1 above). If a man is to be justified on the basis of his obedience, it must not in the least particular fall short of the requirements of the law. But there is no such perfect obedience among men (James 2:10-11; 3:2; Gal. 3:10, 21; Rom. 3:9-10, 19-20, 23).

2) Even if the sinner were to begin to obey God perfectly, his new obedience could do nothing to satisfy the penalty due for past transgressions. Suppose a man convicted of a brutal murder is on death row. The governor notices that while in jail the man's old heart of hatred is replaced by love. The man leads Bible studies which have a transforming effect on the whole prison, persuades his fellow longtime inmates to express their sorrow to those they have hurt, and organizes a national movement to help families victimized by violent crimes. The story of this prison revival spreads across the nation. At length a great cry is raised, pleading with the governor to pardon the man. The governor is perplexed: Should he uphold the law or extend clemency? Herein is his dilemma: he cannot do both. At last he grants the pardon, but reluctantly so, because he knows that the demands of the law have not been satisfied. But God cannot do this. His law must be upheld. If we were to render perfect service for a million years, we could not pay for our past sins (Mic. 6:6-7). The law requires not only the fulfillment of its precepts but also the endurance of its penalties: "without shedding of blood there is no remission" (Heb. 9:22). Calvary is God's answer to the strictness of His law.

---

31. William Gurnall, *The Christian in Complete Armour* (Glasgow: Blackie and Son, 1864; reprint ed., Edinburgh: The Banner of Truth Trust, 1974), 1:516.

3) That we are not justified by the works of the law is the uniform testimony of Scripture (Rom. 3:20, 28; 4:4-8; 9:30-32; 10:3-5; Gal. 2:16; 3:10-12, 21; 5:4; Eph. 2:8-10; Phil. 3:9).

4) Biblical affirmations that we are justified by grace are utterly contrary to the notion that justification is a reward for anything we do. Grace is the bestowal of favor on those who deserve the opposite. This unmerited favor is shown when God justifies those who bring no works for their justification, but believe on Him who justifies the ungodly (Rom. 3:24-28; 4:4-5, 16; 5:15-21; 11:6).

5) Those who in any way seek to be justified by their works render the death of Christ needless and ineffectual. In defending his thesis that "a man is not justified by the works of the law" (Gal. 2:16), Paul declares, "I do not set aside[32] the grace of God: for if righteousness comes through the law, then Christ died in vain" (v. 21). Something is done "in vain" (δωρεάν) when it is done either needlessly or ineffectually.

a) If either a part or a whole of the payment due for our sins can be made by us, it was a needless thing for an infinite sacrifice (Acts 20:28) to be rendered on our behalf. If even part of the payment can be made by us, it was an act of terrible cruelty for the Father to deliver up His Son to the infinite agonies of Golgotha.

b) When we seek either to replace or supplement Christ's death by our own works, we treat His death as if it were ineffectual. According to the Scriptures, Christ's death was effectual for the remission of all of our sins (Matt. 26:28; Heb. 10:11-18; 1 John 1:9) and for the achievement of a righteousness by which we are acceptable to God (Dan. 9:24; 2 Cor. 5:21). It didn't just make it possible for God to replace a hard standard (full payment from us) with an easier standard (partial payment from us). "Christ did not die...to make a hard way to heaven easy; but...to make impossible things *certain*"[33] (cf. Rom. 8:3; Gal. 3:21).

6) The righteousness by which we are justified is the righteousness of *God* (Rom. 1:17; 3:21-24). A righteousness worked out by us (whether acts of penance or evangelical obedience), even if prompted by God, is not a God-righteousness, for it is actually accomplished by us. But the God-righteousness by which we are justified is not our own (Phil. 3:9; Rom. 10:3; cf. 3:20-21).

These six arguments against justification by works are a warning to those who have a damning confidence in their own performances. Take your works and place them in the burning light of God's holiness. You may boast in them all you want, "but not before God" (Rom. 4:2; cf. Heb. 4:12-13). To really be "good" in the eyes of God a work must fully conform to the spiritual and practical demands of His law, be a conscious expression of obedience to His will, spring from absolutely pure motives, be done out of supreme love to God, and aim at God's glory. Not one

---

32. ἀθετῶ—reject, nullify, make invalid, abrogate, make void.

33. Robert Traill, *The Works of Robert Traill* (Edinburgh: George Caw, Printer, 1810; reprint ed., Edinburgh: The Banner of Truth Trust, n.d.), 4:218.

thing you or I have ever done has fully measured up to this standard (Isa. 64:6).

These six considerations also have something to say to those of you who once repudiated your works and trusted in the righteousness of Christ alone, but subsequently have been plagued with a crippling preoccupation with your sins. You are torn between the testimonies of two witnesses: the testimony of your conscience concerning your sins (all of which deserve eternal condemnation) and the testimony of God concerning your justification. You may respond in one of three ways.

1) You may listen to the testimony of each of these witnesses as if they were of equal weight. As long as you do this, you will remain in agony of soul.

2) You may seek to remove the tension by silencing one of the witnesses. You may seek to stifle the voice of your conscience, thereby giving yourself up to increasing hardness of heart. Or you may virtually silence God's testimony by listening more to the voice of your conscience, thereby descending deeper and deeper into despair.

3) You may react to your sin biblically. On one hand, refusing to deny the testimony of your conscience, you make a full and open confession of your sin. On the other hand, you lay hold of God's testimony that there is "no condemnation to those who are in Christ Jesus" and conquer by means of the believing affirmations of Romans 8 (vv. 1, 31-39; cf. 1 John 1:8-9).

2. Positively: It Is Based on Christ

Having denied that our justification is based on anything wrought in us or done by us, the Confession of Faith affirms that we are justified "for Christ's sake alone." It is that righteousness that Christ fully worked out on our behalf during His days on earth and especially while He hung upon the tree (Rom. 3:21-26; 5:6-9; Isa. 53:11), that and that alone, which is the fulfillment of the perfect righteousness God requires. Christ "became for us... righteousness," and we are said to "become the righteousness of God in Him" (1 Cor. 1:30; 2 Cor. 5:21; cf. Jer. 23:5-6). Similar language is used when the righteousness of our justification is said to be "by Him" (Acts 13:38-39), "in Christ Jesus" (Rom. 8:1), "by Christ" (Gal. 2:17), "in Him" (Phil. 3:9) and "in the name of the Lord Jesus" (1 Cor. 6:11).

In order to stress the fact that this righteousness is in no way produced by us but is entirely the work of Christ, Luther called it an "alien righteousness" (*iustitia alienum*), a righteousness entirely "outside of us" (*extra nos*).[34] This righteousness is "nothing whatever in us but is entirely outside of us in Christ and yet becomes truly ours by reason of His grace and gift, and becomes our very own, as though we ourselves

---

34. Martin Luther, *Disputation Concerning Justification*, Thesis 27, in Luther's Works, eds., Jaroslav Pelikan and Helmut T. Lehmann (St. Louis: Concordia Publishing House; and Philadelphia: Muhlenberg Press, 1955-), 34:153 = WA 391:83. Hereafter this English translation, currently 69 volumes, will be abbreviated as LW.

had achieved and earned it."[35] Luther stated this principle even more boldly when he coined that famous formula by which he describes the Christian as "at one and the same time a righteous man and a sinner" (*simul iustus et peccator*). Previously he had thought of the believer as "partly" a sinner and "partly" righteous. But during the winter of 1515–1516, while lecturing on the book of Romans, he spoke of the Christian as "at the same time both a sinner and a righteous man [*simul peccator et iustus*]; a sinner in fact, but a righteous man by the sure imputation and promise of God."[36]

Believers, you must never forget that you are "at one and the same time a righteous man and a sinner"—just as much now as when you first believed. Beginning in 1518–1519, Luther went on to emphasize that the Christian is not only "at one and the same time a righteous man and a sinner" (*simul iustus et peccator*), but *"always* a righteous man and a sinner" (*semper iustus et peccator*). Paul's reference to himself as the chief of sinners (1 Tim. 1:15) is in the present tense. All of his faithfulness and self-denial does not change the fact that, considered in himself, he is still a sinner. His one and only hope of justification is still the same: Christ. There is nothing more fundamental to Christian assurance than this. It is a defense that is impervious to every charge laid against us (Rom. 8:33-34). "Whenever the devil and hell itself come to claim you, show them Christ, and you will be able to silence them."[37]

D. The Method of Justification: Imputation

not by imputing faith itself, the act of believing, or any other evangelical obedience to them, as their righteousness; but by imputing Christ's active obedience unto the whole law, and passive obedience in his death for their whole and sole righteousness,

In common usage "impute" means "reckon" or "regard." Sometimes such reckoning agrees with what is really the case, as with those "counted faithful" in Nehemiah 13:13. But such reckoning may contradict reality, as when an innocent man is thought to be guilty. The Scriptures, however, frequently use the word in a stronger sense, of judicially reckoning either sin or righteousness to one's account as the basis of his condemnation or justification. This may take place in two ways:

1) Merit or demerit that is inherently a man's own may be imputed to him (Ps. 106:31). If he is guilty of a crime, it is reckoned a crime of which he is guilty and is liable for punishment (Lev. 17:4; 2 Sam. 19:19). One of the chief blessings of justification is the non-imputation of sin. "Blessed is the man to whom the LORD does not impute iniquity" (Ps. 32:2; cf. Rom. 4:7-8).

---

35. Luther, *Sermons on the Gospel of John,* on John 16:10 (LW 24:347 = WA 46:44, lines 36-38).

36. Luther, *Lectures on Romans,* on 4:7 (LW 25:260 = WA 56:272, lines 17-18 = Library of Christian Classics, 15:127).

37. Luther, *Sämmtliche Werke,* 67 volume German edition of Luther's works (Erlangen, 1826–1857), 15:60.

2) That which did *not* personally belong to a man prior to its imputation may be imputed to him. It may take place when a man is falsely accused (1 Kings 1:21). But this sort of imputation may be perfectly just in its basis. Based upon the representative relationship that exists between Adam and his posterity, his first sin has been imputed to all those whom he represented (Rom. 5:12-19). Even so, because Christ was constituted the head of all believers, a double imputation was possible: the sins of believers were put to His account and His righteousness was put to their account (2 Cor. 5:21; Rom. 5:19). As was said of Onesimus in Philemon 18, so our Lord said with respect to all of our sins, "If they owe anything, charge it to my account." The imputation involved in our justification is of this second type. That which is imputed is done so by way of *transfer*. a) On one hand, our guilt was debited to Christ's account by way of transfer: "The LORD has laid on Him the iniquity of us all" (Isa. 53:6, 12; cf. Gal. 3:13; 1 Peter 2:24). God "made Him who knew no sin to be sin for us" (2 Cor. 5:21). In what sense? It could not be by way of participation because our Lord "knew no sin." Therefore, it could only be by way of transfer, by laying on Him all of the guilt of His people. b) On the other hand, Christ's righteousness is credited to our account by way of transfer and we are declared righteous (2 Cor. 5:19-21).

Having established the meaning of imputation, we now ask, "When a man is justified, what is it that is imputed to his account?" The Confession answers this question negatively and positively.

1. Negatively: Not by Imputing Faith Itself or Evangelical Obedience

Sinners are justified, the Confession states, "not by imputing faith itself, the act of believing, or any other evangelical obedience to them, as their righteousness." Our justification is:

a. Not by Imputing Faith Itself

Some represent faith as a gospel substitute for works as the ground of our acceptance. Support for this position is sought in the New Testament citations of Genesis 15:6: "Abraham believed God, and it was accounted [ἐλογίσθη][38] to him for righteousness" (Rom. 4:3; Gal. 3:6; James 2:23). In this way a justification based on an inherent righteousness (consisting in faith) is covertly introduced. According to this scheme, the reason why faith is accepted by God is not because of its object (Christ) but because it is a virtue that contains seeds of every other grace. This notion is overthrown by the following considerations:

1) If faith is reckoned to our account as the basis of our justification, we are justified on the basis of a meritorious disposition—which is diametrically opposed to justification by grace and is categorically rejected by the Bible (Rom. 4:4-5; Gal. 2:16, 21). The righteousness by which we are justified is not the righteousness of our faith but the "righteousness of God" (Rom. 3:21-22).

---

38. Λογίζομαι means count, reckon, credit, place to one's account.

2) The idea that faith is reckoned as righteousness is exceedingly derogatory to the character of God expressed in His law. Robert Haldane writes: "That law, which is the transcript of His own unchangeable nature, can acknowledge nothing as its fulfillment but perfect conformity to all its requirements. Nor did the Gospel come to pour dishonor upon it by modifying its demands, or to substitute another law for it, making faith meritorious"[39] (cf. Isa. 42:21; Rom. 3:21-22).

3) Both in Romans 4 and Galatians 3 Paul cites Genesis 15:6 to prove that Abraham was not justified by works but by faith. If his faith was meritorious unto salvation, it was in effect the meritorious work by which he was justified. But this is entirely contrary to Paul's thesis that our justification is a gift of God's grace, not a reward earned by our works (Rom. 3:24; 4:4-5). For Paul to say that Abraham's faith was meritoriously imputed to him as his justifying righteousness (4:3) and then to say that we are not justified by works but by grace (vv. 4-5) would be to contradict himself almost in one breath.

What, then, do the Scriptures mean when they say that Abraham's faith was "reckoned unto him for righteousness"? Here we must remember the two senses in which the Scriptures use the word "reckon" or "impute." Sometimes it is used of that which did not personally belong to a person but is reckoned to his account. But in other cases, "reckon" simply means to recognize something already in existence (cf. Rom. 6:7-11). It is in this second sense that the word is used in the passages under consideration. God "reckoned" or recognized Abraham to have exercised genuine faith. Paul is emphasizing that it was *faith* that was recognized in Abraham, not some good work.

The passages under consideration state that the faith that was reckoned to be faith was reckoned "unto" (*eis*) righteousness. In these verses the Greek preposition *eis* does not properly signify "for" or "in the stead of," but always means "unto" or "in order to." All who are justified, including Abraham, "believe *unto* righteousness" (Rom. 10:10, emphasis added), that is, believe with a view to being justified. The teaching of Romans 4:3 and parallel texts is that 1) Abraham believed God, 2) God reckoned his faith as genuine, and 3) reckoning him to be a believer, God justified him.

4) The notion that our faith is imputed to us as our justifying righteousness is inconsistent with the office ascribed to faith. The New Testament writers commonly use three expressions to describe the relationship of faith to justification. The Christian is said to be justified (a) *pistei*—"by faith" (Rom. 3:28), (b) *ek pisteos*—"from," "out of," or "by faith" (Rom. 3:30; 5:1; Gal. 2:16; 3:24), or (c) *dia pisteos*—"through" or "by means of faith" (Rom. 3:22, 25, 30; Gal. 2:16; Eph. 2:8; Phil. 3:9). But the Scriptures never say that we are justified *dia ten pistin*—"on the ground of" or "on account of faith," thereby making faith the meritorious basis of our acceptance with God.

---

39. Robert Haldane, *An Exposition of the Epistle to the Romans* (reprint ed., Mac Dill AFB, Florida: Mac Donald Publishing Company, n.d.), 164.

These arguments expose the error of those who assert that our faith is our justifying righteousness. Romanists assert that justification rests upon "faith co-operating with good works."[40] The decrees of Trent insist that we are justified by this faith, not because it rests upon the righteousness of Christ, but because of its powerful, fruit-bearing capacity. But error on this point has not been confined to Romanists. Some Arminians hold that God has graciously replaced the demands of the law with an easier requirement: faith, and that this faith is now accepted in the place of perfect obedience as the grounds of justification. Inevitably this leads the anxious inquirer to ask, "Do I have enough faith?" Whereas the trembling Catholic asks, "Have I done enough works?", the sincere Arminian has his own agonizing "enough" questions: "Is my faith strong enough?" "Are the fruits of my faith plentiful enough?"

But such confusion is not limited to Romanists and Arminians. With pastoral insight Robert Traill observed, "There is not a minister that deals seriously with the souls of men, but he finds an Arminian scheme of justification in every unrenewed heart."[41] When a believer falls prey to placing his faith in his faith, every detected inadequacy in his faith makes him tremble. Why? Remaining sin stains, not only his works, but also his faith. Dear doubting believer, if you have begun to trust in your faith rather than Christ, look away from yourself to Him. Joel Beeke says, "Too many Christians live in constant despondency because they cannot distinguish between the rock on which they stand and the faith by which they stand upon the rock. Faith is not our rock; Christ is our rock."[42]

God has chosen to justify us by faith, not because of any inherent virtue in our faith, but because faith looks outside of itself to the righteousness of Another. B. B. Warfield writes, "It is not, strictly speaking, even faith in Christ that saves but Christ that saves through faith."[43] Christ has not chosen to save us through faith because it is morally superior to other virtues, but because the very nature of faith is simple receptivity. We put a gift into a man's hand rather than his ear, not because the hand is better than the ear, but because the hand is the member most adapted to reception. God chose faith to be the instrument of our justification, not because of its moral superiority but because of its humble receptivity.

b. Not by Imputing Evangelical Obedience

Rome teaches that works done by the assistance of divine grace and prompted by the gospel are essential to the justifying process.[44] Many

---

40. Council of Trent, Session 6, Chapter 10 (cf. Ch. 8), in Schaff, *Creeds of Christendom*, 2:99 (cf. 2:97).

41. Traill, *Works*, 1:186.

42. Joel Beeke, "The Relation of Faith to Justification," in ed., Don Kistler, *Justification by Faith Alone* (Morgan, Pa: Soli Deo Gloria Publications, 1995), 93.

43. Benjamin B. Warfield, "Faith," in *Biblical and Theological Studies* (Philadelphia: Presbyterian and Reformed, 1968), 425. This statement is also found in a fuller edition of this article in *The Works of Benjamin B. Warfield*, 10 vols. (New York: Oxford University Press, 1929; reprint ed., Grand Rapids: Baker Book House, 1981), 2:504.

44. Council of Trent, Session 6, Chapter 10, in Schaff, *Creeds of Christendom*, 2:99-100.

Arminians assert that the moral lapses of the believer require the renewal of his justification, and that continuation in a justified state is contingent on continued obedience. Much of what we have already said to refute the notion that our justification is based on anything wrought in us or done by us also refutes this error. Here we merely wish to advert to the fact that it is the testimony of Scripture that the post-conversion works of saints renowned for their godliness (for example, Abraham, Paul) were not the righteousness imputed to them for their justification (Rom. 4:1-16; Phil. 3:4-9).

The root cause of our tendency to look to evangelical obedience as if it were at least part of the righteousness put to our account is pride. Thinking that grace could not be proud, we forget that a man may be proud of his grace. As Gurnall points out, "There is nothing the Christian hath or doth, but this worm of pride will breed in it."[45] Often this pride puts on the guise of humility. This is done in two ways:

1) When poor sinners shrink back from embracing the righteousness of Christ offered in the gospel due to a sense of their own unworthiness, their apparent humility is often a cover for their pride. Assure such a one of the promises of the gospel to all who believe, and he still refuses to be comforted. Why? He refuses to cease from his vain search for something within that will commend him to God. Christ's messengers tell him, "All things are ready" (Matt. 22:4). Pride says, "It is not so, for I am not quite ready." Humility leads you to come to Jesus just as you are.

2) Others of you, having believed some time ago, now are despondent. Why? All of your joy has run out through the cracks of your imperfect performances. Your soul is so dry, your walk is so uneven, and you fall so short of God's law. There you sit at the gospel feast Christ provided, yet you do not know whether you dare eat. Why? Beneath your professed humility lurks pride. If you could pray without wandering, walk without limping and believe without wavering, then you would be happy. Because of that subtle desire to derive comfort from your own performances, you hold back from receiving it purely from Christ. Don't do this! Cease from your efforts to find solace in your own behavior; enfold yourself in the righteousness of Christ alone. Do not rob Christ of the glory due only to Him (1 Cor. 1:30-31).

2. Positively: by Imputing Christ's Active and Passive Obedience

Having repudiated the notion that God justifies sinners by imputing their faith or obedience to them, the Confession affirms that justification is "by imputing Christ's active obedience unto the whole law, and passive obedience in his death for their whole and sole righteousness." The idea that Christ's *passive obedience* consisted in mere suffering and His *active obedience* was confined to His years prior to the cross overlooks the biblical teaching that in both His life and death He was actively engaged in obeying His Father (Phil. 2:8; John 10:17-18; 18:11; 19:30; Luke 23:46; Heb. 5:8-9; 10:5-10; Ps. 40:6-8). Nevertheless, these two terms aptly describe

---

45. Gurnall, *Christian in Complete Armour,* 1:200.

Christ's obedience viewed in two ways. By His obedience He met two conditions necessary for our justification:

a) Our first need was the removal of our guilt. By His "passive" obedience Christ suffered the fullness of the curse and penalty due unto us and thereby provided the basis for the removal of our guilt (Gal. 3:10, 13; 2 Cor. 5:21; Isa. 53:5-6). That part of justification involving our pardon is based on this satisfaction of the penal demands of God's law. Because He rendered this satisfaction as our substitute, it may rightly be said that His passive obedience has been imputed to us. Therefore, our justification is explicitly linked to His redemption (Rom. 3:24), propitiation (3:25-26), blood (5:9), obedience (5:18-19) and becoming sin for us (2 Cor. 5:21).

b) God's law not only has penal sanctions but also positive demands. Therefore, we were also in need of a positive righteousness. If any of us were to be accepted by God, our Substitute must not only endure the penalty due to us but also fulfill all the demands required of us. We not only needed a passive but also an active obedience. Christ met this need by His perfect obedience to all the precepts of the law and all the particular requirements of the will of the Father for Him (Gal. 4:4-5; John 6:38). This obedience was rendered during the entirety of His life and culminated in that great act of obedience when He was obedient even "to the point of death" (Phil. 2:8). By His death He did more than deliver us from hell; He also purchased heaven (Rom. 5:1-2; 15-21; 6:23).

Closely connected to the twofold imputation of Christ's active and passive obedience to us is another "double imputation," in which the sins of believers were imputed to Christ at the cross (Isa. 53:6; 2 Cor. 5:21; Gal. 3:13; 1 Pet. 2:24), and the righteousness and obedience of Christ is imputed to all who believe (Rom. 5:19; 2 Cor. 5:21). What solid ground for assurance is provided by the biblical teaching concerning this mutual transfer! On April 8, 1516, Martin Luther wrote George Spenlein, asking him whether his soul, "tired of its own righteousness, [was] learning to be revived by and to trust in the righteousness of Christ." Luther then pointed his friend to a "sweet exchange": "My dear Friar, learn Christ and him crucified. Learn to praise him and, despairing of yourself, say, 'Lord Jesus, you are my righteousness, just as I am your sin. You have taken upon yourself what is mine and have given to me what is yours.'"[46] Whether in life or death, what greater comfort could there be?

E. The Instrument of Justification: Faith

they receiving and resting on him and his righteousness by faith, which faith they have not of themselves; it is the gift of God.

---

46. LW 48:12 = *Luther: Letters of Spiritual Counsel*, trans. Theodore G. Tappert, in The Library of Christian Classics (Philadelphia: Westminster Press, 1960; reprint ed., Vancouver: Regent College Publishing, 2003), 18:110 = *Dr. Martin Luthers Briefe, Sendschrieben und Bedenken: volständig...*, Wette edition, usually abbreviated WA Br (Berlin: Ben G. Reimer, 1825), 1:17.

1. Its Essence

In this statement, the faith by which we are justified is described with respect to its essential activities, "receiving and resting," and its essential object, "[Christ] and his righteousness."

a. Its Essential Activities

1) Saving faith involves "receiving" Christ (John 1:12; 12:48) and His righteousness (Rom. 10:3, 4). For this reason it has been aptly called the "hand" that receives Christ. Faith is called a "hand," not because it *works* for or *earns* justification, but because it *receives* and *appropriates* Christ as He is freely offered to sinners. It is not a full, working hand but an empty, receptive hand. Faith hears of the pardoning blood and, reaching out, says, "I receive that pardon for myself." It says, "I receive and take Jesus to be mine." "Faith, with arms outstretched joyfully embraces the Son of God given for it and says, 'He is my beloved [*dilectus*] and I am his.'"[47]

2) This faith also involves "resting on" Christ. It is not enough that a man knows the truth of the gospel and even assents unto its truthfulness. His faith must also include the element of trust. In true saving faith the sinner abandons all human resources and rests in Christ alone for his salvation. The Scriptures frequently speak of saving faith in terms of "believing on" Christ. Sometimes this phrase is derived from the Greek words *pisteuein epi,* which express a resting repose or reliance upon the object of faith (Rom. 9:33, 10:11; 1 Peter 2:6; 1 Tim. 1:16). Even more frequently (some forty-nine times) "believe on" translates the Greek phrase *pisteuein eis,* which depicts faith as being reliantly directed away from one's self to Christ (for example, John 3:16, 18, 36; 6:29, 35, 40; 7:38-39; 11:25-26; 14:1; Gal. 2:16). Trusting in Christ is leaning with all our weight upon Him.

b. Its Essential Object

We are justified, the Confession states, by receiving and resting on "him [i.e., Christ] and his righteousness by faith." The object of justifying faith is the person and work of Christ.

1) Justifying faith looks to the person of Christ. Sometimes this is represented as believing on Him as the One sent from God (John 5:38; 6:29) or as God the Son (John 11:27; 20:28-31). But faith characteristically goes directly to Christ Himself. This act is described as "coming" to Christ (John 6:35, 37, 44) or "receiving" Him (John 1:12; 12:48), but most often as "believing on" Him (see the texts cited above). True faith is preoccupied with the object of its gaze: *Christ.* This Christ-centeredness is the hallmark of saving faith. Faith does not look inwardly to itself but outwardly to Christ. Far too many are introspectively preoccupied with examining the character of their faith rather than gazing on that which is outside the sinner: the all-sufficiency of the Redeemer.

2) Saving faith looks not only to Christ Himself but also to "his righteousness," not only to His person but also to His work. The

---

47. LW 34:110 (*Theses Concerning Faith and Law,* thesis 22) = WA 391:46.

righteousness by which sinners are justified is a God-righteousness, a righteousness worked out by God (Rom. 1:17; 3:21-22) through the obedience of Christ (5:17-19), culminating in His death (Phil. 2:8). Because the object of this faith is not only Christ but also Christ's propitiatory work, justifying faith is also described as "faith in his blood" (Rom. 3:24-25, KJV; cf. 5:9). It leads the sinner under the wrath of God to run to the propitiatory covering found in the blood-righteousness of Christ. Faith wraps the soul of the believing sinner in the righteousness of Christ alone (Phil. 3:9; cf. Isa. 64:6; Matt. 22:10-13).

2. Its Source

which faith they have not of themselves; it is the gift of God.

This faith is "not of themselves." It involves "seeing" the truth of the gospel, which is utterly impossible to those who are spiritually blind (John 12:37-40; 1 Cor. 2:14; 2 Cor. 4:3-6). The "hearing" of faith is also beyond the capabilities of deaf sinners (John 9:26-28; 8:43). Faith is also "coming" to Christ, to which sinners are entirely averse (John 5:40). Moreover, those who are "dead" in their sins (Eph. 2:1-3) are powerless to believe. It is impossible for saving faith to originate from ourselves. To the contrary, faith is "the gift of God" (Eph. 2:8). "To you it has been *granted*... to believe on him" (Phil. 1:29, emphasis added). Faith is enumerated among the "fruits of the Spirit" (Gal. 5:22). Apollos is said to have "greatly helped those who had believed through grace" (Acts 18:27).

2. The Exclusive Instrument of Justification (Para. 2)

Faith thus receiving and resting on Christ and his righteousness, is the alone instrument of justification; yet it is not alone in the person justified, but is ever accompanied with all other saving graces, and is no dead faith, but worketh by love.

A. The Exclusive Instrumentality of Faith

Faith thus receiving and resting on Christ and his righteousness, is the alone instrument of justification;

One of the great battle cries of the Reformers was *sola fide* (faith alone). They saw in this slogan one of the great and irreconcilable differences between the Word of God and the Church of Rome. Likewise, when the learned doctors of Rome gathered at Trent to construct a definitive answer to the Protestant Reformation, they saw that this issue was pivotal. Knowing that they could not ignore the many declarations of Scripture that sinners are justified by faith, they had to say something concerning the role of faith in justification. This they did by identifying faith with baptism.[48] Thus, by a subtle shift, the instrument of justification is made to be the "sacrament of faith" (baptism), not faith, pure and

---

48. Council of Trent, Session 6, Chapter 7 (Schaff, *Creeds of Christendom*, 2:95).

simple. Moreover, for those who through sin have "fallen" from their justification there is "a second plank after the shipwreck of grace lost:" the sacrament of penance.[49] And, because justification is not conceived of as a once-for-all judicial declaration but as an ongoing process, it must also be "increased" by good works.[50] For almost five hundred years the question of whether sinners are justified by faith *alone* has been the main theological divide between Catholics and Protestants. This is a call to Christ's faithful soldiers to lift up a banner for the truth and cry, "Here we stand!"

1. The exclusive instrumentality of faith demonstrated.

1) As we have already seen,[51] the only ground of our acceptance is the vicarious righteousness of Christ, and the only instrument by which this righteousness is appropriated is faith (Rom. 3:21-26; Phil. 3:4-9).

2) The Bible repeatedly declares that we are justified by faith, not works (Rom. 3:19-30; 4:4-8; Gal. 2:16; 5:2-6; Phil. 3:3-9). These passages assert that trust in works of any kind, whether of the moral or ceremonial law, contradicts simple faith in Christ. Not only the self-righteousness of do-gooders who think they keep the Decalogue quite well, but also the sacramentalism of those who rely upon dietary taboos, sacraments, rosaries, and masses is condemned.

3) Abraham obtained the blessing of justification by faith alone, prior to his circumcision or the giving of the law (Rom. 4:1-3, 9-18, 22-25). God so ordered the circumstances of Abraham's justification so that no other factor that could be construed as an instrument of his justification was present at the time of his justification. It is the fact that his faith was entirely *alone* as the instrument of his justification that God singles out as qualifying Abraham to be the paradigm for all believers in every age.

2. The exclusive instrumentality of faith explained.

Why has God selected faith and not some other grace as the instrumental means of justification? The reason is not that faith possesses some peculiar virtue not found in any other grace. Of faith, hope and love, Paul says, "the greatest of these is love" (1 Cor. 13:13). If superior virtue were the criterion of God's selection, why do we never read in Scripture of being justified by love? We must look elsewhere for the explanation of God's choice of faith to be the instrumental means of justification.

1) We are justified by faith alone because this is the only method that is consistent with justification being by grace. We are "justified freely by His grace" (Rom. 3:23-24; cf. 4:16). Receiving God's righteousness by *faith* is opposed to earning it by *works* (Rom. 4:3-5; Gal. 2:16; Eph. 2:8-9). God has chosen faith to be the instrumental means because faith is a self-emptying grace. The very act of faith by which the sinner receives Christ is an act of entire renunciation of his own performances and character

49. Ibid., Session 6, Chapter 14 (Schaff, *Creeds of Christendom*, 2:104-106).
50. Ibid., Session 6, Canon 24 (Schaff, *Creeds of Christendom*, 2:115).
51. See I.C. above—"The basis of justification: Christ alone."

as the basis of his acceptance with God. It offers no righteousness of its own and receives the righteousness of Christ as a gift for which it can pay nothing. Faith is the empty hand that receives the unspeakably precious gift of God's Son.

2) God has chosen faith because the principle of justification by faith alone agrees with the fact that there is but one ground of justification, the righteousness of Christ. It is the very nature of faith to trust in and rest upon another. No other grace has this as its distinguishing quality. Faith is "emptiness filled with Christ's fullness; impotency lying down upon Christ's strength."[52]

3) Justification by faith alone gives all the glory to God. When it is seen that the Giver shows kindness to those whose persons and actions have nothing in them to attract and everything to repel His benevolence, it magnifies the freeness and munificence of the grace of God. The doctrine of *sola fide* (faith alone) is the best preparation for the praise of *soli Deo gloria* (to God alone be glory).

B. The Inseparable Accompaniments of Faith

yet it is not alone in the person justified, but is ever accompanied with all other saving graces, and is no dead faith, but worketh by love.

Can a man go on living in wickedness, be utterly bereft of the fruits of holiness and yet, due to his justification, go to heaven at last? The Reformers answered this question with this well-known epigram: "Faith alone justifies, but not the faith that is alone" (*Sola fides justificat, sed fides non est sola*).[53] We must not trust in our godliness for our justification, but we must question a faith that does not lead to godliness. Modern antinomians treat justification as if it were the only essential aspect of salvation, eviscerate the biblical call to repentance of its true meaning, and downplay the observable effects of regeneration. Who can number

---

52. John Girardeau, *Calvinism and Evangelical Arminianism* (Columbia, S.C: W. J. Duffie; New York: Baker & Taylor, 1890), 418; cf. 546.

53. The first instance of this saying in print that I have been able to find is in John Calvin, *Acta Synodi Tridentinae cum antidoto* (1567), 6th session, canon 11—"Fides ergo sola est quae iustificet: fides tamen quae iustificat, non est sola" (*Joanis Calvini opera quae supersunt omnia*, eds. E. Cunitz. J. Baum, and E. Reuss, 59 vols., commonly abbreviated CO [Brunsvigae: C.A. Schwetschke, 1863], 7:477 = "It is therefore faith alone which justifies, and yet the faith which justifies is not alone" (*Acts of the Council of Trent with the Antidote*), in *Selected Works of John Calvin*, ed. and trans. Henry Beveridge, 7 vols. (Edinburgh: Calvin Translation Society, 1851; reprint ed. Grand Rapids: Baker Book House, 1983), 3:152.

A similar statement is found in the *Epitome of the Formula of Concord*, 3.11, drawn up after Luther's death by a group of Lutheran theologians, including Martin Chemnitz, in 1577: "Good works always follow justifying faith and are certainly to be found with it, since such faith is never alone but is always accompanied by love and hope" (article 3, affirmative thesis 8, in *The Book of Concord: The Confessions of the Evangelical Lutheran Church*, trans. and ed. T. G. Tappert, 474 = Schaff, *Creeds of Christendom*, 3:118). Although Luther may have been responsible for coining the epigram, I have not been able to find it in his works. More than once, however, he expressed its basic concept (e.g., LW 34:176 = WA 391:106; LW 34:183 = WA 391:114; and WA 47:114, lines 1-10 = Ewald M. Plass, ed., *What Luther Says: An Anthology*, 3 vols. [St. Louis: Concordia Publishing House, 1959] 1:492, §1469).

the multitudes deceived into thinking that their "decision for Jesus" has secured an eternal place in glory despite evidences to the contrary?

Antinomian "easy-believism" fails to grasp the nexus of justification. Justification does not take place in isolation. Rather, it is interconnected with the other blessings of salvation (Rom. 8:29-30; 1 Cor. 6:11; Gal. 3:24-4:7; Titus 3:5-7). Thus our Confession represents predestination, effectual calling, justification, adoption, sanctification, and perseverance as inextricably linked together in one chain (Chapters 10.1; 11.1; 12; 13.1; 17.1). Justification is part of a whole complex of saving blessings, and justifying faith is always accompanied by every other saving grace.

1. Faith's Accompaniments

Though faith is alone as an instrument of justification, it is not alone as a saving grace. Rather, it "is ever accompanied with all other saving graces," including repentance (Acts 11:17-18; 20:21), humility (Phil. 3:3-9; Rom. 3:27), obedience (Rom. 1:5; 16:26), love (1 Tim. 1:14; 1 Peter 1:7-8), patience (2 Thess. 1:3, 4), hope (1 Thess. 1:3), peace and joy (Rom. 5:1-2; 15:13). Faith is never given apart from its sister graces and is the handmaiden that strengthens each of them.

2. Faith's Operations

Justifying faith, the Confession asserts, "is no dead faith, but worketh by love." While Romanism teaches justification based on the *merits* of good works, easy-believism teaches justification apart from the *existence* of works. But "faith without works is dead" (James 2:26). True faith is a gift of God's regenerating grace (Eph. 2:1-9), not given as a reward for works but as a new principle that will issue forth in good works (v.10). With overflowing joy Luther proclaims the energetic activity of faith: "It is a living, busy, active, mighty thing, this faith." Therefore, "it is impossible to separate works from faith, quite as impossible as to separate heat and light from fire."[54] While it does not justify because it bears fruit, true faith will no more fail to produce good works than the sun can cease to give light.

All of this leads us to say that though we are justified by faith, our faith must be justified (validated) by our works. Stated otherwise, there are two sorts of "justification": *actual* and *declarative* justification.[55] This does not mean that there is more than one way to be justified before God. Only the term "actual justification" refers to one's judicial standing in the presence of God. The other term, "declarative justification," refers to the fact that a man who has actually been justified in God's sight is also justified declaratively in his own conscience or before his fellow men or

---

54. Luther, "Preface to the Epistle of St. Paul to the Romans" (1546), in *Prefaces to the New Testament* (LW 35:370, 371) = D. Martin Luthers Werke. *Die Deutsche Bibel*, commonly abbreviated WA DB (Weimar: Hermann Böhlaus Aachfolger, 1931), 7:11, lines 9-10 and 21-23.

55. See James Buchanan, *The Doctrine of Justification* (Edinburgh: T. and T. Clark, 1867; reprint ed. Grand Rapids: Baker Book House, 1977), 233-39. See also Luther's *Third Disputation Concerning Justification*, thesis 1 (LW 34:151 = WA 391:82).

both. Sometimes the term "justified" is used in a declarative sense with reference to God (Luke 7:29), Christ (1 Tim. 3:16), or wisdom (Matt. 11:19). In other places the Bible depicts the declarative justification of sinners. In Luke's account of the woman who was a "sinner" (cf. 7:37-50) we have a beautiful instance of one whose many outward tokens of love were taken by our Lord as proofs of her forgiveness and justification (vv. 44, 47).

This distinction provides us with an explanation of the apparent discrepancy between the teaching of Paul and James, the former asserting justification apart from works (Rom. 3:28), and the latter insisting that "a man is justified by works, and not by faith only" (James 2:24; cf. v. 21). Careful investigation reveals that there is no real contradiction between the two, since they are addressing different issues. Paul's argument against the works-based justification of the Judaizers has to do with actual justification. However, when we read James, we do not find him opening up the nature and grounds of justification itself, but examining the practical evidences which attest to the genuineness of one's professed faith (2:18). For the actual justification Paul has in view, faith, not works, is the prerequisite; for the declarative justification James has in mind, one's professed faith must be proven genuine by works. The issues Paul and James confronted concern each one of us. You and I must not rest until we are assured that we are truly justified—by faith alone and by a faith that is not alone.

3. The Divine Glory of Justification (Para. 3)

A. Its Basis: The Full Satisfaction of God's Justice

Christ, by his obedience and death, did fully discharge the debt of all those that are justified; and did, by the sacrifice of himself in the blood of his cross, undergoing in their stead the penalty due unto them, make a proper, real, and full satisfaction to God's justice in their behalf;

Here reference is made to the discharge of the "debt of all those that are justified." This debt is twofold: indebtedness to keep the whole moral law of God (Rom. 13:8-9; James 2:8-11) and indebtedness to make full payment for every violation of God's law. This ever-mounting debt is utterly staggering (Matt. 18:27, 32, 34) and we have nothing by which we can pay off or even reduce this debt (v. 25). It is no easy thing for this debt to be removed. God's law is a revelation of His essential character. It is not merely an arbitrary expression of His will. Because God is holy, righteous and good, His law is "holy and just and good" (Rom. 7:12; cf. 1 Peter 1:15-16). Violations of His law may not be dismissed at the wave of a hand—even if it is His hand.

Our Confession puts its finger on the only way the terrible load of our debt can be removed—by the "obedience and death" of Christ, which "did fully discharge the debt of all those that are justified." By the obedience of His life He "fulfilled all righteousness" (Matt. 3:15), and by the physical and spiritual agonies of the death of deaths He made "a proper, real, and full satisfaction to God's justice in [our] behalf" (see Isa. 42:21; Dan. 9:24; Rom. 3:21-26). Nothing has ever so magnified the justice of God as the substitutionary curse-bearing (Gal. 3:13) of the God/man (Acts 20:28) on the cross.

B. Its Motive: The Free Grace of God's Benevolence

yet, inasmuch as he was given by the Father for them, and his obedience and satisfaction accepted in their stead, and both freely, not for anything in them, their justification is only of free grace, that both the exact justice and rich grace of God might be glorified in the justification of sinners.

"It is evident that God *must* either sacrifice his law, his elect, or his Son."[56] Some maintain that the highest expression of God's grace would be a simple forgiveness apart from any satisfaction being made to His justice. They argue that the requirement of such expiation transforms justification into a legal transaction, thereby excluding grace. But the plan these men propose requires that God sacrifice the requirements of His law, which would involve the surrender of His eternal rectitude. His law cannot be sacrificed. What about the elect? They might justly be sacrificed, but what would happen to grace? God chose the third alternative, the sacrifice of His Son. In so doing He not only manifested His justice in an unparalleled fashion but also gave the greatest possible expression of His love and grace. Never is benevolence more conspicuous than when it is costly. Nothing was more costly to God than our justification. When He created the world, He spoke and it was done. But for our justification the Father must pay a dear price: deliver His Son up to the exaction of infinite justice. Likewise, it cost the Son dearly: the excruciations of crucifixion and the wrath of God.[57] But that which was so costly to God costs us absolutely nothing (Isa. 55:1; Rev. 22:17). The Lord will not take anything for it and we have nothing to give. We are "justified freely by His grace" (Rom. 3:24). And that which is a free gift to us is no mere trinket: it is abounding grace (Rom. 5:16-17, 20; 1 Tim. 1:14), rich grace (Eph. 1:7), eternal grace (2:7). Throughout eternity we will never cease to be amazed over the way the same plan that displays the riches of His grace most also magnifies the glory of His justice most. The most intense rays of God's grace and justice find their focal point at the cross (Ps. 85:10).

This truth is of great help to sinners inquiring after salvation and to believers longing for assurance. *Some go through great struggles when it comes to appropriating the grace of God.* When the Holy Spirit begins to work upon their consciences, they are awakened as never before to see the depth, aggravations and multitude of their sins. In anguish of soul such ones cry out:

---

56. A. A. Hodge, *The Confession of Faith* (first publ. 1869; reprint ed., Edinburgh: The Banner of Truth Trust, 1958), 186.

57. cf. Traill, Works, 4:166-67.

> Depth of mercy! Can there be
> Mercy still reserved for me?
> Can my God His wrath forbear?
> Me, the chief of sinners, spare?[58]

In one sense such questions are right. But often they are the expression of a sinful question: "Is not my sin greater than the grace of God?" If such thinking is keeping you from casting yourself on the grace of God for forgiveness and acceptance, let me plead with you to act on what you have just read. In all your dealings with God, fix your eye on His grace. When you plead for justification, plead for it as something offered in grace. When you receive it, receive it as something given by grace. It is a free gift. Why won't you receive it? In the bottom of your heart you do not want to accept something that forces you to confess that nothing you have done can even help deserve such a gift. Give up your proud self-righteousness! Glorify God by casting yourself on His grace.

Others struggle in coming to terms with the justice of God. Two apparently contradictory desires grip such a person's heart: on one hand, he longs for salvation; on the other, having had a glimpse of God's glory, he wants God to be glorified. But there seems to be an inconsistency between the two. His desire that God be glorified seems to be a desire that he himself be damned. But he cannot bring himself to desire his own damnation. Of this heartfelt struggle John Owen writes,

> Which of these desires shall the sinner cleave unto?... Shall he cast off all hopes and desires of his own salvation, and be content to perish for ever? This he cannot do;... Shall he, then, desire that God may part with and lose his glory, so that... he may be saved?... This can be no more in an enlightened mind than it can cease to desire its own salvation. But how to reconcile these things in himself a sinner finds not.[59]

At last, however, God enables faith to harmonize the two. The believing sinner then begins to understand that God is highly glorified when He is seen to be "just and the justifier of the one who has faith in Jesus" (Rom. 3:26; cf. Isa. 45:21).

> What unspeakable peace may dawn upon the soul... when it is enabled to see that the same justice, which might have been glorified in the punishment of the sinner, may now be still more glorified in His pardon...—that all the attributes of God, which were formerly arrayed against us, are now in Christ, the firmest grounds of our confidence and hope,—that the flaming

---

58. Charles Wesley, first published in John and Charles Wesley, *Hymns and Sacred Poems* (London: William Strahan, 1739) with 13 stanzas of 4 lines, under the heading "After a Relapse into Sin." Reprinted in *The Poetical Works of John and Charles Wesley*, 13 vols. (London: Wesleyan-Methodist Conference Office, 1868), 1:271-73.

59. John Owen, *Gospel Grounds and Evidences of the Faith of God's Elect*, in *The Works of John Owen*, 16 vols. (Johnstone & Hunter, 1850–1853; reprint ed., Edinburgh: The Banner of Truth Trust, 1965), 5:416.

sword of justice itself, which once menaced us, has been converted into a shield and buckler for our protection and defense![60]

4. The Temporal Execution of Justification (Para. 4)

God did from all eternity decree to justify all the elect, and Christ did in the fulness of time die for their sins, and rise again for their justification; nevertheless, they are not justified personally, until the Holy Spirit doth in due time actually apply Christ unto them.

A. Its Eternal Decree: God's Decree to Justify the Elect

God did from all eternity decree to justify all the elect,

Paul connects God's decree with our justification: "Whom He predestined, these He also called; whom He called, these He also justified" (Rom. 8:30). Several theologians (for example, Kuyper, Gill, Gadsby, and Philpot) have advocated the doctrine of justification from eternity. This view fails to distinguish between God's eternal decree and its execution in time. In eternity past God determined to create. But this does not mean that creation is an eternal act. We read of the "Lamb slain from the foundation of the world" (Rev. 13:8). But Christ was not crucified in eternity (cf. 1 Peter 1:20). In Romans 8:29-30, among the steps of the *ordo salutis* (order of salvation), justification stands between two steps that take place in time, calling and glorification. One could just as well say that the elect were called or glorified in eternity past as he could say they were justified in eternity. In this text it is clear that the first two steps (foreknowledge and foreordination) took place in eternity past, and the next three (calling, justification, and glorification) take place in time.

B. Its Redemptive Purchase: Christ's Death and Resurrection for Their Justification

and Christ did in the fulness of time die for their sins, and rise again for their justification;

Christ "was delivered up because of [διά] our trespasses and was raised because of [διά][61] our justification" (Rom. 4:25). Some have argued from such texts that the elect must have been justified the moment their debt was paid. But in Paul's assertion that Christ was "raised for [*dia*] our justification," his use of the preposition *dia* need not be interpreted as indicating a retrospective cause and effect, but can be taken in a prospective sense: "in order that we may be justified." The context also favors a prospective interpretation. Paul is not thinking of the justification of the elect *en masse* but of the justification of individuals.

---

60. Buchanan, *The Doctrine of Justification*, 312-13.

61. Διά with the accusative, as in both places in this verse, means "because of," "on account of," or "for the sake of."

They are justified, not at Christ's resurrection, but at the moment when, like Abraham, they believe. The underlying mistake of the justification-at-the-cross view is its failure to distinguish between the accomplishment and application of redemption. In the former, Christ has provided a basis for our justification; in the latter, the Holy Spirit joins sinners to Christ by faith, and they are actually given the justifying righteousness procured by Christ.

C. Its Temporal Execution: The Holy Spirit's Application of Christ for Their Justification

nevertheless, they are not justified personally, until the Holy Spirit doth in due time actually apply Christ unto them.

That sinners are not personally justified until they believe on Christ and are savingly joined to Him by the Spirit may be proven by the following:

1) The Scriptures make it plain that as long as one continues in unbelief he is charged with guilt and exposed to wrath (John 3:18; Gal. 3:10; Eph. 2:3). It cannot be said of those who are "condemned," under the wrath of God, under the curse, and "children of wrath," that they possess the pardon and acceptance of justification.

2) According to the Word of God, faith is antecedent to justification (Gal. 2:16; Rom. 4:3-10, 24; Phil. 3:9). The faith by which sinners are justified consists in believing on Christ that they *might be justified*, not in believing that they are justified already.

3) While it was necessary that Christ do something *for* us, working out a righteousness on our behalf, it was also necessary that the Holy Spirit do a work *in* us, imparting faith to us and uniting us to Christ in order that we might be justified. Both sanctification and justification are connected (though in different ways) with the work of the Spirit as well as the work of Christ (1 Cor. 6:11; Titus 3:4-7). Christ laid the foundation for our justification. But it was equally necessary that the Spirit regenerate our hearts (John 3:5-8, 18), create faith in us (Eph. 2:8), and impart to us a saving knowledge of Christ (1 Cor. 2:7-14). All of this is rendered meaningless if we are not justified at the moment of our conversion.

5. The Subsequent Sins of the Justified (Para. 5)

God doth continue to forgive the sins of those that are justified, and although they can never fall from the state of justification, yet they may, by their sins, fall under God's fatherly displeasure; and in that condition they have not usually the light of his countenance restored unto them, until they humble themselves, confess their sins, beg pardon, and renew their faith and repentance.

A. The Continued Forgiveness of Their Sins

God doth continue to forgive the sins of those that are justified,

Because the justified still sin (1 John 1:8; James 3:2), their prayers are replete with pleas for pardon, and the Bible is filled with assurances that such requests are granted (for example, Ps. 32:1-5; 51:2-5; Matt. 6:11-12; 1 John 1:7–2:2). But confusion has arisen concerning this precious blessing. Luther once spoke of the need for repeated justification.[62] On the other hand, some Antinomians assert that because the sins of a believer are not chargeable to the new man but only to the old, it is unnecessary for them to pray for forgiveness. God doesn't take account of their sins because He sees, not the sins, but the believer in Christ. But most Reformed theologians have charted a course between these two extremes by maintaining that in justification God removes the guilt but not the culpability of sin. In the conscience sensitized by the Scriptures this remaining culpability produces feelings of self-loathing and sorrow over sin (2 Sam. 24:10; Ps. 25:7; 51:3; Ezek. 16:60-63; 2 Cor. 7:9-11; 1 Tim. 1:13-15). Hence, they are driven to confess their sins and seek the comfort and assurance of forgiveness (Ps. 51:1-2, 7-9). This remaining culpability is not merely a subjective matter. In the Bible, saints always view their transgressions as real (Ps. 51:1-5; Rom. 7:15-25; 1 John 1:6-10). Because their sins are real, they provoke God to withdraw the sense of His favor and sometimes to chasten them severely (2 Sam. 12:9-15; Ps. 32:3-5; 51:8-12; 1 John 1:6-7). When they truly confess their sins, the forgiveness they receive is real, as is the corresponding sense of it in their hearts.

B. The Impossibility of Defection Due to Their Sins

and although they can never fall from the state of justification,

According to the Council of Trent, justification may be lost through infidelity or the commission of mortal sin. Once forfeited it may be regained through the sacrament of penance.[63] Likewise, many Arminians insist that only by persevering obedience may believers continue in a justified state.[64] When a man first embraces Christ, he is only conditionally justified—upon the condition that he perseveres to the end. Over against the doctrines of temporary (Rome) and conditional (Arminianism) justification, the Scriptures assert that nothing can be laid to the charge of the justified (Rom. 8:33). Nothing can separate them from the love of

---

62. Luther, *The Disputation Concerning Justification* (1536), in LW, 34:167 = WA 391:98, lines 7-9: "On no condition is sin a passing phase, but we are justified daily [*quotidie*] by the unmerited forgiveness of sins and by the justification of God's mercy."

63. Council of Trent, Session 6, Chapters 14–15, in Schaff, *Creeds of Christendom*, 2:104-07.

64. *The Opinion of the Remonstrants* (1618), Latin text in Acta Synodi Nationalis (Typis Isaaci Elzevir, Societas Dordrechtanae, 1620), 113, 118-19. English translation in Peter Y. De Jong, ed., *Crisis in the Reformed Churches* (Grand Rapids, Michigan: Reformed Fellowship, Inc., 1968), 228-29.

Christ (Rom. 8:35-39). True believers shall never come into condemnation (John 3:16; 5:24; 10:28; Rom. 8:1).

C. The Fatherly Displeasure Due to Their Sins

yet they may, by their sins, fall under God's fatherly displeasure; and in that condition they have not usually the light of his countenance restored unto them, until they humble themselves, confess their sins, beg pardon, and renew their faith and repentance.

The fact that the justified shall never come into condemnation does not mean that God views their sins lightly (Deut. 1:37; 2 Sam. 11:27). Although He no longer punishes them as an angry Judge, He does chasten them as a loving Father (Heb. 12:5-8; Amos 3:2). When believers become careless, they are deprived of the light of His countenance (Pss. 30:5-7; 51:8-12; 89:46; Isa. 54:6-10; Hos. 5:15) and sometimes experience "grievous"[65] chastisements (Heb. 12:11; Ps. 32:3-4; 89:31-32). They do not usually have God's favor restored to them, the Confession states, "until they humble themselves, confess their sins, beg pardon, and renew their faith and repentance" (Ps. 32:5; 51; Matt. 26:75; 1 Cor. 11:30-32).

Two exhortations grow out of this paragraph. 1) Do not use the security of your position to lead you to treat sin lightly. If you don't penitently seek forgiveness, you will incur the hiding of God's face and the wielding of His rod. 2) If you have come to Christ, it is a contradiction of the gospel to shrink back in terror from the God you can only think of as an angry Judge. Remember that there is "no condemnation to those who are in Christ" (Rom. 8:1; cf. 7:15-25). Your sins can never remove the divine Justifier from His throne, the merciful Intercessor from God's courtroom, or the righteous Advocate from your side (Rom. 8:33-34; Heb. 4:14-16; 1 John 2:1-2).

6. The Epochal Unity of Justification (Para. 6)

The justification of believers under the Old Testament was, in all these respects, one and the same with the justification of believers under the New Testament.

Some Dispensationalists have taught that though believers under the new economy are justified by faith, the Mosaic dispensation taught justification by keeping the law. According to Lewis Sperry Chafer, "According to the Old Testament men were just because they were true and faithful in keeping the Mosaic Law."[66] But the Bible clearly teaches that the law was given to lead men to Christ (Gal. 3:21-24) and that the saints in every age are justified by faith alone (Rom. 3:25-26; 4:1-25).

---

65. KJV and ASV in Hebrews 12:11. The word λύπη means "grief," "sorrow," or "pain."

66. Lewis Sperry Chafer, *Systematic Theology*, 8 vols. (Dallas: Dallas Seminary Press, 1948), 7:219. cf. C. I. Scofield, ed., *The Scofield Reference Bible* (New York: Oxford University Press, 1917), 20.

CHAPTER 12[1]

OF ADOPTION

ROB VENTURA

All those that are justified, God vouchsafed, in and for the sake of his only Son Jesus Christ, to make partakers of the grace of adoption,[2] by which they are taken into the number, and enjoy the liberties and privileges of the children of God,[3] have his name put upon them,[4] receive the spirit of adoption,[5] have access to the throne of grace with boldness, are enabled to cry Abba, Father,[6] are pitied,[7] protected,[8] provided for,[9] and chastened by him as by a Father,[10] yet never cast off,[11] but sealed to the day of redemption,[12] and inherit the promises as heirs of everlasting salvation.[13]

Concerning the topic of adoption, Reformed luminary J. I. Packer famously wrote:

> You sum up the whole of the New Testament teaching in a single phrase, if you speak of it as a revelation of the fatherhood of the holy creator. In the same way, you sum up the whole New Testament religion if you describe it as the knowledge of God as one's holy Father. If you want to judge how well a person understands Christianity, find out how much he makes of the thought of being God's child, and having God as his Father. If this is

---

1. This chapter originally appeared in *Growing in Grace* by Reformation Heritage Books, 2020.
2. Ephesians 1:5; Galatians 4:4-5
3. John 1:12; Romans 8:17
4. 2 Corinthians 6:18; Revelation 3:12
5. Romans 8:15
6. Galatians 4:6; Ephesians 2:18
7. Psalm 103:13
8. Proverbs 14:26; 1 Peter 5:7
9. Hebrews 12:6
10. Isaiah 54:8-9
11. Lamentations 3:31
12. Ephesians 4:30
13. Hebrews 1:14; Hebrews 6:12

not the thought that prompts and controls his worship and prayers and his whole outlook on life, it means that he does not understand Christianity very well at all. For everything that Christ taught, everything that makes the New Testament new, and better than the Old, everything that is distinctly Christian as opposed to merely Jewish, is summed up in the knowledge of the fatherhood of God. "Father" is the Christian name for God.[14]

Some Preliminary Matters

1. *Adoption* is Trinitarian in nature. God the Father from before the foundation of the world predestined those who would be adopted into His family (Eph. 1:3-5). God the Son purchased and earned this right for them through His sacrificial death on the cross (Eph. 1:7; Gal. 4:4-5). And God the Holy Spirit gives them the filial privileges as sons, by giving them natures as sons, through regeneration (Ezek. 36:27; John 3:3-8; Rom. 8:14-16; Gal 4:6; Titus 3:5).

2. *Adoption* is a Pauline doctrine. While other authors refer to our sonship, such as the apostle John (cf. John 1:12-13; 1 John 3:1), it is only Paul who actually uses this term. He uses it in five places (Rom. 8:15, 23; 9:4;[15] Gal. 4:5; Eph. 1:5). For the apostle, the word "adoption" symbolized "God's love and grace in accepting believers as His children, intimate members of His family."[16]

3. *Adoption* is rooted in Roman custom.[17] Scholars are almost unanimously agreed on this. In Paul's day, in the context of the Roman Empire, a person could become a son to a father by the father adopting the son into his family, who was not his son by natural procreation. When this happened, it "secured for the adopted child a right to the name and

---

14. J. I. Packer, *Knowing God* (Downers Grove, Illinois: InterVarsity Press, 1973), 182. Of course, this understanding of adoption does not deny the fact that there were Old Testament believers, saints who savingly knew God as Father through faith in Jesus the coming Messiah (Ps. 89:26; Isa. 63:16; 64:8). They knew Him this way, not because of natural generation from Abraham, but because of spiritual regeneration by God, for there was a truly saved "Israel within Israel" (Rom. 9:6-8).

15. In this passage Paul refers to national Israel as receiving "the adoption." In the Old Testament, the Israelites are described as God's sons in some passages (cf. Ex. 4:22; Deut. 14:1; Isa. 1:2). However, in Romans 9:4, he is not speaking about spiritual adoption since not everyone in the entire nation was God's spiritual child. Spiritual adoption only happens when one receives Christ the Messiah by faith alone, which many Old Testament Jews did, but not the nation as a whole (John 1:11-13; Rom. 4:1-8; 11:1-5). Paul, then, in Romans 9:4, is referring to that theocratic adoption of the Israelites as a nation which set them apart as God's own from all the other people groups of the world. In commenting on this matter, Dr. Sam Waldron writes: "Thus, implicitly in Romans 9:4 and explicitly in John 1:11-13, there is a clear contrast between the typical sonship of the Old Testament and the real, substantial and anti-typical sonship conferred by the New Covenant" (Sam Waldron, A Modern Exposition of the 1689 *Baptist Confession of Faith* [Darlington, England: Evangelical Press, 1989], 167). Further, Paul's language here of the adoption of Israel, points forward to the adoption of the true Israel, namely, the church of Jesus Christ, which is made up of both Jewish and Gentile believers.

16. Trent C. Butler, ed., Holman Bible Dictionary (Nashville, Tenn.: Holman Bible Publishers, 1991), 20.

17. While there were examples of people being adopted into families in the Old Testament, such as Moses (Ex. 2:10), and Esther (Esth. 2:7), scholars tell us that adoption was not formally part of Jewish law.

the property of the person by whom he had been adopted."[18] When this occurred, "it carried no stigma; on the contrary, it was special to have been adopted. It meant that someone important had set his love upon you and adopted you to be his son, his heir."[19]

4. *Adoption* is a separate element in our salvation. Sadly, some theologians have not stressed this point enough in their treatments of this subject, making adoption to be merely the positive side of justification, but not a stand-alone topic. However, while the two matters are connected (along with the subject of regeneration), the biblical definitions of each are not the same and should be treated distinctly. John Murray astutely notes: "Justification means our acceptance with God as righteous and the bestowal of the title to everlasting life. Regeneration is the renewing of our hearts after the image of God. But these blessings in themselves, however precious they are, do not indicate what is conferred by the act of adoption. By adoption the redeemed become sons or daughters of the Lord God Almighty; they are introduced into and given the privileges of God's family."[20]

5. *Adoption* is eschatological in its expectation. While it is true that adoption pertains to our lives in the here and now, we must never forget that the New Testament also points forward to a fuller and final adoption with our resurrection unto glory. This is what we might call our consummated adoption, which Paul says, causes us, who are God's children, to groan "within ourselves, eagerly waiting for the adoption, the redemption of our body" (Rom. 8:23). This ultimate aspect of our adoption, of our resurrected, glorified bodies at Christ's return, will "signal our final and full status as the sons of God manifested before all creation"[21] (Rom. 8:17-18; Phil. 3:20-21; 1 John 3:1-3).

The Definition of Adoption

The English term "adoption" derives from the Latin *adoptio* (from *ad*, "to" and *apto*, "choose").[22] The Greek word for adoption (*huiothesia*) is made up of two Greek words and literally means "to place as a son" or "to put in the position of a son," hence, "to adopt a son," or "to give one the status as a son." Foundationally, the word describes the supernatural change of relationship that happens to Christians in salvation from being slaves of sin, to the legal and loved sons and daughters of the living God, which takes place at the moment of conversion by faith (John 1:12; Gal. 3:26;

---

18. D. Martyn Lloyd-Jones, *God's Ultimate Purpose: An Exposition of Ephesians* 1 (Grand Rapids: Baker, 1978), 109.

19. Richard D. Phillips, "The Good News of Adoption," in *Reclaiming Adoption,* ed. Dan Cruver (Adelphi, Md.: Cruciform Press, 2011), 60.

20. John Murray, *Redemption Accomplished and Applied* (1955; repr., Grand Rapids: Eerdmans, 2015), 139.

21. W. R. Downing, *A Baptist Catechism with Commentary* (Morgan Hill, Calif.: PIRS Publications, 2000), 182.

22. Downing, Ibid., 181.

4:3-7).[23] Other definitions concerning adoption abound. The Westminster divines wrote in the Shorter Catechism about this subject.[24] In Question 34, they say, "Adoption is an act of God's free grace, whereby we are received into the number, and have a right to all the privileges of the sons of God."[25]

Dutch Reformed theologian Wilhelmus À Brakel said, "The manner in which believers are children of God is by way of adoption as children."[26] Charles Spurgeon, the well-known Reformed Baptist preacher of the nineteenth century, said, "Adoption is that act of God, whereby men who were by nature the children of wrath, even as others, and were of the lost and ruined family of Adam, are from no reason in themselves, but entirely of the pure grace of God, translated out of the evil... family of Satan and brought actually and virtually into the family of God."[27]

The Reformed Baptists writing in the London Baptist Confession of Faith of 1689[28] write four things about this topic:

The Recipients of Adoption

The writers of the Confession describe those who are adopted by God as "all those that are justified." This is important to understand because while justification and adoption are separate doctrines, as previously mentioned (the former being a legal blessing of salvation, the latter being filial), they are always linked. The point is, all whom God declares "not guilty" and imputes to them "the righteousness of Christ" (justification) become a son or daughter of the living God (adoption). Simply stated, there is not a justified person in all the world who does not receive the tremendous blessing of being brought into God's family. In fact, just as justification is a one-time, immediate, and permanent act, so also is adoption. Hence, John Murray aptly remarks, "The person who is

---

23. It is important to note that contrary to an early heresy in church history known as Adoptionism, the term adoption is never used of Christ even though He is God's Son. This is because He has always been the Son of God by nature, being equal in substance, power and eternity with God the Father and God the Spirit. Additionally, it is vital to note that while the apostle Paul calls unsaved people "the offspring of God" (Acts 17:29), the reference is to that of them being creations of God, not children of God (cf. Mal. 2:10a). Becoming a child of God only happens when one puts personal faith in Christ alone for salvation. As Paul says in Galatians 3:26, "For you are all sons of God through faith in Christ Jesus." Along these lines, John Murray wisely notes, "To substitute the message of God's universal fatherhood for that which is constituted by redemption and adoption is to annul the gospel" (Murray, *Redemption Accomplished and Applied*, 143. cf. Waldron, *A Modern Exposition of the 1689 Baptist Confession*, 166).

24. They also addressed this matter in the *Westminster Larger Catechism* (Q. 74).

25. As to how much the Puritans spoke about the subject, see Joel R. Beeke and Mark Jones, *A Puritan Theology: Doctrine for Life* (Grand Rapids: Reformation Heritage Books, 2016), 537-538.

26. Brakel, *The Christian's Reasonable Service*, 2:416.

27. Charles H. Spurgeon, "An Act of Pure Grace," *Free Grace Broadcaster*, issue 246, Adoption (Winter 2018): 9-10.

28. The parallel statement in the *Westminster Confession of Faith*, Chapter 12, is almost identical.

justified is always the recipient of sonship."[29] He writes: "Adoption is, like justification, a judicial act. In other words, it is the bestowal of a status, or standing, not the generating within us of a new nature or character."[30]

Joel Beeke further observes:

> Justification is the primary, fundamental blessing of the gospel; it meets our most basic spiritual need — forgiveness and reconciliation with God. We could not be adopted without it. But adoption is a richer blessing, because it brings us from the courtroom into the family. "Justification is conceived of in terms of law, adoption in terms of love. Justification sees God as judge, adoption as a father."[31]

The Author of Adoption

God the Father is the Author of adoption. It is He, who, as the Confession states, "vouchsafed" or graciously granted that we would receive this spiritual blessing. In love, He predestined us or literally "marked us off in advance" for adoption as sons (Eph. 1:3-6). In His rich mercies, He ordained that believers would be taken out of the fallen mass of mankind who were headed to hell, and be brought safely into His redeemed, spiritual family on the earth. This was His eternal choice concerning us. For the great I AM said about us, "And I will be a Father to you, and you shall be my sons and daughters says the Lord Almighty" (2 Cor. 6:18). When such a grand truth is set against our great rebellion toward the Almighty, it is astounding. Who can fully comprehend it? Scotty Smith warmly comments,

> Of all the magnificent riches of the gospel, none is more to be treasured and pondered than our adoption in Christ. When the Father lavished his love upon us and made us his children, we weren't just street-wandering orphans looking for a good meal and a warm bed. We were self-absorbed slaves to sin and death. Indeed, we weren't in the orphanage of loneliness; we were in the morgue of hopelessness. Adoption, therefore, is the quintessential freedom for which we long, and for which we've been redeemed.[32]

The Mediator of Adoption

Jesus Christ is the sole Mediator of our adoption (Eph. 1:5; Gal. 4:4-5). The framers of the Confession say this unequivocally when they write that our becoming the supernaturally-born children of God was "in and for the sake of his only Son Jesus Christ." By saying, firstly, that this was done "in... his only Son Jesus Christ," the authors show us that they clearly understood that everything we receive as Christians comes to

---

29. Murray, *Redemption Accomplished and Applied*, 140.

30. Murray, Ibid., 140.

31. Joel R. Beeke, *Heirs with Christ: The Puritans on Adoption*, (Grand Rapids: Reformation Heritage Books, 2008), 28.

32. Scotty Smith, "The Freedom of Adoption," in *Reclaiming Adoption*, ed. Dan Cruver (Adelphi, Md.: Cruciform Press, 2011), 69.

us, not by a natural connection with Abraham or Moses, but exclusively through a spiritual connection with Christ. Richard Muller says: "The concept of *adoptio*, therefore, also rests upon the Reformed teaching of the *unio mystica* (q.v.), or mystical union with Christ: graciously united with Christ, who is Son of God by nature, believers are made sons of God by grace."[33] Dan Cruver further comments,

> ... Paul is revealing that adoption was not given to us *apart from* or *in isolation from* Jesus. Nor was it given to us *in addition to* Jesus. Rather, adoption is nothing less than *the placement of sons in the Son*. These two concepts — adoption unto the Father, and being in Christ — are so necessarily joined to one another as to be inseparable.[34]

The Confession teaches that Jesus is the exclusive source for how we, who are joined to Him by faith alone, become the children of God. For it is only in union with Him, who is the Beloved of God, that we are accepted before God (Eph. 1:6b). All of this is not based on our works, but completely on the sinless life and substitutionary, sin-bearing work of Jesus on our behalf. Consequently, adoption has only one ground— the person and work of Christ. Paul says this explicitly in Ephesians 1:5, when he writes that we have been predestined to adoption as sons "by Jesus Christ."[35] This prepositional phrase can be rendered as "through (*dia*) Jesus Christ," and its use in this verse with the genitive case sets forth Christ as the divine agent through whom our adoption is effected. This is so, because Jesus came to "redeem those who were under the law, that we might receive the adoption as sons" (Gal. 4:5). Dr. Sam Waldron correctly notes, "The whole story of the Bible is the story of how mankind's original, filial relationship with God as their father is restored through the work of Christ."[36]

Secondly, the authors say that God ordained our adoption "for the sake of his only Son Jesus Christ." I take this language to mean that our being adopted into God's family was not only for our sake, but for Christ's also.[37] In fulfillment of what is commonly called "the covenant of redemption,"[38] Christ will see the salvation of His spiritual seed for whom He died and they will be given to Him as spoil (Isa. 53:10, 12; John 6:37-39). He will see the "labor of his soul, and be satisfied" (Isa. 53:11, cf. Heb. 2:11-13). The late R. C. Sproul put it well when he said:

---

33. Richard A. Muller, *Dictionary of Latin and Greek Theological Terms* (Grand Rapids: Baker Academic, 1985), 27.

34. Dan Cruver, "Adoption and Our Union with Christ," in *Reclaiming Adoption*, ed. Dan Cruver (Adelphi, Md.: Cruciform Press, 2011), 51.

35. In commenting on this verse, Clint Arnold helpfully says, "The final purpose of election is then relational. God is bringing together people whom he can delight in and enjoy" (Clinton E. Arnold, *Ephesians, Exegetical Commentary on the New Testament* [Grand Rapids: Zondervan, 2010], 83).

36. Waldron, *A Modern Exposition of Confession of the 1689 Baptist Confession*, 166.

37. R. C. Sproul says something similar in *Truths We Confess: A Systematic Exposition of the Westminster Confession of Faith*, rev. ed. (Sanford, Fla.: Reformation Trust, 2019), 285.

38. See Chapter 7 for a fuller explanation of this.

It is through the grace of God that we are brought into the family of God through adoption. And we, in turn, are the Father's gift to the Son. From all eternity, the Father and the Son were in agreement in this enterprise, and so the Father was pleased to give us to the Son, and the Son was pleased to receive us from the Father. The Son was so pleased about this gift that He laid down His life for us while we were still His enemies, so that we might be His brothers and sisters.[39]

The Blessings of Adoption

1. We Are Received into the Family of God
The Confession says that we are made partakers "of the grace of" or, the undeserved mercy of adoption, by which we are "taken into the number." This means that our Father who is in heaven "cuts us off from the family to which we naturally belong in Adam as children of wrath and of the devil and grafts us into His own family to make us members of the covenant family of God."[40] It means that we who were once "not a people" are "now the people of God" (1 Peter 2:10), since He has delivered us "from the power of darkness, and conveyed us into the kingdom of the Son of His love" (Col. 1:13).

2. We Are Privileged as the Children of God
The writers say that we "enjoy the liberties and privileges of the children of God."[41] Then they put forth four of these liberties and privileges:

First, believers "have his name put upon them."[42] This speaks about ownership. It speaks about possession, as when a stranger is "taken into the family of another, [they] receive the name of the adopter, and those whom God adopts 'are called by a new name, which the mouth of the Lord hath named'" (Isa. 62:2).[43] The point is, Christians now belong to God forevermore. He Himself has marked us out to be His very own cherished ones in Christ. Further, it means that we are no longer our own apart from Him, for our new identity is now in Christ. Our identity is Christian (Acts 11:26; 26:28). Consequently, Thomas Boston says, "Our old name is forever laid aside."[44]

Second, believers "receive the spirit of adoption,"[45] or the spirit who testifies to our spirit, that we are the adopted children of God, which spirit is the Holy Spirit.[46] The Puritan Samuel Willard said it best when he wrote that the Holy Spirit "ratifies our Sonship to be immutable, and

---

39. Sproul, *Truths We Confess*, 285.

40. Beeke and Jones, *Puritan Theology*, 548.

41. John 1:12; Romans 8:17.

42. 2 Corinthians 6:18; Revelation 3:12.

43. Robert Shaw, *An Exposition of the Confession of Faith* (Ross-shire: Scotland: Christian Focus, 1973), 139.

44. Beeke and Jones, *Puritan Theology*, 548.

45. Romans 8:15, 16.

46. John Murray, *The Epistle to the Romans New International Commentary on the New Testament:* (Grand Rapids: Eerdmans, 1968), 296.

confirms our title to all the Promises irreversibly. As such a Spirit, he gives his testimony in us, to ratify all our evidences, and fully assure us of our Sonship and Heirship."[47]

Third, believers "have access to the throne of grace with boldness."[48] This means that the way to God for believers is no longer barred. Rather, we can draw near to Him with great joy and make our requests known to Him because of Jesus' atoning work on our behalf. It means that God's throne is no longer a condemning throne of judgment for us, but one of complete grace. Thus, we can confidently come before Him through Christ, without any fear. John Owen, the great Puritan, affectionately writes, "there is with God in Christ, God on his throne of grace, a spring of suitable and seasonable help for all times and occasions of difficulty. He is 'the God of all grace,' and a fountain of living waters is with him for the refreshment of every weary and thirsty soul."[49]

Fourth, believers "are enabled to cry Abba, Father,"[50] which cry is the result of the Spirit of God in our hearts, for He "not only bestows 'adoption' on us; he also makes us aware of this new relationship."[51] Martin Luther's observations on the believer's use of the word "Abba" are tenderly put:

> This is but a little word, and yet notwithstanding it comprehendeth all things. The mouth speaketh not, but the affection of the heart speaketh after this manner. Although I be oppressed with anguish and terror on every side, and seemed to be forsaken and utterly cast away from thy presence, yet I am thy child, and thou art my Father for Christ's sake: I am beloved because of the Beloved.[52]

3. We Are Cared For as the Redeemed of God

Again, the writers state four examples, saying that God's adopted children are "pitied,"[53] which does not mean that God looks down upon us with disdain and despises us because of our pitiful condition before Him in and of ourselves. God forbid! Rather, it means that as our loving heavenly Father, He cares for us as "a father pities his children" (Ps. 103:13; 1 Peter. 5:7). It means that with divine compassion, He sympathizes with us in our weaknesses for "He knows our frame; He remembers that we are dust" (Ps. 103:14). Jeremiah Burroughs writes, "God, who is the infinite glorious first-being, embraces them with an entirely fatherly love. All the

---

47. Beeke and Jones, *Puritan Theology*, 548.

48. Romans 5:2; Ephesians 2:18; 3:12; Hebrews 4:16.

49. John Owen, *An Exposition of the Epistle to the Hebrews* (Grand Rapids: Baker, 1980), 4:437.

50. Matthew 6:9; Romans 8:15; Galatians 4:6; Ephesians 2:18. Scholars tell us that sense of the word is that of intimacy or endearment. It is the cry of one saying to God, "My dear Father."

51. Douglas J. Moo, *The Epistle to the Romans, New International Commentary on the New Testament:* (Grand Rapids: Eerdmans, 1996), 502.

52. Cited in Moo, *The Epistle to the Romans*, 503.

53. Psalm 103:13.

love that ever was in any parents towards children, is but as one drop of the infinite ocean of fatherly love that there is in God unto his people."[54]

Second, God's adopted children are "protected,"[55] which means that God is always a shield and refuge for His people. He is our mighty fortress, a bulwark never failing. He defends us from the assaults of the world, the flesh and the devil. In the words of Psalm 46:1, "God is our refuge and our strength, a very present help in trouble." Regarding this Psalm, it is said of Luther that there were times in his life which were so dark and dangerous, that when he fell into discouragement he would turn to his close friend and co-worker Philip Melanchthon and say, "Come Philip, let's sing the forty-sixth Psalm."[56]

Third, God's adopted children are "provided for."[57] God knows our needs. He knows them even before we ask (Matt. 6:8). And knowing our needs, He graciously supplies them (Matt. 6:25-32). King David well understood this and said, "I have been young, and now am old; yet have I not seen the righteous forsaken, nor his descendants begging bread" (Ps. 37:25). Matthew Henry expounds:

> Your heavenly father knows ye have need of all these things; these necessary things, food and raiment; he knows our wants better than we do ourselves; though he be in heaven, and his children on earth, he observes what the least and poorest of them has occasion for. You think, if such a good friend did not but know your wants and straits, you would soon have relief: your God knows them; and he is your father that loves you and pities you, and is ready to help you.[58]

Fourth, God's adopted children are "chastened by him as by a Father,"[59] which according to the Bible is a benefit to us, for "God's corrections are our instructions, his lashes our lessons, his scourges our schoolmaster."[60] While God punishes His enemies, He only chastens His children. He does this in love, when we sin, not to break us, but to make us more like Christ, so that "we might be partakers of His holiness" (Heb. 12:10). Therefore, His chastenings are "badges of our sonship and of the Father's love" (Heb. 12:3-11).[61]

---

54. Beeke and Jones, *Puritan Theology*, 550.

55. Proverbs 14:26; 18:10.

56. Cited in James Montgomery Boice, *Psalms* (Grand Rapids: Baker, 1996), 2:388.

57. Psalm 34:10; Matthew 6:30-32; 1 Peter 5:7.

58. Matthew Henry, *Commentary on the Whole Bible* (Peabody, Mass.: Hendrickson, 1991), 5:69.

59. Hebrews 12:6.

60. Thomas Brooks, quoted in *The Complete Gathered Gold*, comp. John Blanchard (Darlington, England: Evangelical Press, 2006), 68.

61. Beeke and Jones, *Puritan Theology*, 549.

4. We Are Preserved by the Power of God[62]

God's adopted children are "yet never cast off,[63] but sealed[64] to the day of redemption."[65] This means that although God disciplines us, He never disowns us (Phil. 1:6; Heb. 13:5; Jude 24). It means that although we must face many tribulations as we enter the kingdom of God (Acts 14:22), as God's adopted children we are eternally secure in the Savior until glory by His eternal decree, seeing "that the gifts and the calling of God are irrevocable" (Rom. 11:29). Thomas Watson wisely remarks: "God's decree is the very pillar and basis on which the saints' perseverance depends. That decree ties the knot of adoption so fast that neither sin, death nor hell can break it asunder."[66]

5. We Are Graced with the Promises of God

God's adopted children also "inherit the promises as heirs of everlasting salvation."[67] This means that as God's children, we have much to look forward to. Our eternal prospects are extremely bright.[68] This is because all of His promises, which are "exceedingly great and precious,"[69] are His "storehouse of blessings and a chest of goodwill" toward us.[70] They are "yes, and in Him Amen,"[71] which means they will certainly come to pass, seeing that "God never promises more than he is able to perform."[72] Moreover, since the Lord "is not a man that he should lie" (Num. 23:19), William Gurnall helpfully counsels us and says, "The wise Christian will store himself with promises in health for sickness, and in peace for future perils."[73]

The Applications of Adoption

Following the reality of the privileges and promises we have as children of God, there are several principles we must apply if we would grow in greater awareness of our adoption as God's children:

1. We must regularly reflect on this stunning teaching of Scripture and all that it means for us personally.

2. We must regularly recall what our new identity is as adopted sons or daughters of God and live in light of it.

---

62. For a further exposition of this matter, see Chapter 17 of *The London Baptist Confession of Faith 1689*, Of The Perseverance of the Saints.

63. Isaiah 54:8; Lamentations 3:31.

64. Ephesians 1:13.

65. Ephesians 4:30; Hebrews 13:5; 1 Peter 1:5; Jude 24.

66. Blanchard, *The Complete Gathered Gold*, 172.

67. Hebrews 1:14; 6:12; 9:15; 10:36; 1 Peter 1:3-4.

68. cf. 1 Corinthians 2:9.

69. 2 Peter 1:4.

70. Joel R. Beeke and James A. LaBelle, *Living by God's Promises* (Grand Rapids: Reformation Heritage Books, 2010), 2.

71. 2 Corinthians 1:20.

72. Matthew Henry, quoted in Blanchard, *The Complete Gathered Gold*, 510.

73. William Gurnall, quoted in Blanchard, *The Complete Gathered Gold*, 510.

3. We must regularly resolve to love all the true people of God who, like us, have been adopted by God.

4. We must regularly reject the ways of the world, which belong to the children of the devil.

5. We must regularly reach out to God in prayer, knowing that His ears are always open to our petitions.

6. We must regularly rejoice, knowing that what awaits us in the eternal state is truly wonderful.

Conclusion

Adoption is a glorious doctrine! It is also a gracious doctrine which tells us that although we do not deserve it, God, in unspeakable love and mercy, has made us members of His family. In His unfathomable kindness and grace, He has bestowed upon us the great honor and status of sons and daughters. Thus, I agree with Packer again, when he said that "The revelation to the believer that God is his Father is in a sense the climax of the Bible."[74] John Murray concurs when he says that this teaching is "surely the apex of grace and privilege."[75] Therefore, may the astonishing nature of this grand theme continually fill our hearts and minds with great joy and praise. May it consume all of our thoughts so that we can happily and habitually say with the apostle John, "Behold what manner of love the Father has bestowed on us, that we should be called children of God!"[76]

---

74. Packer, *Knowing God*, 182.

75. Murray, *Redemption Accomplished and Applied*, 134.

76. 1 John 3:1.

CHAPTER 13

OF SANCTIFICATION

JEFFERY SMITH

1. They who are united to Christ, effectually called, and regenerated, having a new heart and a new spirit created in them through the virtue of Christ's death and resurrection, are also farther sanctified, really and personally,[1] through the same virtue, by his Word and Spirit dwelling in them;[2] the dominion of the whole body of sin is destroyed,[3] and the several lusts thereof are more and more weakened and mortified,[4] and they more and more quickened and strengthened in all saving graces,[5] to the practice of all true holiness, without which no man shall see the Lord.[6]

2. This sanctification is throughout the whole man,[7] yet imperfect in this life; there abideth still some remnants of corruption in every part,[8] whence ariseth a continual and irreconcilable war; the flesh lusting against the Spirit, and the Spirit against the flesh.[9]

3. In which war, although the remaining corruption for a time may much prevail,[10] yet through the continual supply of strength from the sanctifying Spirit of Christ, the regenerate part doth overcome;[11] and so the saints grow in grace, perfecting holiness in the fear of God, pressing

---

1. Acts 20:32; Romans 6:5-6
2. John 17:17; Ephesians 3:16-19; 1 Thessalonians 5:21-23
3. Romans 6:14
4. Galatians 5:24
5. Colossians 1:11
6. 2 Corinthians 7:1; Hebrews 12:14
7. 1 Thessalonians 5:23
8. Romans 7:18, 23
9. Galatians 5:17; 1 Peter 2:11
10. Romans 7:23
11. Romans 6:14

after an heavenly life, in evangelical obedience to all the commands which Christ as Head and King, in his Word hath prescribed them.[12]

The word translated in the New Testament as "sanctification" is sometimes translated, "holiness." It is the word *hagiasmos* (ἁγιασμὸς), the noun form of the verb "to sanctify," "to make holy" (*hagiazo*, ἁγιάζω). The basic meaning of the verb is to set apart from that which is common or unclean and to consecrate unto God. The Hebrew counterpart *qadash* (קָדַשׁ), which is translated by this Greek word in the Septuagint, is sometimes used of inanimate objects. For example, in the Old Testament we read of the holy mount on which the law was given to Moses. Mount Sinai was sanctified in the sense that it was separated from common use and consecrated to God as the special place from which He gave the revelation of His law. We also have reference to holy buildings, vessels, utensils, and other things used in the tabernacle and in the temple. These things were separated from common use and devoted to God's service. In the case of these inanimate objects, they were separated from ceremonial defilement and uncleanness and devoted to God.

In the New Testament, when applied to Christians, to be holy, or to be sanctified, refers primarily to being set apart from sin and uncleanness and devoted to God and righteousness. It is also used to refer to the attitude of heart and walk of life reflecting this separation and devotion. This is the subject of this chapter of the Confession.

Paragraph 1: The Fact of Sanctification

This first paragraph establishes the fact that those who are in Christ undergo the work of sanctification. It also describes the nature of this sanctification of which they are made partakers.

Its Subjects

The subjects of sanctification are described as "they who are united to Christ, effectually called, and regenerated." It should be noted that Chapter 11 on justification begins in a similar way: "Those whom God effectually calleth, he also freely justifieth." Chapter 12 on adoption begins, "All those that are justified, God vouchsafed, in and for the sake of his only Son Jesus Christ, to make partakers of the grace of adoption." And now Chapter 13 describes the subjects of sanctification as "they who are united to Christ, effectually called, and regenerated."

It is not my place to address all the terms used to describe the various elements of the salvation that sinners receive in Christ: effectual calling, regeneration, justification, and adoption. These are addressed in other chapters of this book. However, it is important to see that the writers of the Confession understood that *all* who are in union with Christ receive *all* of these blessings of salvation. Those who are effectually called and regenerated are also justified, those who are justified are also adopted

---

12. Ephesians 4:15-16; 2 Corinthians 3:18; 2 Corinthians 7:1

and those who are adopted are also sanctified. The Confession does not condone a view of salvation in which a believer may be made a partaker of one or more of these blessings without also being made a partaker of all of them.

One reason for this is that the benefits of salvation are never separated in the New Testament from the Savior Himself. Notice, again, that this chapter begins with these words, "They who are united to Christ..." Calling, regeneration, justification, adoption, and sanctification are to be found in Christ and our union with Him. When a sinner is experientially united to Christ by the Spirit through faith, he becomes a partaker of all that Christ has purchased by His blood.

This doesn't mean that every blessing of salvation is the same thing. Justification is not adoption or sanctification, adoption is not justification or sanctification, and sanctification is not justification or adoption. There are important distinctions to be made when it comes to what comprises each of these blessings of salvation and the manner in which we experience them.

For example, consider the distinctions between justification and sanctification. They are not the same thing, and it is, indeed, very important to understand this, and not to confuse them.[13] *Justification* has to do with our forgiveness and acceptance with God for the sake of Christ's righteousness freely put to our account. *Sanctification* has to do with our being made righteous in our own life experience by the power of the Holy Spirit. *Justification* has to do with our bad record being once and for all cleared in heaven. *Sanctification* has to do with our bad hearts and behavior being changed on earth.[14] *Justification* is a finished and completed work, and a believer is perfectly justified forever from the moment he is joined to Christ through faith. *Sanctification* is an imperfect work that begins at conversion and progressively grows and increases and is never perfected until we reach glory. *Justification* is a declaration of God about us, that we are forgiven and accepted by Him as righteous for Christ's sake. *Sanctification* is the work of God within us by which we are more and more conformed to the image of His Son. My point is that there is a sense in which we *must* distinguish between justification and sanctification when it comes to their definitions and in our consciences. They are both vital parts of salvation, but they are two distinct parts that must not be confused or mixed together.

However, there is a danger of separating justification and sanctification in a wrong way by believing or teaching that a person can have one of these blessings without having the other. There are those in the history of the church who have taught this and, in one form or another, this is

---

13. I draw some of the pithy comparisons in this paragraph between justification and sanctification from the similar ones given by J. C. Ryle, *Holiness* (1879 reprint, Durham, England: Evangelical Press, 1991), 29-30.

14. The coupling of "bad record" and "bad heart" is taken from the gospel booklet entitled *A Bad Record and a Bad Heart* based on a sermon with that title by Albert N. Martin (Avinger, Texas: Simpson Publishing Company, 1989).

a popular teaching today in some circles. The idea is conveyed that a man can be a saved man and *only* be justified and not also be sanctified. He can have his bad record cleared in heaven without also having his bad heart and behavior changed and redirected toward the pursuit of holiness here on earth. The Confession is completely opposed to this kind of teaching. In agreement with Scripture, as we'll see, it makes clear that when a sinner is united to Christ by the Spirit and by faith, he is not only justified, he is also sanctified. Sanctification is not an optional extra for Christians. It is an essential part of the salvation God gives to all who are in union with His Son.

Its Beginning in Definitive Sanctification

The Confession goes on to speak of the beginning of sanctification: "They who are united to Christ, effectually called, and regenerated, having a new heart and a new spirit created in them through the virtue of Christ's death and resurrection... " It is evident that this description is intended to describe the *beginning* of sanctification because of the phrase that follows, "are also farther sanctified... " There is an initial sanctification and a "farther" sanctification. There is the inception of sanctification and there is the increase of sanctification.[15] According to the Confession, our union with Christ in His death and resurrection has not only secured our justification, but it is the basis and the effectual cause of there being created within us a new heart and a new spirit. This is initial sanctification.

This may also be called "definitive sanctification."[16] There is a definitive sanctification at conversion followed by progressive sanctification throughout the course of the Christian's life. By "definitive" is meant a decisive, once-and-for-all act. When we speak of sanctification, generally we tend to think of it as a gradual process of moral and spiritual transformation.[17] It is right and biblical to apply the term "sanctification" to this process.[18] But it is often overlooked that in the New Testament sanctification is not only spoken of as a process. It is also often spoken of as a once-and-for-all definitive act.[19] The term "definitive sanctification" is a way of referring to the "basic and radical change that takes place in a sinner's moral and ethical condition when he is united to Christ in effectual calling and regeneration."[20] He is not only justified the moment

---

15. Sam Waldron uses this language of "inception" and "increase" in his outline of this chapter in *A Modern Exposition of the 1689 Baptist Confession of Faith* (Darlington, Co. Durham, UK: Evangelical Press, 1989), 174.

16. I believe this language "definitive" sanctification was first used by John Murray or that it was at least popularized in modern reformed theology by his use of this term to describe the inception of sanctification. See John Murray, *Collected Writings of John Murray, Volume Two: Select Lectures in Systematic Theology* (Carlisle, PA: The Banner of Truth Trust, 1977), 277-84.

17. Ibid., 277.

18. Ibid.

19. Ibid.

20. Waldron. *Modern Exposition of the 1689,* 175.

he believes, he is not only pardoned and accepted by God on the basis
of the merit of Christ put to his account, but there is also a decisive
separation from the reigning dominion of sin and a consecration to God
that occurs at conversion. Let's consider the biblical evidence for this.

The Way the Words for Sanctification Are Often Used in the New Testament
In terms of frequency, the word for "sanctification" in its adjective, verb,
and noun forms is used more often to refer to definitive sanctification
than it is to progressive sanctification. First, there's the *adjective form*
which is translated "holy" or "saint" (*hagios*, ἅγιος). It is often used in the
plural to refer to all Christians, not just to a select few. All believers are
referred to in the New Testament as "saints" or "holy ones" or "sanctified
ones." For example, Paul addresses his epistle to the Philippians, "To
all the saints in Christ Jesus which are at Philippi." "To all the saints,"
literally, "to all the holy ones, the sanctified ones." This implies that at
conversion every believer is made a holy one, a saint. There has been a
definitive separation from common use and separation unto devotion
to God.

Second, we often see the same thing in the way the *verb form* of the
word is used. For example, consider 1 Corinthians 1:2: Paul is introducing
his letter and writes, "To the church of God which is at Corinth, to those
who are sanctified in Christ Jesus, called to be saints." Notice, he refers
to these Corinthian Christians as "those who are sanctified." We have
here a participle in the perfect tense, which could be translated as "those
having been sanctified," or "those who have been sanctified," or simply,
"sanctified." This is something that has already occurred once and for all.
In the New King James translation from which I am quoting, the words
"to be" in the phrase "called *to be* saints" are in italics. This translation
implies that being a saint is a goal they must attain and that would be
true.[21] But in the first part of the verse they are described as already
sanctified and this may be the idea in this last phrase as well. This is
better captured by the New American Standard translation "saints by
calling," instead of "called to be saints." They have been sanctified and
they are saints.

Consider 1 Corinthians 6:11. Paul is describing what happened to
these Corinthian Christians at their conversion and he says, "And such
were some of you. But you were washed, but you were sanctified, but you
were justified in the name of the Lord Jesus and by the Spirit of our God."
Notice two things here. He says, "You *were* sanctified." Again, this is a
sanctification already true of them. Then notice the order. Which comes
first in this verse, sanctification or justification? Sanctification comes
first. This is not progressive sanctification that follows justification. This
is a definitive sanctification. They were washed, through the washing
of regeneration, by virtue of which they were sanctified. They were
set apart from sin unto God and unto holiness. And they were also

---

21. David E. Garland, *1 Corinthians: Baker Exegetical Commentary on the New Testament*
(Grand Rapids, Michigan: Baker Academic, 2003), 27.

justified, declared righteous in their legal standing on the ground of the righteousness of Christ put to their account. All of this had already occurred at their conversion. They weren't being washed, being sanctified, and being justified, they were already washed, sanctified, and justified.

Third, we also often see this in the way the noun form of the word is used. Consider 2 Thessalonians 2:13: "But we are bound to give thanks to God always for you, brethren beloved by the Lord, because God chose you for salvation through sanctification by the Spirit and belief in the truth." Notice the order, "Sanctification by the Spirit and belief in the truth." Sanctification is mentioned first. Then notice something else important here. This sanctification is an operation of the Spirit. It is not simply a change in legal status or a change of position. This is the way that some have interpreted these texts we have been surveying. They agree that these texts are not speaking of the ongoing progressive sanctification of the believer, but then they say that they are speaking of a *positional* sanctification that occurs at conversion.[22] But here in 2 Thessalonians 2:13, Paul is not speaking merely of a positional change, a mere change in legal status or position before God. This initial sanctification is a work of the Spirit. It is a subjective change in the person, and of the person, produced by the Holy Spirit. This is why the term "definitive sanctification," as opposed to "positional sanctification," is much better for describing this initial aspect of sanctification. Now there may, indeed, be a sense in which we can describe this initial sanctification as positional. It does involve a change in our position, in the sense that we are now set apart unto God. But it is not only a positional change. It is a real and subjective change. As the Confession states, it involves "having a new heart and a new spirit created in them."

Consider 1 Peter 1:2. Peter is introducing his letter and he describes those to whom he is writing as "elect according to the foreknowledge of God the Father, in sanctification of the Spirit, for obedience and sprinkling of the blood of Jesus Christ." Peter references the entire Trinity. We have election according to the foreknowledge of God the Father. We have sanctification of the Spirit. And we have sprinkling of the blood of Jesus Christ. Notice the order. This is not a progressive sanctification that follows conversion. This is an initial sanctification that occurs at conversion. Here we have the word "sanctification" followed by the preposition *eis* with the accusative, meaning "into," "unto," or "with this goal or intention," and you'll notice again that this is a work of

---

22. Michael P.V. Barret, *Complete in Him: A Guide to Understanding and Enjoying the Gospel* (Greenville, SC: Ambassador-Emerald International, 2000), 196-97. Dr. Barret writes, speaking of this first dimension of sanctification, "it refers to positional sanctification. This is most likely the sense intended by Paul when he identified the believers in Corinth 'as sanctified in Christ Jesus, called to be saints'...The whole point of the epistle is that in practice, the Corinthians were not acting like saints (literally, holy or sanctified ones), although in reality and fact they were saints. This positional sanctification essentially equates with justification and designates the acceptance the believer has before God in Jesus Christ."

the Spirit. This is not merely a positional sanctification, just a change in status, like justification is. It is a work of the Spirit issuing in obedience. All of these uses of the word in its adjective, verb, and noun forms force us to the conclusion that sanctification is not to be thought of exclusively in terms of a progressive work. Sanctification in one sense *is* to be thought of as a progressive work, as we will see later. But in these texts, the language of sanctification refers to a decisive action or event that occurs at the very inception of the Christian life and one that characterizes all true believers. Let's push a little further. Not only is this definitive sanctification seen in the way the word is often used, it's also seen in...

Key Passages in the New Testament That Describe What Happens in Conversion

There are several passages we could look at, but let us draw our attention to the one that is probably most familiar, Romans 6:1-14:

> What shall we say then? Shall we continue in sin that grace may abound? Certainly not! How shall we who died to sin live any longer in it? Or do you not know that as many of us as were baptized into Christ Jesus were baptized into His death? Therefore we were buried with Him through baptism into death, that just as Christ was raised from the dead by the glory of the Father, even so we also should walk in newness of life. For if we have been united together in the likeness of His death, certainly we also shall be *in the likeness* of *His* resurrection, knowing this, that our old man was crucified with *Him,* that the body of sin might be done away with, that we should no longer be slaves of sin. For he who has died has been freed from sin. Now if we died with Christ, we believe that we shall also live with Him, knowing that Christ, having been raised from the dead, dies no more. Death no longer has dominion over Him. For *the death* that He died, He died to sin once for all; but *the life* that He lives, He lives to God. Likewise you also, reckon yourselves to be dead indeed to sin, but alive to God in Christ Jesus our Lord. Therefore do not let sin reign in your mortal body, that you should obey it in its lusts. And do not present your members *as* instruments of unrighteousness to sin, but present yourselves to God as being alive from the dead, and your members *as* instruments of righteousness to God. For sin shall not have dominion over you, for you are not under law but under grace.

Probably no passage is more instructive when it comes to definitive sanctification than this text. The constraints of this essay will not allow me to give a full and detailed exposition of it but here are the main lines of thought we need to see. Paul has just demonstrated in Romans 3:21–5:21 that the believer's righteous standing and acceptance with God is not based on his own works but on the work of another on his behalf, even the redemptive work of Christ. He has been setting forth the glorious doctrine of justification by grace alone through faith alone in Christ alone. But now in Romans 6:1, he anticipates an objection to this doctrine and a potential abuse of it by wicked men. "But Paul, if, as you say, sinners as sinners are justified by grace alone through faith alone, why not just keep on living in sin that grace may abound? It doesn't matter how we live." This is the error and the objection Paul is anticipating as he begins this chapter.

He writes in verse 1, "What shall we say then? Shall we continue in sin that grace may abound?" Having anticipated the objection, he then answers the objection. He says in verse 2, "Certainly not! How shall we who died to sin live any longer in it?" We have an aorist in the indicative mood. An aorist in the indicative mood normally points to a past time event. There was a specific point in the past when this death occurred. "How shall we who died to sin, live any longer in it?"

Then he goes on to give an extended explanation in verses 3-10. He explains that the believer died to sin in the death of the Lord Jesus. We who are in Christ are united to Him in His death to sin and we are also raised with Him in His resurrection to live a new life. This is symbolized by our baptism.

When did this happen? In one sense, we died with Christ when He died. Jesus was dying as our substitute and representative, even before we existed. In fact, we were chosen *in Him* before the foundation of the world (Eph. 1:4). But we do not actually die with Him in our legal position and standing before God until our conversion. Our old man was crucified with Him as a completed past action in that very moment that we were joined to Him by faith. Sin can no longer condemn us and damn us for we already died in the death of Christ for us.

Furthermore, being joined to Him in His death, we are also raised with Him. Union with Christ in His death always involves union with Christ in His resurrection also. Christ is one, His work is one. His death and resurrection cannot be separated. Notice how Paul brings the two together in verses 3-4: "Or do you not know that as many of us as were baptized into Christ Jesus were baptized into His death? Therefore, we were buried with Him through baptism into death, *that just as Christ was raised from the dead by the glory of the Father, even so we also should walk in newness of life.*" Verse 5: "For if we have been united together in the likeness of His death, *certainly we also shall be in the likeness of His resurrection.*" Verse 8: "Now if we died with Christ, we believe that *we shall also live with Him.*"

Why is it important that being united to Christ in His death, we are also united to Him in His resurrection? Because this is the reason that having died with Christ we are no longer the slaves of sin. Christ, having finished the work of our salvation, rose from the dead. His resurrection takes place by the power of the Spirit. Believers, being united to Him, receive that same Spirit by which Christ was raised from the dead. We enter into a new life by the Spirit, a new spiritual life, in which sin no longer reigns over us. Because our sins have been dealt with and our old man has been crucified with Christ, the barrier that existed between us and God has been removed and we now receive the gift of the Spirit. And by the power of the Spirit we are enabled to walk in newness of life.

Notice, this is exactly the way Paul puts it in Romans 7:6: "We have died to that which we were held by, so that we should serve in the newness of the Spirit." Or in Romans 8:1-2, 4: "There is, therefore, now no condemnation to those who are in Christ Jesus... For the law of the Spirit of life in Christ Jesus has made me free from the law of sin and death... that the righteous requirement of the law might be fulfilled in us who do not walk according to the flesh but according to the Spirit." And he goes on in that chapter to tell us that, if we are in Christ, the Spirit of Christ dwells in us and he describes this new life that the Spirit produces in God's people.

Going back to Romans 6, Paul is telling us that our justification in Christ inevitably produces sanctification also because it brings us into this new realm of the Spirit's power. It was our guilt and our sin that separated us from God and that included the fact that it separated us from the life-giving Spirit of God, who is God. Our old man was separated from the life of God by our sins. Therefore, until our sins were dealt with and we were justified, we remained in bondage, not only to the guilt, but also to the enslaving power of sin. But in Christ our old man was crucified, put to death, and we have been justified from sin (6:7).[23] And just as Christ was raised from the dead, we also are united with Him in His resurrection. Because of our union with Christ, His Spirit dwells within us and we are raised together with Him to walk in newness of life. John Stott gives a helpful illustration.

> Suppose there is a man called John Jones, an elderly Christian believer, who is looking back upon his long life. His career is divided by his conversion into two parts, the old self—John Jones before his conversion—and the new self—John Jones after his conversion. The old self and the new self (or the "old man" and the "new man") are not John Jones' two natures; they are the two halves of his life, separated by the new birth. At conversion, signified in baptism, John Jones, the old self, died through union with Christ, the penalty of his sin borne. At the same time John Jones rose again from death, a new man, to live a new life to God.
>
> Now John Jones is every believer. We are John Jones, if we are in Christ. The way in which our old self died is that we were crucified with Christ.
>
> *A little further on, Stott amplifies his illustration in this way*: Our biography is written in two volumes. Volume one is the story of the old man, the old self, of me before my conversion. Volume two is the story of the new man, the new self, of me after I was made a new creation in Christ. Volume one of my biography ended with the judicial death of the old self. I was a sinner. I deserved to die. I did die. I received my deserts in my Substitute with whom I have become one. Volume two of my biography opened with my resurrection. My old life having finished, a new life to God has begun.[24]

---

23. The word translated "freed" in v.7 of Romans six is *dedikaiotai* (δεδικαίωται), which is a perfect passive form of the verb *dikaioo* (δικαιόω), to justify.

24. John Stott, *Men Made New: An Exposition of Romans 6-8* (Grand Rapids: Baker Book House, 1984), 38-39, as quoted by James Montgomery Boice, *Romans Volume 2: The Reign of Grace* (Grand Rapids, MI: Baker Books, 1992), 655.

This has occurred once and for all for the Christian. This is a definitive sanctification. We have died with Christ, and we have been raised with Christ.

But then Paul follows these statements of fact with exhortations. Definitive sanctification is then the basis of progressive sanctification. Because you have died to sin in the death of Christ and have been raised in union with Christ to newness of life, here is what you must do, verse 11, "Likewise you also, reckon yourselves to be dead indeed to sin, but alive to God in Christ Jesus our Lord." He is not saying reckon this to be so in order to make it so. No, it is so. You are dead, indeed, to sin and alive to God in union with Christ. This is a fact. But now you must believe it and reckon it to indeed be so. Then, in light of this reality, verse 12 tells you what you must do: "Therefore do not let sin reign in your mortal body, that you should obey it in its lusts." You are no longer the old man you once were. Being united to Christ you have been raised with Him to a new life. His Spirit now lives within you. Therefore, in this confidence put away sins and pursue holiness! Do not let sin reign in your mortal body, that you should obey it in its lusts.

The implication is that the old slave master, sin, will be constantly attempting to frighten you and to reestablish his cruel mastery over you. But we are not to give ourselves up to his claims. We are to resist him in the confidence that he is no longer our master. In Christ I am not the same man I once was. I am a new man who has been freed from sin's tyrannical dominion. According to verse 13, you are "not to present your members as instruments of unrighteousness to sin, but present yourselves to God as being alive from the dead, and your members as instruments of righteousness."

Now there are three simple principles that may be derived from this overview of Romans 6. *One*, we learn from this passage that every believer, everyone who has been justified by faith, has also been made spiritually alive in Christ to walk in newness of life; definitive sanctification. *Two*, we learn that every believer who is a new man in Christ must still constantly and deliberately battle with remaining sin; progressive sanctification. *Three*, we learn that every believer who has died and been raised to new life in Christ and must deal with remaining sin, must do so from this perspective and confidence that he is no longer the old man. His old man has died with Christ and he has been made a new person in Christ. In other words, progressive sanctification is to be pursued in the confidence of definitive sanctification.

So with respect to the reality of sanctification, we have reference in this first paragraph to its subjects and to its beginning in definitive sanctification. But then we also have reference to....

Its Increase in Progressive Sanctification

"They who are united to Christ, effectually called, and regenerated, having a new heart and a new spirit created in them through the virtue of Christ's death and resurrection, are also farther sanctified... " Definitive sanctification is just the beginning. It is the inception of sanctification but not the completion of sanctification. The sanctification begun in conversion is subject to increase. The believer in Christ is "farther sanctified, really and personally, through the same virtue." That is by virtue of Christ's death and resurrection. Here we have reference to progressive sanctification.

The Fact of Progressive Sanctification

Earlier, we saw several places where the word "sanctification" in various forms is used to refer to an initial sanctification. But it is also used to refer to something that is still ongoing and progressive. For example, in John 17:17, Jesus is praying for His disciples, "Sanctify them by Your truth." Is He praying for the initial definitive sanctification that occurs at conversion? No, those for whom He is praying are envisioned as already being Christians. They have already undergone an initial definitive separation from evil and from the world and a consecration to God. They are already described in this prayer as those who have kept Your word (v. 6); those who have believed that You sent Me (v. 8); those who are hated by the world (v. 14), and those who are not of this world (v. 16). He is praying for those who are viewed as already converted and He prays that they might be sanctified. In one sense, they are sanctified, but they still need to be sanctified more and more.

We see the word used this way in 1 Thessalonians 5:23 where Paul prays for the Thessalonian Christians: "Now may the God of peace Himself sanctify you completely." They still need to be sanctified more and more. They were not yet sanctified completely, and he prays that, ultimately, they will be. In 1 Thessalonians 4:3, while warning them about sexual sin, he writes: "For this is the will of God, your sanctification, that you should abstain from sexual immorality." Not only have they been sanctified, but they need to be further sanctified. They need to know how to possess their bodies in sanctification (v. 4). "For God did not call us to uncleanness but in holiness," or in sanctification (v. 7). Hebrews 12:14 says: "Pursue peace with all people and holiness without which no one will see the Lord." Sanctification is not only something that occurred in our conversion, but it is also something we are to continually pursue. So, the word is sometimes used to refer to that which is still ongoing and progressive in the life of the Christian.

The Pattern of Progressive Sanctification

Not only is the word itself sometimes used to refer to something ongoing and progressive, there are passages that describe the Christian life in terms of a two-sided pattern of growth and development. This pattern involves the progressive mortification of sin and the progressive cultivating of spiritual graces and Christ-like virtues. Notice how the Confession references this *pattern* of progressive sanctification. It says that "the whole body of sin is destroyed," which is definitive sanctification, "and the several lusts thereof are more and more weakened and mortified, and they are more and more quickened and strengthened in all saving graces, to the practice of all true holiness," which is progressive sanctification. Sin has received its mortal blow but the several lusts thereof still war within us. Thus, this progressive sanctification has both a negative and a positive side to it.

First, there is the negative weakening and mortification, or putting to death, of remaining sin. Romans 8:13: "For if you live according to the flesh, you will die: but if by the Spirit you put to death the deeds of the body, you will live." The verb is in the present tense and may be read as, "If you by the Spirit are putting to death the deeds of the body." This is an ongoing activity of dealing with remaining sin. Colossians 3:5: "Therefore put to death your members which are on the earth: fornication, uncleanness, passion, evil desire, and covetousness, which is idolatry." Colossians 3:8: "But now you yourselves are to put off all these: anger, wrath, malice, blasphemy, filthy language out of your mouth." 1 John. 3:3: "And everyone who has this hope in Him purifies himself (is purifying himself),[25] just as He is pure." 2 Corinthians 7:1: "Therefore, having these promises, beloved, let us cleanse ourselves from all filthiness of the flesh and spirit." The assumption in all of these texts is that there are still remaining sinful tendencies, remaining defilement and corruption, adhering to the believer and this necessitates that we must actively be engaged in cleansing ourselves from that defilement.

Second, there is an emphasis upon the positive enlivening, strengthening and cultivation of every spiritual grace. Again, 2 Corinthians 7:1: "Therefore, having these promises, beloved, let us cleanse ourselves from all filthiness of the flesh and spirit." But it doesn't stop there. We then have the positive, "perfecting holiness in the fear of God." Romans 12:2: "And do not be conformed to this world [that's the negative],[26] but be transformed by the renewing of your mind [the positive]." 1 Thessalonians 4:1: "Finally, then, brethren, we urge and exhort in the Lord Jesus that you should abound more and more, just as you received from us how you ought to walk and to please God." We have this language of process, progression, and growth. 1 Peter 2:2: "As newborn babes, desire the pure milk of the word, that you may *grow thereby*[27]. " 2 Peter 3:18: "*But grow*[28] in the grace and knowledge of our Lord and Savior Jesus Christ." 2 Peter 1:5ff: "giving all diligence, add to your faith virtue, to virtue knowledge; to knowledge self-control, to self-control perseverance, to perseverance godliness, to godliness brotherly kindness, and to brotherly kindness love." In all these verses, we clearly see a progressive sanctification that has both a negative and a positive side to it.

---

25. Parentheses mine.
26. Parentheses in this text mine.
27. Italics mine.
28. Italics mine.

We also saw this when we looked at Romans 6 earlier. In union with Christ, we died to sin and have been raised to newness of life (vv. 1-11). This is definitive sanctification. But it also speaks of progressive sanctification which is based on and grows out of that. "Therefore, do not let sin reign in your mortal body, that you should obey it in its lusts. And do not present your members as instruments of unrighteousness to sin [the negative], but present yourself to God as being alive from the dead, and your members as instruments of righteousness to God [the positive]" (vv. 12-13). We see the same the thing in Colossians 3:9-10: "You have *put off the old man* with his deeds... and have *put on the new man.*" This is definitive sanctification. That's what happened at your conversion. But these indicative verbs are couched on both sides by imperative verbs. Notice the negative aspect in verse 8: "But now you yourselves put off all these: anger, wrath, malice" and so on. Verse 12 gives us the positive: "Therefore as the elect of God, holy and beloved, put on tender mercies, kindness, humility" etc.

The New Testament clearly envisions the Christian life as one that involves progressive sanctification after the pattern described in the Confession: "the several lusts thereof are more weakened and mortified, and they are more and more quickened and strengthened in all saving graces."

The Means of Progressive Sanctification
This first paragraph also mentions the means by which this progressive work of sanctification occurs in the life of the Christian: "are also farther sanctified, really and personally... by his Word and Spirit dwelling in them." We have mention of both the instrumental means and the efficient means.

Let's begin, first, with the efficient means. The term "efficient" means that which makes something effective. The Holy Spirit is the one who causes the work of sanctification in our lives to be effective. It is God alone working in us by the Holy Spirit who sanctifies us. Without the Spirit we can never be sanctified. It is important to understand that. We must never think of holiness as something a man just decides to go in for, something he just decides to pursue of his own initiative and something that he does for himself and acquires by his own natural force of personality or energy. No, it is a supernatural work of God from beginning to end.

Therefore, no one can be sanctified who is not a Christian, who has not been reconciled to God by the death of His Son and indwelt by the Holy Spirit. Sanctification is something that begins with the new birth and our union with Christ.

This also reminds us that truth alone will never sanctify a man. It is God by the Holy Spirit who sanctifies us by His truth. His Word is the instrument, but the Spirit is the one who makes it effectual in our hearts. This is why all of our interaction with the Word of God, whether listening to preaching or personal Bible reading and Bible study, must be joined with earnest prayer for the blessing of God upon it. The Word alone does not sanctify. It is the Spirit who sanctifies.

However, secondly, as the Confession notes, the Word is the instrument the Spirit uses in sanctification. The Word is the *primary* instrumental means. The Word is not the *only* means. God also uses trials to sanctify us.[29] But the Word is the primary means through which the Spirit works to enable us to become progressively sanctified. This does not happen in some kind of magical, mystical way through the mere repetition of Scripture verses. Rather, it is by the Word understood, applied and acted upon. This sanctifying Word of God is full of doctrines to be learned and believed, and commands and exhortations to be obeyed. It is also full of exhortations to diligent effort and painstaking exertion in the living of the Christian life.

We do not remain passive as the Spirit sanctifies us. Rather, He so works in us that we also work. His work in us is evidenced by our diligent application of ourselves to His Word and to what it tells us to believe and commands us to do. His work does not preclude our working. In sanctification the Spirit works and we work. His promised work in us is the basis of our hope of success in the pursuit of holiness. Our work in applying ourselves to God's Word, learning what we are to believe concerning God, and what God requires of us and seeking to do it, is to be the focus of our deliberate effort. They are concurrent realities in the progressive sanctification of the Christian.

Its Necessity

Sanctification is not an option. It is a necessity. The paragraph ends with these words, "without which no man shall see the Lord." This is a quotation from Hebrews 12:14: "Pursue peace with all people, and holiness, without which no one will see the Lord." This sanctification, initial and progressive, is a mark of a true Christian. If we are not pursuing holiness in our lives as defined and described by the Bible, we will be lost in the end. We do not earn salvation by sanctification, but salvation is evidenced in us by and through our sanctification. Indeed, sanctification, like justification, is an essential aspect of true salvation. Therefore, where there is no sanctification, there is no salvation. Does this mean, then, that unless we are perfectly holy and sinless, we are not saved? No, and this leads us to the subject of the next paragraph.

Paragraph 2: The Imperfection of Sanctification

This paragraph begins by asserting that sanctification is "throughout the whole man." It is not that our mind is sanctified but our affections, wills and our bodies are not. Rather, the whole person of the Christian has been definitively sanctified and is being progressively sanctified.

---

29. See, for example, Psalm 119: 67, 71; Romans 5:1-4; 2 Corinthians 4:17-18; James 1:2-4; 1 Peter 1:6-7.

This assertion then leads to the main emphasis of this paragraph. Though sanctification in Christ affects our entire being, "yet" it is "imperfect in this life" and "there abideth still some remnants of corruption in every part." Here we have the reality of remaining sin in the Christian. Of course, this is already implied by the whole concept of progressive sanctification. If it is progressive, it is not yet perfect. Then the Confession describes the consequence of remaining sin in the believer: "whence ariseth a continual and irreconcilable war; the flesh lusting against the Spirit, and the Spirit against the flesh."

Remaining Sin in the Believer

This paragraph opposes the fallacy of any form of Christian perfectionism. Sanctification is "imperfect in this life; there abideth still some remnants of corruption in every part." Though we as believers have died to the *reign* of sin, we still must constantly deal with *remaining* sin. There is always room, and there is always need, for further growth and development. The mortifying of sin and the cultivating and strengthening of Christ-like virtues is a never-ending process until we are glorified in the world to come.

There have been those in the history of the church who have taught that a Christian can arrive at entire sanctification in this life. There are groups who teach that Christians, or at least some Christians, either no longer commit sins, or they no longer have a sinful nature. There are also those who teach that you can receive justification and then sometime later you may receive sanctification as an entire and complete package. They say there is no such thing as progressive sanctification. You are either sanctified or you are not, and if you've received sanctification, you no longer sin. The Confession opposes any such teaching as contrary to the Scriptures.

The latter part of Romans 7 is the classic text addressing the reality of remaining sin. Paul addresses this when he writes: "For the good that I will to do, I do not do; but the evil I will not to do, that I practice. Now if I do what I will not to do, it is no longer I who do it, but sin that dwells in me" (Rom. 7:19-20).

Consider, too, the apostle John. He is the very disciple who leaned on Jesus' breast; the disciple whom Jesus loved; the disciple who was, in a certain sense, closest to our Lord, a man who was there when the Holy Spirit came down in power on the day of Pentecost. He was a man full of the Holy Spirit.

It was this same John who said, (and notice he uses the plural pronoun including himself in what he says): "If *we* say that we have no sin, [no sinful nature, no indwelling sin] we deceive ourselves, and the truth is not in us" (1 John 1:8). In verses 9-10 he says: "If we confess our sins, he is faithful and just to forgive us our sins, and to cleanse us from all unrighteousness. If we say that we have not sinned, [have committed no acts of sin],[30] we make him a liar, and his word is not in us." John wasn't

---

30. Parenthesis mine.

saying this to encourage believers to sin and not be troubled about it. In the very next verse he says: "My little children, these things I write to you so that you may not sin." John was not making light of sin as though it doesn't matter. He was simply acknowledging the fact that sin is still a part of the Christian's experience in this life. More importantly, he is arguing that if you are a true Christian you will be painfully aware of this reality. Those who say they have no sin deceive themselves, he says, and the truth is not in them.

This is the same John who, in this same epistle, also taught the doctrine of definitive sanctification. He could say in 1 John 3:9 that, in one sense, Christians do not commit sin. Specifically, in the context of the concerns of this letter, they do not apostatize from devotion to Jesus Christ as the Son of God who has come in the flesh.[31]

But he also makes it clear here in the first chapter of his epistle that he does not mean that Christians have no more remaining sin. Sin no longer reigns, but it still remains so that every Christian finds the need to still repent and confess sin the rest of his days. And every Christian, as he says also in 1 John 2:2, is still in need of an advocate with the Father, Jesus Christ the righteous who is the propitiation for our sins. This is so not only for the sins we commit before we are converted, but for those sins we struggle with even after we have become Christians.

Now this teaching should guard us from two extremes: Pharisaism on the one hand, and despair on the other. When men try to advocate a doctrine of Christian perfection, they tend to accommodate their understanding of sin to fit their doctrine. Sin is defined as something less than it actually is. So, they focus on outward sins and become blinded to the sins of the heart, sins of thought and attitude, and the depth of the corruption that dwells within them. Their error blinds them even to those visible sins that are more subtle and refined. Therefore, such an understanding of sanctification tends to produce self-deception and pride—a kind of Pharisaism.

At the other extreme, Christian perfectionism tends to produce despair in the heart of the truly sincere and humble child of God. He sees so much sin still clinging to everything he does and sees himself still falling so short of what he ought to be. Therefore, he is caused to feel that he must be some kind of second-class Christian who hasn't discovered *the secret* of the deeper Christian life. Or, he's caused to doubt whether he is a Christian at all. But we must remember that our sanctification is never entire and complete in this life; it is progressive. This fact exposes the fallacy of any form of Christian perfectionism.

Conflict in the Believer
After mentioning the reality of remaining sin in the Christian, the Confession then describes the consequences of remaining sin in the believer: "whence ariseth a continual and irreconcilable war; the flesh lusting against the Spirit, and the Spirit against the flesh." There is

---

31. See 1 John 2:18-23; 4:1-3, 13-16; 5:4-5, 16-18.

struggle and conflict in the Christian life. This is not a bad sign. This is not a sign that a person is not a Christian. This is one of the evidences that you are a Christian. John Murray said:

> If there is remaining indwelling sin, there must be the conflict which Paul describes (for example) in Rom. 7:14ff. It is futile to argue that this conflict is not normal. If there is still sin in any degree in one who is indwelt by the Holy Spirit, then there is tension, yes, contradiction in the heart of that person. Indeed, the more sanctified the person is, the more conformed to the image of his Savior, the more he must recoil against every lack of conformity to the holiness of God. The deeper his apprehension of the majesty of God, the greater the intensity of his love to God, the more persistent his yearning for the attainment of the prize of the high calling of God in Christ Jesus, the more conscious will he be of the gravity of the sin which remains and the more poignant will be his detestation of it. The more closely he comes to the holiest of all, the more he apprehends the sinfulness that is his and he must cry out, "Oh wretched man that I am" (Rom. 7:24).[32]

There are types of holiness teachings and deeper life teachings in evangelical churches that say otherwise. Essentially, they argue that if you are a Christian seeking to live a sanctified Christian life, and you find that you are consciously struggling, laboring, wrestling, fighting, and resisting, you have grieved and quenched the Holy Spirit. You haven't yet learned the secret of victory in the Christian life. They say the trouble with so many Christians is they remain ignorant of this secret. Therefore, they go on fighting and struggling with remaining sin and striving to be holy. What they must do is simply, "let go and let God, and rest by faith in the arms of Jesus and let the Holy Spirit take over." Then, all the struggle will be gone.

Evidently the apostle Paul, and all the other apostles and New Testament writers, were also ignorant of this "secret," because throughout the New Testament, the language of conflict is used to describe the nature of the Christian life. It is language of diligent exertion, struggle, and even violence at times. "Pursue holiness without which no man shall see the Lord" (Heb. 12:14). "If by the Spirit you put to death the deeds of the body you will live" (Rom. 8:13). "Therefore do not let sin reign in your mortal body" (Rom. 6:12). Put off this, put on that. 1 Timothy 6:12: "Fight the good fight of faith." Hebrews 12:4: "You have not yet resisted to bloodshed, striving against sin." The implication is that living a holy life might come to that. This is vigorous language: conflict, struggle, exertion, plucking out the right eye, cutting off the right hand. Progressive sanctification is depicted as a real battle and spiritual warfare.

Does this mean that the Christian is doomed to abject failure? Does it mean that the child of God can never make any real progress in holiness? No! As we've seen, every Christian has been definitively sanctified. There has been a fundamental break with his old life under the dominating power of sin and the beginning of a new life of devotion to Jesus Christ.

---

32. Murray, *Redemption, Accomplished and Applied*, 144-45.

This definitive sanctification is not perfect. The Christian is not sinless. It's not a matter of perfection, but there has been a change of direction.

Furthermore, having been definitively sanctified, the Christian is being progressively sanctified, although not perfectly sanctified in this life. He or she will always battle with remaining sin. But, at the same time, the true Christian will not ultimately be destroyed. In the conflict he will never apostatize and he will grow and increase in Christian virtue. This is the emphasis of the third and final paragraph of this chapter of the Confession.

Paragraph 3: The Certain Progress of Sanctification

A Progress That May Sometimes Experience Setbacks
"In which war, although the remaining corruption for a time may much prevail..." Consider the experiences of Noah falling prey to drunkenness, Abraham lying about his wife Sarah and putting her in danger, Moses striking the rock, David falling into adultery, as well as covering his sin and delaying repentance for a time, and Peter denying the Lord and giving way to the cowardly fear of man. These are all examples of true believers in whom, for a time, remaining corruption prevailed.

A Progress That Will Ultimately Not Be Thwarted
In all the examples just given, none of these saints remained in such a sad spiritual condition indefinitely. Each one of them eventually repented and renewed their faith and devotion to God. It is possible to lose a battle without losing the war. When walking up a long stairway, one may fall or even slide back a few steps, but still persevere and advance toward the top. Sometimes sanctification can give the same appearance of halting progress. But as the Confession goes on to say, "In which war, although the remaining corruption for a time may much prevail, yet through the continual supply of strength from the sanctifying Spirit of Christ, the regenerate part doth overcome."

The Agent of this Progress
It is through the continual supply of strength from the sanctifying Spirit of Christ who indwells every believer that the believer is enabled to overcome.

The Essence of this Progress
The Confession says, "and so the saints grow in grace." This is a concise way of describing progressive sanctification. The language is taken from 2 Peter 3:18: "but grow in the grace and knowledge of our Lord and Savior Jesus Christ." Growing in grace is a common way of describing the gradual increase of those holy virtues that God works in His people through the indwelling Christ.

The Characteristics of this Progress

What does this growing in grace involve? The Confession mentions three interrelated characteristics.

First, it involves "perfecting holiness in the fear of God" (2 Cor. 7:1). In other words, it involves becoming increasingly separated from sin and devoted to God in a spirit of godly fear. To the Christian, the fear of God is not that dread of God that marks the unbeliever and causes him to run from God or to try to suppress God's voice in general and special revelation. Rather, the Confession is referring to a gracious fear of God which is one of the most common ways true godliness is described in the Bible. It is a fear of God that is joined to trust in our Father's love and care for us in Christ, which at the same time counts our Father's frown as our greatest dread and His smile as our greatest joy. We pursue holiness without and within not to impress men, but because we fear God who sees and knows every thought and intent of the heart and because we desire to honor and to please Him who loved us and gave His Son to redeem us.

Second, the Confession says, "pressing after an heavenly life." This progress in sanctification involves seeking to live on earth as a pilgrim-citizen of heaven, with your affections set upon heaven and seeking to do the will of God on earth as it is done in heaven.

Third, the Confession says Christians do this "in evangelical obedience to all the commands which Christ as Head and King in his Word hath prescribed them." This third characteristic might appear simply to be a part of the second. However, there is a comma between the two, so I mention it separately.

What is *evangelical* obedience? This is common language found in the Puritans but it's a concept rarely heard of today. What does it mean? The term "evangelical obedience" includes several important ideas. It is obedience growing out of faith in the gospel, as opposed to a legal obedience that is seeking to obtain salvation as a reward of our efforts. It is obedience that arises from a regenerate heart and is, therefore, marked by a sincere desire to honor and glorify God and our Savior Jesus Christ. And finally, it is an obedience that, though it is not perfect, is also not satisfied with anything less than obedience to *all* that Christ's commands. As the Confession says it aims after obedience "to all the commands which Christ as head and King in His Word hath prescribed them." This is often referred to as *universal obedience*. Universal obedience is not perfect, sinless obedience. Rather, it is *evangelical obedience* which aims for complete compliance to *all* that Christ commands.

This last paragraph teaches that in spite of all the ups and downs and conflict of the Christian life, and in spite of the fact that a Christian may backslide for a time and that remaining corruption may prevail, yet every true Christian will, ultimately, over the course of his life, make progress in sanctification by means of the abiding presence of the Holy Spirit in his heart. Holiness will continue to be perfected in a climate of godly fear. He will continue to press after a heavenly life. And over time, he will grow in evangelical obedience to all the commands of Christ as he becomes aware of them. Some will make greater progress than others. But all of God's true people will ultimately be found in the way of pursuing that holiness "without which no man shall see the Lord" (Heb. 12:14).

CHAPTER 14

OF SAVING FAITH

MARK SARVER

1. The grace of faith, whereby the elect are enabled to believe to the saving of their souls, is the work of the Spirit of Christ in their hearts,[1] and is ordinarily wrought by the ministry of the Word;[2] by which also, and by the administration of baptism and the Lord's supper, prayer, and other means appointed of God, it is increased and strengthened.[3]

2. By this faith a Christian believeth to be true whatsoever is revealed in the Word for the authority of God himself,[4] and also apprehendeth an excellency therein above all other writings and all things in the world,[5] as it bears forth the glory of God in his attributes, the excellency of Christ in his nature and offices, and the power and fullness of the Holy Spirit in his workings and operations: and so is enabled to cast his soul upon the truth thus believed;[6] and also acteth differently upon that which each particular passage thereof containeth; yielding obedience to the commands,[7] trembling at the threatenings,[8] and embracing the promises of God for this life and that which is to come;[9] but the principal acts of saving faith have immediate relation to Christ, accepting, receiving, and resting upon him alone for justification, sanctification, and eternal life, by virtue of the covenant of grace.[10]

3. This faith, although it be different in degrees, and may be weak or

---

1. 2 Corinthians 4:13; Ephesians 2:8
2. Romans 10:14, 17
3. Luke 17:5; 1 Peter 2:2; Acts 20:32
4. Acts 24:14
5. Psalm 27:7-10; Psalm 119:72
6. 2 Timothy 1:12
7. John 14:14
8. Isaiah 66:2
9. Hebrews 11:13
10. John 1:12; Acts 16:31; Galatians 2:20; Acts 15:11

strong,[11] yet it is in the least degree of it different in the kind or nature of it, as is all other saving grace, from the faith and common grace of temporary believers;[12] and therefore, though it may be many times assailed and weakened, yet it gets the victory,[13] growing up in many to the attainment of a full assurance through Christ,[14] who is both the author and finisher of our faith.[15]

Scripture passages abound in which faith is expressly declared as necessary to salvation: "He who believes in the Son has everlasting life; and he who does not believe in the Son shall not see life, but the wrath of God abides on him" (John 3:36; cf. v. 18; Mark 16:16; Heb. 11:6). The presence or absence of saving faith is a matter of supreme and eternal consequence. If faith is so indispensable for our eternal well-being, the immense importance of having scriptural views of the nature of saving faith is obvious. The subject at hand calls for diligent and careful study.

1. The Origin and Growth of Faith (Paragraph 1)

A. The Divine Origin of Saving Faith

> *The grace of faith, whereby the elect are enabled to believe to the saving of their souls, is the work of the Spirit of Christ in their hearts, and is ordinarily wrought by the ministry of the Word;*

In this statement concerning the origin of saving faith we have assertions with respect to its divine source and its instrumental means.

Its Divine Source
While saving faith is exercised by the believing sinner himself, it must always be traced back to its divine source. Our Confession employs several expressions to emphasize this fact:

a). First, it refers to the "grace" of faith. Ultimately, the reason one man believes while another does not is due to divine grace, not human volition. When he came to Ephesus, Apollos "greatly helped those who had believed through grace" (Acts 18:27; cf. Eph. 2:8-9; Phil. 1:29).

b). The Confession also asserts that it is the "elect" who are enabled to believe. The Bible speaks of the "faith of God's elect" (Titus 1:1). Luke gives this explanation of the Gentiles' joyful gospel-reception: "As many as had been appointed to eternal life believed" (Acts 13:48).

c). The third expression in the Confession that points to the divine origin of faith is its assertion that the elect are "enabled to believe" to the saving of their souls. This assertion assumes that, apart from divine enabling, sinners are unable to believe. This inability includes the

---

11. Hebrews 5:13-14; Matthew 6:30; Romans 4:19-20
12. 2 Peter 1:1
13. Ephesians 6:16; 1 John 5:4-5
14. Hebrews 6:11-12; Colossians 2:2
15. Hebrews 12:2

incapacity of their *spiritual perception* and the incapacity of their *spiritual inclination.*

1) Man's natural inability to perceive the glory of Christ and the truths of the gospel is depicted in the Scriptures under the images of seeing and hearing. Sometimes the incapacity of man's spiritual perception is depicted as a spiritual blindness (John 12:37-40; Isa. 42:6-7). In other places this incapacity is depicted as an inability to hear (John 8:43; Isa. 6:9-10).

2) Another aspect of man's natural inability is the incapacity of his spiritual inclination. "There is none who seeks after God" (Rom. 3:11). Why? Because men hate God (Rom. 8:7). Those who hate God also hate God-incarnate (John 15:23-25). Because this settled antagonism runs so deep, they cannot bring themselves to come and entrust themselves to Him (John 5:40; cf. 3:19-20; 8:41-47). Without God's grace no one is able to come to Christ in faith. But when God's efficacious grace is put forth, both the inability of their spiritual perception (2 Cor. 4:3-4) and the inability of their spiritual inclination are overcome (John 6:44-45).

d). The fourth expression in the Confession that stresses the divine origin of faith is its assertion that faith "is the work of the Spirit of Christ in their hearts." The natural man "does not receive" the things the Spirit has revealed and cannot know them "because they are spiritually discerned" (1 Cor. 2:14). But the spiritual man has been given discernment to apprehend the truth and appreciate its excellence (v. 15). This can only be produced by the Holy Spirit.

Faith not only includes spiritual understanding but also a conviction of the truth of the gospel. Man's aversion to the truth is so strong that this bias must be overcome by a persuasive force that is stronger than the prejudice of his own heart. Calvin refers to this persuasion as the "testimony of the Spirit"[16] (cf. John 15:26; 1 John 5:6). Paul asserts that it was not the persuasiveness of human wisdom and eloquence that convinced the Corinthians of the truth, but preaching attended by the "demonstration of the Spirit and of power" (1 Cor. 2:4). The word "demonstration" (*apodeixis*) has the notion of proof, attestation or testimony. Elsewhere Paul calls this omnipotent persuasion of the Holy Spirit *plerophoria* ("much assurance," 1 Thess. 1:5).

In addition to understanding and conviction, the Spirit also produces the whole-souled trust that is essential to saving faith. A man with a disposition of hateful distrust (Rom. 8:7) is incapable of coming to Christ (John 12:32). The glory of Christ is set before him, but has no attraction to him (John 12:37-41). Until the Spirit replaces his stony heart with a heart of flesh (Ezek. 36:26-27), he is coldly indifferent to the message of a crucified Savior and he cannot believe. Only those who are born of the Spirit (John 3:6) are enabled to believe (1:13; 3:8).

---

16. John Calvin, *Institutes of the Christian Religion,* trans. Ford Lewis Battles, 1.7.4, The Library of Christian Classics, 26 vols. (Philadelphia: Westminster Press, 1960), 20:78. Hereafter this edition of the *Institutes* will be abbreviated LCC.

Its Instrumental Means

After emphasizing the divine source of faith, the Confession speaks of its instrumental means: it "is ordinarily wrought by the ministry of the Word." The Word preached is the divinely appointed means by which Christ engenders faith: "How shall they believe in Him whom they have not heard? And how shall they hear without a preacher?... So faith comes from hearing, and hearing by the word of Christ" (Rom. 10:14-15, 17, NAS). A striking feature of this passage is its declaration that Christ Himself is heard when the gospel is being preached. But while He is the One who speaks efficaciously to the heart, He does so by the instrumentality of preaching (cf. v. 8; 1 Cor. 3:5). At Iconium Paul and Barnabas "so spoke that a great multitude... believed" (Acts 14:1; cf. 15:11). In and of itself, preaching is impotent to create faith, but in the hands of God it is "the power of God" (1 Cor. 1:18, 24). When preaching is attended by the testimony of the Spirit it results in saving faith (2:3-5; cf. 1 Thess. 1:5).

B. The Increasing Strength of Saving Faith

by which also [the ministry of the Word], and by the administration of baptism and the Lord's supper, prayer, and other means appointed by God, it is increased and strengthened.

Faith may be "increased and strengthened." Paul thanks God that the faith of the Thessalonians "grows exceedingly" (2 Thess. 1:3; cf. 2 Cor. 10:15). In the same individual, faith may vary in strength (Gen. 12:10-13; 17:17-18; 22:1-10; Matt. 16:16; 14:31; 26:69-74).

The ministry of the Word is the primary means by which faith is increased. In particular, our faith is strengthened as we meditate on the promises of God and on His attributes engaged for their performance— for example, His truthfulness (Heb. 6:17-18), faithfulness (Heb. 10:23; 11:11), immutability (Num. 23:19), holiness (Ps. 89:35) and omnipotence (Rom. 4:20-21; Jer. 32:17, 27).

The Confession adds that faith is also strengthened by "the administration of baptism and the Lord's supper." When at his baptism the new convert gives "the answer of a good conscience" concerning his faith in Christ (1 Peter 3:21; Rom. 10:9), his faith is strengthened. Likewise, our Savior's invitation, "Take, eat; this is My body which is broken for you" (1 Cor. 11:24), has strengthened and comforted many trembling saints down through the ages.

Moreover, faith is strengthened by prayer—sometimes in answer to an explicit petition for faith (Luke 17:5), but usually through the exercise of faith required by prayer (cf. Heb. 11:27) and the confirmation of faith derived from answered prayer (Ps. 116:1-2; cf. 34:6-8).

Faith is also fortified by "other means appointed by God," including the example of others (Heb. 6:12; 11:1-40; 13:7) and the testing of faith through trials (James 1:2-4; 1 Peter 1:6-7).

2. General and Special Faith (Paragraph 2)

"General faith" is faith in the truth of Christianity. More specifically, it is a persuasion of the infallibility of the Scriptures. However, it is not faith in the Bible that saves but faith in Christ. So theologians have identified the act of faith by which the sinner comes to Christ as "special faith."

A. General Faith

By this faith a Christian believeth to be true whatsoever is revealed in the Word for the authority of God himself, and also apprehendeth an excellency therein above all other writings and all things in the world, as it bears forth the glory of God in his attributes, the excellency of Christ in his nature and offices, and the power and fulness of the Holy Spirit in his workings and operations: and so is enabled to cast his soul upon the truth thus believed; and also acteth differently upon that which each particular passage thereof containeth; yielding obedience to the commands, trembling at the threatenings, and embracing the promises of God for this life and that which is to come;

General faith entails believing, trusting and responding to the truth of biblical revelation.

1. Believing the Truth of Biblical Revelation

This paragraph opens with an assertion that faith involves believing "to be true whatsoever is revealed in the Word for the authority of God himself." What do we find when we open up the Bible? A book that claims to be God's Word. Repeatedly throughout Scripture, one part of the Bible will introduce a quote from another part with the words "God says" or "He says," making it plain that when the Scriptures speak, God speaks (e.g., Matt. 19:4-5 with Gen. 2:24; Heb. 1:6 with Deut. 32:43).[17]

Faith in the reliability of the Bible involves believing in the factuality of its message. This may be seen in the use of the Old Testament word *"aman,"* which means to regard something as reliable and true. In the Hiphil it is used to describe "believing in" God's Word (Pss. 106:12, 24; 119:66). Believing in God's Word is particularized by believing its individual declarations—"believing that" such and such is true (Exod. 4:5; Ps. 27:13). It includes "believing in all that the prophets have spoken" (Luke 24:25). It involves a conviction that the assertions of Scripture are true (John 6:69; 10:38; 1 John 4:16; cf. Heb. 11:1). Saving faith involves a firm persuasion of the universal truthfulness and incomparable excellence of biblical revelation.

---

17. For an expanded treatment of the words "God says" and "He says" in quotations, see Benjamin Breckinridge Warfield, *The Inspiration and Authority of the Bible,* ed. Samuel G. Craig (1948; repr., Philadelphia: Presbyterian and Reformed, 1970), 299-348 = B. B. Warfield, *Revelation and Inspiration,* The Works of Benjamin B. Warfield, 10 vols. (Oxford University Press, 1927; repr., Grand Rapids: Baker Book House, 1971), 1:283-332.

a. The Universal Truthfulness of Biblical Revelation

By this faith a Christian believeth to be true whatsoever is revealed in the Word for the authority of God himself,

Its extent: "whatsoever is revealed in the Word." Saving faith reckons every statement of God's Word to be true. When Paul testified concerning his faith before Felix, he said, "This I confess to you, that... I worship the God of my fathers, believing all things which are written in the Law and in the Prophets" (Acts 24:14; cf. 26:27-28). True believers give equal credit to the inspired utterances of the apostles (1 John 4:6; 1 Thess. 2:13). Those who restrict their faith to the words Jesus spoke while He was on earth ignore the fact that Christ regarded the whole Old Testament as authoritative (Luke 24:25, 27). Faith in the entirety of the Bible is inseparable from faith in Christ (John 5:39-40, 46; cf. 2:22).

Its basis: "the authority of God himself." Faith involves giving credence to the testimony of another concerning things we have not seen. Paul declares that at His coming Jesus will be glorified among "those who believe, because our testimony [*marturion*] among you was believed" (2 Thess. 1:10). In human faith we rely upon what *men* say. Divine faith rests on the testimony of *God* (1 Cor. 2:1). No one has proven himself more trustworthy than God.

Occasionally God attested the truthfulness of those who spoke in His name by the testimony of signs (Heb. 2:4). But, while God sometimes accommodates our weakness by giving us external confirmations of His Word, it is not our place to demand such evidences for everything He has said. It is our place to receive the rest of His testimony by faith (1 John 5:10).

b. The Incomparable Excellence of Biblical Revelation

By this faith a Christian... also apprehendeth an excellency therein above all other writings and all things in the world, as it bears forth the glory of God in his attributes, the excellency of Christ in his nature and offices, and the power and fulness of the Holy Spirit in his workings and operations:

This persuasion of the truthfulness of Scripture is not blind credulity. God has borne witness to the veracity of His Word by signs and wonders (Heb. 2:4). The findings of archeologists and historians also confirm the reliability of the Bible. But many biblical assertions can neither be proven nor refuted by external evidence. Recognizing the limitations of extrinsic evidences, the Reformers propounded the principle that the Scriptures are autopistic, or self-authenticating. The most convincing evidence for the divine origin of Scripture is the Bible itself. The Bible bears the *indicia* or marks of its divinity. While Calvin devoted a whole chapter in his *Institutes* (1.8) to the exposition of these marks of divinity, the 1689 Confession singles out the insignia of deity in Scripture that radiates the glory of the triune Godhead.

Saving faith apprehends the supreme excellence of Scripture because of the way in which the glorious attributes of God shine forth from its pages. By this same Book we come to know "the excellency of Christ in his nature and offices." In Christ, apparently incompatible excellencies converge: infinite glory and lowest humility, infinite majesty and transcendent meekness, equality with God and deepest reverence toward God, supreme dominion and unparalleled obedience, absolute sovereignty and perfect resignation, divine self-sufficiency and child-like trust.[18] The Confession adds that the Bible "bears forth... the power and fulness of the Holy Spirit in his workings and operations," including His intimate role in our regeneration, sanctification, illumination, intercession, witnessing, sealing, indwelling, comfort, guidance, gifting, and filling. The more we examine this Book, which continually sparkles with the glory of God, the more our confidence in the Bible grows.

2. Trusting in the Truth of Biblical Revelation
General faith also includes the element of trust. Seeing the incomparable excellence of the Bible, the believer "is enabled to cast his soul upon the truth thus believed." Whatever it says concerning the way of acceptance with God, the path of blessedness in this life, and the rewards of the life to come forms the basis upon which the believer stakes his soul (Ps. 119:41-42).

3. Responding to the Truths of Biblical Revelation

By this faith a Christian... also acteth differently upon that which each particular passage thereof containeth; yielding obedience to the commands, trembling at the threatenings, and embracing the promises of God for this life and that which is to come;

A believing response to the Bible manifests itself in different ways, depending on the nature of the passage in view. In particular, faith in God's Word includes "yielding obedience to the commands" of God. The disobedience of our first parents took place when they doubted the reliability of God's Word (Gen. 3:4-5). Conversely, Abraham's obedience became the pattern for all believers (Heb. 11:8; Gen. 22). It requires faith to see that true blessedness and life lie in the path of obedience and self-denial (Deut. 30:15-20; Prov. 10:17; 12:28; Matt. 7:13-14; 16:24- 27).

Faith also entails "trembling at the threatenings" of God. Unbelievers treat God's warnings as if they were mere idle tales (Jer. 36:21-24; 2 Peter 3:4). But humble believers take God's threats seriously and tremble at His Word (Isa. 66:2, 5; Ezra 10:3; Heb. 11:7).

Faith especially includes "embracing the promises of God for this life and that which is to come." Abraham's justifying faith involved believing

---

18. For a remarkable exposition of these diverse character traits, see Jonathan Edwards' sermon, "The Excellency of Christ," in *The Works of Jonathan Edwards*, ed. Edward Hickman, 2 vols. (Guildford and London: Billing & Sons, 1834; repr., Edinburgh: Banner of Truth Trust, 1974), 1:680-83.

God's promise of an innumerable posterity (Gen. 15:6; 12:1-4; Heb. 11:9). Likewise, his believing descendants all died clinging to unfulfilled promises (Heb. 11:13, 20-22). The true heirs of Abraham are those who lay hold of the promises of the gospel by faith (Rom. 4:13-16; Gal. 3:5-9, 14-22).

B. Special Faith

While faith in the Bible as God's Word is inseparable from a state of salvation, this "general faith" is not the specific act by which sinners are justified. The "special faith" by which we are saved is not faith in the Scriptures but faith in Christ as He is offered to us in the gospel:

but the principal acts of saving faith have immediate relation to Christ, accepting, receiving, and resting upon him alone for justification, sanctification, and eternal life, by virtue of the covenant of grace.

1. The Object of Saving Faith

We fear God as Creator and Judge because of our guilt, but we trust Him as Savior and Redeemer because of His grace. Accordingly, the New Testament ordinarily designates Christ, not His Father, as the object of saving faith. Jesus repeatedly declares that, if they would not be condemned, men must believe on Him (John 3:18; 3:15-16, 36; 6:40, 47-51; cf. Gal. 2:16; 3:24, 26).

A full-orbed Christian faith apprehends Jesus as the Holy One of God (John 6:69), as the Christ, the Son of God (11:27; 6:69; 9:35; 20:30-31), as one with the Father (14:10-11), as the "I am" (8:24; 13:19), in short, as God (20:27-28).

Faith also contemplates Christ as a Savior—as the Messianic Prophet, Priest, and King. This does not mean that genuine faith must have all three offices distinctly in view. But, while faith often eyes the sacrificial work of the High Priest (Heb. 10:1-22), sometimes it views Christ as Prophet (John 4:29; Acts 3:22-23) or King (John 1:49; Acts 5:31; 9:6). True faith never appropriates the benefits of His priestly work while rejecting Christ as the infallible Prophet or supreme King.

Although refusal to submit to Christ's rule is indeed inconsistent with true conversion, Christ crucified and risen is the primary object of saving faith (1 Cor. 15:3-4, 11). Sinners must believe on Him who died, for that is the only basis of their pardon and acceptance. God "set forth" this crucified Savior "to be a propitiation *through faith in his blood*" (Rom. 3:25, KJV, emphasis added; cf. 5:9). Sinners must also believe on Him who rose from the dead, for this assures them that their redemption has been accomplished. The gospel to be believed includes the fact that Christ was "raised for our justification" (Rom. 4:24-25, ASV; cf. 10:9-11; 1 Cor. 15:1-4, 11).

2. The Acts of Saving Faith

The Confession states that the "principal acts" of saving faith are "accepting, receiving, and resting" upon Christ—words which depict a cordial reception of and simple trust in Christ.

The Scriptures represent faith under various metaphors: "receiving" (John 1:12), "coming" (John 6:35-37, 44-45), "fleeing" (Heb. 6:18), "looking" (John 3:14-15), "seeing" (John 6:40), "hearing" (10:26-27), and "eating" and "drinking" (John 6:47-54; 7:37-38). It is as if one's soul has members that correspond to his physical members. Turretin fills out the picture: faith is compared "now to the eye (in respect of the knowledge of Christ), then to the feet (in respect of approach and refuge), then to hands and mouth (in respect of reception and application)."[19] Although the Confession does not give a list all of the biblical representations of faith, its reference to "accepting, receiving, and resting" on Christ highlights the multifaceted nature of saving faith. To "accept" something is to welcome and receive it with a consenting mind—in this case gratefully to receive Christ and His salvation as freely offered in the gospel (1 Tim. 1:15).

While the word "accept" emphasizes the *disposition* by which something is received (consent or favor), the second word, "receive," accentuates the *act* by which something comes into one's possession (John 1:12; 12:48). Faith is the hand by which the sinner actually takes the free gift of Christ's righteousness as his own (cf. Rom. 6:23; Eph. 2:8-9). It is called a "hand," not because it *works* for eternal life, but because it *receives* Christ; it is not a full, working hand, but an empty, receptive hand. And, we must add, it is an appropriating hand. By faith the sinner says, "I receive and take Christ and His righteousness to be mine." As Luther observes, mere historical faith "stands like a lazy man concealing his hand under his armpit and says, 'That is nothing to me.' True faith with arms outstretched joyfully embraces [*amplectitur*][20] the Son of God given for it and says, 'He is my beloved [*dilectus*] and I am his.'"[21]

The Confession also depicts faith as "resting upon" Christ. Here the element of trust is brought into prominence. This aspect of faith appears in those passages that refer to "believing on" (*pisteuein epi*) Christ (e.g., Acts 11:17; 16:31). This phrase portrays a tranquil repose on Christ, sometimes represented as resting on a rock or cornerstone (1 Peter 2:6). Trusting in Christ is resting on Him with your whole weight; it is falling down and lying on the Rock of Ages.

---

19. Francis Turretin, *Institutes of Elenctic Theology*, trans. George Musgrave Giger, ed. James T. Dennison, Jr., 3 vols. (Phillipsburg, N.J.: P & R Publishing, 1994), 2:559.

20. *Amplector* means "to twine around," "embrace with love," or "cling to."

21. Martin Luther, "Theses Concerning Faith and Law," theses 21–22, in *Luther's Works*, eds., Jaroslav Pelikan and Helmut T. Lehmann (St. Louis: Concordia Publishing House; and Philadelphia: Muhlenberg Press, 1955–), 34:110. Hereafter this English translation, currently 69 volumes, will be abbreviated as LW. cf. the Latin text in *D. Martin Luthers Werke. Kritische Gesamtausgabe* (Weimar, 1883–), 391:46, lines 1-4). Hereafter the Latin and German Weimarer Ausgabe (German for "Weimar Edition") of Luther's works, currently 121 volumes, will be abbreviated WA.

These descriptions of faith—"accepting, receiving and resting" upon Christ—all imply an act of personal appropriation. It will not do merely to smell or admire the gospel meal. Unless you "eat the flesh of the Son of Man and drink His blood," unless you take His shed blood for the removal of your sins in particular, "you have no life in you" (John 6:53). On Paul's affirmation that Christ "loved me and gave Himself for me" (Gal. 2:20), Luther writes, "Read therefore with great vehemency these words 'ME' and 'FOR ME,' and so inwardly practice with thyself that thou... mayest conceive and print this 'ME' in thy heart... not doubting but that thou art of the number of those to whom this 'ME' belongeth."[22]

The Confession's description of the acts of faith as "accepting, receiving, and resting" prompts us to say something about the Protestant teaching that saving faith is comprised of three constituent elements: knowledge (*notitia*), assent (*assensus*) and trust (*fiducia*).

a). First, saving faith includes *knowledge*. We do not trust a person unless what we know of him convinces us that he is worthy of our confidence. What we know of Christ engenders the confidence that He is equal to the task of saving us from sin and its eternal consequences.

John assumes a virtual interchangeability between faith and knowledge (11:42; 17:3, 8, 21). Paul assumes that certain things must be known as the basis of faith, especially the death and resurrection of Christ (Rom. 4:24-25; 10:9-10; 1 Cor. 2:1-5; 15:1-4; Col. 2:12).

The Bible often highlights this aspect of faith by employing the phrase "believe that" followed by a proposition to be known and believed. John says that the signs included in his account were written "that you may believe that Jesus is the Christ, the Son of God, and that believing you may have life in His name" (20:31, cf. 6:69; 8:24; 14:10--11; 1 John 5:1, 5; Rom. 10:9). The New Testament also often uses the parallel construction "know that" followed by a proposition that is known and believed (e.g., John 4:42; 6:69; 10:38; 16:30; Gal. 2:16; 1 John 5:13, 20). In some places the "know that" and "believe that" are joined together (John 6:69; 10:38; 16:30; 17:8).

The evidence for knowledge as an element of faith overthrows the notion of "implicit faith," the Catholic doctrine that, as long as the "faithful" implicitly accept the church's teaching, it is not essential that they know the content of that "faith." This is also a healthy antidote to the tendency of some to conceive of faith as a mystical experience that bypasses intellectual propositions and rational processes.

How much of the gospel must a man know to be saved? Ultimately, this question can only be answered by God. Who but God can discern whether a man's attitude toward Christ, expressed poorly in words, represents genuine faith? But in general it may be said that, with the

---

22. Martin Luther, *A Commentary on St. Paul's Epistle to the Galatians*, ed. Philip S. Watson, translation based on the "Middleton" English version of 1575 (Cambridge and London: James Clarke, 1953), 179-80 = LW 26:179 = WA 401:299, lines 29-34. This passage represents Luther's distinctive emphasis on faith apprehending Christ's sacrificial love "FOR ME," accentuated in the Latin original with capital letters, "PRO ME"—with the result, *Christus pro me.*

coming of the Redeemer, the contents of this knowledge came to be known as the "gospel," the message of the God-man who died and rose again for the salvation of sinners (1 Cor. 15:1-4).

Having emphasized the *content* of this knowledge, we must also say something about its *spiritual nature*. It is not merely the transcription of biblical data upon the mind; it also includes a spiritual apprehension of the glory of Christ. In the new creation God "has shone in our hearts to give the light of the knowledge of the glory of God in the face of Jesus Christ" (2 Cor. 4:6). "Everyone who sees the Son and believes in Him may have everlasting life" (John 6:40). It is possible to see Christ with the eye of flesh without seeing Him with the eye of faith (v. 36).

The knowledge by which spiritual things are beheld must be a perception that is suited to behold them: it must be spiritual (1 Cor. 2:14). Because the "natural man" is incapable of this spiritual perception, it must come from the Spirit (v. 13). As Thomas Goodwin observes, a man may be able to look at a printed piece of music and learn its harmony artificially by the rules of music theory, but be incapable of understanding the real harmony of the song because he doesn't have an ear for music. Likewise, in a rational manner the natural man is able to perceive the meaning of the words that set forth spiritual realities, but is unable to understand them "purely and nakedly" apart from an impression from the Spirit.[23] The Spirit must impart a *new understanding*, a new ability to see the glory of Christ (John 16:14; 1 John 2:20, 27). Once He has imparted this new understanding to the sinner, the Spirit also comes with *new light* upon this understanding, conveying the image of spiritual things to the mind. If the angels who have seen Christ in glory were to use all of their rhetorical or artistic skills, they could not impart such a sight of Christ as that which comes by faith through the illumination of the Holy Spirit.[24]

b). Secondly, saving faith includes *assent*—the conviction that one's knowledge of Christ is true and the persuasion that the provisions of the gospel are suited to meet our deepest needs.

1) By this assent the believer not only knows the contents of the gospel but also believes they are *true* (the intellectual element of assent). "Faith is assurance of things hoped for" (Heb. 11:1, ASV; cf. 3:14; 2 Cor. 11:17). Just as physical eyesight produces evidence of visible things, faith is the "conviction of things not seen" (Heb. 11:1; cf. v. 27). Saving faith involves "believing that" (*pisteuo hoti*) certain unseen realities are true (John 6:69; 20:31; Rom. 10:9).

This element of saving faith is also indicated by the verb *pisteuo* ("believe") followed by a noun in the dative case—the person or proposition believed. When the object of the word "believe" is a person, frequently the One believed is Jesus (John 10:37-38; 14:11; 2 Tim. 1:12).

2) By this assent the sinner not only believes the gospel is true but also that Christ is *suitable and sufficient* for his case (the emotional element

---

23. Thomas Goodwin, *The Object and Acts of Justifying Faith*, 2.1.1, in *The Works of Thomas Goodwin*, 12 vols. (1861–1866; repr., Eureka, Calif.: Tanski Publications, 1996), 8:259.

24. Ibid., 8:260.

of assent). He ceases to consider the object of faith in a cold, detached manner. Now he sees his desperate need for Christ and the wonderful way the Savior is suited to meet that need. Seeing in Christ a way of salvation that perfectly upholds the righteous demands of God's law (Acts 13:38-39), he now delights in the way of forgiveness set forth in the gospel. "There is something common to all gracious persons... and this is the heart's satisfaction with God's plan of salvation by Christ."[25] This is what it means to "accept" Christ—to grant Christ and His accomplished righteousness a welcome in our hearts (1 Tim. 1:15; cf. Rom. 5:17).

In saving faith the sinner also views Christ as an *all-sufficient* Savior. He sees in the cross an "abundance of grace" (Rom. 5:17; cf. Ps. 130:7) sufficient to cover his many sins, and in the risen Savior, One who is "able to save to the uttermost those who come to God through Him" (Heb. 7:25). Therefore, he ceases to regard any other ceremony or work as contributing, even in the least, to his acceptance with God (Phil. 3:3-9; Gal. 2:16; Heb. 4:10).

Having seen that Christ is such a suitable and all-sufficient Savior, the sinner coming to faith *desires* Christ for himself. He "hungers and thirsts" for that righteousness that can be found only in Christ (Matt. 5:6; cf. John 6:35, 50-58; contrast Isa. 53:2-3). Christ is the treasure for which he is willing to "sell all that he has and buy" (Matt. 13:44-46).

The sinner now sees how *he in particular* may be saved. Not content with approving this way of salvation in general, he applies its truth unto himself, saying, "It is God's way, fitted, and suited, and able to save me, who am the chiefest of sinners"[26] (cf. 1 Tim. 1:15). He sees that if he were the only sinner on earth, Christ could not be more adapted to meet his needs.

c). In addition to knowledge and assent, faith includes *trust*. Of these elements, trust is saving faith's most definitive act. The faith of demons includes knowledge and assent: they know there is one God and begrudgingly assent to His existence—even to the point of trembling (James 2:19). But they do not trust Christ as their Savior. While knowledge and assent are necessary, it is by the act of trust that we receive Christ as our Savior.

In a nutshell, trust is an implicit reliance upon Christ alone for one's salvation. It is a whole-souled engagement of the person of the sinner as lost to the person of Christ as able and willing to save. In this engagement the sinner abandons all reliance on himself and all other human resources, and rests in Christ alone for his salvation.[27]

---

25. William Guthrie, *The Christian's Great Interest* (1658; repr., Inverness, Scotland, 1969), 69.

26. John Owen, *Gospel Grounds and Evidences of the Faith of God's Elect*, in *The Works of John Owen*, ed. William H. Goold (1850–53; repr., Edinburgh: The Banner of Truth Trust, 1976), 5:419.

27. John Murray, *Redemption Accomplished and Applied* (Grand Rapids: Wm. B. Eerdmans, 1955), 111.

The Old Testament often employs the word אמן (*aman*) to designate this trustful repose. The Hiphil form of this word means "to regard as firm or trustworthy." It is often followed by the preposition ב (*be*, "in"), which introduces the person or thing on which one confidently rests: the words and works of God (Pss. 106:12; 78:32), and God Himself (Gen. 15:6; 2 Chron. 20:20; Ps. 78:22). Another Hebrew word for trust is בטח (*batach*), "confide in," "lean upon," or "trust." It often describes confidence in God in times of distress and danger (Pss. 22:4-5; 28:7-8; 56:4, 11).

The New Testament employs the word *pisteuō* (πιστεύω) with various prepositions to express the sinner's trustful reliance on Christ and the gospel. *Pisteuō en* ("believe in") indicates a firm, fixed confidence in its object (Mark 1:15; John 3:15). *Pisteuō epi* ("believe upon") with the object of faith in the dative case expresses a calm reliance and restful repose on its object (1 Tim. 1:16; Rom. 9:33). *Pisteuō epi* ("believe upon'" with its object in the accusative case depicts the movement of the mind and heart toward the object of faith, as in Acts 16:31, "Believe on the Lord Jesus Christ," that is, "Turn with confident trust to the Lord Jesus Christ" (cf. Rom. 4:5, 24).

Pisteuō eis ("believe into") with its object in the accusative case is the most frequent phrase denoting this aspect of faith. In every use of this phrase (except one) the object toward which faith is directed is a person— usually Christ (John 3:16, 18, 36; 6:35). The preposition *eis* ("into"), with its emphasis of movement toward its object, expresses "an absolute transference of trust from ourselves to another, a complete self-surrender to Christ."[28]

In addition to these Hebrew and Greek words, the Bible depicts trust by the use of several illustrative expressions which highlight various analogies between faith and the human body. Faith is the *eye* that looks to the object of its trust. As the Israelites were to look to the brass serpent, sinners must look away from themselves to the uplifted One (John 3:14-15). Faith is also the *hand* that receives, grasps and appropriates Christ (John 1:12; 13:20). It hears of Christ's blood and says, "I receive it for the pardon of my sins" (cf. Acts 10:43). It hears of imputed righteousness and gratefully receives the "gift of righteousness" freely offered to sinners (Rom. 5:17). Therefore, take what God offers. You will not be a thief, for you have a divine permit: "Whosoever will, let him take of the water of life freely."[29] Faith is also the *mouth* that feeds upon and drinks of Christ (John 6:35, 47-54; 7:37-38). Has God begun to create in you a hunger for Christ? Then, just as you take bread into yourself and it becomes your own, receive Christ by faith as your very own (cf. Rom. 10:8; Matt. 5:6).

28. Benjamin B. Warfield, *Biblical and Theological Studies* (Philadelphia: Presbyterian and Reformed, 1968), 437-39 = B. B. Warfield, *Biblical Doctrines*, The Works of Benjamin B. Warfield, 10 vols. (New York: Oxford University Press, 1929; repr., Grand Rapids: Baker Book House, 1981), 2:476-78.

29. C. H. Spurgeon, *All of Grace* (Chicago: Moody Press, n.d.), 50-51; citation from Rev. 22:17.

The Bible also uses several expressions that illustrate this aspect of faith by drawing parallels between trust and various actions common to human experience. Just as children trustingly come when called (Matt. 18:2-3; 19:13-14), by faith we are to *come* to Christ when He calls (John 6:35, 37, 64-65; 7:37). As the man-slayer fled to the city of refuge, believers have "fled for refuge to lay hold of the hope set before [them]" (Heb. 6:18; cf. Ps. 71:1-3; Prov. 18:10). Faith is also described as *resting* or *leaning* upon God (2 Chron. 14:11; Isa. 26:3; 48:2; cf. Amos 5:19). Again, committing oneself to Him involves *rolling* oneself on the Lord: "He trusted in the LORD" (lit., "He *rolled himself* on the Lord," Ps. 22:8; cf. 37:5; Josh. 10:18). A man entrusts his money to the care of a banker, implicitly trusting the solvency of the bank. Even so, the believer declares, "I know whom I have believed and am persuaded that He is able to keep what I have committed [*parathēkē*, 'deposit'] to Him until that Day" (2 Tim. 1:12).

In general terms faith is the means of commerce between the sinner in his emptiness and the Savior in His fullness (John 1:12-16; Col. 1:19). But the consciousness of his need shapes the particular manner in which the sinner entrusts himself to the Savior. The hungry, thirsty soul *eats and drinks* (John 6:35; 7:37–38). The sinner pursued by the claims of the law *flees* to Christ as to the city of refuge (Heb. 6:18). The sinner needing pardon *receives* Christ and His atonement as his own (John 1:12; Rom. 5:11, 17). Whatever spiritual need is uppermost in the sinner's mind finds an answer in Christ, and that which faith finds in Christ it appropriates as its very own.

In addition to personal appropriation, the biblical words and metaphors for faith inform us that trust involves an act of commitment or entrustment to Christ: 1) The use of *pisteuō eis* ("believe into") with its object in the accusative case emphasizes the movement of the soul toward the object of faith (e.g., John 3:16, 18, 36; 6:35); it is "an absolute transference of trust from ourselves to another, a complete self-surrender to Christ."[30] 2) In 2 Timothy 1:12 Paul describes faith as a committal or deposit (*parathēkē*). 3) The metaphor of fleeing to Christ as to a city of refuge is based on the analogy between a man-slayer entrusting himself to the protection of a city and a sinner entrusting himself to the protection of his Savior (Heb. 6:18).

Our observations concerning faith as an act of commitment lead us to conclude that trust is an act of the will: (1) The frequent instances of *pisteuō eis* ("believe into") and *pisteuō epi* ("believe upon") with the accusative, both of which depict a movement of the heart toward the object of faith, assume a volitional inclination in the direction of the object of faith. (2) The scriptural commands to believe call for a decision on the part of the sinner (1 John 3:23; Mark 1:15; Acts 16:31; Rom. 16:26). (3) The biblical analogies for trust (a hand that receives Christ, feet that come or flee to Christ, and a mouth that eats or drinks of Him) all assume an act of the will.

---

30. Warfield, *Biblical and Theological Studies*, 439 = Warfield, Biblical Doctrines, 2:478.

The sinner must not wait around until he feels an emotional attraction to Christ. The gospel summons him to surrender his stubborn refusal to believe and to comply willingly with its demand: "Believe on the Lord Jesus Christ." Refusal to believe is blatant disobedience: "He who *believes* in the Son has eternal life; but he who *does not obey* the Son shall not see life, but the wrath of God abides on him" (John 3:36, NASB, emphasis added; cf. Rom. 10:16; 1 Peter 4:17). No language could be plainer: unbelief is disobedience. Therefore, you must trust in Christ *at once*.

3. The Aim of Saving Faith

Saving faith has certain practical ends in view. It involves receiving and resting upon Christ "for justification, sanctification, and eternal life." Paul refers to believers as those who "seek to be justified by Christ" (Gal. 2:16-17; cf. Rom. 4:5, 24-25; Phil. 3:9). The Confession also speaks of receiving Christ "for... sanctification." Believers long for deliverance, not only from the guilt of sin, but also from its power. Therefore, they are said to be sanctified by faith in Christ (Acts 26:18; cf. 15:7-9). The Confession adds that believers also rest upon Christ "for... eternal life." The Son of Man was lifted up "that whoever believes in Him should not perish but have eternal life" (John 3:14-15; cf. vv. 16, 36; 6:40, 47; 1 John 5:13; 1 Tim. 1:16; Titus 3:7). Jesus offers a life that becomes the immediate possession of all who believe (John 3:15-16, 36; 5:24) and culminates in the complete enjoyment of the life and blessedness of God in eternity (Rev. 22:1-4; John 12:25; Rom. 6:22; Titus 3:7). In summary, faith rests upon Christ for a *complete salvation*: "for salvation not only from wrath, but also from sin— not only for salvation from the guilt of sin, but also from its pollution and power—not only for happiness hereafter, but also for holiness here."[31]

4. The Warrant of Saving Faith

This paragraph in the Confession concludes with the assertion that saving faith involves resting upon Christ alone "by virtue of the covenant of grace." Chapter 7 of the Westminster and 1689 Confessions refers to the "covenant of grace; wherein [God] freely offereth unto sinners life and salvation by Jesus Christ, requiring of them faith in him" (cf. Westminster Shorter Catechism, Q. 86). Hence, we conclude that the framers of both Confessions were saying that the warrant of saving faith is the covenant of grace, that is, the free offer of the gospel. Four considerations assure the believer that he has a warrant for coming to Christ for pardon and deliverance:

a). *An unrestricted invitation.* Christ's invitation is so broad that the most unworthy sinner may know he is not merely permitted but also welcome to come. Who can conceive of more indiscriminate language than the invitation of our Lord in Matthew 11:28, "Come to Me, all you who labor and are heavy laden, and I will give you rest"? (cf. John 7:37; Rev. 22:17; Isa. 45:22).

---

31. Robert Shaw, *An Exposition of the Westminster Confession of Faith* (1845; Fearn, Ross-shire, Scotland: Christian Focus Publications, 1992), 150-51.

b). *An unbounded command.* The texts we have just cited are more than invitations; they carry the force of urgent commands: "Look unto Me," "Come to Me and drink," etc. Appealing to the highest interests of sinners, God entreats, He pleads, He implores: "Why will you die?" But, knowing that men procrastinate, He also couches His exhortations with the urgency of a warning and a command: "Turn from your evil ways!" "Flee the wrath to come!" "Do not boast about tomorrow!" (Ezek. 33:11; Matt. 3:7; Prov. 27:1; cf. 1 John 3:23; John 3:18).

c). *An unfailing promise.* Among the promises that have been used to encourage trembling souls are these: "The one who comes to Me I will by no means cast out" (John 6:37; cf. Matt. 11:28). "Whoever calls upon the name of the Lord shall be saved" (Rom. 10:13; cf. 4:5; John 3:14-16). In order that timid souls might be emboldened to entrust themselves to the Lord, He has confirmed these promises with a covenant (Heb. 6:13-18). When Jesus gave the cup to His disciples, He said, "This is My blood of the new covenant, which is shed for many for the remission of sins" (Matt. 26:28; cf. Heb. 8:6, 12). This blood-ratified covenant provides sinners with a warrant for boldly laying hold of all of the promises included in the gospel.

d). *An unstinting Savior.* To stint is to limit one's expenditures, often unduly. Sinners have no reason to imagine that Christ is under constraints to dispense His grace in such a manner. With Him is "abundant pardon," pardon for great and numerous sins, pardon for every sinner who believes (Ps. 130:7; Isa. 55:7; 1:18; Acts 13:38-39; Col. 2:13; 1 Tim. 1:15; 1 John 1:7, 9).

3. The Distinctiveness and Prevalence of Faith
(Paragraph 3)

A. Its Distinctive Nature

This faith, although it be different in degrees, and may be weak or strong, yet it is in the least degree of it different in the kind or nature of it, as is all other saving grace, from the faith and common grace of temporary believers;

1. It Is Not Distinguished from Weak Faith.
That which distinguishes saving from spurious faith is not its relative strength. The Bible records instances of great and little faith (Matt. 8:10, 26; 14:31; 15:28; 16:8; 17:20), strong and weak faith (Rom. 4:19-20; 14:1-2), and of growing and declining faith (2 Thess. 1:3; 2 Cor. 10:15). Even within the same believer faith fluctuates. Fully aware of the deadness of his own body and of Sarah's womb, Abraham was "strengthened in faith, giving glory to God" (Rom. 4:20, 17-21; cf. Gen. 22:1-10). Yet on other occasions his faith gives way (Gen. 12:10-13; 16:1-4; 20:2-13). In the heart of true believers there is often a mixture of faith and unbelief, as with the man who cried out, "Lord, I believe; help my unbelief!" (Mark 9:24; cf. Luke 24:41). As Calvin observes, "Some portion of unbelief [*incredulitas*] is always mixed

[*semper mixta*] with faith in every Christian."[32] Therefore, true faith is not distinguished from spurious faith by its strength. Let this encourage those with weak faith. So that your heart might be at rest, let me remind you of a few things:

a). *A weak faith may grasp a strong Savior.* The hand of a little child may grasp the hand of her father ever so feebly, but it is the tenacity of the father that keeps her safe. As one languid look at the uplifted serpent in the wilderness engaged the life-giving power of God (Num. 21:8-9), one faint look at the Crucified One secures eternal life (John 3:14-15; cf. Mark 5:25-30).

b). *It is not the strength of our faith but the strength of Christ's obedience that justifies us.* Joel Beeke argues, "If we start qualifying our faith, we destroy the gospel. Our faith may be weak, immature, timid, even indiscernible at times, but if it is real faith it is justifying faith... Faith's value in justification does not lie in any degree in itself but in its uniting us to Christ and His glorious achievement."[33]

c). *The promises of the gospel are not made to strong faith but to true.* "Whoever believes" will not perish but have everlasting life (John 3:15-16, 36). As Watson notes, "The promise says not whoever has a giant-faith, that can remove mountains, that can stop the mouths of lions, shall be saved; but whosoever believes, be his faith ever so small."[34]

d). *Those whose faith is weak are the special objects of the care of our dear Shepherd.* Every instance of weak faith in the Gospels pertains to Christ's true disciples (Matt. 6:30; 8:26; 14:31; 16:8; UBS reading of 17:20). In each case Christ did not respond to their weakness with the withering denunciations reserved for Pharisees, but with the nurturing care of gentle reproofs.

e). *Finally, weak faith may grow stronger.* Faith usually springs up by degrees: "first the blade, then the head, after that the full grain in the head" (Mark 4:28). Is your faith small? He who began this good thing in you "will complete it until the day of Jesus Christ" (Phil. 1:6).

2. It Is Distinguished from Temporary Faith.

Even when saving faith is weak, "yet it is in the least degree of it different in the kind or nature of it, as is all other saving grace, from the faith and common grace of temporary believers." This reference to "temporary believers" seems to be drawn from Christ's description of the stony ground hearer who receives the Word with joy but only endures for a while (Matt. 13:20-21). "Miracle faith" is often of this sort. Based on His

---

32. John Calvin, *Institutes of the Christian Religion,* trans. John Allen, 6th ed., 3.2.4 (1813; Philadelphia: Presbyterian Board of Education, 1902), 1:493 = Ioannis Calvini, *Opera quae supersunt omnia,* eds. G. Baum, Eduard Cunitz, and Eduard Reuss, vol. 2 (Brunsvigae: C. A. Schwetschke et filium, 1864), in *Corpus Reformatorum,* 30:400. Hereafter this Latin edition of the Institutes will be abbreviated CR.

33. Joel R. Beeke, "Justification by Faith Alone," in *Justification by Faith Alone,* ed. Don Kistler (Morgan, Pa.: Soli Deo Gloria Publications, 1995), 93-94.

34. Thomas Watson, *A Body of Divinity* (1890; repr., Edinburgh: The Banner of Truth Trust, 1958; rev. ed., 1965; repr. 1974), 220.

miraculous signs, many believed Christ was the promised Prophet (John 2:23; 6:14; Deut. 18:15-19). But their "faith" merely admired the temporal benefits or spectacular powers of the kingdom (John 4:48; 6:29-36; Acts 8:9-19). Temporary impressions are also felt by persons exposed to grave danger. But with the return of safety they relapse into their former unbelief (Judg. 3:7-12). Spurious professions are also made by those who temporarily have a relish for good preaching (Ezek. 33:31–32; Matt. 13:20), are enlightened, and taste the "powers of the age to come" (Heb. 6:4-5). But when persecution or temptation arises (Matt. 13:21; Luke 8:13), they fall away.

One difference between true and false faith is that the false is temporary. But, as Waldron notes, if this were the only difference, two consequences would follow.[35] First, there could be no assurance until a person had persevered to the end, which contradicts biblical exhortations to seek assurance (e.g., Heb. 6:11-12; 10:22). Second, such ones would be temporarily forgiven, justified and adopted, which is contrary to Scripture (Isa. 43:25; Rom. 5:1-2; 8:15-17, 30).

If faith differs from its counterfeit in "kind or nature," what are its distinctive features?

a). *Saving faith involves an unrivaled attachment to Christ.* When Jesus said, "Follow Me," His disciples "left all, rose up, and followed Him" (Luke 5:28; Matt. 4:18-22; 19:27). But when faith is tested, its true attachment is revealed. Therefore, Christ stressed that money, loved ones and even life itself must not rival one's attachment to Him (Mark 8:34-35; Luke 14:26; 18:22).

b). *In saving faith a sinner embraces a whole Christ.* He does not receive Him as a Priest to procure his pardon, while rejecting Him as an infallible Prophet to be his guide in all things (Acts 3:22; Deut. 18:15-19), or as a King to rule over him in everything (Acts 22:10; Luke 19:14). Careless professors would do well to take Alliene's discriminatory word seriously:

> The unsound convert takes Christ by halves. He is all for the salvation of Christ, but he is not for the sanctification... Jesus is a sweet name, but men do not love the Lord Jesus in sincerity. They will not have Him as God offers, "to be a Prince and a Savior" (Acts 5:31). They divide what God has joined, the King and the Priest... Every man's vote is for salvation from suffering, but they do not desire to be saved from sinning. They would have their lives saved, but still would have their lusts... [But] the sound convert takes a whole Christ... without exceptions, without limitations, without reserve.[36]

c). *Faith also produces repentance.* Repentance and faith are inseparable twins that always come forth from the womb of conversion together (Acts

---

35. Samuel E. Waldron, *A Modern Exposition of the 1689 Baptist Confession of Faith* (Durham, England: Evangelical Press, 1989), 192.

36. Joseph Alliene, *An Alarm to the Unconverted*, ed. Thomas E. Watson (Wilmington, Del.: Cornerstone, 1975), 25; in this edition the English of the original 1672 edition has been modernized. cf. J. Alliene, *An Alarm to the Unconverted, with an Introductory Essay by Andrew Thomson*, 2nd ed. (Glasgow: Chalmers and Collins, 1824), 127-28.

20:21; cf. 10:43-44 with 11:17-18). A believing reception of Christ implies a penitential rejection of sin (Luke 7:38, 50).

d). *True faith is marked by and results in obedience.* The same faith that is an act of obedience at one's conversion goes on to manifest itself in a life of obedience (Heb. 11:8). "Faith is not an idle grace; as it has an eye to see Christ, so it has a hand to work for him. It not only believes God's promise, but obeys his command."[37]

e). S*aving faith also leads to holiness of heart and life.* God bore witness to the validity of the Gentiles' conversion, "purifying their hearts by faith" (Acts 15:8-9; cf. 26:18). Faith in Christ crucified does not take away the life of sin, but it does take away the love of sin.[38] The holiness of true believers is distinguished by its universality. "Universal holiness does not mean perfect holiness. It means that we do not pick and choose among Christ's commands. [It means] that there is not a knowing and impenitent refusal to obey any command of Christ"[39] (contrast Mark 10:17-22 with Ps. 119:128).

f). *Saving faith also manifests itself in good works.* "What does it profit," James asks, "if someone says he has faith but does not have works?" If you send a needy brother away hungry, of what use is that kind of profession of faith? Don't you know that faith without works is dead? (2:14-20, 26; cf. 1 Thess. 1:3; Titus 3:8). Martin Luther vigorously declares:

> O it is a living, busy, active, mighty thing, this faith. It is impossible for it not to be doing good works incessantly. It does not ask whether good works are to be done, but before the question is asked, it has already done them, and is constantly doing them... Faith is a living, daring confidence in God's grace, so sure and certain that the believer would stake his life on it a thousand times... Because of it, without compulsion, a person is ready and glad to do good to everyone, to serve everyone, to suffer everything, out of love and praise to God who has shown him this grace. Thus it is impossible to separate works from faith, quite as impossible as to separate heat and light from fire.[40]

g). *Saving faith is marked by persevering fruitfulness.* The fault of thorny ground hearers is not that they do not continue, but that they "bring no fruit to maturity." But true believers, having heard the gospel, "hold it fast, and bear fruit with perseverance" (Luke 8:14-15, NAS; cf. John 15:4-5).

These are some of the distinguishing marks of saving faith. This side of glory no believer bears all these marks in perfect form. But at least in seed form they are present in every believer.

---

37. Watson, *A Body of Divinity*, 219.

38. Ibid.

39. Waldron, *Exposition of the 1689 Baptist Confession*, 192.

40. Martin Luther, "Preface to the Epistle of St. Paul to the Romans," in LW 35:370–71 = WA DB 7:11.

B. Its Prevailing Tendency

therefore, though it may be many times assailed and weakened, yet it gets the victory, growing up in many to the attainment of a full assurance through Christ, who is the author and finisher of our faith.

1. Its Certain Victory in All

Faith may be "assailed and weakened" by means of a condemning conscience, the accusations of Satan, adverse circumstances, physical pain, or mental depression—as may be seen in the cases of Abraham, Job and Peter. When everything around him seems to be God's "no" in contradiction to the "yes" of God's promise, the faith of the believer is sorely tried.

Since biblical times, perhaps no one has had his faith assailed more than Luther. Often he referred to his *Anfechtungen,* a German word that connotes a spiritual assault, accompanied by a sense of foreboding doom. Under this terror, "every corner of the soul is filled with the greatest bitterness, dread [*horrore*],[41] trembling [*pavore*],[42] and sorrow in such a manner that all these last forever."[43] One source of assault was the devil: "He easily creates hell and damnation for you because you take one drink too many or sleep too long, and soon you become sick with conscience, scruples and despondency and practically die of grief."[44] Most difficult were those times when Satan tormented him with doubts concerning God's grace: "God hates sinners. You are a sinner. God hates you." Perhaps no depression was as severe as that which he experienced in 1527: "For more than a week I was cast into death and hell, so that in my whole body I was so afflicted that I trembled [*tremam*] in all my members. Christ was totally lost. I was driven by floods and tempests of desperation [*desperationis*][45] and blasphemy of God."[46]

But, as the Confession says, though faith is often assailed, "yet it gets the victory." While Satan did his utmost to blow Peter's faith away like chaff, it did not fail, due to Christ's prayers. From the year of Luther's deepest depression we have the battle hymn of the Reformation, "A Mighty Fortress Is Our God." The forces of darkness and light make the soul the arena of deadly strife. But "this is the victory that has overcome the world—our faith" (1 John 5:4).

How does faith prevail? Its strength is in the Word (Rom. 10:17; Gal. 3:2, 5). "Where this Word enters the heart in true faith, it fashions the heart like unto itself, it makes it firm, certain, and assured [*sicher*]. It

---

41. From *horror,* shaking, trembling, quaking, dread, terror, horror.

42. From *pavor,* trembling, quaking, shaking, terror, anxiety, fear, dread, alarm.

43. Luther, *Explanations of the Ninety-Five Theses,* in LW 31:129 = WA 1:557, lines 6-8.

44. Luther, *Exposition of Selected Psalms III,* on Ps. 118:16-18, in LW 14:84 = WA 311:148, lines 6-9, 24-26.

45. From *desperatio,* hopelessness, despair, desperation.

46. Luther's letter to Melanchthon on August 2, 1527, no. 887, in WA Br 4(3):189 (my translation).

becomes buoyed up, rigid, and adamant over against all temptation [*anfechtung*], devil, death... it defiantly and haughtily despises and mocks everything that inclines toward doubt, despair [*zagen*], anger, and wrath; for it knows that God's Word cannot lie to it."[47] Robust faith, "looking through the gloom of tempest, death and hell, recognizes even the God who abandons as Protector, recognizes the God who persecutes as Helper, and recognizes the God who damns as Savior."[48] How is faith able to see through the darkness of the storm and trust the God who seems to be doing the opposite of His promise? The answer is found in the supreme embodiment of God's promise (2 Cor. 1:20). It is faith in God's final "yes" to us—Christ—that overcomes the apparent opposition of God's providential "no."

2. Its Full Assurance in Many

The prevailing tendency of faith also includes "growing up in many to the attainment of a full assurance through Christ." Usually the word "assurance" refers to the confidence that one has been forgiven, has passed from death to life, and is an heir of glory (1 John 5:13; 3:14).

In this connection the question has arisen as to whether assurance belongs to the essence of saving faith, or is an additional blessing not included in faith. Rome asserts that even the faithful cannot experience assurance, except rare individuals to whom it is given by special revelation. Reacting against this teaching, Calvin writes, "No man is a believer, I say, except him who, leaning upon the assurance [*securitati*][49] of his salvation, confidently triumphs over the devil and death."[50] Such statements, however, are tempered by others which stress that assurance is often contested by doubt (e.g., *Institutes*, 3.2.4, 7, 15, 17, 20). But where Calvin qualifies himself, the Heidelberg Catechism unambiguously asserts that saving faith includes assurance. "True faith is... an assured confidence... that not only to others, but to me also, remission of sin, everlasting righteousness, and salvation are freely given by God... " (Q. 21).

The 1689 and the Westminster Confessions stake out an intermediate position on this question. In their chapters on faith, both speak of faith "growing up in many to the attainment of a full assurance," which allows the possibility that in this life some believers may never experience this comfort. In Chapter 18 of these Confessions, paragraph three asserts, "This infallible assurance doth not so belong to the essence of faith, but that a true believer may wait long, and conflict with many difficulties before he be a partaker of it." These words preclude assurance from "so" belonging to faith that all believers are immune to struggles over their assurance.

---

47. Luther, *Treatise on the Last Words of David,* in LW 15:272 = WA 54:32, lines 27-32.

48. Luther, *Operationes in Psalmos,* 1519–1521, on Ps. 3:3 (Vulgate, Ps. 3:4), in WA 5:82, lines 14-17.

49. From *securitas,* security, safety, freedom from anxiety.

50. *Institutes,* 3.2.16; LCC 20:562 = CR 30:411.

In arriving at a carefully nuanced theology of faith and assurance, we must distinguish between objective and subjective assurance. *Objective assurance* is a certitude concerning the object of faith, the "conviction that Christ is all He professes to be, and will do all He promises"[51] (cf. Heb. 10:22; 11:6). Most agree that this is essential to saving faith. *Subjective assurance* is experiential: the believer's conviction that he or she is saved. This distinction goes hand in hand with another: objective assurance pertains to the *primary* or *direct* act of faith (trust in Christ that we might be saved); subjective assurance relates to the *secondary* or *reflexive* act of faith (the peace that results from an assurance that we are saved). Having believed on Christ so that we might be saved, we reflexively believe He will keep His promise to save all who believe.

In his *Exposition of the 1689 Baptist Confession* Sam Waldron makes two statements that encapsulate the intermediate position of the Confession: faith is not assurance; and faith is inseparable from assurance.[52] We shall arrange our observations under these two points.

a). *Faith is not assurance.* While faith has the tendency to lead to assurance, the two are not the same:

1) The biblical basis of faith is God's Word. The Scriptures nowhere assert that Mark Sarver is already saved. The gospel commands me to believe in Christ in order that I might be saved (Acts 16:31; John 3:15-18), not to believe that I have already been saved.

2) The object of saving faith is Christ, not the fact that He has saved me. Its focus is not inward, looking within to see if faith is there, but outward, looking to Christ that I might be saved. To say that assurance belongs to the essence of faith posits an object of faith other than Christ.

3) The Scriptures everywhere set forth faith, not assurance, as the instrumental means of salvation. To insist upon assurance as a constituent element of saving faith is to say that a person must believe that he is saved in order to be saved. This is a logical contradiction.

4) We have examples in the Bible of those who, in the very exercise of faith, experienced no assurance—including a woman of Canaan (Matt. 15:22-28) and a tax collector (Luke 18:9-14).

5) The Scriptures also give us examples of those with true saving faith who went through periods when they felt that God had utterly deserted them. One such example is found in Psalm 88, which records the words of godly Heman (cf. 1 Kings 4:31). Even though he experienced no assurance of God's acceptance and repeatedly spoke of himself as being cut off from God (Ps. 88:3-5, 14), he continued to cling to God in faith (v. 1).[53] David, Asaph and Job had similar experiences (Pss. 31:22; 77:2; Job 30:20-23).

6) Finally, we may deduce that one may have genuine saving faith without full assurance from the biblical injunctions to believers to

---

51. Robert L. Dabney, *Lectures in Systematic Theology* (1878; repr., Grand Rapids: Zondervan, 1976), 611.

52. Waldron, *Exposition of the 1689 Baptist Confession*, 189-90.

53. cf. Goodwin, *The Object and Acts of Justifying Faith*, 2.1, in *The Works of Thomas Goodwin*, 8:341.

cultivate assurance (1 John 5:13; 2 Peter 1:1, 5-10). The Bible contains examples of true believers who went through seasons in which they agonized over their relationship with God (e.g., Job 23:3-16; Pss. 51:8-12; 77:1-10; John 21:15-17).

b). *Faith is inseparable from assurance.* Although faith and assurance are not the same, assurance is produced and strengthened by faith as one of its normal effects:

1) Saving faith does not exist without its effects. The subjective effects of justifying faith include "peace with God through our Lord Jesus Christ, through whom also we have access by faith into this grace in which we stand, and rejoice in hope of the glory of God" (Rom. 5:1-2). The first effect mentioned here is peace with God. Peace arises from a sense of reconciliation. "As soon as the minutest particle of faith is instilled into our minds, we begin to behold the face of God placid, serene, and propitious; far off indeed, but still so distinctly as to assure us that there is no delusion in it."[54] Second, Paul speaks of "access by faith into this grace in which we stand" (v. 2; cf. Eph. 2:18; 3:12). No longer a condemned criminal, the believer may boldly enter the "Holiest" by the blood of Jesus and "draw near... in full assurance of faith" (Heb. 10:19, 22). The third effect Paul lists in Romans 5 is also bright with the sunshine of assurance: we "rejoice in hope of the glory of God" (v. 2). Hope is the expectation of a future good—identified here as "the glory of God," which is "that state of 'God-like-ness' which has been lost because of sin, and which will be restored in the last day to every Christian"[55] (cf. 8:17-18, 29-30; Phil. 3:21). Here hope is given a climactic place. From quiet peace to exultant hope, faith leads the soul to confidence, not only in its acceptance with God, but also in its participation in His glory.

2) The association between the terms used for hope and faith in the Bible underscores the inseparable relationship between assurance and faith. In forty-six places the Septuagint translates the Hebrew word for trust, בָּטַח (*batagh*), with ελπίζω (*elpizo*), the primary Greek word for hope. However, when *batagh* is rendered *elpizo*, the connotation in view is almost always trust in the face of danger (e.g., Ps. 21:5-6 = ASV 22:4-5) rather than expectant hope for some future good. None of these texts focus on the notion we usually associate with hope: an expectation of a future good. Of even greater significance is the fact that the Hebrew word for justifying faith, אָמַן(*aman*), is frequently rendered *pisteuo* (believe) but never *elpizo* (hope).

In the New Testament, the Septuagint's use of *elpizo* to refer to trust is overtaken by its use to describe hope as an expectation of future good—hope in the resurrection, eternal life, the "hope of glory," etc. (e.g., Acts 24:15; Rom. 5:2; 8:23-25; Col. 1:27; 1 Thess. 5:8; Titus 1:2). By its very nature

54. Calvin, *Institutes of the Christian Religion*, trans. Henry Beveridge, 2 vols., 3.2.19 (Grand Rapids: Wm. B. Eerdmans, 1966), 1:486 = CR 30:413.

55. Douglas Moo, *The Epistle to the Romans,* The New International Commentary on the New Testament (Grand Rapids: William B. Eerdmans, 1996), 302.

this expectation of glory includes the element of assurance. Wherever saving faith is present, its sister graces of hope and love are also there (1 Thess. 1:3-4; cf. 5:8). Wherever saving faith exists, hope is always present, along with the assurance that is so integral to the nature of hope—even if only in its tender beginnings (cf. 1 Peter 1:3).

In Hebrews 11:1 faith is portrayed as giving rise to the assurance of hope: "Faith is assurance of things hoped for, a conviction of things not seen" (ASV). The "hope" of unbelievers is vague, wishful thinking. But the hope of believers is characterized by certainty and assurance, because it is founded upon the promises of God. With respect to the word *hupostasis*, translated "assurance" in the ASV and NAS, various connotations are possible,[56] but its use elsewhere (Heb. 3:14; 2 Cor. 9:4; 11:17) favors the meaning, "confident assurance," and this sense fits the context. It is the confident assurance of faith that certifies the reality of the object of hope (cf. Titus 1:1-2; 3:7).

In some sense, then, the assurance that characterizes hope also characterizes the faith from which it has arisen. But the assurance that is said to characterize one's faith and hope may not in every instance pertain to one's subjective assurance that he is saved. In many places it has to do with one's certainty concerning the object of faith and hope— the Savior, His intercession, and His manifestation in glory. But it is the nature of hope to anticipate some future good, and the one who exercises this hope envisions himself participating in that good. To the extent that he has this "assurance of hope," he will also enjoy the "assurance of faith."

3) The inseparable relationship of faith and assurance also underlies the phrases "full assurance of faith" and "full assurance of hope" in Hebrews 10:22 and 6:11. The former phrase occurs in the exhortation, "Having boldness to enter the Holiest by the blood of Jesus... and having a High Priest over the house of God, let us draw near with a true heart in full assurance of faith... " (10:19, 22). We are to draw near with "fullness" (*plerophoria*) of faith, with "the fullest and most assured belief."[57] Here the "full assurance of faith" is primarily objective in nature—the assurance that our High Priest has entered heaven, and that the presentation of His blood is efficacious. But objective assurance concerning the efficacious sacrifice and intercession of Christ is never divorced from its subjective counterpart. By this "full assurance of faith" in Christ, the believer may enter God's presence with boldness and assurance.

This link between the objective and subjective aspects of assurance is very instructive. The believer's subjective assurance of his own salvation is not strengthened by an introspective examination of the genuineness of his faith but by looking outside of himself to Christ, whose sacrifice and intercession have opened the way into the presence of God. If the "full

56. See Philip Edgecumbe Hughes, *A Commentary on the Epistle to the Hebrews* (Grand Rapids: Wm. B. Eerdmans, 1977), 439-40.

57. John Brown, *Hebrews,* The Geneva Series of Commentaries (1862; repr., Edinburgh: The Banner of Truth Trust, 1976), 460.

assurance of faith" in Hebrews 10:22 is assurance concerning the object of faith, the "full assurance of hope" in Hebrews 6:11 is the assurance of final salvation. This "full assurance of hope" will be ours as we "imitate those who through faith and patience inherit the promises" (v. 12). The faith that continues to cling to God's promises also carries within its womb the "full assurance of hope."

4) The inseparability of faith and assurance may also be seen in the relationship of saving faith to its evidences:

One such evidence is a changed view of God's law. Formerly the law provoked his hatred for God. Now the believer sees that which is "holy and just and good" (Rom. 7:12) in those commands that once provoked him. Even when he is engaged in an agonizing struggle with his indwelling sins, the believer loves the law as an expression of the character and heart of God (v. 22; Ps. 119:68, 77, 137).[58]

Faith also produces repentance. It is a soul-melting grace. Believers look on Him whom they have pierced, and mourn (Zech. 12:10). Even a glimpse of his Savior made Peter weep for his sins, because he saw Him with the eye of faith and love (Matt. 26:75; cf. Luke 7:44).

Saving faith is a world-conquering power. "This is the victory that has overcome the world—our faith" (1 John 5:4). "Faith overcomes the frowning world, the fawning world, the tempting world, and the persecuting world."[59] It conquers the world by out-bidding it. By faith Moses esteemed the reproach of Christ greater riches than all the honors and treasures of Egypt (Heb. 11:26; cf. Matt. 13:45-46). Faith also outbids the world by looking forward to the reward (v. 26; Ps. 16:5, 8, 11; cf. Gen. 14:21-15:1).

Faith also fills the heart with love. What true believers have seen of Christ with the eye of faith (John 6:40) ravishes their hearts with love. Your faith, now tested by fire, will be honored at the revelation of Christ, "whom having not seen you love. Though now you do not see Him, yet believing, you rejoice with joy inexpressible and full of glory" (1 Peter 1:7-8). Robert Leighton notes three elements of this love: 1) *goodwill* toward Christ, a longing that His glory would be spread and known (Phil. 2:21); 2) *delight* in Christ, a joyful admiration of Him (Ps. 45:1-8; 2 Thess. 1:10); and 3) *desire* for Him, a longing for communion with Him in this life (Phil. 3:10; Luke 24:29-32) and a yearning to be with Him in heaven (Phil. 1:23; 2 Cor. 5:8).[60]

The same faith that produces love for Christ also engenders love for the brethren (1 John 3:23). Patterned after the love of Christ for His own, true believers have a distinguishing love for the brethren (John 13:34). The character of every believer reflects the image of Christ (2 Cor. 3:18; Rom. 8:29), and it is this that attracts the eye and wins the heart.

---

58. See Owen, *Evidences of the Faith of God's Elect,* 5:422-36.

59. Thomas Brooks, *Heaven on Earth,* in *The Works of Thomas Brooks,* ed. Alexander B. Grosart (1861–67; repr. Edinburgh: The Banner of Truth Trust, 1980), 2:458 = Brooks, *Heaven on Earth,* Puritan Paperbacks (1654; repr. London: The Banner of Truth Trust, 1961), 212.

60. Robert Leighton, *Commentary on First Peter* (formerly published as *A Practical Commentary on the First Epistle of St. Peter,* 1853; repr., Grand Rapids: Kregel, 1972), 54.

Thus, we see how saving faith has its evidences. Assurance is thereby strengthened, and so the role of faith in producing these evidences is further proof of the inseparability of faith and assurance.

5) The biblical teaching that those who believe receive the Spirit of adoption confirms the inseparability of faith and assurance. This teaching may be presented as a biblical syllogism:

Major premise: when sinners believe they receive the Spirit (Gal. 3:2, 14; Eph. 1:13).

Minor premise: the Spirit imparts assurance to those to whom He has been given. "You did not receive the spirit of bondage again to fear, but you received the Spirit of adoption by whom we cry out, 'Abba, Father'" (Rom. 8:15). The Spirit replaces our pre-Christian fear with that instinct by which we address God with child-like familiarity: "Abba" (cf. the word "daddy," Gal. 4:6). The Spirit "bears witness with our spirit that we are children of God" (Rom. 8:16).

Conclusion: at least in seed form, a Spirit-wrought assurance is given to everyone who believes in Christ. It is inconceivable that those who have received the Spirit will never know any of the assurance so integral to His presence in the heart of every believer (Rom. 5:1, 5).

c). We have given several reasons why faith is not assurance, and reasons why faith is inseparable from assurance. *With these perspectives in mind, we are in a position to make several practical observations regarding the relationship between faith and assurance.*

1) An appreciation of the first perspective, that faith is not assurance, relieves the trembling believer of one unnecessary source of spiritual anxiety. If he is told that the essence of faith is assurance, then every time he questions his salvation, his struggles with assurance only intensify. But this source of angst is alleviated by the knowledge that faith is not assurance.

2) An understanding of the fact that faith is not assurance delivers us from the tendency of "easy-believism" to discourage any attempt to test the reality of one's profession by the presence or absence of the evidences of saving faith. To such teachers doubting one's salvation is tantamount to doubting the Word of God. But often tender souls are not so much doubting God's Word as doubting themselves. For those whose faith is spurious, such self-doubt may be the first step in the direction of genuine faith (2 Cor. 13:5).

3) The inseparability of faith and assurance also has practical relevance. If assurance is the by-product of faith, our assurance is increased by the increase of our faith. To this end: a) Begin by pleading with God to increase your faith (Mark 9:24; Luke 17:5; cf. Heb. 12:2). b) Lay hold of God's promises by faith (e.g., John 6:37; Rom. 10:13; Isa. 43:25; Ezek. 36:25). c) When you go to a promise, fix your gaze on the character of the Promiser. Abram was "strengthened in faith... being fully convinced that what He had promised He was able to perform" (Rom. 4:18-21). d) Finally, your faith and assurance will be strengthened as you act in faith. Faith is strengthened by its exercise. Abraham was "strengthened in faith"

(Rom. 4:20) through a series of tests, beginning with his departure for the land of promise (Gen. 12:1-5; Heb. 11:8-10), and culminating in the near-sacrifice of his son (Gen. 22:1-14; Heb. 11:17-19). To cultivate assurance, "walk by faith" (2 Cor. 5:7), giving practical expression to your faith by your baptism (Mark 16:16; cf. 1 Tim. 6:12), witness (1 Thess. 1:8), speech (2 Cor. 4:13), battles with temptation (Eph. 6:16; 1 Tim. 6:12), choice of Christ over the world (Heb. 11:24-27; 1 John 5:4), service (1 Thess. 1:3), persecutions (2 Thess. 1:4) and trials (1 Peter 1:7).

3. Its Glorious Completion in Christ

Full assurance may be ours "through Christ, who is both the author and finisher of our faith." Hebrews 12:1-2 urges us to run with endurance, looking unto Jesus, the "author and finisher" of our faith. The word ἀρχηγόν (*arkegon*), usually translated "author" (originator) by the more literal versions, may also be rendered "leader" or "pioneer" (RSV), thereby portraying the Savior as our "trail-blazer or pathfinder."[61] In 2:10, it is said that God made "the captain [ἀρχηγόν] of [our] salvation perfect through sufferings." Christ is the "captain" or "pioneer" who has blazed the trail to perfection through increasingly difficult tests of faith (5:7-9).

In Hebrews 12:2 Jesus is also called the *teleioten*, "perfecter," of our faith. He was "made perfect" through His sufferings (Heb. 2:10; 5:8-9), and one aspect of this perfection was His faith. His faith was tried by ever greater tests, culminating in the agonies of Gethsemane (Matt. 26:39) and the cross (Matt. 27:43, 46). His process of becoming "perfect" (Heb. 2:10) is integral to the perfection of His people, with whom He is one (v. 11). One aspect of that perfection is our faith (v. 13).

He who was perfected in faith is the perfecter of our faith. As we first "put on Christ" by faith (Gal. 3:26-27), we must continue to do so (Rom. 13:14), thereby drawing all our strength from Him (Eph. 4:15; Phil. 4:13), ever praying, "Lord, increase our faith" (Luke 17:5).

How this should encourage us to persevere in faith! There is coming a day in which He who first won our faith to Himself will at last present it "faultless before the presence of His glory with exceeding joy" (Jude 24; cf. Phil. 1:6). He who was able to gaze upon His finished work *for us* with undiminished satisfaction also will be able to inspect His work *in us* with triumphant jubilation, exclaiming, "It is finished!"

---

61. F. F. Bruce, *The Epistle to the Hebrews*, The New International Commentary on the New Testament, ed. F.F. Bruce (Grand Rapids: Wm. B. Eerdmans, 1978), 351.

CHAPTER 15

OF REPENTENCE UNTO LIFE AND SALVATION

JEREMY WALKER

1. Such of the elect as are converted at riper years, having sometime lived in the state of nature, and therein served divers lusts and pleasures, God in their effectual calling giveth them repentance unto life.[1]

2. Whereas there is none that doth good and sinneth not,[2] and the best of men may, through the power and deceitfulness of their corruption dwelling in them, with the prevalency of temptation, fall into great sins and provocations; God hath, in the covenant of grace, mercifully provided that believers so sinning and falling be renewed through repentance unto salvation.[3]

3. This saving repentance is an evangelical grace,[4] whereby a person, being by the Holy Spirit made sensible of the manifold evils of his sin, doth, by faith in Christ, humble himself for it with godly sorrow, detestation of it, and self-abhorrency,[5] praying for pardon and strength of grace, with a purpose and endeavour, by supplies of the Spirit, to walk before God unto all well-pleasing in all things.[6]

4. As repentance is to be continued through the whole course of our lives, upon the account of the body of death, and the motions thereof, so it is every man's duty to repent of his particular known sins particularly.[7]

5. Such is the provision which God hath made through Christ in the covenant of grace for the preservation of believers unto salvation; that

---

1. Titus 3:2-5
2. Ecclesiastes 7:20
3. Luke 22:31, 32
4. Zechariah 12:10; Acts 11:18
5. Ezekiel 36:31; 2 Corinthians 7:11
6. Psalms 119:6; Psalms 119:128
7. Luke 19:8; 1 Timothy 1:13, 15

although there is no sin so small but it deserves damnation;[8] yet there is no sin so great that it shall bring damnation on them that repent;[9] which makes the constant preaching of repentance necessary.

The place of the chapter on repentance in the sequence of the Confession should be noted. In the overarching sequence it follows on from the saving acts of God, stepping on from His sovereign and merciful deeds to the responses and engagements of those who are the recipients of His effectual call and its consequences. It also follows immediately upon the section which deals with saving faith. Professor John Murray says that "repentance is the twin sister of faith—we cannot think of one without the other, and so repentance would be conjoined with faith [in the order of salvation]. Conversion is simply another name for repentance and faith conjoined and would therefore be enclosed in repentance and faith."[10] Faith and repentance can be distinguished, but cannot be divided, and no one should attempt to do so; true faith is always bathed in—suffused with—true repentance. Christ saves through faith, and we should not give that place to repentance. Nevertheless, a faith that knows nothing of sorrow for sin, with a yearning for holiness and increasingly complete obedience to the will of God in Christ, is not a saving faith. It is, therefore, both proper and helpful to have faith and repentance standing together in the Confession.

It is worth noting that, although we often like to divide up sins into categories or degrees, the repentance dealt with here is repentance for any and all sin. While it is true that there are some particularly vile, scandalous, distasteful, or great sins (1 Cor. 5:1), and that some people can be accounted great sinners, no sin in itself is small (Rom. 3:23). Each sin requires covering with the blood of Jesus Christ. Every sin is grievous, an offense against God's holy law, and to stumble in one point is to be guilty of all (James 2:10). The repentance required of sinners is repentance for sin generally and particularly, and we should continue with that in mind. Every sin is damnable: a single sin not dealt with would be sufficient to take us to hell.[11]

As we consider this topic, we should be clear that repentance is not virtuous in and of itself. Repentance does not merit God's favor or oblige Him to pardon: repentance is not the effective cause of God pardoning our sins. Repentance itself is not a satisfaction for sin: that is the work of Christ alone. While this might seem to be splitting hairs, it is vital that we do not fall into the error of attributing to sinful man what belongs to God and Christ, His Messiah. To rely upon our repentance as in any way entitling us to, or meriting, God's favor would be to take the glory from Christ, and to make our salvation depend upon a good work. It is true to

---

8.   Romans 6:23

9.   Isaiah 1:16-18; Isaiah 55:7

10. John Murray, *Redemption Accomplished and Applied* (Edinburgh: Banner of Truth, 1961), 87.

11.   See the consideration of paragraph five below for more on these issues.

say that even our repentance is marred by sin. Not one of us truly realizes the gravity and awfulness of our sin. That failure dishonors God. If we saw our iniquity the way that the all-holy God perceives it, we would be utterly crushed. Though the Holy Spirit might be pleased to make a man "sensible of the manifold evils of his sin" (paragraph 3), we fall short of the glory of God even in realizing what an offense sin is in itself when compared with His holiness and majesty.

Early in the life of the church of Christ, not long after the time of the apostles, some began to make the mistake of replacing the concept of "repenting" in the biblical sense with the idea of "doing penance." These concepts are not the same. To "do penance" implies that we can somehow atone for our own sins, that there are works that we can do to make up for or counterbalance our sinfulness and sins. But true repentance is not a system of weights and balances whereby we can somehow atone, by ourselves and in our own right, for an equal and opposite weight of sin. Our repentance is *not* the ground upon which we rest for the satisfaction of divine justice. Some—the Roman Catholic Church, for example, as well as others—make penance a virtue by means of which God's favor is merited by man. This is not at all the biblical doctrine of repentance unto life. Salvation is not of works—not even of works that are good in themselves—lest any man should have grounds for boasting (Eph. 2:8-9). Such an attitude would make repentance an enemy of faith, rather than its twin grace. Repentance is a grace given by God.

Having said that, as we shall soon see, no man is saved unless he repents. True repentance is necessary before God will pardon our sins because such sorrow for sin and turning from sin is the response of the regenerate heart. When God, in sovereign mercy, creates the heart of man anew, the Spirit of God invariably works both faith and repentance in the heart of that man. So, although we are saved through faith in Christ's glorious person and finished work and not because of repentance as the effective cause of our salvation, we are not saved apart from both faith in Christ and repentance unto life.

The two opening paragraphs of this chapter situate the treatment of this topic within the Confession, tying in repentance unto life (alongside saving faith) with effectual calling and the covenant of grace (see Chapter 7 of the Confession). The paragraphs contain incidental counsels and exhortations of warning and encouragement concerning repentance, before the authors go on to deal with the nature of repentance itself. We must avoid possible misinterpretations of these two paragraphs, making sure that we understand repentance in the light of the whole counsel of God, and the summary here in the Confession of Faith.

Paragraph 1

Such of the elect as are converted at riper years, having sometime lived in the state of nature, and therein served divers lusts and pleasures, God in their effectual calling giveth them repentance unto life.

The first paragraph does *not* mean that only old sinners who have lived for many years in gross or scandalous sins (such as those indicated in Titus 3:3) need to repent, nor that you need to be a gross sinner in order to be sorry for sin. We are all sinning sinners. All people are sinners by nature and by deed, and all need to repent of their sins. Neither should we imagine that it is a pleasant, good, or helpful thing to have lived a life full of gross sin before repenting; instead, we should consider that it was our sin that took Christ to the cross. Some people seem to think that you need a record of extravagant sin in order really to know and feel yourself sinful, but this is far from the case. The least sin appears abhorrent to the scripturally-trained conscience under the influence of God's Spirit.

The second paragraph is *not* a warrant or license for the people of God to sin, or go on sinning, because God has provided a remedy. Paul thought that the idea of continuing in sin that grace might abound to be repulsive and spoke against it in the strongest terms in Romans 6:1-14. Neither does it mean that a Christian no longer needs to bother repenting of sin, as is made quite clear.

Rather, these paragraphs might be read as counsels of warning, instruction and encouragement to particular types or kinds of people. The emphasis of the first paragraph falls on the fact that sinners are granted repentance in connection with their effectual calling (see Chapter 10, "Of Effectual Calling"). It is a function of gracious divine power. Writing to Titus, Paul reminds him that "we ourselves were also once foolish, disobedient, deceived, serving various lusts and pleasures, living in malice and envy, hateful and hating one another. But when the kindness and the love of God our Savior toward man appeared, not by works of righteousness which we have done, but according to His mercy He saved us, through the washing of regeneration and renewing of the Holy Spirit" (Titus 3:3-5).

Many men and women have spent many years of their life dead in trespasses and sins (sometimes terrible and vile sins) before being converted. Examples include Manasseh, the king of Judah who went so far as to sacrifice his children to idols, but who repented and believed after God took him into exile (2 Chron. 33:1-20); the apostle Paul, the violently arrogant blasphemer who persecuted the church of Jesus Christ until the risen Lord confronted him on the road to Damascus, saving him as a pattern of divine patience and mercy (Acts 9:1-9; 1 Tim. 1:12-16); and the Philippian jailer, who was about to commit suicide at the prospect of his prisoners having escaped, but was prevented from doing so by Paul, who preached to him salvation in Christ, after which he believed, rejoicing (Acts 16:25-34).

The encouragement of this paragraph lies in the fact that those who have been spiritually dead in trespasses and sins for many years— including the most heinous transgression and appalling iniquity—are not beyond the saving power of God in Christ. Paul was saved as a very pattern of divine longsuffering (1 Tim. 1:16): old sinners, seemingly set in their sinful ways, can and should be preached to, warned, and exhorted to flee from the wrath to come, in the confidence that God can and will call them, and that Christ is willing and able to save all who come to Him for salvation. The instruction of this paragraph lies in the implication that, though such of the elect as are saved after a long life of wickedness are granted repentance unto life, not all of the elect are converted after long years of ungodliness. A child raised in a Christian home might early experience the light of salvation dawning like the day, rather than flashing like lightning upon their soul in later years. Someone may sit under preaching for a long time and come slowly to a saving knowledge of Christ; others might hear one sermon and be immediately converted. A crisis experience (like the exile of Manasseh, or the earthquake that awoke the Philippian jailer to his need of salvation, or similar to Christ's direct confrontation with Saul) might be a *legitimate* part, but is not a *necessary* part of any man's salvation. We should not demand it either of ourselves or of others. Some who are drawn gradually to faith in Christ might agonize over their lack of such a rapid and distinctive experience of salvation, though they should not be building their hopes upon any felt experience in themselves, but rather upon the Christ of salvation. On the other hand, we observe that not everyone who experiences some sort of deep emotional or spiritual crisis (even one that issues in a profession of faith) is necessarily saved. There are other indications of new life in Christ that *must* go alongside any such experience. The issue is one of God's effectual call by His Word and Spirit out of death and into life. All to whom that experience occurs receive the grant of repentance.

Paragraph 2

Whereas there is none that doth good and sinneth not, and the best of men may, through the power and deceitfulness of their corruption dwelling in them, with the prevalency of temptation, fall into great sins and provocations; God hath, in the covenant of grace, mercifully provided that believers so sinning and falling be renewed through repentance unto salvation.

Paragraph two further situates the provision of repentance within the covenant of grace. This language was first introduced in the seventh chapter of the Confession, concerning God's covenant. There it was used to identify the free and sovereign determination of God to save His people from their sins in accordance with His most holy, wise, and good purposes. The same language is found in the second paragraph of Chapter 14 on saving faith, where it has precisely the same connection. Believing and repenting are mercies found within the provisions of God's gracious covenant with His people, and cannot be understood or experienced outside of the provisions of that covenant.

The second paragraph contains a warning and an encouragement for believers falling into sin. The authors probably had in mind two biblical examples. First, that of David, who committed adultery with Bathsheba, but repented of his sin (2 Sam. 11:11-12:15; Ps. 51). Second, that of Peter who denied the Lord Jesus three times, even with cursing, but was pierced to his soul by Christ's look, wept bitterly in true repentance, and was subsequently restored by our Lord (John 13:36-38; 18:15-27 cf. Luke 22:54-62; John 21:15-19). We are reminded here that "the best of men are men at best': every person sins and has sinned, even the best and most sanctified of men (Prov. 20:9; Eccl. 7:20), except Christ. Sin no longer *reigns* in the Christian because the power of sin is broken (Rom. 6:11, 17-18); but sin does *remain* in the Christian, and temptation stirs up that sin and it breaks forth in thought, word, and deed (James 1:13-15). This is what happened with both David and Peter, who were redeemed men. Observe, too, that though David and Peter sinned awfully (adultery and murder in the former, and the denial of the Lord Jesus in the latter), the principles of repentance taught here are true for *every* believer regarding *any* sin.

This is not told us so that we can relax about the prospect of falling into sin. Rather, there is an encouragement to the penitent saint who grieves over sin (sometimes truly grievous sin): God has mercifully provided in the covenant of grace that believers who sin might be renewed through repentance unto salvation. The new covenant in Christ is an everlasting covenant, in which the Almighty so puts His fear into the hearts of His people that they will not depart from Him (Jer. 32:40). Our Lord Himself prayed for Peter, that his faith should not fail (Luke 22:31-32). But notice that the sinning and falling saint is renewed *through repentance unto salvation:* this is the only path back.

While there is encouragement for the believer who truly repents over sin, there is a fearful warning for those who simply become dull to sin, or who sin and resist all the means that God has provided for their restoration. This is not preservation of the saints regardless of their activity; it is preservation by means of perseverance. A man who goes on in sin without repentance calls into question his profession. It does not matter what he has been in the past: the mark of a true saint under such circumstances is renewed and ongoing repentance for sin, joined with faith in Christ. Then, and only then, can there be any confidence of God's favour (1 John 1:9–2:2). Someone who goes on in sin without such repentance calls into question the genuineness of his or her profession of faith. Observe, too, that no believer is bound to fall into some great and public sin; it is not inevitable. Many believers go through life without committing such sins (and every believer will desire and aim to live without such sin breaking out). Great sins and great repentance are not required to validate Christian experience. True repentance is repentance, regardless of the sin or sins over which someone grieves.

Paragraph 3

This saving repentance is an evangelical grace, whereby a person, being by the Holy Spirit made sensible of the manifold evils of his sin, doth, by faith in Christ, humble himself for it with godly sorrow, detestation of it, and self-abhorrency, praying for pardon and strength of grace, with a

*purpose and endeavour, by supplies of the Spirit, to walk before God unto
all well-pleasing in all things.*

The Confession goes on in the third paragraph to deal more particularly
with what repentance is, and with its place, practice, and relative
priority in the life of the child of God. First of all, "saving repentance
is an evangelical grace." This language simply means a grace genuinely
connected with the gospel and God's power revealed in it. The Confession
connects it with "the Spirit of grace and supplication" poured out on
those who look on the Pierced One of Zechariah 12:10, emphasizing the
divine grant of repentance (Acts 11:18).

This also implies that there is a repentance that is not saving, that is,
something that appears to be or might be called repentance, but which
has no connection with the power of the gospel, is not joined to faith,
and does not issue in salvation. We see such false or empty "repentance"
in the lives of men like King Ahab, who humbled himself before God so
that the punishment for his wickedness was postponed, but was never
a man of faith, and never tasted salvation (1 Kings 21:17-29). We see it
in Judas Iscariot, who was filled with remorse because of his betrayal
of Christ, but who hanged himself (Matt. 27:3-5), and was called "the
son of perdition" (John 17:12). Such false repentance may involve grief
and remorse, a desire to avoid the consequences of sin, a terror of hell,
and even outward reformation of life. However, if it does not involve a
hatred of sin as offensive and odious to the righteous God of heaven and
earth, it is lacking something necessary. Furthermore, true repentance
involves more than merely a true recognition of sin; it also involves an
apprehension (a real appreciation and grasp) of the mercy of God in
Christ.

Saving repentance, then, grows in gospel soil: it is an evangelical
grace. It is not just a natural terror stirred up by the law. It is not a
merely human response caused by fear of retributive justice to which
the Almighty God is obliged to respond. Rather, it is the gift of God,
a product of gospel grace. It is something worked by the sovereign
God in the heart of the regenerate man (Acts 5:31; 11:18). Although true
repentance does not consist *solely* in a sense of sin, we must realize that
a true sense of sin is a fundamental part of true repentance. Such a sense
of sin is something worked in a man by God's Holy Spirit, who opens
his spiritual eyes (1 Cor. 2:14) to understand something of the horror of
transgressing God's law. Older writers spoke of "the sinfulness of sin,"
calling sin "the plague of plagues"[12] and "the evil of evils,"[13] in an attempt
to communicate something of how foul a thing is sin. When a person
is "made sensible of the manifold evil of his sins" (when he knows and
feels the profound and varied evil of his own sins), he has more than
merely an intellectual grasp of what sin is, and what its consequences
are. To understand something of what a man feels like when he sees his

12. Ralph Venning, *The Sinfulness of Sin* (Edinburgh: Banner of Truth, 1993).
13. Jeremiah Burroughs, *The Evil of Evils* (Philadelphia: Soli Deo Gloria, 1992).

sin, look at the biblical examples: David's groaning over his iniquity (Ps. 51); the psalmist's appreciation of his vileness and guilt (Ps. 130:1-3); Job's sense of the abhorrence of his sin before God (Job 42:5-6); the sense of unworthiness of the prodigal son (Luke 15:18-19); the deeply wounded hearts of the men of Jerusalem when Peter's sermon was used to convince them that they had crucified Jesus, whom God had made both Lord and Christ (Acts 2:36-38).

To be sure, different people might respond differently, according to their God-given character or temperament, or the usual indications of grief in their culture. Some might be evidently full of outward weeping and groaning; others might have a less evident but no less real sense of these things. We should also say (see below) that some believers might arrive at a greater sense of their sin after conversion than before. However, something of this "godly sorrow, detestation of [sin], and self-abhorrency" will be true for every truly repentant person, however it is manifested.

But alongside the grieving sinner's sense of sin, and arising out of it, is a casting of oneself, in faith, upon God for mercy. Here, again, is that intimate and necessary connection with faith. Observe that in most, if not all, of the examples above, there is also an explicit or implicit conviction that there is forgiveness with God (Ps. 130:4). David's confession in Psalm 51 is a cry for mercy to the very God whom he has offended, and who alone is able to deal with his sin! The psalmist calls upon God's people to hope in Him because there is mercy and abundant redemption with Him (Ps. 130:7-8). Job abhors himself and repents because he has seen the might and mercy of God.

The prodigal son, convinced of his unworthiness, nevertheless casts himself upon the forgiving love of his father. Peter's congregation, cut to the heart, nevertheless ask "What shall we do?" and Peter calls on them to repent. God hates sin, but a sense of sin should not drive us *from* God, but *to* God, through faith in Christ. This is because the God whom we have offended extends mercy to us in the gospel, and it is He alone who has devised a remedy for our sins in the death of Jesus Christ, His Son. Satan often twists our guilt to make us feel that we cannot approach God, but true repentance contains this comprehension of the mercy of God in Christ which carries us to the gracious Lord to be cleansed of our transgressions and washed thoroughly from our sins. True repentance therefore involves a crying out to God in faith for pardon of sins, on the basis of His promises in Christ Jesus.

The heart of repentance is a turning from sin to God. It is more than simply being sorry for our sins. It is a fundamental and radical change of perspective, feeling, and desire (involving the intellect, emotions, and will). Our perspectives on God, ourselves, sin, and righteousness undergo a radical transformation from what was perverse and flawed to what is right and true. The repentant person turns *from* sin with grief and sorrow over sin, and hatred for it, because it offends a holy God. He turns *to* a merciful God with a heart that desires to walk no longer in the paths of sin, but to be found in the ways of righteousness, and to walk in holiness in dependence upon the Spirit of God (Phil. 2:12-13). This is why alongside "praying for pardon" goes praying for "strength of grace."

The repenting sinner who has a true sense of sin appreciates his or her own weakness and inability to walk pleasing to God by natural strength and gift. He mourns over every manifestation of sin, crying out wholeheartedly for deliverance (Rom. 7:24). He cries to "the Spirit of grace and supplication" (Zech. 12:10) to grant the grace and strength to walk in the newness of life to which he has been delivered and to work out salvation by God's strength and grace. In prayerful dependence on the Spirit of God, he undertakes to put off the old man with his deeds and to put on the new man, who is renewed in knowledge according to the image of the Lord who created him new (Col. 3:9-10). We cannot "walk before God unto all well-pleasing in all things" without the grace of God enabling us to do so. This heartfelt pursuit of obedience is always joined with the heartfelt renunciation of sin.

We see all this worked out in the Thessalonian Christians, who had turned to God from idols to serve the living and true God (1 Thess. 1:9): it was a complete reversal of attitude and lifestyle (Ps. 119:59, 128); theirs was a true repentance. Note that the prodigal son of Luke 15 did more than become convinced of the vileness of his sin; he did more than recognize his father's mercy. Having come to his spiritual senses, he got up, returned to his father, and placed himself back under his father's loving care and rule. The law of the Lord is now written on the heart of the believing and repenting disciple (Ps. 119:6).

Paragraph 4

As repentance is to be continued through the whole course of our lives, upon the account of the body of death, and the motions thereof, so it is every man's duty to repent of his particular known sins particularly.

The Confession goes on in paragraph four to speak of the ongoing nature of this repentant life as that which is to continue through "the whole course of our lives." Again, we must not imagine that in order to remain justified we must keep repenting of our sins, as if every time we sin or think of a sin not confessed and repented of, we lose our justification. Justification is a once-for-all declaration concerning the believer by Almighty God. The faith, which He gives, receives and rests on Christ and is the sole instrument of this justification. Nevertheless, while it is true that we are justified once and once-for-all, the work of repentance in a believer's life does not end with his justification, but is also a part of his sanctification (see Chapter 11, "Of Justification," especially paragraph five of that chapter).

The reason that the authors give for this ongoing repentance is "the body of death, and the motions thereof." In other words, although we have been redeemed from sin and death and hell—although the reign or dominion of sin in the Christian has been ended—there is sin remaining in the Christian which needs to be mourned over and mortified. We still have inclinations towards sin and towards actions which are sinful. Repentance, therefore, is a lifelong task. The Christian is a saved sinner who is a new creation in Christ, one who has put off the old man and put on the new. However, the habits of the old man still need to be put to death and the habits of the new creature cultivated and protected. Grievously, there is remaining sin, and will be until either the believer dies and his soul is made perfect, or until Christ returns and glorifies the saints at the resurrection.

On the one hand, the Confession seeks to steer us clear of self-deception: there must be an ongoing forsaking of sin in the life of a true saint of God. Someone who is consistently unwilling to acknowledge, confess, and forsake sin shows few indications of walking in newness of life (Mark 1:4-5; Ps. 51:1-4; Matt. 3:8; 1 Thess. 1:9-10). On the other hand, we are steered away from unbiblical and unreasonable expectations of perfection in this life. Forsaking sin is not the same as perfect obedience: it is the pursuit of and desire after full obedience, out of love for God with all one's heart and mind and soul and strength, with repentance over our failings and shortcomings.

A wise Christian once said, "There's nobody perfect—that's the believer's bed of thorns; that's the hypocrite's couch of ease."[14] The Christian is not perfect, but would be if he could, and mourns over his imperfections. Hypocrites do not care about full and heartfelt obedience. A Christian is concerned not to sin at all, rather than not to sin too much.

Observe also that the authors bring their exposition of God's Word right to the heart of the individual. Repentance is much more than a general change of mind or a vague awareness of sin. It is relatively easy to assault sin generally, to speak with fervor against sins in the plural, but true repentance deals with particular, individual, specific sins. Charles Hodge writes that "no man has any right to presume that he hates sin in general unless he practically hates every sin in particular; and no man has any right to presume that he is sorry for and ready to renounce his sins in general unless he is conscious of practically renouncing and grieving for each particular sin into which he falls."[15]

True repentance, then, involves dealing not simply with sin in general, but with *our* sins in particular. Most of us have what might be called "constitutional sins." These are sins which, in their form, occasion, regularity, or manifestation, are peculiar temptations to ourselves, and to which we might be particularly prone. In some, it might be envy; for others, covetousness; others struggle with sexual lust; and some struggle with gluttony. The list could go on and on. For most of us, it is likely to be several such sins. Our Bible is particular about sin: it does not allow vague

14. John M. Brentnall (ed.), *"Just A Talker": Sayings of John ("Rabbi") Duncan* (Edinburgh: Banner of Truth, 1997), 129.

15. Charles Hodge, *The Westminster Confession: A Commentary* (Edinburgh: Banner of Truth, 2002), 216.

concepts of sin to float around "out there." Sin is brought to bear upon our individual consciences with regard to its particular manifestations in us. Before their conversion, the Thessalonian believers had been well-known for their idolatry. Their repentance was demonstrated in their turning *to* God *from* idols. The evidence of their alienation from God was idolatry, and the specific sphere of their repentance was in turning from that specific sin (1 Thess. 1:9-10). So it must be with us at the beginning of our Christian life and as we go through it. Though truly redeemed, we engage in a battle with sin and must identify, repent of, and mortify the particular sins to which we are particularly prone, naming them and seeking God's grace to fight free of them and kill them.

Here, then, is a forsaking of sin that is both comprehensive and specific, particular and ongoing. Repentance is a turning from all known sin generally and every known sin particularly, with faith in Christ for mercy from God. Every Bible-minded Christian knows the reality of this ongoing battle. The redeemed person sets out to be well-pleasing to God in all things, but soon discovers much with which God is not pleased: old sins are recalled; new sins come to light. New circumstances create new temptations, and new spiritual awareness and insight reveals not just the breadth of sin but the depth of sin. An instructed conscience identifies more and more what is ungodly, and strips away our ignorance about sin (Ps. 19:12-13). Repentance is a continual, daily experience for the God-aware, sin-hating, Christ-centered Christian.

There may be incidents that call forth or demand particular and focused acts of repentance. This might be the old sinner who comes to a recognition of his lifelong wickedness, or the believer who falls into particularly grievous sin. Or, it may be the Christian who is reforming in his faith and life and comes to see that there is some area of his doctrine or lifestyle that has been largely untouched by Scripture, or a particular demand for repentance on the part of a church or nation. However, repentance is not a one-off or temporary experience (see 1 John 1:9, in which the language implies an ongoing and constant work). Christian experience holds a biblical hatred of sin alongside a biblical understanding of the mercy of God in Christ. To be unaware of the horror and just punishment of sin that is not dealt with is delusional and ruinous; to be unaware of the glorious mercy of God held out to the repentant sinner is crushing and destructive. Awareness of divine punishment and divine mercy must go hand in hand. Sadness and sorrow arise out of our convictions of sin; joy and gladness arise out of our thankfulness for the mercy and goodness of God. Weeping endures for a night, but joy comes in the morning (Ps. 30:5), and there must be a night of repentance as well as a morning of gladness (Ps. 32:3-5).

We might summarize what we have considered so far by using the illustration of a tree. True repentance grows in the gospel soil of God's sovereign grace working in the lives of sinful men and women, effectually calling them from death to life. The roots of true repentance are this biblically-informed grief over sin on the one hand, and a biblically-informed apprehension of God's mercy in Christ on the other. The trunk and branches of true repentance are this turning from sin and turning to God. The fruit of true repentance is this pursuit of, and endeavor after, new obedience, in dependence upon the Holy Spirit.

Paragraph 5

Such is the provision which God hath made through Christ in the covenant of grace for the preservation of believers unto salvation that although there is no sin so small but it deserves damnation; yet there is no sin so great that it shall bring damnation on them that repent; which makes the constant preaching of repentance necessary.

The Confession completes its treatment of repentance with some particular and searching counsel about the necessity of preaching repentance in the light of what we know about sin. As we noted when we began, every sin is grievous, and the least sin (as men perceive it)— any single sin—is sufficient for the condemnation of any man. However, that God is willing to forgive the sins of those who come to Him in faith and repentance is the hope of the sinner, and must therefore be preached to sinners fully and freely. This is the teaching of paragraph 5 of this chapter.

Let us never underestimate sin: there is no sin so small but it deserves damnation. The wages of sin—all sin, each and every sin—is death (Rom. 6:23). In this sense, no sin should be considered small, as it brings so great a condemnation. The holy law of God is like a great and fragile object, perhaps a beautiful window or some other work of art, all made of one piece. If I make a crack in this great and fragile thing, no one accuses me of breaking only a part of it. The entire object is no longer whole. Thus it is with the law of God: to break it at all is to break it all (James 2.10). To stumble in any point is to become a lawbreaker, and therefore to be guilty and deserving of punishment.

When David cries out for forgiveness in Psalm 51, there is a comprehensiveness in his desperate request: he is concerned for sins, yes, but also with every particular sin. He wants God to cleanse him from sin in its totality and sins in their plurality. He desires a complete cleansing (for example, Ps. 51:2, 7, 9), because he knows that one sin is fatal to peace with God. All this means that when we look at any man or woman, boy or girl, we are looking at someone who is a lawbreaker, who has offended the gracious and holy God, and is therefore liable to the just and fearful punishment of that God for the transgression of His revealed will. The proper and righteous punishment is death and hell. This is the awfulness of sin in all its horrible sinfulness.

But, as we should not underestimate sin, neither should we underestimate the Christ who saves us from sin. Here is cause for great praise and thanksgiving! Such is the provision which God has made through Christ in His covenant of grace for the preservation of believers unto salvation, that there is no sin so great that it shall bring damnation on them that repent.[16] The blood of Christ is sufficient to wash away the deepest stain of iniquity—His blood can make the foulest clean. The gospel offer, the gospel provision, for repenting sinners is that those whose sins are like scarlet shall be made as white as snow through the blood of the Lamb; though our sins are red like crimson, they shall be as pure new wool (Isa. 1:18). All upon whom God has set His love are so provided for by the atoning blood of Christ in His propitiating sacrifice that each sin, all sin, and every sin can be covered, and every transgression swept away as far as the east is from the west (Ps. 103:12). Again, this is no ground for sinning with impunity, but is rather the great motivation to holiness of life and fleeing every sin.

We should also be very clear in our minds and hearts, and in our preaching, about the certainty of forgiveness where true repentance is demonstrated. As we should ourselves repent with an "apprehension of the mercy of God in Christ," so we should preach to others. God is always pleased to forgive those in whom He is working faith in Christ and repentance unto life. The one follows on from the other as night follows day: those whom God predestines and calls (a sovereign, mighty, and effectual call) are invariably justified (Rom. 8:30). God's effectual calling works newness of life, which issues in faith and repentance in the heart of man.

God is then graciously pleased to forgive and justify that man, declaring him righteous in His sight. Although repentance does not oblige God to forgive us, true repentance always issues in true forgiveness, and we should assure men that it does. We do not call on men in our preaching to know that they are regenerate before they believe and repent. We call upon them to believe in Christ and to repent of their sins. We trust that God will work His salvation in those people by His effectual call, which will be manifested in them by their faith and repentance.

To put it concisely, in order for men to be saved, they must repent and believe, and *this makes the preaching of repentance absolutely, vitally, and constantly necessary.*

Much contemporary preaching demands faith. This is right insofar as it goes, but it is not all because preachers should not demand faith *only.* We are saved by faith in Christ, yes, but Christ saves us, through faith, *from sin.* He was called Jesus (literally, Savior) because He was going to save His people *from their sins* (Matt. 1:21). If the preaching of salvation through Christ has no reference to sin, then the people to whom we preach are robbed of the whole context of sin which gives penitent faith in Christ its significance. It is easier, even pleasant, to preach faith in Christ as the only necessary response to the proclamation of gospel truth, but it is sin to which sinners are attached.

---

16. We do not have space here to deal with the unforgivable sin of blasphemy against the Holy Spirit (Matt. 12:31-32), except to say that those who commit such sin never truly repent of it: it is bound up with such hardness of heart that it does not enter this equation. Rather we should note that this same passage reminds us that, for the truly repentant sinner, "every sin and blasphemy will be forgiven." True repentance always brings forth true forgiveness from our merciful Father in heaven.

So-called "faith in Christ" that is divorced from any recognition of sin, and any turning from sin to God through faith in Christ, is not the saving faith of which the Bible speaks. To preach faith without repentance waters down the gospel demands addressed to men and women who are wedded to their sins. But to preach repentance in its proper relation to faith is not a pleasant task, and usually calls forth the anger and hatred of sinful men (although some may later repent), and it can therefore be tempting to avoid preaching in this way. Nevertheless, it is necessary for the gospel preacher to preach repentance in its proper relation to faith. If you do not marry faith and repentance in your preaching, you will never see men divorced from their sins. Men might make all manner of accusations, and charge the preacher with "legalistic preaching," or of not preaching the gospel, but repentance unto life is an evangelical grace (paragraph 3), and calls to such repentance must therefore be an indispensable element of evangelical preaching (paragraph 5). There is no hope for pardon without repentance of sin, and to fail to preach the necessity of repentance is, to some extent, to abandon the souls of those to whom we preach and to bring condemnation upon ourselves (Ezek. 3:18-19).

The Old Testament men of God called upon their hearers to repent of their sins, turning to God in faith and with repentance, and practiced such repentance themselves (see Isa. 6:5 and 55:7; Joel 2:12-13; Ezek. 1:28 and 33:11; Job 42:5-6; Jer. 3:12-13; 8:6). We find precisely the same pattern and language in the servants of God in the New Testament, pre-eminently in Jesus Christ Himself, the great Servant of the Most High (who Himself needed to repent of no sins, being perfect in obedience). The opening note of Christ's preaching ministry was repentance (Matt. 4:17; Mark 1:15). It was a constant theme in our Lord's public teaching and in His own understanding of His mission (Luke 5:32; 13:3, 5; 15:7, 10). It was the note sounded by His forerunner, John the Baptist (Matt. 3:2, 8, 11; Mark 1:4; Luke 3:3, 8; Acts 13:24; 19:4). It was the command that the Christ issued to His disciples (Luke 24:46-47; Acts 26:16-18); it was a command that they obeyed, from their first public ministry (Mark 6:12) to their ongoing efforts to spread the gospel of God abroad (Peter in Acts 2:38; 3:19; 8:22; Paul in Acts 17:30; 20:21; 26:20). The writer to the Hebrews puts "repentance from dead works" alongside "faith toward God" as part of the foundation of the truth as it is in Jesus (Heb. 6:1).

The nature of the gospel ministry itself, the requirement for obedience to the command and example of Christ, and the absolute necessity of true repentance, alongside faith, for the salvation of lost sinners all demand that we preach a full-orbed and biblical gospel. That means that repentance must be preached. The apostle Peter said that God has exalted Christ to His right hand as Prince and Savior to give repentance to Israel and forgiveness of sins (Acts 5:31). The present heavenly ministry of our Lord involves His giving of repentance unto the forgiveness of sins.

Therefore, if we would be well-pleasing to God as we undertake the awesome privilege of laboring together with Him (2 Cor. 5:9-11;

6:1), if we would be faithful ambassadors of Christ in our ministry of reconciliation (2 Cor. 5:18-21), then our pleading with men must include the gospel demand for repentance from their sins. It is necessary for the unconverted, as an indispensable element in their initial experience of salvation; it is necessary for the converted, as an indispensable element in their ongoing experience of salvation.

As faith is not a momentary experience of dependence, but a constant and ongoing attitude of trust and confidence toward Christ, so repentance is not a momentary experience of sorrow, but a constant and ongoing activity, a heartfelt contrition over our sinfulness and our sins. God does not despise the broken spirit, the broken and the contrite heart (Ps. 51:17). This is a picture of the attitude of the faithful follower of the Lord Jesus.

A Christian cannot look at the cross of Christ, and the awful blood-price paid for our deliverance from sin, without grief over the sin that took Christ to the cross and demanded of Him the full price of forsakenness from God. Christ's blood pours out as an overflowing and ever flowing fountain for the cleansing of sin and uncleanness (Zech. 13:1), one to which the believer goes repeatedly and continually. The cross is where repentance begins, and the cross is where repentance continues.

The principled pursuit of holiness, the life of heart obedience to all the revealed will of God as a bondservant of Jesus Christ, is a life of unparalleled peace through the mercy of God. This life has within it as a foundational element that true gospel repentance, whereby a sinner, out of a true sense of his sin and apprehension of the mercy of God in Christ, does, with grief over and hatred of his sin, turn from that sin to God with full purpose of and endeavor after new obedience.

CHAPTER 16

OF GOOD WORKS

JEFFERY SMITH AND GARY HENDRIX

1. Good works are only such as God hath commanded in His Holy Word,[1] and not such as without the warrant thereof are devised by men out of blind zeal, or upon any pretence of good intentions.[2]

2. These good works, done in obedience to God's commandments, are the fruits and evidences of a true and lively faith;[3] and by them believers manifest their thankfulness,[4] strengthen their assurance,[5] edify their brethren, adorn the profession of the gospel,[6] stop the mouths of the adversaries, and glorify God,[7] whose workmanship they are, created in Christ Jesus thereunto,[8] that having their fruit unto holiness they may have the end eternal life.[9]

3. Their ability to do good works is not at all of themselves, but wholly from the Spirit of Christ;[10] and that they may be enabled thereunto, besides the graces they have already received, there is necessary an actual influence of the same Holy Spirit, to work in them to will and to do of His good pleasure;[11] yet they are not hereupon to grow negligent, as if they were not bound to perform any duty, unless upon a special motion of the Spirit, but they ought to be diligent in stirring up the grace of God that is in them.[12]

---

1. Micah 6:8; Hebrews 13:21
2. Matthew 15:9; Isaiah 29:13
3. James 2:18, 22
4. Psalm 116:12-13
5. 1 John 2:3, 5; 2 Peter 1:5-11
6. Matthew 5:16
7. 1 Timothy 6:1; 1 Peter 2:15; Philippians 1:11
8. Ephesians 2:10
9. Romans 6:22
10. John 15:4-5
11. 2 Corinthians 3:5; Philippians 2:13
12. Philippians 2:12; Hebrews 6:11, 12; Isaiah 64:7

4. They who, in their obedience attain to the greatest height which is possible in this life, are so far from being able to supererogate, and to do more than God requires, as that they fall short of much which in duty they are bound to do.[13]

5. We cannot by our best works merit pardon of sin or eternal life at the hand of God, by reason of the great disproportion that is between them and the glory to come, and the infinite distance that is between us and God, whom by them we can neither profit nor satisfy for the debt of our former sins;[14] but when we have done all we can, we have done but our duty, and are unprofitable servants; and because as they are good they proceed from his Spirit,[15] and as they are wrought by us they are defiled and mixed with so much weakness and imperfection, that they cannot endure the severity of God's punishment.[16]

6. Yet notwithstanding the persons of believers being accepted through Christ, their good works also are accepted in him;[17] not as though they were in this life wholly unblameable and unreprovable in God's sight, but that He, looking upon them in His Son, is pleased to accept and reward that which is sincere, although accompanied with many weaknesses and imperfections.[18]

7. Works done by unregenerate men, although for the matter of them they may be things which God commands, and of good use both to themselves and others;[19] yet because they proceed not from a heart purified by faith,[20] nor are done in a right manner according to the word,[21] nor to a right end, the glory of God,[22] they are therefore sinful, and cannot please God, nor make a man meet to receive grace from God,[23] and yet their neglect of them is more sinful and displeasing to God.[24]

Introduction
This chapter of the Confession addresses the crucial topic of good works which accompany true salvation. Before this, the Confession spoke about the blessings of salvation given to us by God in our effectual calling

13. Job 9:2, 3; Galatians 5:17; Luke 17:10
14. Romans 3:20; Ephesians 2:8, 9; Romans 4:6
15. Galatians 5:22-23
16. Isaiah 64:6; Psalm 143:2
17. Ephesians 1:6; 1 Peter 2:5
18. Matthew 25:21, 23; Hebrews 6:10
19. 2 Kings 10:30; 1 Kings 21:27, 29
20. Genesis 4:5; Hebrews 11:4, 6
21. 1 Corinthians 13:1
22. Matthew 6:2, 5
23. Amos 5:21, 22; Romans 9:16; Titus 3:5
24. Job 21:14, 15; Matthew 25:41-43

(Chapter 10), our justification (Chapter 11), our adoption (Chapter 12), and in our sanctification (Chapter 13). Then we are told about the graces exercised by us in salvation, which are faith (Chapter 14), repentance (Chapter 15), good works (Chapter 16), and perseverance (Chapter 17). Lastly, the Confession treats the assurance that we are meant to enjoy in salvation (Chapter 18).

Good works are the fruit of effectual calling, justification, adoption, and sanctification, and they proceed from true faith in Christ and repentance from sin. You will notice that this is a long chapter. This should not surprise us because this matter of good works and its relationship to salvation has often been a controversial subject in church history.[25] This was particularly the case during the Reformation. Consequently, a great deal of attention is given to this subject. The seven paragraphs of this chapter can be divided under the following headings:[26]

Paragraph 1: The Identity of Good Works
Paragraph 2: The Importance of Good Works
Paragraph 3: The Cause of Good Works
Paragraph 4-5: The Limitations of Good Works
Paragraph 6-7: The Acceptance of Good Works

The Identity of Good Works

What determines whether a work is good? How are good works identified, and what is the standard by which they are defined? The Confession answers these questions in paragraph 1 with both a positive and a negative answer. Notice it says, positively, that "good works are only such as God has commanded in His Holy Word." Negatively, it says, "and not such as, without the warrant thereof, are devised by men out of blind zeal, or upon any pretence of good intentions."

The Positive:
"Good works are only such as God has commanded in His Holy Word." *Good,* according to the Greek words chosen by the Holy Spirit in the New Testament, speaks primarily of that which is beneficial, valuable, and morally beautiful. God, who alone is good (Mark 10:18), has shown us what is good. He has shown us this in His Holy Word. Only God knows what is truly good, and only God can show us what is good. In the Bible, God tells us all we need to know in order to identify and be equipped for every good work. Second Timothy 3:16, 17 says that "All Scripture is given by inspiration of God, and is profitable for doctrine, for reproof, for correction, for instruction in righteousness, that the man of God may be complete, thoroughly equipped for every good work." Moreover, Micah

---

25. R. C. Sproul, *Truths We Confess: A Systematic Exposition of the Westminster Confession of Faith* (Sanford, FL: Reformation Trust Publishing, 2019), 355.

26. This outline borrows from that of Sam Waldron in *A Modern Exposition of the 1689 Baptist Confession of Faith,* 5th Edition: Revised and Corrected (Darlington Co. Durham, UK: Evangelical Press, 2016), 246.

6:8 says, "He has shown you, O man, what is good; and what does the Lord require of you but to do justly, to love mercy, and to walk humbly with your God."

Careful attention must be given to the context in which we find the word *good* in Scripture. Additionally, it should be noted that the Confession uses the term *good* at times as a synonym for right or righteous. Such is the case when reference is made to actions that conform to the law of God or the Word of God. In general, then, we can say that good works are those works that conform to the law of God as revealed in Scripture.[27]

The Negative:

"And not such as without the warrant thereof (that is, without the warrant of Scripture) are devised by men out of blind zeal, or upon any pretence of good intentions."[28] Here, the Confession underscores an important truth, that works finding no warrant in Scripture are not in the category of what are called good works, even if they are done from zeal for God, or even good intentions. If there is no warrant in Scripture for them, then they are not truly good works in the eyes of God. In speaking to the Scribes and Pharisees of His day, Jesus confronted this issue by quoting from Isaiah 29:13 and said this about them in Matthew 15:9: "in vain they worship Me, teaching as doctrines the commandments of men." Our Lord's point was that these religious leaders elevated the commandments of men to the level of God's Word, and they expected people to obey these man-made rules as if they were good works, works that were required by God and pleasing to Him.

Further, in Colossians 2:21-23, Paul referred to a kind of asceticism that required one to subject oneself to various regulations abstaining from this or from that, "according to the commandments and doctrines of men." He said, "These things indeed have an appearance of wisdom in self-imposed religion, false humility and neglect of the body, but are of no value against the indulgence of the flesh." They are the commandments and doctrines of men which find no warrant in Holy Scripture.

Such man-made rules and practices are attempts to make oneself right before God or to commend oneself to God. Again, this was common among the Jews in Jesus' day so that, for example, going through a particular ritual of washing one's hands before eating was considered a good work (Matt. 15:2). Of course, there is nothing wrong with washing our hands. It is good, in one sense, but the Jews had wrongly elevated human rules such as this to the status of a command of God, a good work required by God and to be done in order to please Him. The Scribes and Pharisees had many requirements like this, as many people do today.

A primary concern in this chapter of the Confession is related to the Roman Catholic view of justification. The Council of Trent (1545–1563) was Roman Catholicism's response to the Protestant Reformation. The

27. Waldron, 247.
28. Italics ours.

Council formulated a rather comprehensive statement on the doctrine of justification. Part of it reads as follows:

> CANON XX. If any one saith, that the man who is justified and how perfect soever, is not bound to observe the commandments of God and of the Church, but only to believe; as if indeed the Gospel were a bare and absolute promise of eternal life, without the condition of observing the commandments; let him be anathema.

> CANON XXIV. If any one saith, that the justice received is not preserved and also increased before God through good works; but that the said works are merely the fruits and signs of Justification obtained, but not a cause of the increase thereof; let him be anathema.

> CANON XXXII. If any one saith, that the good works of one that is justified are in such manner the gifts of God, as that they are not also the good merits of him that is justified; or, that the said justified, by the good works which he performs through the grace of God and the merit of Jesus Christ, whose living member he is, does not truly merit increase of grace, eternal life, and the attainment of that eternal life, if so be, however, that he depart in grace,-and also an increase of glory; let him be anathema.[29]

The Roman Catholic Church plainly states in these canons at least two doctrines which the Reformers repudiated in the strongest of terms: (1) that good works are meritorious in gaining justification and an increase of grace; and (2) that the obedience which constitutes good works must involve obedience both to the commandments of God and the Church.

The opening paragraph of this chapter declares that good works consist exclusively in compliance with what "God has commanded in his Holy word." God alone determines what is good. That which He commends as good does not originate with humans, even those humans who occupy lofty positions in recognized religion. We must go to God and, more specifically, to the Bible if we are to judge correctly between good and evil, right and wrong. Sadly, many people think that, by doing what the Church of Rome requires them to do, they will be declared not guilty before God in the final day. They think, for example, that pilgrimages to Rome, vows of celibacy, vows of poverty, acts of penance, the purchasing of indulgences, kissing the rosary, and so on, will earn them favor with God. These are all presented as *good works*. However, none of them are commanded in Scripture. Rather, they are "devised by men out of blind zeal," as the Confession puts it.

When the last phrase in paragraph 1 of this chapter speaks about "any pretence of good intentions," it should be noted that good intentions alone do not make a good deed. One can be sincere, yet be sincerely wrong. In fact, Scripture speaks of those who thought that they were doing good, but who were actually doing terrible evil. This is seen in John 16 when Jesus was preparing His disciples for the persecution they would experience. He said to them in verse 2 of that chapter concerning

---

29. http://www.thecounciloftrent.com/ch6.htm.

unbelievers that "They will put you out of the synagogue; yes; the time is coming that whoever kills you will think that he offers service to God." In other words, they will think they are pleasing God. However, it does not matter what they think or what their intentions are, what they are doing is wicked because what pleases God is not defined by us; it is only defined by His Word.

The Importance of Good Works

The Bible is clear that our good works are not the basis of our justification before God. Romans 3:20 plainly states that "by the deeds [or works] of the law no flesh [no person whatsoever] will be justified." Romans 4:5 states, "But to him who does not work but believes on Him who justifies the ungodly his faith is accounted for righteousness." These passages and many others show that, before God, our good works are in no way the basis or ground of our title to eternal life. Romans 6:23 states, "For the wages of sin is death, but the gift of God is eternal life in Christ Jesus our Lord." Eternal life is a free gift of God's grace to those who trust in Jesus alone for life and salvation. It is not something we merit either in whole or in part by our good works. However, at the same time, the New Testament is very clear that good works are important and necessary for us who have been saved by free grace through faith in Jesus Christ alone. Paul instructs Titus, for example, in Titus 3:8, "to affirm constantly, that those who have believed in God should be careful to maintain good works." But why are good works important?

Beginning in paragraph 2, this chapter of the Confession answers this question unequivocally when it states that "These good works, done in obedience to God's commandments, are the fruits and evidences of a true and lively faith." We are justified by faith alone, in Christ alone (Rom. 5:1), but according to the Bible, that faith is itself never alone. It will always produce good works. This is the emphasis of the apostle James in James 2:17: "Faith by itself, if it does not have works, is dead." In other words, it is a dead faith, not a real and saving faith. James goes on to write in verse 18: "But someone will say, 'You have faith, and I have works.' Show me your faith without your works, and I will show you my faith by my works." What is James saying? It is this: merely saying that we have faith proves nothing. Where true faith in Christ exists, it will always be shown by good works. In summary, then, while good works are the fruit of our salvation, they are not the root of our salvation. This is the biblical teaching on this subject which was held by the Reformers. Justification is not based on our works. We are justified by Christ and His work alone, which we receive and rest on by faith alone. By being united to Christ through faith alone, good works will inevitably follow because the believer in Christ has also been given the gift of the Spirit and now desires to live for and in obedience to the One who has saved him.

Second, good works are one of the ways true Christians express their thankfulness to God. The Confession goes on to say, "and by them believers manifest their thankfulness." We are to thank God for His saving mercies to us, not only with our lips but by our deeds. 1 Peter 2:9 states, "But you are a chosen generation, a royal priesthood, a holy nation, His own special people, that you may proclaim the praises of Him who called you out of darkness into His marvelous light." How do we proclaim the praises of Him who called us out of darkness into His marvelous light? One of the ways we do so is by our good works.

Third, the Confession says that good works "strengthen our assurance." How do good works do this? This takes us back again to the fact that good works are one of the evidences of faith. They do not strengthen our assurance by accumulating merit before God. However, they help us see that our faith in the Savior is not a sham. They show us that being *in Christ* by faith means that Christ is now *in us* by His Spirit. First John 2:2 states, "Now by this we know that we know Him, if we keep His commandments." This is one of the ways we know that we belong to Jesus. We are not saved because we keep His commandments. However, we are saved unto the keeping of His commandments. In other words, the salvation which God gives as a free gift, and is received through faith alone, is a salvation that causes us to want to obey God and keep His commandments. As we see this desire in our hearts, our assurance is strengthened.

Additionally, when we as Christians struggle with assurance, the best approach is not to keep examining ourselves repeatedly but to cast ourselves afresh upon Christ for mercy. We must keep believing and resting in the free gift of God in Jesus Christ. Then, from this posture of believing and resting in the good news of the gospel, we serve and work for Him. As we do this, our assurance is strengthened. Peter speaks to this in 2 Peter 1. In verse 10 of that chapter, he exhorts us to "be even more diligent to make your call and election sure." The infinitive verb "to make" is in the middle voice in the Greek text, showing us that we are to make this matter sure for ourselves. Peter is talking about having a genuine assurance of our salvation. But how do we make our calling and election sure to ourselves? He tells us beginning in verse 5 of that chapter:

> But also for this very reason, giving all diligence, add to your faith virtue, to virtue knowledge, to knowledge self-control, to self-control perseverance, to perseverance godliness, to godliness brotherly kindness, and to brotherly kindness love. For if these things are yours and abound, *you will be* neither barren nor unfruitful in the knowledge of our Lord Jesus Christ. For he who lacks these things is shortsighted, even to blindness, and has forgotten that he was cleansed from his old sins. Therefore, brethren, be even more diligent to make your call and election sure, for if you do these things you will never stumble; for so an entrance will be supplied to you abundantly into the everlasting kingdom of our Lord and Savior Jesus Christ (vv. 5-11).

Peter says we are to give diligence to add to our faith by way of pursuing and growing in obedience and good works. This is the pathway of making our call and election sure to ourselves. He says that without this, our spiritual eyes will be dim, and we will be like men in the dark who cannot see the forgiveness of their past sins or the certainty of their heavenly inheritance in the future.

Fourth, the Confession says, good works "edify our brethren." Simply stated, they build up and encourage the saints, God's people. Further, when we see our brethren doing them, they motivate us to "go and do likewise."

Fifth, they "adorn the profession of the gospel." In Titus 2:9, Titus exhorts servants in their relationships to their masters (or we might say the relationship of employees to their employees) to please them well in their work and to be faithful and trustworthy, "that they may adorn the doctrine of God our Savior in all things." Simply stated, good works enhance the beauty of the gospel and make it more attractive to people.

Sixth, good works "stop the mouths of adversaries." 1 Peter 2:15 says, "For this is the will of God, that by doing good you may put to silence the ignorance of foolish men." The good works of believers make it difficult for those who are lost to find fault with the gospel. Good works silence our critics. 1 Peter 2:12 states, "Having your conduct honorable among the Gentiles, that when they speak against you as evildoers, they may, by your good works which they observe, glorify God in the day of visitation."

This points to a seventh reason the Confession mentions that good works are so important: they "glorify God." Matthew 5:16 says, "Let your light so shine before men, that they may see your good works and glorify your Father in heaven." The good works of believers show forth God's glory. They reveal the beauty and majesty of His glorious perfections, especially the glory of His grace, which takes sinners like us and causes us to be new creations in Christ who do good works for His glory. As the Confession states, our good works "glorify God, whose workmanship they are, created in Christ Jesus thereunto."

Of course, here, the writers are thinking of that wonderful statement of the apostle Paul in Ephesians 2:8-9: "For by grace you have been saved through faith, and that not of yourselves; it is the gift of God, not of works, lest anyone should boast." Our salvation is not based on our works; if it were, we would have something to boast about. Instead, "It is the gift of God, not of works, lest anyone should boast." But does that mean good works do not matter, or that they are not important? No, not at all. In fact, in the next verse, Ephesians 2:10, we are told, "For we are His workmanship, created in Christ Jesus for good works, which God prepared beforehand that we should walk in them."

Eighth, the last phrase of the second paragraph states that believers have been created in Christ Jesus for good works, "that having their fruit unto holiness they may have the end eternal life." The writers of the Confession are referring here to Romans 6:22, which states, "But now having been set free from sin, and having become slaves of God..." This is what happened in our conversion. Being united to Christ by faith, we were set free from the guilt and condemnation of our sin, and we became the servants of God. So, Paul says, "But now having been set free from sin, and having become slaves of God, you have your fruit to holiness, and the end, everlasting life." Notice three things here that always go together: being set free from sin and becoming slaves of God (conversion), we have our fruit to holiness (good works), and the end, everlasting life (glory). Again, we cannot separate those three things.

Remember the illustration Jesus uses in the Sermon on the Mount. He speaks of the narrow gate and the narrow way that leads to life. The gate and the way cannot be separated. If you are *not* in the narrow way that leads to life, you *never* entered the gate, and if you have entered the narrow gate, you will be in the narrow way. The way, the gate, and the end, eternal life, are inseparable. Good works are not the narrow gate of conversion. We enter the gate of conversion by faith in Christ's person and work alone, not by our good works. Further, we do not merit the eternal life that is at the end of the road by good works, but good works are the appointed way upon which we arrive there. Faith in Christ (entering the narrow gate) leads to good works (walking in the narrow way) which ends in eternal life. In that sense, we can even say that although good works do not save, there is no salvation where there are no good works.

The Cause of Good Works

Paragraph 3 underscores two essential, interrelated truths. The first is that the ability to do good works is caused by the influence of the Holy Spirit who indwells believers. Only those individuals who are joined to Christ are qualified to please God, and even these individuals require the Holy Spirit in order to do good works. The second truth is that while the working of the Holy Spirit in us is the ultimate cause of the good works, at the same time our working requires deliberate effort.

First, the Holy Spirit is the source and the cause of the good works of believers. The Confession says: "Their ability to do good works is not at all of themselves, but wholly from the Spirit of Christ; and that they may be enabled thereunto, besides the graces they have already received, there is necessary an actual influence of the same Holy Spirit, to work in them to will and to do of his good pleasure." When the writers speak of the insufficiency of the graces we have "already received," they are underscoring that our need of the Holy Spirit's enablement is a continual, ongoing need.

We are not simply to live on the grace received at our conversion. Rather, the point is that we are in constant need of grace. We are daily and continually in need of the ongoing influence of the Holy Spirit, for without the Holy Spirit's working in us, we will not be able to will or to do works that are in any true and real measure good works. This reminds us how important it is that we are regularly praying for the help of the Spirit in our efforts to do good works. As Paul writes in 2 Corinthians 3:5, "Not that we are sufficient of ourselves to think of anything as being from ourselves, but our sufficiency is from God." But the fact that good works are caused by the Holy Spirit and that our ability to do good works is completely dependent on Him does not mean that we are at liberty to just be passive and to wait for the Spirit to move us before we seek to do any good works.[30] If we draw this conclusion, we are wrong.

To guard against this, the Confession goes on, secondly, to say, "yet they are not hereupon to grow negligent, as if they were not bound to perform any duty, unless upon a special motion of the Spirit, but they ought to be diligent in stirring up the grace of God that is in them." We could look at many passages in this regard, but one of the clearest passages in which we see this balance is Philippians 2:12, 13. Here Paul writes, "Therefore, my beloved, as you have always obeyed, not as in my presence only, but now much more in my absence, work out your own salvation with fear and trembling; for it is God who works in you both to will and to do for His good pleasure." The apostle Paul is writing here to people who are already Christians. He refers to them as "my beloved." Only Christians are referred to in this way by Paul in his epistles. He is writing to Christians in the church of Philippi, those who are referred to in Chapter 1 of this book as "all the saints in Christ Jesus who are in Philippi." He exhorts these Christians, these born again, justified, forgiven believers in the Lord Jesus, to: "work out your own salvation with fear and trembling." What is Paul implying?

Negatively, he is not implying that these people are not converted. He is not implying that they were to earn salvation by their working. Positively, he is telling them to *work out*, not *work for*, the salvation they already have in Christ. He is speaking regarding the working out of their new Christian life in a life of gospel holiness with increasing conformity to Christ. He is speaking about living a life of doing good works by the power of the Holy Spirit, as we are commanded in the Word of God. The individual Christian is responsible for making progress in the Christian life and to be active in pursuing these things.

But then this is followed by a wonderful promise and statement of fact in Philippians 2:13, when Paul writes: "For it is God who works in you both to will and to do for His good pleasure." If you are a Christian, then God is working in you the very thing Paul commanded us to do. He does not say, if we believe enough, God is working in us. Or, if we will only let Him, God is working in us. There is no condition here. He simply states it as a matter of fact and as a promise to be trusted. If we are true believers, then God, by the Holy Spirit, is working in us "both to will and to do for His good pleasure."

There are four vital principles regarding the doing of good works in this passage.[31] The *first one* is that, when it comes to good works, our working and the work of the Spirit in us happen together at the same time. In verse 12, Paul commands us to work. In verse 13, he tells us that

---

30. Waldron, *Exposition of 1689 Baptist Confession*, 250-51.

31. I first heard these four principles laid out in a sermon by Albert N. Martin over twenty years ago.

God is working in us both to will and to do for His good pleasure. And so, which is it? Does God work, or do we work? Well, it is not an either/or proposition. Rather, it is both/and. They happen at the same time. God's working does not stop, nor is it in some way hindered because we work. On the other hand, God's working does not at all remove the absolute necessity of our working.

A second principle is that the underlying and ultimate cause of our working is God, by the Spirit, working in us. This is our hope and our confidence. If we are in Christ, the Spirit of God is working in us to will and to do of God's good pleasure. This is the ultimate cause of our good works.

A third principle is that while God's working in us is the ultimate cause of our good works and is the basis of our hope and confidence (v. 13), our actual obedience and the working out of our salvation is to be the focus of our deliberate, personal effort (v. 12). Understand the balance: the promise of God working in us is the source of our confidence and ability in this matter; but our conscious, obedient conformity to His Word is the means by which He brings it to pass. We are commanded to work out our salvation with fear and trembling. The fact that God is working in us both to will and to do for His good pleasure does not change this at all.

The fourth principle is that the evidence that the Spirit of God is working in us is the fact that we are working. Good works are caused by the Holy Spirit, without whom we can do no work that is truly good and pleasing in God's sight. However, at the same time, the Holy Spirit does not do the good works Himself. *We* must do the good works. We must seek to do them prayerfully and with a sense of our dependence upon Him. But we are never to be passive, waiting for something to happen to us or for some special feeling to come over us to move us in this direction. No, we must act and be diligent in seeking to do what is good as God calls us to do.

The Limitations of Good Works

Although we are to give ourselves with all diligence to doing good works, we must remember to keep our good works in their proper perspective and to understand what they cannot do. Paragraph 4 in this chapter deals with this. The Confession says:

> They who in their obedience attain to the greatest height which is possible in this life, are so far from being able to supererogate, and to do more than God requires, as that they fall short of much which in duty they are bound to do.

What are works of supererogation? The second phrase helps to explain. It says, "and do more than God requires." The terminology of "supererogation" is a way of referring to works that are above and beyond what is necessary. Here again, the writers of our Confession have Roman Catholic teaching in their crosshairs. Concerning this matter, R. C. Sproul says,

According to Roman Catholic teaching there have been a few saints who have lived lives of such extraordinary righteousness that they accumulated more merit than they needed in order to gain direct entrance into heaven. Their excess merit was then deposited in the treasury of merit, where it is available to others.[32]

Roman Catholic theology teaches that a person can do so many good works, and live a life of such great righteousness, godliness, and obedience to God's commands, that he accumulates more merit than he needs, i.e., works of supererogation. Then this excess merit is deposited in some kind of heavenly vault or treasury of merit to be meted out to ordinary saints who meet certain conditions. You may recall that one spark that lit the flame of the Reformation was Luther's objections to the way Johann Tetzel was selling indulgences in Saxony. Quoting Sproul again, "As a representative of the church, Tetzel was promising the peasants that the more money they gave, the sooner their dead relatives would exit purgatory and enter heaven."[33] This was based on the idea that by giving money, they could draw on the treasury of merit on behalf of their dead relatives. Luther had begun to question the whole system of indulgences and this whole idea of a treasury of merit.[34] Eventually, such teaching was totally rejected as contrary to Scripture by the Reformers.

Works of supererogation are impossible because no mere human being has done all that God requires perfectly, much less more than God requires. The Scriptures are clear that all have sinned and fall short of the glory of God (Rom. 3:23). Also, the good works that are required of us are determined and defined by God's Word, as we have seen. Therefore, there are no good works beyond what God's Word requires. Even if we did all that God requires in His law personally, perpetually, and perfectly, inwardly and outwardly all the time, without fail, which we do not, we have only done what God requires, *not more* than what God requires. This brings us now to paragraph 5 in this chapter, still under this heading of the limitations of good works. Not only are works of supererogation impossible, but:

We cannot by our best works merit pardon of sin or eternal life at the hand of God, by reason of the great disproportion that is between them and the glory to come, and the infinite distance that is between us and God, whom by them we can neither profit nor satisfy for the debt of our former sins; but when we have done all we can, we have done but our duty, and are unprofitable servants; and because as they are good they proceed from his Spirit, and as they are wrought by us they are defiled and mixed with so much weakness and imperfection, that they cannot endure the severity of God's punishment.

32. Sproul, *Truths We Confess*, 371.
33. Ibid.
34. Ibid.

The Confession says, "We cannot by our best works merit pardon of sin or eternal life at the hand of God." Why is that? The framers mentioned several reasons.

First, it says, "by reason of the great disproportion that is between them and the glory to come, and the infinite distance between us and God." The glory to come is so splendid, valuable, weighty, and eternal that there is nothing any mortal could ever do to merit it. It would be like a person coming to your house with a handful of pennies expecting this should be enough to purchase your home. It would be insulting to you. When it comes to our good works and the glory to come, the disproportion is infinitely greater than that, especially when we consider that the chief blessing of the glory to come is God Himself, who is infinite in value and worth.

Second, our good works do not somehow "profit" God. In other words, we are not doing God a favor when we do good works. We are not benefitting Him in some way, for He is entirely sufficient in Himself. Additionally, our good works do not "satisfy for the debt for our former sins." Even if we started from this day forward never to sin again but obeyed all of God's commands perfectly (which none of us will ever do in this life), we still would not make up for any of our past sins. We would still have earned and deserved hell for all the sins we committed in the past.

Third, even when we have done all we can, as the Confession says, "We have done but our duty and are unprofitable servants." The Confession is quoting Luke 17:10, where Jesus says, "So likewise you, when you have done all those things which you are commanded, say, 'We are unprofitable servants. We have done what was our duty to do.'" Whatever we do as Christians in this world in service and devotion to Christ is nothing more than our duty. So, our good works cannot merit pardon and eternal life because by them we do not satisfy divine justice for the debt we owe to Him for our sins.

The Confession mentions a fourth reason we cannot, even by our best works, merit pardon and eternal life from God. It says because "as they are good they proceed from his Spirit." In other words, whatever real and actual good is in our works is only the result of His Spirit enabling us to do them.

And then, fifth, as they come from us, even our best works are still defiled by sin. The Confession says, "and as they are wrought (or done) by us they are defiled and mixed with so much weakness and imperfection, that they cannot endure the severity of God's punishment."

Our best works are always mixed with sin and imperfections. Our motives are never entirely pure; thus, our highest and best works could never meet God's acceptance or approval apart from the mediation of Christ. As the Scripture says, "All our righteousnesses are like filthy rags" (Isa. 64:6). This is especially evident when our works are held up to the perfect standard of God's law. Therefore, the Scriptures say that "there is none righteous, no, not one" (Rom. 3:10). The Psalmist writes,

"Do not enter into judgment with Your servant. For in your sight no one living is righteous" (Ps. 143:2). When carefully examined under the all-seeing eye of God and by the perfect standard of His law, all of our best works are greatly stained with many deficiencies.

In summary, paragraphs 4 and 5 focus on the limitations of good works. We cannot merit the pardon of sin and eternal life even by our best works. Only Christ and His work completely justify us before God. Hence, when He died on the cross in our place, He cried out saying, "It is finished" (John 19:30). Now, if this is all that the Bible has to say about the good works of believers, it could be a bit discouraging. Can God's believing children do nothing that pleases Him? The fact that our good works cannot merit salvation and even at their best are still defiled with sin is not the final word about them. The final paragraphs of the Confession make this plain.

The Acceptance of Good Works

Paragraph 6 speaks of God's acceptance of the good works of believers. And then paragraph 7 speaks of His rejection of the apparent good works that unbelievers do.

The Good Works of Believers Are Accepted by God in Christ

> Yet notwithstanding the persons of believers being accepted through Christ, their good works also are accepted in him; not as though they were in this life wholly unblameable and unreprovable in God's sight, but that he, looking upon them in his Son, is pleased to accept and reward that which is sincere, although accompanied with many weaknesses and imperfections.

This paragraph puts forth an important truth. It tells us that because the believer is in Christ, he is entirely accepted by God. Therefore, our efforts to do good works are pleasing to Him. The Almighty is pleased with our good works, even though they are not perfect, and are tainted with sin. Looking upon us in union with Christ and justified on the basis of His perfect righteousness alone, God is pleased to accept and even reward our sincere efforts to obey and to honor Him, though our works are accompanied with many weaknesses and imperfections.

In terms of our legal standing before God, we need a perfect, sinless righteousness to be justified in His sight. That righteousness has been provided for us in Jesus. When it comes to standing up to the perfection required in God's law, we are thoroughly undone in ourselves. But in union with Christ, God completely accepts us (Eph. 1:6) and is pleased with our sincere, though imperfect, efforts to serve Him. We can—and do—please God through Jesus! Sometimes, as Christians, we can have a hard time saying or believing that, but it is true nonetheless. So, regarding the acceptance of good works, this sixth paragraph explains that the good works of believers are accepted by God and pleasing to Him in Christ.

This brings us now to the last paragraph, still under the heading of the acceptance of good works.

The Good Works of Unregenerate Men are Not Accepted by God or Pleasing to Him

> Works done by unregenerate men, although for the matter of them they may be things which God commands, and of good use both to themselves and others; yet because they proceed not from a heart purified by faith, nor are done in a right manner according to the word, nor to a right end, the glory of God, they are therefore sinful, and cannot please God, nor make a man meet to receive grace from God, and yet their neglect of them is more sinful and displeasing to God.

Unregenerate people are individuals who have not been born again and who have not repented of their sins and trusted in Christ. They are not in union with Christ and have not been justified by faith in Him. What does the Confession say about their efforts to do good works?

First, it tells us that unregenerate men may do works that, from one perspective, may be called good. The Confession says specifically that, "works done by unregenerate men, although for the matter of them they may be things which God commands and of good use to themselves and others. . ." Thus, we see that while the Bible says, "there is none who does good, no, not one," at the same time, it acknowledges that there is another sense in which even unconverted men do good things.

Paul tells us, for example, in Romans 2:12 that even though the heathen do not have God's law, they by, nature, do the things in the law, "being a law to themselves." Jesus likewise says in Matthew 7:11 that earthly fathers, being evil, know how to give good gifts to their children. They have a natural affection for their children, and they do good things for them. Many nice people in the world do a lot of nice things. There may even be unbelievers who in some ways are nicer than some Christians from one perspective. Thus, even though man is fallen and dead in his trespasses and sins (Eph. 2:1), he is capable of doing many things that we might call relatively good, or civil good.[35] He may exercise love for his family, be a good citizen, give large sums of money to charitable institutions, or abstain from the practice of certain vices. He may be friendly and easy to get along with, and he may help people who are in need.

Further, when, for example, an adult child takes care of his aging parents, it is a good thing. When a person takes a meal to a neighbor who has had a death in the family, that is a good thing. When a father works hard to provide for his children, that is a good thing. When he is kind and faithful to their mother, that is good. When a soldier throws

---

35. Some of the examples of the good unregenerate men may do are taken from a sermon by Ted Donnelly, "Total Depravity" – https://www.sermonaudio.com/sermoninfo. asp?SID=570910234310.

himself upon a grenade to protect his platoon, that is heroic. These are all good things which we should encourage, and we should show our appreciation for them when people do them.

However, as the Confession goes on to tell us, outside of Christ none of these things can establish a right relationship with God, nor are they pleasing to Him. In fact, they are all wholly defiled and corrupted by evil. Why is that? The Confession says, "Yet because they proceed not from a heart purified by faith, nor are done in a right manner according to the Word, nor to a right end, the glory of God, they are therefore sinful, and cannot please God." When it comes to what people do, it is not enough to look at actions or at outward appearances (1 Sam. 16:7).

We must consider the matter of our reasons and motivations for such works, and of our attitude toward and our relationship to God as we do them. According to the Confession, a work must involve at least three things to be truly good:

First, it must proceed from "a heart purified by faith." A heart purified by faith is a believing, regenerated, repentant heart. It is a new heart given to a person by Christ, which results in a purity that otherwise does not and cannot exist. It is the heart of a person who is justified by faith in Christ alone and indwelt by His life-giving, sanctifying Spirit.

Second, to be a truly good work, it must be according to a right rule. That rule is "according to the Word." This is God's rule by which He expresses His will for His creatures. For example, the love of the believing husband, insofar as it is a truly good work, is an attempt to imitate Christ in His love for His church, which means that the husband will lay down his life for his wife. He will deny himself in ways that are sacrificial, and even painful, in order to bless his wife as Christ commands (Eph. 5:25-33). And part of his motivation will be the demonstration of the gospel to his wife, children, and the watching world.

Third, there must also be a right end in view which, as the Confession states, is "the glory of God." There is the whole question of why a person does what he does. A person may have many legitimate ends in view for anything he does. There are many good motives identified in the Word of God. However, the ultimate and essential motive that must be supreme in order to constitute a truly good work is the desire to glorify God. The Shorter Catechism says it best in answer to the question, "What is man's chief end?" The answer is, "Man's chief end is to glorify God and to enjoy him forever."

So true goodness flows from a right, regenerated heart. It is done according to a right rule and with a right end in view. When we view anything that man does in his natural, unregenerate, unrepentant, unbelieving state by this standard, what is the conclusion? It is that even his best works may be good in a social and civil sense as between men, yet before God (to use words attributed to Augustine), "they are but splendid sins."[36] They do not please God.

---

36. G. I. Williamson, *The Westminster Confession: For Study Classes* (Philadelphia, PA: Presbyterian and Reformed Publishing Company, 1964), 124.

Andrew Fuller has a helpful illustration of this. He said something along these lines:[37]

> Imagine a ship's company that has risen in mutiny against their rightful captain. They take command of the ship themselves and they leave the captain on some deserted island. Then they sail to a distant port, intending to dispose of their cargo and to divide the profits among themselves, and then to continue using the ship in a career of merchant shipping. Now this group of mutineers, for the sake of self-preservation and tranquility on the ship, establish several good laws. There's no lying or stealing on the ship. There's no fighting, no killing. They're very impartial and very fair in the distribution of their profits. They're all very courageous men in the face of danger. They're hard workers and they share with one another and take care of one another if someone gets sick or has a need. They do many things that, in one sense, are good. But, you see, there's something fundamentally wrong with all their supposed goodness, isn't there? All of that goodness is not truly good, because it's all part of a life of rebellion against their rightful captain. It's all just so many expedients by which they enable themselves to continue on in their mutinous lives with peace and tranquility. Therefore, none of their supposed goodness is truly good, it's evil.

So it is with unregenerate men. Ultimately, all their good works are done from a heart in rebellion against God. Therefore, they are but splendid sins in God's eyes. Because this is so, this paragraph points out that the works of unbelievers cannot "make a man meet," or following a modern version, "they cannot qualify anyone to receive grace from God." Here the Confession refutes the kind of theology that teaches that if an unregenerate man does his best to do good, God will reward him with grace. As has already been mentioned, the problem with this is that his good works are ultimately sinful and do not please God.

Finally, the Confession underscores in the last sentence of this paragraph that it is still better for unregenerate men to do what is at least good in form than to neglect doing so at all. It says, "and yet their neglect of them is more sinful and displeasing to God." There are degrees of sin, according to the Scriptures (Matt. 11:24; John 19:11). Some sins are worse than others and will receive greater punishment than others if the person enters eternity still lost.

So, it is better for an unregenerate, unbelieving person to be kind to people than not to be, for even though being kind to someone cannot save him or please God, it is not as displeasing to God as neglecting to be kind. Children for example, should still be brought to church and taught to pray, even though they may not yet be believers and may lack a right attitude and a converted heart, because it is more sinful to neglect going to church and praying altogether.[38] However, at the same time, we must teach our children not to be content to just go through the motions.

---

37. Andrew Fuller, *The Complete Works of Andrew Fuller,* Vol. 3 (Revised by Joseph Belcher, American Baptist Publication Society, 1845; reprint, Harrisonburg, Virginia: Sprinkle Publications, 1988), 673.

38. Waldron, *Exposition of 1689 Baptist Confession,* 252.

Instead, we must exhort them to pray, not unbelievingly, but believingly, believing the gospel and trusting in Jesus to save them.

Conclusion

The primary lessons of this chapter are:

1. God determines which works are good in His sight.

2. The works that God sees as good are the works that He Himself commands and commends.

3. Works contrived and commanded by men, including those people who are considered to be leaders and authorities in the church, are of no value unless they are clearly rooted in the Word of God.

4. For any human being to behave in a manner that God accepts as good, that human must be accepted in Christ and moved and empowered by the Holy Spirit.

5. Persons who are not Christ-followers are void of the Holy Spirit and unable to perform works that God would consider good. Even when their outward works appear to conform to God's Word, those works are unacceptable to God because they are ruined by heart sins and are not presented to Him by individuals who are pardoned and justified before God on the merits of Jesus Christ. Christ alone makes the unclean to be clean in God's sight.

CHAPTER 17

OF THE PERSERVERANCE OF THE SAINTS

CALVIN WALDEN

1. Those whom God hath accepted in the beloved, effectually called and sanctified by his Spirit, and given the precious faith of his elect unto, can neither totally nor finally fall from the state of grace, but shall certainly persevere therein to the end, and be eternally saved, seeing the gifts and callings of God are without repentance, whence he still begets and nourisheth in them faith, repentance, love, joy, hope, and all the graces of the Spirit unto immortality;[1] and though many storms and floods arise and beat against them, yet they shall never be able to take them off that foundation and rock which by faith they are fastened upon; notwithstanding, through unbelief and the temptations of Satan, the sensible sight of the light and love of God may for a time be clouded and obscured from them,[2] yet he is still the same, and they shall be sure to be kept by the power of God unto salvation, where they shall enjoy their purchased possession, they being engraven upon the palm of his hands, and their names having been written in the book of life from all eternity.[3]

2. This perseverance of the saints depends not upon their own free will, but upon the immutability of the decree of election,[4] flowing from the free and unchangeable love of God the Father, upon the efficacy of the merit and intercession of Jesus Christ and union with him,[5] the oath of God,[6] the abiding of his Spirit, and the seed of God within them,[7] and the nature of the covenant of grace;[8] from all which ariseth also the certainty and infallibility thereof.

1. John 10:28-29; Philippians 1:6; 2 Timothy 2:19; 1 John 2:19
2. Psalm 89:31-32; 1 Corinthians 11:32
3. Malachi 3:6
4. Romans 8:30; Romans 9:11, 16
5. Romans 5:9, 10; John 14:19
6. Hebrews 6:17-18
7. 1 John 3:9
8. Jeremiah 32:40

3. And though they may, through the temptation of Satan and of the world, the prevalency of corruption remaining in them, and the neglect of means of their preservation, fall into grievous sins, and for a time continue therein,[9] whereby they incur God's displeasure and grieve his Holy Spirit,[10] come to have their graces and comforts impaired,[11] have their hearts hardened, and their consciences wounded,[12] hurt and scandalize others, and bring temporal judgments upon themselves,[13] yet shall they renew their repentance and be preserved through faith in Christ Jesus to the end.[14]

In John 10, the Lord is speaking in the temple to a group of Jews who have gathered around Him. These Jews have made an inquiry of the Lord concerning His true identity: "How long dost thou make us doubt? If thou be the Christ, tell us plainly" (John 10:24 KJV). In replying to the inquiry, Christ sets before them the contrast that exists between the Christian and the non-Christian. "My sheep hear my voice, and I know them and they follow me" (John 10:27). This statement is followed by two benefits that come to those who hear His voice and follow Him: "I give them eternal life and they shall never perish" (John 10:28). These benefits are stated as a twofold proposition so that there is no mistaking their implication. A. W. Pink writes: "Quite impossible is it for a sheep to become goat, for a man who has been born again to be unborn."[15]

The certainty of the truth is declared through two statements that Jesus makes: "neither shall any man pluck them out of my hand... No man is able to pluck them out of my Father's hand" (John 10:28-29). The hands of Christ are under His sheep, and the hands of the Father are over His sheep. "Thus we are secure in the clasped hands of Omnipotence."[16]

J. C. Ryle puts it this way:

> Christ declares that His people "shall never perish." Weak as they are, they shall all be saved. Not one of them shall be lost and cast away: not one of them shall miss heaven. If they err, they shall be brought back: if they fall, they shall be raised. The enemies of their souls may be strong and mighty, but their Savior is mightier; and none shall pluck them out of their Savior's hands.[17]

---

9. Matthew 26:70, 72, 74

10. Isaiah 64:5, 9; Ephesians 4:30

11. Psalm 51:10, 12

12. Psalm 32:3-4

13. 2 Samuel 12:14

14. Luke 22:32, 61-62

15. A.W. Pink, *Exposition of the Gospel of John* (Grand Rapids Michigan: Zondervan Publishing House, 1975, reprint 1978), 143.

16. Ibid. 144.

17. J. C. Ryle, *Expository Thoughts on the Gospel, St. John. Vol. II.* (Cambridge: James Clarke & Co, Ltd., reprinted 1976), 230.

John 10:28-29 is one of the clearest passages guaranteeing the absolute security of every true child of God. This doctrine is opened up in detail in the seventeenth chapter of the Confession. In the paragraphs of this chapter, there are three features concerning the doctrine of the perseverance of the saints: the explanation of this doctrine, the foundation upon which the doctrine rests, and the qualification that must be addressed from this doctrine.

The Explanation of This Doctrine
In the first paragraph of this chapter, there is a twofold explanation about the perseverance of the saints: the reality stated and the reality enlarged.

The Reality Stated
In stating the reality of the perseverance of the saints, the writers of the Confession focus upon two features: the recipients and the significance. Those who persevere are identified as "Those whom God hath accepted in the beloved"; they are found to be in Christ. In writing to the church at Ephesus, Paul tells his readers that God's favor comes to them freely "in the Beloved" (Eph. 1:6). Peter T. O'Brien writes: "the expression 'in the Beloved' continues the notion that all of God's blessings come to us in Christ... 'Beloved' marks out Christ as the supreme object of the Father's love."[18] In Ephesians 2, Paul sets down the contrast between our ruin and God's remedy. He describes our sad condition left to our natural state: "by nature the children of wrath" (Eph. 2:1-3). Paul goes on to declare that they have come to a new life with Christ in His death and resurrection. "Even when we were dead in sins, hath quickened us together with Christ, (by grace you are saved) and hath raised us up together, and made us sit together in heavenly places in Christ Jesus" (Eph. 2:5-6).

The Confession goes on to explain that those who are "accepted in the beloved" have become so because they were "effectually called and sanctified by the Spirit and given the precious faith of his elect." They are "effectually called." It is this call that brings men to salvation. "Moreover whom he did predestinate, them he also called" (Rom. 8:30). They are "sanctified by the Spirit"—that is, they are people who have experienced a transformation of life by the work of the Spirit. Paul, when expressing thanks to God for the church at Thessalonica, describes them as "brethren beloved of the Lord, because God hath from the beginning chosen you to salvation through the sanctification of the Spirit and belief of the truth" (2 Thess. 2:13). And finally, they are "given the precious faith of his elect." Paul says, "If thou shalt confess with thy mouth the Lord Jesus, and shalt believe in thy heart that God hath raised him from the dead, thou shalt be saved" (Rom. 10:9). Dr. Waldron writes, "Faith, on the

---

18. Peter T. O'Brien, *The Letter of the Ephesians* (Grand Rapids, Michigan: Wm. B. Eerdmans Publishing Company, 1999), 104.

other hand, is commitment to the Christ of the gospel. Commitment here means the act of entrusting ourselves to Christ."[19]

The recipients of this grace of perseverance are not all those who profess to be Christians, but only those who have, by the grace of God, been effectually called, sanctified by the Spirit, and given this precious faith. Only these are "accepted in the beloved." These are the true saints, and those who are the recipients of the work of perseverance.

The writers go on to give their readers the substance of this doctrine. What is perseverance? The Confession states, "Those whom God has accepted in the beloved ... can neither totally nor finally fall from the state of grace, but shall certainly persevere therein to the end, and be eternally saved." The substance of this doctrine is the reality that God, having begun a work of grace, continues that work in the life of a true believer to the very end. "Being confident of this very thing, that he which hath begun a good work in you will perform it until the day of Jesus Christ" (Phil. 1:6). Michael Bentley writes: "Paul was confident, not only that God would care for them, but that the Lord would bring them safely to the 'day of Christ Jesus'... When God writes your name in his book, it is there forever."[20]

When writing on Romans 8:28-30, Stuart Olyott notes:

> Every person whom God so predestined He called by the gospel, justified, and glorified. It is all in the past tense, because it is so certain that it has as good as happened. Not one of those on whom God has set His love will fail to arrive in heaven (see John 6:37-39). However many are our present sufferings, and however intense, we can rejoice that we are certain to arrive at our heavenly destination.[21]

Every true believer will persevere to the end.

The Reality Enlarged

This is a reality because the true believer has the Spirit of God and His fruit in their hearts. That fruit is stated in the Confession as: faith (1 John 5:1-5), repentance (1 John 1:7-9), love (1 John 3:14-15), hope (Col. 1:23), and joy (Matthew 13:44). "Though the Christian may become insensible to these graces in himself and though they may become invisible to others, these graces are never completely eradicated even when a Christian sins grievously."[22]

Such a reality is not without its opposition. Paul exhorts the believer to "put on the whole armor of God that you may be able to stand against the wiles of the devil" (Eph. 6:11). The Confession acknowledges that the Christian's life is confronted with "many storms and floods that arise and beat against them." Paul refers to this opposition as the "wiles of

---

19. Samuel E Waldron, *A Modern Exposition of the 1689 Baptist Confession of Faith* (Evangelical Press, 1989), 185.

20. Michael Bentley, *Shining in the Darkness* (Evangelical Press, 1997), 27.

21. Stuart Olyott, *The Gospel as It Really Is* (Evangelical Press, 2001), 80.

22. Waldron, *A Modern Exposition of the 1689 Confession of Faith*, 217.

the devil." Paul wants us to know that the enemy opposes the genuine believer with specific schemes having intended purposes of defeat, destruction, and discouragement toward the believer. Paul wrote to the church at Corinth, "We are not ignorant of his devices" (2 Cor. 2:11). The apostle Paul's own testimony was, "I have fought the good fight, I have finished my course, I have kept the faith" (2 Tim. 4:7). The believer is described in the Scriptures as a runner, a boxer, a soldier, and an athlete. All face struggles, challenges, and obstacles, but none of these things change what the believer is in Christ. The writers of the Confession state: "they shall never be able to take them off that foundation and rock which by faith they are fastened upon." The true believer will go through periods of unbelief, experience the temptations of Satan, and seasons that cloud the presence of God, but none of them changes what they are in Christ.

There are three certainties that guarantee such to be the case. As the true believer passes through such occasions, he can find himself secure in who he is because he is kept by the power of God. Peter confirms this to the believer when he declares that the elect are "kept by the power of God" (1 Pet. 1:5). In John 10:29, Jesus describes the Father as "greater than all; and no man is able to pluck them out of my Father's hand." Leon Morris states, "This shepherd is all-powerful and the sheep in His hand have nothing to fear."[23]

Not only is the believer kept by the power of God, but he also has the certainty of having been engraved upon the palm of God's hand. Isaiah assures his readers that God has continual concern and attention over His own: "Behold I have graven thee upon the palms of my hands; thy walls are continually before me" (Isa. 49:16). Matthew Henry, when writing about such imagery, has stated: "His setting them thus as a seal upon his arm denotes his setting them as a seal upon his heart and his being ever mindful of them and their interest."[24]

The final certainty addressed in the Confession is the fact that every true believer's name has been written in the book of life from all eternity (Rev. 13:8). This is the heavenly register of those ordained to new life through the person and work of Christ. Their names were written in the book before the foundation of the world. "In the midst of persecution and the immense power of the Beast, the saints may find security in God's guarantee of their heavenly citizenship."[25]

The Foundation of This Doctrine
The second paragraph of this chapter states, "this perseverance of the saints depends," directing the reader to the fact that this doctrine rests upon certain key biblical truths. The writers begin this section by

---

23. Leon Morris, *The Gospel According to John* (Wm. B. Eerdmans Publishing Company, 1971,) 522.

24. Matthew Henry, *Matthew Henry Commentary, Volume IV, Isaiah to Malachi* (MacDonald Publishing Company), 279.

25. Vern S. Poythress, *The Returning King* (P & R Publishing Company, 2000), 143.

pointing out that one of those truths is not, as some assume, "their own free will." The Scriptures teach that "free will" is not the decisive factor of man's salvation, but rather the free grace of God. We read in Philippians 2:13: "for it is God which worketh in you both to will and to do of his good pleasure." Romans 9:16: "So then it does not depend on the man who wills or the man who runs, but on God who has mercy." Olyott makes this clear:

> So then, if you are in favour with God it is not because of inward intention, nor because of your outward exertion. There is not one atom of praise that you can take to yourself. It is all because God has shown you mercy. Nobody is in favour with Him, except on this basis. His people are composed solely of those upon whom He has had mercy.[26]

There are, however, six factors or pillars upon which this doctrine rests as pointed out in the Confession.

1. Immutability of the Decree of Election
Man is brought to faith in God only by the divine selection of God. Paul, writing to the people of God in Thessalonica, says of them, "God hath from the beginning chosen you to salvation" (2 Thess. 2:13). God divinely chose them for salvation. Paul again points to this divine selectivity in Ephesians 1:4: "According as he hath chosen us in him before the foundation of the world, that we should be holy and without blame before him in love." Because men are divinely selected by God's immutable decree, they will continue living by faith until the end.

2. The Efficacy of the Merit and Intercession of Jesus Christ and Union with Him.
In Romans 8, Paul argues that no one can bring a charge against God's elect and the believer stands in the place of no condemnation. His argument is built upon the truth that "He that spared not his own Son, but delivered him up for us all... It is Christ that died, yea rather, that is risen again, who is even at the right hand of God, who also maketh intercession for us" (8:32, 34). It is by the work and intercession of Christ for those united to Him by the effectual call of God that the believer is kept in grace.

3. The Oath of God
The third pillar upon which this blessed doctrine rests is the oath of God. In Hebrews 6:16-20, we read of the oath which God made toward His people. Abraham was a recipient of the promise of God and the certainty of God's Word was given to him by an oath. It is so with the child of God who is called an heir of the promise. God not only gives a promise, but also confirms that promise with an oath. Waldron says:

> The God who always keeps his promises, and thus has no obligation to

---

26. Olyott, *The Gospel as It Really Is*, 86.

confirm his promises by swearing an oath – the God who has no one greater than himself by whom to swear an oath – has confirmed his promises by swearing an oath by himself. The single reason for all this seemingly needless effort and superfluous oath-taking on God's part is the comfort of true believers. It is to give us "strong encouragement," "an anchor of the soul," and "a hope both sure and steadfast."[27]

4. *The Abiding of His Spirit*

Paul tells the Christians in Ephesus that they "were sealed with the Holy Spirit of promise" (Eph. 1:13). This seal was a pledge of the complete expression of God's redemptive purpose in His creatures (Eph. 1:14). Paul states that there were two sides to the redemption that the Gentile believers experienced: "... having also believed..." and they were "sealed with the Holy Spirit of promise" (Eph. 1:13). The "seal" carries the idea of ownership and protection. Their owners, to indicate to whom they belonged, branded cattle and even slaves with a seal. It was a means to protect their own against those who may desire to snatch them away.

The Holy Spirit is a deposit, guaranteeing our inheritance. O'Brien comments, "Their longing for a heavenly dwelling results from the certainty that they have been provided with an advance installment of the Spirit...God is not simply promising us a final inheritance, but actually providing us with a foretaste of it."[28] God "hath also sealed us, and given the earnest of the Spirit in our hearts" (2 Cor. 1:22). The thought that a true believer who possesses the seal of the Spirit may completely and ultimately fall from grace suggests that God may default on His solemn pledge.

5. *The Seed of God within Them*

This fifth pillar is very much tied to the fourth pillar. The Holy Spirit not only works as a pledge for the believer, but also indwells the believer. "Whosoever is born of God doth not commit sin; for his seed remaineth in him: and he cannot sin because he is born of God" (1 John 3:9). John goes on to state that the one born of God "overcometh the world" and is kept by God, and "he that is begotten of God keepeth himself, and that wicked one toucheth him not" (1 John 5:4, 18).

6. *The Nature of the Covenant of Grace*

The language of the New Covenant gives assurance of salvation and perseverance to those who are a part of it. "This is the covenant that I will make with them after those days, says the Lord: I will put my laws into their hearts, and in their minds I will write them." He then says, "and their sins and iniquities will I remember no more" (Heb. 10:16-17). That which is accomplished through the one offering of Christ comes with the assurance that "their sins and lawless deeds I will remember no more." The nature of the covenant of grace assures more than just

---

27. Waldron, *A Modern Exposition of the 1689 Baptist Confession of Faith*, 220.

28. O'Brien, *The Letter of the Ephesians*, 121.

the forgiveness of sins, for the reality is that God will remember them no more. All those who are part of the Covenant of Grace are promised absolute forgiveness. Waldron remarks, "The idea that anyone who really is in the New Covenant may fail to continue and persevere in it and finally perish is foreign to the Bible."[29]

With these pillars holding up this doctrine of the perseverance of the saints, the conclusion is drawn: it is certainly and absolutely true.

The Qualification of This Doctrine

The writers of the Confession give a word of qualification. The qualification comes by way of a certain actuality: while every true believer will persevere, true believers "do fall into grievous sins." In dealing with this reality, the writers note in particular: the causes, the consequence, and the conclusion of this sad reality.

The Causes

There are four causes given that may lead a true believer "into grievous sins, and for a time continue therein."

a. The Temptation of Satan

Peter describes Satan as the devil who "walks about like a roaring lion, seeking whom he may devour" (1 Pet. 5:8). In writing about this, Thomas Brooks penned:

> He is but a titular Christian that hath not personal experience of Satan's stratagems, his set and composed machinations, his artificially moulded methods, his plots, darts, depth, where by he outwitted our first parents, and fits us a pennyworth still, as he sees reason.[30]

b. The World

James exhorts the believer to "keep himself unspotted from the world" (James 1:27). John Blanchard writes:

> No Christian should take his cue from the moral and ethical standards presented to him by the mass media of radio, television and press, nor any social group of his fellow men. We are to repulse its lies; the world makes many fulsome promises, of happiness, fulfillment and satisfaction, but the truth of the matter is at the end of the day it can give none of these...We are to resist its temptation: the fact that "everybody is doing it" can easily weaken the Christian's resolve to take a stand on many issues.[31]

c. The Prevalence of Corruption Remaining in Them

Paul warns the Church at Rome concerning this corruption: "Therefore, brethren, we are debtors, not to the flesh, to live after the flesh. For if ye live after the flesh, ye shall die: but if ye through the Spirit do mortify

---

29. Waldron, Ibid., 220.

30. Thomas Brooks, *Precious Remedies Against Satan Devices* (Carlisle: PA, Banner of Truth Trust, 1984), 26.

31. John Blanchard, *Truth For Life* (Hertfordshire, England: Evangelical Press, 1979), 111.

the deeds of the body, ye shall live" (Rom. 8:12-13). Paul is telling his
readers that in light of the glorious realities (liberation, redemption, and
transformation) that they possess in Christ, they are obligated to "mortify
the deeds of the body" and not allow remaining corruption to prevail. No
genuine believer has yet experienced the complete annihilation of sin in
this life. The believer is not to let the remaining corruption of the flesh
be dominant but is to be diligently putting those things to death. Olyott
says, "Whatever stirs up sin in your members is to be cut out! Paul tells
us bluntly that this sort of painful surgery is essential to life."[32]

d. The Neglect of the Means of Their Perseverance
The believer has been given that which he needs to be kept from grievous
sins. These things are prayer, the Word, and fellowship. Neglecting these
things will lead to backsliding and grievous sins. Paul admonishes, "But
refuse profane and old wives' fables, and exercise thyself rather unto
godliness" (1 Tim. 4:7). Ryle remarks, "None but a fool or fanatic would
think of building a house without a ladder and scaffolding, and just so no
wise man will despise the means, especially when ordained by God."[33]

The Consequences
The writers of the Confession set before the reader six sobering and sad
consequences experienced when the believer falls into grievous sins,

1. God's displeasure (Ps. 38:1-8)
2. Grieving of the Spirit (Eph. 4:30; 1 Thess. 5:19)
3. Graces and comfort are impaired (Ps. 51:10-12)
4. Hearts hardened and conscience wounded (Ps. 32:3-4)
5. Others are hurt and scandalized (Rom. 14:13-18)
6. Bring about temporal judgment (1 Cor. 11:27-32)

Each of these consequences is a lasting reminder for every believer not to
take sin lightly, but to recognize that their fall will lead to serious harm.

The Conclusion
The writers of the Confession end this chapter by stating a truth
concerning the genuine believer: "Yet shall they renew their repentance
and be preserved through faith in Christ Jesus to the end." The truth is
that whatever pleasure a Christian finds in sin is short-lived, and that by
the grace of God, he is brought to turn from it (Luke 22:31-32). Paul makes
it clear, "But when we are judged, we are chastened of the Lord, that
we should not be condemned with the world" (1 Cor. 11:32). Spurgeon
summarizes:

> You will not be lost, for he who owns you is able to keep you. If you were to
> perish who would be the loser? Why, he to whom you belong, and "ye are
> not your own", ye belong to Christ. My hope of being preserved to the end

32. *Olyott, The Gospel as It Really Is*, 75.
33. J. C. Ryle, *Thoughts For Young Men* (Amityville, NY: Calvary Press, 1993), 71.

lies in that fact, that Jesus Christ paid far too much for me ever to be let go. Each believer cost him his heart's blood. Stand in Gethsemane, and hear his groans: then draw near and mark his bloody sweat, and tell me, will he lose soul for whom he suffered thus? See him hanging on the tree, tortured, mocked, burdened with an awful load, and then beclouded with the eclipse of his Father's face, and do you think he suffered all that and yet permit those for whom he endured it to be cast into hell. He will be a greater loser than I if I perish, for he will lose what cost him his life: surely he will never do that. Here is your security, you are the Lord's portion, and he will not be robbed of his heritage. We are in a hand that bears the scar of the nail; we are hidden in the cleft of a rock – a rock that was riven for us near nineteen hundred years ago. None can pluck us from that hand that redeemed us; its pressure is too warm with love and strong with might for that.[34]

---

34. C. H. Spurgeon, *Metropolitan Tabernacle Pulpit*, Vol.26 (Banner of Truth Trust, 1971), 476.

CHAPTER 18

OF THE ASSURANCE OF GRACE AND SALVATION

JEFFERY SMITH

1. Although temporary believers, and other unregenerate men, may vainly deceive themselves with false hopes and carnal presumptions of being in the favor of God and state of salvation, which hope of theirs shall perish;[1] yet such as truly believe in the Lord Jesus, and love him in sincerity, endeavoring to walk in all good conscience before him, may in this life be certainly assured that they are in the state of grace, and may rejoice in the hope of the glory of God,[2] which hope shall never make them ashamed.[3]

2. This certainty is not a bare conjectural and probable persuasion grounded upon a fallible hope, but an infallible assurance of faith[4] founded on the blood and righteousness of Christ revealed in the Gospel;[5] and also upon the inward evidence of those graces of the Spirit unto which promises are made,[6] and on the testimony of the Spirit of adoption, witnessing with our spirits that we are the children of God;[7] and, as a fruit thereof, keeping the heart both humble and holy.[8]

3. This infallible assurance doth not so belong to the essence of faith, but that a true believer may wait long, and conflict with many difficulties before he be partaker of it;[9] yet being enabled by the Spirit to know the things which are freely given him of God, he may, without extraordinary

---

1. Job 8:13, 14; Matthew 7:22-23
2. 1 John 2:3; 1 John 3:14, 18-19, 21, 24; 1 John 5:13
3. Romans 5:2, 5
4. Hebrews 6:11, 19
5. Hebrews 6:17, 18
6. 2 Peter 1:4, 5, 10, 11
7. Romans 8:15, 16
8. 1 John 3:1-3
9. Isaiah 50:10; Psalm 88; Psalm 77:1-12

revelation, in the right use of means, attain thereunto:[10] and therefore it is the duty of every one to give all diligence to make his calling and election sure, that thereby his heart may be enlarged in peace and joy in the Holy Spirit, in love and thankfulness to God, and in strength and cheerfulness in the duties of obedience, the proper fruits of this assurance;[11]—so far is it from inclining men to looseness.[12]

4. True believers may have the assurance of their salvation divers ways shaken, diminished, and intermitted; as by negligence in preserving of it,[13] by falling into some special sin which woundeth the conscience and grieveth the Spirit;[14] by some sudden or vehement temptation,[15] by God's withdrawing the light of his countenance, and suffering even such as fear him to walk in darkness and to have no light,[16] yet are they never destitute of the seed of God[17] and life of faith,[18] that love of Christ and the brethren, that sincerity of heart and conscience of duty out of which, by the operation of the Spirit, this assurance may in due time be revived,[19] and by the which, in the meantime, they are preserved from utter despair.[20]

The subject of this eighteenth chapter of the Confession is described as the assurance of grace and salvation. The writers are referring to the personal certainty that I am in a state of grace, saved, and will be saved on the last day. They speak of this in paragraph 2 as "an infallible assurance of faith," that is, an assurance growing out of faith that will not deceive us.[21] It is the assured conviction that I am now and forever will be saved and have eternal life. I will refer to this in short throughout this chapter as "the assurance of salvation." The focus of the first paragraph is the possibility of assurance in this life.

Paragraph 1: Believers May Have Assurance in This Life

The Historical Background
In the history of the church, there have been those who argue that assurance of salvation is not possible in this life. For example, the Roman

---

10. 1 John 4:13; Hebrews 6:11-12

11. Romans 5:1, 2, 5; Romans 14:17; Psalm 119:32

12. Romans 6:1,2; Titus 2:11, 12, 14

13. Song of Solomon 5:2, 3, 6

14. Psalm 51:8, 12, 14

15. Psalm 116:11; Psalm 77:7-8; Psalm 31:22

16. Psalm 30:7

17. 1 John 3:9

18. Luke 22:32

19. Psalm 42:5, 11

20. Lamentations 3:26-31

21. Sam Waldron, *A Modern Exposition of the 1689 Baptist Confession of Faith* (Durham, England: Evangelical Press, 1989), 226.

Catholic Council of Trent declared that the assurance of being in a state of grace and final salvation is impossible, except by special revelation to select saints.[22] This special revelation is something very rare and not to be enjoyed by the ordinary Christian. In fact, Rome not only views assurance as ordinarily impossible, or extremely rare, it also regards it as undesirable and dangerous in most cases. The thought is that if a person is sure he has eternal life, it will lead to presumption and to careless living. By denying the possibility of assurance, Rome maintains the power of the priests over ignorant consciences and, in Dabney's words, "they make gain of their absolutions, masses, indulgences... "[23] It is in Rome's interest to keep her devotees in a state of uncertainty.

Likewise, Arminianism leads to a form of the same error because it denies the doctrine of the preservation and perseverance of the saints. According to this perspective, a man may be saved today and lost tomorrow. While there may be a present assurance that you are presently saved, there can be no assurance in this life that you will remain saved and be finally saved in the end.

Sadly, this error of denying the possibility of assurance is not confined to Romanists and Arminians. There is even a kind of Calvinist who tends to be very nervous about the whole idea of assurance and to regard it as presumption. Spurgeon describes in his own colorful manner who were around in his day. He says:

> I have seen their long faces. I have heard their whining periods, and read their dismal sentences in which they say something to this effect – "Groan in the Lord always, and again I say groan! He that mourneth and weepeth, he that doubteth and feareth, he that distrusteth and dishonoureth his God, shall be saved." That seems to be the sum and substance of their very ungospel-like gospel.[24]

These are hyper-Calvinists who are so afraid of a false assurance, they've swung to this opposite extreme.

In opposition to these denials of assurance, this first paragraph argues for the possibility of enjoying the full assurance of salvation in this life. The paragraph contains a concession and an assertion.

A Concession

"Although temporary believers and other unregenerate men, may vainly deceive themselves with false hopes and carnal presumptions of being in the favor of God and state of salvation, which hope of theirs shall perish...."

Though the main concern of paragraph 1 is to assert that true believers may have assurance in this life, it begins by conceding the fact that there

22. See *The Council of Trent: The Sixth Session: Canon XV, XVI.* This may be accessed at https://history.hanover.edu/texts/trent/ct06.html

23. Robert Dabney, *Systematic Theology* (1871; reprint, Carlisle, PA: Banner of Truth Trust, 1985), 701.

24. Spurgeon, "Full Assurance," 535.

is also the danger of a false assurance.[25] It speaks of "temporary believers and other unregenerate men."

Temporary believers are those who have a kind of faith that is not saving faith. It is not the faith of those who are regenerate. Notice the language, "temporary believers and *other* unregenerate men" (emphasis added). These temporary believers are included in the category of those who are not regenerate.

The New Testament, in several places, speaks of a kind of faith men may have that is not saving. For example, we see this in the second soil in the parable of the sower.[26] These hearers of the word are described as believing in some sense, and as even being very emotional about it, but theirs was a spurious faith that never brought forth saving fruit. There is the example of Simon the sorcerer in his initial response to the preaching of Philip.[27] Also some of the crowds who followed Christ are described as believing in some sense but, at the same time, they turned away from Him when confronted with the true nature of the salvation He came to give.[28] They were looking to Christ for bread or for temporal blessings or miracles, not for the salvation from sin Christ came to accomplish and to provide for sinners. Therefore, their faith was a false and temporary faith.

There are other kinds of false faith besides temporary faith. There can be an intellectual understanding and acceptance of the facts of the gospel that is void of repentant trust in the Christ of the gospel.[29] In addition to "temporary believers," the Confession also refers to "other unregenerate men" who "may vainly deceive themselves with false hopes and carnal presumptions of being in the favor of God and state of salvation, which hope of theirs shall perish." Those who have a false assurance are not always "temporary" professors of faith. They may continue in their false hope even to the day of judgment. It is a scary prospect, but Jesus tells us in Matthew 7:22-23 that "Many will say to Me in that day, 'Lord, Lord, have we not prophesied in Your name, cast out demons in Your name, and done many wonders in Your name?' And then I will declare to them, 'I never knew you; depart from Me, you who practice lawlessness.'"

An Assertion

After making this concession, we then come to the main assertion of the first paragraph:

> ...yet such as truly believe in the Lord Jesus, and love him in sincerity, endeavoring to walk in all good conscience before him, may in this life be certainly assured that they are in the state of grace, and may rejoice in the hope of the glory of God, which hope shall never make them ashamed.

---

25. Waldron, *Modern Exposition*, 227.

26. Luke 8:13

27. Acts 8:9-23

28. John 2:23-25; John 8:31-47

29. Acts 26:27

Here, the Confession asserts that it is possible to have full assurance of salvation in this life. It speaks of *the proper subjects* of this assurance: "such as truly believe in the Lord Jesus, and love him in sincerity," and who give evidence of their faith and love for Christ by "endeavoring to walk in all good conscience before him."

Then it speaks of *the present and eternal scope* of this assurance: "may in this life be certainly assured that they are in the state of grace." And not only may they be assured that they are presently in the state of grace, but it says: "and may rejoice in the hope of the glory of God, which hope shall never make them ashamed." What scriptural evidence may be given to support this assertion of the Confession?

First, there are many examples in the Bible of persons who possessed this assurance. Job says in Job 19:25-26: "For I *know*[30] that my Redeemer lives, and He shall stand at last on the earth; and after my skin is destroyed, this I *know*, that in my flesh I shall see God." When Job said this, he had assurance of his salvation. David, though it appears he had his assurance shaken after his backsliding and sin with Bathsheba, could say later in Psalm 32:1, speaking of himself: "Blessed is he whose transgression is forgiven, whose sin is covered." He knew his sins were forgiven and covered.

What about the apostle Paul? Listen to Paul in 2 Timothy 4:6-8: "For I am already being poured out as a drink offering, and the time of my departure is at hand. I have fought the good fight, I have finished the race, I have kept the faith. Finally, there is laid up for me the crown of righteousness, which the Lord, the righteous Judge, will give to me on that Day, and not to me only, but also to all who have loved His appearing."

J.C. Ryle points out that in this passage we see Paul looking three ways: downward, backward, and forward.[31] He looks *downward* to the grave without fear: "For I am already being poured out as a drink offering and the time of my departure is at hand." He looks backward to his life as a gospel minister without shame: "I have fought the good fight, I have finished my course, I have kept the faith." And he looks *forward* to the great day of reckoning without doubt: "There is laid up for me a crown of righteousness, which the Lord, the righteous Judge, will give to me on that day." Paul had a full assurance of his salvation. In 2 Timothy 1:12, he says: "I know whom I have believed and am persuaded that He is able to keep what I have committed to Him until that Day." That's assurance.

Speaking not only of himself, but with reference to the believers in Corinth, Paul says: "For we know that if our earthly house, this tent, is destroyed, we have a building from God, a house not made with

---

30. Italics mine. The same when any word or phrase in a Scripture quote is in italics in this chapter.

31. J.C. Ryle, "Assurance," chapter seven in *Holiness* (1879; reprint, Darlington, Co. Durham, England: Evangelical Press, 6th ed., 1991), 98-100. This paragraph adapted from his comments on this text.

hands, eternal in the heavens."[32] Consider what he wrote to the Roman Christians, again, not merely with reference to himself, but with reference to them as well. Romans 8:16: "The Spirit Himself bears witness with our spirit that we are children of God." Romans 8:31-34a: "What then shall we say to these things? If God is for us, who can be against us. He who did not spare His own Son, but delivered Him up for us all, how shall He not with Him also freely give us all things? Who shall bring a charge against God's elect? It is God who justifies. Who is he who condemns?" Romans 8:38-39: "I am persuaded that neither death nor life, nor angels nor principalities nor powers, nor things present, nor things to come, nor height nor depth, nor any other created thing, shall be able to separate us from the love of God which is in Christ Jesus." These are all strong assertions of assurance.

John speaks of this often in his first epistle. He had assurance, and he assumes that many of his readers have it or should have it. "Now by this *we know* that we know Him" (1 John 2:3); "*We know* that we have passed from death to life" (1 John 3:14); "*We know* that we are of God, and the whole world lies under the sway of the wicked one" (1 John 5:19).

Now, this assurance was not merely confined to the days of the apostles. There have been many throughout the history of the church who have given every evidence of being true Christians and have also known this same assurance. There are those who have marched to the stake to be burned for their faith with a full assurance of their salvation. There are many who have known this assurance in the past and many who know it in our own day.

Second, not only are there many examples of persons who enjoyed assurance; we are also exhorted and commanded in the Bible to get this assurance if we don't have it and to preserve it if we do. For example, Hebrews 6:11: "And we desire that each one of you show the same diligence to the full assurance of hope until the end;" and 2 Peter 1:10: "Therefore, brethren, be even more diligent to make your calling and election sure." The infinitive translated "sure" is in the middle voice. The idea is to make yourself sure.

Think again of the first epistle of John where John tells us that one of the reasons he wrote it was to help believers to have assurance. "These things I have written to you who believe in the name of the Son of God, *that you may know* that you have eternal life, and that you may continue to believe in the name of the Son of God" (1 John 5:13).[33] One of the purposes for which John wrote his epistle is that those who believe in the name of the Son of God may know that they have eternal life. He writes to promote and confirm the believer's assurance of salvation. The assumption, therefore, is that a true believer can and should have assurance.

---

32. 2 Corinthians 5:1
33. Italics mine.

Paragraph 2: The Three-Fold Basis of Assurance

The focus of the second paragraph is on the threefold basis of assurance, or the three roots of a biblical assurance of salvation. The paragraph begins by once more asserting that there is such a thing as an "infallible" assurance, an assurance that does not deceive. "This certainty is not a bare conjectural and probable persuasion." In other words, it is not a mere wish or hope-so-maybe-so, or a mere probability, falling short of a full certainty. Why? It is not built on "a fallible hope." The word "hope" seems to be used here objectively to refer to that which is the basis of one's hope. So the Confession asserts that this assurance available to the Christian is not built upon something fallible, something that is subject to failure. Then, the Confession proceeds to lay out the threefold basis of this assurance. It is also helpful to think of these as three roots that feed the flower of assurance.[34] What are they?

The Objective Foundation of Assurance

The first root of assurance, according to the Confession, is something totally outside of ourselves. I refer to it as the objective foundation of assurance. The Confession says that this "infallible assurance of faith" is "founded on the blood and righteousness of Christ revealed in the gospel."

Interestingly, the earlier Westminster Confession refers to this first root as "the divine truth of the promises of salvation." It seems this is a different way of saying much the same thing.[35] The promises of salvation have reference to the atoning blood and righteousness of Christ revealed in the gospel; and, in a real sense, the blood and righteousness of Christ and their implications for sinners form the content of the gospel promises of salvation.[36] The emphasis in both Confessions is on the fact that the first root of assurance is totally outside of us in the realities and promises of the gospel; namely, Christ and His work for us freely extended to us in the gospel, and the promises of salvation to all who trust in Him and His work alone. This is the taproot of assurance, the primary source, the objective foundation of assurance in the heart of the believer. There are many texts we could look at, but space allows us to look at only one that sufficiently illustrates and demonstrates this.

Paul writes in Roman 8:33-34: "Who shall bring a charge against God's elect? It is God who justifies. Who is he who condemns? It is Christ who died, and furthermore is also risen, who is even at the right hand of God, who also makes intercession for us." Consider closely verse 34 which begins with these words, "Who is he who condemns?" This is a defiant expression of assurance of salvation. It comes as part of a series of confident challenges. This one is connected to the last words of verse 33, and to the first part of verse 34. Paul says in verse 33b, "It is God who

---

34. Waldron, *A Modern Exposition*, 228.

35. Ibid.

36. Ibid.

justifies." It is God who declares the believing sinner righteous in his sight. Verse 34a says, "Who is he who condemns?" Then Paul goes on to describe the basis of this confidence.

The confidence Paul expresses is based on Christ and His saving accomplishment for us. "Who is he who condemns? It is Christ who died, and furthermore is also risen, who is even at the right hand of God, who also makes intercession for us." All four of the things he mentions about the work of Christ have to do, not with Christ's work in us, but with Christ's work for us. "It is Christ who died," making full atonement for our sins. "Furthermore," it is Christ who "is also risen," confirming that His sacrifice was sufficient and accepted by God. It is Christ "who is even at the right hand of God," the supreme place of acceptance and authority, having successfully finished the work the Father gave Him to do. And it is Christ "who also makes intercession for us."

If there is any lingering fear that, though I may not presently be condemned, I still could be in the future, the last aspect of Christ's saving work which Paul mentions effectively expels it. An Arminian friend comes along and says, "Well, yes, it's possible to have a present assurance of being in a present state of salvation, but it is not possible to be presently assured that you will always be saved and that you will finally be saved on the last day. It is possible a true Christian might fall away and apostatize and, therefore, be condemned in the end." What kind of assurance is that? What do we say to this man? Among many other things, we say this: "...who also makes intercession for us." What's the connection? The Bible tells us that the Lord Jesus not only offered up Himself as the sacrifice for sin once and for all upon the cross, but having been raised from the dead, and ascended to the right hand of the Father, He ever lives to make intercession for all who come to God by Him. And what is the end secured by our Lord's intercession? Hebrews 7:25 says: "Therefore He is also *able to save to the uttermost* those who come to God through Him, since He always lives to make intercession for them."[37] The end secured is salvation to the uttermost, or uttermost salvation. In other words, He is able to save completely and to bring us safely all the way to glory. This is the end secured by the ongoing intercession of Christ for His people, an intercession that is based on our Lord's finished, all sufficient, substitutionary, curse-bearing death for our sins on the cross.

The assurance expressed by the apostle and for which he is arguing belongs to every Christian. It is grounded in gospel facts and realities that are totally outside of himself. He says nothing about himself, nothing about who he is, and nothing about what he has or has not done. He says nothing about what he feels or does not feel. He looks away from and out of himself to Christ and His work for us and there he rests his case. This is the primary source and taproot of assurance of salvation. I let all my fears, doubts and uncertainties drive me afresh, constantly, and repeatedly to Christ and His work for us as my only trust, saying,

---

37. Italics mine.

"Nothing in my hand I bring—simply to thy cross I cling." Spurgeon gives this very helpful illustration:

> A great monarch was accustomed on certain set occasions to entertain all the beggars of the city. Around him were placed his courtiers, all clothed in rich apparel. The beggars sat at the same table in their rags of poverty. Now it came to pass, that on a certain day, one of the courtiers had spoiled his silken apparel, so that he dared not put it on, and he felt, "I cannot go to the king's feast today, for my robe is foul." He sat weeping till the thought struck him, "Tomorrow when the king holds his feast, some will come as courtiers happily decked in their beautiful array, but others will come and be made quite as welcome who will be dressed in rags. 'Well, well,' said he, 'so long as I may see the king's face, and sit at the royal table, I will enter among the beggars.' So without mourning because he lost his silken habit (costume), he put on the rags of a beggar, and he saw the King's face as well as if he had worn his scarlet and fine linen.[38]

Spurgeon then goes on to make the application: "My soul has done this full many a time, when her evidences of salvation have been dim; and I bid you do the same when you are in like case. If you cannot come to Jesus as a saint, come as a sinner; only do come with simple faith to Him; and you shall receive joy and peace."[39]

You see, no matter how low I may be and no matter how dull and dry and dark I may feel in my soul, Christ is still the same. He and all the benefits of His saving work for sinners are still as free to me now, just as I am, as He has always been to me from the beginning and will always be. Therefore, if my evidences of grace are so dim that I wonder if I even have any and I feel that I can't come to Jesus with any confidence that a true work of grace has been wrought in my soul, I can still come as a sinner and nothing but a sinner, looking out of myself to Him and His work alone. His promise will always be true that "Him who comes to me I will by no means cast out" (John 6:37b).

The Subjective Supports of Assurance
The Confession goes on to mention a second root of assurance. It says that this assurance is, "founded on the blood and righteousness of Christ revealed in the gospel; *and also upon the inward evidence of those graces of the Spirit unto which promises are made.*"[40] The subjective supports of assurance are the evidences of Christ's work in us, or what are sometimes called the evidences of grace, or the marks of the new birth. The salvation Christ gives to sinners includes two major and inseparable components. It includes a change of status and standing before God, which is solely based on Christ's work for us, and it includes a change of nature, which is the result of Christ's work in us. And both a change of status and a

---

38. Charles Spurgeon (1834–1892), *Spurgeon's Sermon Illustrations: Choice Selections from the "Prince of Preachers,"* compiled and edited by David O. Fuller (Grand Rapids: Kregel Publications, 1990), 23-24.

39. Ibid.

40. Italics mine.

334 A New Exposition of The London Baptist Confession of Faith of 1689

change of nature will always come together. Our acceptance with God and status before God as His justified children are not *based* on a change of nature. But at the same time, they are never separated from a change of nature. Where there is faith in Christ alone for acceptance with God, there has also occurred the new birth. Where there is justification, there is also regeneration and ongoing sanctification.

Now there are various evidences of the new birth and of ongoing sanctification referred to in many different places in the New Testament. But one of the most succinct and helpful references to this source of assurance is in the epistle mentioned earlier in this chapter, the first epistle of John. You remember John says in 1 John 5:13: "These things I have written to you who believe in the name of the Son of God, that you may know that you have eternal life." The phrase "These things" is not merely a reference to that verse; it refers to his entire letter.[41] John is saying that one of the main reasons he wrote the things he has written in this epistle is in order that believers might have assurance. One of the things John does in this letter is to set forth various marks of grace, or

---

41. This may be questioned. Here are some exegetical considerations. The verse begins with the Greek word *tauta* (Ταῦτα) translated "these things." A question raised is whether *tauta* refers to preceding material or to what follows. I think it clearly refers to what John has written preceding this for the following reasons. The phrase, "these things I have written to you who believe on the name of the Son of God," is followed by a *hina* (ἵνα) clause giving the purpose for the writing. It is *in order that* you may know that you have eternal life. However, the next verse introduces an entirely different subject, the subject of prayer (v. 14).

Then the question becomes, does "these things I have written" refer to what John just wrote immediately before this in verses 1-12, perhaps, or in verses 11-12, or does it refer to everything he has written before this in the entire epistle? There are different opinions among commentators. I think the phrase refers to the entirety of the letter or, at least much of the entirety of the letter, for the following reasons:

First, the structure of 1 John betrays a kind of cyclical structure throughout the letter, in which John keeps repeating the same things over, though in slightly different ways. Therefore, if the phrase refers to what precedes it, it really refers to most all of what precedes it.

Second, a comparison between the statement of purpose near the end of 1 John and a similar statement near the conclusion of the gospel of John further supports the understanding that the statement of purpose in 1 John is referring to the whole epistle preceding it. This is because the similar statement in John's gospel is, without doubt, referring to the entirety of his gospel account. Note in John 20:31, he writes, "These are written that you may believe that Jesus is the Christ, the Son of God, and that believing you may have life in His name," referring to all that he has written already in his gospel record. In our text in 1 John, the statement, "These things I have written to you who believe in the name of the Son of God, that you may know that you have eternal life," is clearly parallel in purpose and language. Therefore, it is most natural to understand 1 John 5:13 in the same way, to refer to all that has preceded it.

Third, it has been argued, and I think rightly, that the phrase *tauta egrapha humin* (Ταῦτα ἔγραψα ὑμῖν) "these things I have written to you," forms an *inclusio* with 1 John 1:4, *kai tauta graphomen hemeis* (ταῦτα γράφομεν ἡμεῖς), "And these things we write to you that your joy may be full." An inclusio is a literary device that serves like brackets, or a frame, around a similar body of material. So John tells us near the beginning of his letter what his purpose is in writing it, i.e., that our joy may be full. Then he says it again in our text near the end of the letter, just in different words, "These things I have written that you may know that you have eternal life." Obviously, these two ideas are intimately related. How can your joy be full if you are uncertain that you have eternal life? In short, John's reference in 1 John 5:13 to "These things I have written" refers to the whole of the preceding letter.

evidences of the new birth, by which we can test ourselves. For example, consider four things John mentions.

First, the true children of God see and feel that they are sinners in need of Christ and seek to deal honestly with God about their sins. By nature, the unregenerate walk in darkness and falsehood before God, justify themselves, and seek to keep up a good opinion of themselves. But those who have come to know and to trust Jesus Christ walk in the light of truth, which includes being honest and truthful before God about their sins. A key text is 1 John 1:6–2:2:

> If we say that we have fellowship with Him, and walk in darkness, we lie and do not practice the truth. But if we walk in the light as He is in the light, we have fellowship with one another, and the blood of Jesus Christ His Son cleanses us from all sin. If we say that we have no sin, we deceive ourselves, and the truth is not in us. If we confess our sins, He is faithful and just to forgive us our sins and to cleanse us from all unrighteousness. If we say that we have not sinned, we make Him a liar, and His word is not in us. My little children, these things I write to you, so that you may not sin. And if anyone sins, we have an Advocate with the Father, Jesus Christ the righteous. And He Himself is the propitiation for our sins, and not for ours only but also for the whole world.

Do you see the contrast being made in that passage? There are those who walk in darkness, and there are those who walk in the light. One of the ways that true Christians who walk in the light are known is they do not try to cover or minimize the reality of their sins. They do not try to justify themselves before God. They seek to deal honestly and truthfully with God about their sins. They walk in the light, not in pretense, willing to have their sins exposed by God's truth. Their hearts echo the sentiments of the psalmist when he cried, "Search me O God and know my thoughts, try me, and know my anxieties, and see if there is any wicked way in me" (Ps. 139:23, 24). They know and confess that they are sinners constantly in need of Christ as their advocate and of His blood to cleanse them.

Second, a person who has been born again is marked by repentance from sin. He is looking to Christ alone for salvation, but he is also endeavoring to turn from and to forsake all of his sins as he is made aware of them. "Whoever is born of God does not sin, for His seed remains in him, and he cannot sin, because he is born of God" (1 John 3:9). John does not mean that one who is born again is sinless in the absolute sense. This is the same John who just said over in 1:8: "If we say that we have no sin, we deceive ourselves, and the truth is not in us." And, "If we say that we have not sinned, we make him a liar, and His word is not in us" (1 John 1:10). This is the same John who speaks to Christians about confessing our remaining sins as we become aware of them and of the Lord Jesus being the Christians' advocate before the Father when the Christians sin. John clearly is not speaking of sinlessness here. But he is underscoring a fundamental difference between the regenerate man and the unregenerate man. The regenerate man, the man who is born of the

Spirit, no longer lives and walks in the ways of sin as a lifestyle. The verb is in the present tense. He is neither committing nor practicing sin. More specifically, in the context of this letter, it may be that John especially has in mind the sin of apostasy.[42] The genuine believer never apostatizes from the faith and returns to a life of unbelief and impenitence. He has a repentant heart and lifestyle.

A third infallible evidence of salvation is the desire and endeavor to obey God's commandments. This includes not only a turning from the pursuit of sin, but also the turning to the pursuit of obedience to God's commandments. "By this we know that we know Him, if we keep his commandments" (1 John 2:3). The person who is born again is a person who endeavors to live according to God's will. He wants to do the things that please God. Though he often fails, he is grieved about his many failures because his heart's desire and serious endeavor is to obey his Heavenly Father in everything, without exception.

Fourth, John tells us that those who belong to Christ have a practical affection and attachment to God's people. "We know that we have passed from death to life, because we love the brethren" (1 John 3:14). A person born of the Spirit has a special love and attraction to all those who evidence themselves to be true disciples of Jesus Christ. He loves the brethren because they are God's people and because of what he sees of the grace of God in them. He wants to be part of and share his life with them. As John goes on to explain, this love is a practical love causing us to seek to serve them. We never love them perfectly or sinlessly, but we count God's people as our people, our special family in Christ.

These are four simple marks or evidences of grace. There is often a great difference in the depth and strength of these marks among the true children of God.[43] The Bible speaks of degrees of maturity in the spiritual life. It speaks of growth in grace. But still, making every allowance, God has given us simple clear-cut marks like these that will, in at least some measure, be evident in every soul born of the Spirit. And as we see them in any real measure in our lives, they serve as supports to the believer's assurance. This brings us now to the third root that feeds the flower of assurance.

The Divine Agent of Assurance

The Confession next mentions "the testimony of the Spirit of adoption, witnessing with our spirits that we are the children of God." This brings us back to Romans 8. Paul writes in verses 15-16: "For you did not receive the spirit of bondage again to fear, but you received the Spirit of adoption by whom we cry out, 'Abba, Father.' The Spirit Himself bears witness with our spirit that we are children of God." This is the key passage with reference to this third root of assurance. There is also Galatians 4:6: "And

---

42. Cf. 1 John 2:19 and 1 John 5:16-18

43. Some of the language in this paragraph is paraphrased or adapted from a gospel tract by J.C. Ryle (1816–1900) entitled, "Are You Born Again" (reprint, Berryville, VA: Hess Publications, 2012), 7.

because you are sons, God has sent forth the Spirit of His Son into your hearts, crying out, 'Abba, Father.'" And we might also add 1 Corinthians 2:12: "Now we have received, not the spirit of the world, but the Spirit who is from God, that we might know the things that have been freely given to us by God." The New Testament does, indeed, teach that one of the sources of assurance is the Spirit of Adoption bearing witness with our spirit that we are the children of God (Rom. 8:16). There is no doubt about that. But now the question is, what exactly is the witness of the Spirit and what is its relationship to the other two sources of assurance? There are two major errors we need to avoid.

One error that some have argued is that the witness of the Spirit is simply the witness given by the marks of the new birth in God's people. We see the marks and evidences of the work of the Spirit in our hearts and lives and this is the witness of the Holy Spirit. This view simply joins together two of the three roots of assurance already mentioned in the Confession and makes them one. The marks of the new birth are the witness of the Holy Spirit.

There are problems with this interpretation of Romans 8:15-16. It is true Paul has been talking earlier in the chapter about the Spirit's work of sanctifying us; His enabling us to walk not after the flesh but after the Spirit, and so on. In verses 13-14, he speaks of the Spirit's work of leading us and enabling us to be putting to death our remaining sin. This is one of the marks of grace. This is in the category of the evidences of salvation we considered earlier. Then in verse 15, he speaks of the Spirit's work of producing in us a childlike disposition toward God, as opposed to a tormenting dread of God; a childlike disposition that comes to the level of our consciousness by inclining us to cry to God about the needs of our soul. "For you did not receive the spirit of bondage again to fear, but you received the Spirit of Adoption by whom we cry out, 'Abba, Father.'"

The word translated "cry" is often used in the New Testament to denote a cry of distress.[44] One of the marks of the believer is that he no longer characteristically runs from God or draws back from Him in times of difficulty. He has a childlike disposition toward God by which he cries to Him in his distresses. He cries to God as a Father about the needs of his soul. I would argue that this is indeed one of the evidences of grace, an evidence of faith. These are things *we do* by the power and influence of the indwelling Spirit in our hearts, and these are all evidences of His work in us.

But what we have in verse 16 is something in addition to that. The text describes, not what we do by the Spirit's power which evidences His work in our lives, but it describes what the Spirit Himself does in addition to that. Notice the emphatic way Paul puts this. We have received the Spirit of Adoption by which we cry, Abba, Father. And then he says, "The Spirit *Himself* bears witness with our spirit." Literally, it reads in the Greek text, "Himself, the Spirit bears witness." He could have simply

---

44. Matthew 9:27, 14:26; Luke 9:39

said, "The Spirit bears witness," or, "the Spirit bears witness with our spirit." But that's not what he said. He deliberately put it this way: "The Spirit *Himself* bears witness with our spirit." This way of putting it guards us from thinking that he is merely talking about the evidences of the work of Spirit in our lives. No, it is the person of the Spirit Himself witnessing together with our spirit.

You see, the Holy Spirit is not only instrumental in *making us* God's children by awakening within us faith in Christ and producing new life. There is also the Spirit's work of *making us aware* that we are God's children. This is the Spirit Himself making us aware, causing us to know, that we are the children of God.

But there is a *second way* this has been understood, and this understanding can be dangerous. Recognizing what has just been pointed out, there have been some who have gone on to argue that this text is referring to some secret revelation of the Spirit to your heart. In some mysterious way the Spirit, as it were, inwardly speaks to a man by a kind of inward voice, or impression, and assures him that he is a child of God. Therefore, in reality, according to this view, the witness of the Spirit amounts to some kind of new extrabiblical revelation of the Spirit. He inwardly tells you, or inwardly reveals to you that you are a child of God, not in, or by, or together with the Word of God and the marks of grace, but in a kind of direct special communication.

I agree with Jonathan Edwards who said that such a notion of the witness of the Spirit is dangerous and delusive and produces "many mischiefs," as he puts it, that have arisen from it. Edwards' comments:

> Many mischiefs have arisen from that false and delusive notion of the witness of the Spirit, that it is a kind of inward voice, suggestion, or declaration from God to a man, that he is beloved, pardoned, elected, or the like.... It is to be feared that multitudes of souls have been eternally undone by it.[45]

In paragraph 3 of this chapter, our Confession states that this assurance is "without extraordinary revelation."[46] In other words, this is not any direct revelation from the Spirit detached from the Word of God.

If the witness of the Spirit is not simply the witness to our sonship given by the marks of the new birth, and if it is not some secret inward voice or special revelation in your heart telling you that you are a Christian, what is it? I agree with the greater part of credible, respected, and Reformed exegetes and theologians that the Spirit witnesses with our spirit, not by some special revelation, but by enabling us *clearly to discern* from the scriptures the evidence of His work in our hearts and by making the promises of the gospel precious to us and by working faith in us to lay firm hold of them.

---

45. Jonathan Edwards, "Treatise Concerning Religious Affections" in *The Works of Jonathan Edwards,* Vol. 1 (1834; reprint, Carlisle, PA: Banner of Truth Trust, 1987), 274.

46. See near the middle of paragraph 3 in the Confession.

Remember the other roots of assurance: the promises of the gospel and the evidences of grace. These two roots nourish the flower of assurance. But what is it that makes all that work, so to speak, to produce a felt sense of assurance in my heart? It is the Holy Spirit. He applies the promises to my soul by giving me faith to believe them. And He shines, as it were, upon the work He has done and is doing in my soul. And He so does this that I have a felt confidence in my status as an adopted child of God. I agree with the comments of Joel Beeke:

> At every point in true assurance, the activity of the Holy Spirit is essential. Without the Spirit's application the promises of God will never affect us, and without the enlightening of the Spirit, self-examination tends to nothing but morbid introspection, bondage, and legalism.[47]

This second paragraph ends with a reference to the effects of assurance in the heart of a true believer. Contrary to the Roman Catholic fear that assurance produces presumption and careless living, the Confession states that a biblical assurance, "as a fruit thereof," keeps "the heart both humble and holy." The Confession will have more to say on the fruits of assurance later, as we shall see.

Paragraph 3: The Lack of Full Assurance in a True Believer

A True Believer May Be Lacking a Full Assurance

Previously, we considered those who deny that a believer can have assurance in this life. Here in the first part of this third paragraph, the Confession seeks to guard us from the opposite extreme. There have been those who teach that if you do not have a full assurance of salvation, this proves you're not a believer at all. In opposition to this error, the Confession states at the beginning of this paragraph: "This infallible assurance doth not so belong to the essence of faith, but that a true believer may wait long, and conflict with many difficulties, before he be partaker of it." Maybe you have heard preachers who have said something like this from the pulpit: "If you don't have full assurance, you're not converted, and you don't have faith." I used to hear this kind of thing from the pulpit sometimes in the church settings in which I grew up: "Do you know that you know that you know that you know that you are saved, and if you died right now, you will go to heaven?" Then it is implied that if you ever have any doubts about it at all, this means you do not have faith and you are not saved.

Let me also mention that this idea that there is no faith in Christ where there is not a full assurance of salvation has sometimes been attributed to the sixteenth century Reformers. Then, the attempt is made to contrast their teaching with that of the late sixteenth-century and seventeenth-century Puritans. Now, this is partly based on the way the

---

47. Joel Beeke, *Assurance of Faith: Calvin, English Puritanism, and the Dutch Second Reformation* (New York: Peter Lang Publishing, Inc. 1991), 173.

Reformers defined saving faith. They rightly included in their definition the assurance of God's benevolence toward each believer in Christ.[48] They were properly concerned to emphasize that saving faith involves personal appropriation of the gospel and its promises to oneself. They were also concerned to combat what had been for a long time the prevailing Roman Catholic notion that assurance is not possible in this life. In contrast, many of the Puritan treatments of this subject are written on a more pastoral level to help struggling believers, rather than on a polemic level to combat Rome.

However, a more careful study of the Reformers shows that they also allowed for the fact that true believers sometimes struggle with assurance of salvation. When defining saving faith, they often defined faith as it is considered independently and alone. And, of course, defined that way, faith is the opposite of doubt and uncertainty. But they also understood that faith, as it dwells in the heart of the believer, is dwelling in a heart still plagued with remaining sin. Therefore, our faith in Christ and the believing appropriation of the promises to ourselves can vary in strength and must battle with remaining darkness of mind and unbelief. For example, Calvin wrote: "While we teach that faith ought to be certain and assured, we cannot imagine any certainty that is not tinged with doubt, or any assurance that is not assailed by some anxiety." [49] The fact is, there is no real substantial difference between the Reformers and the Puritans here. There is a difference in emphasis, perhaps, because of a different context, and because of fighting different battles, but not a real difference theologically. For a definitive demonstration of this, I would highly recommend Joel Beeke's *Assurance of Faith: Calvin, English Puritanism, and the Dutch Second Reformation.*[50]

What do we say to those who really would argue that it is not possible for a true believer to be lacking a full assurance of salvation? Consider again the text that has already been referenced several times, 1 John 5:13. What does John say? "These things I have written to you." To whom? "To you who believe on the name of the Son of God." These were believers, true believers. But he says to them, "These things I have written to you who believe in the name of the Son of God," not *because* you know, but in order *"that* you may know that you have eternal life." The implication is that it is possible for a true believer not to know; to be lacking in the certainty that he has eternal life. If faith automatically brings full

---

48. For example, Calvin in his *Institutes* defines saving faith as "a firm and certain knowledge of God's benevolence toward us, founded upon the truth of the freely given promise in Christ, both revealed to our minds and sealed upon our hearts through the Holy Spirit." John Calvin, *Institutes of the Christian Religion*, ed. by John T. McNeil and trans. by Ford Lewis Battles (Philadelphia: The Westminster Press, 1960; reissue, Louisville: Westminster John Knox Press, 2006), Vol. 1, Book 3, Chapter 2, Section 9, 551.

49. Ibid. Vol. 2, Book 3.2.17, 562.

50. Beeke, *Assurance of Faith: Calvin, English Puritanism, and the Dutch Second Reformation.* This is a revision of his Ph.D. dissertation for Westminster Seminary. Another version was later published under the title: *Quest for Full Assurance: The Legacy of John Calvin and His Successors* (Carlisle, PA: Banner of Truth Trust, 1999).

assurance, then John's words are nonsense. Indeed, much of 1 John would be nonsense. In addition to what's implied in this text, consider the following:[51]

First, it is evident that faith is not assurance of salvation because the basis of faith is the Word of God. Faith is being convinced of the truth of the gospel message and entrusting myself to the Christ of the gospel to save me. And the basis of that faith is the statements and propositions of God's Word. The Scriptures nowhere declare that Jeff Smith possesses eternal life. If they did, then it would be an act of faith for me to have assurance.[52] But the Scriptures never assert that any one of us by name is a Christian. Therefore, faith is not assurance. The gospel says, whoever believes in Christ shall be saved. And if I believe in Christ, I am saved and can know that I am saved. But then the question might come, "Am I really believing on Christ?" This is where the matter of assurance comes in.

Second, to say that faith is assurance of salvation is a logical contradiction.[53] If you say that saving faith includes the assurance that I am saved, that would be saying that a person must believe he is saved in order to be saved. But faith is not the belief we have been saved. It is instead the entrusting of oneself to Christ in order to be saved. A sinner goes to Christ for salvation because he is afraid that he is not saved, not because he believes he is saved.[54] Therefore, "if it is by faith that we receive salvation, faith cannot be the assurance that we are saved."[55] Here is a poor soul under conviction of sin and desiring to come to Christ. If I tell him faith is the assurance of salvation, I put up a roadblock between him and Christ. He might reason in this way, "I must believe that I am saved in order to be saved, but I feel that I am a lost sinner in need of salvation." Thus, such instruction has the tendency to leave him in that dismal spiritual condition. Instead of going to Christ just as he is *in order to be saved,* he is waiting for God, as it were, to zap him and to give him assurance, when the only way he can begin to have assurance is by first coming to Christ as a sinner who has no assurance.

Third, to say that faith is inseparable from a full assurance of salvation is to contradict the experience of some of God's people throughout the ages; and it also contradicts the experience of some of God's people in Scripture.

Consider, for example, 2 Peter 1:10: "Therefore, brethren, be even more diligent to make your call and election sure." As mentioned earlier, the infinitive "to make" in this text is in the middle voice. The idea is to make sure for yourselves; for yourselves make sure your calling and election. Do not rest short of being personally assured that you are one

---

51. The first two of the following arguments are found briefly mentioned by Sam Waldron, *A Modern Exposition of the 1689 Baptist Confession of Faith,* 189-90.

52. Ibid., 190.

53. Ibid.

54. Ibid.

55. Ibid.

of those God has effectually called and chosen. The command to make their calling and election sure implies that some were not sure, or at least the possibility that some might not be sure. Who are the people to whom this exhortation was directed? They are the people described in verse 1 of that same chapter: "Simon Peter, a bondservant and apostle of Jesus Christ, to those who have obtained like precious faith with us by the righteousness of our God and Savior Jesus Christ." To whom is he writing? He is not writing to people who are unbelievers and who need to be told how to be converted. He is writing to people who have already believed the gospel. And he says to them, though you have obtained like precious faith with us, though I have every reason to believe this is true of you (v. 1), give diligence, (v. 10), to make your calling and election sure to yourselves. So a person may have saving faith and still not have a rock-solid assurance of salvation.

There are many other examples of this that could be pointed to in the Scriptures. Read through the Psalms. In several instances, you see the psalmists, though they had faith, struggling with a sense of insecurity regarding their standing before God. At other times, they have full assurance. Read church history and Christian biographies and you will find that some of God's choicest saints sometimes struggled with assurance.

And then also consider, if faith is assurance of salvation, all the exhortations to believers in Scripture to attain assurance would be nonsense. 2 Peter 1:10 again: "Therefore, brethren, be even more diligent to make your call and election sure." This is given as a command to believers. What is the point in commanding believers to make their calling and election sure to themselves if being sure is automatically of the essence of faith? 2 Corinthians 13:5 says, "Examine yourselves as to whether you are in the faith. Test yourselves. Do you not know yourselves, that Jesus Christ is in you?" If faith equals assurance of salvation, what's the point in commanding professing believers to examine themselves whether they are in the faith?

These considerations show us that there may still be genuine faith, even where there is little assurance of salvation. Understanding this immediately delivers us from at least one unnecessary source of struggle about assurance.[56] If someone really believes that faith in Christ is inseparable from assurance, then what will happen if at any time he has any struggles with assurance? His very struggles will only take away any measure of assurance he does have. The very fact that, from time to time, he has any measure of doubt about his salvation will become another argument that he is not saved and will be viewed as a proof he is not saved. But even as there is weak faith and strong faith, and faith can be strengthened, so assurance can be increased as well. It is not an all or nothing matter. A true believer may presently be lacking a sense of full assurance but that does not mean he is not a true believer.

---

56. Ibid., 190-91.

But there is a balancing truth that we must not miss. This is not a chapter on saving faith, so I will not go into this in detail, but it is important to understand that, though faith is not assurance, it is the seed out of which assurance grows. Faith does have a measure of assurance in it. It does contain at least the seed of assurance.[57] Notice the Confession does not say "assurance is *not of* the essence of faith,"[58] as though there is absolutely no assurance in faith or any necessary connection between assurance and faith. Instead, it says "assurance *doth not so belong* to the essence of faith."[59] Those who believe the gospel do not just believe the facts of the gospel are true. They are looking to Christ for mercy, being moved to do so by the promises of the gospel. They are trusting in Christ to save them and appropriating the promises of the gospel to themselves.

This is what the Reformers were concerned to emphasize. Faith may struggle against unbelief, and there may be a painful conflict, but saving faith wrought in the heart by the Holy Spirit is never ultimately and fully overcome. Every believer is marked, at the very least, by the grace of hope, by some measure of expectation of good from Christ, as opposed to complete despair.[60] Also, the faith that receives Christ, also obtains with Him the gift of the Holy Spirit who dwells in the believer's heart as the Spirit of Adoption.[61] Therefore, the believer, even at his worst and when most in doubt, is never back in the state he was in as an unbeliever; a state in which he was at enmity with God and had no personal hope in God's mercy to sinners in Jesus Christ.

Therefore, since the seed of assurance is there in the heart of the believer, we may grow in our assurance of salvation. It's not all or nothing.[62] A person may have faith in Christ and be a true Christian and not be certain he is. A person may have a degree of assurance at one time that is stronger than what he has at another time. Some come immediately at the moment of their conversion to a full assurance and rarely have it shaken all of their days. Others, in the words of the Confession, "may wait long for it."

Assurance Should Be Pursued
In the second part of this third paragraph, the Confession speaks of the duty of using means to pursue and obtain assurance if you do not have it. Though a Christian may conflict with many difficulties, "yet being enabled by the Spirit to know the things which are freely given him of God, he may, without extraordinary revelation, in the right use of means, attain thereunto: and therefore it is the duty of everyone to give all diligence to make his calling and election sure…" We have already seen that the New Testament calls believers to pursue assurance. It is, as

57. Ibid., 190.
58. Italics mine.
59. Italics mine.
60. Waldron, *A Modern Exposition of the 1689 Baptist Confession of Faith*, 190.
61. Ibid.
62. Ibid., 191.

the Confession states, "the duty of everyone" to do so. But how does a professing Christian who is lacking assurance do that? The Confession says, "in the right use of means." We are to use biblical means to pursue assurance. It can be very helpful here to think again about the three roots of assurance. If we think of assurance as a flower, how do we feed the three roots that nourish and produce that flower?

First, give diligence to obtaining clearer and fuller views of the gospel. Think deeply about the gospel. Seek to make sure you properly understand the gospel. Be learning more about Christ: His goodness, His mercy, the work He has accomplished for sinners by His obedience and death, His promises to all who look to Him in faith. Meditate upon them. Feed your soul upon the promises and truths of the gospel of Jesus Christ. If one of the roots (the primary root) through which the Spirit works to produce assurance is a believing grasp upon the object of faith, Christ and His work for sinners as revealed in the gospel and its promises, this tells us that defective or constricted views of the gospel are one of the great causes of a lack of assurance.

Second, give diligence to grow in grace and in practical godliness. What's the second root of assurance? The evidences of grace in the heart and life. Therefore, a person lacking assurance needs to nurture and cultivate that root. This means I must apply myself to the means of grace: the regular sustained habit of private prayer, the devotional intake of God's word, faithful and careful attendance at church and upon the public means of grace. It means I need to be seeking to put to death remaining sin and to cultivate positive Christ-like virtues in my life. It means I must not be grieving the Holy Spirit by having a known controversy with God in some area of my life (Eph. 4:30). This is the way the Christian grows in grace and practical godliness. The Bible makes it clear that there is an inseparable connection between the diligent pursuit of practical godliness and a stable, well-grounded assurance.

2 Peter 1 is, again, a key passage here. We are told in verse 10 to give diligence to make our call and election sure. But how do we do that? Peter tells us in verses 5-11:

> But also for this very reason, diligently add to your faith, virtue; to virtue, knowledge; to knowledge, self-control; to self-control, perseverance; to perseverance, godliness; to godliness, brotherly kindness; and to brotherly kindness, love. For if these things are yours and abound, you will be neither barren nor unfruitful in the knowledge of our Lord Jesus Christ. For he who lacks these things is shortsighted, even to blindness, and has forgotten that he was cleansed from his old sins. Therefore, brethren, be even more diligent to make your call and election sure, for if you do these things you will never stumble; for so an entrance will be supplied to you abundantly into the everlasting kingdom of our Lord and Savior Jesus Christ.

Peter says we are to give diligence to add to our faith in this way: to grow in grace and godliness. And he says that this is the pathway of making our call and election sure to ourselves. But he says, without this our spiritual eyes will be dim and we will be like men in the dark who cannot plainly see the forgiveness of their past sins or the certainty of their future heavenly inheritance.

Sometimes, this is the problem with those who have constant struggles with assurance. They are grieving the Holy Spirit by chronic slackness and slothfulness, or there is some controversy with God, some sin they have been holding on to and for which they need to repent. They may keep examining themselves and crying to God, but it is no use as long as that is the real problem. Listen to Jonathan Edwards speaking to this very case:

> Many persons in such a case spend time in a fruitless labor in pouring over past experiences, and examining themselves by signs which they hear laid down from the pulpit, or read in books. There is other work for them to do, which, while they neglect, all their self-examinations are like to be in vain, if they should spend never so much time in them. The accursed thing is to be destroyed from their camp, and Achan to be slain, and until this be done they will be in trouble. It is not God's design that men should obtain assurance in any other way, than by mortifying corruption, increasing in grace, and obtaining the lively exercises of it. And although self-examination be a duty of great use and importance, and by no means neglected; yet it is not the principal means by which the saints do get satisfaction of their good estate. Assurance is not to be obtained so much by self-examination as by action.[63] The Apostle Paul maintained it chiefly this way, even by forgetting the things that were behind, and reaching forth unto those things that were before, pressing towards the mark for the prize of the high calling of God in Christ Jesus.[64]

Third, give diligence to proper and prayerful self-examination. Self-examination while you are grieving the Holy Spirit because of a controversy with God, as Edwards says, will probably not help you. You have an Achan in your camp. The accursed thing is covered and buried and hidden away in your tent and must be addressed. But that does not mean, as he also says, that self-examination is not important. Second Corinthians 13:5 says: "Examine yourselves as to whether you are in the faith. Test yourselves. Do you not know that Jesus Christ is in you?" We are expected to examine ourselves as to whether we are in the faith.

Self-examination serves at least two purposes in this matter of assurance. Since the Word of God has set forth various marks of a Christian, how can you possibly be made aware that you have them if you do not know what they are, and you do not examine yourself by them? Self-examination also drives us back again and again to Christ. For if we honestly examine ourselves, the true Christian will always find that, even though there seems to be evidences of grace there, we are far, far from what we ought to be. We will always see much sin and failure even at our best. Therefore, far from leading us to build our hope

---

63. Italics mine.
64. Edwards, *Works*, Vol. 1, "Religious Affections," 263.

on a self-righteous foundation, there are few things more useful than honest self-examination to keep us humble, to keep us from trusting in our own righteousness, and to cause us to build our hope of acceptance with God more firmly and exclusively upon Christ alone and what He has done for us.

Fourth, give diligence to praying for the witness of the Holy Spirit. It is the Spirit who makes these things effectual to produce a conscious and strong assurance of salvation. It is the Spirit who enables us to understand the gospel. It is the Spirit who makes the promises precious to us and convinces us of their trustworthiness. It is the Spirit who gives faith to believe them and strengthens faith. It is the Spirit who helps us to see from the Bible the marks of His saving work in our lives. He Himself bears witness together with these things, and with our spirits, that we are the children of God. Therefore, surely if we would know more assurance, we need to pray for greater measures of the operations of the Holy Spirit in our lives. Do not believe the error that all Christians have all the Holy Spirit they may ever expect to have. He is not limited. His fullness is inexhaustible. There is always more of His power, more of His gracious operations in the soul to be known. And there can be more of His bearing witness with my spirit that I am a child of God.

It was with reference to the work of the Holy Spirit in our hearts and lives that Jesus said in Luke 11:9ff, "Ask and it shall be given you; seek and you shall find; knock and it shall be open to you... If you then being evil, know how to give good gifts to your children; how much more will the heavenly Father give the Holy Spirit to those who ask him?" The gift of the Spirit, though in one sense already given to every believer, continues to be given in fuller and increasing measures as we seek more of Him from the Father in persistent and expectant prayer.

Benefits of Assurance

The latter part of this third paragraph mentions several benefits of assurance to motivate us not to be content without it. It mentions three categories of benefits, or what it calls "proper fruits of this assurance."

The "Heart" is "Enlarged in Peace and Joy in the Holy Spirit." Few things present a poorer testimony for the gospel than a gloomy, depressed Christian. The world looks at such a Christian and says, "What good has this man's Christianity done for him? Why would I ever want it?" But the assured Christian will be marked by peace and joy in the Holy Spirit.

The Heart is Enlarged "in Love and Thankfulness to God." The assured Christian will have a greater sense of love and affection for the God who saved him. And he will be a praising Christian with a heart full of gratitude. Assurance produces heart-felt exuberant worship.

The Heart is Enlarged "in Strength and Cheerfulness in the Duties of Obedience." A heart enlarged in peace and joy, and in love and thankfulness to God, will also be motivated and strengthened in holiness and obedience to God. It will not be a grudging obedience, but a cheerful obedience to the commands and duties God has given to us. The assured

Christian will tend to be much more zealous and diligent in his service to God than the Christian who is constantly plagued by uncertainty.

Finally, the third paragraph ends much the same way the second did by underscoring that these positive effects of assurance are contrary to any notion, such as is taught by Rome, that assurance promotes loose living. Rather, it promotes all these benefits and more, "so far is it from inclining men to looseness."

Paragraph 4: The Decrease and Recovery of Assurance

The focus of the fourth and final paragraph of this chapter of the Confession is on the variable nature of assurance in believers. It addresses the fact that assurance in a true believer may decrease for various reasons, while assurance decreased may be revived.

Assurance Can Be Decreased

The Possibility of Decreased Assurance
"True believers may have the assurance of their salvation divers ways, shaken, diminished and intermitted." The situation envisioned here is that of a true believer who has enjoyed the assurance of salvation, but the sense of assurance is no longer what it once was. "Shaken" seems to speak of a sudden jolt. Think of the panicky fear that came over the disciples in the boat when an unexpected and sudden windstorm fell on the lake.[65]

The word "diminished" speaks of something being lessened or reduced. It is not *entirely* gone, but it is not as strong and steady as it once was. "Intermitted" means caused to cease for a time or suspended. Whether or not assurance can be *completely and totally* lost in a true believer may be a matter of debate. Certainly, a believer is never back in the same position he was in before coming to faith in Christ. He is never unregenerate and entirely unbelieving. Where the Spirit indwells and faith exists, at least the seed of assurance remains. As the Confession asserts later in this paragraph, "they" are "never destitute of the seed of God and life of faith." At the very least, the believer knows who to turn to in his fears, the Lord Jesus. However, there is no question the Scriptures recognize the fact that a true believer may, indeed, have his assurance shaken or greatly diminished and, perhaps, so diminished that it appears to have been completely lost.

Causes of Decreased Assurance
The Confession mentions a number of ways a true believer's assurance may be decreased.

"*By Negligence in Preserving It.*" Assurance can be likened to a delicate flower which needs cultivation. As we saw earlier, slackness in our

---

65. Matthew 14:22-33; Mark 4:33-41; Luke 8:22-25

pursuit of practical godliness and in our use of the means of grace can damage or weaken it.

"By Falling into Gross Sin." The Confession says, "by falling into some special sin which woundeth the conscience and grieveth the Holy Spirit." Think of David when he committed adultery with Bathsheba and was accessory to the murder of her husband Uriah. Writing about the state of his heart in his psalm of repentance, Psalm 51, David prays in verse 8: "Make me hear joy and gladness, that the bones You have broken may rejoice." He writes in verse 12, "Restore to me the joy of my salvation." David's assurance had been severely diminished.

As we saw earlier, it is the Holy Spirit who is the divine agent of assurance in the heart of the believer. But, according to Ephesians 4:30, we can grieve the Holy Spirit. When we do, because we have a controversy with God, His assuring ministry in our hearts may in large part be withdrawn.

None of this is to say that every time a Christian sins, he loses, or should lose, assurance. The Christian life will always be an ongoing conflict with remaining sin. However, gross, scandalous sins or sins left remaining on our consciences unconfessed and not repudiated, can hinder and diminish assurance.

"By Some Sudden or Vehement Temptation." Think again of the disciples on the stormy sea. They were overcome with panicky fear and even began to question whether the Lord cared. "Teacher, do You not care that we are perishing?"[66]

"By God's Withdrawing the Light of His Countenance." The Confession is not being redundant here but goes on to explain, "and suffering even such as fear him to walk in darkness and to have no light." The writers are arguing that sometimes, for His own good reasons, God withdraws the sense of assurance from the heart of a believer and, in this case, it is not because of negligence, scandalous sin or sudden and vehement temptation. No, this sometimes happens even with those who "fear him." The reference seems to be those who are living lives of careful and even exemplary devotion to God. The text referenced is Isaiah 50:10: "Who among you fears the Lord? Who obeys the voice of His Servant? Who walks in darkness and has no light? Let him trust in the name of the Lord and rely upon his God." Why would God withdraw a sense of assurance from an exemplary Christian? Perhaps it is to teach the child of God to trust Him more exclusively and not to be overly dependent upon his or her feelings. We sometimes forget that our faith is not in our feelings of assurance, but in Christ. Feelings can fluctuate, but Christ is always the same. God would have us learn this lesson. God may have other reasons, as well, for withdrawing the comforting sense of His presence for a time. One may be to cause us to examine ourselves in order that we might discover hidden sins of the heart. Perhaps it is to enable us in the future to be better able to minister to others in their struggles. Or, He may use

---

66. Mark 4:38

times of seeming desertion to humble us and prepare us to receive some blessing He has purposed for us without it puffing us up with pride.

Assurance Decreased May Be Recovered

According to the Confession, assurance decreased may be recovered and revived. As mentioned earlier, the child of God is never back in the old unregenerate state he was in before his conversion. He remains in union with Christ and indwelt by the Holy Spirit. He never becomes an unbeliever in the absolute sense. However dark his way, he is never left to complete despair. As the Confession puts it, the Christian is never completely "destitute of the seed of God and life of faith, that love of Christ and the brethren, that sincerity of heart and conscience of duty out of which, by the operation of the Spirit, this assurance may in due time be revived, and by the which, in the meantime, they are preserved from utter despair."

Has there been negligence in preserving assurance? Repent and give diligence to make your calling and election sure. Has there been scandalous sin or sin hidden in your tent like Achan, unconfessed and not repudiated? Repent and put it away and run by faith to Christ for mercy. Have you been overcome by sudden temptation or affliction? Be still and know that the Lord is God. Cast yourself upon Him, knowing that He cares for you. Does it seem that for no apparent reason your soul is in a period of dryness and God seems distant? Wait upon the Lord and trust Him nonetheless. "When the eye of faith is dim, hold to Jesus, sink or swim."[67] Keep on in this way and assurance will in due time be revived.

---

67. This line is quoted in a sermon by Charles Spurgeon, "The True Position Of Assurance," in *Metropolitan Tabernacle Pulpit, Vol. 10* (1864 reprint, Albany, OR: The Ages Digital Library), 699.

CHAPTER 19

OF THE LAW OF GOD

JOHN REUTHER

1. God gave to Adam a law of universal obedience written in his heart, and a particular precept of not eating the fruit of the tree of knowledge of good and evil;[1] by which He bound him and all his posterity to personal, entire, exact, and perpetual obedience;[2] promised life upon the fulfilling, and threatened death upon the breach of it, and endued him with power and ability to keep it.[3]

2. The same law that was first written in the heart of man continued to be a perfect rule of righteousness after the fall,[4] and was delivered by God upon Mount Sinai, in ten commandments, and written in two tables, the four first containing our duty towards God, and the other six, our duty to man.[5]

3. Besides this law, commonly called moral, God was pleased to give to the people of Israel ceremonial laws, containing several typical ordinances, partly of worship, prefiguring Christ, His graces, actions, sufferings, and benefits;[6] and partly holding forth divers instructions of moral duties,[7] all which ceremonial laws being appointed only to the time of reformation, are, by Jesus Christ the true Messiah and only law-giver, who was furnished with power from the Father for that end abrogated and taken away.[8]

---

1. Genesis 1:27; Ecclesiastes 7:29
2. Romans 10:5
3. Galatians 3:10, 12
4. Romans 2:14-15
5. Deuteronomy 10:4
6. Hebrews 10:1; Colossians 2:17
7. 1 Corinthians 5:7
8. Colossians 2:14, 16-17; Ephesians 2:14, 16

4. To them also He gave sundry judicial laws, which expired together with the state of that people, not obliging any now by virtue of that institution; their general equity only being of moral use.[9]

5. The moral law doth for ever bind all, as well justified persons as others, to the obedience thereof,[10] and that not only in regard of the matter contained in it, but also in respect of the authority of God the Creator, who gave it;[11] neither doth Christ in the Gospel any way dissolve, but much strengthen this obligation.[12]

6. Although true believers be not under the law as a covenant of works, to be thereby justified or condemned,[13] yet it is of great use to them as well as to others, in that as a rule of life, informing them of the will of God and their duty, it directs and binds them to walk accordingly; discovering also the sinful pollutions of their natures, hearts, and lives, so as examining themselves thereby, they may come to further conviction of, humiliation for, and hatred against, sin;[14] together with a clearer sight of the need they have of Christ and the perfection of his obedience; it is likewise of use to the regenerate to restrain their corruptions, in that it forbids sin; and the threatenings of it serve to shew what even their sins deserve, and what afflictions in this life they may expect for them, although freed from the curse and unallayed rigour thereof. The promises of it likewise shew them God's approbation of obedience, and what blessings they may expect upon the performance thereof, though not as due to them by the law as a covenant of works; so as man's doing good and refraining from evil, because the law encourageth to the one and deterreth from the other, is no evidence of his being under the law and not under grace.[15]

7. Neither are the aforementioned uses of the law contrary to the grace of the Gospel, but do sweetly comply with it,[16] the Spirit of Christ subduing and enabling the will of man to do that freely and cheerfully which the will of God, revealed in the law, requireth to be done.[17]

This subject of the Law of God is close to the heart of God because His Law relates not only to His righteousness, but also to His love. If we love God, we will keep His commandments (John 14:15). The Law of God is

---

9. 1 Corinthians 9:8-10
10. Romans 13:8-10; James 2:8, 10-12
11. James 2:10-11
12. Matthew 5:17-19; Romans 3:31
13. Romans 6:14; Galatians 2:16; Romans 8:1; Romans 10:4
14. Romans 3:20; Romans 7:7, etc.
15. Romans 6:12-14; 1 Peter 3:8-13
16. Galatians 3:21
17. Ezekiel 36:27

a gift to mankind as a revelation of His will and His love. Carl Henry expressed this well:

> The Bible is the superlative propositional revelation of God; in defining man's duties it is the repository of the world's noblest ethical ideals. It is the supreme evidence that God has not withheld from individuals and nations the moral instruction they need for the perfect fulfillment of their calling. Those who exhibit its moral claims assert them to be more than human representations; indeed, we do not hesitate to identify them as the very will of God, revealed and written. The Torah gained its hold on Hebrew life because it was considered to be revealed instruction. The reverence Jesus held for the Law in written form is clear in Matthew 5:18, "not the smallest letter or stroke shall pass away from the Law." This implies that He appealed to the Old Testament as authoritatively containing the Divine command. Paul declares the glory of the Hebrews to be that they alone knew God's will (Romans 2:17), possessing the very oracles of God.[18]

Psalms 1, 19, and 119 are the three psalms which praise, applaud, and commend the Law of God. Though the Confession does not mention Psalm 119 here, the Christian should not think about God's Law without turning his or her thoughts to this acrostic poem, a masterpiece of Hebrew poetry by one who exclaimed, "Oh, how I love Your law! It is my meditation all the day" (Ps. 119:97). Spurgeon said: "The law is God's law, and therefore it is our love. We love it for its holiness, and pine to be holy; we love it for its wisdom, and study to be wise; we love it for its perfection, and long to be perfect. Those who know the power of the gospel perceive an infinite loveliness in the law as they see it fulfilled and embodied in Christ Jesus."[19] Psalm 19 says: "More to be desired are they than gold, Yea, than much fine gold; Sweeter also than honey and the honeycomb" (Ps. 19:10). And Psalm 1 sets the tone for the collection of psalms by describing the man of God in this way: "his delight is in the law of the Lord, And in His law he meditates day and night" (Ps. 1:2).

When the Bible speaks about the Law of God, it refers to the commandments specifically and the Word of God generally. For an Israelite to say that he loved God's Law meant that he loved the Ten Commandments. They were (and are) the basis for God's guidance for life. This is because the "commandment is exceedingly broad" (Ps. 119:96). This means that God's commandments are applicable to all life's situations, the simple and the complex. The Law (Hebrew torah) in Israel was understood as the gift of guidance from God for everyday life:

> Psalm 1 is the first of several torah psalms strategically placed within the book of Psalms (1; 19; 119). These psalms exhort the hearers/readers to pay close attention to God's commandments and to be faithful in their response to them. At the same time, however, the wisdom understanding of torah prevents easy limitation to the five books of the Torah. Biblical

---

18. Carl F. H. Henry, *Christian Personal Ethics* (Grand Rapids: Eerdmans, 1957), 265-66.

19. C. H. Spurgeon, *The Treasury of David*, Volume 3, Psalms 111–119 (Grand Rapids: Zondervan, 1976), 330.

wisdom literature had already begun to identify torah (the life-giving commandments of Yahweh) with the life-giving insights given by Yahweh through the wisdom tradition. Thus, most likely torah here implies the traditional commandments of God in the Torah – commandments Israel is expected to obey – as well as the life-giving guidance God gives elsewhere in Scripture. Brevard Childs is undoubtedly right when he observes that the function of this exhortation in the introductory psalm of the Psalter is to encourage the readers to meditate on the book of Psalms as Scripture and to seek there God's message that guides and establishes the life of faith.[20]

All the things we love about the Psalms, and all the spiritual and physical help we receive from each of them (for we view every psalm as applicable to the Christian life in our everyday experience and use them in our prayers) are derived from their basis in the Law of God! The theme of the book of Psalms is "the Lord reigns" (Ps. 47:8; 93:1; 95:3; 96:10; 97:1; 99:1).[21] He is "King over all the earth" (Ps. 47:2). The King is sovereign over His domain. He rules by His Law (though His grace is always operative). Psalm 1 sets the tone for the entire psalter, and it sets forth the Law of God as the object of meditation for the godly. The God of the Psalms is the God of the Testaments, Old and New. A Christian must not take a cavalier attitude toward the place which law still has for believers under the New Covenant. He must not view grace as abolishing God's law. He must not relegate the Law of God to the life of the Old Testament believer and deny its permanent place in Christian living. Naturally, he does recognize that the distinctions between the moral, civil, and ceremonial laws must always be maintained.

The Confession deals with this subject using a simple progression. Paragraph 1 talks about God's law to Adam in the Garden of Eden. Paragraph 2 explains the delivery of the Law on Mount Sinai in the Ten Commandments. Paragraph 3 explains ceremonial law given for the worship of God in Israel. Paragraph 4 briefly comments on the judicial or civil laws in Israel. Paragraph 5 is crucial because it establishes the binding nature of the moral law before and after Christ's coming. Paragraph 6 is the longest paragraph and explains the Law's usefulness to the believer as a rule of life, and also that promises and blessings attend our obedience to it. Paragraph 7 briefly states the harmony between the Law and the gospel, and how the uses explained in Paragraph 6 "do sweetly comply" with the grace of the gospel.

Follow the Confession on the historical and theological tour of God's Law in the history of man, from creation to Israel to Christ to the Christian life.

---

20. Gerald H. Wilson, The NIV Application Commentary, *Psalms,* Volume 1 (Grand Rapids: Zondervan, 2002), 96.

21. Psalms 93–99 are a micro collection called the "Kingship of Jehovah Psalms." Kingship is also taught in Psalms 2, 24, 29, 45, 68, 72, 84, 89, 145, 149, and in numerous verses throughout the book of Psalms.

Paragraph 1: Creation Law

The opening paragraph takes us back to Genesis 2, although this chapter is not listed in the references cited. Having created Adam, "God planted a garden eastward in Eden, and there He put the man whom He had formed" (Gen. 2:7-8). Then, "the Lord God commanded the man, saying, 'Of every tree of the garden you may freely eat; but of the tree of the knowledge of good and evil you shall not eat, for in the day that you eat of it you shall surely die'" (Gen. 2:16, 17). It is this verse to which the paragraph in the Confession is referring. "Universal obedience" is explained in the words "personal, entire, exact, and perpetual obedience." Adam was bound by the Law of God for his entire life. But the commandment to which he was initially bound was the "precept of not eating the fruit of the knowledge of good and evil." He and his posterity were bound to this commandment in the Garden of Eden. There was a promise of life attached to that obedience, and the threat of death upon disobedience, "for in the day that you eat of it you shall surely die" (Gen. 2:17).

Since God had provided everything for Adam in the Garden, the Confession says that God "endued him with power and ability to keep it." Chapter 4, paragraph 2, of the Confession used this language but added the important truth, "having the law of God written in their hearts, and power to fulfill it, and yet under a possibility of transgressing, being left to the liberty of their own will, which was subject to change." Adam was not confirmed in holiness, a blessing which we now enjoy through Christ. Nevertheless, he was created in sinlessness and integrity. Richard Barcellos says: "Being the image of God for Adam, then, meant that his mind was stocked with and able to process true knowledge of God. His heart was morally pure; he was made upright. His will acted in accordance with the law of God. Romans 2:14-15 teaches us that all men have the law of God written on their hearts due to being created."[22]

The Confession cites Ecclesiastes 7:29: "Truly, this only I have found: That God made man upright, But they have sought out many schemes." Our first parents came up with the first scheme and sinners have been scheming ever since. Barcellos explains: "It is best to understand this as referring to man's original moral uprightness. Man was originally holy. He had integrity of soul. The devices we all seek are sinful devices, sinful ways. This seeking 'out many devices' is wrong. It is not in accord with man's original state of integrity. Man was made morally upright but something happened. Creation *imago Dei* included moral integrity."[23] God is not to be blamed for the sins of man according to this verse.

James taught this:

> Let no one say when he is tempted, "I am tempted by God"; for God cannot be tempted by evil, nor does He Himself tempt anyone. But each one is tempted when he is drawn away by his own desires and enticed. Then, when desire has conceived, it gives birth to sin; and sin, when it is full-grown,

22. Richard C. Barcellos, *Better than the Beginning* (Palmdale, CA: RBAP, 2013), 98.
23. Ibid., 97.

brings forth death. Do not be deceived, my beloved brethren. Every good gift and every perfect gift is from above, and comes down from the Father of lights, with whom there is no variation or shadow of turning (James 1:13-17).

For Adam, this "law of universal obedience" is called a "covenant of works."[24] True believers are not under the Law "as a covenant of works, to be thereby justified or condemned" (paragraph 6). But Adam was, and he "and all his posterity" were bound to fulfill this covenant with "personal, entire, exact, and perpetual obedience," with the promise of life or the threat of death attending it. And when Adam disobeyed the commandment and broke that covenant, all men sinned in him since he was the representative head of the human race.

Paul taught this in a strategic passage: "Therefore, just as through one man sin entered the world, and death through sin, and thus death spread to all men, because all sinned" (Rom. 5:12). Adam's sin is imputed to us. The phrase "because all sinned" establishes that all sinned in Adam. It does not say (as you might expect) "because *Adam* sinned," but "because *all* sinned." Adam's sin, as the representative head of the race, is imputed to his posterity.

Imputation is the same principle in view from the standpoint of salvation in Christ. Christ's righteousness is imputed (charged) to the sinner's account when he or she repents and turns to Christ. "And the gift is not like *that which came* through the one who sinned. For the judgment which came from one offense resulted in condemnation, but the free gift which came from many offenses resulted in justification" (Rom. 5:16). The imputation of Christ's righteousness is "the gift of righteousness" (Rom. 5:17). Through His one "righteous act" we have "justification of life" (Rom. 5:18) through the imputation (reckoning) of Christ's righteousness to our account.

Man has been united to God by Law and love from the beginning of His creation. Creation in God's image constitutes us, among other things, moral creatures in a moral universe of right and wrong, good and evil. Law therefore is intrinsic to our relationship with God. This is why I began by saying that the subject of the Law of God is close to the heart of God: "If you love me, keep my commandments" (John 14:15).

The first eleven chapters of Deuteronomy join the Law and the love of God. Here are some verses:

Showing mercy to thousands, to those who love Me and keep My commandments (Deut. 5:10).

You shall love the Lord your God with all your heart, with all your soul, and with all your strength. And these words which I command you today shall be in your heart (Deut. 6:5-6).

The Lord did not set His love on you nor choose you because you were more

24. See two chapters in Richard C. Barcellos, *Getting the Garden Right* (Cape Coral, FL: Founders Press, 2017), 38-78. In Chapter 4, Barcellos covers the confessional statement we are considering here. In Chapter 5, he develops the scriptural formulation of the doctrine.

in number than any other people, for you were the least of all peoples; but because the Lord loves you, and because He would keep the oath which He swore to your fathers, the Lord has brought you out with a mighty hand, and redeemed you from the house of bondage, from the hand of Pharaoh king of Egypt. Therefore know that the Lord your God, He is God, the faithful God who keeps covenant and mercy for a thousand generations with those who love Him and keep His commandments (Deut. 7:7-9).

Then it shall come to pass, because you listen to these judgments, and keep and do them, that the Lord your God will keep with you the covenant and the mercy which He swore to your fathers. And He will love you and bless you and multiply you; He will also bless the fruit of your womb and the fruit of your land, your grain and your new wine and your oil, the increase of your cattle and the offspring of your flock, in the land of which He swore to your fathers to give you (Deut. 7:12-13).

And now, Israel, what does the Lord your God require of you, but to fear the Lord your God, to walk in all His ways and to love Him, to serve the Lord your God with all your heart and with all your soul, *and* to keep the commandments of the Lord and His statutes which I command you today for your good? Indeed heaven and the highest heavens belong to the Lord your God, also the earth with all that is in it. The Lord delighted only in your fathers, to love them; and He chose their descendants after them, you above all peoples, as *it is* this day (Deut. 10:12-15).

He administers justice for the fatherless and the widow, and loves the stranger, giving him food and clothing. Therefore love the stranger, for you were strangers in the land of Egypt. You shall fear the Lord your God; you shall serve Him, and to Him you shall hold fast, and take oaths in His name. He is your praise, and He is your God, who has done for you these great and awesome things which your eyes have seen (Deut. 10:18-21).

Therefore you shall love the Lord your God, and keep His charge, His statutes, His judgments, and His commandments always (Deut. 11:1).

And it shall be that if you earnestly obey My commandments which I command you today, to love the Lord your God and serve Him with all your heart and with all your soul (Deut. 11:13).

For if you carefully keep all these commandments which I command you to do—to love the Lord your God, to walk in all His ways, and to hold fast to Him (Deut. 11:22).

God is holy and righteous and perfect in all His attributes. God created man. Man was created to reflect His holiness. Law is given as the expression of that reflection of the image of God in man. We also learn from Scripture that grace is also operative and the sovereign work of God on behalf of sinners. But that is a subject for another place.

Paragraph 2: The Ten Commandments in Israel

Paragraph 2 speaks of the *continuity* of the Law given to Adam (verbally and written on his heart), and the *propagation* of that law in the form delivered to Moses on Mt. Sinai; two tablets of stone contained the Ten Commandments, divided into two parts. The first part contained the first four commandments that outline our duty toward God and the second part contained the last six commandments that outline our duty toward man.

Question 44 in *The Westminster Shorter Catechism* explains the continuity: "The moral law is summarily comprehended in the Ten Commandments."[25] David Jones says: "In short, then, it can be said that the moral law was present before Sinai, at Sinai, and after Sinai. Indeed, the moral law is present throughout Scripture. As a revelation of God's character, the moral law is timeless, unchanging, and the standard by which God judges man."[26]

This timeless Law came to Moses on Mt. Sinai in a form that is remarkable. I call it the *foundation* form for righteousness, holiness, ethics, and morality. It is the unchanging standard of right and wrong. Each commandment stands for a category of sins. *The Westminster Larger Catechism*, Question 99, explains this rule of interpretation: "That under one sin or duty, all of the same kind are forbidden or commanded; together with all the causes, means, occasions, and appearances thereof, and provocations thereunto." For example, the first commandment forbids the sins of atheism, idolatry, self-love, unbelief, hypocrisy, pride, tempting God, and more. The third commandment forbids the sins of blasphemy, perjury, false oaths, violating lawful vows, maintaining false doctrine, and more. The sixth commandment forbids sinful anger, hatred, envy, desire for revenge, immoderate use of food and drink, oppression, striking, wounding, and more. The seventh commandment forbids adultery, fornication, rape, incest, homosexuality, unnatural lusts, unclean thoughts, filthy speech, immodest apparel, polygamy, desertion, gluttony, drunkenness and more. The eighth commandment forbids theft, human trafficking, removing landmarks, unjust contracts, unjust depopulations, gambling, prodigality, and more.[27] The point here is that the Decalogue is foundational; upon it is built the structure of right living in a sinful world.

The Ten Commandments were given to the redeemed people and are therefore not a means of justification. Paul said: "For if there had been a law given which could have given life, truly righteousness would have been by the law" (Gal. 3:21). It is the standard of righteousness to which we adhere in obedience to the command: "You shall therefore be holy, for I am holy" (Lev. 11:45). The theme of the Ten Commandments is holiness, separation to God from sin. "And Moses said to the people, 'Do not fear; for God has come to test you, and that His fear may be before you, so that

---

25. In *The Shorter Catechism: A Modest Revision for Baptists Today* (Grand Rapids: Truth for Eternity Ministries), and *The Shorter Catechism: A Baptist Version* (Avinger, TX: Simpson Publishing Co. 2003), question 44.

26. David W. Jones, *An Introduction to Biblical Ethics* (Nashville: B&H, 2013), 59-60.

27. Many of these examples are taken from *The Westminster Larger Catechism* in its extensive treatment of the Ten Commandments. This is a valuable resource.

you may not sin'" (Exod. 20:20). This is still the requirement for this age: "My little children, these things I write to you, so that you may not sin" (1 John 2:1). The basic form has two parts, love to God and love to man, and each of these channels in which love is to flow contains ethical categories.

Righteousness in Scripture refers to the standard. God Himself is the standard in this moral universe. *Holiness* means to be separate, sacred, as opposed to common, profane. God is holy. He is *separate*, which means *transcendent*. Yet the Creator is *immanent* and *involved* with the creation through His providence. But He calls us, as His spiritual, moral, rational creatures, to be separate from sin, consecrated to Him, and adhering to the righteous standard set forth in His Law. Walter C. Kaiser Jr. presents the Ten Commandments under the scriptural theme, "holiness as a way of life." He shows how this theme is developed through the commandments: holiness in worship (commandments 1–4), holiness in work and worship (commandment 4), holiness in family and society (commandment 5), holiness in regard for life (commandment 6, the sanctity of life), holiness in marriage and sex (commandment 7), holiness in wealth and possessions (commandment 8, the sanctity of possessions), holiness in obtaining and using truth (commandment 9), and holiness in motive and heart (commandment 10).[28]

But what is the nature of this Law of commandments given on Mt. Sinai? Is it merely a set of rules which God devised, not necessarily arbitrarily (for God is never arbitrary), but a set of rules outside of Himself? David W. Jones sets forth three views in his book *An Introduction to Biblical Ethics:*[29]

> The first is called "The Authority over Law Paradigm" (42f). This view states that the law is right and good simply because God commanded it… "God said it. I believe it. That settles it… What makes the law right and good – rests on God's ability to espouse moral legislation." The second view is called "The Authority Under Law Paradigm" (45f). In this view the law is loved because it is holy… God's laws are right and true because God commanded what is right and true… the true power of the law rests within the law's own fundamental intrinsic rightness and goodness… In this view the law is external and antecedent to God.[30]

Jones holds the third view (which I also hold), "the authority is law" paradigm of the nature of God's Law:

> This view of the nature of law teaches that the law is right and true simply because it reflects and reveals God's moral character, which is right and

---

28. Walter C. Kaiser, Jr., *Toward Old Testament Ethics* (Grand Rapids: Zondervan, 1983), viii, ix. David W. Jones presents it this way: no other God (1, whom we worship), no graven images (2, how we worship), no misuse of God's name (3, verbal worship of God), keep the Sabbath (4, our temporal worship of God), the sanctity of human authority (5), the sanctity of human life (6), the sanctity of relational intimacy (7), the sanctity of material stewardship (8), the sanctity of truth (9), the sanctity of motives (10). David W. Jones, *An Introduction to Biblical Ethics,* from the summaries on pages 169, 170, 197–99.

29. David W. Jones, *An Introduction to Biblical Ethics,* 41.

30. Ibid., 42, 45.

true. According to this position, then, the true power of the law rests in the fact that it is a revelation of God's moral character. To be clear, under this paradigm the law itself is not God; the law is ontologically separate from God, as it appears in Scripture. Yet, according to this view, the content of the law is a faithful representation and expression of God's moral character.[31]

However, if the law reflects God's holiness and moral character, as believers keep the law, they naturally will become like him. Under this paradigm, then, the process of sanctification is as follows: God gives his self-reflecting law to mankind and calls believers to be sanctified; in obedience believers keep the law of God and consequently become holy like God. As will be explored in the following chapter, Protestants have traditionally referred to this as the third or proper use of the law.[32]

If "sin is the breaking of the law" (1 John 3:4), and the law is a reflection of God's moral character, then God himself can make propitiation for man's sin. When men sin, the law is broken, and God is offended. While God's justice will not allow sin to be overlooked, in his mercy and grace God can atone for man's sin by paying the penalty for sin himself. That the law is an expression of God's own character is one of the factors that make the substitutionary atonement possible. As the writer of the book of Hebrews explains, Jesus voluntarily chose to become "like His brothers in every way, so that He could become a merciful and faithful high priest in service to God, to make propitiation for the sins of the people" (Heb. 2: 17). Indeed, given man's lost condition, not only can God provide substitutionary atonement, but this is the only way man can be saved (cf. Acts 4:12). Just as sin is man substituting himself for God, so salvation is God substituting himself for man.[33]

The Law delivered to Moses on Mt. Sinai, "written with the finger of God" (Ex. 31:18), reflects His Being, perfections, and attributes in the lives of His moral creatures who obey it. It is the standard of righteousness and the way of holiness.

The Ten Commandments were also summarized into the first and second commandment, or, "The Great Commandment" and "the second." Jesus was asked,

"Teacher, which is the great commandment in the Law?" He replied: "You shall love the Lord your God with all your heart and with all your soul, and with all your mind. This is the great and foremost commandment. The second is like it, 'You shall love your neighbor as yourself'" (Matt. 22:37-39).

The Ten Commandments are the summarizing system of righteousness, ethics, and morality, and yet this summarizing system is itself further summarized into two commandments by Jesus. This does not mean that the two commandments—"just love God and love your neighbor" —are sufficient! No, the Decalogue gives us the map for loving God

---

31. Ibid., 47, 48.

32. Ibid., 49.

33. Ibid., 51.

and neighbor, and the rest of Scripture expounds on and applies these fundamental commandments. God's Word declares that divine law is a good thing. Paul expressed, "I agree with the law that it is good" (Rom. 7:16). It is good because it requires and promotes love to God and love to our fellow man.

Paragraph 3: The Ceremonial Law in Israel

Paragraphs 3 and 4 state the distinction between the moral, ceremonial, and civil laws given to Israel. Paragraph 3 explains the ceremonial laws, and there are two important features to note.

Ceremonial laws are "typical ordinances," meaning that these laws are types or prefigurements of things to come. These are the laws given in Exodus and Leviticus concerning the tabernacle, the priesthood, the sacrifices, and purity in approaching God. The types are structures, official persons, actions, offerings, and rituals, which have counterparts that will be manifested in the future. When we speak of a "type," we are referring to the picture proclaimed in the structure (tabernacle, holy of holies), the official persons (priests), actions (setting up and taking down the tabernacle, building altars), offerings (burnt, grain, peace, sin, guilt), and rituals (ordaining the priests, cleansing after defilements). The ceremonies, therefore, are types of things to come: "For the law, having a shadow of the good things to come, *and* not the very image of the things, can never with these same sacrifices, which they offer continually year by year, make those who approach perfect" (Heb. 10:1). These "are a shadow of things to come, but the substance is of Christ" (Col. 2:17).

The Confession states that these were appointed only "to the time of reformation," that is, the time when Jesus the Messiah would come and fulfill these types. The relationship of these typical ordinances to their fulfillment in Christ is seen in the offices of prophet, priest, and king and in the ministries and accomplishments of Christ. They were ceremonies that Israel performed as acts of worship in anticipation of the grace, the actions, the sufferings, and the benefits that would be bestowed by Christ in the fullness of time. Sinners then drew near to God through the shedding of the blood of spotless animal sacrifices. Sinners now draw near to God through Christ, the spotless and sinless Lamb of God. In Israel, God ordained the priesthood to lead sinners to Himself. In Christ we have the perfect High Priest who not only brings us to God through the offering, but who is Himself the offering: "Who does not need daily, as those high priests, to offer up sacrifices, first for His own sins and then for the people's, for this He did once for all when He offered up Himself" (Heb. 7:27). In the tabernacle, there was a table upon which was placed the lampstand and the bread of the presence. Christ is the Light of the world and the Bread of Life.

The ceremonial laws were "abrogated and taken away." This is explained in Hebrews, which portrays Christ as "better" than the Old Testament rituals because He fulfills them all in His Person and work. Now that He has come, they are no longer needed.

The second feature explained here is that these ceremonial laws possess moral instruction that God uses to teach truth throughout history. Reference is made to 1 Corinthians 5:7: "Therefore purge out the old leaven, that you may be a new lump, since you truly are unleavened. For indeed Christ, our Passover, was sacrificed for us." The Passover is abrogated, but the truths embodied in the Passover and the symbolism of the Passover give moral instruction and illustrate timeless truths for the New Covenant believer.

Paragraph 4: The Civil Law in Israel

Here is a simple (and obvious) statement regarding the civil laws given to Israel when God was their King and they were the nation which He redeemed and established in the earth to declare His praise. Notice the words, "expired with the state of that people." Israel today is no longer constituted as the people of God as they were under the Old Testament. Jesus declared: "Therefore I say to you, the kingdom of God will be taken from you and given to a nation bearing the fruits of it" (Matt. 21:43). The church is that nation (1 Pet. 2:9).

Two points are made here. The first is that which was just expressed, that we are not obliged to their keeping "by virtue of that institution." We are not national Israel, we do not live in a theocracy; we are Christians, citizens of the spiritual, multi-national Kingdom and live under world governments (although here in America we have a Christian heritage for which we thank God). And this leads to the second point, that even though we are not obliged now by those civil laws, there are principles of general equity which remain as moral principles that apply to believers today.

Consider some examples from the civil law:

You shall not see your brother's ox or his sheep going astray, and hide yourself from them; you shall certainly bring them back to your brother. And if your brother is not near you, or if you do not know him, then you shall bring it to your own house, and it shall remain with you until your brother seeks it; then you shall restore it to him (Deut. 22:1, 2).

A woman shall not wear anything that pertains to a man, nor shall a man put on a woman's garment, for all who do so *are* an abomination to the Lord your God (Deut. 22:5).

When you build a new house, then you shall make a parapet for your roof, that you may not bring guilt of bloodshed on your household if anyone falls from it (Deut. 22:8).

You shall not oppress a hired servant who is poor and needy, *whether* one of your brethren or one of the aliens who is in your land within your gates. Each day you shall give *him* his wages, and not let the sun go down on it, for he *is* poor and has set his heart on it; lest he cry out against you to the Lord, and it be sin to you (Deut. 24:14, 15).

You shall not muzzle an ox while it treads out *the grain* (Deut. 25:4).

All of these are legislation for the civil life of the nation of Israel. In their form, we are not required to keep them. But there is a spirit or a principle and in two of these illustrations the New Testament gives specific application. The principle in Deuteronomy 22:1, 2 is that we are to regard our neighbor's property, possessions, and livelihood. The principle in Deuteronomy 22:5 is the God-ordained distinction between male and female, even in their dress. The principle in Deuteronomy 22:8 is to have regard for our neighbor's life by not placing him in a potentially dangerous situation on our property. The principle in Deuteronomy 24:14, 15 is applied specifically by James: "Indeed the wages of the laborers who mowed your fields, which you kept back by fraud, cry out; and the cries of the reapers have reached the ears of the Lord of Sabaoth" (James 5:4). The principle in Deuteronomy 25:4 is specifically applied by Paul to ministerial compensation: "Let the elders who rule well be counted worthy of double honor, especially those who labor in the word and doctrine. For the Scripture says, 'You shall not muzzle an ox while it treads out the grain,' and, 'The laborer *is* worthy of his wages'" (1 Tim. 5:18; cf. 1 Cor. 9:9).[34]

Jones explains:

Biblical civil laws are simply the application of God's moral standards to a particular time and culture. Behind each civil law, then, is a moral law. In fact, as Augustine famously noted, a civil law apart from a moral law is no law at all. Said differently, the civil law is the moral law applied. For example, a memorable Hebrew civil law is, "Whoever strikes his father or his mother must be put to death" (Exod 21:15). Yet this civil law is simply a time-bound, cultural application of the moral duty to honor one's parents (cf. Exod 20:12). So, then, to question whether the command to kill disobedient children applies in modern society is to misunderstand the nature of civil law. While God's moral standards do not change, their application (and penalty for violation) in each time and culture is unique and ever changing. A benefit, then, of studying the civil law is that the civil law shows the breadth of the moral law as well as the different ways in which the moral law has been applied in various ages.[35]

Paragraph 5: The Abiding Moral Law in the Christian Life

Having already (1) established the biblical teaching that God is King, (2) the fundamental place of law in our relationship to the Creator, (3) the scope of the Ten Commandments as the standard for righteousness, and (4) the way of holiness in this sinful world, it is clear that "the moral law doth for ever bind all." And "the authority of God the Creator" and "Christ in the Gospel" does not dissolve this obligation, but rather strengthens it.

Examples are found in these references:

Owe no one anything except to love one another, for he who loves another has fulfilled the law. For the commandments, "You shall not commit

---

34. Paul refers to 1 Corinthians 9:9 here, as well in this verse.
35. David W. Jones, *An Introduction to Biblical Ethics*, 58-59.

adultery," "You shall not murder," "You shall not steal," "You shall not bear false witness," "You shall not covet," and if *there is* any other commandment, are *all* summed up in this saying, namely, "You shall love your neighbor as yourself." Love does no harm to a neighbor; therefore love *is* the fulfillment of the law (Rom. 13:8-10).

If you really fulfill *the* royal law according to the Scripture, "You shall love your neighbor as yourself," you do well; but if you show partiality, you commit sin, and are convicted by the law as transgressors. For whoever shall keep the whole law, and yet stumble in one *point*, he is guilty of all. For He who said, "Do not commit adultery," also said, "Do not murder." Now if you do not commit adultery, but you do murder, you have become a transgressor of the law. So speak and so do as those who will be judged by the law of liberty (James 2:8-12).

Do not think that I came to destroy the Law or the Prophets. I did not come to destroy but to fulfill. For assuredly, I say to you, till heaven and earth pass away, one jot or one tittle will by no means pass from the law till all is fulfilled. Whoever therefore breaks one of the least of these commandments, and teaches men so, shall be called least in the kingdom of heaven; but whoever does and teaches *them*, he shall be called great in the kingdom of heaven (Matt. 5:17-19).

Do we then make void the law through faith? Certainly not! On the contrary, we establish the law (Rom. 3:31).

Paul explains the weakness of the Law: "For what the law could not do in that it was weak through the flesh, God *did* by sending His own Son in the likeness of sinful flesh, on account of sin: He condemned sin in the flesh" (Rom. 8:3). Then Paul sets over against this the power of the indwelling Spirit of God that enables us to keep the Law: "that the righteous requirement of the law might be fulfilled in us who do not walk according to the flesh but according to the Spirit" (Rom. 8:4). As a result of Christ's sinless accomplishments, and His perfect law-keeping, we are enabled by His Spirit to fulfill the requirement of the Law, as Paul said in that crucial statement in Romans 8:4; He said that the requirement of the Law might be *fulfilled* in (or *by*) us (not forgotten because "Christ did it for us"). The Confession states that "neither doth Christ in the Gospel any way dissolve, but much strengthen this obligation."

Philip Hughes wrote: "The Christian is still under solemn obligation to keep the law of God, but with this difference, that he now has the power, the power of Christ by the Holy Spirit within himself, to keep it."[36]

Paragraph 6: The Christian and the Moral Law
This is the longest paragraph in the chapter. The first statement emphasizes the "great use" of the Law in contrast to any idea of a believer being under the Law "as a covenant of works, to be thereby justified or condemned." That is not the purpose of the Law. The Confession already

---

36. Philip Edgcumbe Hughes, *Paul's Second Epistle to the Corinthians* (Grand Rapids: Eerdmans, 1986), 90.

explained the Law as a covenant of works in the Garden of Eden. It also established the continuity of the Law before, at, and after Sinai. Again, Paul is clear about the issue of whether the Law imparts life (that justifies sinners in the eyes of God): "if there had been a law given which could have given life, truly righteousness would have been by the law. But the Scripture has confined all under sin, that the promise by faith in Jesus Christ might be given to those who believe" (Gal. 3:21, 22). Consequently, the Law is emphasized here as being useful, in addition to already being established as both obligatory and as a "rule of life."

David W. Jones issues a needed caution:

> In the Protestant tradition theologians have commonly identified three uses of the moral law for Christians, the first of which is the *social use*. This is sometimes called the civil use (not to be confused with the interpretive category of civil law) or the political use of the moral law. When functioning in this manner, the law serves as a barricade or a bridle that restrains men from sin – believers and unbelievers alike... A second use of the moral law is the *convictional use*, which is sometimes referred to as the evangelical, proper, or theological use of the moral law. Paul summarized this function of the law when he wrote, "For no one will be justified in His sight by the works of the law, because the knowledge of sin comes through the law" (Rom 3:20; cf. 4:15; 5:20; 2 Cor. 3:7). When serving in this capacity, then, the law convicts men of sin by becoming a mirror that reflects man's sinful condition in light of God's holiness and moral standards... The third use of the moral law is the *normative use*, which is also referred to as the didactic or pedagogical use of the law. This use of the law is identified by most Protestant thinkers as the main use of the moral law. When the law functions in this capacity it acts as a lamp to instruct believers in righteousness. Since the law is holy, just, good, and spiritual (cf. Rom 7:12, 14), this use of the law by Christians is not unexpected.

He goes on to clarify:

> In sum, understanding the law is an important component in the correlation of the law and the gospel. When the term law appears in Scripture, Bible readers must first identify which interpretive category of law is under discussion: the civil law, the ceremonial law, or the moral law. Second, if the moral law is in view, the interpreter must discern how it is being used: the social use, the convictional use, or the normative use. Confusion may enter into a discussion about the relationship between the law and the gospel if the law is misidentified in regard to either category or use. Moreover, given these dynamics, it is understandable how biblical writers may make seemingly contradictory statements about the law within the same epistles.[37]

The first use set forth is in this long sentence, "informing them of the will of God and their duty, it directs and binds them to walk accordingly; discovering also the sinful pollutions of their natures, hearts, and lives, so as examining themselves thereby, they may come to further conviction of, humiliation for, and hatred against, sin." Therefore, the Law is useful

---

37. David W. Jones, *An Introduction to Biblical Ethics*, 60-2.

for the discovery of sin in the heart to the end that confession of sin, followed by repentance, results in forgiveness granted and received.

David shows this pattern in Psalm 19. After extolling the revelation of God in creation (Ps. 19:1-6), and then setting forth the perfections of God's Law (Ps. 19:7-11), he turned his thoughts inward to see the sin there and the dangers lurking in his heart and in his environment:

> Moreover by them Your servant is warned,
> *And* in keeping them *there* is great reward.
> Who can understand *his* errors?
> Cleanse me from secret *faults.*
> Keep back Your servant also from presumptuous *sins;*
> Let them not have dominion over me.
> Then I shall be blameless,
> And I shall be innocent of great transgression (Ps. 19:11-13).

David broadly refers to three categories of sins. The first is "errors" which, in the Old Testament, refers to inadvertent sins where a person sins and does not realize that he has sinned. Next, he mentions "secret *faults.*" This refers to the hidden aspects of our hearts, a reminder that we do not always understand what is lurking in our hearts. Finally, he mentions the category found in the Old Testament of "high-handed sins," called here "presumptuous sins." This one can lead to "the great transgression" which he obviously fears. Whether this great transgression is adultery, or idolatry, or the unpardonable sin, David sees it as the most serious.

The second use set forth is, "together with a clearer sight of the need they have of Christ and the perfection of His obedience: it is likewise of use to the regenerate to restrain their corruptions, in that it forbids sin; and the threatenings of it serve to shew what even their sins deserve, and what afflictions in this life they may expect for them, although freed from the curse and unallayed rigor thereof." The Law is useful for showing us our need of Christ, His virtue, His example, and His justifying grace. Christ endured the curse for us (Gal. 3:13): "Christ has redeemed us from the curse of the law, having become a curse for us (for it is written, 'Cursed is everyone who hangs on a tree')." This shows us what sin deserves. Joined to the perfections which are in Christ, we are further helped in a life of evangelical obedience to the Law of God.

The Confession is pointing us to Christ. We glory in the *imputation* of Christ's righteousness and perfect law-keeping received in justification. We also look to Him for the *impartation* of the Christlikeness that will enable us to keep the Law through His Spirit in the progress of sanctification:

> Till we all come to the unity of the faith and of the knowledge of the Son of God, to a perfect man, to the measure of the stature of the fullness of Christ; that we should no longer be children, tossed to and fro and carried about with every wind of doctrine, by the trickery of men, in the cunning craftiness of deceitful plotting, but, speaking the truth in love, may grow up in all things into Him who is the head—Christ (Eph. 4:13-15).

The paragraph concludes with the reminder, "The promises of it likewise shew them God's approbation of obedience, and what blessings they may expect upon the performance thereof." This is qualified in the words which follow, "though not as due to them by the law as a covenant of works; so as man's doing good and refraining from evil, because the law encourageth to the one and deterreth from the other, is no evidence of his being under the law and not under grace." The modern language version of the Confession is a bit easier to read here:

> In similar manner the promises attached to the law intimate God's approbation of obedience and set forth the blessings which flow from the fulfillment of the law, but with the proviso that those blessings do not accrue to men from the law viewed as a covenant of works. The fact that a man does good and refrains from evil because the law encourages the former and deters from the latter, is no evidence that the man is under the law and not under grace. [38]

Paragraph 7: Christ and the Law

The harmony of the Law and the gospel is asserted. The indwelling Spirit of God enables the believer to do "freely and cheerfully" that which the Law requires. So there is *power and divine presence* and the *will* to do it. The Spirit writes the Law on our hearts in Christ since He has been poured out at Pentecost. God spoke through Jeremiah: "But this *is* the covenant that I will make with the house of Israel after those days, says the Lord: I will put My law in their minds, and write it on their hearts; and I will be their God, and they shall be My people" (Jer. 31:33). He spoke similarly through Ezekiel: "I will put My Spirit within you and cause you to walk in My statutes, and you will keep My judgments and do *them*" (Ezek. 36:27). Solomon earlier spoke a proverb to his son with this same idea of writing the commandments (of father and mother) on the heart: "Keep my commands and live, And my law as the apple of your eye. Bind them on your fingers; Write them on the tablet of your heart" (Prov. 7:2-3).

Barcellos comments:

> Jeremiah clearly teaches that the law of God under the New Covenant is a law that was written on stone by God and that will be written on hearts by God. Exodus 24:12 identifies the "tablets of stone" with "the law and commandments which I have written." This is a very important verse, for it uses the Hebrew word *torah* [law] as a synonym for what God wrote on stones.
> The word *law (torah)* is used 306 times in the Hebrew text in 214 verses. It normally refers to the law revealed by God though Moses to Israel. It does have other uses…. Its uses include: the law of the Old Covenant as a whole, the book of the covenant, the Decalogue, the words of a prophet, the providence of God, and the instruction of parents. [39]

---

38. *A Faith to Confess: The Baptist Confession of Faith of 1689 Rewritten in Modern English* (Leeds: Carey Publications, 1997), 46, 47.

39. Richard C. Barcellos, *In Defense of the Decalogue* (Enumclaw, WA: Winepress, 2001), 21, n14.

From stone to heart. This is one of the glorious features of the New Covenant. Now that we have the Spirit of the resurrected, exalted Christ, we have the Law written on our hearts. This means presence, power, and the will to do, and we genuinely love His Law. This is not to say that Old Covenant believers did not love God this way, for there were many who did, like Zacharias and Elizabeth (Luke 1:6). However, it was not the characteristic of the entire nation. But in the New Covenant "all shall know me" (Jer. 31:34). With these Old Covenant saints Zacharias and Elizabeth, for example, we see *continuity.* In the New Covenant, continuity and discontinuity are both seen in the change of administration from Israel to the Church. The preparatory and provisional features of the Old Covenant are now abolished and replaced with New Covenant worship. Jesus described New Covenant worship in John 4:24: "God is Spirit, and those who worship Him must worship in spirit and truth." Paul described it in Philippians 3:3: "For we are the circumcision, who worship God in the Spirit, rejoice in Christ Jesus, and have no confidence in the flesh."

Jesus spoke of the continuity of the Law from the Old Testament to the New in Matthew 5. Poythress comments on Matthew 5:17-19:

> The whole law points to Him, and its purposes find their realization in Him. All the commandments of the law are binding on Christians… but the way in which they are binding is determined by the authority of Christ and the fulfillment that takes place in His work… Since Jesus commands us to practice and teach even the "least of these commandments" of the law (5:19), we are bound to do so. But we do so as disciples who have learned how to discern the function of the law of Moses as a pointer to the realities of Jesus Christ the Lord.[40]

Christians keep the law by evangelical obedience. Law-keeping is the natural response to the justifying grace shown us in Christ, as well as the response to the indwelling Spirit who is the source of our sanctification. But our obedience to the Law of God is the foundation of our ethical, moral, righteous living. And while the New Testament says more about ethics and righteous living, all that it says is based on this foundation form delivered on Mt. Sinai.

Carl Henry is worth pondering:

> The transcendent basis of biblical ethics in special Divine revelation is the consistent affirmation of the whole sacred literature of the Hebrew-Christian movement… The whole of Scripture carries forward the correlation of ethics with the God of creation… The Decalogue is bound up with God's election of the Hebrews… Jesus did not modify the theological orientation of ethics. He reinforced it. Neither expediency, nor considerations of pleasure or prudence, nor the utilitarian concern with the greatest happiness of the greatest number, nor the appeal to the constitution of man and his ideal self-fulfillment gave Him the fundamental touchstone of morality… In disentangling the inner meaning of the Law from the accretions of tradition,

---

40. Vern S. Poythress, *The Shadow of Christ in the Law of Moses* (Phillipsburg, NJ: P&R, 1991), 268-69.

Jesus correlated the ethical claim with the Word of God... The Pauline ethic bears the same theological stamp... the moral life is conceived of as the spiritual reign of God in the lives of believers... The idea of God's rule in the heart is as central in his teaching as in that of Jesus.[41]

Two verses in the book of Revelation highlight the inseparable connection between keeping the commandments of God and our faith in Jesus Christ. The first is Revelation 12:17: "And the dragon was enraged with the woman, and he went to make war with the rest of her offspring, who keep the commandments of God and have the testimony of Jesus Christ." The second is Revelation 14:12: "Here is the patience of the saints; here are those who keep the commandments of God and the faith of Jesus." The law and the gospel are friends and allies when understood and applied correctly!

I close this exposition of Chapter 19 with the exhortation of John Calvin:

The third and principal use, which pertains more closely to the proper purpose of the law, finds its place among believers in whose hearts the Spirit of God already lives and reigns. For even though they have the law written and engraved upon their hearts by the finger of God [Jer. 31:33; Heb. 10:16], that is, have been so moved and quickened through the directing of the Spirit that they long to obey God, they still profit by the law.

Here is the best instrument for them to learn more thoroughly each day the nature of the Lord's will to which they aspire, and to confirm them in the understanding of it. It is as if some servant, already prepared with all earnestness of heart to commend himself to his master, must search out and observe his master's ways more carefully in order to conform and accommodate himself to them. And not one of us may escape from this necessity. For no man has heretofore attained to such wisdom as to be unable, from the daily instruction of the law, to make fresh progress toward a purer knowledge of the divine will.

Again, because we need not only teaching but exhortation, the servant of God will also avail himself of this benefit of the law: by frequent meditation upon it to be aroused to obedience, be strengthened in it, and be drawn back form the slippery path of transgression. In this way the saints must press on; for, however eagerly they may in accordance with the Spirit strive toward God's righteousness, the listless flesh always so burdens them that they do not proceed with due readiness.[42]

The testimony of Scripture to the goodness and foundational permanence of God's moral Law, summarized in the Decalogue and expanded and applied throughout Scripture, is overwhelming. Man's laws are a mixture of good and evil. Citizens of any country are protected by good laws, but governments create harmful laws that take away the freedom of citizens and cater to special interest groups. The whole Law of God is good and

---

41. Carl F. H. Henry, *Christian Personal Ethics* (Grand Rapids: Eerdmans, 1957), 197-99.

42. Calvin: *Institutes of the Christian Religion,* The Library of Christian Classics Volume XX, ed. John T. McNeill, translated by Ford Lewis Battles (Philadelphia: The Westminster Press, MCMLX), 360, 361.

His people love His Law because they know it comes from a righteous and holy God whose providence cares for His creation and His creatures, especially His own blood-bought children.

Law is not antithetical to love, and it will not do to say that love replaces law. Even in the greatest passage on love in the Bible, 1 Corinthians 13 (the "love chapter"), love is shown by keeping commandments. Keeping these commandments gives substance to love:

> Love suffers long *and* is kind; love does not envy; love does not parade itself, is not puffed up; does not behave rudely, does not seek its own, is not provoked, thinks no evil; does not rejoice in iniquity, but rejoices in the truth; bears all things, believes all things, hopes all things, endures all things. Love never fails (1 Cor. 13:4-8).

What is *descriptive* of love here is also *prescriptive*. We may call these the negative commandments of love: "be longsuffering," "do not envy," "do not be a show-off," "do not behave rudely," "do not seek your own things," "do not be provoked," "do not think the worst about someone," "do not rejoice when someone sins or falls." And the positive side of love is that love "rejoices in the truth; bears all things, believes all things, hopes all things, endures all things." These are positive commands given along with the negative commands.

As the Confession said in paragraph 7 of this chapter: "Neither are the aforementioned uses of the law contrary to the grace of the Gospel, but do sweetly comply with it." Christ does not give us a new law, but the law of pure and simple love. The Ten Commandments show us how to love God and how to love our neighbor. And, most importantly, they show us how to be holy.

CHAPTER 20

OF THE GOSPEL, AND THE EXTENT OF THE GRACE THEREOF

STEVEN E. HOFMAIER

1. The covenant of works being broken by sin, and made unprofitable unto life, God was pleased to give forth the promise of Christ, the seed of the woman, as the means of calling the elect, and begetting in them faith and repentance;[1] in this promise the gospel, as to the substance of it, was revealed, and [is] therein effectual for the conversion and salvation of sinners.[2]

2. This promise of Christ, and salvation by Him, is revealed only by the Word of God;[3] neither do the works of creation or providence, with the light of nature, make discovery of Christ, or of grace by Him, so much as in a general or obscure way;[4] much less that men destitute of the revelation of Him by the promise or gospel, should be enabled thereby to attain saving faith or repentance.[5]

3. The revelation of the gospel unto sinners, made in divers times and by sundry parts, with the addition of promises and precepts for the obedience required therein, as to the nations and persons to whom it is granted, is merely of the sovereign will and good pleasure of God;[6] not being annexed by virtue of any promise to the due improvement of men's natural abilities, by virtue of common light received without it, which none ever did make, or can do so;[7] and therefore in all ages, the preaching of the gospel has been granted unto persons and nations, as to the extent or straitening of it, in great variety, according to the counsel of the will of God.

---

1. Genesis 3:15
2. Revelation 13:8
3. Romans 1:17
4. Romans 10:14-15, 17
5. Proverbs 29:18; Isaiah 25:7; Isaiah 60:2, 3
6. Psalm 147:20; Acts 16:7
7. Romans 1:18-32

4. Although the gospel be the only outward means of revealing Christ and saving grace, and is, as such, abundantly sufficient thereunto; yet that men who are dead in trespasses may be born again, quickened or regenerated, there is moreover necessary an effectual insuperable work of the Holy Spirit upon the whole soul, for the producing in them a new spiritual life;[8] without which no other means will effect their conversion unto God.[9]

Introduction
How has it come to pass that we have been forgiven of our sins and granted pardon and acceptance with God? The answer is because of God's electing love which He set upon us in eternity past. He is the One who has made us to differ. Then again, it is through faith alone in the person and work of Jesus Christ alone who paid for our sins in His atoning sacrifice on the cross. This is the clear answer of the heart of the Christian and of this Confession.

But in our own life history, how did we come to learn of Christ that we might trust in Him? Someone brought us the gospel! "How then shall they call on Him in whom they have not believed? And how shall they believe in Him of whom they have not heard? And how shall they hear without a preacher? And how shall they preach unless they are sent?" (Rom. 10:14-15a). We ought to thank God greatly that we have been privileged to hear the gospel, and that preachers have been sent to us. This is the topic of this chapter of the Confession of Faith.

1. The Initial Revelation of the Gospel
The first thing to be noticed in paragraph 1 is that *the gospel is given in the context or setting of sin.* Adam's fall is referred to in the opening sentence, where it speaks of the Covenant of Works being broken by sin. Without getting into the question of whether Adam's pre-fall relationship with God is best described by this language (which is not the topic of this chapter!), the point here is clearly that after the fall, man cannot please God by works. It is now impossible for him to attain life by any means of his own making. He is lost in sin, and if he is to be restored to communion with God, the initiative must come from God alone. The natural man, whose mind is set on the flesh, cannot please God (Rom. 8:6-8). The effects of sin on the human race must not be minimized. No man can come to God by a way of his own invention. In all evangelism, no matter the exalted moral condition or seeming enlightenment of the people to whom we go, we must recognize that they cannot attain life without the gospel. They are dead in trespasses and sins. This theme is repeated over and over again in this chapter.

The next thing to be observed in this first paragraph is the *initial promise of the gospel.* The first announcement of the good news to sinful men comes immediately after Adam and Eve fell. It is given in the midst

---

8. Psalm 110:3; 1 Corinthians 2:14; Ephesians 1:19, 20
9. John 6:44; 2 Corinthians 4:4, 6

of the curse on the serpent: "And I will put enmity between you and the woman, and between your seed and her seed; he shall bruise your head, and you shall bruise his heel" (Gen. 3:15). The woman's seed refers to Christ and the elect people of God. The people are to be rescued from an unholy alliance with the devil and brought back to friendship and fellowship with God. Whereas Adam and Eve have now sided with Satan against God, that bond between God and man has been broken and replaced with enmity. The enmity with God, by inference, will be taken away, and replaced with peace. In other words, reconciliation will take place between God and sinners. How will this take place? By means of the (singular) seed of the woman who will bruise or crush Satan's head, thus gaining victory over the enemy. This will prove costly to the Redeemer, however, as the serpent is said to bruise His heel. Who is this champion who will conquer the serpent? It is Jesus, born of a woman, "offspring of the virgin's womb."

Then, too, *the purpose of the first gospel revelation* is declared. The gospel is revealed from the first as the means of calling the elect. It is only by the means of this revelation that sinners will be saved. It is to call men to repentance and faith. This is no mere acknowledgment that there is a seed of the woman who will crush Satan's head, but it also involves trust in that promised One that He alone would be able to deliver from bondage to sin and Satan. And if He is to *deliver from* the serpent, then the *works of* the serpent must be repented of; namely, sin and disobedience. The gospel is clearly stated as the means of calling the elect. They are not called apart from means. The necessity of the gospel unto salvation is emphasized from the very entrance of sin into the world.

Furthermore, *the sufficiency of the first gospel revelation* is emphasized. Although this first promise of the gospel does not contain all the rich detail found in its fulfillment, the revelation of a Savior is still sufficient to bring salvation to all who believe it. There is much more to be revealed about the seed of the woman who was also the Son of God, as well as of His atoning work. However, the Confession makes clear that there was enough revealed in this first promise for those who sinned from Adam's time onward to lay hold of, to believe, and to be saved from their sins. It is fruitless to speculate about how clearly they may have understood this, or what conception they had of the work of Messiah. But one thing is clear: they could see that salvation would only come by grace from God alone, through the work of One sent by Him, and that they must put their trust in the promised One alone. The only way for sinners to be saved, from Adam to Moses to David to the coming of Jesus until now, is by the gospel of Jesus, the seed of the woman who crushed the serpent's head.

Taken as a whole, this first paragraph is emphasizing that from the very beginning of the entrance of sin into the world, there is only one way of salvation. It repeats the emphasis of Chapter 7, paragraph 3, which states:

This covenant is revealed in the gospel; first of all to Adam in the promise of salvation by the seed of the woman, and afterwards by farther steps, until the full discovery thereof was completed in the New Testament; and it is founded in that eternal covenant transaction, that was between the Father and the Son, about the redemption of the elect; and it is alone by the grace of this covenant, that all of the posterity of fallen Adam, that ever were saved, did obtain life and a blessed immortality; man being now utterly incapable of acceptance with God upon those terms, on which Adam stood in his state of innocency.

Contrary to what some may misunderstand about the relation of the Old Testament to the New, the only way any sinner has ever been saved, from Adam until now, is through faith in God's Messiah: "But when the fullness of the time had come, God sent forth His Son, born of a woman, born under the law, to redeem those who were under the law, that we might receive the adoption as sons" (Gal. 4:4-5).

2. The Necessity of the Gospel for Salvation
The necessity of the revelation of the gospel for salvation is stated in no uncertain terms in the opening words of paragraph 2. The only way to know Christ, and obtain His promised salvation, is through the revelation contained in Scripture. The word only is an emphatic addition, which serves to repeat the doctrine of *sola Scriptura*—by Scripture alone. "For since, in the wisdom of God, the world through wisdom did not know God, it pleased God through the foolishness of the message preached to save those who believe" (1 Cor. 1:21). Men will not be saved unless they come into contact with the gospel revealed in Scripture. Against the views that the light of nature, the works of creation and providence, or even man's own ability to discover truth, are sufficient for salvation, this paragraph declares that men need the gospel, which is revealed in the Word of God, to be saved.

What is the *implication of this necessity?* If men are only saved by coming into contact with the gospel as revealed in Scripture, then the implication is that, without the Word of the gospel, no one is saved, not even one. Whether men have more or less light by nature or common grace, or whether they have a view of God that approximates the Christian view, does not matter at all. We ask again the question found in Romans 10:15: "How shall they believe on him whom they have not heard?" The fact is that the nations sit in darkness. The burden is on those who have the light to bring it to those who lack any knowledge of it.

Contrary to the proclamations of philosophers, "enlightened heathen," and misguided Christians who think that the sincere man of whatever religion will find his way to God, the Scriptures make it clear that all men apart from Christ are under the condemnation of the law. The light of nature and the general revelation found in creation declare the power and majesty of God. This is enough to make men accountable to judgement, but it is not enough to bring them to salvation. All men are justly condemned for being disobedient to the light of nature and for worshiping and serving the creature rather than the Creator (Rom. 1:25).

They know something of God and have heard of Him in the creation. Paul responds to the objection that they should not be condemned if they have never heard of God by quoting from Psalm 19:4: "But I say, have they not heard? Yes indeed: 'Their sound has gone out to all the earth, and their words to the ends of the world'" (Rom. 10:18). Even though they know something of God's eternal power and Godhead, they suppress the truth in unrighteousness (Rom. 1:18ff.). Therefore, because they are condemned by general revelation, they will not be saved without the special revelation of the gospel.

Consider Cornelius. He is called "a devout man and one who feared God with all his household, who gave alms generously to the people, and prayed to God always" (Acts 10:2). Peter even concluded when he went to Cornelius' house, "In truth I perceive that God shows no partiality. But in every nation whoever fears Him and works righteousness is accepted by Him" (vv. 10:34-35). The question is, how is that man to be reconciled to God? He needs to hear the gospel, which is why the angel directed Cornelius to send for Peter, "saying, 'Send men to Joppa, and call for Simon whose surname is Peter, who will tell you words by which you and all your household will be saved'" (11:13-14). If Cornelius was to be saved just by fearing the God that he knew something about and doing what was right, why was it necessary to hear from Peter? In fact, the angel told him that it was only through the words Peter was going to speak that he would be saved. The point is that when God in His sovereign prerogative determines to save, He does so by sending the gospel to those whom He has chosen.

3. The Sovereign Dissemination of the Gospel (or, God's Determination of the Extent of Its Spread)

Paragraph 3 opens with *a declaration that the spread of the gospel in history has been according to God's sovereign direction.* The Confession acknowledges that God is sovereign over the spread of His own gospel in the actual outworking of His decrees in history. In Old Testament times, the Word was revealed in various portions and ways, mainly to the Jewish nation. This is based on the statement of Hebrews 1:1-2: "God, who at various times and in various ways spoke in time past to the fathers by the prophets, has in these last days spoken to us by His Son, whom He has appointed heir of all things, through whom also He made the worlds." Formerly, God spoke almost exclusively to the Hebrew fathers. The Gentiles that came to a saving relationship with the living God were exceptions and not the general rule. The salvation of Nineveh under the reluctant ministry of Jonah comes to mind, as well as Naaman the Syrian in the time of Elisha. However, even during the times of the New Testament, not all nations have benefitted equally from the light of the gospel. The Confession acknowledges that in this, as in all matters, God has been sovereign. We may not understand the reasons why one nation is blessed abundantly with gospel preaching, and another seems to be passed by, but the fact remains for all to see.

One implication of this truth is that those who do not receive the gospel cannot be saved. Many in our day are unwilling to believe in the exclusivity of the scriptural way of salvation in Christ. They would like to allow room for sincere Hindus, animists, Muslims, Buddhists, etc., to be saved by being faithful to the light they have. They would like to think that all the other religions of the world are different paths to the same goal, but in fact they are damnable delusions. There is no promise given to us in the Bible that would allow us to believe that men can be saved unless God sends the gospel to them. In fact, the Scripture is clear: "Nor is there salvation in any other, for there is no other name under heaven given among men by which we must be saved" (Acts 4:12). The Confession gets somewhat repetitive with this emphasis, but it was evidently needed then, and we candidly admit that it is still needed now. As a matter of fact, no one has ever improved his "natural abilities, by virtue of common light" and no one can do so because of the effects of the fall on man's mind and will. None do good, and none by nature seek for God (Rom. 3:10ff).

Notice also the result of God's sovereign direction of the spread of the gospel. Because God has sovereignly directed the spread of the gospel, not all nations have the same degree of gospel light. To trace this out in church history, we note that Europe was blessed early on with the truth, but this happy condition soon gave way to the deadness of the Dark Ages and the development of Roman Catholicism. Though the gospel quickly spread from the Middle East to Asia and Northern Africa, the Muslim onslaught brought great darkness to many of those lands. As a result of the Protestant Reformation, northern Europe was illuminated brightly with the truth, especially in Great Britain. During the colonial period, Europeans spread the gospel to new lands. Sadly, this was accompanied by much that was not good. Greedy men oppressed the indigenous peoples, and some unwise missionaries replicated the errors of their imperfect denominations rather than spreading the unadulterated message of the pure gospel. But, for various reasons, many lands had their first contact with the saving knowledge of Christ as a result of missionaries following the tracks laid down by colonial businessmen and explorers. In the case of North America, the gospel was spread because of Christians fleeing religious persecution and coming to the New World. As a result, the Gospel came to many parts of the world that had never before heard the joyful sound. The point is well taken that there is "great variety" in the degree of gospel light in various parts of the world, and we acknowledge that God is sovereign even over this.

4. The Sufficiency of the Gospel unto Salvation

In the final paragraph of this chapter, the sufficiency of the gospel unto salvation is clearly stated. Although there is only one gospel, that is enough. This gospel is abundantly sufficient unto salvation. We should be confident in the sufficiency of the gospel preached. "For I am not ashamed of the gospel of Christ, for it is the power of God to salvation for everyone who believes, for the Jew first and also for the Greek" (Rom.

1:16). It is because of Paul's confidence in this gospel that he tells us, "So, as much as is in me, I am ready to preach the gospel to you who are in Rome also" (v. 1:15). The word here translated "ready" (πρόθυμος) can also be translated "willing" or "eager."[10] Paul had every confidence that, if he proclaimed the good news clearly, then it would do the work for which God had purposed to send it.

We need this same confidence. Today, some churches have invented all sorts of gimmicks to attract people to them. In many places, entertainment with gospel bands, movies, or stand-up comedy acts have replaced the plain, heart-to-heart declaration of the truth. But the apostle Paul had great confidence that this gospel, directly declared, was powerful to save.

However, the paragraph closes with a balancing truth. *The sufficiency of the gospel unto salvation is carefully qualified.* In addition to the Word (and not divorced from it), there needs to be an effectual, powerful work of the Holy Spirit on the soul of the hearer to produce new life and open their heart to receive the gospel. The Word apart from the Spirit's powerful work will not save. Men are dead in their sins and cannot hear. Like Lydia, they need to have their hearts opened by God to heed and receive the things spoken by God's messengers (Acts 16:14). This destroys all carnal confidence in the ability of the preacher or evangelist to convert. Unless the Spirit moves, no good will be done to the souls of men. This should drive us to our knees in all gospel endeavors.

Our Confession of Faith is wonderfully balanced here to avoid the extremes of Arminianism on the one hand and hyper-Calvinism on the other. Arminians, such as Charles Finney, believe and teach that, by creating the proper conditions for the preaching of the Word, and properly declaring it, the results of conversion are assured. Proper use of the proper means brings certain results, they say. Thus, "revival meetings" are programmed to manipulate men to a psychologically dictated decision. But we can guarantee no *genuine* results, because "the wind blows where it wishes, and you hear the sound of it, but cannot tell where it comes from and where it goes. So is everyone who is born of the Spirit" (John 3:8). "Man-produced conversions" may result, but that they are not the real thing is seen by the appalling statistics of "backsliding" of those who went forward in mass crusades. In reality, they are not backsliding, but going back to the mud or vomit from which they came (2 Pet. 2:22).

On the other hand, the Confession also guards against hyper-Calvinism. There are those who teach that the Spirit regenerates and gives life apart from the means of the hearing of the word of the gospel. This makes gospel preaching unnecessary, and some would even say wrong. However, the Scriptures declare that the Word is necessary to the new birth. "Having been born again, not of corruptible seed but incorruptible, through the word of God which lives and abides forever... Now this is

---

10. William Arndt, Frederick W. Danker, and Walter Bauer, "πρόθυμος," A Greek-English Lexicon of the New Testament and Other Early Christian Literature, 2nd ed. (Chicago: University of Chicago Press, 1979).

the word which by the gospel was preached to you" (1 Pet. 1:23, 25). The gospel preached is the means by which they are declared to have been born again. Consider also James 1:18: "Of His own will He brought us forth by the word of truth, that we might be a kind of firstfruits of His creatures." It is by the word of truth that we were brought forth, that is, born again. It is sovereign, yes, but it is by means. The instrumentality of the gospel is seen in other passages such as Acts 14:21, 1 Corinthians 4:15, Ephesians 1:13, and James 1:21.

An Additional Concern

There is one matter that should be considered in addition to the material presented in the Confession of Faith. Although the London Baptist Confession has ably stated the necessity of the gospel for the salvation of sinful man, and the sovereignty of God exercised in its dissemination, it has not placed emphasis on the mandate given to the church to bring that gospel to the world. The Confession was written in a time of the defense of the truth against the errors of Rome and of Romanizing tendencies in the Church of England. The emphasis on the spread of the gospel to the unconverted nations did not come until the end of the next century, more than a hundred years later. However, the church must not hide behind the sovereignty of God as an excuse for laziness in failing to fulfill the commission of our Lord Jesus to "make disciples of all the nations" (Matt. 28:19). For example, while we acknowledge that it was God who sovereignly decreed that India should not receive the gospel until the very end of the eighteenth century,[11] this should not excuse the fact that the church failed in its mission to bring the glad tidings to every land. There is no explicit declaration in the Confession as a whole, nor in this chapter in particular, that the church is obligated to bring the gospel to the world, which is an unfortunate omission. In order to redress this omission, we must consider what the Scripture teaches on this vital matter.[12]

Is there a *mandate* for the work of missions and evangelism? What gives us the warrant for going to other lands to "proselytize"? This is the challenge hurled at missionaries in this era. What right do we have to go to convert the heathen? Even the term "heathen" seems to have a condescending and imperialistic ring in our day. Without a clear divine mandate for missions, we would be lost in the subjectivism of this generation. But the Bible does give us a mandate, and that from Genesis to Revelation. God who created all deserves the worship of all. The Psalms speak of the nations praising Jehovah. The prophets speak of Messiah being a light to the nations. But the clearest warrant for missions is found in the "Great Commission" passage of Matthew 28:16-20. This is

---

11. Whether or not Thomas went to India with the gospel is a matter of historical uncertainty which does not affect the point being made.

12. For a further discussion of this matter the editor points the reader to Andrew Fuller's: *The Gospel Worthy of all Acceptation*. And William Carey's monumental missionary manifesto: *An Enquiry into the Obligations of Christians to use Means for the Conversion of the Heathens*.

a well-known "missionary" passage, and rightly so, for it contains many key concepts regarding the great work of missions.

> Then the eleven disciples went away into Galilee, to the mountain which Jesus had appointed for them. When they saw Him, they worshiped Him; but some doubted. And Jesus came and spoke to them, saying, "All authority has been given to Me in heaven and on earth. Go therefore and make disciples of all the nations, baptizing them in the name of the Father and of the Son and of the Holy Spirit, teaching them to observe all things that I have commanded you; and lo, I am with you always, even to the end of the age." Amen.

First, there are *several prerequisites* given before the commission. There is a prerequisite condition: the command is given to obedient disciples. There is a prerequisite attitude: worship. Before they were witnesses, the disciples were worshipers. They saw Him and worshiped Him. There is also a prerequisite authority: Christ's. He tells us to make disciples, and we are bound to obey. Modern objections notwithstanding, we have His authority to evangelize people of every nation, tribe, and tongue.

Then, there is *the essence of the command:* to make disciples. The only verb in the imperative mood—that is, the only direct command—in the whole passage is: "make disciples of all the nations." A disciple is a learner, a pupil, one who sits at the feet of his master and learns of him all he has to teach. He is a follower. This shows the error of an easy-believism which produces decisions but not true disciples.

Furthermore, we have *the scope of the command:* all the nations. Jesus has not sent the message of His salvation to Jews only, but rather this gospel is for the whole world, and for every nation in the world. Although this seems overwhelming, we must not be daunted by the size of the task, for all authority is given to Jesus over all things in heaven and on earth. There are no bounds to His kingdom, and no earthly authority can effectually shut out the banner of King Jesus.

The command comes with some *accompanying activities:* baptizing and teaching. These are two subordinate participles speaking of activity subordinate to and contingent upon the main verb. As such, they relate to us what should be done with those who are made disciples. First, they should be baptized; that is, initiated into the local church by this ordinance of immersion into water signifying death to sin, cleansing from sin, and new life in Jesus. This activity at the outset of discipleship demonstrates that the work of missions involves church planting, for baptism is the initiatory rite into the church.

Then, the disciples should also be taught. New converts are not left to their own imagination as to who God is, nor as to what He would have them do. The whole counsel of God is given to them that they may live a full-orbed Christian life in doctrine and application, faith and experience, belief and practice. This again alludes to the necessity of church-planting in the fulfillment of the commission, for teaching falls within the province and responsibility of the church. The risen Lord Jesus gave to His church the continuing gift of pastor-teachers (Eph. 4:11).

The commission also delineates *the duration of this command:* to the end of the age. Although some say that this command no longer applies to us, that it is already fulfilled, the truth of the matter is that we have not yet brought the word of Christ to the whole world! There are vast areas without a Christian witness. There are inhabited islands in the Philippines without an evangelical church of any kind. The same is true of extensive areas in China, many Muslim countries, and certain lands previously under communist control. To this day, many of the nations sit in darkness. The work is not done.

Others say that this was only for the apostles, the twelve. But Jesus indicates by His promise that His command is relevant unto the end of the age. The life of the apostles certainly did not extend until the end of the age. Therefore, we must continue to labor to make disciples by proclaiming Christ until He comes.

Finally, in this passage note *the accompanying promise:* "Lo, I am with you always, even to the end of the age." Here is a precious promise especially applicable to those involved in the work of missions, church planting and evangelism. There are times of discouragement when little fruit appears, or when opposition is intense, or when loneliness is poignantly painful. There are tragedies, such as the loss of a wife or child, which could perhaps have been avoided in the better medical facilities of the home country. Besides these burdens, there are times when the tempter makes you feel his power. At times like these, the promised presence of the Savior is especially precious.

Conclusion
The 1689 Confession of Faith ably states the necessity and sufficiency of the gospel for the salvation of the elect. It declares God's sovereign direction of the spread of the gospel in history. These truths are good and necessary for us to know. In addition, however, it is vital for us to consider our responsibility to declare God's glory unto the nations. With confidence in the authority of Christ, and assured of the presence of Christ, let us boldly make Him known, trusting that the Spirit will work through the Word to effectually call all whom He has chosen to be His by grace.

CHAPTER 21

OF CHRISTIAN LIBERTY AND LIBERTY OF CONSCIENCE

JIM SAVASTIO

1. The liberty which Christ hath purchased for believers under the gospel, consists in their freedom from the guilt of sin, the condemning wrath of God, the rigor and curse of the law,[1] and in their being delivered from this present evil world,[2] bondage to Satan,[3] and dominion of sin,[4] from the evil of afflictions,[5] the fear and sting of death, the victory of the grave,[6] and ever-lasting damnation:[7] as also in their free access to God, and their yielding obedience unto him, not out of slavish fear,[8] but a child-like love and willing mind.[9] All of which were common also to believers under the law for the substance of them;[10] but under the New Testament the liberty of Christians is further enlarged, in their freedom from the yoke of a ceremonial law, to which the Jewish church was subjected, and in greater boldness of access to the throne of grace, and in fuller communications of the free Spirit of God, than believers under the law did ordinarily partake of.[11]

2. God alone is Lord of the conscience,[12] and hath left it free from the doctrines and commandments of men which are in any thing contrary to his word, or not contained in it.[13] So that to believe such doctrines, or obey such commands out of conscience, is to betray true liberty of

---

1. Galatians 3:13
2. Galatians 1:4
3. Acts 26:18
4. Romans 8:3
5. Romans 8:28
6. 1 Corinthians 15:54-57
7. 2 Thessalonians 1:10
8. Romans 8:15
9. Luke 1:73-75; 1 John 4:18
10. Galatians 3:9, 14
11. John 7:38, 39; Hebrews 10:19-21
12. James 4:12; Romans 14:4
13. Acts 4:19, 29; 1 Corinthians 7:23; Matthew 15:9

conscience;[14] and the requiring of an implicit faith, an absolute and blind obedience, is to destroy liberty of conscience and reason also.[15]

3. They who upon pretence of Christian liberty do practice any sin, or cherish any sinful lust, as they do thereby pervert the main design of the grace of the gospel to their own destruction,[16] so they wholly destroy the end of Christian liberty, which is, that being delivered out of the hands of all our enemies, we might serve the Lord without fear, in holiness and righteousness before him, all the days of our lives.[17]

The subject of Christian liberty, to the modern mind, is primarily one of practice or applied biblical ethics. The term itself has come to be almost entirely associated with the *adiaphora,* or "things indifferent." What may I practice as a Christian? Is a certain practice forbidden in God's Word? If not, I am free to practice it. The mere mention of "Christian liberty" causes the mind to run to questions of alcohol, movies, clothing, make-up, certain holidays and traditions, and the like. It is refreshing, then, to see how the framers of our Confession understood and applied the subject of liberty to the believer.

The matter of Christian liberty is far more doctrinal, spiritual, and glorious than it is often seen to be. The word "liberty" means to be free of constraints, to be in command of one's life and actions, to be in bondage to no one and nothing. To be at liberty is to live without restraints, bars, chains, or prisons. It is the opposite of being enslaved or hindered.

For the Christian, this liberty is more than bodily or political freedom. It is more than the ability to think, speak, or do as one desires. At its core, Christian liberty is freedom purchased by Christ, delineated in Scripture, and enjoyed under the present influence of the Holy Spirit.

It is troubling, then, to see that which ought to bring unbridled joy to the church is the source of so much contention and judgment among believers. Several chapters in the New Testament are given over to this subject, speaking firmly of the liberty that we do have in Christ, as well as warning us strongly about abusing that liberty. Paul spoke of those who were strong judging the weak. He also spoke of the weak either judging the strong or being led away by them, thus, sinning against their own consciences. In light of the inherent dangers that this subject poses to a congregation, we must be careful in approaching it. The chapter before us is a very careful treatment of the matter of the conscience and Christian liberty. As we examine these truths in this chapter, we will do so under two primary headings: first, our freedom in Christ defined; second, our freedom in Christ defended (defended against legalism and license).

14. Colossians 2:20, 22-23
15. 1 Corinthians 3:5; 2 Corinthians 1:24
16. Romans 6:1, 2
17. Galatians 5:13; 2 Peter 2:18, 21

1. Our Freedom in Christ Defined
Three questions will be asked and answered under this heading. From what are we freed? For what are we freed? Is this freedom in Christ unique to new covenant believers?

(1) From What Are Christians Freed?
This chapter begins with these words, "The liberty which Christ hath purchased for believers under the gospel, consists…" There then follow six glorious statements declaring the spiritual freedom found for the believer through the work of Jesus Christ:

1. Freedom from the Guilt of Sin
This is what the angel meant when he said to Joseph in Matthew 1:21 that the coming Messiah would save His people from their sin. He would save from the guilt of sin, the power of sin, and one day finally, fully, and forever from the presence of sin. In John 8:36, Jesus promised that those whom the Son has made free are free indeed. The crushing guilt, stain, and weight of sin is removed from the believer in the death of Jesus. Jesus is the ultimate guilt offering; He is the scapegoat: the means by which the guilt and burden of our sin is sent away.

2. Freedom from the Condemning Wrath of God
The beginning of God's work of grace is ever and always tied to the work of the Spirit convicting us of sin and judgment. Before faith in Christ, we were children of wrath, just as the others (Eph. 2:3). Jesus taught that unbelievers had the "wrath of God abiding on them" (see John 3:36). It is by the work of the Spirit that we see that we are "not well", but truly in need of the Divine Physician. But this gracious work not only informs the soul of its guilt before a holy God, it also allows the cleansed conscience to know that, just as the angel of death passed over the bloodied door post of the Israelites, so too does the wrath of God pass over those who are washed in the blood of the Lamb (Rom. 5:9).

3. Freedom from the Rigor and Curse of God's Law
In Christ, the believer is not under the law as a covenant of works. That is, they are not using the law as the means of earning or maintaining a righteous standing before God. If we look to the law for our righteousness, it will only become the means of our condemnation. By the works of the law, we are assured by the apostle Paul, no flesh shall be justified in His sight (cf. Rom. 3:20). The same apostle declares to us in Galatians 3:10-13 that the law, apart from the blood and righteousness of Christ, will only bring condemnation. However, a proper understanding and application of the death of Jesus shows that Jesus removed the curse of the law by becoming a curse for us upon the cross.

But note that the Confession not only states the believer's liberty from the curse of the law, but also from the rigor of the law. There is a bondage that comes by looking at the law as the means of our righteousness before God, for the law demands complete and unblemished obedience to all its commands at all times (Gal. 3:19). The child of God who has found a righteousness in Christ is able to live a life pleasing to God, even though their works are not done perfectly.

4. Freedom from Our Great Spiritual Enemies
Here, the framers speak to the issue of the world, the flesh, and the devil. The world would woo and enslave the saint, the great adversary would hold us in bondage, and the flesh, left to itself, would have us under its dominion.

The power of these enemies to bind the believer is addressed clearly in the Word of God. We are not of the world, but chosen out of the world (John 15:19). We are no longer enslaved to the desire to be in the world and conformed to the world. In Christ, the great enemy of our soul has been defeated. He has been bound and his house plundered (Mark 3:27). The believer may yet know his temptations, but he can be resisted, and when resisted he will flee from the believer. And what of our own sin? Though the presence of sin has yet to be fully done away, the believer is no longer under the dominion of sin (Rom. 6:14, 17). Whom the Son has made free, is free indeed. By the power of the Holy Spirit, stubborn patterns of sin need not hold sway on the blood-bought child of God. We are dead to sin and alive to Christ.

5. Freedom from the Evil of Afflictions
This statement does not mean that the child of God, under the New Covenant, will lead a life free from trials, and distress, harm, or persecution. The believer, free from the curse of the law and the wrath of God, interprets the providence that befalls them in the light of their new identity in Christ. God is not an enemy who is against them, but a reconciled Father who is for them and who loves them and who will utilize every trial for their good and not for their harm (Rom. 8:28).

6. Freedom from the Fear of Death and of the World to come
Hebrews 2:15 speaks of those who were all their life subject to the bondage of the fear of death. What is it about death that makes one fearful? Some would say it is fear of the unknown. The Word indicates that what truly troubles men's soul is the fear of the known—the knowledge of standing before a holy God and giving an account for their lives. It is appointed unto men once to die and after this the judgment (Heb. 9:27). In Christ, the believer is able to face the king of terrors, to be loosed from the bondage of the fear of death, knowing that when they depart, they will be with Christ which is far better (Phil. 1:23).

(2) For What Are Christians Freed?
If you went from living in prison to living in a little room where you locked the door and stayed inside all day long, you would have missed the point of liberty. We are not merely freed from that which held us in bondage; we are free to enjoy a new vigorous life in Christ.

Our Confession states, "as also in their free access to God, and their yielding obedience unto Him, not out of slavish fear, but a child-like love and willing mind." Too often, obedience to the Lordship of Christ is cast in terms that are antithetical to the gospel. The Christian who strives to take his duty seriously and who embraces a biblical view of the seriousness of sin can, at times, find these views a straitjacket to the enjoyment of his identity in Christ. Just as the law is no longer a source of condemnation to the believer, so too the pursuit of holiness ought not to be a source of grief. Instead, holiness is pursued with the confidence of a child accepted in the Beloved.

The liberty we have in Christ is furthermore not a self-centered or selfish liberty. We are freed from the condemnation of the law, not from the essence of God's law or will for our lives. That is to say that the freedom from the condemnation of the law due to our sin is not a freedom from the clear command that we love God with all our heart, mind, soul, and strength and our neighbor as we do ourselves. We do not view the law as that which will damn us, but as the words coming from a loving Father to His children who want to please Him.

(3) Is Freedom in Christ Unique to New Covenant Believers?

The third question to answer under this heading has to do with the connection between the believer's liberty under the Old and New Covenants. Here the Confession states:

> All which were common also to believers under the law for the substance of them; but under the New Testament the liberty of Christians is further enlarged, in their freedom from the yoke of a ceremonial law, to which the Jewish church was subjected, and in greater boldness of access to the throne of grace, and in fuller communications of the free Spirit of God, than believers under the law did ordinarily partake of.

Did believers under the Old Covenant enjoy what we call Christian liberty? That is, were the benefits of Christ's life and death and resurrection applied to them in spiritual and practical ways so that there existed among our Jewish brethren a true sense of their freedom from the guilt of sin, the terrors of the law, etc.? The answer is yes and no. As believers in the grace of God, who looked upward for a righteousness outside of themselves, they did enjoy the liberty and freedom which Christ has purchased for His people. However, their enjoyment of this liberty was as those under the influence of a tutor as is laid out in Galatians 3:23ff. The New Covenant is truly a better covenant. The shadowy types have given way to the fuller light of the gospel. The fuller revelation of the New Testament demonstrates the unfathomable riches we have in Christ.

This brings us to our second major consideration.

2. Our Freedom in Christ Defended

One of the prime concerns of our brethren in addressing this subject in the second paragraph of Chapter 21 was the question: Who is "Lord of the conscience?" Who or what rules over the consciences of God's people, compelling them to embrace right belief and to take right action? This burden was not unique to the time of the Reformation, but it is present in Paul's writings as well. If Christ is our liberator and our king, then we must not become the slaves of men or of traditions.

There is all the difference in the world between faithful allegiance to the duties laid out in Scripture (too often called legalism) and a slavish adherence to the rules and regulations of society, or some teacher or organization. Who has sway over you and why? At the time this document was written, there were many who had the Roman Catholic Church and its traditions as Lord of the conscience. There were others who said, "No, the Lord of the conscience is the state." There were some who lived as though, "My tradition or my church group is the Lord of my conscience and I follow them no matter what they say." And then there were others who were saying, "No one and nothing is over my conscience other than the dictates of my own heart."

Against these extremes our brethren took up their Bibles and their pens to speak the truth of Holy Scripture and defend freedom in Christ against legalism and license.

(1) Against Legalism

I want to say a word about what legalism is. Legalism *is not* a strict and conscientious life of obedience to the commands of Scripture. Legalism is not pressing biblical duty upon a person. To expound the Word of God and then apply that Word to the hearts and consciences of the people of God is not browbeating and it is not legalism.

Legalism, biblically speaking, has three prongs to it. First, it is the mentality of a works righteousness—that is, the idea that my good works earn my salvation or secure my salvation before God. Second, and this is closely related, it is enforcing into practice regulations which God has fulfilled in Christ. This was part and parcel of the Galatian heresy —dietary laws, circumcision, feast days, and sacrifices were added to the work of Christ to ensure that one was truly saved. Third, legalism is when those in authority preach their own traditions in place of the Word of God. In Matthew 15:9, Jesus calls this, "teaching as doctrines the commandments of men."

Our Confession clearly states in paragraph 2:

> God alone is Lord of the conscience, and hath left it free from the doctrines and commandments of men which are in any thing contrary to his word, or not contained in it. So that to believe such doctrines, or obey such commands out of conscience, is to betray true liberty of conscience; and the requiring of an implicit faith, an absolute and blind obedience, is to destroy liberty of conscience and reason also.

These truths are well summarized in the words of Paul in 1 Corinthians 7:23: "You were bought at a price; do not become slaves of men." This truth is emphasized again in the words of Galatians 5:1: "Stand fast therefore in the liberty by which Christ has made us free, and do not be entangled again with a yoke of bondage."

(2) Against License

The work of the enemy and the presence of remaining sin in our hearts is such that if we will not be brought low by legalism, we will destroy ourselves with license. The framers of the Confession were wise then to add in paragraph 3:

> They who upon pretence of Christian liberty do practice any sin, or cherish any sinful lust, as they do thereby pervert the main design of the grace of the gospel to their own destruction, so they wholly destroy the end of Christian liberty, which is, that being delivered out of the hands of all our enemies, we might serve the Lord without fear, in holiness and righteousness before him, all the days of our lives.

The New Testament's warnings against such license are many: "What shall we say then? Shall we continue in sin that grace may abound? Certainly not! How shall we who died to sin live any longer in it?" (Rom. 6:1, 2). "For you, brethren, have been called to liberty; only do not use liberty as an opportunity for the flesh" (Gal. 5:13).

Peter expressed his deep burden in 1 Peter 2:15-16: "For this is the will of God, that by doing good you may put to silence the ignorance of foolish men—as free, yet not using liberty as a cloak for vice, but as bondservants of God." And then again in 2 Peter 2:19: "While they promise them liberty, they themselves are slaves of corruption; for by whom a person is overcome, by him also he is brought into bondage." The doctrine of Christian liberty is never an excuse to sin. To claim God as the Lord of one's conscience is to walk in the light of the revelation that He has given and in accordance with the indwelling Spirit of holiness.

What then do we make of the *adiaphora*? By what standard is the believer to judge whether or not he can participate in certain matters not expressly forbidden in the Word of God?

Several questions ought always to be considered in the practical application of these doctrines. Is what I am about to do a matter of faith? Can I pray about it? Can I ask God's blessing on it? Will what I am about to do bring me into bondage? Am I already under bondage? Can I live without it? Has this thing become an obsession with me? Will what I am about to do put a stumbling block before one of my brothers or sisters?

The answers to these questions may not forbid the practices, but they may affect when and where I practice them. Will what I am about to do affect my witness to my neighbor? Will my refraining from or my participating in a certain activity prove an obstacle in my witness to the lost? Has the practice I am embracing proven to be good or harmful to my never-dying soul? Christian liberty does not mean that I am free from such prayerful concerns. We ought to bring all of the practical questions concerning life, what we will and will not do, under the light of the Word of God.

We are to act in faith at all times; we are to seek the glory of God at all times; we are to follow our consciences at all times; we are to guard our own hearts at all times; we are to defer to our brethren at all times; we are to remember our witness to the world at all times.

CHAPTER 22

OF RELIGIOUS WORSHIP AND THE SABBATH DAY

SAM WALDRON

1. The light of nature shews that there is a God, who hath lordship and sovereignty over all; is just, good and doth good unto all; and is therefore to be feared, loved, praised, called upon, trusted in, and served, with all the heart and all the soul, and with all the might.[1] But the acceptable way of worshiping the true God, is instituted by Himself,[2] and so limited by His own revealed will, that he may not be worshiped according to the imagination and devices of men, nor the suggestions of Satan, under any visible representations, or any other way not prescribed in the Holy Scriptures.[3]

2. Religious worship is to be given to God the Father, Son, and Holy Spirit, and to Him alone;[4] not to angels, saints, or any other creatures;[5] and since the fall, not without a mediator,[6] nor in the mediation of any other but Christ alone.[7]

3. Prayer, with thanksgiving, being one part of natural worship, is by God required of all men.[8] But that it may be accepted, it is to be made in the name of the Son,[9] by the help of the Spirit,[10] according to His will;[11] with understanding, reverence, humility, fervency, faith, love, and perseverance; and when with others, in a known tongue.[12]

---

1. Jeremiah 10:7; Mark 12:33
2. Deuteronomy 12:32
3. Exodus 20:4-6
4. Matthew 4:9, 10; John 6:23; Matthew 28:19
5. Romans 1:25; Colossians 2:18; Revelation 19:10
6. John 14:6
7. 1 Timothy 2:5
8. John 14:13-14
9. Psalm 95:1-7; Psalm 65:2
10. Romans 8:26
11. 1 John 5:14
12. 1 Corinthians 14:16, 17

4. Prayer is to be made for things lawful, and for all sorts of men living, or that shall live hereafter;[13] but not for the dead,[14] nor for those of whom it may be known that they have sinned the sin unto death.[15]

5. The reading of the Scriptures,[16] preaching, and hearing the Word of God,[17] teaching and admonishing one another in psalms, hymns, and spiritual songs, singing with grace in our hearts to the Lord;[18] as also the administration of baptism,[19] and the Lord's supper,[20] are all parts of religious worship of God, to be performed in obedience to Him, with understanding, faith, reverence, and godly fear; moreover, solemn humiliation, with fastings,[21] and thanksgivings, upon special occasions, ought to be used in an holy and religious manner.[22]

6. Neither prayer nor any other part of religious worship, is now under the gospel, tied unto, or made more acceptable by any place in which it is performed, or towards which it is directed; but God is to be worshiped everywhere in spirit and in truth;[23] as in private families[24] daily,[25] and in secret each one by himself;[26] so more solemnly in the public assemblies, which are not carelessly nor wilfully to be neglected or forsaken, when God by His word or providence calleth thereunto.[27]

7. As it is the law of nature, that in general a proportion of time, by God's appointment, be set apart for the worship of God, so by his Word, in a positive moral, and perpetual commandment, binding all men, in all ages, He hath particularly appointed one day in seven for a sabbath to be kept holy unto Him,[28] which from the beginning of the world to the resurrection of Christ was the last day of the week, and from the resurrection of Christ was changed into the first day of the week, which is called the Lord's day:[29] and is to be continued to the end of the world

---

13. 1 Timothy 2:1-2; 2 Samuel 7:29
14. 2 Samuel 12:21-23
15. 1 John 5:16
16. 1 Timothy 4:13
17. 2 Timothy 4:2; Luke 8:18
18. Colossians 3:16; Ephesians 5:19
19. Matthew 28:19-20
20. 1 Corinthians 11:26
21. Esther 4:16; Joel 2:12
22. Exodus 15:1-19; Psalms 107
23. John 4:21; Malachi 1:11; 1 Timothy 2:8
24. Acts 10:2
25. Matthew 6:11; Psalm 55:17
26. Matthew 6:6
27. Hebrews 10:25; Acts 2:42
28. Exodus 20:8
29. 1 Corinthians 16:1, 2; Acts 20:7; Revelation 1:10

as the Christian Sabbath, the observation of the last day of the week being abolished.

8. The Sabbath is then kept holy unto the Lord, when men, after a due preparing of their hearts, and ordering their common affairs aforehand, do not only observe an holy rest all day, from their own works, words and thoughts, about their worldly employment and recreations,[30] but are also taken up the whole time in the public and private exercises of His worship, and in the duties of necessity and mercy.[31]

Introduction

The Importance of the Chapter
The subject of this chapter brings forward two of the distinctive tenets of the Puritan movement. Its presence in the 1689 Baptist Confession shows clearly that our Baptist forefathers were Puritans. Those two tenets are, of course, the regulative principle of worship stated in paragraph 1, and the Sabbath Day expounded in its last two paragraphs.

The regulative principle of worship embodies the Reformed approach to *sola scriptura* as opposed to the more limited views of the Lutheran and Anglican churches. The Reformed churches extended *sola scriptura* to include the worship and government of the church.[32] Lutherans and Anglicans wished to limit it to what they called "doctrine" and did not wish to be governed by it when it came to the worship and government of the church.

The doctrine of the Christian Sabbath is the emblem and mark of the Puritan understanding of the Law of God. Though widely disregarded in our day, its exposition in this chapter deserves both careful attention and renewed practice in the contemporary church.

The Outline of the Chapter
This chapter, like many others in the 1689, may be outlined in different ways with some justification. In this exposition of the chapter, I will follow the division suggested by the title itself. We will divide the chapter into its teaching on religious worship and its teaching on the Sabbath Day and expound it accordingly: (1) Of Religious Worship (Paragraphs 1-6); (2) Of the Sabbath Day (Paragraphs 7-8)

1. Of Religious Worship

1. Its Regulative Principle (Para. 1)
This chapter follows very closely the Savoy Declaration's minor revisions of the Westminster Confession. The only change of note from the Savoy is the addition of the phrase, "teaching and admonishing one another in

---

30. Isaiah 58:13; Nehemiah 13:15-22

31. Matthew 12:1-13

32. John Calvin, "The Necessity of Reforming the Church," *Selected Works* (Grand Rapids: Baker Book House, 1983), 1:128-129.

psalms, hymns and spiritual songs" in paragraph 5. This alteration, which seems to have originated with the authors of the 1689 Confession, takes the place of the phrase "of psalms" in the Westminster Confession and Savoy Declaration. The immediate historical occasion of this paragraph was the debate between Puritans and Anglicans about the church and its worship in the late sixteenth and seventeenth centuries. The twentieth article of the Church of England's Thirty-Nine Articles states, "The Church hath power to decree rites or ceremonies and authority in the controversies of the faith. And yet it is not lawful for the church to ordain anything contrary to God's Word written."[33]

James Bannerman helpfully contrasts the Puritan doctrine on this matter (contained in our Confession) and the Anglican doctrine:

> In the case of the Church of England, its doctrine in regard to Church power in the worship of God is that it has a right to decree everything, except what is forbidden in the Word of God. In the case of our own church, its doctrine in reference to church power in the worship of God is that it has a right to decree nothing, except what expressly or by implication is enjoined by the Word of God.[34]

G. I. Williamson helpfully illustrates the difference between the Anglican and Puritan understandings of the regulative principle with the following diagrams.[35]

The Regulative and Normative Principles Contrasted

The Anglican View

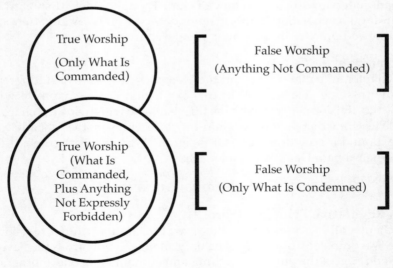

33. James Bannerman, *The Church of Christ*, vol. I (Edinburgh, The Banner of Truth Trust, 1960), 339.

34. Ibid., 339, 340.

35. G. I. Williamson, *The Westminster Confession of Faith for Study Classes*, 160.

The Puritan View

The difference between the Puritan and Anglican views of the regulation of worship may be helpfully illustrated by means of two builders intent on building the temple of God. Mr. Anglican must use the materials of the Word of God, but he has no blueprint and may use other materials. Mr. Puritan must use only materials of the Word of God and has a blueprint. It takes no special genius to discern that the two completed buildings will differ drastically or to discern which will be more pleasing to God.

Four biblical arguments for the Puritan regulative principle of worship may be presented.

First, it is the prerogative of God alone to determine the terms on which sinners may approach Him in worship. Bannerman eloquently states this:

> The fundamental principle that lies at the basis of the whole argument is this, that in regard to the ordinance of public worship it is the province of God and not the province of man, to determine both the terms and the manner of such worship... The path of approach to God was shut and barred in consequence of man's sin: it was impossible for man himself to renew the intercourse which had been so solemnly closed by the judicial sentence which excluded him from the presence and favour of his God. Could that path ever again be opened up, and the communion of God with man and of man with God ever again be renewed? This was a question for God alone to determine. If it could, on what terms was the renewal of intercourse to take place and in what manner was fellowship of the creature with his Creator again to be maintained? This, too, was a question no less than the former for God alone to resolve.[36]

But not only does God possess this prerogative, the Bible shows that He exercises it! Genesis 4:3-5 records the first instance of formal worship in the Bible:

> And in the process of time it came to pass that Cain brought an offering of the fruit of the ground to the Lord. Abel also brought of the firstborn of his flock and of their fat. And the Lord respected Abel and his offering, but He did not respect Cain and his offering. And Cain was very angry, and his countenance fell.

It is clear from this passage that it is not merely the persons of Cain and Abel that determined God's acceptance of Abel's offering and the rejection of Cain's. The text is clear. It is both Abel and his offering that are accepted and Cain and his offering that are rejected. Sometimes it is assumed that, because there are no previously mentioned requirements for such offerings, there could have been nothing more acceptable about Abel's offering than Cain's. But there are several problems with this assumption. First, the slaughter of animals to provide skin coverings for Adam and Eve in Genesis 3:21 is suggestive of the appointment of animal sacrifice. Second, the mention in Genesis 4:4 of "the firstborn of the flock and of their fat" anticipates later appointments of the sacrificial laws. For

---

36. James Bannerman, *The Church of Christ,* vol. I, 340, 341.

the sacrificial significance of the firstborn, notice Leviticus 27:26. For the sacrificial significance of the fat, notice Exodus 23:18; 29:13, 22; Leviticus 3:3-4, 9-10; 7:3-4, 23-24. The likelihood is that Moses intends us to think of these later appointments. Thus, it is not implausible to understand Moses in Genesis 4:4 as intending us to conclude that both Cain himself and his sacrifice were unacceptable to God (1 John 3:12).

Exodus 20:4-6 is often cited as one of the key passages as grounding the regulative principle in the Reformed tradition. It also makes clear that God exercises His prerogative to control how human beings bring worship to Him. How arrogant for man to think that he has the right to determine how God will be worshiped and served!

Second, the introduction of extra-biblical practices into worship inevitably tends to nullify and undermine God's appointed worship.

Matthew 15:3 suggests the inevitable tendency of following human traditions: "And He answered and said to them, 'Why do you yourselves transgress the commandment of God for the sake of your tradition?'" 2 Kings 16:10-18 is a penetrating moral tale and striking illustration of what happens to the ordinances when human invention intrudes itself into the ordained worship of God. If you read the story, you will notice that the altar of the Lord is not replaced by the king with the new altar. It is only displaced. This is the usual subtlety of human error. "We would never dream of getting rid of God's ordinances. We will treat them with great respect. But they will not have the central place in our worship. That will be occupied by the inventions of our wisdom." This tendency is illustrated in some evangelical churches today where mundane or silly announcements in the middle of worship, the unwise tradition of hand-shaking in the middle of worship, badly organized testimony times, clown shows, mime, liturgical dance, movies, and drama completely replace or severely restrict the clearly ordained parts of worship. These and other traditions of men often leave only fifteen to twenty minutes for preaching. Similarly, worship bands and the predominance of special music can push congregational singing, not to mention preaching, into the corner of corporate worship.

Third, the wisdom of Christ and the sufficiency of the Scriptures is called into question by the addition of un-appointed elements into worship.

The reasoning behind the addition of un-appointed elements in worship illustrates how this happens. John Owen remarks:

> Three things are usually pleaded in the justification of the observance of such rites and ceremonies in the worship of God: First, That they tend unto the furtherance of the devotion of the worshippers; secondly, That they render the worship itself comely and beautiful; thirdly, that they are the preservers of order in the celebration thereof. And therefore on these accounts they may be instituted or appointed by some, and observed by all.[37]

---

37. John Owen, *The Works of John Owen*, vol. XV (London, the Banner of Truth Trust, 1960), 467.

Reasoning such as Owen describes impugns the wisdom of Christ. With all our weakness, sin, and folly, will Christ leave us without an adequate guide in this most important matter of worship? Has He left us who are natively in such a poor spiritual condition without a sufficiently devotional, beautiful, and orderly worship of God? Says another Puritan: "For he that is the wisdom of the Father, the brightness of his glory, the true light, the word of life, yea truth and life itself, can he give unto his Church (for the which he paid the ransom of his blood) that which should not be a sufficient assurance for the same?"[38]

Not only is such reasoning out of accord with our needy spiritual condition; and not only does it, therefore, bespeak not a little spiritual pride; but such reasoning also impugns the sufficiency of Scripture (2 Tim. 3:15-17). Dr. John Tulloch, an opponent of the regulative principle, attempts to evade this charge that his view denies the sufficiency of Scripture by arguing (in a way typical of Anglicans) that the Bible was never intended to be a rule of church polity. He remarks: "The Christian Scriptures are a revelation of divine truth, and not a revelation of church polity. They not only do not lay down the outline of such a polity, but they do not even give the adequate and conclusive hints of one."[39]

The key biblical text on the sufficiency of Scripture provides us with explosives necessary to destroy Dr. Tulloch's view. 2 Timothy 3:16-17 is that text. The sufficiency of the Scriptures spoken of in this text is its sufficiency precisely for the man of God. The man of God is the person charged to order and lead the people of God. 2 Timothy 3:16-17 requires us to raise this question to those who think like Dr. Tulloch. Is ordering the church for the glory of God a good work which the man of God is peculiarly required to perform? If so, then the Scriptures are indeed able to thoroughly equip the man of God for this task. They teach the man of God an adequate form of biblical church order and the essential elements of the worship of the church.

Fourth, the Bible explicitly condemns all worship that is not commanded by God (Lev. 10:1-3; Deut. 17:3; 4:2; 12:29-32; Josh 1:7; 23:6-8; Matt. 15:13; Col. 2:20-23).

Three of these passages deserve special comment. Deuteronomy 12:29-32 in its original context is addressed precisely to the question of how God should be worshiped (v. 30). The rule given here in answer to this issue is very clear. "Whatever I command you, you shall be careful to do; you shall not add to nor take away from it" (v. 32). This clearly implies that it is a great temptation for God's people to see how the world worships and to allow that to have a formative impact on our attitudes about worship. Such an attitude is explicitly forbidden for God's people.

Colossians 2:23 condemns what may be literally translated as "will worship." Herbert Carson states the unavoidable implication of this

---

38. *The Reformation of the Church,* selected with introductory notes by Iain Murray (London: The Banner of Truth Trust, 1965), 75.

39. *The Reformation of the Church,* 44.

phrase: "The words… imply a form of worship which a man devises for himself."[40]

Leviticus 10:1-3 is the frightening account of what happened to Nadab and Abihu when they displeased God in the way they worshiped Him. What was it that brought upon them such a shocking judgment? Verse 1 is explicit. They "offered strange fire before the Lord." The meaning of the phrase, "strange fire," is expounded in the following clause. It is not fire which God had forbidden. The Hebrew clearly and literally reads that it was fire "which He had not commanded them." The mere fact that they dared to bring "unauthorized fire" (the translation of the NIV) brought fiery death upon them.

With this ample biblical support, why are men so lenient in their worship? It is because the God of modern men is not a God to be feared. Of all that is not appointed by God in His worship, we must hear Jesus saying, "Take these things hence!" Thus, the child of God will not respond to the regulative principle as if it were an intolerable straitjacket! Rather, he will pray, "O Lord, teach me to worship you acceptably."

Before leaving the subject of the regulative principle, a couple of concluding observations are important.

The first observation has to do with an important clarification of the regulative principle. Chapter 1, paragraph 6b, of the Confession speaks of the worship and government of the church. In so doing it says: "… there are some circumstances concerning the worship of God, and government of the church, common to human actions and societies, which are to be ordered by the light of nature, and Christian prudence, according to the general rules of the Word, which are always to be observed." When we say, therefore, that what is not commanded is forbidden, we are speaking of the substance and parts of worship (see paragraphs 2-6), not its circumstances. Minor circumstantial details God has left to be determined by the light of nature, Christian prudence, and general rules of Scripture. 1 Corinthians 14 contains two examples of such general rules which God demands that we apply to our specific circumstances. They are the rules of edification and order (vv. 26, 40). God demands that these two rules be followed, but He has not given us a detailed list of what they mean in every situation. Churches may differ as to where the line is drawn between circumstances and substance and parts. As long as each church holds seriously to the regulative principle, reasonable differences should not be made the source of division. We must be charitable in such things, while clearly insisting on the regulative principle.

The second observation has to do with the ecclesiastical framework of the regulative principle. The contents of this chapter strongly suggest that the regulative principle of worship has primary reference to the worship of the church in its formal gatherings. This is also suggested by the qualifying statement of the Confession in 1:6b which speaks of the worship of God and the government of the church together. It is

40. Herbert Carson, *Tyndale New Testament Commentaries: The Epistles of Paul to the Colossians and Philemon* (Grand Rapids: Wm. B. Eerdmans, 1976), 79.

specifically and primarily the sacred life of the church that is governed by the regulative principle. The church is holy in a sense that the rest of life is not (1 Tim. 3:15; Matt. 18:20). Thus, its government and worship are governed by the Word of God with a specificity that the rest of life is not (1 Tim. 3:14; Matt. 18:15-20; 2 Cor. 5:1-13).[41]

2. Its Restricted Presentation (Para. 2)

This paragraph speaks of two aspects of the presentation of worship. Both of these aspects had been compromised by Roman Catholic tradition at the time of the Reformation.

Regarding the object of worship, Roman Catholicism has compromised worshiping the Triune God alone. This was done by means of fine distinctions according different levels of worship to God, the Virgin Mary, the saints, and their images. A. A. Hodge begins his rebuttal of these fine distinctions by saying: "The objections to this entire system are … that it has neither as a whole nor in any element of it a shadow of support in Scripture." He then proceeds to lodge six more objections against the Roman Catholic distinctions.[42] Hodge is, of course, right. The unified response of Scripture to worship offered to any but God is complete and outright rejection (Acts 14:11-15; Rev. 19:10; 22:8-9; cf. Isa. 42:8; 48:11).

Regarding the mediation of worship, Roman traditions have also led to grievous detraction from the glory of Christ as the sole mediator. The practice of invoking the saints and their merits was one such practice. Once more, then, the Confession insists that true worship must be offered only through the mediation of the one Mediator between God and man, the man Christ Jesus (John 14:6; 1 Tim. 2:5).

3. Its Constituent Elements (Paras. 3-5)

Several practical observations on paragraphs 3-5 are necessary. First, these paragraphs speak of the various parts of worship. Note the reference to prayer as a part of worship in paragraph 3 and the statement that the several things mentioned in paragraph 5 are "all parts of religious worship of God." This reference is to the parts of worship which must be specifically appointed by God according to paragraph 1. This is to be contrasted with the circumstances of the worship and government of the church mentioned in Chapter 1, paragraph 6b: "… there are some circumstances concerning the worship of God, and government of the church, common to human actions and societies, which are to be ordered by the light of nature, and Christian prudence, according to the general rules of the Word, which are always to be observed."

Second, there is no reason to think that the Confession intends to be exhaustive regarding the listing of the various parts of worship. Paragraph

---

41. I provide a longer and more detailed treatment of the regulative principle of the church in *Going Beyond the Five Points* (Rob Ventura, 2015); *The Regulative Principle of the Church* (Pensacola, Chapel Library).

42. A. A. Hodge, *The Confession of Faith* (London, the Banner of Truth Trust, 1983), 273-75.

5 in particular only mentions several parts of worship without asserting that this list is exhaustive. Personally, I think there is an argument for other parts of worship not mentioned.

Third, the Confession assumes in paragraph 5 that churches under the leadership of their elders have the authority to appoint special days of fasting and humiliation as well as special days of rejoicing and thanksgiving. This assumption is noteworthy. It suggests that a degree of freedom of application is consistent with the strict practice of the regulative principle.

Fourth, the Confession reflects the plain teaching of 1 Corinthians 14:16-17 when it says in paragraph 3 that prayer must be made "when with others, in a known tongue." This is important because it exposes the lack of biblical basis for the Charismatic Movement today. Even supposing for the sake of argument that the gift of tongues is still given today, Paul gives three very clear rules in 1 Corinthians 14 that must govern its exercise in the formal meetings of the church. Each of these rules is widely ignored in Charismatic churches. Tongues must be translated (1 Cor. 14:16-17); tongues must be limited to two or three tongues-speakers (1 Cor. 14:27); and tongues must not be exercised by women in the assembly (1 Cor. 14:34-35). If Charismatic churches simply followed the apostle's rules, they would eliminate most modern, tongues-speaking practices in their churches!

Fifth, often some curiosity is expressed about the statement in paragraph 5 that prayer must not be made "for those of whom it may be known that they have sinned the sin unto death." The Confession is simply reflecting the language of the cited proof text, 1 John 5:16. I do not know that anything more profound than a simple attempt to be faithful to Scripture should be made of this. 1 John 5:16 is no doubt speaking of the Gnostic false teachers that troubled the churches to which the apostle John was writing. As in Matthew 12:31-32 and Hebrews 6:4-6, it appears that these false teachers had rejected a miraculously attested gospel in favor of a satanic counterfeit. Such rejection of miraculous light attesting the gospel was fatal—a sin unto death from which there was no spiritual recovery. It should go without saying that believers today need not fear that they have committed such a sin unless they claim to have seen actual miracles attesting the gospel and have then turned their back on it.

4. Its Appropriate Locale (Para. 6)

The phrase "under the gospel" reveals that there is an implied contrast in this paragraph with the situation "under the law." Since this is so, we shall look first at the appropriate locale of worship "under the law" and then "under the gospel." In the period of the Mosaic covenant, worship was tied to a definite geographical location and physical structure (Ex. 25:8, 9, 22; 40:34-38; 1 Kings 8:38, 48-49; Ps. 5:7; 2 Chr. 6:38; Dan. 6:10). This connection of worship with a physical structure and geographical location was typical and ceremonial and thus was abolished in Christ (John 4:21-23; 1 Tim. 2:8; Mal. 1:11). Worship must not be tied to, nor sanctity be attributed to, any particular locations or structures in the New Testament period. The historical rationale for this paragraph was Rome's attributing special sanctity to certain structures and places, i.e., cathedrals, Jerusalem, Rome.

The abolition of such geographical localization of the worship of God does not mean, however, that there is no appropriate locale for worship in the New Covenant. That locale is now not geographical, but spiritual. In a sense there is an extension of the idea embodied in the temple and tabernacle. They were the place of worship, because they were the place of God's special presence. There is a still a place in which God is especially present, but according to the New Testament, the church is the new temple and its assemblies are the place of God's special presence (Matt. 18:20; 1 Cor. 3:16; 14:25; Eph. 2:21-22). The assemblies of this new, spiritual temple are to be prized by the people of God now just as much as the people of God in the Old Testament prized the worship at the physical temple. Both are the place of God's special presence (Ps. 84:1, 2, 10). The public assemblies of the church "are not carelessly nor willfully to be neglected or forsaken" (Heb. 10:25; Acts 2:42). The principle that God's special presence is the place of worship also has its application, as the Confession implies, to secret and family worship. This is the case because the believer himself is the temple of God (1 Cor. 6:19)—the place of God's special presence.

2. Of the Sabbath Day (Paras. 7-8)

The thrust of paragraph 1 of this chapter is that God has and exercises the right to appoint how He will be worshiped. Man does not have the right to intrude his ideas, his opinions, or his authority into divine worship. It is only in this framework and from this perspective that we can appreciate the biblical and Puritan teaching on the Sabbath. Just as every other major element of worship is appointed by God and not by ecclesiastical authority, even so the day of public worship is not left for man to decide. By a positive, moral, and perpetual commandment, God appoints the day.

Now in treating the appointed day of worship, the Confession expounds its institution (para. 7) and its sanctification (para. 8). We will take these up in order.

1. Its Institution (Para. 7)
The Confession first mentions the *natural necessity* of an appointed day of worship. The Confession teaches that the law of nature requires an appointed day for worship. Several things should be evident by the light of nature.

- First, God must be worshiped by men. Of course, the light of nature makes this clear.

- Second, God should be worshiped publicly and corporately by men. Mankind is corporate. There is human society. Worship, therefore, must be corporate and social.

- Third, such public and corporate worship requires a corporately agreed upon proportion of time. Such a proportion of time must be appointed by God, because the only alternative (that men should appoint it) would violate the prerogatives of God in His worship.

The *positive enactment* of the appointed day is next mentioned. Although general revelation (the law of nature) makes it clear that an appointed day of worship is necessary, the law of nature does not and cannot specify which day that should be. Resting for worship on the seventh day or first day is not written by creation on the hearts of men. Since the law of nature did not specify the right proportion or the specific part of our time for public worship, there must be a positive commandment by God to specify that time. The term "positive" used here in the Confession means something appointed by God in addition to the law of nature and general revelation. The appointed day must be revealed by special revelation. Some have asked, "If the Sabbath is a moral law, why are not Gentiles without special revelation indicted for breaking it in the Bible?" The reason is evident. It is a positive commandment revealed only by special revelation. Positive commandments, as the Confession makes clear, may also be moral. Thus, the specially revealed character of the Sabbath does not mean that it is ceremonial.

But not only is this commandment called positive because it is something in addition to the law of nature, it is also called moral and perpetual. This commandment of one day in seven as a Sabbath may be seen to be moral and perpetual for at least three good reasons:

- It was instituted at creation (Gen. 2:3; Exod. 20:8-11; Mark 2:27-28). What was instituted at creation has significance for as long as the creation continues. Thus, both Jesus and Paul ground ethical duty on the fact that something was instituted at creation (Matt. 19:4-8; 1 Tim. 2:13; 1 Cor. 11:8-9).

- It was included in the Decalogue (Exod. 20:8-11). God saw fit to include the Sabbath ordinance in the Ten Commandments. The Ten have an importance that transcends the other Old Testament laws. (Note Chapter 19 of the Confession.) They alone were directly spoken by God. They alone were written on stone by the finger of God. They alone were placed in the Ark of the Covenant. They are said to be written in the hearts of New Covenant believers (Jer. 31:33). They are repeatedly cited as fundamental moral laws of perpetual significance in the New Testament (Rom. 13:8-10; Matt. 22:18,19; 1 Tim. 1:8-10). The idea that the Sabbath is a ceremonial and temporary law flatly contradicts these biblical facts.

- It is continued in the Lord's Day. The Lord's Day of the New Covenant embodies the sabbath principle instituted at creation. This is proved by the many conspicuous parallels between the sabbath and the Lord's Day.

  (1) The designation, "Lord's Day," alludes to biblical phrases descriptive of the sabbath: "my holy day," "the Lord's holy day" (Isa. 58:13); "The Lord of the sabbath" (Matt. 12:8).

  (2) Like the sabbath and unlike any other religious observance, the Lord's Day is the celebration of one day of weekly recurrence.

  (3) Like the sabbath and unlike any other religious observance, the Lord's Day thus presupposes the seven-day week of creation.

  (4) Like the sabbath and unlike any other religious observance, the Lord's Day is a memorial of both creation and redemption. Even as the sabbath memorialized the first creation and the exodus of Israel from Egypt, so also the Lord's Day memorializes a new creation and a greater redemption.

  (5) Like the sabbath, the Lord's Day is a day belonging especially to God. Sixteen times God speaks of "my sabbaths."

  (6) The Lord's Day is a holy day and must be kept holy. The sabbath was a holy day. It was sanctified and was to be kept holy (Gen. 2:3; Exod. 20:8). The Lord's Day is also a holy day. The word "holy" means to set apart to God from common use. Something that is set apart to God is His special possession; it is holy. To be holy and to belong especially to God are equivalents (Exod. 13:2; Num. 16:3-7). Is the Lord's Day God's special possession in a sense that other days are not? Yes. Then, it is holy and must be sanctified. We must then remember the Lord's Day, to keep it holy.

  (7) Like the sabbath, the Lord's Day is a day of corporate, public worship (Acts 20:7; 1 Cor. 16:1,2). But if it is a day appointed for public worship, it must be a day of rest or sabbath. This is so for three reasons. First, all days of public, corporate worship are sabbaths in the Bible. A day of worship which was not a sabbath would have been incomprehensible to the Jewish disciples of Jesus. Secondly, the Lord's Day is a holy day and, therefore, must be set apart from ordinary labors and set apart to worship. That is what sanctifying the day requires. Such a day is, however, clearly a day of rest. Thirdly, no one can engage in public worship without, at least for an hour or two, resting from his secular labors.

It is now evident why the Lord's Day must be viewed as the Christian Sabbath. The institution of the Sabbath at creation, the inclusion of the Sabbath in the Decalogue and the continuation of the Sabbath principle in the Lord's Day demands this. This is why when someone says, "The term, Sabbath, always refers to the Jewish Sabbath in the New Testament," it need not bother us. Of course, the Sabbath in the Bible referred to the seventh-day Sabbath. It had referred to that ordinance for four thousand years. On the basis of the evidence just cited, however, we must distinguish between the Jewish, seventh-day Sabbath ordinance which is abolished and the concept of the Sabbath which is continued on the Lord's Day. This distinction between the ordinance of the Sabbath and the concept of the Sabbath is demanded by its institution at creation, its inclusion in the Ten Commandments and the very meaning of the term, "Lord's Day."

In the last part of paragraph 7, the epoch-making alteration of the appointed day from the seventh to the first day of the week is discussed. Many have felt that this is the weak point in the Confession's doctrine of a Christian Sabbath. At first glance, their criticism seems plausible. It is argued that if the Sabbath commandment is a moral law, it could not be altered. Two different conclusions have been drawn from this premise. Some, like Seventh Day Adventists, have concluded from this premise that the day has not been changed and that the appointed day of worship is still the seventh day of the week. Others have concluded that since the day is changed, the Sabbath could not possibly be a moral law.

The answer to the dilemma posed by this premise is found in the peculiar character of the Sabbath commandment implied in the language used by the Confession to describe it. It is called "a positive moral and perpetual commandment." This particular moral law is composed of two separate elements: the law of nature and the positive enactment. The law of nature cannot be and is not altered. The positive enactment may be and is altered. Thus, the alteration of the day is no argument against the morality and perpetuity of the Sabbath commandment.

A further issue may be raised at this point. The Sabbath commandment is a positive commandment instituted at creation. How can a creation ordinance be altered? The answer is, of course, that only a new creation could alter a creation ordinance. Christ has, however, inaugurated a new creation (2 Cor. 5:17; Gal. 6:15). Hence, one would expect a change in the creation ordinance of the Sabbath.

That the observation of the last day of the week is abolished is proved by Colossians 2:16, 17. While this text is not speaking of the concept or principle of the Sabbath, it is teaching that the old creation and old covenant "seventh day" Sabbath ordinance is abolished.

Another difficulty people have about the alteration of the day is that they can find no mention in the Scriptures of this change of the day. If this problem is to be resolved, one must first understand the principle by which the day of worship is appointed in the creation ordinance. The designation principle must be understood. In Genesis 2:3, it says that God set apart the seventh day because He rested on that day. Recognizing that what God did in redemption was so great that nothing less than the concept of a new creation could describe it, we must understand that God in the new creation uses the same designation principle. The new creation Sabbath is designated on the same principle as that of the old creation Sabbath. It is the day of God's rest. The first day of the week is the day upon which Christ's labors to atone for the sins of His people came to an end and He entered His rest in resurrection glory. The Lord's

Day is the first day, the day of new beginnings. As the seventh day was associated with and memorialized the old work of creation, so the first day is associated with and memorializes a new creation.

2. Its Sanctification (Para. 8)

The substance of the Fourth Commandment is "Remember the Sabbath day to keep it holy." The above defense of the institution of the Christian Sabbath makes abundantly clear that we may also say with clear biblical warrant: "Remember the Lord's Day to keep it holy." The Lord's Day is a day that is holy because it is a day that belongs especially to God. Thus, the essence of Lord's Day keeping is the same as the essence of Sabbath keeping. The day must be kept holy.

Without fear of contradiction, we may say that there is a holy day in the New Covenant. Just as there is a holy meal (the Lord's Supper, 1 Cor. 11:20), so there is a holy day (the Lord's Day, Rev. 1:10). The notion that there is no holy, special day that belongs to God in the New Covenant is nonsense and betrays ignorance of the New Testament Scriptures. You must remember the Lord's Day to keep it holy. The Fourth Commandment in this way applies to you.

But who is going to teach us how to keep a day holy? Are we allowed to make this up out of the imaginations of our own hearts? Of course not. We must allow the Scriptures to teach us how to keep the Lord's Day holy. That means we must look at its observance by Jesus and its moral observance in the Old Testament. The Confession does an admirable job of summing up the practical teaching of Scripture.

Preparations Must Be Made to Keep the Day Holy. The Confession reads: "when men, after a due preparing of their hearts and ordering their common affairs aforehand." If there is a day upon which we must do certain things as a matter of religious obligation to the Lord Jesus, then it stands to reason that we should prepare on the other days of the week. Preparation is just common sense if we believe in keeping the Lord's Day holy. Thus, it was a common understanding among the Jews that Friday was the preparation day for the Sabbath. Five times in the New Testament it is mentioned that Jesus was crucified on the day of preparation. Listen to Luke 23:54, for instance: "It was the preparation day, and the Sabbath was about to begin." Ignatius, the early church Father writing of the early Christians, speaks of how they began to live according to the Lord's Day.[43] We cannot simply wake up on Lord's Day morning and say, "Oops! It is the Lord's Day. I have to keep it holy." We have to prepare to do so. If we are to keep it holy, we cannot spend the day mowing the lawn and shopping for groceries. We have to do such things on another day. Just as our mentality about our money changes when we become Christians, so also our mentality about our time has to change. We have to plan in order to give God the firstfruits. We also have to plan in order to keep the Lord's Day holy.

---

43. Ignatius, *Magnesians* 9:1.

But all of this assumes some things which I actually have not said yet. This brings me to *specifics:* keeping the Lord's Day holy involves specific concepts and duties. The Confession says that the keeping of the Lord's Day requires that we "do not only observe an holy rest all day, from their own works, words and thoughts, about their worldly employment and recreations, but are also taken up the whole time in the public and private exercises of his worship and in the duties of necessity and mercy."

The idea of holiness, as I said, is separation or *set-apart-ness.* The idea of holiness is, then, two-sided. We set apart from, and we set part to. This is also the idea of rest. We rest from, and we rest to. All of this is a consequence of the fact that the day belongs to God. This means that it must be focused away from our ordinary lives in the world and focused on God. Again, there is a *from* and a *to.*

Now the problem with all this is that contemporary Christianity has almost entirely lost the sacred-secular distinction. The term, secular, suggests something that belongs to this age or the world. The term, sacred, refers to something that is associated with God and thus the age or world to come. But contemporary Christianity insists on its blind and one-sided notions that "all of life is worship," that "Christianity is not a religion," and that "every day is holy." With these blinders on, it has lost sight of the distinction between the sacred and the secular. We must get this back because the whole keeping of the Lord's Day holy is built squarely on this distinction.

When we do recover this crucial distinction, then what it means to keep the Lord's Day holy is plain. It means to set aside the business and the amusements of this age and focus on the business and pleasures associated especially with God. It means we turn our faces from this life to the life to come. It means that we turn from the world to Christ, the Word of Christ, Christ's appointed worship, and the things of Christ's kingdom.

This is what is in the mind of the prophet Isaiah in Isaiah 58:13-14. The Lord's Day, then, is a day dedicated to the corporate worship of God. It is a day dedicated to the reading of God's Word. So, you are behind in your reading of the Scriptures. The Lord's Day is a day to catch up. You never do get enough time to read those good Christian books that you want to read and that will help you in your walk with God. The Lord's Day is for that. You never have enough time to fellowship with Christian friends and speak with them about the things of God and their lives and show them love. The Lord's Day is for that. You have little time to minister or get over to the nursing home to see the folks there. The Lord's Day is for that. But, you will not do any of those things if you don't stop with all the worldly business and amusements and nonsense, and set apart the day to God.

Now, of course, there are other things which must be attended to besides the holy business of the Lord that we have been discussing. There are works of necessity that must be done. Police, corrections officers, soldiers, nurses, doctors, and other people must work on the Lord's Day.

Meals must be prepared, and people must eat on the Lord's Day. The other common functions of life that must be done every day must be done on the Lord's Day. The notion that no work of any kind may be done on the Lord's Day is wrong. If it were true, it would make our Lord Himself a sinner. The works of piety, necessity, and mercy are allowed on the Lord's Day. There is no sin in them. Perhaps the one passage which illustrates this best is Matthew 12:1-14. Notice the works of necessity, mercy, and piety in this passage. Notice the work of necessity. The disciples were eating on the Sabbath as they walked through the fields. Notice the work of piety. The priests labor in the temple and are guiltless. Notice the work of mercy. Jesus commonly and frequently healed on the Sabbath. Even the Pharisees when they were in their right minds and not under the influence of their murderous hatred for Jesus pulled their sheep out of the pit on the Sabbath.

There are, of course, many practical questions about Lord's Day observance that cannot be answered in this brief exposition of the Confession. But the doctrine of the Christian Sabbath does not depend on unanimity among genuine lovers of the Christian Sabbath about these questions. Situations differ. Cultures differ. Such differences may affect the applications of the Christian Sabbath, but they do not change the responsibility of the Christian to keep the Lord's Day holy.[44]

---

44. Many fine defenses of the confessional doctrine of the Sabbath are available. I urge those with a desire to know more and who have questions to read those treatments. Among them are my own *Lectures on the Lord's Day* available from Chapel Library in Pensacola, FL; Robert Martin, *The Christian Sabbath* (Trinity Pulpit Press, 2015); Joseph A. Pipa, Jr., *The Lord's Day* (Christian Focus Publications, 1997); Richard Barcellos, *Getting the Garden Right* (Reformed Baptist Academic Press, 2017).

CHAPTER 23

OF LAWFUL OATHS AND VOWS

JEFFREY B. JOHNSON

1. A lawful oath is a part of religious worship, wherein the person swearing in truth, righteousness, and judgement, solemnly calleth God to witness what he sweareth,[1] and to judge him according to the truth or falseness thereof.[2]

2. The name of God only is that by which men ought to swear; and therein it is to be used, with all holy fear and reverence; therefore to swear vainly or rashly by that glorious and dreadful name, or to swear at all by any other thing, is sinful, and to be abhorred;[3] yet as in matter of weight and moment, for confirmation of truth, and ending all strife, an oath is warranted by the word of God;[4] so a lawful oath being imposed by lawful authority in such matters, ought to be taken.[5]

3. Whosoever taketh an oath warranted by the Word of God, ought duly to consider the weightiness of so solemn an act, and therein to avouch nothing but what he knoweth to be truth; for that by rash, false, and vain oaths, the Lord is provoked, and for them this land mourns.[6]

4. An oath is to be taken in the plain and common sense of the words, without equivocation or mental reservation.[7]

5. A vow, which is not to be made to any creature, but to God alone, is to be made and performed with all religious care and faithfulness;[8] but

---

1. Exodus 20:7; Deuteronomy 10:20; Jeremiah 4:2
2. 2 Chronicles 6:22, 23
3. Matthew 5:34, 37; James 5:12
4. Hebrews 6:16; 2 Corinthians 1:23
5. Nehemiah 13:25
6. Leviticus 19:12; Jeremiah 23:10
7. Psalms 24:4
8. Psalm 76:11; Genesis 28:20-22

popish monastical vows of perpetual single life,[9] professed poverty,[10] and regular obedience, are so far from being degrees of higher perfection, that they are superstitious and sinful snares, in which no Christian may entangle himself.[11]

Some of us were taught that it is wrong to swear. It was not so much about using foul language. We were taught that we should not swear in the most technical sense of the word. We were never to say, "I swear that... " The rationale for the instruction probably had something to do with what our Lord said in Matthew 5:34: "But, I say unto you, do not swear at all." There you have it. Jesus' authoritative words should settle it. It is simply wrong ever to take an oath. I wonder how many others have interpreted and applied that command in the same way? It is that misunderstanding of oaths and vows which makes this chapter of the Confession both interesting and practically relevant.

Historically, this chapter is a response to the Anabaptists, who taught that any form of swearing is absolutely forbidden and to the Roman Catholic Church, who perverted it. Our spiritual forefathers have provided us with a balanced perspective on swearing to steer us clear of those two errors.

Swearing Lawfully

There are two types of oaths. There are those in which we affirm that we are telling the truth and those where we promise to do something.[12] "A lawful oath" indicates that it is lawful (not inherently sinful) to give such affirmations and make such promises (Gen. 21:22-24; Num. 30:1-2; Josh. 2:12-21; Ruth 1:16-17; Neh. 10:1-31; 2 Cor. 1:23; 1 Thess. 5:24). Consider the following features of a "lawful oath" that are set forth in the first paragraph:

A part of religious worship. This is not to be interpreted to mean that oath taking is an element of public worship when the church gathers on the Lord's Day. A lawful oath is a religious act in that it is set apart and distinct from the common communications of everyday life, because, as is stated in the second paragraph, an oath is to be sworn in God's name (Ex. 20:7).[13]

---

9. 1 Corinthians 7:2, 9

10. Ephesians 4:28

11. Matthew 19:11

12. "When a person swears to facts past or present, this is called an *assertory* oath. When a person swears that he will perform a certain deed or deeds in time to come, this is called a *promissory* oath." Robert Shaw, *The Reformed Faith: An Exposition of the Westminster Confession of Faith* (Fearn, Ross-shire, Scotland: Christian Focus, 2008), 304.

13. One reality that makes this scriptural theme difficult is that swearing in the Old Testament is explicitly tied to the worship and service of God. Expounding the third commandment, Calvin commented on this, writing, "That an oath, when duly taken, is a species of divine worship, appears from many passages of Scripture, as when Isaiah prophesies of the admission of the Assyrians and Egyptians to a participation in the covenant, he says, 'In that day shall five cities in the land of Egypt speak the language of Canaan, and swear to the Lord of hosts' (Isaiah 19:18). Swearing by the name of the Lord

Truth, righteousness, and judgment.[14] "Truth" can be a reference both to content and motive. What is said is to be in accordance with reality, and the one taking the oath is to be sincere. There is no hidden agenda. To swear in "righteousness and judgment" is to commit oneself to do that which is right, just, and fair in the sight of God (Gen. 18:19). We should never swear to do evil and we are never bound to follow through with such an oath (Acts 23:12-14).

Calling upon God as witness. "The eyes of the Lord are in every place keeping watch on the evil and the good" (Prov. 15:3). He sees and hears all that we do, even when others do not (Lev. 19:14). To call upon God as witness is to express that we are keenly conscious that He is omnipresent and omniscient and is the only One who can infallibly know if we are sincere and communicating the truth (2 Cor. 1:23).

Calling upon God as judge. The most sobering aspect of a lawful oath is invoking God to judge us based upon the truth or falsity of what we communicate. We are calling upon God to curse us if we are lying or fail to follow through with what is promised. This is what Peter did when he denied knowing Christ (Matt. 26:72-74).

Swearing Exclusively

The name of God. Deuteronomy 10:20 declares: "You shall fear the Lord your God; you shall serve Him, and to Him you shall hold fast, and take oaths in His name." What does it mean to swear by God's name? Think of how people often swear. Someone might say, "I swear on my mother's grave."[15] The person is connecting something of honor to the oath. If the truth and nothing but the truth is communicated by the oath, then Mom's grave (memory) is honored. If it is a lie or there is no follow through with the promise, then Mom's grave is dishonored. The idea is that a person would certainly not desecrate his mother's grave. Therefore, he or she

---

here means, that they will make a profession of religion. In like manner, speaking of the extension of the Redeemer's kingdom, it is said, 'He who blesseth himself in the earth shall bless himself in the God of truth: and he that sweareth in the earth shall swear by the God of truth' (Isaiah 65:16)." John Calvin, *Institutes of the Christian Religion,* trans. Henry Beveridge (Gainesville, FL: Bridge-Logos, 2005), 2.8.23 (352). Therefore, in one sense, at least under the Old Covenant, a lawful oath was part of worship in that it was to swear to serve and worship Jehovah only. Calvin argues, therefore, that the third commandment only addresses swearing for that purpose and that it does not address swearing with reference to men's dealings with one another. This is not correct. Rather, once men swore to serve and worship God alone, they were to swear all oaths in their dealings with others exclusively in God's name (2 Chron. 6:22-23).

14. Jeremiah 4:2 is used as the proof text for this phrase in the Confession. Again, Calvin restricts "swearing" in this verse to the worship and service of God. Those who penned the Confession do not, but rather apply it to oath-taking among men. However, Calvin's comments on this text are helpful in understanding the meaning of "truth, righteousness and judgement." The Reformer defines "truth" as "integrity" and "sincerity of heart" in the worship of God. He says that this sincerity toward God is "especially known by *judgment and righteousness;* that is, when men deal faithfully with one another, and render to all their right, and seek not their own gain at the expense of others." John Calvin, *Commentaries on the Prophet Jeremiah and the Lamentations* (Grand Rapids, MI: Baker, 2003), 1:201.

15. John Piper, "Should Christians Swear on the Bible?" Desiring God. March 28, 2016, https://www.desiringgod.org/interviews/should-christians-swear-on-the-bible

must be telling the truth or be definitely committed to what has been promised. To swear by God's name is to attach His honor to the oath. If we are lying or not committed to what is promised, we have desecrated His name. "You shall not take the name of the Lord your God in vain, for the Lord will not hold him guiltless who takes His name in vain" (Ex. 20:7) not only forbids using God's name as a curse word, but it also requires us carefully to honor His name when taking an oath. Commenting on the meaning of the third commandment, R. C. Sproul wrote,

> When we hear that, our first thought is that it prohibits blasphemy or cursing. Certainly it does prohibit those things, by extension, but mainly it has to do with using the name of God in an oath or a vow. The third commandment protects the sanctity of truth, which is vitally important to human relationships, and doing the truth – keeping our promises.[16]

This is why it is a grievous sin to "swear vainly or rashly by that glorious and dreadful name."

The name of God only. Why must we swear by God's name exclusively? First, Scripture reveals this to be a universal duty of all men and to swear by any other name is a form of idolatry, stealing honor that belongs only to Him (Isa. 65:16; Jer. 12:16). Second, to swear by someone other than God is to essentially ascribe to that person those divine attributes mentioned in the first paragraph that belong to God alone—the ability to infallibly know the truth or falsity of the oath taken and to judge the person swearing the oath. Third, to swear by something other than God's name can open the door to justifying dishonesty because the moral pressure to be absolutely truthful is lessened. It is lessened because there is not the sense of seriousness that comes from knowing that God will curse those who swear falsely by His name (Lev. 19:12). This was a huge problem in Jesus' day. This is why He says: "But I say to you, do not swear at all: neither by heaven for it is God's throne; nor by earth, for it is his footstool; nor by Jerusalem, for it is the city of the great King. Nor shall you swear by your head, because you cannot make one hair white or black" (Matt. 5:34-36). Jesus is not forbidding swearing an oath in all circumstances. He is forbidding and condemning the frivolous oath-taking that was taught and practiced by the religious leaders of His day. John MacArthur explains this practice of oath-taking:

> People would swear by heaven, by earth, by the Temple, by the hairs on their heads, and by any other thing they thought would impress those they wanted to take advantage of. That kind of routine oath-making was usually lie-making; and it was considered by those who practiced it to be perfectly acceptable as long as it was not in the name of the Lord. The command "You shall not swear falsely by My name" (Lev. 19:12) was conveniently interpreted to mean that swearing falsely by any other name was allowed.[17]

---

16. R.C. Sproul, *Truths We Confess, A Layman's Guide to the Westminster Confession of Faith:* Volume Two, Salvation and the Christian Life (Phillipsburg, New Jersey: P & R Publishing, 2007), 352.

17. John MacArthur, *The MacArthur New Testament Commentary: Matthew 1-7* (Chicago:

Furthermore, in Calvin's view their scheme did not protect them from swearing falsely in God's name. Concerning the perversion of the Jewish leaders, the Reformer wrote:

> For part of the error consisted in their supposing, that when they swore by the heaven and the earth, they did not touch the name of God. The Lord, therefore, after cutting off the principal source of prevarication, deprives them of all subterfuges, warning them against supposing that they escape guilt by suppressing the name of God, and appealing to heaven and earth. For it ought here to be observed in passing, that although the name of God is not expressed, yet men swear by him in using indirect forms, as when they swear by the light of life, by the bread they eat, by their baptism, or any other pledges of the divine liberality towards them. Some erroneously suppose that our Savior in that passage, rebukes superstition, by forbidding men to swear by heaven and earth, and Jerusalem. He rather refutes the sophistical subtlety of those who thought it nothing vainly to utter indirect oaths, imagining that they thus spared the holy name of God, whereas that name is inscribed on each of his mercies.[18]

Swearing Reservedly

Swearing an oath should be reserved for *matters of weight and moment* (matters of great importance), when much is at stake and the recipient of the promise needs an extra added confirmation of truth (Gen. 25:29-34). For example, marriage is a covenant (Mal. 2:14) in which promises are made between the man and woman. Considering the weightiness of that commitment (till death do us part), both parties are entitled to the assurance that swearing an oath is meant to offer. God Himself provides the great example of this principle: we have so much riding on His gospel promise, He condescends to confirm it with an oath (Heb. 6:13-19). There are also occasions when a conflict arises where one's integrity is in question. Depending on the details, swearing an oath in situations like that can be legitimate for the "ending of all strife" (v. 13).

Reserving oaths for these serious matters helps us understand the import of Christ's words when He says, "But let your 'Yes' be 'Yes' and your 'No' be 'No.' For whatever is more than these is from the evil one" (Matt. 5:37). Again, our Lord is not forbidding swearing oaths absolutely. The point is that swearing oaths should not be a part of everyday conversation regarding the routine affairs of life. When it comes to such, we are to simply speak what is true. Commenting on our Lord's words, Dr. Martyn Lloyd-Jones wrote, "He calls for simple veracity, the speaking of truth always in all ordinary communications and conversations and speech."[19] Any idea that it is not as important to be accurate with our words, or that we are somehow less obligated to do what we have said because we did not swear an oath, is evil. Even though God has sworn

Moody Press, 1985), 323.

18. Calvin, *Institutes of the Christian Religion*, 2.8.26 (352).

19. D. Martyn Lloyd-Jones, *Studies in the Sermon on the Mount, One-Volume Edition* (Grand Rapids, MI: Inter-Varsity Press; Eerdmans, 1989), 268-69.

oaths, He would have fulfilled His word just the same had He not done so because He is the God who cannot lie (Titus 1:2; Heb. 6). We are to reflect this as His image bearers, conscious that the ninth commandment is to regulate all of our verbal interactions with others. Our word should suffice without the need of an oath. If a person characteristically says, "I swear," in everyday conversation, that may be an indication that he is not trustworthy. A truthful person generally feels no need to do anything other than to speak the truth.

Swearing Submissively

The Anabaptists believed that oaths were commanded in the Old Testament, but Christ, who took the Law to its fullest purpose and meaning, forbade oath-taking of any kind, whether true or false. The seventh article of The Schleitheim Confession of Faith of 1527, written by Michael Sattler, the Anabaptist, states,

> The oath is a confirmation among those who are quarreling or making promises. In the Law it is commanded to be performed in God's name, but only in truth, not falsely. Christ, who teaches the perfection of the Law, prohibits all swearing to His [followers], whether true or false, – neither by heaven, nor by earth, nor by Jerusalem, nor by our head, – and that for the reason which He shortly thereafter gives, For you are not able to make one hair white or black. So you see that it is for this reason all swearing is forbidden: we cannot fulfill that which we promise when we swear, for we cannot change [even] the very least thing on us. Christ also taught us along the same line when He said, Let your communication be Yea, yea; Nay, nay; for whatever is more than these cometh of evil. He says, Your speech or word shall be yea and nay. [However] when one does not wish to understand, he remains closed to the meaning. Christ is simply Yea and Nay, and all those who seek Him simply will understand His word. Amen.[20]

As a practical result of this conviction, the Anabaptists refused to swear an oath when civil authorities required it. However, if indeed, swearing oaths in "matters of weight and moment" is "warranted by the Word of God," a believer has no scriptural grounds to conscientiously refuse to do so when it is "imposed by lawful authority in such matters."[21] For example, a believer may be called to bear witness in a legal proceeding such as a court trial where he or she will be "placed under oath." It is entirely appropriate to swear an oath in that situation, because a person's statements can make the difference between someone's freedom or incarceration, or even life and death.

---

20. "The Schleitheim Confession of Faith of 1527" translated by J.C. Wenger, https://courses.washington.edu/hist112/SCHLEITHEIM%20CONFESSION%20OF%20FAITH.htm.

21. We have an example of this in Nehemiah 13:25 when Nehemiah, a civil ruler, imposed an oath on the Jews. "So I contended with them and cursed them and struck some of them and pulled out their hair, and made them swear by God, 'You shall not give your daughters to their sons, nor take of their daughters for your sons or for yourselves.'"

Swearing Cautiously

A logical conclusion from the first two paragraphs in this chapter of the Confession is that before swearing an oath one "ought duly to consider the weightiness of so solemn an act" making sure that one "avouch nothing but what he knoweth to be truth." It should never be done lightly. In fact, if and when we have the option, not swearing an oath is generally the wisest choice because "by rash, false, and vain oaths, the Lord is provoked, and for them this land mourns." It appears that this is the point the apostle James makes when he instructs us: "But above all, my brethren, do not swear by heaven or by earth or with any other oath; but your yes is to be yes, and your no, no, so that you may not fall under judgment" (James 5:12). James not only echoes our Lord's command not to swear "by heaven or by earth," he also forbids us to swear "by any other oath." That prohibition is so broad that it seems to include swearing by God's name. In what sense? As we have already seen, it must not be interpreted as an absolute prohibition. The key phrase is, "so that you may not fall under judgment." We fall under judgment when we swear by His name falsely. Simon Kistemaker captures James' warning well when he writes: "That is, God's judgment strikes anyone who carelessly swears an oath and fails to uphold the truth."[22]

Remember, a lawful oath is one in which we call upon God as witness and judge. So, when what we verbally communicate in an oath is not accurate, or when we fail to follow through with the promise, we invite a divine curse. So, it seems that James is saying that our "yes" should be "yes" and our "no" should be "no," not only because our word should be good, but because we risk great danger to ourselves when we swear an unnecessary oath. By multiplying oaths in everyday conversations, we increase the potential of judgment because we increase the possibility of communicating something that is inaccurate or committing ourselves to do something we are unable to fulfill. If in reading this you are thinking, "I only want to take an oath when it is absolutely necessary," then you have gotten the message.

Swearing Sincerely

'Who may ascend to the hill of the Lord? Or who may stand in His holy place? He who has clean hands and a pure heart, who has not lifted up his soul to an idol, nor sworn deceitfully" (Ps. 24:3-4). One form of swearing deceitfully is to use words in any other way than their "plain and common sense." When accused of lying, the dishonest person will defend himself by exclaiming, "You misunderstood what I was saying." He then will put a spin on his words to prove how he did not lie. "What I meant was…" Swearing an oath sincerely is when we intend to be understood according to the widely accepted meaning of the words we speak.

22. Simon J. Kistemaker, *New Testament Commentary, Exposition of James, Epistles of John, Peter, and Jude,* (Grand Rapids: Michigan: Baker Books, 1986), 172.

Another form of swearing deceitfully is "equivocation," using unclear language to conceal the truth. Again, the purpose of that sort of unclear communication is to make it difficult for someone to charge us with lying. It is the same with "mental reservation." "Mental reservation" is defined as "a tacit withholding of full assent or an unexpressed qualification when one is taking an oath, making a statement, etc."[23] Consider the following example of mental reservation. A man and a woman take the traditional wedding vows, "in sickness and health, for richer or poorer, etc." He files for divorce after only a year of marriage because she burns the toast. She reminds him of the promise he swore to her. He explains that as he was taking the wedding vows he had the qualification, "only if she is a good cook," *in his mind* as he made those promises to her. Again, this is a deceitful effort to get out of the commitment while avoiding the charge of lying.

The overarching point is that sincerity in swearing an oath demands that we use our words according to how the other person will normally and legitimately interpret what is said. Anything less than that is to swear deceitfully.

Swearing Biblically

The language changes in the fifth paragraph from "oath" to "vow." This is not a mere change of terminology to avoid monotony. There is a difference. The Hebrew term in the Old Testament translated "vow" is always used to refer to commitments made to God,[24] so the Confession is correct when it asserts that a vow *is not to be made to any creature, but to God alone.*[25] Surveying the biblical testimony concerning vows is eye-opening because it reveals that it is even proper to make commitments to God based on answered prayer as in the case of Hannah when pleading with the Lord for a child (1 Sam. 1:10-11). Perhaps we, as Reformed Baptists, have not taught and emphasized the legitimate place of making vows to the Lord. It would be an interesting study, but there is not enough space allotted here to address it in detail.

There are a couple of important notes to consider, however, that are brought out in the Confession. First, a vow is voluntary, but once made it is to be "performed with all religious care and faithfulness" (Deut. 23:21-23). Second, since it is a sin to make a vow to the Lord and fail to fulfill the vow,[26] it is better not to make it than to make it and fail to keep it. As with swearing an oath, we should give much thought before we make

23. *The Free Dictionary,* s.v. "Mental reservation," https://www.thefreedictionary.com/mental reservation.

24. Gen. 28:20; 31:13; Lev. 27:8; Num. 6:2, 21; 21:2; 30:2-3,10; Deut. 12:11, 17; 23:21-23; Judg. 11:30, 39; 1 Sam. 1:11; 2 Sam. 15:7-8; Pss. 76:11; 132:2; Eccl. 5:4-5; Isa. 19:21; Jer. 44:25; Jonah 1:16; 2:9; Mal. 1:14.

25. Numbers 30:2 is a text that clearly distinguishes between a vow and an oath. "If a man makes a vow to the Lord, or swears an oath to bind himself by some agreement, he shall not break his word; he shall do according to all that proceeds out of his mouth."

26. Mosaic legislation allowed one to be released from obligation to fulfill a vow or an oath under certain circumstances (Num. 30:3-15).

a vow to the Lord (Eccl. 5:1-5). Third, a vow must be *biblical*. In contrast to the Anabaptists, the Roman Catholic Church had no issues with swearing oaths or vows. Their problem is that they take vows outside the boundaries of Scripture. Rome teaches that those who join a religious order are to make "popish monastical vows" to God. The vow of:

- "Perpetual single life;" a commitment to remain in an unmarried state.
- "Professed poverty;" a commitment to live simply with only the bare necessities of life.
- "Regular obedience;" a commitment to a life separated from the world (monastic life) and a voluntary commitment to submit to their superiors in this type of life which results in being connected more closely to the church.[27]

Those three vows are supposedly committing oneself to "degrees of higher perfection" that cannot be attained when the "ordinary Christian" is involved in the mundane affairs of everyday life. Because we are natively "superstitious," this kind of life may seem commendable and that it aids consecration to God. In reality, it undermines true gospel holiness. These vows are "sinful snares, in which no Christian may entangle himself." A vow to remain unmarried can leave one vulnerable to sexual immorality (1 Cor. 7:1-9). Vows of poverty and of regular obedience, which are based on the idea that minimal contact with the world produces greater levels of spirituality, are useless in the process of sanctification. They feed the pride we need to mortify, as do all man-made doctrines (Col. 2:18-23).

Applications

1. The scriptural testimony regarding oaths and vows underscores the importance of truthfulness and fulfilling our commitments. The apostle Paul declares in Romans 1:31 that one of the distinguishing features of a reprobate society is that the people are "untrustworthy," which can literally mean "covenant breakers." For people to lie or purposefully fail to fulfill commitments is surely sinful. But it is especially evil when a society is full of people who are unfaithful to what they swear.

2. This chapter is a good reminder to be careful in the use of our tongue and to think before we speak (James 1:19), knowing that the Lord is recording every word. "But I say to you that every idle word men speak, they will give an account of it in the day of judgment. For by your words you will be justified, and by your words you will be condemned" (Matt. 12:36-37). As we have seen from the Scripture, swearing oaths and vows brings us under even closer scrutiny. We cannot afford to be careless and play fast and loose with words.

3. A vital lesson from all of this is that truthfulness and faithfulness are not merely good core values and best policies. They are rooted in the

---

27. Code of Canon Law, Section I: Institutes of Consecrated Life, Title I: Norms Common to All Institutes of Consecrated Life (canons 573-606), http://www.vatican.va/archive/ENG1104/_P1Y.HTM.

fear of God and a desire to have the approbation of the One who hears all we say and sees all we do.

Conclusion

In sum, Scripture teaches us that, on the one hand, taking oaths and vows should not be our daily practice. On the other hand, there are times when it is entirely appropriate, necessary, and God-honoring.

CHAPTER 24

OF THE CIVIL MAGISTRATE

JOHN PRICE

1. God, the supreme Lord and King of all the world, hath ordained civil magistrates to be under Him, over the people, for His own glory and the public good; and to this end hath armed them with the power of the sword, for defence and encouragement of them that do good, and for the punishment of evil doers.[1]

2. It is lawful for Christians to accept and execute the office of a magistrate when called thereunto; in the management whereof, as they ought especially to maintain justice and peace,[2] according to the wholesome laws of each kingdom and commonwealth, so for that end they may lawfully now, under the New Testament wage war upon just and necessary occasions.[3]

3. Civil magistrates being set up by God for the ends aforesaid; subjection, in all lawful things commanded by them, ought to be yielded by us in the Lord, not only for wrath, but for conscience sake;[4] and we ought to make supplications and prayers for kings and all that are in authority, that under them we may live a quiet and peaceable life, in all godliness and honesty.[5]

The Christian's relationship to the civil magistrate is an all-important aspect of his witness in the world. A proper understanding of governing authorities is vital to being the salt of the earth and the light of the world (Matt. 5:13-16). The New Testament assumes every believer lives under a civil magistrate and therefore every Christian should have a great interest in this subject.

---

1. Romans 13:1-4
2. 2 Samuel 23:3; Psalm 82:3-4
3. Luke 3:14
4. Romans 13:5-7; 1 Peter 2:17
5. 1 Timothy 2:1, 2

Some Preliminary Matters

1. The Confession does not advocate any particular form of civil government, but recognizes that under the New Testament many different forms will be found in the world. A. A. Hodge notes in his commentary on the Westminster Confession of Faith that

> he (God) has left every people free to choose their own form of government in their own way, according to their various degrees of civilization, their social and political condition, their historical antecedents, and as they are instructed by his Word, and led and sustained by providence.[6]

2. Many Christians today place their hope for impacting culture in civil government by engaging in political activism, lobbying, demonstrations, and other measures, including civil disobedience. Such efforts often require great expenditures of time and money, often to the neglect of the church and the preaching of the gospel. Our hope for a more righteous society will only come through the power of Christ changing hearts. Righteous legislation will be a by-product of such transformed lives. The writers of the Confession recognized our duties as Christians to the civil magistrate while not encouraging us to place our hope in him for a more righteous society.

John MacArthur writes on this subject:

> Even social and political activities that are perfectly worthwhile can deplete the amount of a believer's time, energy, and money that is available for the central work of the gospel. The focus is shifted from the call to build the spiritual kingdom through the gospel to efforts to moralize culture – trying to change society from the outside rather than individuals from the inside. When the church is politicized, even in support of good causes, its spiritual power is vitiated and its moral influence diluted.[7]

3. In this chapter on the civil magistrate, the writers of the London Baptist Confession of Faith omitted a paragraph contained in the Westminster Confession of Faith. The missing paragraph dealt with the role of the magistrate in exercising various powers to preserve the order, peace, truth, worship, and discipline of the church. Our Baptist forefathers desired to uphold the religious liberty of the church. They did not believe it was the role of the magistrate to dictate such matters, and therefore, they left out that paragraph.[8]

This chapter contains three paragraphs, and I will expound each in their order:

6. Archibald Alexander Hodge, *A Commentary on the Westminster Confession of Faith* (Edinburgh: Banner of Truth Trust, 2002), 294.

7. John MacArthur, *The MacArthur New Testament Commentary on Romans 9–16* (Chicago: Moody Press, 1994), 207.

8. For a more thorough discussion of this issue, see Samuel E. Waldron, *A Modern Exposition of the 1689 Baptist Confession of Faith* (Durham, England: Evangelical Press, 1989), 293.

Paragraph 1
Note the following things from Paragraph 1:

The Supreme Authority of God
The writers of the Confession begin paragraph 1 with a description of the nature of God. He is "God, the supreme Lord and King of all the world." As Creator of all things in heaven and on earth, He is the highest authority in all the universe and all subordinate authority proceeds from Him. As the Sovereign Lord and King, He has the right to establish and delegate authority to men as He pleases.

The Civil Magistrate as Ordained by God
The main point of paragraph 1 of the Confession is: God "hath ordained civil magistrates." The apostle Paul states concerning the civil government: "For there is no authority except from God, and those which exist are established by God" (Rom. 13:1b). The office of the civil magistrate does not exist by human invention as if men experimented throughout human history and decided this would be the best social arrangement to live under. Neither does the authority of the magistrate come from the will of a majority, or "the consent of the governed" as stated in the American Declaration of Independence. The office and authority of the civil magistrate exists because God has ordained it. In his classic passage on civil authority in Romans 13:1-7, Paul writes concerning the Roman Emperors who surely did not derive their authority from "the consent of the governed." Jesus said to Pilate, the Roman governor, "You could have no power at all against Me unless it had been given you from above" (John 19:11).

The Divinely Ordained Position of the Civil Magistrate
The Confession states the position God has given to the civil magistrate in two short phrases: "to be under him, over the people." "To be under him" means the magistrate is under obligation to obey God's will and purpose in the exercise of his authority. He is not free to do whatever he pleases but is responsible to God for his conduct in his office (Prov. 16:12). Jesus said: "For everyone to whom much is given, from him much will be required; and to whom much has been committed, of him they will ask the more" (Luke 12:48). In Romans 13:2, 4, 6, Paul's descriptions of the civil magistrate as "the ordinance of God," "a minister of God," and a "servant of God," all underscore his authority as derived from God and his accountability to Him.

The civil magistrate is also "over the people", which refers to the authority God has given him over the people and the subjection they owe to him. Paul says: "Let every person be in subjection to the governing authorities" (Rom. 13:1). "Every person" includes believers and unbelievers, so no one should regard himself as exempt or ignore the authority of the civil magistrate. The word "subjection" which the apostle uses involves not only an outward obedience which one may give grudgingly. It also involves an inward and willing recognition of one's place of submission to the magistrate.[9] Every person is responsible to recognize God's will in placing the civil magistrate over him regarding the civil laws of government.

The Divinely Ordained Purpose of the Civil Magistrate

God's good and wise purpose in ordaining the civil magistrate is "for his own glory and the public good." Rulers are responsible to uphold law and order in human society and to maintain peace and safety for those under their rule. In 1 Timothy 2:1-2, Paul exhorts the church to pray for all civil magistrates that they may fulfill their God-given purpose and preserve the tranquil order of society. He contemplates the benefit of such good rule: "that we may lead a quiet and peaceable life in all godliness and reverence." This is to the glory of God in the spread of the gospel and for the general happiness of the human race.

God's ordained purpose for the civil magistrate is also given at the end of paragraph 1: "for defense and encouragement of them that do good and for the punishment of evil doers." Because of the harmful and disordering effects of sin, God established the civil magistrate to preserve the order of society and the well-being of those who live in it. Rulers are to defend and protect those who do good and to bring punishment upon those who do evil. Paul writes in Romans 13:3-4: "For rulers are not a terror to good works, but to evil. Do you want to be unafraid of the authority? Do what is good, and you will have praise from the same. For he is God's minister to you for good. But if you do evil, be afraid; for he does not bear the sword in vain; for he is God's minister, an avenger to execute wrath on him who practices evil."

If we compare the dangerous state of the world before the flood in Genesis 6:11, "The earth also was corrupt before God, and the earth was filled with violence," with that contemplated in 1 Timothy 2:2, in which believers can live "a quiet and peaceable life in all godliness and reverence," we may ask, what is it that brings about this great difference? The answer is not found in men overcoming their sinful nature over the centuries, but in God's institution of civil government which is responsible for the peace and order we so often enjoy in human society today. We see how quickly men fall back into chaos and violence in places where civil government has collapsed. Even in nations where civil governments are corrupt, much peace and order still result from it. No one desires to live in the anarchy and danger which comes from the dissolution of civil government. Many in western nations have perhaps become too accustomed to the peace and order which comes from a stable civil government. No wonder Paul tells us thanksgiving should be made for God's blessing of the civil magistrate (1 Tim 2:1-2).

Robert Haldane comments:

---

9. John Murray, *The Epistle to the Romans, Vol II* (Grand Rapids, Michigan: Wm. B. Eerdmans Publishing Co., 1959), 148.

The institution of civil government is a dispensation of mercy, and its existence is so indispensable, that the moment it ceases under one form, it re-establishes itself in another. The world, ever since the fall... has been in such a state of corruption and depravity, that without the powerful obstacle presented by civil government to the selfish and malignant passions of men, it would be better to live among the beasts of the forest than in human society. As soon as its restraints are removed, man shows himself in his real character. When there was no king in Israel, and every man did that which was right in his own eyes, we see in the last three chapters of the Book of Judges what were the dreadful consequences.[10]

The Divinely Ordained Power of the Civil Magistrate
The Confession states that in order to fulfill His purpose, God has given power to the magistrate: "and to this end hath armed them with the power of the sword." The sword is mentioned in Romans 13:4: "But if you do evil, be afraid; for he does not bear the sword in vain; for he is God's minister, an avenger to execute wrath on him who practices evil." The sword is an instrument of death and represents the full power of the magistrate to carry out punishment on evil doers up to and including execution (Prov. 16:14; 20:2).[11]

Paragraph 2
Note the following points from paragraph 2:

The Lawfulness of a Christian Fulfilling the Office of Civil Magistrate
The main concern of this paragraph is to assert that a Christian may lawfully hold the office of a civil magistrate and carry out its functions. The Confession states: "It is lawful for Christians to accept and execute the office of a magistrate when called there unto." The need to address this concern has roots in the history of the church. There have been sects of Christians who have denied that a believer should have any involvement in civil government. The followers of Menno Simmons in the Netherlands in the sixteenth century would not allow the members of their churches to perform any office in the civil government.[12] Others, such as the German Anabaptists of the sixteenth century, rejected the usefulness of civil government to the Christians and believed it was "of the devil."[13] There are believers today who regard the civil government as a corrupt and worldly institution in which the Christian should have no involvement. Some even refuse to exercise their privilege to vote in elections. However, the lawfulness of the Christian participating in and

10. Robert Haldane, *Commentary on Romans* (Grand Rapids: Kregel Publications, 1992), 589.

11. For discussions on capital punishment see: Waldron, *A Modern Exposition of the 1689 Baptist Confession of Faith*, 286-87; G. I. Williamson, *The Westminster Confession of Faith* (Philadelphia: Presbyterian and Reformed Publishing Company, 1964), 242.

12. Robert Shaw, *An Exposition of The Westminster Confession of Faith* (Fearn, Scotland: Christian Focus Publications, 1992), 241.

13. Cited in Samuel E. Waldron, *A Modern Exposition of the 1689 Baptist Confession of Faith*, 288.

even holding the office of the civil magistrate can be confirmed by several lines of argument from Scripture.

First, the apostle uses exalted descriptions of the civil magistrate in Romans 13:2, 4, 6 such as "the ordinance of God," "a minister of God," and "servant of God."[14] These descriptions imply God's favor upon the office of the magistrate and the lawfulness of those who occupy it and execute its functions. In Romans 13, this would include the duties of bringing praise upon those who do good and punishment upon those who do evil, up to and including the use of the sword.

Second, some of the godliest men have exercised the office of the civil magistrate under clear divine guidance and approval. When Joseph was elevated to rule over all the land of Egypt with only Pharaoh above him, he said to his brothers in Genesis 45:7-8: "God sent me before you to preserve a posterity for you in the earth, and to save your lives by a great deliverance. So now it was not you who sent me here, but God." We should note that Joseph accepted this position after he had been wrongfully imprisoned for two years by the same civil magistrate for something he had not done. When called upon to serve, he did not respond with bitter resentment declaring the civil magistrate to be an evil office, but he willingly took the responsibility and carried it out for the good of his fellow man with divinely given wisdom. The Bible also gives examples of good and godly men who served in public office such as David, Daniel, Nehemiah, Josiah, and Hezekiah, among others. Such men not only prove that believers can serve as civil magistrates, but they can do so while maintaining their own personal integrity. In the cases of Joseph and Daniel, they did so in the pagan and godless societies of Egypt and Babylon, respectively.

Third, in various passages in the Pentateuch, God commanded "judges and officers" how they were to enforce the civil laws of the nation of Israel (Ex. 22:7-8; Deut. 16:18-20). Many of these judges and officers would have been believers who performed their duties under God's approval.

Fourth, the lawfulness of the civil magistrate is confirmed by frequent favorable statements of its functions in the book of Proverbs (14:35; 16:10, 12; 20:26, 28; 25:2; 28:15-16; 29:4, 14; 31:4-5).

The Main Duty of the Civil Magistrate

The Confession addresses the main duty of the civil magistrate by the statement, "in the management whereof, as they ought especially to maintain justice and peace, according to the wholesome laws of each kingdom and commonwealth." The main duty of the magistrate to uphold justice and peace is supported by many passages of Scripture (Ex. 18:25-26; 21:6; 22:7-9; Deut. 16:18-20; 17:8-13; 19:14-21; 2 Chron. 19:5-6; Ps. 82:2-3; Rom. 13:1-6; 1 Tim. 2:1-2). The goal of every magistrate is found in Deuteronomy 16:20: "Justice, and only justice, you shall pursue."[15]

---

14. Quoted from the *New American Standard Bible* (Chattanooga: AMG Publishers, 1977).

15. Quoted from the *New American Standard Bible*.

The Confession speaks of "the wholesome laws of each kingdom and commonwealth." The writers of the Confession recognized that in the New Testament there is no theocracy as there was in the Old Testament in which the civil laws of the nation were given directly from God. Under the New Testament, there will be kingdoms[16] and commonwealths[17] which will have "wholesome laws." The word "wholesome" refers to that which is "favorable to morals, religion, or prosperity; conducive to public happiness, virtue, or peace."[18] Wherever such wholesome laws exist, it is the duty of the magistrate to uphold and carry them out, according to his office and authority.

The Right of the Civil Magistrate to Wage War

The Confession asserts that the civil magistrate under the New Testament has the prerogative to wage war given certain conditions: "so for that end they may lawfully now, under the New Testament wage war upon just and necessary occasions."[19] Biblical support for this is found in Luke 3:14, where John the Baptist had been preaching a baptism of repentance for the forgiveness of sins. Some Roman soldiers repented at this message, and desiring to live a new life of obedience to God, they asked John: "And what shall we do?" Even though waging war was the essence of being a soldier, John did not tell them to lay down their weapons and cease their soldiering. Rather, he instructed them how to continue their work in a way pleasing to the Lord: "Do not intimidate anyone or accuse falsely, and be content with your wages" (Luke 3:14). Jesus did not require the Roman centurion to leave his profession when He healed his servant (Matt. 8:5-13). We should also note that the first Gentile convert to Christianity was Cornelius, who was a Roman centurion. When Cornelius believed, Peter did not demand he give up his position in the Roman army before being baptized (Acts 10:47-48).

In Romans 13:4, Paul states that the civil magistrate has the power of "the sword." The sword was a military weapon used to suppress seditious rebellions against the Roman Emperor. By asserting the right of the magistrate to carry the sword as a weapon of war, the apostle affirms his right to wage war. Sam Waldron writes: "The use of the sword in Romans 13:4 has direct reference to military actions to put down rebellion… Thus it is used of a form of war."[20]

---

16. A kingdom is defined as "a government, country, state, or population that is nominally or actually ruled by a king or queen" *The American Heritage Dictionary of the English Language* [Boston: Houghton Mifflin Company], 1976.

17. A commonwealth is a broader term than kingdom which includes other forms of government and is defined as "the people of a nation or state; or other political entity" *The American Heritage Dictionary of the English Language*.

18. *American Dictionary of the English Language* (San Francisco: Foundation for American Christian Education, facsimile ed., 1985).

19. The Confession is focused on the civil magistrate's prerogative to wage war under the New Testament. Under the Old Testament, God explicitly commanded wars (Deut. 7:1-2; 9:1-3; Judg. 1:4). We know that God can never command anything which is morally wrong.

20. Waldron, *A Modern Exposition of the 1689 Confession of Faith*, 287.

For these reasons, we conclude it is lawful for a Christian to be a soldier and to wage war. If it is lawful for a Christian to wage war, then it must also be lawful for a Christian magistrate to do the same.

The Confession states that the magistrate may lawfully wage war "upon just and necessary occasions." There will be differing opinions on what these occasions are. A distinction can be made between offensive and defensive wars. An offensive war is when one nation seeks to conquer another out of ambitious desire for land, wealth, power, or worldly glory. Most people agree such wars are unjustified. A defensive war is when a nation is attacked and must defend its own people, territory, and way of life. Most agree such a war can be called "just and necessary."

The Christian pacifist argues that war cannot be justified upon any grounds, and he points to two main passages of Scripture to support his view. The first is found in the Sermon on the Mount where Jesus said: "But I tell you not to resist an evil person. But whoever slaps you on your right cheek, turn the other to him also" (Matt. 5:39); and "You have heard that it was said, 'You shall love your neighbor and hate your enemy.' But I say to you, love your enemies, bless those who curse you, do good to those who hate you, and pray for those who spitefully use you and persecute you, that you may be sons of your Father in heaven" (Matt. 5:43-45). The answer to this objection is found in an important biblical distinction between the private duty of an individual and the public duty of the magistrate. There may be duties which belong to a public magistrate but not to a private individual. For example, the magistrate has the duty of taking vengeance upon evildoers while the individual does not. In this passage, Jesus is dealing with the private duty of the individual, not with the public duty of the magistrate. By keeping this distinction in mind, we understand that Jesus' words do not support pacifism. The same distinction can be found in Romans 12:19 where Paul addresses the duty of the individual: "Beloved, do not avenge yourselves, but *rather* give place to wrath; for it is written, 'Vengeance is Mine, I will repay,' says the Lord." Only a few verses later, Paul states it is the duty of the magistrate to exercise God's wrath against the evildoer: "for he is God's minister, an avenger to *execute* wrath on him who practices evil" (Rom. 13:4).

A second passage used by Christian pacifists is found in the sixth commandment: "You shall not murder" (Ex. 20:13). The pacifist argues if it is wrong to commit murder then it must be wrong to wage war. However, two times in the very next chapter, God commands the taking of a life: "He who strikes a man so that he dies shall surely be put to death" (Ex. 21:12); and, "But if *any* harm follows, then you shall give life for life" (Ex. 21:23). How do we reconcile these passages? The answer is found in the distinction between the duty of the private individual and the duty of the magistrate. In the sixth commandment, God is addressing the duty of the individual while, in Exodus 21, He is addressing the duty of the magistrate. The civil magistrate has duties which belong to him that do not belong to the individual, and among them is capital punishment and the waging of war.

Paragraph 3
Note the following points from Paragraph 3:

The Ground of a Christian's Duty to the Civil Magistrate
The Confession begins by stating that our duty to the civil magistrate is grounded in God's ordination of the office and the good purposes for which He ordained it: "Civil magistrates being set up by God for the ends aforesaid." This refers to God's purposes in giving the civil magistrate which are found in paragraph 1: "for his own glory and the public good," and in paragraph 2: "to maintain justice and peace, according to the wholesome laws of each kingdom and commonwealth." God's ordination of the civil magistrate and His good purpose in doing so imply the two duties which follow: 1) subjection to all lawful commands of the civil magistrate; and 2) prayer for him in performing his office.

The Extent of Subjection to the Civil Magistrate
The extent of the Christian's submission to the civil magistrate is stated as "subjection, in all lawful things commanded by them, ought to be yielded by us in the Lord, not only for wrath, but for conscience sake." The duty of subjection is clearly taught by two main passages in the New Testament. The first is found in Romans 13:1: "Let every soul be subject to the governing authorities." Romans 13:1-7 should be viewed as part of the larger context beginning in Romans 12:1-2 in which Paul is instructing believers concerning practical matters in the Christian life. The Christian's subjection to the civil magistrate is part of "presenting our bodies a living and holy sacrifice acceptable to God" (Rom. 12:1) and being "transformed by the renewing of your mind, that you may prove what is that good and acceptable and perfect will of God" (Rom. 12:2).

In ancient Rome, as is the case today, some viewed civil government with contempt, belligerence, or even hostility. Such attitudes may develop because of various influences or experiences in one's past. But when one becomes a believer, his starting point regarding civil authority is to be one of subjection, and this is part of the transformation of his mind into the good and acceptable and perfect will of God.

A second important passage is found in 1 Peter 2:13-14: "Therefore submit yourselves to every ordinance of man for the Lord's sake, whether to the king as supreme, or to governors, as to those who are sent by him." The Christian's submission to civil authorities is part of his testimony before the onlooking world, as Peter makes clear in the previous verse: "having your conduct honorable among the Gentiles, that when they speak against you as evildoers, they may, by your good works which they observe, glorify God in the day of visitation" (1 Pet. 2:12). Peter wrote these words while living in Rome under the oppressive and tyrannical

Roman Emperor Nero. Submission to the civil magistrate is due even when he is an unbeliever, morally corrupt, and harsh.[21]

The Confession gives two motives for our subjection to the civil magistrate in the phrase, "not only for wrath, but for conscience sake," which comes from Romans 13:4-5. The first motive is to avoid God's wrath which comes through the penalty of the civil magistrate upon disobedience. The second motive is out of conscience toward God in desiring to obey Him by recognizing the civil magistrate as ordained by Him and invested with His authority. Peter writes in 1 Peter 2:13: "submit yourselves to every ordinance of man for the Lord's sake," which means out of conscience to the Lord and a sense of obligation to obey Him through the authorities He has ordained.

Wayne Gruden comments on the extent of submission to civil authorities: "we obey except when commanded to sin. This is the Christian's responsibility toward all forms of rightful human authority, whether the individual Christian agrees with all the policies of that authority or not."[22]

The Limits of Subjection to the Civil Magistrate

The authority of the civil magistrate is not absolute. The Confession states subjection to civil authorities is limited to "all things lawful." The Christian is to submit to commands of the civil magistrate so long as they do not violate the commands of God. When the commands of the magistrate require him to disobey God, the believer is bound to obey God rather than man. The phrase "in the Lord" means our subjection is yielded out of conscience to the Lord. Any obedience to the civil magistrate which violates the will of God can no longer be "in the Lord." Conscience toward God is our motive for obedience when the magistrate gives lawful commands. But conscience toward God is also our motive for disobedience when he gives unlawful commands.

Various examples of disobedience to civil authorities are found in the Scripture (Ex. 1:17; Dan. 1:8; 3:4-6, 16-18; 6:5-10, 22; Acts 4:19-20; 5:29). In each of these cases, it was not a matter of disagreement or opinion which led to the believer's resistance, but a clear biblical command which he was being asked to violate. Resistance to such demands is the Christian's duty. Even when a believer must decline obedience to the magistrate, his resistance must be respectful and not belligerent or provocative.

Charles Hodge writes on the disobedience of the apostles to civil authorities,

> ...the same inspired men who enjoin, in such general terms, obedience to rulers, themselves uniformly and openly disobeyed them whenever their commands were inconsistent with other and higher obligations. "We ought to obey God rather than men," was the principle which the early Christians avowed, and on which they acted. They disobeyed the Jewish and heathen

---

21. See also Titus 3:1-3.

22. Wayne Gruden, *Tyndale New Testament Commentaries, 1 Peter* (Grand Rapids: William B. Eerdmans Publishing Company, 1992), 118.

authorities, whenever they required them to do anything contrary to the will of God. There are cases, therefore, in which disobedience is a duty.[23]

The Duty of Prayer for the Civil Magistrate

The Confession states this duty in the second half of paragraph 3: "and we ought to make supplications and prayers for kings and all that are in authority, that under them we may live a quiet and peaceable life, in all godliness and honesty." These words come from 1 Timothy 2:2-3 where the apostle exhorts the Ephesian church to pray for the Roman Emperor who was at that time the cruel and ungodly Nero. Our duty to the magistrate does not depend on his competence, moral character, or disposition.

Even when kings persecute believers, they are to pray for them and it is an opportunity to fulfill the Lord's command in Matthew 5:44-45: "But I say to you, love your enemies, bless those who curse you, do good to those who hate you, and pray for those who spitefully use you and persecute you, that you may be sons of your Father in heaven." Churches in peaceful and orderly societies are prone to forget to pray for their civil magistrates. But this is a sin of neglect, and we cannot presume that such peace and orderliness will continue indefinitely.

Paul urged the church to pray for kings and all in authority because God is pleased to answer such prayers. The church prays to the King of kings and Lord of lords who has absolute sovereignty over all earthly kings. "The king's heart is in the hand of the Lord, *like* the rivers of water; He turns it wherever He wishes" (Prov. 21:1). The King of heaven declares: "Counsel *is* mine, and sound wisdom; I *am* understanding, I have strength. By me kings reign, and rulers decree justice. By me princes rule, and nobles, all the judges of the earth" (Prov. 8:14-16).

Donald Guthrie writes:

> The Christian attitude towards the State is of utmost importance. Whether the civil authorities are perverted or not they must be made the subjects of prayer, for Christian citizens may in this way influence the course of national affairs, a fact often forgotten except in time of special crisis.[24]

The church should always pray for the conversion of civil magistrates. Paul writes, "For this is good and acceptable in the sight of God our Savior, who desires all men to be saved and to come to the knowledge of the truth" (1 Tim. 2:3-4). There are times when under tyrannical and persecuting kings, imprecatory prayers may also be appropriate. The Lord has power to take down ungodly kings from their thrones whenever it pleases Him (Dan. 4:31-33; Acts 12:23).[25]

---

23. Charles Hodge, *Romans* (Edinburgh: The Banner of Truth Trust, 1989), 413.

24. Donald Guthrie, *Tyndale New Testament Commentaries, The Pastoral Epistles,* (Grand Rapids: William B. Eerdmans Publishing Company, 1990), 80.

25. Opinions differ as to whether a Christian should be involved in the revolutionary overthrow of a tyrannical ruler. For opinions opposed to such involvement, see G. I. Williamson, *The Westminster Confession of Faith,* 241; Waldron, *A Modern Exposition of the 1689 Baptist Confession of Faith,* 290; and John MacArthur, *The MacArthur New Testament*

Prayer for the civil magistrate often brings the blessing of a peaceful society so believers may live in godliness and honesty which is for the spread of the gospel and the glory of God. When Christians live godly lives, they are seen as peacemakers who are full of moral goodness and virtue. The church is seen not as people caught up in the turmoil and trouble of the kingdoms of this world, but as a transcendent people whose eyes are fixed on a heavenly kingdom.

John MacArthur states,

> Believers are to be model citizens, known as law abiding not rabble-rousing, obedient rather than rebellious, respectful of government rather than demeaning of it. We must speak against sin, against injustice, against immorality and ungodliness with fearless dedication, but we must do it within the framework of civil law and with respect for civil authorities. We are to be a godly society, doing good and living peaceably within an ungodly society, manifesting our transformed lives so that the saving power of God is seen clearly.[26]

Applications of the Confession's Teaching on the Civil Magistrate

1. We should give thanks to God for His good gift of the civil magistrate in providing order and peace in society.

2. We should be in submission to all lawful demands of the civil magistrates.

3. We should pray that our civil magistrates would have the wisdom to fulfill God's good purpose in upholding law and order that we may live a life of tranquility and peace in all godliness and dignity.

4. We should be prepared to obey God rather than man if the demands of the civil magistrate violate the will of God.

Conclusion

The civil magistrate has been ordained by God with divinely delegated authority for the good and welfare of the nations. God's purpose in giving civil authority is for the defense and protection of those who do good and the punishment of those who do evil. Believers should see God's authority in the magistrate and therefore offer willing submission to him as to the Lord. Because the magistrate is a good gift of God, believers may accept and perform the office when called to it. The church is responsible to pray for the civil authorities that they might enforce good laws which are consistent with the Word of God and for the peace and order of society. When the magistrate violates his God-given responsibility and enacts laws which are contrary to the Word of God, it is the duty of Christians to respectfully obey God rather than man.

Commentary on Romans 9-16, 206. For opinions which support such involvement under certain conditions, see Shaw, *An Exposition of the Westminster Confession of Faith*, 243; Hodge, *The Confession of Faith*, 299; Stuart Olyott, *The Gospel as It Really Is* (Hertfordshire, England: Evangelical Press, 1979), 122.

26. MacArthur, *The MacArthur New Testament Commentary on Romans 9-16*, 213.

CHAPTER 25

OF MARRIAGE

LEE MCKINNON

1. Marriage is to be between one man and one woman; neither is it lawful for any man to have more than one wife, nor for any woman to have more than one husband at the same time.[1]

2. Marriage was ordained for the mutual help of husband and wife,[2] for the increase of mankind with a legitimate issue,[3] and the preventing of uncleanness.[4]

3. It is lawful for all sorts of people to marry, who are able with judgment to give their consent[5]; yet it is the duty of Christians to marry in the Lord;[6] and therefore such as profess the true religion, should not marry with infidels, or idolaters; neither should such as are godly, be unequally yoked, by marrying with such as are wicked in their life, or maintain damnable heresy.[7]

4. Marriage ought not to be within the degrees of consanguinity or affinity, forbidden in the Word;[8] nor can such incestuous marriages ever be made lawful, by any law of man or consent of parties, so as those persons may live together as man and wife.[9]

In Holy Scripture, Genesis is the book of beginnings. It is the record of first instances and first institutions. It is the revelation of human life

---

1. Genesis 2:24; Malachi 2:15; Matthew 19:5-6
2. Genesis 2:18
3. Genesis 1:28
4. 1 Corinthians 7:2, 9
5. Hebrews 13:4; 1 Timothy 4:3
6. 1 Corinthians 7:39
7. Nehemiah 13:25-27
8. Leviticus 18
9. Mark 6:18; 1 Corinthians 5:1

as originally intended by its Creator. In Genesis 1, we are told at each stage in God's creating work, "God saw that it was good." In Genesis 2, however, by God's own testimony, we find the first thing in creation that is "not good." He declares, "It is not good that man should be alone" (Gen. 2:18). This statement does not mean that there was fault or failure in God's work, but only that the work was incomplete. He supplied what was lacking that very day by giving Adam what he most needed: not a pet, or a fishing buddy, but a woman to be his wife. Thus, God not only created a "helper comparable" to Adam, but also instituted the marriage relationship (Gen. 2:22-24).

Chronologically, this was on the sixth day of creation (Gen. 1:26-28), and it is after this that we are told, "Then God saw everything that He had made, and indeed it was very good"[10] (Gen. 1:31). That includes the marriage relationship and is in marked contrast to that incomplete state of "not good" described in Genesis 2:18.

When God instituted marriage, He gave instructions concerning it: "Therefore a man shall leave his father and mother and be joined to his wife, and they shall become one flesh"[11] (Gen. 2:24). This verse shows that marriage is a shared life, even as if two become "one flesh" or one person. It is the closest human relationship, even closer than parent and child.

Though the words found in Genesis 2 about marriage are few, God has given us directions throughout His Word on this important subject. The Bible describes the duties attached to the relationship, the respective roles in the relationship, and the conduct of husbands and wives to make the relationship what it is supposed to be.

Much of this instruction was necessitated by the fall of Adam and Eve into sin (Gen. 3). God's words to Eve show that sin's entrance especially impacted marriage. This is the point of God's pronouncement: "Your desire shall be for your husband, and he shall rule over you" (Gen. 3:16). That desire which Eve would have was not a good and commendable desire. Rather, the word is to be understood in the same sense as when used in the next chapter where it refers to sin's desire to rule over Cain (Gen. 4:7). As a consequence of sin's entrance into the world, this would be Eve's desire with reference to Adam. As for her husband, when God said, "he shall rule over you," it means that now this fallen, sinful, selfish man will rule, rather than the sinless, loving man that Adam had been before his fall. The obvious point is that sin's entrance introduced all the problems that can be seen in marriage, especially the selfish attitudes, self-serving actions, and failures to think and act as "one flesh." This is why God has so often and so pointedly addressed marriage in His Word, and it shows how important it is that we know what He has said in this connection.

---

10. Emphasis added, but this simply reflects the emphasis intended in the original by inserting the word "very" here in contrast to the previous use of the phrase in Genesis 1.

11. Professor John Murray demonstrates that this verse is part of the "revelatory data" given to Adam in his state of innocence, Murray, *Principles of Conduct* [Grand Rapids: Wm. B. Eerdmans Publishing Company, 1957, reprinted 1984], 28-29.

In light of all that the Bible says about marriage, Chapter 25 of the Confession is very brief. In fact, marriage is not even defined here. It's as if the framers assumed readers would know what is set before them in God's Word: that marriage is a formal, binding, and permanent commitment of one man and one woman to be joined in a shared life. We are not told specifically that it is an institution created by God, though the word "ordained" in the second paragraph certainly points in that direction. Neither did the authors say anything about the nature of the marriage relationship, which is both a covenant commitment and a companionship, as seen throughout Scripture, and explicitly stated in Proverbs 2:17 and Malachi 2:14. Although Genesis 2:24 is included in the proof texts, no mention is made in the Confession of the priority and closeness of the union as emphasized in that verse. Further, nothing is said about the roles of husband and wife or the many responsibilities that God Himself has attached to marriage in His Word. Neither is the matter of divorce discussed in these paragraphs. This particular omission will be addressed at the end of our examination of Chapter 25. Since our concern is with what the Confession does say, rather than what it doesn't say, we now proceed to the following considerations.

1. The Divine Pattern for Marriage (Paragraph 1)

This is the only paragraph in Chapter 25 which is identical in the London Confession, the Westminster Confession of Faith (Westminster Confession) and the Savoy Declaration, including the proof texts. These texts point to what marriage was intended to be from the beginning. The Lord Jesus used this same description of marriage as an argument against divorce in Matthew 19:5-6.

There can be no question from the original paradigm that marriage was designed to be monogamous, or "between one man and one woman." The words of Genesis 2:24 about a man leaving his father and mother prove this was not simply the case for the first marriage, as neither Adam nor Eve had parents to leave. This statement could only apply to successive generations of their progeny.

In our day, the emphasis on "one man and one woman" speaks clearly to the issue of "same sex marriage." In addition to what God's Word says about homosexual practices (for example, Leviticus 18:22; 20:13; Romans 1:26-27; 1 Corinthians 6:9), the very pattern from the beginning shows that marriage is not a same sex relationship. God unmistakably and unambiguously created Adam as a male and Eve as a female, thereby establishing marriage as a special relationship between a man and a woman. Regardless of what is practiced in a culture, or is allowed by the laws of a nation, or is tolerated in some religious organizations, heterosexual marriage was God's design and intention at creation, and, as such, is the model for all time. What is said of "incestuous marriages" in paragraph 4 of this chapter applies no less to so-called "marriages" between those of the same sex: "nor can such…ever be made lawful, by any law of man or consent of parties, so as those persons may live together as man and wife." If this is true of those living together as "man and wife," how much more is it true of those living together as "man and man" or "wife and wife"?

The framers of the seventeenth-century Confessions did not have to deal with this. Their focus seems to be more on the matter of polygamy, which is having more than one spouse "at the same time." Genesis 2:24 is rightly given as a proof text here since the pattern established in the beginning is a relationship of two and only two individuals becoming one flesh. A man (singular) leaves his father and mother and is joined to his wife (singular) in an exclusive union which takes precedence over all other human relationships.

That being so, it begs the question: what about the multiple wives of the patriarchs or David and Solomon? It is important to note that the first instance of multiple marriage partners in the biblical record is in the ungodly line of Cain, in the seventh generation after Adam's creation (Gen. 4:19). This shows polygamy to be not only a deviation from God's original order, but also an apparent casting off of what had been the recognized universal norm for several hundred years. The originator was a man named Lamech. He later boasted of another wrongdoing: "Then Lamech said to his wives: 'Adah and Zillah, hear my voice; wives of Lamech, listen to my speech! For I have killed a man for wounding me, even a young man for hurting me'" (Gen. 4:23). The proud ungodliness of this man hardly recommends the practice of having more than one spouse. As Professor Murray observed, "The context suggests, to say the least, that the taking of two wives is co-ordinate with the other vices which appear so conspicuously in this case."[12]

It is also important to note that the patriarchs, Abraham and Jacob, did not initiate having more than one spouse as if it were their own idea. In Abraham's case, it was at the request, or even demand, of childless Sarai that he take her maid, Hagar, and have children by her. Sarai's plan to use a proxy was an expression of unbelief or impatience or both (Gen. 16:1-3).

As to the multiple marriage partners of Jacob, not only was this not his idea, it was contrary to his original desire. He had worked seven years for Rachel, but because Leah was the older sister, Laban deceived Jacob on his wedding night and substituted her instead. Jacob didn't discover the deception until the next morning. To appease Jacob's anger, Laban then promised him Rachel in exchange for seven more years of labor (Gen. 29:15-30). Later, because Rachel was barren, she insisted Jacob take her maid, Bilhah, as his wife in order that Rachel might have children by her (Gen. 30:3-4). When Leah had for a time stopped bearing children, she then gave her maid, Zilpah, to be Jacob's wife so that she might also continue to have children by her maid (Gen. 30:9). So, while Jacob ended up with four wives, we see that it was not at his initiating, not his original intention, and not done as the normal practice of the time.

---

12. Murray, *Principles*, 45.

Furthermore, we find no indication that polygamy was common among Jacob's twelve sons.

Also, in connection with the patriarchs, it is noteworthy that the relationship of Isaac and Rebekah was monogamous, even when she was unable to bear children for more than twenty years (Gen. 25:20-26). This again underscores that polygamy was not the norm, and that there was no divine sanction for it. Even the burial practice of the patriarchs suggests that a monogamous relationship was recognized as the proper order. Notice the words of Jacob in reference to where he wished to be buried: "There they buried Abraham and Sarah his wife, there they buried Isaac and Rebekah his wife, and there I buried Leah" (Gen. 49:31).

David's case was very different from that of Abraham and Jacob. He deliberately took multiple wives (at least seven, not to mention concubines, who were sometimes regarded as wives but having a lower status). Why would David do this? It seems he married different women for different reasons. In the case of Abigail, it was his appreciation for the character and appearance of this woman who was recently widowed. Taking Bathsheba as his wife, however, was the result of the well-known and heinous sins David had previously committed (2 Sam. 11). Perhaps the precedent set by Abraham, Jacob, and others, including King Saul, also factored into his thinking. For whatever reason, David took multiple wives for himself, although it certainly was not by divine instruction or with divine approval.

What about Solomon's many wives? According to 1 Kings 11:3, he had seven hundred wives and three hundred concubines. What was Solomon's motive for such blatant and egregious polygamy? It's true that having multiple wives to show one's prosperity was in keeping with the practice of monarchs in that day. It may also have been a means for establishing alliances between Israel and other nations. But, whatever Solomon's reasons, none of them made it right. In fact, Solomon's many marriages went against the command God had expressly given kings in His law: "Neither shall he multiply wives for himself, lest his heart turn away" (Deut. 17:17). These are words which Solomon would have written out for himself from the copy of God's Word belonging to the priests (Deut. 17:18). He was to study this personal copy diligently "all the days of his life, that he may learn to fear the Lord his God and be careful to observe all the words of this law and these statutes" (Deut. 17:19). We know that the troubles that befell Solomon in his life and reign were of his own making because he failed to obey God's Word (1 Kings 11:3-39).

Since polygamy is contrary to God's design, why did He allow it? We might just as well ask, "Why did God allow any evil in His creation?" That inquiry obviously goes far beyond the scope of our present purpose. But why did God not give explicit prohibitions against the practice and why did He not immediately rebuke those who did take more than one spouse? Instead, we find Him simply giving instructions regarding conduct where there are multiple marriage partners (for example, Ex. 21:10; Deut. 21:15-17).

This is very similar to how God dealt with divorce. Moses gave instructions about divorce in Deuteronomy 24:1-4, not because divorce has divine approval, but, as the Lord Jesus said, "because of the hardness of [people's] hearts" (Matt. 19:8). The directives concerning divorce were given especially to protect the wife so that she could remarry. This helped keep her from being subject to various problems such as permanent destitution. Although this is described as "permitted" in Matthew 19:8, permission is not approval.

As this is true with divorce, so it is true with polygamy. Although it was tolerated in that Old Testament period, and God gave laws for the protection of those who might be harmed by this aberration from the divine pattern, that does not mean it was right or had divine approval. What John Murray said of divorce applies also to polygamy: "It is highly necessary...to distinguish between this sufferance or toleration, on the one hand, and divine approval or sanction, on the other. Permission, sufferance, toleration was granted. But underlying this very notion is the idea of wrong. We do not properly speak of toleration or sufferance as granted or conceded in connection with what is intrinsically right or desirable."[13]

To again quote Murray, referring to our Lord's words in Matthew 19:8, "As it was in the case of divorce that 'from the beginning it was not so,' so it is that in the matter of...polygamy from the beginning it was not so."[14] We can add to this that it was not universal and there is no indication that it was the more common practice in Old Testament Israel.

Robert Shaw, a nineteenth-century commentator on the Westminster Confession of Faith, demonstrated that polygamy is a clear violation of the seventh commandment, "You shall not commit adultery" (Ex. 20:14). Referring to Matthew 19:9, he observed: "The words of Christ plainly imply a prohibition of polygamy; for if whosoever putteth away his wife [except it be for incontinence[15]], and marrieth another, committeth adultery, he who marrieth another without putting away the first, must be no less guilty of adultery."[16]

The closing words of paragraph 1 in Chapter 25 of the Confession, "at the same time," remind us of the Scripture's teaching that marriage is only for this world, and that death ends it (Matt. 22:23-30). That being so, a widowed wife or husband is free to remarry, and under those circumstances, he or she will still have only one spouse at that time, the former marriage being dissolved (Rom. 7:2-3; 1 Cor. 7:39).

---

13. John Murray, *Divorce* (Philadelphia: P & R Publishing, 1961), 8-9.

14. Murray, *Principles,* 30. For more on this see 14-19, 27-30, 45-49.

15. As used here, *Webster's Dictionary of 1828* defines "incontinence" as "Want of restraint of the sexual appetite; free or illegal indulgence of lust; lewdness...." *Webster's Dictionary 1828 Online Edition,* www.webstersdictionary1828.com/Dictionary/. Accessed February 10, 2020.

16. Robert Shaw, *The Reformed Faith* (Inverness, Scotland: Christian Focus Publications, 1974, first printed in 1845), 254-55.

2. The Distinct Purposes of Marriage (Paragraph 2)

The Confession mentions three specific purposes for the institution of marriage:

1) Marriage was ordained "for the mutual help of husband and wife." We've seen from Genesis 2:18 that Adam's aloneness was not good. It was, therefore, a great kindness for God to provide "a helper comparable to him." This phrase is used twice in Genesis 2, giving it a special emphasis. The Hebrew word translated here as "helper" is most often used to describe the help that God is to His people. Doesn't that point to the power of this word and underscore the genuine help the wife is to the husband? This is all the more true since she is "comparable" to Adam, being "taken out of man" and made of the same substance.

Adam acknowledged this suitability in his happy response when Eve was presented to him: "This is now bone of my bones and flesh of my flesh" (Gen. 2:23). It is notable that these are the first words from Adam recorded in the Bible. He recognized the great contrast between the woman and all the animals he had named in Genesis 2:20. He realized that he had been given a truly special gift from God! Being so "comparable" to him, she was in every way suited to be just what he needed and to do him "good... all the days of her life" (Prov. 31:12).

This was fine for Adam and his sons, but the Confession says marriage is for "the *mutual* help of husband *and* wife." Where do we see this reciprocal theme in Genesis 2? It could be inferred from the words in verse 24 about the two becoming "one flesh." This phrase certainly suggests a shared life in which all that is the husband's is also the wife's and in which he is to love and treat her as he would himself. That this is the correct inference is clear from Paul's use of the statement in Ephesians 5, strengthening what he had just said about husbands: "So husbands ought to love their own wives as their own bodies; he who loves his wife loves himself. For no one ever hated his own flesh, but nourishes and cherishes it, just as the Lord does the church... For this reason a man shall leave his father and mother and be joined to his wife, and the two shall become one flesh" (Eph. 5:28-29, 31). The appeal to Christ's relationship with His church clarifies even more that marriage is also for the wife's help. We see this concept elsewhere in Scripture, such as when Peter admonishes: "Husbands, likewise, dwell with them with understanding, giving honor to the wife, as to the weaker vessel, and as being heirs together of the grace of life, that your prayers may not be hindered" (1 Pet. 3:7).

Notice further the beneficial reciprocity in Paul's statement in 1 Corinthians describing the norms for both husbands and wives: "He who is married cares about the things of the world—how he may please his wife... She who is married cares about the things of the world—how she may please her husband" (1 Cor. 7:33-34). In the context of this chapter of Paul's epistle, he is writing about the advantage single Christians enjoy in service for the Kingdom, being freed from certain domestic distractions. The apostle is not criticizing a husband or wife for giving attention to "the things of the world" for their spouse's sake. He is simply stating as a fact that they have legitimate responsibilities toward each other which require attention. For our purpose, notice that this responsibility is mutual, and is the expected standard for husband and wife equally. Their mutual aim is to "please" each other, which, in some way, parallels pleasing the Lord (cf. 1 Cor. 7:32). These verses also speak of giving real thought and carefulness to that end, not even neglecting one another while in service to Christ's Kingdom.

This "mutual help" involves all areas of the couple's shared life, including both the practical and the emotional realms. They not only help each other in the ordinary issues of daily living, but also in giving comfort, encouragement, joy, and in making it their aim to truly "please" each other (1 Cor. 7:33-34, and for husbands, 1 Pet. 3:7, and for wives, Prov. 31:12).

Of all the ways in which husbands and wives are to be of "mutual help," the context in Genesis points to one matter especially: "So God created man in His own image; in the image of God He created him; male and female He created them. Then God blessed them, and God said to them, 'Be fruitful and multiply; fill the earth *and subdue it; have dominion* over the fish of the sea, over the birds of the air, and over every living thing that moves on the earth'" (Gen. 1:26-27). It goes beyond the scope of our present study to consider all that is entailed in subduing the earth and having dominion over it. We can see, though, even on the face of it, that men and women, working together as husbands and wives, are to engage primarily in doing what God has commanded them, and doing so for His glory in the earth. For this great end is each wife to be a help to her husband and each husband a help to his wife. How imperative it is, then, for each to follow the teaching of God's Word to make their marriage what it is supposed to be.

Since marriage is for the very desirable "mutual help of husband and wife," does this mean that an unmarried person suffers some great disadvantage? And what are we to make of Paul's statements in 1 Corinthians where he seems to commend singleness over being married (1 Cor. 7:1, 7-8, 28, 32-34, 40)? Does this mean it is better in every sense to be single? Not at all. In 1 Corinthians 7:8-9, Paul refers to at least one example where this is not the case. However, there are indeed some instances when being unmarried offers advantages, as is seen in 1 Corinthians 7:32-35. Here, Paul speaks of being free from marriage responsibilities in order to "serve the Lord without distraction." Also, 1 Corinthians 7:25-26 suggests that in certain providential circumstances, singleness is more suitable. All of this demonstrates that being without a spouse does not mean one is less than a whole person or suffers some vital deficiency.

It should be noted, though, that in 1 Corinthians 7:7, Paul refers to each person having his own gift in this regard, and in 1 Corinthians 7:17, to God distributing to each person his or her particular state. This is written especially with reference to being single, and it reminds us that in Matthew 19:11, our Lord speaks of celibacy as being "given" to some.

That being so, it indicates special grace must be required of, and is given to, those whom the Lord would have to remain unmarried. Does this not underscore how much spouses need the "mutual help" that the marriage relationship is designed to provide? At the same time, no single person needs to feel incomplete because Christ's grace is certainly sufficient for every need. Thus, attention should be focused on pleasing the Lord both in the advantages of the marriage partnership and in the advantages that singleness affords.

2) Marriage was ordained "for the increase of mankind with a legitimate issue." In making all living creatures, it was God's intention that they "be fruitful and multiply" (Gen. 1:22), and God physiologically equipped those creatures to fulfill that purpose. God also gave this blessing to humankind (Gen. 1:28), although there is a clear difference. For human beings, this multiplying is to take place only within the framework of a recognized and permanent commitment to a shared life, the institution of marriage. There is no other God-ordained context for human propagation or the sexual activity that leads to it. Thus, the Confession calls the issue from such a relationship "legitimate," meaning it conforms to God's rule and law for humanity.

The distinctiveness of human procreation and its being a purpose for marriage underscores that children are not only to be brought into this world but are to be trained and equipped for life here (Prov. 22:6; Eph. 6:4). This training, in the normal order of Providence, is to take place in a home where there is a mother and a father committed to one another in marriage and committed to the greater good of their children, especially with a view to their everlasting good through faith in the Lord Jesus Christ.

3) Marriage was ordained for "the preventing of uncleanness." This wording in the Confession recognizes the teaching throughout Scripture that sexual activity outside the context of the marriage relationship is unmistakably wrong. Such activity is moral "uncleanness," regardless of the form it takes (including not only adultery and fornication, but also other ways of gratifying immoral sexual lusts, for example, viewing pornography, etc.). Marriage provides for the prevention of these sins by furnishing a legitimate way to satisfy proper sexual desire. In light of God's provision for spouses, how inexcusable is adultery! Here the Confession cites 1 Corinthians 7:2, where Paul clearly states, "because of sexual immorality, let each man have his own wife, and let each woman have her own husband." Another proof text is 1 Corinthians 7:9, where Paul advises the unmarried who cannot exercise self-control to marry, "for it is better to marry than to burn with passion."

To those who are married, Paul writes: "Do not deprive one another except with consent for a time, that you may give yourselves to fasting and prayer; and come together again so that Satan does not tempt you because of your lack of self-control" (1 Cor. 7:5). This instruction speaks to the strength of the sexual drive in both men and women, and also affirms that the desire itself, as well as its gratification, is not sinful in the God-ordained context of marriage (compare Hebrews 13:4). It also demonstrates that having children is not the only valid purpose for sexual relations in marriage. In 1 Corinthians 7:2-9, Paul never mentions procreation.

Simply stating that "preventing uncleanness" is a purpose of marriage falls short of the biblical emphasis placed on the mutual joy and delight of marital intimacy. In Proverbs, when Solomon warns his son against adultery, he didn't merely say, "Have sexual relations with your wife." Rather, we read, "Let your fountain be blessed, and rejoice with the wife of your youth. As a loving deer and a graceful doe, let her breasts satisfy you at all times; and always be enraptured with her love" (Prov. 5:18-19). This word "enraptured" is also used in the next verse to describe the pleasure or exhilaration which is sinfully sought with an immoral woman. That pleasure is legitimately enjoyed only in the marriage bed and is for both the husband and wife (cf. Heb. 13:4). This shared enjoyment is illustrated by Paul's words in 1 Corinthians 7:3. Here, the apostle writes that both husband and wife are to render unto each other the "affection due" their spouse. Paul's exhortation points to that mutual delight in this aspect of the marriage relationship which is so beautifully and poetically expressed in the Song of Solomon. And surely, for this facet of marriage to be "the preventative of uncleanness," there ought to be that proper delight in one another found in sexual intimacy as indicated by Solomon's words, "always be enraptured."

Recognizing these three purposes for God-ordained marriage should cause us to see marriage as the rich blessing it is for those who enjoy this divine arrangement. Husbands and wives should seek mutual benefit from it, and they should thank God not only for the institution of marriage, but for the one they enjoy themselves.

3. The Distinguished Participants for Marriage (Paragraphs 3 and 4)

In considering the proper candidates for marriage, the Confession recognizes two all-encompassing groups.

1) Those who may lawfully marry. The Confession makes a very broad statement in this connection, initially limiting it only by personal capacity. As the wording indicates, marriage should be by "consent," or voluntary and not forced. We see this even in the Old Testament, for example in Genesis 24:58 and 1 Samuel 25:40-42. But it is not unqualified consent. It must be with "judgment," obviously indicating the ability to make a reasonable and mature decision. There is a good reason why each of the United States has some kind of age requirement for entering into marriage and requires parental consent below that age. Marriage is so serious and so permanent that it is not to be entered into lightly. Such a commitment calls for careful thought and due "judgment." For young people still living at home, the counsel of parents should certainly be sought and taken to heart (in keeping with the Bible's language of "giving in marriage," 1 Cor. 7:38; Deut. 7:3).

The framers did not say marriage is lawful for "all people," but for "all sorts of people." This is an important distinction in light of the restrictions referred to in this paragraph and the next of Chapter 25. However, we must not diminish the force of the words, "all sorts." Within the stated restrictions, all kinds of people may marry all kinds of other people, including those with disabilities, or from different cultures, backgrounds, and races, or from different social, educational, and economic levels. Neither is any stipulation made relating to age differences between those who want to marry, although, as mentioned above concerning the legal requirements of states, common sense should prevail. The phrase, "all sorts of people," embraces these distinctions and more.

It must be recognized, however, that there is a substantial difference between what is lawful and what is wise or advisable. Recall how Paul spoke of circumstances in which it is better not to marry (1 Cor. 7:26). Some distinctions, including major doctrinal differences, might present such obstacles to living as "one flesh" that they render marriage impractical or unadvisable. This further underscores the significance of requiring consent "with judgment."

The first proof text here states, "Marriage is honorable among all" (Heb. 13:4). "All" includes those who do not know the Lord. Marriage is not just for Christians, but for everyone, and it is to be universally esteemed as a rich blessing from our Creator. Even when two unbelievers marry, Christians should acknowledge that union as honorable. When one spouse is converted by Christ after marriage, that marriage, too, is still to be regarded as honorable. This seems to be what Paul is addressing in 1 Corinthians 7:12-16 (cf. 1 Pet. 3:1-7).

In addressing this matter, the framers of the seventeenth-century Confessions probably had the mandatory celibacy of Roman Catholic Church leaders in mind. That requirement is contrary to God's Word and to the practice of the church in the days of the apostles (1 Cor. 9:5; 1 Tim. 3:2-5; Titus 1:6). In fact, it is so contrary to biblical teaching that it is labeled a doctrine of demons: "Now the Spirit expressly says that in latter times some will depart from the faith, giving heed to deceiving spirits and doctrines of demons...forbidding to marry" (1 Tim. 4:1-3). So, when the Confession says, "It is lawful for all sorts of people to marry," it most definitely includes "clergy" (cf. 1 Tim. 3:2). How right that this should be the assumed norm for pastors since they are to be mature Christians and will be shepherding believers, the majority of whom are married. Dr. Sam Waldron notes, "The Bible contains no further restrictions on lawful marriage than those mentioned in these paragraphs."[17] But there are indeed restrictions mentioned and we will now address them.

2) Those who cannot marry. A short summation of the latter part of paragraph 3 is simply that believers in Christ must not marry any unsaved person, regardless of the form that person's unbelief takes. This includes "infidels," which simply means unbelievers, whether atheists,

17. Samuel E. Waldron, *A Modern Exposition of the 1689 Baptist Confession of Faith* (England: Evangelical Press, 1989), 303.

agnostics or any other persons who do not believe the truth of Scripture and deny the living God. The Confession mentions next "idolaters," that is, any persons believing in or worshiping a false god rather than He who alone is revealed in the Bible and in His Son, Jesus Christ. Marriage is also prohibited between believers and "such as are wicked in their life," meaning those whose consistent conduct and tenor of life as a whole are that of an unsaved person, even if they seem to be religious (Titus 1:16; 1 John 2:3-4; Matt. 7:21-23). Finally, to these are added those who "maintain damnable heresy." This does not simply mean that they are of a different persuasion in certain teachings of the Bible, but rather what they believe is so contrary to the Bible that no genuine believer could embrace and continue in it (1 John 2:26-27; Jude 3-4). While there are differences between these named categories, they all have this in common: each describes those who are very obviously not true Christians.

The Westminster Confession and the Savoy Declaration also add "Papists," or those adhering to Roman Catholicism in these proscriptions. The Baptists do not address this separately, perhaps because they are including it under "damnable heresy."[18] Specific mention of "Papists" in the other Confessions underscores that being religious and holding to *some* truths of Scripture does not necessarily signify salvation. If there is no clear understanding of the gospel and no embracing of the Savior by faith, or if eternal hope is built on something other than or in addition to the person and work of Jesus Christ, then that individual is unsaved, notwithstanding any similarities to true Christians in creed or appearance. Such a one is not suitable as a marriage partner for a true believer.

The expression "unequally yoked" is taken from 2 Corinthians, where we read, "Do not be unequally yoked together with unbelievers. For what fellowship has righteousness with lawlessness? And what communion has light with darkness?" (2 Cor. 6:14). The original context of these words has to do with local church life, but they also apply to marriage and other kinds of relationships. The idea behind this language may be taken from the Law: "You shall not plow with an ox and a donkey together" (Deut. 22:10). This gives a graphic illustration why Christians are not to be unduly bound up with the unsaved. It's like two entirely different creatures, with contrary temperaments and dispositions, which simply cannot do well in a shared yoke. Therefore, God forbids it. If this is true in other close relationships (like church membership), it is certainly true in the closest human relationship, marriage. As Paul goes on to write, "What part has a believer with an unbeliever?" (2 Cor. 6:14).

In the Confession, there are two relevant proof texts affirming this qualification. The first deals with Christian widows: "She is at liberty to be married to whom she wishes, only in the Lord" (1 Cor. 7:39). Any future husband must clearly be a true Christian, in union with the Lord Jesus

18. We are speaking here of the major distinctives of Romanism, intelligently embraced and not merely a vague understanding or mere nominal attachment to an institution.

by faith. Paul was surely not insisting on this only for godly widows, but for all of the Lord's people who would enter into marriage.

The second proof text is Nehemiah 13:25-27, which is a rebuke to those who returned from the Babylonian captivity and entered into marriages with non-Jews or had allowed their children to do so. This rebuke strongly reflects that oft repeated prohibition to Old Testament Israel about marrying Gentiles (Ex. 34:13-16; Deut. 7:3-4; Josh. 23:11-13, etc.). Nehemiah argues against this from one very well-known case in history: "Did not Solomon king of Israel sin by these things? Yet among many nations there was no king like him, who was beloved of his God; and God made him king over all Israel. Nevertheless pagan women caused even him to sin" (Neh. 13:26). This example alone should persuade us that God's people must not marry the unsaved. The words of the next verse drive this home even more: "Should we then hear of your doing all this great evil, transgressing against our God by marrying pagan women?" (Neh. 13:27). What possible reason do we have to think that such marriages today are not just as great an evil or transgression against our God?

John Murray's words are insightful here: "Married life is to be guided, not by impulse or fancy, but by considerations which conserve and promote the interests of godliness."[19] This perspective makes consent "with judgment," in the opening part of paragraph 3, very relevant words. How careful believers must be to make sure the person being considered as a potential marriage partner is truly converted. And further, how careful believers must be to avoid romantic involvement, or even entertaining the notion of it, with the unsaved.

Paragraph 4 deals with a different kind of restriction: "Marriage ought not to be within the degrees of consanguinity or affinity, forbidden in the Word; nor can such incestuous marriages ever be made lawful, by any law of man or consent of parties, so as those persons may live together as man and wife" (Lev. 18; Mark. 6:18; 1 Cor. 5:1).

Stated simply, this means that some persons cannot marry because of previously existing relationships. "Consanguinity" means related by blood, such as those biological relationships listed in Leviticus 18 (father, mother, sister, half-sister, grandchild, aunt, uncle). These are all described as "near of kin" (Lev. 18:6), and sexual activity with such blood relatives is strictly prohibited (Lev. 18:6-14; 20:11-21; Deut. 22:20; 27:20-23). If sexual activity is forbidden, then obviously marriage to any blood relative closer than a first cousin is also excluded.

"Affinity" refers to relatives by marriage. These are also included in the prohibitions of Leviticus 18 (father's wife or one's stepmother, a stepmother's daughter, aunt by marriage, daughter-in-law, sister-in-law, step-grandchildren; Deuteronomy 27:23 includes mother-in-law). Although these are not blood relatives, sexual activity and marriage are prohibited just as if they were because they are "near of kin" by affinity

---

19. Murray, *Principles,* 46.

(Lev. 18:17). Thus, the Confession labels marriage to any such persons "incestuous," a word describing a relationship which is morally repugnant to most people (1 Cor. 5:1), and which is certainly an abomination to God (Lev. 18:26-30). Such unions can never be "made lawful" before God by any means.

This paragraph of the Confession raises several questions, though. What about the immediate offspring of Adam and Eve? Undoubtedly, Adam and Eve's children did marry among themselves. Who else could they wed? It was the responsibility of those first people to "be fruitful and multiply" (Gen. 1:28). To fulfill that divine mandate, they had to marry, and the only persons available to marry were siblings. What G. I. Williamson said of humanity's duty generally was certainly true of them in particular: it was "conditioned by divine provision."[20] As Williamson explains: "It was the duty of human beings to marry beyond the degrees of consanguinity and affinity, but not before there was a sufficiently wide development of the human race to permit the operation of this duty."[21] Such marriages were not prohibited in that first generation, but neither were the choice of partners for those first marriages normative for all time.

What about Abraham and Sarah, though? We see from Genesis 20:12 that Sarah was Abraham's half-sister, being the daughter of his father but not his mother. What are we to make of this? It is important to realize that they were already married when they are first mentioned in Scripture (Gen. 11:31). This was before God spoke the gospel to Abraham (Gen. 12:1-3; Gal. 3:8), and at that time in his life, he was a pagan whose family worshiped idols (Josh. 24:2). It is no great marvel that pagans should act like pagans and marry within the degrees of consanguinity (Lev. 18:24). The marvel is that God deals with fallen human beings in sovereign grace, bringing salvation to sinners such as Abraham and Sarah.

Was it acceptable for Jacob to marry both Leah and Rachel (Gen. 29:22-30)? Although it's true Jacob married within degrees of affinity by marrying his wife's sister, as previously noted, he neither initiated nor desired this arrangement. Jacob's situation was created by the unrighteous father of these women (Gen. 29:27). Again, this is clearly not normative, and it was also before the prohibition of such marriages had been clearly codified for God's people in Leviticus 18.

Is it possible that these prohibitions are simply Old Testament Law, only for the Jews at that time and no longer applicable? The proof texts for paragraph 4 include Mark 6:18, referring to Herod taking his brother's wife. Even if this was not simply a case of adultery, but an incestuous relationship, it doesn't answer the question of whether these laws apply in New Testament times because Herod and Herodias were still living under the Old Covenant (Jer. 31:33; Matt. 26:28).

---

20. G. I. Williamson, *The Westminster Confession of Faith For Study Classes* (Philadelphia: P & R Publishing, 1964), 185.

21. Ibid., 185.

However, we do find a clear instance of such a prohibited relationship in the New Testament. It is the incident in the Corinthian church of the man who had taken his father's wife. Because Paul does not call her "his mother" in 1 Corinthians 5:1, it is reasonable to suppose that she was the man's stepmother.[22] This, then, is a case of affinity, where those involved are related by marriage rather than by blood. Whether this man had married his stepmother or only had sexual relations with her, their relationship was a violation of the Law as recorded in Leviticus 18, etc. This indicates that these proscriptions are permanently binding and not limited to those under the Old Covenant.[23]

That they are intended for everyone without distinction and not just for Jews is at least hinted at in 1 Corinthians 5:1. Here, Paul refers to the Gentiles among whom this kind of sexual immorality "is not even named," being regarded as wrong and abhorrent.

The universality of these prohibitions is also seen in their Old Testament contexts. For example, after defining the proscribed relationships in Leviticus 18, the Lord commands, "You shall therefore keep My statutes and My judgments, and shall not commit any of these abominations, either any of your own nation or any *stranger* who dwells among you" (Lev. 18:26). Even more enlightening are the verses immediately preceding these: "Do not defile yourselves with any of these things; for by all these the nations are defiled, which I am casting out before you. For the land is defiled; therefore I visit the punishment of its iniquity upon it, and the land vomits out its inhabitants" (Lev. 18:24-25). The Gentiles inhabiting the Promised Land were guilty of those sins described and were punished for them, even though they were not recipients of the Law of Moses. This plainly indicates the prohibitions were not limited to the Jews even in the Old Covenant period.

Why would God establish such strict prohibitions? One explanation is that, although the people in that day surely didn't understand genetics and the possibility of birth defects in the offspring of close genetic kin, God did. It is clear, however, that the reason for these divine prohibitions goes beyond that. Sexual relations within these degrees of consanguinity and affinity are denounced as "wickedness" (Lev. 18:17), warranting the most severe punishment in Old Testament Law (Lev. 20:11-21). Furthermore, it is still considered so wicked that it warrants the most severe consequence in the New Covenant community: excommunication (1 Cor. 5:1-13). What accounts for this intense disapprobation?

In Leviticus 18 and its parallel passages, the word "marriage" is not found. Instead, emphasis is on "uncovering nakedness," the wording used in every verse in Leviticus 18:6-19. In Ezekiel 16:35-37, this same language denotes the activity of harlots, obviously referring to illicit

---

22. John Murray writes, "The woman in question here is undoubtedly the step-mother," which he then demonstrates in a footnote (*Principles*, 51, footnote 6).

23. Noting it was a relationship of affinity rather than consanguinity, John Murray observed: "the bearing of the Mosaic prohibitions in their entirety upon the ethic of the New Testament is more apparent" (Murray, *Principles*, 52).

sexual intercourse. This shared connotation is the point of repeating the phrase in Leviticus. Whereas marriage with the persons described there is clearly forbidden, the language emphatically forbids sexual relations with them, whether married or not.[24] This emphasis on sexual activity shows why these relationships are condemned in such strong terms in Leviticus and Deuteronomy, even beyond other forms of sexual immorality.

What can be said in defense of those for whom sexual gratification and even illicit lusts so control their minds, overriding any sense of propriety, respect, and natural affection, that they are driven to incest? Considering what is said of the nations who committed such sins wholesale and were vomited out of the land before Israel, these people may be fairly characterized as "sex crazed." Those whom God drove out of Canaan would have sex with anyone, regardless of gender or how closely they were related. Even animals were not excluded from their immorality. This is indeed such "wickedness" that even many among the Gentiles found it appalling (1 Cor. 5:1).[25]

All of this shows that the framers of the seventeenth-century Confessions were very right to include this paragraph when addressing the subject of marriage.

Chapter 25 of the Confession closes with a reminder that God alone has the authority to say who can and cannot marry, even as it is His prerogative to tell us what marriage is and how we must conduct ourselves in the relationship.

Why Doesn't the Confession Say Anything About Divorce?

Looking at this chapter through modern eyes, we might wonder if not discussing divorce is a glaring omission or oversight, especially when comparing the London Confession with the Westminster Confession. The title of the corresponding chapter in the Westminster Confession is "Of Marriage *And* Divorce," and includes two additional paragraphs, dealing with the latter subject. Why was this omitted in the London Confession? It certainly wasn't because it is unimportant or because Scripture is silent on the subject. Neither is it likely that the absence of the additional paragraphs is due to perceived error or disagreement with what they contain. Indeed, those paragraphs in the Westminster Confession give a very good summation of the Bible's teaching on divorce, and on remarriage. The interested reader is encouraged to carefully consider what is said there.

But, the question remains: Why aren't these paragraphs in the London Confession? It is probably for much the same reason they are absent from

---

24. John Murray argues, "There can be no doubt but that the main purpose is to prohibit marriages within these degrees of consanguinity and affinity. This is shown by Leviticus 18:18, 20:14, 21. The expression 'take a wife' indicates that more is involved than an act of sexual intercourse" (Murray, *Principles*, 49-50, footnote 3).

25. For more on this subject, see Murray, *Principles*, 49-55. In this same work, Murray also addresses the command in Deuteronomy 25:5 for a man to marry his widowed sister-in-law if his brother died childless. See Appendix B, 250-56.

the Savoy Declaration. It is because these paragraphs are also absent in the version of the Westminster Confession which was given final approval by the English Parliament in 1648.[26] This omission probably reflects the belief in Parliament that divorce is a civil rather than a religious matter and should not be included in a Confession of Faith.

In the preface to the Savoy Declaration,[27] those Divines stated that the version of the Westminster Confession used for their purposes was that which was approved by Parliament. However, they did make reference to the omitted paragraphs on divorce, including them in what they called "doubtful assertions," and thus "unsuitable to a Confession of Faith." Did the framers of the London Confession also regard these paragraphs as "doubtful assertions"? Whether they did or not, they must have thought them "unsuitable to a Confession of Faith," or at least they were content to follow the version of the Westminster Confession approved by Parliament and followed by the Savoy Divines.[28]

In any event, it is right that our focus should not be so much on the tragedy of divorce, which God hates (Mal. 2:16), but on the precious gift that He intended marriage to be. Those who conduct themselves in that "one flesh" relationship to the praise and glory of God will find it an exquisite treasure indeed!

---

26. What is now recognized as the Westminster Confession of Faith in the Westminster Standards is the original work of the Westminster Divines, adopted by the Church of Scotland in 1647 and later ratified by the Scottish parliament without amendment.

27. Philip Schaff, "The Savoy Declaration," in *The Creeds of Christendom* (Grand Rapids: Baker Book House, 1977, first published in 1877), Volume 3, 715.

28. I am greatly indebted to two excellent articles treating this matter: Dr. James Renihan, *IRBS Theological Seminary*. https://irbsseminary.org/frequently-asked-symbolics-questions-divorce (accessed February 11, 2020) and Dr. Samuel Renihan, "Why does 2LCF omit WCF 24.5-6 on Divorce?" *Petty France*. https://pettyfrance.wordpress.com/2019/11 (accessed February 11, 2020).

CHAPTER 26

OF THE CHURCH

SAM WALDRON

1. The catholic or universal church, which (with respect to the internal work of the Spirit and truth of grace) may be called invisible, consists of the whole number of the elect, that have been, are, or shall be gathered into one, under Christ, the head thereof; and is the spouse, the body, the fullness of Him that filleth all in all.[1]

2. All persons throughout the world, professing the faith of the gospel, and obedience unto God by Christ according unto it, not destroying their own profession by any errors everting the foundation, or unholiness of conversation, are and may be called visible saints;[2] and of such ought all particular congregations to be constituted.[3]

3. The purest churches under heaven are subject to mixture and error;[4] and some have so degenerated as to become no churches of Christ, but synagogues of Satan;[5] nevertheless Christ always hath had, and ever shall have a kingdom in this world, to the end thereof, of such as believe in Him, and make profession of His name.[6]

4. The Lord Jesus Christ is the head of the church, in whom, by the appointment of the Father, all power for the calling, institution, order or government of the church, is invested in a supreme and sovereign manner;[7] neither can the Pope of Rome in any sense be head thereof, but is that antichrist, that man of sin, and son of perdition, that exalteth

---

1. Hebrews 12:23; Colossians 1:18; Ephesians 1:10, 22-23; Ephesians 5:23, 27, 32
2. 1 Corinthians 1:2; Acts 11:26
3. Romans 1:7; Ephesians 1:20-22
4. 1 Corinthians 5; Revelation 2; Revelation 3
5. Revelation 18:2; 2 Thessalonians 2:11-12
6. Matthew 16:18; Psalm 72:17; Psalm 102:28; Revelation 12:17
7. Colossians 1:18; Matthew 28:18-20; Ephesians 4:11, 12

himself in the church against Christ, and all that is called God; whom the Lord shall destroy with the brightness of his coming.[8]

5. In the execution of this power wherewith He is so intrusted, the Lord Jesus calleth out of the world unto Himself, through the ministry of His word, by His Spirit, those that are given unto Him by His Father,[9] that they may walk before Him in all the ways of obedience, which He prescribeth to them in His word.[10] Those thus called, he commandeth to walk together in particular societies, or churches, for their mutual edification, and the due performance of that public worship, which he requireth of them in the world.[11]

6. The members of these churches are saints by calling, visibly manifesting and evidencing (in and by their profession and walking) their obedience unto that call of Christ;[12] and do willingly consent to walk together, according to the appointment of Christ; giving up themselves to the Lord, and one to another, by the will of God, in professed subjection to the ordinances of the Gospel.[13]
H
7. To each of these churches thus gathered, according to his mind declared in His word, He hath given all that power and authority, which is in any way needful for their carrying on that order in worship and discipline, which He hath instituted for them to observe; with commands and rules for the due and right exerting, and executing of that power.[14]

8. A particular church, gathered and completely organized according to the mind of Christ, consists of officers and members; and the officers appointed by Christ to be chosen and set apart by the church (so called and gathered), for the peculiar administration of ordinances, and execution of power or duty, which He intrusts them with, or calls them to, to be continued to the end of the world, are bishops or elders, and deacons.[15]

9. The way appointed by Christ for the calling of any person, fitted and gifted by the Holy Spirit, unto the office of bishop or elder in a church, is, that he be chosen thereunto by the common suffrage of the church itself;[16] and solemnly set apart by fasting and prayer, with imposition of

---

8. 2 Thessalonians 2:2-9
9. John 10:16; John 12:32
10. Matthew 28:20
11. Matthew 18:15-20
12. Romans 1:7; 1 Corinthians 1:2
13. Acts 2:41, 42; Acts 5:13, 14; 2 Corinthians 9:13
14. Matthew 18:17-18; 1 Corinthians 5:4-5; 1 Corinthians 5:13; 2 Corinthians 2:6-8
15. Acts 20:17, 28; Philippians 1:1
16. Acts 14:23

hands of the eldership of the church, if there be any before constituted therein;[17] and of a deacon that he be chosen by the like suffrage, and set apart by prayer, and the like imposition of hands.[18]

10. The work of pastors being constantly to attend the service of Christ, in His churches, in the ministry of the word and prayer, with watching for their souls, as they that must give an account to Him;[19] it is incumbent on the churches to whom they minister, not only to give them all due respect, but also to communicate to them of all their good things according to their ability,[20] so as they may have a comfortable supply, without being themselves entangled in secular affairs;[21] and may also be capable of exercising hospitality towards others;[22] and this is required by the law of nature, and by the express order of our Lord Jesus, who hath ordained that they that preach the Gospel should live of the Gospel.[23]

11. Although it be incumbent on the bishops or pastors of the churches, to be instant in preaching the word, by way of office, yet the work of preaching the word is not so peculiarly confined to them but that others also gifted and fitted by the Holy Spirit for it, and approved and called by the church, may and ought to perform it.[24]

12. As all believers are bound to join themselves to particular churches, when and where they have opportunity so to do; so all that are admitted unto the privileges of a church, are also under the censures and government thereof, according to the rule of Christ.[25]

13. No church members, upon any offence taken by them, having performed their duty required of them towards the person they are offended at, ought to disturb any church-order, or absent themselves from the assemblies of the church, or administration of any ordinances, upon the account of such offense at any of their fellow members, but to wait upon Christ, in the further proceeding of the church.[26]

14. As each church, and all the members of it, are bound to pray continually for the good and prosperity of all the churches of Christ,[27] in all places, and upon all occasions to further every one within the bounds

17. 1 Timothy 4:14
18. Acts 6:3, 5-6
19. Acts 6:4; Hebrews 13:17
20. 1 Timothy 5:17, 18; Galatians 6:6-7
21. 2 Timothy 2:4
22. 1 Timothy 3:2
23. 1 Corinthians 9:6-14
24. Acts 11:19-21; 1 Peter 4:10-11
25. 1 Thessalonians 5:14; 2 Thessalonians 3:6, 14-15
26. Matthew 18:15-17; Ephesians 4:2-3
27. Ephesians 6:18; Psalm 122:6

of their places and callings, in the exercise of their gifts and graces, so the churches, when planted by the providence of God, so as they may enjoy opportunity and advantage for it, ought to hold communion among themselves, for their peace, increase of love, and mutual edification.[28]

15. In cases of difficulties or differences, either in point of doctrine or administration, wherein either the churches in general are concerned, or any one church, in their peace, union, and edification; or any member or members of any church are injured, in or by any proceedings in censures not agreeable to truth and order: it is according to the mind of Christ, that many churches holding communion together, do, by their messengers, meet to consider, and give their advice in or about that matter in difference, to be reported to all the churches concerned;[29] howbeit these messengers assembled, are not intrusted with any church-power properly so called; or with any jurisdiction over the churches themselves, to exercise any censures either over any churches or persons; or to impose their determination on the churches or officers.[30]

Introduction

The Uniqueness and Importance of the Chapter

Chapter 26 of the 1689 Confession is one of the chapters in which it differs most widely from the Westminster Confession of Faith. The chapter entitled "On The Church" in the Westminster Confession of Faith has six paragraphs, whereas the 1689 Confession has fifteen. The doctrine of the church separates the Baptist Puritans from the Presbyterian Puritans. Baptists, however, were not the only ones to differ from the Westminster Confession of Faith on this issue. Many of the paragraphs in this chapter are derived from similar statements in a platform of church polity published with the Savoy Declaration of Faith by the Congregationalist Puritans in 1658. The ideas found in this chapter are, then, not exclusively those of Baptists, but ideas advocated by such Congregationalist Puritans as Thomas Goodwin, John Owen, and John Cotton. The polity of our Baptist forefathers derives from and is very similar to such Congregationalist Puritans. Only the idea of placing them in the Confession itself is unique to the Baptists. This shows the importance of the doctrine of the church for our Baptist forefathers.

The Analysis and Outline of the Chapter

This chapter is clearly divided into two distinct sections. Paragraphs 1-4 deal with the universal church, while Paragraphs 5-15 deal with the local church. This division is indicated not only by the respective emphases of the two parts of the chapter, but by their respective origins. Paragraphs 1-4 are substantially derived from the Savoy revision of the

---

28. Romans 16:1, 2; 3 John 8-10
29. Acts 15:2, 4, 6, 22, 23, 25
30. 2 Corinthians 1:24; 1 John 4:1

Westminster Confession's chapter on the church which deals with the universal church. Paragraphs 5-15 are, on the other hand, substantially derived from the platform of local church polity published with the Savoy Declaration. In the exposition of this chapter, the outline provided above will generally be followed.

1. The universal church

1. Its Identity (Paragraphs 1-2)

The Universal Church as Invisible
There are three key words in paragraph 1. The term "catholic" simply means universal. When we speak of the catholic church, we mean the universal church and not the Roman Church which calls itself universal, or catholic. The term "invisible" can be very easily misunderstood as it is used here. You will notice that it is very carefully qualified by the Confession: *which may be called invisible.*

The term "elect" is the third key word. The universal church as invisible consists *of the whole number of the elect that have been, are, or shall be gathered into one.* This paragraph, by means of these key words, teaches at least three things. Firstly, there is a universal church. Secondly, this universal church consists of all the elect. Thirdly, as such, this universal church is invisible.

Does the Bible teach that there is a universal church? The New Testament uses the word "church" one hundred and fifteen times. Most of those occurrences do not refer to the universal church, but to a local church or to local churches (2 Cor. 8:23-24; Gal. 1:2). Nevertheless, the New Testament does speak of a universal church (Matt. 16:18; 1 Cor. 12:28; Eph. 1:22; 4:11-15; 5:23, 24, 25, 27, 29, 32; Col. 1:18, 24; Heb. 12:23). Such passages refute Landmarkism and its denial of a universal church.

Does the Bible teach that this universal church consists of all the elect? Here a distinction is crucial. We must distinguish between the visible church as it has existed in different periods of history from the ideal or invisible church.

The visible church was typified in the church or assembly of physical Israel created by the Old Covenant. The type began to be fulfilled in the church as a spiritual organism and institution created by the New Covenant. When the New Covenant is consummated in the age to come, all the elect will be a part of it in the glory of resurrected life. There is a distinction implied here which enables us to do justice to portions of the New Testament which are frequently misinterpreted.

There was, on the one hand, a very important sense in which the church *began* as an institution and organism in the complex of events surrounding Christ's first advent. There was a sense in which historically the church as the final organized expression of the people of God began in the events of Christ's early ministry, death, resurrection and pouring out of the Spirit. The apostles of Christ are the historical foundation upon which Christ is now building His church (Matt. 16:18; Eph. 2:20; Heb 12:18-24). The future tense in the statement of Christ, "I will build my church," may, therefore, be given its natural force. Though Israel was a type of the church (Rom. 2:28-29; 1 Cor. 10:18; Gal. 6:16; Phil. 3:3) and though the church is the new Israel of God and the fulfillment of prophecy (Acts 2:16; 15:14-18; 1 Cor. 10:11; Gal. 6:16; Eph. 2:12-19; Heb. 8:7-13), it is true that the church as the institution and organism it is today did not exist in the Old Testament. These truths contradict the tendency of some strains of Covenant Theology to flatten the difference between the church and Israel in the interest of paedo-baptism.

On the other hand, the church can be considered invisibly in Scripture. Thus, language is frequently used which equates the church with all those in union with Christ. The church is the body and bride of Christ (Eph. 1:22; 4:11-16; 5:23-27, 29, 32; Col. 1:18, 24). Furthermore, the bride of Christ is composed in the last day of the saved from every age (Eph. 5:27; Rev. 21:9-14; note also Matt. 8:11-12; John 10:14-17; Heb. 11:39, 40). Thus, the visible church will one day be composed of all the redeemed. As the people of God, the church does consist *of the whole number of the elect.* These considerations refute Dispensationalism with its church/Israel distinction and its denial that the Old Testament saints are part of the church.

Does the Bible teach that this universal church is invisible? If we use the term "invisible," we must, like the Confession, use it very carefully, because there is no invisible church absolutely distinct from the visible church. In other words, the universal church is always also a visible, organized institution. John Murray says, "There is no evidence for the notion of the 'church' as an invisible entity distinct from the church visible."[31] The universal church is always visible, even if it is not perfectly or completely visible. The universal church spoken of in Ephesians is visible (Eph. 1:22; 3:10, 21; 4:4, 11-13 cf. 1 Cor. 12:28). The universal church could be persecuted and so had to be visible (Acts 8:1, 3; 9:1-2; 9:31; cf. Gal. 1:13; Phil. 3:6). One may not credibly profess to be a member of the invisible church while despising membership and fellowship in the visible church.

In what sense, then, is the church "invisible"? It is invisible because we cannot directly see the work of the Spirit which joins a person to Christ. It is invisible because we cannot perfectly judge the truth of another person's grace. It is invisible because the church as a whole is not yet a perfected, earthly reality.[32]

The Universal Church as Visible
The universal church is not simply or completely invisible. Paragraph 2 teaches that it is visible. It asserts two things about this visible, universal church.[33] The identity of the visible church is described as those only who

31. John Murray, *Collected Writings Vol. II* (Banner of Truth Trust, 1982), 234.
32. A. A. Hodge, *The Confession of Faith* (Edinburgh: Banner of Truth Trust, 1983), 312.
33. The 1689 Confession does not use the phrase, visible church, speaking instead

profess to believe the gospel and obey Christ and who do not contradict this profession by holding foundational errors or practicing ungodliness (1 Cor. 1:2; Rom. 1:7-8; Acts 11:26; Matt. 16:18; 28:15-20; 1 Cor. 5:1-9). The relation of the universal, visible church to local churches is that only visible saints should be members of local churches (Matt. 18:15-20; Acts 2:37-42; 4:4; 1 Cor. 5:1-9). While the universal church is not perfectly or completely visible, it is practically visible. There is no true Christian who does not confess Christ's name and obey Him outwardly. Any profession of faith, no matter how glowing, is contradicted by impenitence in any heresy or path of ungodliness.

Particular notice must be given to the phrase in paragraph 2, *everting the foundation.* The old English word "evert" may mean to turn something inside out. Here, however, because of its use with the word "foundation" it rather means to turn something upside down or to overthrow it. Thus, it speaks of errors which overthrow the foundations of Christian doctrine. This is why I have spoken of heresy. There is a distinction between lesser errors which are consistent with a profession of faith and greater errors which overthrow the foundation of the Christian faith and must be called heresy. It is very important practically and for the sake of Christian charity to distinguish between lesser errors from such error or heresy which overthrows the foundation.

2. Its Perpetuity (Paragraph 3)

1. Its Seeming Improbability
The perpetuity of the universal, visible church is introduced by a reference to certain realities which might seem to make such perpetuity implausible or doubtful. Those realities are that local churches can sin (1 Cor. 1:11; 5:1; 6:6; 11:17-19; 3 John 9, 10) and even apostatize (Rev. 2:5 with 1:20; 1 Tim. 3:14-15). We must not blindly follow the examples of any church or its leaders. We must watch carefully against corporate sin and apostasy. If you love your church, you must pray for your church, watch against sin, and exhort those in sin.

2. Its Actual Certainty
In spite of such realities which may befall individual local churches, the universal church will always visibly continue (Matt. 16:18; 24:14; 28:20; Mark 4:30-32; Ps. 72:16-18; Isa. 9:6-7). Both the Scriptures and the Confession are speaking of the indestructibility of the visible, universal church. Christ will always "have a kingdom... of such as... make profession of his name." We need not fear that the name and church of Christ will ever vanish. Atheists predict it. Novelists write about it. Voltaire prophesied it, but his home was turned into a place where Bibles

---

of "visible saints." It does suggest the phrase, visible church, by speaking of "particular congregations" later in the paragraph. The writers may have avoided the term, "visible church," in order to avoid the impression that a visible, universal church exists with earthly officers which have authority over more than one congregation. Note the assertion of the independence of the local church in paragraph 7.

were printed.[34] We may claim these promises in our prayers for our own local church. While we have no absolute promise that our own local church will continue, we do know that Christ's universal church will always visibly continue. The way in which He has appointed for that to happen is in local churches like ours. Thus, we may pray that He would build His church and defeat the forces of Satan through us!

3. Its Authority (Paragraph 4)

The main point of paragraph 4 is that the Lord Jesus is the head or authority of the universal church. Secondarily, it is deduced from this that the pope of Rome is not in any sense the head of the church. Many who hold staunchly to the 1689 Confession doubt the value of its dogmatism regarding the pope being the antichrist. This writer is among these. Such doubts are commonly viewed as consistent with full subscription of the Confession. This is one of those statements which might be qualified in the Confession. Such a qualification must be made, however, not because of any weakening of our convictions about the apostate condition of the Church of Rome or the wicked and heretical character of the claims of the pope, but out of the exegetical conviction that the statement of the Confession is without adequate biblical basis.[35]

Christ is repeatedly asserted to be the head of the church (Col. 1:18; Eph. 4:11-16; 1:20-23; 5:23-32; 1 Cor. 12:27-28; John 17:1-3; Matt. 28:18-20; Acts 5:31; John 10:14-16). Someone might say, however, "All this sounds great, but how does this work out practically? Christ is in heaven, not on earth. No living person on earth has literally spoken to Him face to face in almost twenty centuries. What really can such a headship mean? How is it exercised?" The answer to this latter question is actually very simple. Christ exercises His headship by the Holy Spirit working through His appointed representatives on earth.

The Holy Spirit is the Vicar of Christ. He is sent to carry on and carry out Christ's work (John 14:16-18, 26; 15:26-27; 16:7-13; Acts 16:6-10; 2 Cor. 3:17-18). The apostles of Christ are "universal overseers" of the church and through their witness are its foundation (Matt. 16:16-18; Eph. 2:19-22; Acts 1:20-26; Rev. 21:14). Thus, the work of the ascended Christ is carried on through their "witness" (Acts 5:31-32). These "witnesses" still rule Christ's church through their inscripturated testimony (the New Testament). The Spirit is present to apply that Word to the end of the age.

The apostles of Christ, the universal overseers of the church, were not content to have local groups of believers without definition or leadership. Here, they again had the mind of Christ who was giving gifts to the church. Hence, they appointed local overseers in the individual churches (Eph. 4:11; Acts 14:23; 13:1; 20:28; 1 Pet. 5:1; Titus 1:5-9). These leaders, who

---

34. https://crossexamined.org/voltaires-prediction-home-and-the-bible-society-truth-or-myth-further-evidence-of-verification/

35. The writer's own conviction is that 2 Thessalonians 2 is speaking of an individual destroyed at the second coming of Christ, not a line of popes. Of course, it is possible that a future pope could be that individual.

are variously called elders, overseers, pastors or teachers, exercise a real, but only a local and fallible authority, in the particular church where they are appointed. Yet, in those churches they do exercise Christ's authority and rule over His church.

If what we have said about the headship of Christ and its earthly representatives is true, then the claims of the pope are false and so also are the claims of any person or persons who would claim authority over all or even many local churches. The true Vicar of Christ is the Holy Spirit, not the pope. The pope does not possess the qualifications to be an apostle. The only genuine apostolic succession is that present in the writings of the New Testament. The only earthly representatives of Christ's authority are local overseers. Their authority is strictly local, while the pope wrongly claims universal authority.

2. The Local Church

Having examined the universal church in paragraphs 1-4, and having concluded that examination by an assertion that the Lord Jesus Christ is its living head, the Confession comes now, in paragraph 5, to apply the truth of this headship to the particular, individual expression of the universal church, which is the local church. Having just spoken to how Christ as the head of the church *is invested with all power for the calling, institution, and order or government of the church,* the Confession now shows how Christ exercises that power in the origin of local churches.

1. Its Originating Mandate (Paragraph 5)
This paragraph teaches that the local church originates from Jesus Christ, its living and powerful head. Jesus Christ originates the church by His saving power and His authoritative mandate. His saving power is the foundation of that mandate.

1. The Foundation of the Mandate
The first step in the origin of any local church is that Christ powerfully and effectually brings men to Himself by calling them through His Word and Spirit. This effectual calling takes place by means of the Word, through the power of the Spirit and according to the pattern of God's electing purpose (John 10:16, 27-28; 12:32; 17:2; Acts 5:31-32; see Chapter 10 of the Confession). The call to salvation comes to us in the context and framework of the Great Commission (Matt. 28:18-20). Its goal, stated in verse 20 of that passage, is that those called should be taught to observe all that Christ commanded the apostles.

2. The Substance of the Mandate
Christ's command to His people to walk together in particular churches is not merely another one of His precepts. This precept creates the structure or context in which the Great Commission (especially the third part alluded to in the Confession) is carried out. Jesus desires that His disciples be taught to observe all that He commanded. How shall this

be accomplished? By the creation of local churches, with local teacher-elders. Jesus commands such churches in Matthew 18:15-20. If Jesus commands that offenses be brought to the church and commands the church to rebuke such offenses and ultimately to exclude the impenitent, then necessarily He commands the existence of these local churches. In this passage, the stated purpose of the church is to teach one of Christ's commands to an erring member by calling him to repentance and, if necessary, by disciplinary action.

Jesus also gives a mandate to such local churches through the example of His apostles. The apostle Paul, Christ's personal representative, fulfilled the Great Commission everywhere he went by forming local churches and appointing local teacher-elders in those churches. Three instructive examples of this may be mentioned. In Lystra, Iconium and Antioch in Pisidia, Paul personally founded such churches and appointed such local teachers (Acts 14:21-23). In the cities of Crete, Paul again established such churches, but part of their organization was left to his representative, Titus (Titus 1:5). In Ephesus there was again a combination of Paul's initial personal activity and, later, solidification through his apostolic representatives (1 Tim. 1:3; 3:14-16; 5:17-22).

What were these elders? They were official teachers appointed to carry on the work, especially of the third part of the Great Commission, while Paul moved on to new fields (1 Tim. 3:2; 5:17; Titus 1:9-11; Eph. 4:11-13).

The central manward ministry of the local church is the building up of believers in their obedience to all the commands of Christ. Ordinarily and normatively, teaching the disciples of Christ to observe all His commands demands the existence of officially recognized teacher/elders in the local church. The church may exist, but it cannot be well, without such pastor-teachers. It is often said that while one church may be strong in the teaching of God's Word to God's people, other churches may be strong in music, fellowship, social concerns, or evangelism. Such assertions are false. Teaching the Word is an essential and central manward function of every church (1 Tim. 3:15).

The necessity of church-planting as an essential, integral part of fulfilling the Great Commission is also underscored by the above. It is often argued for one reason or another that the church cannot fulfill the Great Commission. In fact, only the church can fulfill the Great Commission because that commission assumes and demands the creation of local churches.

2. Its Defined Membership (Paragraph 6)
Discipleship, baptism, and church membership are intimately connected in the Great Commission. Discipleship, therefore, demands baptism, church membership, and submission to the elders/teachers of the church. Church membership presupposes and demands discipleship manifesting itself in obedience to the Lord—obedience manifested specifically in the acts of baptism and submission to the Word in the teaching ministry of the church. Baptism is not to be divorced from discipleship and church

membership. A further implication of all this is that baptized disciples who leave one local church ought not to be and ought not to expect to be gullibly or automatically received by another local church. They ought willingly to provide that church and its elders with proof of their discipleship by verbally relating their experience of Christ, letters of recommendation from their former church and their manifest good conduct and submission to the Lord and His church (Acts 9:26-30; Jude 4; Rev. 2:2, 14-15).

3. Its Authoritative Power (Paragraph 7)

1. Its defined recipients
2. Its complete sufficiency
3. Its reiterated origin
4. Its specified purpose
5. Its regulated execution

Clearly, the subject of paragraph 7 is the power and authority possessed by the local church. In dealing with this paragraph, we must first examine the description of this power in the Confession. The five points of this description are set out in the outline above. The scriptural evidence for this description may be found in two passages which explicitly mention or support every one of the points made by the Confession about this power given to the local church (Matt. 18:15-20; 1 Cor. 5:1-13, especially vv. 4-5). In these passages, *the defined recipient* of this power is the local church. Even the local church at Corinth, with all its problems, possesses this power. *Its complete sufficiency* is suggested by the mention of the keys of the kingdom in Matthew 18:18-19. In 1 Corinthians 5, this sufficiency is suggested by the assertion that in their assembly the power of the Lord Jesus was present (v. 4) and by the command to remove the wicked man in verses 7 and 13. *The reiterated origin* of this power is clearly Christ Himself (Matt. 18:20; 1 Cor. 5:3-5). *The specified purpose* of this power includes even the excommunication of a member of the church (Matt. 18:17; 1 Cor. 5:7, 13), but worship is also suggested by Matthew 18:20. *Its regulated execution* is clearly indicated by the detailed rules given in Matthew 18:15-17 and 1 Corinthians 5:4, 11, with 2 Corinthians 2:6-8.

In the letters to the seven churches of Asia in Revelation 2 and 3, the subject of church discipline is repeatedly emphasized by Christ, but each church is held solely responsible for its own members and their discipline. Christ never asserts, assumes, or implies that the other churches may exercise church discipline by intervening in another church's affairs. The entire group is not held responsible or told to act for the discipline of Laodicea.[36]

Presbyterians object to such independence for each local congregation under Christ on many different grounds. The key and classic passage,

---

36. Note Wardlaw's remarks cited in James Bannerman's *Church of Christ* (Edinburgh: The Banner of Truth Trust, 1960), vol. II, 300.

however, upon which their arguments depend is Acts 15.[37] Essentially, the Presbyterian argument rests on two points. First, the gathering in Jerusalem exercised authority over many different local churches. This point is certainly correct (Acts 15:28; 16:4). Second, the gathering in Jerusalem was a church council or synod constituted by elders representing many different local churches. It is this point which must be disputed.

While it is true that "elders" were subordinately involved in the authoritative decision (Acts 15:23; 16:4), it is not true, nor can it be proved, that this gathering was composed of the elders of many churches or even two churches. There is no evidence that even Paul and Barnabas were among "the apostles and elders" who made the decision (Acts 15:2, 4, 6, 22-23; 16:4). Acts 15:2, 4, and 16:4 especially exclude Paul and Barnabas from the elders in view. There is absolutely no proof that any of the elders of the many other churches to whom the decrees were delivered were present.

The authority of the council of the church at Jerusalem is rather based on factors unique to that church. For many reasons, the church of Jerusalem had a unique authority in redemptive history unparalleled by any other church. Hence, it cannot be made an example for other later and lesser churches:

- It was the church where the twelve apostles dwelt. Their influence and presence would give her official statements great authority. This was probably the definitive reason for the authority of this council.

- It was also the first church of Christianity.

- Its leaders (even without counting the Twelve) were the original disciples and followers of Christ. Elders like James, the half-brother of our Lord, though not among the original twelve apostles, yet exercised an authority that can only be called apostolic (Gal. 2:9; 1 Cor. 15:7).

It exercised an authority for all the reasons stated above akin to the Jewish Sanhedrin's (the council of the seventy elders of Israel) authority over Jewish synagogues everywhere.

Several practical lessons are underscored by paragraph 7. We learn the high authority of the true local church. We see the solemn privilege of being a member of it and under its authority. We note the solemn responsibility of the local church not to abuse its power. We understand the glorious liberty of the true local church. There is no higher religious authority instituted among men. Finally, we observe the vital origin of the power of the local church – the special presence of Christ.

---

37. James Bannerman, *The Church of Christ* (Edinburgh: The Banner of Truth Trust, 1974), vol. II, 325, 326.

4. Its Appointed Government (Paragraphs 8-13)

1. The Identity of Its Government (Paragraph 8)
The point of paragraph 8 is that Christ has appointed only two continuing offices in the local church—elders and deacons. According to the Confession, elders, bishops, and pastors occupy exactly the same office. It may be helpful to collate the evidence for this assertion. Paragraph 8 speaks of "bishops or elders and deacons." Paragraph 9 speaks of "the office of bishop or elder in a church." Paragraph 11 speaks of "the bishops or pastors of the churches." The statements of this chapter put beyond all reasonable doubt that it views the office of elder, bishop, or pastor as one and the same. It was common for those Puritans to argue that all elders were bishops and reject the distinction between bishops and elders assumed by those who held an episcopal form of church government.[38]

More might be said, but the main, biblical assertions important to this (two-office) view of church government are these:

- First, only these two offices are mentioned in the classic New Testament passages on the continuing offices of the local church (Phil. 1:1; 1 Tim. 3:1-13). The implication is that there were no other offices.

- Second, the office of elder or presbyter, overseer or bishop, and pastor or shepherd are one and the same (Acts 20:17, 28; Titus 1:5-7; 1 Peter 5:2; and 1 Tim. 3:2, with Eph. 4:11). It is common today to draw a distinction between pastors and elders. In Acts 20:17 and 28 and 1 Peter 5:2 the elders are commanded to shepherd or pastor the church. In 1 Timothy 3:2, it is required that all elders be able to teach. The pastor-teachers of Ephesians 4:11 are simply elders. There are not three offices in the church—pastor, elder, and deacon. There are only two offices—overseer-elder-pastor and deacon. Pastors and elders are the same. The biblical teaching should not be subtly undermined by unbiblical terminology.

- Third, the norm is a plurality of elders in each local church. This is the clear implication of both the Bible and the Confession. No instance of a New Testament church with only one elder exists. Universally, a plurality of elders is mentioned (Acts 14:23; 20:17; Phil. 1:1, 1 Thess. 5:12; Titus 1:5; Heb. 13:17; James 5:14).

---

38. While the evidence for the two-office view of church government in the Confession is clear, there are remaining questions that are raised by but remain unanswered in the Confession. Paragraph 10 speaks of the financial support of "pastors." Furthermore, it seems to imply that all such pastors should be supported as the church has ability. This seems, however, both unlikely in itself and contrary to Scripture (1 Tim. 5:17-18; Acts 20:33-35). Perhaps the interpretation which does the most justice to the language of the Confession emphasizes the qualifying phrase in paragraph 10, "according to their ability." In the original Scripture proofs of the Confession, 1 Timothy 5:17-18 is cited at this point. Perhaps, the Confession is asserting that "ideally" all elders should be supported, but this phrase adds the thought that this support must be according to the priorities for pastoral support stated in the Bible.

- Fourth, though these elders hold the same office and thus have the same authority, this does not mean that they are and must be equal in every respect. There is, first, legitimate diversity as to spiritual gifts (1 Cor. 12:11; 1 Pet. 4:10-11). There are different gifts in the eldership (Rom. 12:7-8) and different degrees of these gifts (Matt. 25:14-15). There is, second, legitimate diversity as to financial support (1 Tim. 5:17-18). There is, third, different degrees of actual influence. This was true of the highest office in Christ's church—the office of apostle. Paul labored more than all the apostles and had a greater influence (1 Cor. 15:10). Peter exercised a greater influence than many of the other apostles (Matt. 16:18; Acts 1:15; 2:14, 38; 3:1). What is true of the extraordinary office of apostle certainly must be true of the ordinary office of the pastor or elder.

2. The Appointment of Its Government (Paragraph 9)

The spiritual prerequisite for appointment to office in the church is stated in the words "fitted and gifted by the Holy Spirit" (Eph. 4:11; 1 Tim. 3:1-13). The church has no right to appoint any man to an office for which God has not fitted him.

The essential features of this appointment are two: election and ordination. I use both words to describe paragraph 9 with some hesitation.

Election is used with some reservation. To modern ears, an election connotes several things which clearly deviate from what the Word of God teaches. There is no scriptural instance in which two or more men compete for votes in order to be elected to office in the church. There is no basis for the idea that election is an act of sovereign and autonomous authority or that it is the ultimate source of power in the church. Again, such an idea contradicts the scriptural teaching. We have no biblical right before Christ to vote for whomever we please. We have a duty to vote for the one Christ is giving as a gift to His church. The term, election, is used only to epitomize what is meant by the Confession when it asserts that calling to an office in the church must be "by the common suffrage of the church itself." No one may be appointed to any office in the church without the consent of the church itself. The elders of the church may not appoint a man to be a fellow elder without the consent of the church. No supposed higher authority may do this, whether that authority is a bishop, a denomination, or a pope.

This "common suffrage of the church" is deduced from the teaching of paragraph 7. Since God has given all needful power to the local church to carry on that order He has ordained, and if this authority extends even to the excommunication of its members, and if excommunication may only be enacted by the consent of the assembled church (Matt. 18:15-17; 1 Cor. 5:1-13), then this suggests that no officer may be appointed without the consent of the congregation. Further confirmation of this comes from the account of the selection of deacons in Acts 6. That account shows that the authority of the church extends to the election of officers. The requirement of Acts 14:23 may also suggest this act of election. The Greek word used here originally meant to vote by stretching out the hand. Luke may have used this word to suggest "the common suffrage of the church." More relevant to this matter may be the description of the church as a royal priesthood (1 Pet. 2:5, 9; Rev. 1:6; 5:10). An indication of the church being a royal priesthood is that it is permitted to recognize and consent to the leadership given by its head.

Ordination is also used only with reservation. It means many things in contemporary religious circles which I do not intend by its use here. Baptist polity does not permit the notions of permanent or universal ordination. Ordination, if it is used to describe anything biblical, must be used to succinctly describe the formal installation of a man into a biblical church office by means of "the imposition of hands of the eldership of the church." Both this paragraph and the Bible mandate such *ordination* for elders and deacons. The Seven in Acts 6:6 were so ordained as deacons of the church at Jerusalem. Though no explicit text in the New Testament records elders laying hands on men who are being set apart to the eldership, there is every reason to think that this is right. There are instances of elders ordaining and elders being ordained. There is, therefore, biblical warrant for elders being set apart through the laying on of hands by the already constituted eldership of a church. This *ordination* is a necessary part of the process. An important implication of this is that no man on whom the elders of the church cannot in good conscience lay hands may be ordained to the eldership (1 Tim. 5:22). The church and its elders must therefore agree in the setting apart of any new officer.[39]

Notice the table below which collates the biblical instances of "ordination."

Scripture Reference	Who Ordained?	Who was Ordained?
1 Timothy 4:14	Eldership	Timothy
1 Timothy 5:22	Timothy	Elders
Acts 6:6	The Twelve	The Seven
Acts 13:3	Prophets and Teachers	Paul and Barnabas
2 Timothy 1:6	Paul	Timothy

3. The Cornerstone of Its Government: the Ministry of the Word (Paragraphs 10-11)

The Confession moves now to the ministry of the Word in its treatment of the government of the church. This is significant because Christ rules the church by the Word of God. The church's highest continuing office has as its unique requirement the ability to teach (1 Tim. 3:2; 5:17). The first deacons were appointed to be servants of the servants of the Word

---

39. John Cotton in *The Keys of the Kingdom* (San Diego: Thaddeus Publications, 2018) is seminal and vastly important for Congregational Puritan polity and the Particular Baptist polity which descends from it. He argues that both the authority of the eldership and the liberty of the membership are necessary for the bringing to the completion of any church act.

so that this central function would not be neglected even for so noble a purpose as feeding widows (Acts 6:2, 4). The church's central function is the proclamation of the Word (1 Tim. 3:15). Hence, the ministry of the Word is the cornerstone of its government.

The official ministry of the Word by pastors is the subject of paragraph 10. The thrust of paragraph 10 is the material support of elders in the local church. Thus, I want to isolate and concentrate attention on that subject. Such concentrated attention is, perhaps, especially warranted because only this paragraph of this chapter appears to have no precedent in any of the previous Confessions from which the authors drew.

There are, of course, not a few who have denied that an elder in the local church ought to be supported regularly. Since such a view can have devastating results for the church, it is important to focus our attention on this point. The biblical evidence is mainly to be found in three classic passages.

- 1 Timothy 5:17-18 describes material support as "honor." *What is double honor?* Honor here means financial support. The Greek word translated as "honor" in the New Testament frequently designates something of material value (Matt. 27:6-9; Acts 4:34; 5:2-3; 7:16). Honor is used of material support in the immediate context of 1 Timothy 5:17-18 (cf. 3 and vv. 4-8, 16). 1 Timothy 5:18 supports the statement of verse 17 (note the conjunction, "for") with verses used elsewhere in the New Testament to describe material support (1 Cor. 9:9; Matt. 10:10; Luke 10:7).

  What, then, is double honor? Two clues unlock the meaning of this unusual phrase. The first is the use of honor in verse 3. Note the connection with verse 17. Widows are to be honored (financially). Elders are to be doubly-honored (financially). The second clue is the use of "double" in the New Testament (Rev. 18:6; Matt. 23:15). Double is used figuratively to indicate amplitude or great extent. Double honor, then, is ample material or financial support.

  Who are to be doubly-honored? The answer is clearly elders who rule well, but especially those who labor in the Word and teaching — the public ministry of the Word. Paul's thought may be illustrated by means of two concentric circles. The outer circle encompasses all elders who rule well. The inner circle encompasses those elders who (are gifted to) "work hard at preaching and teaching." Financial support must be focused on the inner circle and then radiate outward as the necessity and ability of the church makes this appropriate.

- Galatians 6:6 describes material support as "sharing." Three questions again must be put to this text. *What is to be shared?* The answer is: "all good things." The "good things" of verse 10 are clearly material blessings. The emphasis on "all good things" indicates an open-hearted generosity. *With whom are they to be shared?* They are to be shared with the one who teaches the

Word. The word translated as "teach" in this verse is the one from which the English word "catechize" is derived. It designates formal, regular, or systematic instruction (Rom. 2:18). *What are the consequences of such sharing of all good things?* The consequences of the duty stated in Galatians 6:6 must be emphasized. There are great spiritual consequences, for better or for worse, depending on the performance of this duty (Gal. 6:7-9). The wicked and oppressive failure of most evangelical churches to support their pastors amply is at the root of much of the dearth and curse which is upon the professing church of Jesus Christ. Those who highly value the labor of the servant of God will find themselves blessed with highly valuable labor.

- 1 Corinthians 9:14 describes material support as "a living." Two questions again enable us to understand its significance. *Who should have a living?* The one who preaches (solemnly proclaims) the gospel. *What is to be earned?* "A living" or "livelihood." This designates such a sufficient supply of this world's goods as to have a decent life, as opposed to such an insufficiency as makes life a slow death.

Other data may be found in Matthew 10:10; Luke 10:7; Philippians 4:10-20; and 2 Timothy 2:4-6. Gospel ministers should be so supported as not to be necessarily entangled or distracted by worldly needs. 1 Peter 5:2 shows that the early church was marked by the custom of so comfortably supporting their teachers as to open the possibility that some would rule for the sake of sordid gain (cf. 1 Timothy 6:5).

Several important conclusions may be drawn from this biblical data. The first is that elders in the local church are to be supported materially. No hair-splitting distinctions are to be found in these passages. The Bible does not fastidiously restrict support only to some rare class of teachers or itinerant missionaries. Its wording is broad. 1 Corinthians 9:14 speaks of "those who proclaim the gospel." Galatians 6:6 speaks of "him who teaches." 1 Timothy 5:17 speaks of "the elders who rule well… especially those who work hard at preaching and teaching."

The second conclusion is that the focus of material support should be upon those elders who engage in the public ministry of the Word. This again underscores the pre-eminence of the Word in the church.

The third conclusion is that the extent of material support given to such elders by the church ought to be generous and ample. It ought to be "a living," "all good things," and "double honor" (1 Cor. 9:14; Gal. 6:6; 1 Tim. 5:17). The Confession's language is admirable. Churches are "to communicate to them of all their good things, according to their ability, so as they may have a comfortable supply, without being themselves entangled in secular affairs; and may also be capable of exercising hospitality toward others."

The auxiliary ministry of the Word by others is the theme of paragraph 11. The prohibition of preaching by non-ministers is usually associated with an exaggerated distinction between ministers and elders. There is, however, no precept forbidding any Christian to preach the gospel as he may have opportunity. There are examples of Christians preaching the Word who were not ordained elders (Acts 8:5; 11:19-21; 1 Pet. 4:10). There are precepts and principles which require him to avoid pride and to submit to the church and its overseers in the estimate and exercise of his gifts (Rom. 12:3; Heb. 13:17).

The teaching of the 1689 here, regarding the administration of the ordinances (28:2), is in contrast to that of the Westminster Confession, which frequently speaks of ministers of the Word as alone competent to preach and administer the sacraments (Chapters: 15:1; 27:4; 28:2; 29:3). Particularly revelatory of the restrictive, Presbyterian view of this matter is the statement of 27:4 (WCF): "There be only two sacraments ordained by Christ our Lord in the Gospel; that is to say, baptism, and the Supper of the Lord: neither of which may be dispensed by any, but by a minister of the Word lawfully ordained."

4. The Extent of Its Government (Paragraphs 12-13)

These paragraphs deal with that aspect of church government which concerns the discipline of the local church. My use of the term "discipline" may require explanation since it is not used in these paragraphs. The Bible teaches that the local church is neither a loose-knit social club, nor merely a preaching center. The Bible teaches that the local church is a society dedicated to teaching men to observe all that Christ commanded. It is, therefore, a religious order characterized by mutual accountability. God has commanded the church to exercise a certain authority or discipline over its members in order to bring them to the observance of all Christ's commands. He has even given the church power to publicly censure, admonish, and ultimately expel those who impenitently or grossly violate Christ's commands. It is this authority and these actions which are commonly called the discipline of the local church.

Paragraphs 12 and 13 concentrate on one main point: the duty of subjection to the discipline of the local church. As the outline makes clear, according to the Confession this discipline extends to all the members of the church and all church problems.

Paragraph 12 asserts that all believers are bound to join a local church ("when and where they have opportunity so to do") and, when they join, to submit themselves to its discipline. This is assumed because it has already been stated in paragraph 5. The implication of this duty is that Christians ought to submit to the government of their churches. Biblical support for the duty to join and submit to the discipline of the local church is found in 1 Thessalonians 5:14; 2 Thessalonians 3:6, 14, 15; 1 Corinthians 5:9-13; and Hebrews 13:17.

Paragraph 13 pointedly addresses a sin against the government of the church, which is very common today.

The situation envisioned is that certain church members have been offended by another person in the church. They have performed the duty required in Matthew 18:15-17. The person has not satisfied them by his repentance. At this point, the Confession is not clear. Perhaps the people have not yet taken the matter to the church. Perhaps they have, but the church has not yet acted; at least, not to their satisfaction. The Confession assumes that these people belong to a church that has a manifested commitment to church discipline. The Confession also is assuming that the church is led by faithful, though, of course, fallible, pastors. The great question facing these people is what do they do now?

The prohibition issued informs such church members as to what they should not do! The substance of the Confession's prohibition is that there must be no anarchy, no revolution against the discipline of the church. There must be no disturbance of the church-order by public demonstrations, whispering or letter-writing campaigns, or gossip. There must be no absenting of themselves from the church's meetings or abstinence from the church's ordinances.

The direction required informs such members of what they should do! If they have not told the church, they should. If they have told the church and the church has not yet acted, they should wait upon Christ in the further proceeding of the church. They should do the one thing that people in such a situation are least likely to do. They should pray. They should continue to believe that there is someone higher than the elders in every true church—the Lord Jesus Christ—and wait on the orderly proceeding of the church.

In our day, when the situation envisioned in this paragraph would be viewed as a clear warrant for a church split, the teaching of this paragraph is radical. "What!" someone says, "Just wait? What about how offended I am? You mean I do not have the right to just leave for another church?" Such attitudes require that the scriptural warrant for the statements of the Confession be examined.

The regulative importance of Christ's directions in Matthew 18:15-17 for our conduct in the church must be remembered. The principles taught there are underscored in Ephesians 4:2-3; Colossians 3:12-15; and 1 John 2:7-11, 18-19. If you love your brother, you will not leave his fellowship without the greatest grief, reluctance, and hesitation. If you are endeavoring diligently to maintain the unity of the Spirit, you will not in selfish petulance disturb the unity of the church. If you are humble, you will not be arrogantly positive that your perspective on your brother and the Scripture is without defect. You will carefully and slowly re-examine yourself, if the church refrains from exercising discipline. You will remember that, even if you are right this time, you have been slow to see the right before. Therefore, you will exercise forbearance and longsuffering.

The regulative importance of Christ's presence for our conduct in the church must also be remembered (Matt. 28:20). The precise words of the Confession are that we should "wait upon Christ in the further proceeding of the church." Is Christ present? Are you in a true church with qualified pastors? Then, even if the church has temporarily delayed or even miscarried in its obedience to Christ, should not your posture be one of prayerful waiting on Christ to vindicate you? Hastily disturbing the peace of the church and precipitously leaving it are a manifestation that you are held in the grip of unbelief. You are saying that Christ is not present in His Church!

5. Its Fraternal Relations: the Communion of Local Churches (Paragraphs 14-15)

The duty which the Confession seeks to expound in its treatment of the relations of the local church is the duty of holding communion with other churches. This is emphasized by the occurrence in both paragraphs of the phrase "hold (or holding) communion." The notion of "formal associations" or "informal associations" in connection to the phrase "holding communion" has been much debated among Reformed Baptists in recent years. Nevertheless, it seems clear to me now that the most natural interpretation of the Confession is that it assumes formal associations in Chapter 26, paragraphs 14-15.[40]

1. Its Divine Authorization (Paragraph 14)

a) Its Significant Backdrop (Para. 14a)

The divine authorization for this duty of local churches to hold communion must begin with the presupposition that the churches of Jesus Christ are already (legally) one in their mediatorial head and apostolic foundation. They simply recognize and regulate a pre-existing unity. Also important here is the love and oneness in Himself, which Christ desires for His people (John 13:34-35; 17:11, 21-23; Eph. 4:11-16). The first requirement of such unity and communion is prayer for each other (Eph. 6:18; Ps. 122:6). Its scriptural precedents are: occasional support of gospel workers from other churches (Rom. 16:1-3; 3 John 8-10 with 2 John 5-11), frequent communication with other churches (Col. 2:1 with 1:3, 4, 7 and 4:7, 12) and combined benevolence for needy saints in other churches (Rom. 15:26; 2 Cor. 8:1-4, 16-24; and 9:12-15).

b) Its Specific Obligation (Para. 14b)

There appear to be scriptural illustrations of regional communions of local churches. Such communions illustrate both the scriptural duty of local churches holding communion and its necessary providential limitations. For examples of regional associations in the Bible compare the churches of Galatia (Gal. 1:2), churches of Judea (Gal. 1:22), and the communication between Colosse and Laodicea (Col. 4:16). Possibly the clearest illustration of such communion is that of the seven churches of Asia (Rev. 1:4). The

---

40. For further discussion on this topic, I point the reader to *Edification and Beauty* (Wipf and Stock, 2009), and *Denominations or Associations?* (Calvary Press Publishing, 2001) by James M. Renihan.

angels of these churches are probably their messengers. Notice the co-action, co-operation and communication involved in their acting together with John.

c) Its Spiritual Benefits (Para. 14c)

The Confession speaks of benefits of such associations for churches as "their peace, increase of love and mutual edification." Why is communion necessary for these things? Because knowledge and communication are pre-requisites to love and edification, while lack of knowledge breeds suspicion and division (1 John 4:1-3; 2 John; 3 John). These passages shows that communication and knowledge are prerequisites for love and edification. Testing must precede receiving (Rom. 16:1-3; 2 Cor. 9:12-15). The events of Joshua 22 teach that lack of knowledge can breed suspicion, division, and strife. Communion, which has for its by-products communication and mutual understanding, is necessary in order to avoid such contradictions of Christian love. It is, therefore, a solemn duty.

2. Its Special Advantage: Advisory Meetings (Para. 15)

The possible reasons for such assemblies are difficulties, differences, and injuries between churches or in one church. The *biblical basis* for such assemblies is the biblical doctrine of seeking counsel and not being wise in our own conceits (Gal. 2:2; Prov. 3:5-7; 12:15; 13:10). Such assemblies are also required by the biblical necessity of endeavoring to preserve unity (Eph. 4:1-3). The *strict limit* of such an assembly is that it is merely advisory. In the Bible, counsel is often not authoritative, even if it comes from an apostle (1 Cor. 7:25, 40). Hebrews 13:17 equates the leaders of the church with governors, given charge by a King over a province of His kingdom. Such governors may seek advice from one another, but they are legally responsible only to the King.

Conclusion

There are few greater blessings in this life than the privilege of being part of a well-ordered church where both the faith and the love which are in Christ Jesus are manifestly present. There are few writings more helpful and weightier than this chapter of the Confession in constructing, with the help of God, such a church. Its balanced teaching about the nature of the universal church, its clear teaching about the character of the local church and its government, and its useful guidance about how local churches should relate to one another is still proving its immense worth today.

CHAPTER 27

OF THE COMMUNION OF THE SAINTS

VICTOR CLAUDIO

1. All saints that are united to Jesus Christ, their head, by His Spirit, and faith, although they are not made thereby one person with Him, have fellowship in his graces, sufferings, death, resurrection, and glory;[1] and, being united to one another in love, they have communion in each other's gifts and graces,[2] and are obliged to the performance of such duties, public and private, in an orderly way, as do conduce to their mutual good, both in the inward and outward man.[3]

2. Saints by profession are bound to maintain an holy fellowship and communion in the worship of God, and in performing such other spiritual services as tend to their mutual edification;[4] as also in relieving each other in outward things according to their several abilities, and necessities;[5] which communion, according to the rule of the gospel, though especially to be exercised by them, in the relation wherein they stand, whether in families,[6] or churches,[7] yet, as God offereth opportunity, is to be extended to all the household of faith, even all those who in every place call upon the name of the Lord Jesus; nevertheless their communion one with another as saints, doth not take away or infringe the title or propriety which each man hath in his goods and possessions.[8]

Introduction
The communion of the saints has been an important doctrine of the Christian Church throughout its history. It appears in the Apostles' Creed, which confesses, *"I believe in the Holy Spirit, the holy catholic Church,*

---

1. 1 John 1:3; John 1:16; Philippians 3:10; Romans 6:5-6
2. Ephesians 4:15, 16; 1 Corinthians 12:7; 1 Corinthians 3:21-23
3. 1 Thessalonians 5:11, 14; Romans 1:12; 1 John 3:17-18; Galatians 6:10
4. Hebrews 10:24-25; Hebrews 3:12-13
5. Acts 11:29-30
6. Ephesians 6:4
7. 1 Corinthians 12:14-27
8. Acts 5:4; Ephesians 4:28

the communion of saints." This chapter details our Baptist forefathers' understanding of the Bible's teaching on this subject. But what is meant by the term "communion of the saints"? The term refers to the spiritual bond that Christians have one with another by virtue of their union with Christ. The word "communion" comes from koinonia in Greek, which is often translated in the New Testament as "communion," "participation," or "fellowship." The idea is that of close fellowship between church members who genuinely love and care for one another.

Notice how naturally this chapter flows from the previous one. In Chapter 26, the Confession gives an overview of the nature and structure of the universal and local churches of Jesus Christ. Then, in Chapter 27, the focus changes from the universal church to the personal, spiritual communion that God's people have with each other within the context of local congregations. Of course, this does not negate fellowship Christians have with believers in other places. We will consider this paragraph under three main headings: the Christian's union with Christ, the Christian's communion with other Christians, and the Christian's communion obligations to other Christians.

Paragraph 1

1. The Christian's Union with Christ

The Confession affirms that all saints *are united to Jesus Christ,* their head, highlighting the union that true Christians have with Christ and that He has with them. The Scripture speaks of this spiritual union between the Lord Jesus and His people in many places and describes it in at least two ways: first, as believers being *in* Christ; second, as Christ being *in* believers.

For example, Paul teaches that Christians who are in union with Christ are raised *with* Him, and their lives are now hidden in Him (Col. 3:1-3). Additionally, Paul declares that there is no condemnation for those who are found *in* Christ (Rom. 8:1). Our position in Christ is not based on what we have done but solely on what Christ has done. Thus, the Christian is said to be "accepted in the Beloved" (Eph. 1:6). God is no respecter of persons, nor is there any difference in value among God's elect, for all are united and are now "one in Christ Jesus" (Gal. 3:28).

The apostle Paul also rejoiced in the reality that the risen Christ lived *in him* (Gal. 2:20)—that is, Christ dwelt in him by the Holy Spirit. This was the same truth that Paul sought to make known to Christians: that Christ, the hope of glory, dwells in them as well (Col. 1:26-27). In fact, Paul encouraged believers to examine themselves in order to determine whether they were in the faith and if Christ resided in them (Rom. 8:10; 2 Cor. 13:5).

The Lord Jesus Christ Himself spoke of this mutual union. In John 15:4-5, He told His disciples, "Abide in Me, and I in you. As the branch cannot bear fruit of itself, unless it abides in the vine, neither can you, unless you abide in Me. I am the vine, you *are* the branches. He who abides in Me, and I in him, bears much fruit; for without Me you can do nothing."

The Scriptures provide other illustrations describing the union that Christians have with Christ, including the unity displayed in the human body (Eph. 4:15-16), the marriage union between a husband and wife (Eph. 5:31), and the merging of a foundation with the superstructure built upon it (1 Pet. 2:4-6).

"... united to Jesus Christ, their head, by his Spirit, and faith..."

The Confession goes on to explain how this union between Christ and the Christian is established: "by His Spirit, and faith." The Holy Spirit is a necessary agent in the salvation of the elect. There is no redemption for sinners apart from His regenerating work. In John 3:3-5, Jesus informs Nicodemus of this reality: "Most assuredly, I say to you, unless one is born again, he cannot see the kingdom of God... Most assuredly, I say to you, unless one is born of water and the Spirit, he cannot enter the kingdom of God."

The Holy Spirit convicts and draws sinners to Christ (John 16:8). He unites believers to Christ and His body, the Church (1 Cor. 12:13). Therefore, merely claiming union with Christ is insufficient. If one is not indwelt by the Holy Spirit, he or she does not belong to Christ (Rom. 8:9). To such persons, Christ will declare on the final day, "I never knew you; depart from Me" (Matt. 7:23). There can be no true union with Christ without the Holy Spirit first establishing it. Further, the Spirit's work is essential, not only in the regeneration and engrafting of the elect into Christ, but also in sanctifying and preserving them (1 Pet. 1:2; 2 Thess. 2:13; Phil. 1:6; Rom. 8:11).

The Spirit unites believers to Christ through the instrumentality of *faith.* It is through faith that Christ dwells in the hearts of His people (Eph. 3:16-17). Now, this faith is not of one's own making, but is rather a gift from God by the working of the Holy Spirit in the elect: "For by grace you have been saved through faith, and that not of yourselves; it [faith being the closest antecedent] is the gift of God" (Eph. 2:8). While sinners may be able to comprehend something of the gospel intellectually, none will ever have saving *faith* without God first graciously bestowing it. Robert Shaw writes that "Christ apprehends His people by His Spirit, and they receive Him by faith, which His Spirit produces in them."[9] It is by the quickening power of the Holy Spirit that the elect are enabled to lay hold of Christ by faith in order to be in saving union with Him.

"although they are not made thereby one person with Him"

The Confession now qualifies the phrase "union with Christ" by stating what it does not imply. For further clarification, this statement should be paralleled with Chapter 26, paragraph 3, of the Westminster Confession

9. Robert Shaw, *The Reformed Faith: An Exposition of the Westminster Confession of Faith* (Inverness, Scotland; Christian Focus Publications, 2008), 346.

which states: "This communion which the saints have with Christ, doth not make them in any wise partakers of the substance of his Godhead; or to be equal with Christ in any respect: either of which to affirm is impious and blasphemous." The framers of the Westminster Confession strongly rejected the idea that a Christian's union with Christ implies being equal with Him or divine in any aspect. Sam Waldron states: "This was an important qualification in the seventeenth century. Different sects were interpreting union with Christ in a mystical, pantheistic sense. It is a necessary distinction in our day."[10] Waldron makes a great point. In our day, we have cults, like Mormonism, which teach that people are made divine after death. Additionally, Pentecostal charismatics from the *Word of Faith* movement teach their adherents that union with God causes them to become "little gods." Such teaching is responsible for the heretical "name it and claim it" theology and the "prosperity gospel" of our day.

R. C. Sproul states:

> All we have is humanity. We may have reborn humanity, but it is humanity in the process of sanctification. We may be indwelt by the Holy Spirit, but we never participate in his substance of deity, even though we are created in the image of God. To be the image of God does not mean that we participate in his essence, his deity. It means that there are aspects which God imparts that are similar to his own being.[11]

However, the Confession goes on to define what union with Christ does imply.

"That we have fellowship in Christ's graces, sufferings, death, resurrection, and glory..."

Union with Christ implies that we become partakers of His special grace and life. Christians who are in union with Christ receive all of the benefits of Christ's suffering which He endured on behalf of His people. Because of Christ's sufferings, believers themselves do not have to suffer the condemnation of sin (Rom. 8:1-4). Because of the death of Christ, Christians will not have to endure the second death (Heb. 2:9). Because of the resurrection of Christ, believers are now justified and will also be resurrected like Christ (1 Cor. 15:20, 23; 1 Thess. 4:16). All that Christ has done on our behalf has been credited to our account.

Furthermore, Christians who are spiritually united to Christ share in the same experiences of Christ to some extent. Those who would live godly lives will suffer persecution (2 Tim. 3:12). Christ warned His disciples that "If they persecuted Me, they will persecute you as well" (John 15:20). Those who endure sufferings in this present age are considered to be "partakers of Christ's sufferings" (1 Pet. 4:13; Col. 1:24).

---

10. Samuel E. Waldron, *A Modern Exposition of the 1689 Baptist Confession of Faith* (Grand Rapids, MI: Evangelical Press, 2013), 416.

11. R.C. Sproul, *Truths We Confess: A Layman's Guide to the Westminster Confession of Faith*, *vol.* 3 (Phillipsburg, NJ: P&R Publishing), 73.

Sproul adds: "So important is that concept, in terms of our union with Christ, that the apostle Paul says that unless we are willing to participate in his suffering and death, we will not enter into his exaltation (2 Tim. 2:11-12). If we do enter into the afflictions of Jesus, and embrace his humiliation, we participate in his exaltation and in his glory."[12]

Christ has been seated on His throne at the right hand of the Father (Heb. 1:3), where God has made us alive and has seated us in Him (Eph. 2:6). On the last day, God will vindicate His saints and present them without spot or wrinkle (Eph. 5:27). On that day, we too shall be glorified with Christ (Rom. 8:17, 29-30). As Sam Waldron writes: "Everything Christ did and everything he now possesses as the Mediator belongs to us."[13] What a glorious reality that "God has blessed us in Christ with every spiritual blessing" (Eph. 1:3).

2. The Christian's Communion with Other Christians

"... being united to one another in love, they have communion in each other's gifts and graces..."

The outgrowth of union with Christ is the communion and fellowship of the saints with each other. Christians who are in union with the Lord Jesus Christ are now part of the same body and share a common purpose because they have a common union with Christ.

A. A. Hodge enlarges upon this:

> They have a common Head, and common duties with respect to him; a common profession, a common system of faith to maintain, a common gospel to preach, a common worship and service to maintain. They have a common life, and one Holy Ghost dwelling in and binding together in one the whole body.[14]

The Confession highlights *love* as one of the bonds that joins believers together. Christian love is the mark of a true disciple of Christ, which distinguishes us from all other people (John 13:35; 1 John 3:14). Our Savior Himself commanded us to "love one another; as I have loved you" (John 13:34). The apostle Paul further instructed that "over all these virtues put on love, which binds them all together in perfect unity" (Col. 3:12-14).

"... they have communion in each other's gifts and graces"

Another outcome of Christian fellowship is sharing in the benefits of each other's gifts and graces. God is the source of all spiritual gifts and disperses them within the church as He sees fit (1 Cor. 7:7; 12:11). They are given for the common good of all believers. Within the church, Christ gives specific gifts and graces for ministering His Word to instruct and

---

12. R. C. Sproul, Ibid., 65, 66.

13. Waldron, Ibid., 417.

14. A. A. Hodge, *The Westminster Confession: A Commentary* (Edinburgh, UK: The Banner of Truth), 324.

edify the church (Rom. 12:7-8; Eph. 4:11-12). Others are granted gifts of serving, hospitality, or generosity to further profit the body (Rom. 12:6-8; 1 Cor. 12:7-10). All Christians within the church have been entrusted with spiritual gifts "according to the measure of Christ's gift" (Eph. 4:7). Thus, Christ provides the means of mutual edification, gifts and graces which strengthen the body as members share their allotment with each other.

3. The Christian's Communion Obligations to Other Christians

"... are obliged to the performance of such duties, public and private, in an orderly way, as do conduce to their mutual good, both in the inward and outward man."

The Confession now presses upon Christians their obligations to serve one another with the gifts and graces that God has bestowed upon them. It is not enough for a believer to merely possess these graciously conferred abilities. There is a divine obligation to diligently exercise them for the mutual good of the church.

Christians are not at liberty to "bury their talents." Communion does not involve coasting. If one has been given the gift of preaching, then he is obligated to preach diligently. If another has been granted the gift of teaching, then he is obliged to teach conscientiously. Likewise, those who have received gifts of service or hospitality are compelled to exercise those skills to serve their brethren (Rom. 12:8, 13). Gifts are to be regarded as God-given capabilities that must be exercised for the church's edification (Eph. 4:11-16).

The Heidelberg Catechism wonderfully addresses this point when it asks, "What do you understand by 'the communion of saints'?" The second half of the answer replies, "that everyone must know it to be his duty, readily and cheerfully to employ his gifts, for the advantage and salvation of other members."[15] Christians are to be good stewards of their gifts by being faithful to employ them within the local church (1 Pet. 4:10-11).

The gifts and graces which God has bestowed upon His people can be exercised in a variety of ways within the local church. Publicly, they may be exercised by means of the preaching and teaching of God's Word. In this way, the body is edified as a whole through exhortation or rebuke (1 Tim. 4:13; 5:20). Privately, they may be exercised by means of one-on-one admonishment, encouragement, and prayer (Rom. 1:12; 1 Thess. 5:11, 14; Eph. 4:29). Such gifts may be the means which the Lord uses to restore our brethren (Matt. 18:15; Gal. 6:1; Jam. 5:19-20). Each believer has the ability to contribute for the good of the whole church.

It is also important to note that we should not only love our brethren in "word or in tongue, but in deed and in truth" (1 John 3:18). The Confession states that Christians are to be concerned for the good of their brethren not only in reference to their souls, but also with respect to the *outward*

---

15. The Heidelberg Catechism of 1563, Q. 55.

man. This would include practical deeds of love calculated to minister to their temporal needs. Here is where the gifts of service and hospitality come into play. Through the multifaceted gifts and graces that God has given to His people, Christians are able and ready to help relieve both the inward and outward needs of their brethren.

Applications

Although many applications could be drawn from this paragraph, the first is obviously the supremacy of union with Christ; for without it there is no spiritual life and no genuine Christian fellowship. Union with Christ makes a person a Christian. Else, a person is "Christian" in name only and their interactions with others are merely social, never rising to the level of Christian communion. Union with Christ imparts spiritual life and enables shared life with other true Christians.

Second, it is imperative that each believer commits himself or herself to a local body of Christ. Union with Christ inherently unites believers with each other. Therefore, there is no option for anyone to be in union with Christ and yet abandon the local body of believers. If one is truly in union with Christ, then he is to be committed to the local church.

Paragraph 2:

We will consider this paragraph under three heads: the expressions of Christian Communion, the recipients of Christian Communion, and the limitations of Christian Communion.

1. The Expression of Christian Communion

"Saints by profession are bound to maintain a holy fellowship and communion in the worship of God..."

Christians who profess faith in the gospel are bound to preserve a *holy fellowship and communion in the worship of God.* In Scripture, God, who is majestic in holiness, is exalted as "holy, holy, holy" (Ex. 15:11; Rev. 4:8). Therefore, anyone who is to draw near to God in worship must be holy; for we are to "worship the Lord in the beauty of holiness" (Ps. 96:9). The worship of God and holy fellowship go hand-in-hand; for the Lord says, "be holy for I am holy" (Lev. 19:2; 1 Pet. 1:16). If Christian communion is to flourish in the special presence of God, then Christians are to hold fellowship in a holy manner.

"performing such other spiritual services as tend to their mutual edification; as also in relieving each other in outward things according to their several abilities, and necessities."

Those brought together in the bond of the Spirit as members of one body under Christ, are to render service for mutual edification. Expressions of Christian communion are evident when saints are rendering *spiritual and practical service* toward one another.

We are to be genuinely concerned for our brethren's spiritual needs and do what we can to alleviate them. We can serve each other spiritually by encouraging and building up one another (1 Thess. 5:11). In Hebrews 10:24, we are commanded to "consider one another in order to stir up love and good deeds." Where there is spiritual carelessness or overt patterns of sin, we are to warn each other of the dangers of backsliding. When meeting attendance is neglected, we are to exhort each other not to forsake the gathering of the local church (Heb. 10:25). This world is full of temptations which seek to draw us away from the living God. Therefore, we are to watch over one another daily, while it is called today, because of the hardening effect that sin's deceitfulness has on the heart (Heb. 3:12-13). If Christ prayed that the apostle Peter's faith would not fail, how much more do we need to pray the same for one another? (Luke 22:32; Jam. 5:16).

There are also implications for the believer who is in spiritual need. If we are distressed in spirit, we should be willing to share our inward struggles with our pastor or some other mature, trustworthy brother or sister, so they might be able to provide the spiritual service in view. The Christian life comes with many common spiritual challenges, yet how frequently are we unwilling to admit our struggles! Should we bury our burdens when the Lord has given us legitimate means to unburden our souls? Of course not! We ought, rather, cast them at the feet of Christ and confide in mature brethren who may be able to help bear those burdens with us (Gal. 6:2). In this way, communion is enhanced. For we commune in both directions; in making the need known and then in relieving it.

Christians are to also be actively concerned for the practical needs of their brethren. The Confession states, "also in relieving each other in outward things according to their several abilities, and necessities." We should seek to help our brethren materially or financially if needed. Some Christians have an abundance of the world's goods while others do not (Rev. 2:9; 3:17). Christians are not only to pray that God meets the needs of their brethren, they themselves are to also help provide relief as they are able (James 2:15-16; 1 John 3:17-18). In Acts 2:44-46, we see the members in the early church selling some of their property to help their needy brethren. As God's people, we are to demonstrate love and compassion for our brethren and remember those who suffer or who lack some of life's basic necessities. Sproul nicely summarizes the point when he writes: "The confession is developing the principle that when we see a person weeping, we weep with him or her. When someone in our fellowship is going through extreme need or want, it is the duty of the congregation to help that person."[16] As the Lord has blessed us in our need, so also must we use our gifts and abilities, whether spiritual or practical, to bless our brethren who are in need. We thus mirror His character, display His heart toward His people, and become instruments of His ministry to them.

16. Sproul, Ibid., 71.

2. The Recipients of Christian Communion

"... though especially to be exercised by them, in the relation wherein they stand, whether in families, or churches."

Some of the first recipients of a Christian's charitable deeds should be those of his own household. The Confession states, "in the relation wherein they stand, whether in families... " One who professes to believe the Gospel of Christ must also be one who provides for the needs of his own family. Anyone who willfully neglects such obligations is considered to be "denying the faith" and "worse than an unbeliever" (1 Tim. 5:7-8).

Along with concern for meeting their practical needs, we are also to be concerned for the spiritual needs of those under our roof. This has particular applicability for parents toward their children. According to Scripture, we are commanded to "bring up our children in the discipline and admonition of the Lord" (Eph. 6:4). We are to labor in making our children mindful of the things of Christ. Husbands are also to be concerned for the spiritual well-being of their wives, loving them as Christ loved the church (Eph. 5:25-26) and encouraging them with the Word of God. Such labors first practiced at home will more readily extend to relationships in the Church.

"yet, as God offereth opportunity, is to be extended to all the household of faith, even all those who in every place call upon the name of the Lord Jesus."

The Confession affirms that our charitable deeds ought to be carried outside of our family and into our local congregations. In the days of the early church, many local congregations would send financial contributions to brethren living in different regions (Acts 11:29-30; Rom. 15:25-27). What might this look like in our day? A wealthy congregation can assist a church elsewhere which cannot fully support itself. When possible, they may be able to contribute to the pastor's salary or to any other need of that flock. Such aid is especially helpful to churches in impoverished areas.

All Christians are to take part in this work. Sam Waldron writes: "In efforts of the church physically or spiritually to assist saints in the other places, the individual Christian does not have the right to stand aloof and unconcerned. According to one's ability all believers ought to be interested, concerned participants."[17] One congregation's small contribution may turn out to be a great blessing to brethren who receive it.

---

17. Waldron, Ibid., 418.

3. The Limitations of Christian Communion

"nevertheless, their communion one with another as saints, doth not take away or infringe the title or propriety which each man hath in his goods and possessions."

The Confession does highlight the limitations of Christian communion by affirming an individual's right to private property. At first glance, one might imagine that the Confession supports some form of socialism. Some may point to Acts 2:44-45 and Acts 4:32-35 as examples of communal socialism practiced within the early church. Others may highlight how early Christians "sold their possessions and goods" so that the proceeds would be divided among their brethren in order "that they [might] hold all things in common" (Acts 2:44-45). However, in Acts 5, we see through the examples of Ananias and Sapphira that none of these actions were mandated by any in the early church. When the apostle Peter questioned Ananias and Sapphira about their behavior, the apostle clearly indicated that both their property and the proceeds from its sale were under their own control, for them to use as they wished. In Acts 5:4, there is no indication that Ananias and Sapphira were compelled or forced to sell their property to the early church. Ananias and Sapphira were not condemned for withholding the proceeds but rather for their lying hypocrisy (Acts 5:8). Christian fellowship does not infringe upon an individual's right to private property.[18]

The corporate sharing in the early church in Acts 2–4 is a picture of Christians voluntarily doing what they can to meet the needs of their brethren. No one in Christ's church is forced to sell their possessions in order to hold all things in common with their brethren. Saints are only encouraged to be generous toward brethren in need as a way to show love practically to them. In this way, both the right to private property and the virtue of charity are preserved. In the churches of Christ, those who are poor are not to envy the wealth of their brethren (Ex. 20:17). On the other hand, those who are wealthy are not to hoard their goods, but rather to be generous to their brethren who are in need (1 Tim. 6:17-19).

Applications

First, God in His mercy has equipped believers with a variety of gifts to have a place within the local body.[19] When it comes to our loving service to one another, we as Christians should remember that we are to be concerned for the spiritual and practical well-being of our brethren. When our brethren are in need, we are to be quick not only to assist in spiritual matters, but also in practical and financial ones. We are to be careful not to view the variety of gifts with which God has entrusted

---

18. For a helpful online resource on this topic, I point the readers to Art Lindsley's article: *Does the Book of Acts Command Socialism?*: https://www.thegospelcoalition.org/article/does-the-book-of-acts-command-socialism/ published May 28, 2013.

19. Of course, this does not mean that we do not use our gifts more broadly in the universal church.

each of us as for our own self-interest. Rather, we are to view them as a means of building up our brethren within the church.

Second, an authentic expression of the church's communion has a direct impact on the spiritual health of the local body. Where there is self-serving and disinterest in the hardships of our brethren, there is disunity and detachment of believers. The conduct of the fellowship of believers within the local church can either glorify or shame the name of Christ. Therefore, let us glorify the Name of Christ in wholeheartedly serving one another.

CHAPTER 28

OF BAPTISM AND THE LORD'S SUPPER

JIM SAVASTIO

1. Baptism and the Lord's Supper are ordinances of positive and sovereign institution, appointed by the Lord Jesus, the only lawgiver, to be continued in his church to the end of the world.[1]

2. These holy appointments are to be administered by those only who are qualified and thereunto called, according to the commission of Christ.[2]

Chapter 28 is the briefest of the thirty-two chapters of our Confession of Faith. In many ways, it can be seen as a preparatory statement for the two chapters which follow. Even so, it is interesting to note how condensed these remarks are compared to the four, fuller paragraphs in the Confession's parent documents. Both the Westminster and the Savoy devote four fuller paragraphs that the framers of our Confession deemed unnecessary.

1. The Meaning of Ordinances
Our Confession states that baptism and the Lord's Supper are *ordinances.* The London Baptist Confession of Faith is the third in the line of the British Reformed confessions of the seventeenth century. The "grandfather" is the Westminster, the "father" is the Savoy. The other two Confessions utilize the term *sacrament* to describe baptism and the Lord's Supper. The term "sacrament" essentially means that which is sacred or set apart for religious use. In the Westminster Confession of Faith we read:

> 1. Sacraments are holy signs and seals of the covenant of grace, immediately instituted by God, to represent Christ and his benefits, and to confirm our interest in him: as also to put a visible difference between those that belong unto the Church and the rest of the world; and solemnly to engage them to the service of God in Christ, according to his Word.

---

1. Matthew 28:19, 20; 1 Corinthians 11:26
2. Matthew 28:19; 1 Corinthians 4:1

2. There is in every sacrament a spiritual relation or sacramental union, between the sign and the thing signified; whence it comes to pass that the names and the effects of the one are attributed to the other.

The authors of our Confession chose to use the term *ordinance,* which means a practice established by authority. This choice was not accidental. "Ordinance" not only emphasizes that a sacrament is *ordained* by the head of the church, but it also distances the framers of this Confession from both the seven sacraments of the Roman Catholic Church and from the dangers of sacerdotalism.

2. The Number and Identity of the Ordinances

The Roman Catholic Church established seven sacraments (baptism, confirmation, the Eucharist, penance, marriage, anointing of the sick, and holy orders). The authority behind these sacraments is not that of the Scriptures; it is the authority of the popes and councils of the Roman Catholic Church, mentioned above. A careful study of the Word of God demonstrates that Christ has authoritatively given two ordinances to be perpetuated in His churches till the end of time—baptism and the Lord's Supper. Some baptistic Confessions have added foot washing as an ordinance. This conviction is rooted in the actions and words of Jesus in John 13. However, the Lord's example demonstrated the necessity of servanthood as a mark of God's people; it was not the establishment of foot washing as an ongoing church ordinance.

The command of Jesus to baptize disciples as a part of the Great Commission (Matt. 28:18-20), a commission to be carried on till the end of the age, shows that baptism is clearly ordained by Jesus Himself. We find the same truth regarding the institution of the Lord's Supper (Matt. 26:26ff).

3. The Nature of the Ordinances

Baptism and the Lord's Supper are of a positive and sovereign institution. The term "positive" refers to that which might not necessarily be inferred from the law of nature or the perpetual moral law yet is plainly and formally instituted by our sovereign Lord. Jesus clearly commands His followers to make disciples and to baptize them. Jesus clearly commands His people to remember Him in the bread and the wine. These ordinances did not exist in these forms until the Lord Jesus commanded them to be done by His people. Though religious washings and the baptism of John existed prior to this command, Christian baptism is expressly Trinitarian and done in obedience to Jesus, and not merely as an imitation of something we see historically. There are things in the Bible which are described but are not clearly prescribed. Baptism and the Lord's Supper are prescribed.

4. The Author of the Ordinances

This truth has already been asserted, but here it is clearly laid out. The sovereign of the church is the Lord Jesus. When the church baptizes disciples and when the church takes the bread and the wine in remembering the body and blood of Jesus, they are clearly and decisively obeying the explicit commands and will of the Lord Jesus.

It was the risen Savior who commanded His servants to go among the nations with the gospel. Jesus commanded them to baptize newly made disciples and to gather them into churches for instruction in all the things that He had taught them. It is Jesus who presents the bread and the cup to His disciples. It is Jesus who lays forth the significance of the bread in relation to His body and the cup in relation to the blood of the New Covenant. If the Lord were to ask His people, "Who has asked this of you?" we can answer simply, "You have, Lord."

5. The Sphere of the Ordinances
This is the most offensive element of the Confession to many modern evangelicals. This is due to a fundamental misunderstanding and lack of appreciation for biblical ecclesiology. It is common for modern evangelicals to misuse the words of Jesus in Matthew 18:20 which states, "For where two or three are gathered together in My name, I am there in the midst of them." It is not uncommon to hear a group of believers gathering together for any purpose at all to declare, "We are the church." In such a setting, it is not, therefore, uncommon for believers to partake of the Lord's Supper in a conference context or even casually when they are meeting together for fellowship. It is this view that often promotes a spontaneous baptism service or the baptism of a believer outside of the context of the gathered church with little to no connection between the one baptized and a local organized body of believers.

6. The Duration of the Ordinances
To date, churches have been celebrating baptism and the Lord's Supper for some two thousand years. The Word of God tells us that both institutions of Christ will endure till the end of the age.

We read at the conclusion of Matthew's gospel these words of the Savior: "All authority has been given to Me in heaven and on earth. Go therefore and make disciples of all the nations, baptizing them in the name of the Father and of the Son and of the Holy Spirit, teaching them to observe all things that I have commanded you; and lo, I am with you always, even to the end of the age. Amen" (Matt. 28:18-20). The duration of baptism is tied together with the evangelistic labors of the church and the presence of Christ with those laborers "even to the end of the age." We find a similar statement made by Paul concerning the Lord's Supper: "For as often as you eat this bread and drink this cup, you proclaim the Lord's death till He comes" (1 Cor. 11:26).

There is coming a day when there will be no need for baptisms to celebrate the new life that a believer has been given in Christ. There will be no need for baptism because there is coming a day when the last of the elect will be called by the gospel. There is coming a day when the day of grace will be over. We are exhorted to labor while it is called "today."

The apostle urges people to be reconciled to God "now" because "today is the day of salvation." One day the last gospel plea will be made and embraced. In the words of Luke 13:25, the master of the house will arise and shut the door. Just as the door to the ark was closed on a day of sovereign appointment, so too the open door of gospel invitation will one day be shut.

The Lord's Supper will also come to an end. Whenever the body of Christ (His gathered local church) takes the bread and the cup, they are called upon to "remember" His person and work on the cross. These elements offered in the supper are a means of grace to point the faith of the believer back to the reality and hope of their salvation. But this ordinance is held by the believer only "till He (Christ) comes." The reason why there will be no Lord's Supper following the second coming of Christ is that our "faith will be made sight." A man may gaze at a photo of his wife while they are parted from one another, but he does not gaze at the photo when they are together. There is coming a day when "every eye" will see him. There is coming a time when we will "ever be with the Lord" and the need for remembering what we are prone to forget will no longer be necessary.

7. The Administration of the Ordinances

Here, we find differences with the Westminster Confession of Faith and the Savoy Declaration as well as with the First London Confession of 1644. In the previous Baptist Confession, we read these words: "The persons designed by Christ, to dispense this ordinance, the Scriptures hold forth to be a preaching Disciple, it being nowhere tied to a particular church, officer, or person extraordinarily sent, the commission enjoining the administration, being given to them under no other consideration, but as considered Disciples."

The Westminster Confession and the Savoy Declaration say this about the ones who administer the sacraments:

> The grace which is exhibited in or by the sacraments, rightly used, is not conferred by any power in them; neither doth the efficacy of a sacrament depend upon the piety or intention of him that doth administer it, but upon the work of the Spirit, and the word of institution, which contains, together with a precept authorizing the use thereof, a promise of benefit to worthy receivers.

Having said that, the Confession continues in the next paragraph:

> There be only two sacraments ordained by Christ our Lord in the Gospel, that is to say, Baptism and the Supper of the Lord: neither of which may be dispensed by any but by a minister of the Word lawfully ordained...

The framers of the Westminster Confession of Faith and the Savoy Declaration clearly believed that only an ordained gospel minister was to perform baptisms and lead in the celebration of the Lord's Supper. The first London Confession indicates that a "preaching disciple" is fit to oversee the ordinances. The 1689 seeks to stride between the two in saying, "These holy appointments are to be administered by those only who are qualified and thereunto called, according to the commission of Christ."

This language begs the question: To whom do the framers refer? It would seem to refer to pastors or elders. The use of "qualified" and "called" seems to indicate someone other than an indiscriminate man in the church. There are explicit qualifications for those who would attain the office of an elder, a task to which they must be called—inwardly by Christ and outwardly by the local church. This raises the question of churches that have no such officers. Can a church without an elder conduct baptisms and enjoy the regular observance of the Supper? Is baptism only valid if done in the church and by a pastor? Must a church forego the blessings and benefits of the Lord's Supper until such time as the head of the church is pleased to grant overseers? These questions can be difficult to deal with in a real-world situation. Are the ordinances given to the church or to the elders of the church? If given to the church, then it would seem reasonable that a church without an established eldership could appoint men whom they deemed to be fit and qualified to lead the members in these ordinances. Churches without qualified leadership should make the pursuit of qualified men a priority. It is often wise and prudent to seek the aid of a like-minded church to help in the administration of baptism and the Lord's Supper until such men are appointed in such congregations.

CHAPTER 29

OF BAPTISM

JIM SAVASTIO AND MIKE RENIHAN

1. Baptism is an ordinance of the New Testament, ordained by Jesus Christ, to be unto the party baptized, a sign of his fellowship with Him, in His death and resurrection; of His being engrafted into him;[1] of remission of sins;[2] and of giving up into God, through Jesus Christ, to live and walk in newness of life.[3]

2. Those who do actually profess repentance towards God, faith in, and obedience to, our Lord Jesus Christ, are the only proper subjects of this ordinance.[4]

3. The outward element to be used in this ordinance is water, wherein the party is to be baptized, in the name of the Father, and of the Son, and of the Holy Spirit.[5]

4. Immersion, or dipping of the person in water, is necessary to the due administration of this ordinance.[6]

In 1644, the first London Baptist Confession of Faith was published. Two years later, the Westminster Confession of Faith was presented to the world. Some twelve years later, the latter document would be modified and published by a group of Congregationalists in England as the Savoy Declaration. It was in response to the Westminster and the Savoy that the Baptists brought forth a new, second London Baptist Confession in 1677. Due to political pressures and persecution, it would take another

---

1. Romans 6:3-5; Colossians 2; 12; Galatians 3:27
2. Mark 1:4; Acts 22:16
3. Romans 6:4
4. Mark 16:16; Acts 8:36-37; Acts 2:41; Acts 8:12; Acts 18:8
5. Matthew 28:19, 20; Acts 8:38
6. Matthew 3:16; John 3:23

twelve years before it would be published and gain its shortened name, "the 1689."

A comparative study of the Westminster, the Savoy, and the Second London Confession of Faith demonstrates the general unity that existed doctrinally among the Reformed Churches. In fact, the authors of the 1689 wrote in the appendix:

> Whosoever reads, and impartially considers what we have in our forgoing confession declared, may readily perceive, that we do not only concenter with all other true Christians on the Word of God (revealed in the Scriptures of truth) as the foundation and rule of our faith and worship. But that we have also industriously endeavored to manifest, that in the fundamental Articles of Christianity we mind the same things and have therefore expressed our belief in the same words, that have on the like occasion been spoken by other societies of Christians before us.

This agreement shared by Presbyterians, Congregationalists, and Baptists was clearly and confessionally demonstrated in the great unity displayed across a vast array of topics as expressed in their Confessions of Faith. While the Savoy modified certain aspects of the Westminster, the two were in substantial agreement in the matter of baptism. It is preeminently in the chapter now under consideration that the Baptists stamped their unique contribution to their Confession.

It is interesting to note in light of their departure from the two previous Confessions that this chapter is more succinct in its declarations concerning the meaning, recipients, and mode of Christian baptism. This may be due to the fact that the arguments for believers' baptism by immersion appear to be more straightforward and on the surface of the text. Most paedobaptists will admit that their conclusions regarding infants being baptized are based upon a more multipart series of arguments which they think is essential for tying the sacraments in the two testaments more tightly together.

The point of this chapter is not primarily to refute paedobaptism. That will be done by way of necessity, but it is not the burden of this chapter. Our desire in our exposition of this chapter is to give a defense and explanation of "credo baptism" or "believers' baptism" as rooted in the Bible and the explanatory statements of our Particular Baptist forefathers.

The authors of our Confession and of this chapter hold their Presbyterian and Reformed brethren who differ with them in high esteem. We are thankful for the great contributions of pastors, past and present, who differ with us fundamentally on these issues. However, for us, we are convinced that a thorough investigation of the relevant biblical material supports the 1689's doctrine of believer's baptism (just as the paedobaptists feel equally convinced about the 1640's doctrine of infant baptism as presented in the Westminster Confession and catechisms).

In working through the material, we will consider five matters for analysis:

Paragraph 1: The Origin and Meaning of Baptism

"Baptism is an ordinance of the New Testament, ordained by Jesus Christ, to be unto the party baptized, a sign of his fellowship with Him, in His death and resurrection; of his being engrafted into Him; of remission of sins; and of giving up into God, through Jesus Christ, to live and walk in newness of life."

1. The Origin of Baptism

There was a time in history when Christian baptisms began to occur. While there were among Old Covenant Jews various rituals involving water and washing, it was not until the arrival of John the Baptist that we begin to read about baptism. The baptism under discussion in this chapter is not the baptism associated with John, but rather that "ordained by Jesus Christ" and especially His post-resurrection command given to His disciples.[7]

Soon after our Lord began His public ministry, His disciples began baptizing other disciples in association with Jesus Himself. John had proclaimed Christ to be "the Lamb of God who takes away the sin of the world" (John 1:29). These disciples were not merely expressing repentance and hope in the coming kingdom of God, but they were expressing their belief that this Jesus of Nazareth was the long-promised Messiah. We read about this in John 4:1, 2: "Therefore, when the Lord knew that the Pharisees had heard that Jesus made and baptized more disciples than John (though Jesus Himself did not baptize, but His disciples)."

The baptisms we perform and celebrate today are rooted in the clear command of Jesus found in what we commonly call the Great Commission. These are our Lord's words in that commission:

> And Jesus came and spoke to them, saying, All authority has been given to Me in heaven and on earth. Go therefore and make disciples of all the nations, baptizing them in the name of the Father and of the Son and of the Holy Spirit, teaching them to observe all things that I have commanded you; and lo, I am with you always, even to the end of the age (Matt. 28:18-20).

Here, we find the risen Christ commanding His apostles to take the message of the gospel to all the nations. This command is rooted in the authority of the Son of God over the nations. The act of baptism is to be done in obedience to a command given by the Lord Jesus Christ to His disciples. It is to be practiced until the end of the age. Jesus is the Lord of His spiritual kingdom on the earth. He has the right to insist on His will. The command consists of the church going to the nations and making disciples. What was to be done with these new disciples? Two things are articulated. The first is to baptize them in the name of the Father, the Son, and the Holy Spirit (Matt. 28:19). Second, His disciples were to instruct these new converts in all the commandments of the Lord Jesus (v. 20). It

---

7. See The Antecedents of Christian Baptism in *Baptism In The New Testament* by G.R. Beasley-Murray, (Eerdmans, 1973), Chapter One.

is in obedience to this commission that we find the apostles and disciples of Jesus baptizing those who had come to faith in Christ.

The first example is found in Acts 2. After Peter had preached to the multitudes gathered for the feast of Pentecost, there was a wonderful response granted by the power of the Holy Spirit. We read in verse 41, "Then those who gladly received his word were baptized; and that day about three thousand souls were added *to them.*" There was an embrace of the message (faith expressed in it) followed by water baptism. These new converts joined the other disciples. This pattern of preaching, response, and baptism is repeated throughout the book of Acts.

Acts 8 gives two accounts of baptisms among new converts. The first being found in verse 12: "But when they believed Philip as he preached the things concerning the kingdom of God and the name of Jesus Christ, both men and women were baptized." The second is the record of the conversion and baptism of the eunuch from Ethiopia (Acts 8:27-40).

Chapter 9 records the conversion and baptism of Saul of Tarsus (Acts 9:18), and Chapter 10 showcases the beginning of the work of God among the Gentiles with the conversion of Cornelius and his family along with their baptisms (vv. 44-48). We see further instances of baptisms in Acts 16 wherein Luke recounts the saving work of Christ in Lydia and the Philippian jailer along with their households (vv. 11-15, 31-34). We read in Acts 18:8, that "Crispus the ruler of the synagogue, believed on the Lord with all his household. And many of the Corinthians, hearing, believed and were baptized."

Christian baptism, then, is rooted in the revelation of the New Testament and is done in obedience to the clear command of the Lord Jesus Christ. Both the Westminster and Savoy state the same truth in their first paragraphs. Their justification for infant baptism, however, is not rooted in the New Testament teaching, nor in a clear command of Jesus, nor in the pattern of the book Acts, but rather in the ancient Jewish practice of circumcision and the covenant God made with Abraham and his seed.[8]

The Baptists, in contrast to this, were standing on solid ground in teaching that the rite of baptism was rooted firmly in the New Covenant and performed in strict obedience to the command of Jesus to baptize "disciples."

2. The Meaning of Baptism

"...to be unto the party baptized, a sign (given by God which points to the spiritual reality) of his fellowship with Him, in hHis death and resurrection; of his being engrafted into Him; of remission of sins; and of giving up into God, through Jesus Christ, to live and walk in newness of life."

---

8. This connection is one which no New Testament writer clearly makes, or uses to teach infant baptism.

The primary meaning and significance of baptism is set forth in personal terms. It is "unto the party baptized." There is also in Scripture a corporate nature to baptism, showing union with the people of God (Acts 2:40-47). Baptism is a gateway into the fellowship of the local church, but this reality is not the emphasis of this chapter.

It is interesting to note here that the Westminster and Savoy say essentially the same thing. The Savoy states in its first paragraph:

> Baptism is a sacrament of the New Testament, ordained by Jesus Christ to be unto the party baptized a sign and seal of the covenant of grace, of his ingrafting into Christ, of regeneration, of remission of sins, and of his giving up unto God through Jesus Christ to walk in newness of life; which ordinance is by Christ's own appointment to be continued in his Church until the end of the world.

There are at least four things highlighted about the meaning of baptism from our Confession: (1) It is a sign to the one being baptized of their fellowship with the Lord Jesus; (2) It is a sign to the one being baptized of their union with Christ in His death and resurrection; (3) It is a sign to the one being baptized that they have had their sins forgiven; (4) It is a sign to the one being baptized that declares their determination to walk in newness of life.

First, baptism is a sign of fellowship with the Lord Jesus. Baptism is associated with the person and work of Christ. It is "Christian baptism" ordained by Jesus and done *in* obedience to Jesus. Baptists root their practice (as best they can) in the reality of one's possession of salvation, while the paedobaptist practice of baptism is performed in hope of a future embrace of the faith. However, scripturally speaking, there can be no baptizing of an individual apart from a saving connection with Jesus. Baptism is a sign of one's discipleship to the Lord. To be a disciple is to be a follower of Jesus. It is the preeminent commitment of the heart and soul to the person of Christ (cf. Luke 14:26).

Second, baptism is a sign of union with Christ in His death and resurrection. Paul says to the believers at Rome, in Romans 6:3-5:

> Or do you not know that as many of us as were baptized into Christ Jesus were baptized into His death? Therefore we were buried with Him through baptism into death, that just as Christ was raised from the dead by the glory of the Father, even so we also should walk in newness of life. For if we have been united together in the likeness of His death, certainly we also shall be in *the likeness* of His resurrection.

Many people see an open parable in the manner of baptism. In that act of immersion, the party being baptized is literally plunged beneath the waters and then lifted from the waters. The plunging into the waters is a picture of the believer's death to his old self and union with Christ in His death. The rising from the water is a portrait of new, resurrected life.

The third aspect of baptism is a sign of the forgiveness of sins. This is clear from several passages of Scripture. In fact, the statements at times are so vivid that the sign and the thing signified are sometimes conflated into one, leading some to the grievous error of baptismal regeneration. In Acts 2:38, Peter declares, "Repent, and let every one of you be baptized in the name of Jesus Christ for[9] [or with a view to] the remission of sins;[10] and you shall receive the gift of the Holy Spirit." Paul uses this language of cleansing in association with his own baptism, recounting in Acts 22:16: "And now why are you waiting? Arise and be baptized, and wash away your sins, calling on the name of the Lord."[11]

The fourth aspect associated with baptism for the person undergoing it is that it is a sign declaring their determination to follow Christ as a life-long disciple. In a real sense, believers are declaring in the waters, "I now belong to Jesus! I am His disciple. I will go where He tells me to go and be what He calls me to be!" This is the practical outworking of discipleship. Jesus asked, "Why do you call Me, 'Lord, Lord,' and do not do the things I say?" (Luke 6:46). As we have quoted earlier from Romans 6:4, baptism is a sign of "newness of life." The one coming to Christ has become a new creation. Old things have passed away and new things have come (2 Cor. 5:17).

One way to incorporate these truths can be in the actual baptism ceremony itself. When the candidate for baptism comes forward, a series of questions can be asked to highlight these truths. For instance, the pastor may ask, "Are you declaring today that you are a sinner who was on their way to hell?" "Is your hope of eternal life and peace with God in Jesus alone?" "Is it your testimony that having come to Christ, you now enjoy the blessedness of forgiveness and peace with God?" "Is it your determination to follow the Lord Jesus in obedience all the days of your life?"

Paragraph 2: The Proper Recipients of Baptism

"Those who do actually profess repentance towards God, faith in, and obedience to, our Lord Jesus Christ, are the only proper subjects of this ordinance."

This is a core matter that divides Reformed Baptists from many of their other Reformed brethren. Interestingly, it is not so much *the meaning* of baptism as it is *the recipients* and to a lesser degree *the proper mode* of baptism which does this. While paedobaptists happily recognize the need to "baptize" new believers without a Christian background upon a profession of faith, they assert clearly, "Not only those that do actually profess faith in and obedience unto Christ, but also the infants of one or both believing parents are to be baptised, and those only" (WCF 28:4).

---

9. The Greek preposition *eis* is best understood like this.

10. Acts 3:19 makes it clear that the remission of sins is connected to the repenting of them, not baptism.

11. It is clear from the Greek text that the "washing away of one's sins" is connected to "calling on the name of the Lord," and not with the baptism.

Baptists, however, cannot agree with this because they do not see this practice in their Bibles. As it has already been demonstrated, baptism is an ordinance of the New Covenant and rooted in obedience to the command of Christ. These matters, along with a proper exposition of the relevant historical passages, coupled with the actual meaning of baptism itself, is why Baptists say, "only those who actually profess faith in Christ [or have a credible profession of faith] are the proper recipients of baptism."

But it should be first asked, "What is meant by a 'credible' profession?" Two primary characteristics must be present. The first is an understanding of the gospel and the second is an ability to convey one's testimony of faith in Christ. What does this person profess to believe? Who is Jesus to them? Are they hoping and trusting in their works or in Christ alone? Have they cried out to Him in faith? Is there evidence of new life? New birth? New desires? A break with sin and a commitment to holiness? A love for and commitment to the gathering of God's people?

Second, it should be asked, "Why do Baptists insist on only baptizing those who make a credible profession of faith?"

The first reason is that Jesus commanded that disciples, and only disciples, be baptized, as was mentioned earlier. If baptism is an ordinance of the New Testament and if Jesus is the founder of baptism, then we must look to His words and commands regarding whom to baptize. Throughout His ministry, Jesus defined who and what He meant by the term "disciple." They are those who found Him to be the pearl of great price (Matt 13:46). They are those who have counted the cost and counted their lives and other relationships as nothing compared to their love to Him (Luke 14:27ff). They have denied themselves and taken up their cross and followed Him (Matt. 10:38).

The second reason is that we see a pattern in the New Testament, especially in the book of Acts. In the book of Acts, faith always precedes baptism. This is well summarized by the words of Luke in Acts 2, "Then those who gladly received his word were baptized...." (v. 41).

The final consideration for only baptizing one with a credible profession of faith is to be seen in the essence of baptism itself. What does baptism signify to the person being baptized? It is that they have had their sins forgiven, that they are in union with Christ, and that they have determined to walk in newness of life. These truths are not a sign *prospectively* of the one being baptized, rather they are a sign *actually* of the baptismal candidate.

Paragraph 3: The Element and Proper Formula of Baptism

"The outward element to be used in this ordinance is water, wherein the party is to be baptized, in the name of the Father, and of the Son, and of the Holy Spirit."

The first matter here is obvious: baptism utilizes water. The first description of baptism in the Bible shows that it was done in the Jordan

River (cf. Matt. 3:6). Water is the element used for cleansing, and when done by immersion, baptism clearly symbolizes cleansing, burial, and resurrection. The more controversial matter stated here is in relation to the baptismal formula itself.

The command of Jesus is to baptize disciples in "the name of the Father and of the Son and of the Holy Spirit." This is the Trinitarian formula for baptism, and it shows that the union expressed in baptism is with the Father and the Spirit as well as with the Son. The Father planned our salvation, the Son accomplished our salvation, and the Holy Spirit applied our salvation. When we are saved, we are in union with the Godhead and our baptism celebrates and depicts this fact.

There is a controversy though, which arises from the fact that we have Peter telling his audience in Acts 2 to be baptized "in the name of Jesus." This is repeated in Acts 18:13 and 19:5. You could add to this the phrase that Paul uses in Romans 6:3 that we are baptized "into Christ." There are sects of Christians who boast of baptism in "Jesus' name" only.

Must we, who administer baptism, verbally recite the words "in the name of the Father and of the Son and of the Holy Spirit" or is it permissible to use the verbal shorthand "In the name of Jesus?" The primary meaning of "in the name of Jesus" is "in or under the authority of Jesus" or "in obedience to Jesus" or "in association with Jesus." When submerging the new disciple into the water, it is a long-standing tradition amongst Baptists and Reformed believers to utilize the literal formula containing the words of the Lord Jesus found in Matthew 28. This is how we baptize "in Jesus' name." It is in obedience to the words of Jesus that baptism is properly done.

Paragraph 4: The Proper Mode of Baptism

"Immersion, or dipping of the person in water, is necessary to the due administration of this ordinance."

This statement is in direct response to the Westminster and the Savoy. In those documents we read, "Dipping of the person into the water *is not necessary*; but baptism is rightly administered by pouring or sprinkling water upon the person."

Why the difference and does it really matter? We believe that it can be argued that this is the least matter of concern regarding baptism. Who and why a person is baptized coupled with the meaning of the ritual is our primary concern. There are times, when in the actual act of baptism, a portion of the body may not be fully submerged (the head may not go all the way under or the hand may stay above the water, etc.). A full immersion may not be possible in the case of an invalid or an elderly person. The writers responsible for the Didache (an early church document dated from the first century, describing church life and practice) allowed for pouring if living or running water was unavailable.

Nevertheless, we affirm as Baptists the necessity of immersion on the basis of three primary realities.

The first is the clear meaning of the word *baptizo*. Words matter to us. We who hold to a biblical doctrine of inspiration assert that the very words of Scripture and all the words of Scripture are inspired by God. There are words in the Greek language that convey sprinkling or pouring. These words are not utilized in association with Christian baptism. In the Septuagint (the Greek translation of the Hebrew Old Testament), we find the words for dipping and sprinkling used in the same passage (cf. Leviticus 4:6: "The priest shall dip his finger in the blood and sprinkle some of the blood seven times before the Lord, in front of the veil of the sanctuary"). The word translated "dip" is associated with the word baptism and the word for "sprinkle" is associated with the word from which we get our English word "rain." The clear definition in any Greek Lexicon or dictionary will show that the word given by the Spirit through the writers of the Scripture carries the meaning of dipping or immersing. It was a word used for the dyeing of materials and even of sunken ships. Even when the word is used metaphorically as in Luke 12:50, "I have a baptism to be baptized with…," it shows that immersion or plunging is in view.

The second argument for immersion is found in what we can determine from the actual baptisms performed in the New Testament. Though less conclusive than the first argument, we do find it recorded in Matthew 3:16 that Jesus "came out of the water." The same sort of language is used in Acts 8:39 speaking of the baptism of the Ethiopian: "they came up out of the water."

The final argument is that of meaning—especially the symbolic meaning of cleansing and of resurrection. The plunging of the body into water properly showcases the nature of the provision of the cleansing blood of Jesus and the body rising from the waters is a vivid picture of the believer's resurrection in Christ (Rom. 6:4-5).

Conclusion

This chapter of the Confession demonstrates the determination of the seventeenth-century Baptists to be what some have called "thorough Reformers." While affirming their fellowship with those who differ from them, our Baptist forefathers could see no way around the clear teaching of Jesus regarding the subjects, meaning, and mode of baptism. We who stand in their tradition can likewise express our great appreciation for the labors of our paedobaptist brethren. However, we ought not to be ashamed in any degree for differing with them on this vital issue. If we are going to be those who truly believe as our Confession states that "The Holy Scripture is the *only sufficient, certain, and infallible rule of all saving knowledge, and faith and obedience*," then we feel that we can hold to no other position (every bit as strongly as our paedobaptist friends do).

We must remember that the emphasis of this chapter is an exhortation to respond properly and joyfully to the work and the Word of Jesus in the lives of His saved people, and not to attack infant baptism. There would be no baptisms if Jesus Christ were not seeking and saving that which is lost. There would be no baptisms unless the Son of God had died for sinners. The reason we have baptisms is that Jesus Christ is building His church. This means that we are seeing evidence of His saving work among us and the beginning of His sanctifying work in the lives of His redeemed people by the Word and His Spirit.

May the Lord Jesus so bless the ministry of the Word in our churches that we will regularly turn to this chapter in our Confession when preparing a new disciple to obey our Lord in all that He has commanded.[12]

---

12. For further reading, I recommend: Paul K. Jewett, *Infant Baptism and the Covenant of Grace*, (Grand Rapids: Eerdmans, 1978); Jeffery D. Johnson, *The Fatal Flaw*, (Free Grace Press, Conway, AK 2017); Mike Renihan, *Antipaedobaptism in the thought of John Tombes*, (B and R Press, Auburn, MA, 2001); David Kingdon, *Children of Abraham*, (Carey Publications, 1973); Fred Malone, *The Baptism of Disciples Alone*, (Cape Coral, FL: Founders Press, 2003).

CHAPTER 30

OF THE LORD'S SUPPER

DAVE CHANSKI

1. The supper of the Lord Jesus was instituted by Him the same night wherein He was betrayed, to be observed in his churches, unto the end of the world, for the perpetual remembrance, and shewing forth the sacrifice of himself in His death,[1] confirmation of the faith of believers in all the benefits thereof, their spiritual nourishment, and growth in Him, their further engagement in, and to all duties which they owe to Him; and to be a bond and pledge of their communion with Him, and with each other.[2]

2. In this ordinance, Christ is not offered up to His Father, nor any real sacrifice made at all for remission of sin of the quick or dead, but only a memorial of that one offering up of Himself by Himself upon the cross, once for all;[3] and a spiritual oblation of all possible praise unto God for the same.[4] So that the popish sacrifice of the mass, as they call it, is most abominable, injurious to Christ's own sacrifice the alone propitiation for all the sins of the elect.

3. The Lord Jesus hath, in this ordinance, appointed His ministers to pray, and bless the elements of bread and wine, and thereby to set them apart from a common to a holy use, and to take and break the bread; to take the cup, and, they communicating also themselves, to give both to the communicants.[5]

4. The denial of the cup to the people, worshiping the elements, the lifting them up, or carrying them about for adoration, and reserving

---

1. 1 Corinthians 11:23-26
2. 1 Corinthians 10:16-17, 21
3. Hebrews 9:25-26, 28
4. 1 Corinthians 11:24; Matthew 26:26-27
5. 1 Corinthians 11:23-26, etc.

them for any pretended religious use, are all contrary to the nature of this ordinance, and to the institution of Christ.[6]

5. The outward elements in this ordinance, duly set apart to the use ordained by Christ, have such relation to Him crucified, as that truly, although in terms used figuratively, they are sometimes called by the names of the things they represent, to wit, the body and blood of Christ,[7] albeit, in substance and nature, they still remain truly and only bread and wine, as they were before.[8]

6. That doctrine which maintains a change of the substance of bread and wine, into the substance of Christ's body and blood, commonly called transubstantiation, by consecration of a priest, or by any other way, is repugnant not to Scripture alone,[9] but even to common sense and reason, overthroweth the nature of the ordinance, and hath been, and is, the cause of manifold superstitions, yea, of gross idolatries.[10]

7. Worthy receivers, outwardly partaking of the visible elements in this ordinance, do then also inwardly by faith, really and indeed, yet not carnally and corporally, but spiritually receive, and feed upon Christ crucified, and all the benefits of His death; the body and blood of Christ being then not corporally or carnally, but spiritually present to the faith of believers in that ordinance, as the elements themselves are to their outward senses.[11]

8. All ignorant and ungodly persons, as they are unfit to enjoy communion with Christ, so are they unworthy of the Lord's table, and cannot, without great sin against Him, while they remain such, partake of these holy mysteries, or be admitted thereunto;[12] yea, whosoever shall receive unworthily, are guilty of the body and blood of the Lord, eating and drinking judgment to themselves.[13]

History and mystery. These are two significant words related to the subject of the Lord's Supper. *History* is important because, while there are only a few Scripture texts on this subject, there is a lengthy history of theological controversy and debate surrounding it. Therefore, engagement with historical theology is vital in order to reach an understanding of the teaching of God's Word regarding this sacrament. We will notice

6. Matthew 26:26-28; Matthew 15:9; Exodus 20:4-5
7. 1 Corinthians 11:27
8. 1 Corinthians 11:26-28
9. Acts 3:21; Luke 14:6, 39
10. 1 Corinthians 11:24-25
11. 1 Corinthians 10:16; 1 Corinthians 11:23-26
12. 2 Corinthians 6:14-15
13. 1 Corinthians 11:29; Matthew 7:6

that much of that history is reflected in the language of this chapter of the Confession.

Mystery has also been an integral part of the doctrine of the Lord's Supper since the early centuries of the church. Mystery clouds much of the thinking of even faithful and mature Christians regarding this matter. Consequently, the more we come to a clear understanding of the Bible's teaching on this sacrament, the more the clouds of mystery will dissipate, and the more we will benefit from this symbolic, gospel ordinance.

1. The Institution and Purposes of the Lord's Supper (Paragraph 1)

1. Institution of the Lord's Supper

The opening part of paragraph 1 restates what is asserted in paragraph 1 of Chapter 28, which reads: *"Baptism and the Lord's Supper are ordinances of positive and sovereign institution, appointed by the Lord Jesus, the only lawgiver, to be continued in His church to the end of the world."* Notice four particulars regarding the institution of the Lord's Supper:

1. Author: "the Lord Jesus." The author, or founder, of the Lord's Supper is Christ, the Eternal Son of God and the head of the Church (Eph. 1:22). It was His absolute right to establish this memorial ordinance, and He did so as an act of gracious condescension to His church. Reformed theology places greater emphasis upon what *God* does in the Lord's Supper than upon what *we* do. That emphasis is biblical, and it begins with the institution of the Lord's Supper by the Lord Himself, for He alone has the right to enact such "orders" for the worship of His church.

2. Time: "the same night wherein He was betrayed." The words here echo the words of Paul in 1 Corinthians 11:23: "The supper of the Lord Jesus was instituted by Him the same night wherein He was betrayed." On that night, less than twenty-four hours before His body would be broken and His blood spilled out for His people, our Lord uttered the words theologians have called the "words of institution" of the Lord's Supper: "This is My body;" "This is My blood." For us, these words point back to the cross and all that led up to it; while, for the apostles, on that night, they pointed ahead to the cross.

3. Beneficiaries or Receivers: "the churches." The word "beneficiaries" means "those who benefit from something," and in the case of the Lord's Supper, the beneficiaries are obviously Christ's people: the church. We may also refer to the beneficiaries as the "receivers" of this ordinance, reflecting Paul's words in 1 Corinthians 11:23: "For I received from the Lord that which I also *delivered* to you."

The Particular Baptists followed the wording of the Congregationalists in the Savoy Declaration by making the word "church" plural ("in the church*es*") as a distinction from the singular in the Westminster Confession. This reflects the Baptists' and Congregationalists' shared emphasis on "particular" churches and their "independence" (see Chapter 26).

The Confession's wording, therefore, reflects the fact that Scripture teaches that the Lord's Supper, like baptism, is a church ordinance. Unlike prayer and reading of the Bible, it is not an element of worship that can form a part of Christian fellowship in just any setting. It is to be observed "in the churches," that is, when the church has gathered together for worship (see 1 Cor. 11:18, 20, 23).

One practical implication of this teaching is that the Lord's Supper, as a rule, is to be restricted to the normal worship services of the church, as opposed to the common Roman Catholic practice of distributing "Holy Communion," or the "Eucharist," in private homes, hospitals, or nursing homes.

4. *Duration: "unto the end of the world."* The Quakers, while not denying that Jesus gave the Lord's Supper to His church, have taught that the ordinances of baptism and the Lord's Supper were not intended to be observed continuously throughout this age. They claim that the ordinances were concessions to the infant church during the period of transition from the types and shadows of the Old Covenant to the pure spiritual worship of the New Testament. Such thinking betrays a blindness to the church's weak condition and true needs. It also demonstrates an unsubmissive attitude toward the Word of God which makes it clear that we are to continue to observe this Supper until Jesus comes again. It is to be a "perpetual remembrance" of our Lord in His death.

2. Purposes of the Lord's Supper

1. Remembrance of "the Sacrifice of Himself"

The first purpose of the Lord's Supper asserted in the Confession is *"for the perpetual remembrance... [of] the sacrifice of [Christ] in His death."* When Jesus instituted the Supper, He directed the apostles, and us through them, to observe it "in remembrance of Me" (Luke 22:19; 1 Cor. 11:24-25). In the Lord's Supper, the focus of our mental, emotional, volitional, and spiritual powers is to be upon Christ Himself ("in remembrance of *Me*"), and upon Him particularly in His death for us (*"for the perpetual remembrance ... [of] the sacrifice of Himself in His death"*). The symbolism of the bread and the cup points us to the death of our Lord. His body was "broken" and "given" for us (Luke 22:19; 1 Cor. 11:24); His blood was "shed" for us (Luke 22:20); when we eat and drink, we "proclaim the Lord's *death*" (1 Cor. 11:26).

The bread and the wine, representing the body and blood of Jesus, are not merely intended to remind us that Jesus Christ was a real man with flesh and blood. They are to remind us of the fact that He laid down His true humanity in a once-for-all sacrifice to deliver us from our sins. We are to *remember* historical facts, historical realities—a God-man who walked the face of this earth in Palestine; events that occurred in His life, culminating on a Roman cross at Golgotha. The gospel message, pictured so simply in the Lord's Supper, is rooted in things that truly happened, particularly the incarnation and the suffering of the sinless Son of God. We are to remember *Him*, in His *death*.

Although we may think of remembering as primarily an activity of the mind, our process of remembering is not to be a mere academic or intellectual exercise. It is indeed that, but it is to be far more than that. It is to be a remembering that grips our souls. We might observe a monument in a park or an exhibit in a museum and say, "I remember that from history class," and then simply move on to the next exhibit. We are not to remember Jesus' death in that way. We are to remember Him in a way that stirs us in the inner man to love our Savior more and moves us to serve Him more wholeheartedly. We are to remember Him the way an American soldier fighting in the Mexican-American War would "remember the Alamo," or a Marine fighting in the Pacific Theater during World War II would "remember Pearl Harbor."

Furthermore, our remembering is an exercise of *faith*. When prompted by the symbolism of the bread and the cup, we look upon our Lord in His death, it is an act of faith—an affirmation of all we believe about Christ's death and an appropriation of all that is in Christ. This assumes that we are intellectually and spiritually engaged. We are not simply going through the motions or presuming upon the grace of God in a way that someone might who views the Lord's Supper through the Roman Catholic doctrine of *ex opere operato* (the idea that a sacrament imparts grace simply by virtue of its having been performed, whether the recipient is exercising faith or not).

We must exert ourselves spiritually in order to profit from the Lord's Supper, but this does not obscure the fact that the ordinance is a means of grace—that is, one of "the delivery systems God has instituted to bring grace"[14] (see Chapter 14, paragraph 1). This means that God has committed Himself to making this ordinance a means by which we experience spiritual communion with Jesus Christ and receive every blessing that He died to obtain on our behalf. As Calvin wrote regarding the Lord's Supper:

> There can be no doubt that God grants within us by His Spirit that which the sacraments figure [symbolize] to our eyes and the other senses. That is: that we may receive Christ, as the fountain of all good, both that we may be reconciled to God by means of His death and renewed by the Spirit to holiness of life, and that we may obtain righteousness and finally salvation.[15]

As already noted, this remembrance is to be "perpetual." The church is to remember her Lord "until He comes." Remembering our Lord in this symbolic way is an act of solemn worship in which we are to engage

---

14. Richard Barcellos, *The Lord's Supper as a Means of Grace: More than a Memory* (Fearn, Ross-shire, Scotland: Christian Focus Publications, 2013), 23.

15. Consensus Tigurinus in James T. Dennison, Jr., Editor, *Reformed Confessions of the 16th and 17th Centuries in English Translation: Volume 1, 1523-1552* (Grand Rapids: Reformation Heritage Books, 2008), 540-41.

throughout the entirety of this age. It is a means of grace that God has ordained for our good. It is a means that is perfectly suited to our needs, since we are physical creatures who, even in the New Covenant, benefit from a tangible, visible element of worship (Ps. 103:13-14). And this element is ordained by our God to bring Jesus Christ and His saving work regularly before us.

2. Shewing Forth of the Sacrifice of Himself

The phrase *"shewing forth"* which was not included in the Westminster Confession's statement was included by the Congregationalists and also by the Baptists. It is most likely taken from the statement of Paul in 1 Corinthians 11:26 in the King James Version, "ye do shew the Lord's death till he come." To shew (or show) is the translation of the Greek word *katangello*, which means "to preach or proclaim." The word is used ten times in the book of Acts to describe the preaching of the apostles. Most of the more modern English versions translate the word as "proclaim" in 1 Corinthians 11:26. Here, the assertion of the Confession is the same as Paul's in his epistle: the church *proclaims* Christ in His death in the Lord's Supper.

How do we proclaim the Lord's death in the Lord's Supper, and to whom are we proclaiming it? Certainly, we are proclaiming His death in our actions of eating and drinking and, no doubt, in the entirety of the "communion service." In a sense, we are preaching the gospel in a non-verbal manner. We could say, first, that we are proclaiming it to God, since observing the Lord's Supper is an act of worship. All worship is the worship of God, and we should perform it conscious that we are in His presence and that whatever we do in worship has Him as its primary referent. We are "making known His deeds" and "talking of all His wondrous works" (Ps. 105:1-5). Although not using words, we are using a symbolic ordinance that God Himself has given us for this purpose.

Second, we are proclaiming it to one another, to our fellow believers. As we have seen, the Lord's Supper is not an ordinance for individual or private worship. It is for a corporate setting (1 Cor. 11:17-18, 33; 10:16-17). Just as our singing during corporate worship is done for the benefit of those around us, even though it is directed primarily to God (Col. 3:16), so, in like manner, is our proclaiming of Christ to the brethren around us in the Lord's Supper.

Third, we are proclaiming Christ's death to unbelievers who are present. When we eat and drink in the Lord's Supper, we are proclaiming, in a visible, symbolic way, that Christ died in His people's place and that we live by faith in Him. Therefore, it is a true preaching of the gospel to unbelievers. We could call the Lord's Supper a God-appointed, congregational preachment of the gospel of Christ to sinners.

3. Confirmation, Nourishment, Growth

The next purpose of the Lord's Supper is the "confirmation of the faith of believers in all the benefits thereof, their spiritual nourishment, and growth in Him." The first clause, *confirmation of the faith of believers in all the benefits thereof,* asserts that God intends the Lord's Supper to assure true believers that we really are His children, partakers of His grace in Christ. This clause replaces "the sealing all benefits thereof unto true believer" in the Westminster Confession of Faith and the Savoy Declaration. The function of a seal is to verify the genuineness of something, as in the case of a king's seal (Dan. 6:17). To the believer who partakes of the Lord's Supper in faith in Jesus Christ and in obedience to His command, God assures him that it is right to receive this bread and this cup, since he is a disciple of Christ and a child of God. Our faith is confirmed, or assured.[16]

What are the benefits of partaking of the Lord's Supper? They are communion with Christ and all the benefits He died to gain for His people. A parallel statement to this paragraph in *The Westminster Larger Catechism* says we "feed upon Christ crucified, and all the benefits of His death." One effect of the Lord's Supper is the encouragement and assurance that the partaker is truly in communion with Jesus Christ and that he is a legitimate partaker of every blessing for which Christ died (1 Cor. 10:16).

Additionally, the Lord's Supper is a means of the believers' "spiritual nourishment, and growth in Him." This reflects the reality that God uses this sacrament, or ordinance, in a similar way to how He uses His Word, to build us up in our faith and to grant us spiritual growth (Jude 20; 2 Pet. 3:18). This is *spiritual nourishment* because in the Lord's Supper we "really and indeed... spiritually receive, and feed upon Christ crucified, and all the benefits of His death"[17] (cf. John 6:55). This is genuine spiritual nourishment, which results in genuine spiritual growth.

4. Further Engagement in Duties

Another purpose of the Lord's Supper is for believers' "further engagement in, and to all duties which they owe to Him." If the Lord's Supper is a sign of our being in fellowship with Christ, testifying that we are His disciples, then it imparts encouragement to us because it reminds us of our Savior's dying and continuing love for us. That remembrance should also stimulate us to love and good works (Ps. 116:12-14; Heb. 10:19-25). We are debtors to Christ, and the regular contemplation of His sacrifice for us in the Lord's Supper should serve as a reminder and motivator in our service to Him (Rom. 8:12; 12:1). Jesus said that the cup of the Lord's Supper is "the new covenant in His blood" (Luke 22:20; Matt. 26:28; Mark 14:24). When we partake of this Supper, is there not a sense in which we ought to be "renewing" our covenant vows to serve our Lord with all our heart (cf. 2 Chron. 34:30-31)? This seems to be what the Confession is suggesting here.[18]

---

16. *The Westminster Confession of Faith* at 27:1 says that the purposes of sacraments include "to represent Christ, and His benefits; and *to confirm our interest in Him.*"

17. LBCF, ch. 30, para. 7

18. Barcellos, Ibid., 36.

The fact that the Lord's Supper is a means of grace tells us it is something that God has ordained and graciously extends to us for our benefit. But the means of grace also have implications for believers. We are to receive them with humility, gratitude, and faith, and it is our responsibility to "engage" ourselves in wholehearted obedience to our Lord as a response.

5. Bond and Pledge
A continuation of this idea is contained in the following statement: the Lord's Supper is "to be a bond and pledge of their [believers'] communion with Him, and with each other." Participating in the Lord's Supper represents the bond believers have with their Savior and should also serve to "cement" that bond, so to speak. Similarly, it is a pledge to our Lord and to His people. In baptism, believers publicly testify of their union with Christ and of their allegiance to Him; the same is true of the Lord's Supper. Notice that the Confession speaks of the union and communion we have with Christ and of the union and communion we have with our fellow believers. Both aspects of communion are true, and both are expressed in Scripture in 1 Corinthians 10:16-17. We testify that we are all together in union and communion with our Savior as well as with one another. As we have seen, the Lord's Supper is a church ordinance, which emphasizes our union and communion as a body, with Christ's body.

2. The Nature of the Lord's Supper (Paragraph 2)

This paragraph focuses specifically on whether the Lord's Supper is a literal sacrifice of the body of Jesus Christ.

1. Denial of Error: Not a Real Sacrifice
Because the Reformation was a rejection of many Roman Catholic doctrines and practices, Reformed Confessions are marked by many statements that repudiate those false teachings. Paragraph 2 begins with such a statement. It is a denial of the Roman Catholic doctrine that, in the Mass, the bread and wine become the actual body and blood of Jesus and that these are then "sacrificed" to God. Rome also asserts that, by that sacrifice, atonement is made for the sins of the living and the dead.[19] The paragraph thus begins with an emphatic denial of this error. Christ is not offered up to God in the Lord's Supper, and no sacrifice is made to remit the sins of anyone. The only sacrifice that ever has availed for

---

19. "As often as the sacrifice of the Cross by which 'Christ our Pasch has been sacrificed' is celebrated on the altar, the work of our redemption is carried out." "The sacrifice of Christ and the sacrifice of the Eucharist are *one single sacrifice:* 'The victim is one and the same... [O]nly the manner of offering is different.' 'In this divine sacrifice which is celebrated in the Mass, the same Christ who offered himself once in a bloody manner on the altar of the cross is contained and is offered in an unbloody manner.'" *Catechism of the Catholic Church* (Liguori, MO: Liguori Publications, 1994), 343, 344. "This sacrifice [of the mass] is truly propitiatory... both for the living and the dead." Council of Trent (1562), 22nd Session, Chapter II.

the forgiveness of sins is the once-for-all sacrifice of Jesus upon the cross two thousand years ago.

2. Statement of Its True Nature

1. Memorial of Christ's Sacrifice

The positive statement about the nature of the Lord's Supper opposes the Roman Catholic view that it is an actual re-sacrificing of Christ's actual body. Rather, the Supper is "only a memorial" of Christ's one-time offering of Himself on the cross. Our Lord said we are to observe the Lord's Supper "in remembrance" of Him. Thus, the church is to constantly remember her Lord's sacrifice by means of the Lord's Supper, but not to repeat it. That sacrifice is never to be repeated and it is not repeatable. It was "once for all" (Heb. 7:27; 9:12, 25-28).

The Confession notes that Jesus' offering was *"of Himself by Himself."* From one perspective, it was the Father who offered up the Son. Romans 8:32 speaks of the Father "who did not spare His own Son, but delivered Him up for us all." But Jesus also asserted that He laid down His own life, which is the point the Confession makes: "Therefore My Father loves Me, because I lay down My life that I may take it again. No one takes it from Me, but I lay it down of Myself. I have power to lay it down, and I have power to take it again. This command I have received from My Father" (John 10:17-18). By offering up Himself, He acted as our high priest (Heb. 8:3). One of the things that makes His sacrifice so unique is that He is both the *offerer* and the *offering*. It was an "offering up of *Himself by Himself."*

By using the phrase *"only* a memorial", the Confession is not saying that the Lord's Supper is only a mental exercise on the part of the worshipers. It does not mean that the church simply meets together to engage in fellowship on a horizontal level as they focus upon the past. It does not mean that the Lord's Supper is not a means of grace in which God acts to bless His people, or that, in the Lord's Supper, Christ does not visit and commune with His people. Rather, the phrase *"only* a memorial" here emphasizes the radical distinction between the Roman Catholic view, here denied, and the biblical view of the Reformers.

My reason for emphasizing this point is that some Protestant Christians, in order to completely distance themselves from Roman Catholic error, have taught that the Lord's Supper is literally nothing more than a memorial; that it is not a means of grace as Reformed Christians understand it. This view has come to be called a "Zwinglian" view of the Lord's Supper, after the Swiss Reformer Huldrych Zwingli, who had intense debates with Luther in the early sixteenth century. It is true that, in his teaching, Zwingli did not emphasize the spiritual presence of Christ or the acting of God in the Lord's Supper, as did the Reformers who followed him. But his impassioned rejection of the Roman Catholic and Lutheran doctrine of the *physical, bodily* presence of Christ should not be understood as a rejection of Christ's *spiritual* presence. Therefore, it is not a fair characterization of this Reformer to equate his teaching with that of Christians who hold to what has been called a "bare memorial" view of the Lord's Supper.

Zwingli was an early Reformer, who died before Calvin even came upon the Reformation scene.[20] Because of the focus of his debates with Rome and Luther—the denial of the *physical* presence of Christ in the Supper—his view came to be represented as one in which the bread and wine are signs of what is *absent*. It is not that Zwingli never thought at all beyond this issue of the relation of the signs (bread and wine) to the things signified by them (Christ's body and blood). But he was not part of the discussions, disagreements, and debates that subsequently led to the more fully developed Reformed view on the Lord's Supper. Calvin himself apparently understood that Zwingli's doctrine was not unbiblical, but only less full-orbed than the Reformers who followed him.[21]

2. Spiritual Oblation of Praise

In addition to being a memorial, the Lord's Supper is a "spiritual oblation." An oblation is an offering or a sacrifice. If oblation is a synonym for sacrifice, why does the Confession say that the Lord's Supper is an oblation in the same sentence in which it denies it to be a sacrifice? Likely, the authors of the Westminster Confession wanted to avoid the use of the word "sacrifice" in reference to the Lord's Supper since that designation is made by Rome to represent their "abominable" doctrine of the Mass. The authors were saying that there is a sense in which the Lord's Supper can be called a sacrifice, or oblation, but it is only in the same sense that our praise *can be called a sacrifice (Heb. 13:15). It is an element of our* worship that has been ordained by God and is pleasing to Him (Phil. 4:18).

In Calvin's words, "This kind of sacrifice has nothing to do with appeasing God's wrath, with obtaining forgiveness of sins, or with meriting righteousness; but it is concerned solely with magnifying and exalting God."[22] In calling this element of worship a *spiritual* sacrifice, the

---

20. Zwingli died in 1531 at the relatively young age of forty-seven, around a year before Calvin's conversion.

21. Calvin said regarding the Consensus Tigurinus: "If Zwingli and Oecolampadius, these most excellent and illustrious servants of Christ, were now alive, they would not change a word in it." Quoted in William Cunningham, *The Reformers and the Theology of the Reformation* (Edinburgh, Scotland and Carlisle, PA: The Banner of Truth Trust, 1979), 231. Geoffrey Bromiley wrote regarding Zwingli: "A valuable feature of Zwingli's teaching is that by his sharp repudiation of all forms of belief in a literal presence of Christ in the Supper he prepared the ground for a far more satisfying doctrine of the sacramental presence and efficacy. His contribution in this respect was largely negative: his denials were more prominent than his assertions. But the medieval insistence upon one extreme almost inevitably demanded a more persistent emphasis upon the other, and it was left to Zwingli's successors to draw out more fully the positive implications of his teaching. Zwingli did not deny either the true presence of Christ after his deity, or the possible conjunction of sign and thing signified by virtue of the valid administration of the rite. And it was necessary that these denials be made if superstitious notions were to be cleared away and a more scriptural doctrine constructed." G. W. Bromiley, *Zwingli and Bullinger* (Philadelphia: The Westminster Press, 1953), 39.

22. John Calvin, *Institutes of the Christian Religion*, (Philadelphia: The Westminster Press, 1960), IV:xvi.

authors underscore that it's not an offering of anything *physical*—whether of the elements themselves, or, as Rome teaches, of Christ's actual body.

3. Denial of Error: The Mass Abominable

In light of the claims and the doctrine of Rome regarding the Eucharist and the Mass, the Confession states that the *"sacrifice of the mass... is most abominable."* In particular, it is abominable because it blasphemously contradicts the plain teaching of Scripture: Jesus Christ's sacrifice on the cross was the only, once-for-all, completely efficacious offering that atones for sins (Heb. 9:12-14, 23-28; 10:1-4, 10, 12-14). If this is not blasphemous and abominable heresy, it is difficult to imagine that anything could ever be so designated.

Confessions and catechisms of the Reformation use terms similar to "abominable" to describe the Roman Mass: blasphemy, detestable, intolerable abomination, abhorrent, dreadful idolatry, pagan and heathen, wicked, manifest profanation, Papist delirium, devilish, and ungodly, to name several. The Heidelberg Catechism (1563) states that *"the mass, at bottom, is nothing else than the denial of the one sacrifice and sufferings of Jesus Christ, and an accursed idolatry"* (Question 80). In light of the Bible's clear teaching, twenty-first century Christians would do well to ask whether or not these are overstatements. And they would do well to ask whether they should feel the liberty to attend Roman Catholic Masses on any occasion.

3. Administration of the Lord's Supper (Paragraphs 3 and 4)

Paragraphs 3 and 4 address the subject of how the Lord's Supper is to be administered by gospel ministers. It was not just an ordinance for Jesus' close friends, the apostles. It was intended for all His disciples throughout this age—"until He comes."

How are pastors of churches to conduct the observance of this ordinance? They are to do just as Jesus did when He instituted it, in obedience to His command: "Do *this.*"

The Confession specifies the actions of prayer, blessing the elements, breaking the bread, taking the cup, and distributing both elements to the communicants, and all then partaking of both elements. The list of actions is simply a recounting of what Jesus did on the night before He died: "And as they were eating, Jesus took bread, blessed and broke it, and gave it to the disciples and said, 'Take, eat; this is My body.' Then He took the cup, and gave thanks, and gave it to them, saying, 'Drink from it, all of you'" (Matt. 26:26-27).

1. Proper Administration

1. Praying, Blessing, Setting Apart

When the Confession says that the ministers *"bless the elements... and thereby set them apart,"* it is not suggesting that anything happens to or changes in the bread and the wine. The blessing does not transform them, infuse them with any supernatural energy, or surround them with a heavenly aura. It simply means what the Confession asserts: prayer, in the form of thanksgiving and petition for the blessing of God, is how the elements are "set apart from a common to a holy use." The Confession is again distinguishing a Scriptural observance of the Lord's Supper from the Roman Catholic observance of the Mass. The bread and wine do not become materially or inherently different from other bread and wine, or from the bread and wine that were present before the prayer. They are simply now "set apart" for this special use.

The nineteenth-century Presbyterian Robert Shaw wrote:

> Nor is there any more difficulty in apprehending how Jesus blessed the bread, than in apprehending how God blessed the seventh or the Sabbath-day – Gen. 2:3; Exod. 20:11... God blessed the seventh day by setting it apart to a holy use, or appointing it to be a day of sacred rest; Christ blessed the bread, by setting it apart from a common to a holy use, or appointing it to be the visible symbol of his body.[23]

There is no suggestion of any mysterious or supernatural process.

2. Breaking
The breaking of the bread as part of the observance of the Lord's Supper should most likely be understood as a symbolic act. It represents the broken body of our Lord, as opposed to simply a pragmatic procedure performed in order to facilitate the distribution of the bread. But the breaking of the bread does not imply any kind of dramatic or ostentatious performance arising from any sort of veneration of the elements. This is the concern of the next paragraph.

3. Communicating
The words *"communicating"* and *"communicants"* refer to the partaking of "communion" and of those who partake of it. The reason for specifying that *both* of the elements are to be received by *all* of the communicants is due to another of Rome's perversions of this ordinance: their practice of denying the cup to the laity, or non-clergy. It is again directly addressed in the beginning of paragraph 4.

2. Rejection of Roman Catholic Errors (Paragraph 4)

1. Denial of the Cup
Besides the blasphemies of the Mass and of transubstantiation, other erroneous practices of the Roman Catholic Church constitute abuse of this ordinance of Christ. Paragraph 4 addresses some of them. First is *the denial of the cup to the people*. In A.D. 1415, Rome officially denied the cup to the people; the priest alone partook of it on his own behalf and on

---

23. Robert Shaw, *An Exposition of The Westminster Confession of Faith* (Fearn, Ross-shire, Scotland: Christian Focus Publications, reprinted 1992), 299.

behalf of the people.[24] This was its policy for over five hundred years, well into the twentieth century. It was a flagrant disregard for Jesus' words in Matthew 26:27, "Drink from it, *all of you*." Further, it was of a piece with Rome's rank clericalism; the practical despising of the "laity" on the part of the Church's leadership and priesthood.

2. *Veneration of the Elements*

In addition to this denial of the cup, the Confession rejects "worshiping the elements, the lifting them up, or carrying them about for adoration, and reserving them for any pretended religious use." It follows from the doctrine of transubstantiation (see paragraph 6) that the consecrated bread is the very body of Christ, so Roman Catholicism sees this as grounds to justify worshiping it. Rome's own official statements explain:

> Because Christ himself is present in the sacrament of the altar, he is to be honored with the worship of adoration.... In the liturgy of the Mass we express our faith in the real presence of Christ under the species of bread and wine by, among other ways, genuflecting or bowing deeply as a sign of adoration of the Lord. The Catholic Church has always offered and still offers to the sacrament of the Eucharist the cult of adoration, not only during Mass, but also outside of it, reserving the consecrated hosts with the utmost care, exposing them to the solemn veneration of the faithful, and carrying them in procession.[25]

These errors are all rejected by this paragraph, because they "are all contrary to the nature of this ordinance, and to the institution of Christ." Further, the Romish errors at this point are a patent violation of the second commandment (Ex. 20:4-5).

4. Relation of the Signs to the Things Signified (Paragraphs 5 and 6)

When we speak of the "relation of the signs to the things signified," we are discussing how it is, precisely, that the bread and the wine in the Lord's Supper are related to the body and the blood of Christ which they represent. This question revolves around how we interpret the words of Jesus when He instituted the Supper, particularly the words "This is My body" and "This is My blood." The Roman Catholic interpretation of these words, both at the time of the Reformation and today, is that they must mean the bread actually becomes the very physical body of Jesus and the wine actually becomes His physical blood. Rome teaches that, in the Mass, the transformation from bread to body and wine to blood occurs when the priest consecrates the elements, even though the elements retain the appearance of mere bread and wine to our senses.

---

24. Loraine Boettner, *Roman Catholicism* (Philadelphia: The Presbyterian and Reformed Publishing Company, 1962), 181.

25. *Catechism of the Catholic Church,* 347, 356.

On this point of transubstantiation, Luther and the Reformed both rejected the doctrine of Rome. However, there was not entire agreement between Luther and the Reformed. Although Luther rejected transubstantiation, he still insisted that Jesus' words, "This is My body" and "This is My blood" must be interpreted literally. Therefore, he believed the physical body of Jesus must be present in the Lord's Supper. Luther did not teach that the bread and wine *become* the body and blood of Christ, but, in some way, His physical body and blood become present "in, with, or under" the symbolic elements, which remain what they were and remain only symbols themselves. This view has been called "consubstantiation." Against both Rome and Luther, the Reformed argued that Jesus Christ is *truly* and *really* present in the Lord's Supper, but His presence is not physical, rather it is only spiritual.

1. Positively Stated (Paragraph 5)

With the background and explanation of paragraph 4 in view, let's briefly consider paragraph 5. The main point of paragraph 5 deals with the relation of the signs to what they symbolize. The bread and the wine remain what they were—bread and wine—and therefore are only symbols of Christ's body and blood. The language in Jesus' words of institution is to be understood *figuratively*, not literally. Jesus' actual body and blood are in heaven, not on earth.

What does the Confession mean by the assertion that "the outward elements in this ordinance... have such relation to Him crucified, as that truly... they are sometimes called by the names of the things they represent?" First, and most obviously, this would refer to the words of Jesus when He said, "This is My body" and "This is My blood." Jesus very clearly and very legitimately used language that seemed to identify the bread with His body and the wine with His blood. But if we understand the words as figurative and not literal, the words are perfectly intelligible. Further, speaking in such a way is not shocking, even though Rome and Luther insisted that the language demanded that Jesus' literal physical body and blood must be present. Jesus spoke in such ways about Himself on other occasions: in John 10:9, "I am the door"; in John 15:5, "I am the vine"; and in several places in John 6, "I am the bread." He used the same kind of speech in instituting the Lord's Supper, and in the same way, the use of the state of being verb ("is" or "am") is not intended to be taken literally, but symbolically. The bread *represents or symbolizes* His body; it does not become His body.

But the Confession is saying more than just this when it says that the elements "*truly* are called by the names of the things they represent." In view of the Reformed conviction that the elements represent not simply what is absent (Christ's body in heaven) but also what is *present* (Christ truly present *spiritually*), the Confession states that Jesus' words speak of a genuine relationship between the elements and His body and blood; a relationship that goes beyond merely "figurative" language. In terms of the actual relationship of the bread to Christ's physical body, and the cup to Christ's physical blood, the connection is only symbolic (the point of paragraph 2). But at the same time, there is a relationship between the symbols and something that is truly present.[26]

How is this so? Such a virtual identification of the sign with what it symbolizes is fitting for a number of reasons. First, since the Lord's Supper is a means of grace, the elements are vehicles by which God "presents" Christ to us and "delivers" Him, and all the blessings He earned by His death, to us. Second, we must remember that the Lord's Supper is a memorial, a symbolic part of the church's worship that is ordained by God to be a vital part of that worship throughout this age. If God has ordained it, it is not a mere empty or vain symbol. As the Belgic Confession states, "Now as it is certain and beyond all doubt that Jesus Christ hath not enjoined to us the use of His sacraments in vain, so He works in us all that He represents to us by these holy signs" (Article 35). Further, these symbols represent to us, not only great spiritual truths, but also *present* spiritual realities. When Christ's people partake of the Lord's Supper, the elements and actions represent the true presence of Christ as He communes with and nourishes His people with His own flesh (John 6:55-57). As Calvin says, "There is nothing more absurd than to call something a Sacrament which is empty and does not truly offer us the matter signified."[27]

One great concern and aim of the Reformers in their controversy with Luther and Rome was to underscore their belief in Christ's true presence in the Lord's Supper. They took great pains in stressing that to believe that Christ's presence in the Lord's Supper is *spiritual* does not mean that one also believes His presence is not real, true, and genuine. They desired to promote their genuine convictions regarding the true presence of Christ, the power of the Holy Spirit, and the glory of God in this means of grace. They did this by using such language as is echoed here in the Baptist Confession.

2. Negatively Stated: Denial of the Error of Transubstantiation (Paragraph 6)

The Roman Catholic doctrine of transubstantiation has been in the crosshairs of the Confession throughout this chapter. Although, it is the underlying error behind the abomination of the "popish sacrifice of the mass" mentioned in paragraph 2, it is explicitly mentioned for the first time here in paragraph 6.

---

26. "Therefore although we draw a distinction, as we must, between the signs and the things signified, yet we do not disjoin the truth from the signs." *Consensus Tigurinus* in Dennison, ed., *Reformed Confessions*, 541. "[I]t is not a bare figure, but [is] joined to its reality and substance. It is therefore with good reason that the bread is called body, since not only does it represent it to us, but also presents it to us." John Calvin, "Short Treatise on the Lord's Supper," in ed. J. K. S. Reid, *Calvin: Theological Treatises* (Philadelphia: The Westminster Press, 1954), 147.

27. David W. Torrance and Thomas F. Torrance, editors, *Calvin's New Testament Commentaries, Volume 3: A Harmony of the Gospels, Matthew, Mark and Luke, Volume III, James and Jude* (Grand Rapids: Wm. B. Eerdmans, reprinted 1980), 314.

1. Explanation of Transubstantiation

First, what is transubstantiation? It is the doctrine which maintains that, in the Mass, the priest consecrates the host (bread) and the host becomes the very body of Jesus Christ. The Catholic Church officially explains:

> "[B]y the consecration of the bread and wine there takes place a change of the whole substance of the bread into the substance of the body of Christ our Lord and of the whole substance of the wine into the substance of his blood. This change the holy Catholic Church has fittingly and properly called transubstantiation."
>
> "By the consecration the transubstantiation of the blood and wine into the Body and Blood of Christ is brought about. Under the consecrated species of bread and wine Christ himself, living and glorious, is present in a true, real, and substantial manner: his Body and his Blood, with his soul and his divinity (cf. Council of Trent: DS 1640; 1651)."[28]

2. Repugnance of the Doctrine of Transubstantiation

This doctrine is "repugnant" in several ways. First, as we saw immediately above in paragraph 5, the best way to interpret Jesus' words of institution regarding the sacrament is to take them to mean that "This [the bread] represents My body" and "This [the cup] *represents* My blood." Second, according to Acts 3:21, one of the Confession's proof texts for this paragraph, Jesus' body is presently in heaven. It has been there since His ascension (Luke 24:51; Acts 1:9), and it will remain there until He comes again in glory: *"whom heaven must receive until the times of restoration of all things,* which God has spoken by the mouth of all His holy prophets since the world began" (Acts 3:21; cf. Ps.110:1).

Third, the Bible's doctrine of the Person of Christ does not allow for the conversion or confusion of His two natures (see the Confession, Chapter 8, paragraph 2). That is, the omnipresence that belongs to Christ's divine nature is not communicated to His human nature so that His physical body could be present in Roman Catholic Masses in many places in the world at the same time.

Fourth, the Confession states that transubstantiation is repugnant to common sense and reason. This idea takes into account that when Jesus said to the apostles, "This is My body," they would have never dreamed of anything like the doctrine of transubstantiation because they would have seen that Jesus was already present in His body. They never would have understood Him as saying that what looked and tasted like bread was actually His body.

Fifth, the Confession states that the doctrine of transubstantiation overthrows the nature of the ordinance. We saw in paragraph 2 that the nature of the ordinance of the Lord's Supper is symbolic and commemorative; it is not a sacrifice, which is what the doctrines of the Mass and of transubstantiation make it out to be.

Finally, paragraph 6 says that this false doctrine of transubstantiation *"is the cause of manifold superstitions, yea, of gross idolatries."* Some of those

---

28. *Catechism of the Catholic Church*, 347, 356.

were specified in paragraph 4. Others likely include the kind of legends and old wives' tales that I heard from nuns during my elementary school days at the Roman Catholic Church school I attended. They are akin to the ghost stories told around campfires, except blasphemous and not to be repeated here.[29]

5. Reception of the Lord's Supper (Paragraphs 7 and 8)

Paragraphs 7 and 8 address the subject of who can rightfully partake of the Lord's Supper and how they ought to receive it. Paragraph 7 addresses the worthy reception of the Supper and paragraph 8 the unworthy reception of it.

1. Worthy Receivers (Paragraph 7)

1. Who Are "Worthy Receivers"?
Only true believers who are also members of particular churches of Christ may partake of this ordinance. This is implied from the statements in paragraph 1 which say that the Supper was instituted by Jesus to be observed "in His churches," for the purpose of confirming "the faith of believers." The Baptists greatly abbreviated their chapter on the sacraments (Chapter 28: *"Of Baptism and the Lord's Supper"*). One of the statements in the longer chapter of the Westminster Confession of Faith (Chapter 27: *"Of the Sacraments"*) indicates that one purpose of these ordinances is *to put a visible difference between those that belong unto the Church, and the rest of the world* (paragraph 1).

Another implication also exists: true believers who receive the elements of the Lord's Supper must do so in a worthy way, including the present exercise of faith in Christ as they partake. The Confession speaks of those who receive Christ "inwardly by *faith*," and states that He is "spiritually present to the *faith* of believers." By speaking in this way, the Confession makes two points.

First, grace is not received "automatically" in the Lord's Supper. We do not receive it simply because it is scripturally administered and we are physically present. No, we must exercise faith as we eat and drink if we are to benefit. We must avoid a practical adoption of the Roman Catholic doctrine of the sacraments working *ex opere operato*. To use Jesus' words, according to our faith it will be to us (Matt. 9:29).

Second, "worthy receiving" means we must avoid the kinds of sinful attitudes and conduct which Paul calls "eating and drinking in an unworthy manner" in 1 Corinthians 11:27-34. This includes the kinds of sins mentioned in that chapter: (1) sins of rudeness and unkindness toward our brethren (vv. 21-22, 33-34); (2) sins of thoughtlessness and irreverence toward our Lord and Savior who laid down His life for us, and in whose presence we are eating this sacred meal (vv. 27, 29).

---

29. See also Philip Schaff, ed., *The Creeds of Christendom, Vol. I: The History of Creeds* (Grand Rapids: Baker Book House, reprint, 1983), 284-85.

Therefore, Paul urges us to examine ourselves lest we be guilty of such unworthy partaking (1 Cor. 11:28). Several things should be borne in mind so that we avoid common errors associated with such self-examination.

First, we should not let self-examination turn the Lord's Supper into an exercise of gloom and doom. As this very chapter states in paragraph 2, the Supper *is a spiritual oblation of all possible praise unto God.*

Second, we should remember that the self-examination we engage in to prepare our hearts for the Lord's Supper is not to be regarded as peculiar to or limited to the Lord's Supper. As Jesus taught in Matthew 5:23-24, we should take care to have a good conscience any time we are about to engage in the worship of God, and not just before the Lord's Supper. In fact, self-examination should not be limited to times when we are preparing to worship God; it should be a regular part of our daily Christian life (Acts 24:15-16; Ps. 139:23-24).

Third, such self-examination is not limited to our relationships with our brethren. As 1 Corinthians 11:29 indicates, it is necessary in our vertical relationship, not just our horizontal ones (Acts 24:16).

Fourth, the goal of such self-examination is not to prevent our participation in the Supper should we detect any sin in our hearts or lives. We must remember that the Lord's Supper is what has been called a "sinners ordinance." As the Heidelberg Catechism states in Question 81: "For whom is the Lord's Supper instituted?"

Answer: *For those who are truly sorrowful for their sins, and yet trust that these are forgiven them for the sake of Christ; and that their remaining infirmities are covered by His passion and death; and who also earnestly desire to have their faith more and more strengthened, and their lives more holy; but hypocrites, and such as turn not to God with sincere hearts, eat and drink judgment to themselves.*[30]

2. What Do Worthy Receivers Receive?

The Confession mentions the reception of "the visible elements in this ordinance," but only in such a way as to make clear that those elements —the bread and wine—are not the main things received in this means of grace. However, some comments are in order regarding this mention of the visible elements. The Roman Catholic Church argues that everyone who partakes of the Eucharist, irrespective of faith, receives both the very body of Christ and also the grace of Christ.[31] Lutherans say that both believers and unbelievers actually receive the body of Christ orally

---

30. "[T]he Supper would be not only useless to us all, but also pernicious, if we had to bring an integrity of faith or life in which there was nothing with which to find fault... For if we allege as pretext for not coming to the Supper, that we are still weak in faith or in integrity of life, it is as if a man excuse himself from taking medicine because he is sick." Calvin, "Short Treatise," 152-53.

31. "If any one saith, that by the said sacraments of the New Law grace is not conferred through the act performed [*ex opere operato*], but that faith alone in the divine promise suffices for the obtaining of grace: let him be anathema." Council of Trent, Seventh Session (1547), Canon VIII.

(*manducatio oralis*),[32] although only believers receive Him spiritually and receive the grace of Christ. The Reformed argued against both Rome and Luther and said that Christ is truly received in any sense only through faith, and it is this conviction that is expressed here in the Confession.

The paragraph states that worthy receivers "really and indeed... spiritually receive, and feed upon Christ crucified, and all the benefits of His death." The wording here is significant. It specifies that in the Lord's Supper we receive and feed upon both Christ Himself and all the benefits of His death. The Reformers insisted upon this as well: that the grace received in the Lord's Supper does not consist only in the benefits Christ purchased for us, but in Christ Himself. As the Second Helvetic Confession (1566) stated it, *"Christ Himself... is that special thing and substance of the Supper"* (Chapter XXI). The main blessing received is communion with Christ Himself. Every other blessing comes in, or through, Christ. This is a truth not simply forged through the Reformation debates regarding the Lord's Supper, but it is founded in Scripture itself. The Bible nowhere states that we receive any blessings other than *"in Christ"* (e.g. Eph. 1:3). In John 6, Jesus emphasized that we partake of *Him* by faith, not just of His gifts, for He is the bread of life (vv. 35, 48, 50-58). Similarly, in the words of institution, Jesus said, "This is *My body*," not "This represents all the things I will gain for you by My death." As we sing in a familiar hymn:

> We taste *thee*, O thou living Bread,
> And long to feast upon *thee* still;
> We drink of *thee*, the Fountainhead,
> And thirst our souls from *thee* to fill.[33]

3. Spiritually Feeding upon Christ

It is worth noting that although the Confession asserts that worthy partakers "really and indeed... spiritually receive, and feed upon Christ," such an assertion does not mean that this feeding upon Christ only occurs during the Lord's Supper. Henry Bullinger wrote in the Second Helvetic Confession, commenting on Jesus' words about eating His flesh and drinking His blood in John 6 (Chapter XXI): "And the eating of the flesh and drinking of the blood of the Lord is so necessary to salvation that without it no man can be saved. But this spiritual eating and drinking takes place also without the Supper of the Lord, even so often as, and wheresoever, a man does believe in Christ." Calvin said, "[A]ny man is deceived who thinks anything more is conferred upon him through the sacraments than what is offered by God's Word and received by him in true faith."[34]

---

32. Richard A. Muller, *Latin and Greek Theological Terms*, p. 183.

33. "Jesus, Thou Joy of Loving Hearts," by Bernard of Clairvaux, translated by Ray Palmer. #549 in the Trinity Hymnal.

34. Calvin, *Institutes*, IV: xvii: 14.

This begs a question: If we receive everything we receive in the Lord's Supper *apart* from the Lord's Supper, why then do we have this ordinance?

For an answer, Calvin states it this way: "It is indeed true that this same grace is offered us by the gospel; yet... in the Supper we have a more ample certainty and fuller enjoyment."[35] In other words, the Lord's Supper is not a means of our receiving a different kind of grace, but it is simply a different kind of means of grace—a symbolic one. God gives us a tangible way of receiving grace from Him because He knows our frame and remembers that we are dust; He pities us (Ps. 103:13-14). We are not purely spiritual creatures as the Quakers would like to think. We are "of the earth, earthy" (1 Cor. 15:47, KJV). So God gives us a tangible ordinance, if you will, to meet us in our need. This serves not to give us a different kind of fellowship with Christ, but to enhance the communion we already enjoy with Him.

Consider how a wedding band, a mere piece of metal that is not love itself, enhances the experience of marital love (especially for a woman). Further, consider that the Lord's Supper is a special meal, ordained by God Himself, for the special purpose of nourishing us through communion with His Son in His Son's special presence. It's as if God has invited us to a great banquet; the greatest of banquets we can possibly enjoy this side of glory. Therefore, it is unthinkable that we should compare it to eating breakfast alone at the local diner. The diner meal may nourish us as effectively as the banquet, but God gives us the banquet of the Lord's Supper in order to enhance our spiritual benefit, our enjoyment and intimacy of communion with Him, and to deepen our gratitude to Him.

4. Presence of Christ

The last part of paragraph 7 speaks of Christ's "presence to the faith of believers" in the Lord's Supper. It denies that He is "corporally or carnally" present; that is, He is not bodily present, as both Rome and Luther asserted. It is true that Christ is present to the faith of believers in terms of His being received by them and His communing with them as they look to Him in faith. However, the statement does not say all that could be affirmed about Christ's presence in the Lord's Supper.

There is a proper sense in which we could say that Christ is present in the Supper in an objective way, irrespective of the faith of any individual who is partaking. Perhaps the easiest way to understand this is to compare the observance of the Supper to the preaching of the Word. When the Word of God is preached, Christ is present regardless of whether anyone believes that Word or not. As we sing in one of our hymns, "Christ in his Word draws near." However, only those who believe the Word receive Christ into their souls and commune with Him. Nevertheless, it is still true that Christ was present to everyone who heard the preaching (2 Cor. 2:14-16).

35. Calvin, "Short Treatise," 145.

In a similar way, we could say that Christ "draws near" whenever the Supper is observed. He is present. Consider the case of a believer who is in attendance at the Supper but is harboring sin and is unrepentant. In fact, during both the preaching and the Lord's Supper, he is savoring in his mind his last episode of his sin and fondly anticipating his next. In a foolish act of formalism, he carelessly takes the elements and eats and drinks. Did he receive Christ into his soul? No. But was Christ *present*, both in the preaching and in the Supper, admonishing, convicting, wooing, inviting, and offering Himself to this erring disciple? Yes. Calvin put it this way in the *Institutes:* "And truly [Christ] offers and shows the reality there signified to all who sit at that spiritual banquet, although it is received with benefit by believers alone, who accept such great generosity with true faith and gratefulness of heart."[36] This underscores the seriousness of eating without "discerning the body" and the resulting judgment one may bring upon himself (1 Cor. 11:27-34), which is the subject of the next paragraph.

It highlights the importance of a proper knowledge about this ordinance and of coming to the table with our minds and hearts fully engaged. We should take pains to understand the Lord's Supper from the Bible's perspective and we should gird up the loins of our minds whenever we are at the table. We must avoid coming to the table expecting to be sovereignly visited with a wonderful emotional experience irrespective of our own cognitive activity. Just as with our using the Word of God as a means of grace, *thinking* is required. As Jesus said, we are to *remember* Him.

2. Unworthy Receivers (Paragraph 8)
Paragraph 7 addressed worthy receivers of the Lord's Supper. Paragraph 8 addresses unworthy receivers, acknowledging that there are two types, or kinds, of unworthy receivers.

1. Ignorant or Ungodly Persons
First, are mentioned *all ignorant or ungodly persons.* By this, the Confession means unbelievers: those who do not know Christ and have never known Him. These are, by definition, those who are not in fellowship with Christ. As a proof text, the Confession offers 2 Corinthians 6:14-15:

> Do not be unequally yoked together with unbelievers. For what fellowship has righteousness with lawlessness? And what communion has light with darkness? And what accord has Christ with Belial? Or what part has a believer with an unbeliever?

Such attendants are not believers and are therefore not qualified to partake of the Lord's Supper. They are also unqualified to partake since they are not members of the church. As the Confession states, *they are unfit to enjoy communion with Christ, so are they unworthy of the Lord's table.*

---

36. Calvin, *Institutes*, 4.17.10.

But what if an unbeliever does partake of the Lord's Supper? The Confession's answer is that he commits great sin against Christ. Further, he therefore ought not be admitted to the Lord's table. The pastor, or pastors, of a church therefore should not permit unbelievers to partake of the Lord's Supper. They should "fence" the table; that is, they should state clearly at the beginning of the Supper's observance that unbelievers are not welcome to partake of the elements of bread and wine.

2. Other Unworthy Recipients

The last part of the paragraph speaks of *anyone* (*"whosoever"*) who receives the elements of the Lord's Table unworthily. The *"whosoever"* means not only unbelievers, but also any believers who might receive the Lord's Supper in an unworthy manner. We know that believers and church members can be unworthy receivers based on Paul's warnings in 1 Corinthians 11. In verses 27 to 34, he warns believing members of the church in Corinth of the danger they face in taking the Lord's Supper unworthily. These are serious warnings against serious sins which can incur serious judgments from the Lord. Even though true believers who are members in good standing of a well-ordered church should come with eagerness and boldness to the Lord's Supper, no one should come carelessly and flippantly. We should come with regard for our Lord (1 Cor. 11:29) and with loving respect for our brethren (1 Cor. 10:17; 11:21-22, 33-34). Otherwise, we risk incurring the judgment of God, "eating and drinking judgment to ourselves" (cf. Heb. 10:29).

6. Concluding Observations

1. The Reformed Doctrine of the Lord's Supper

I believe it is fair to say that the teaching of our Confession represents the Reformed doctrine of the Lord's Supper. It is true that the Particular Baptist authors withheld some of the clearer and more emphatic expressions of that view, most notably through their significant abbreviation of Chapter 28. They achieved that abbreviation by eliminating much of the material in the parallel chapters of the Westminster Confession of Faith (Chapter 27) and the Savoy Declaration (Chapter 28). Therefore, for further study of the subject of the Supper, in addition to the relevant passages of Scripture, I commend the study of Calvin's writings on the Lord's Supper and the study of the other Reformed Confessions, especially those referenced above in this chapter.

2. The Heart and Message of the Lord's Supper

If there is one thing that stands out above all else in the Confession's—and in the Bible's—teaching on the Lord's Supper, it is the vital connection between the Supper and Christ crucified. This is obvious from the way in which Jesus instituted this ordinance just before He went to the cross, from the words of institution that He spoke, and from the very symbolism of the elements and actions of the ordinance. It is all about Christ and the cross.

A believer who partakes of the Lord's Supper ought to remember that he is "proclaiming" something when he eats and drinks (1 Cor. 11:26). What exactly is he proclaiming? Essentially, he is saying that Christ has died in his place; that he deserved to be punished on the cross, but that Christ, who did *not* deserve it, was punished there in his place. He is testifying that, as a Christian, his whole life is Christ (Phil. 1:21), and the church of which he is a part exists only because of Christ and His death. "Christ died for me; I live by faith in Him" is the proclamation.

Then, from the standpoint of God, it is obvious that His great intention is to keep that very message, the gospel itself, constantly before His people. That is why He has given us this symbolic ordinance. In the Lord's Supper, God has put the gospel in a visible form that is very simple, but very profound. We could say that God has, in a sense, put the gospel in a nutshell. And He has given the Supper to us in order to keep that gospel constantly before our eyes. It is the same with the Son (John 10:30). It is Christ's desire that we constantly focus our attention directly upon Him in His death for us, and commune with Him in that remembrance. It was His earnest desire to commune with His apostles in the most intimate of ways when He observed the Passover with them and instituted the Lord's Supper (Luke 22:15). It is His desire today to commune in the same way with His church on the earth.

Calvin expressed this focus upon Christ and the cross in this way:

> Here, then, is the peculiar consolation we receive from the Supper, that it directs and conducts us to the cross of Jesus Christ and to his resurrection, in order to assure us that, whatever iniquity there may be in us, the Lord does not cease to regard and accept us as righteous; whatever material of death may be in us, he does not cease to vivify us; whatever the wretchedness we may have, yet he does not cease to fill us with all felicity.[37]

In the Lord's Supper, God directs and conducts us to the cross of Jesus Christ, in a visible and symbolic way, as often as we partake of it.

---

37. Calvin, "Short Treatise," 145.

CHAPTER 31

OF THE STATE OF MAN AFTER DEATH, AND OF THE RESURRECTION OF THE DEAD[1]

JIM DOMM

1. The bodies of men after death return to dust, and see corruption;[2] but their souls, which neither die nor sleep, having an immortal subsistence, immediately return to God who gave them.[3] The souls of the righteous being then made perfect in holiness, are received into Paradise, where they are with Christ, and behold the face of God in light and glory, waiting for the full redemption of their bodies;[4] and the souls of the wicked are cast into hell; where they remain in torment and utter darkness, reserved to the judgment of the great day;[5] besides these two places, for souls separated from their bodies, the Scripture acknowledgeth none.

2. At the last day, such of the saints as are found alive, shall not sleep, but be changed;[6] and all the dead shall be raised up with the selfsame bodies, and none other;[7] although with different qualities, which shall be united again to their souls forever.[8]

3. The bodies of the unjust shall, by the power of Christ, be raised to dishonor; the bodies of the just, by His Spirit, unto honor, and be made conformable to His own glorious body.[9]

---

1. Much of the material in this chapter comes from Samuel E. Waldron's *A Modern Exposition of the 1689 Baptist Confession of Faith* (Welwyn Garden City: Evangelical Press, 1989, 2016), 439-80.

2. Genesis 3:19; Acts 13:36

3. Ecclesiastes 12:7

4. Luke 23:43; 2 Corinthians 5:1, 6, 8; Philippians 1:23; Hebrews 12:23

5. Jude 6-7; 1 Peter 3:19; Luke 16:23-24

6. 1 Corinthians 15:51, 52; 1 Thessalonians 4:17

7. Job 19:26-27

8. 1 Corinthians 15:42, 43

9. Acts 24:15; John 5:28-29; Philippians 3:21

The final two chapters of the Confession are concerned with eschatology (the doctrine of last things).[10] The eschatology of the Confession, as well as the Bible, is simple. It consists of three main historical events: the return of Christ, the resurrection of the dead, and the final judgment. Another item that is usually included in the department of eschatology is what is called the intermediate state. The items treated in the Confession in connection with last things and the world to come include the intermediate state and the resurrection of the dead (Chapter 31), and the return of Christ and the final judgment (Chapter 32).[11]

Over the centuries, eschatology has become a hotly debated issue, sometimes leading to bitter divisions among professing Christians. We must note that the Baptists saw no reason to disagree with anything the Presbyterians and Congregationalists had to say about these subjects in their Confessions. The lesson from this is clear. Eschatology need not become an occasion for division among God's people. Let us therefore seek, with the help of God, to keep focused on the most important and practical issues in the study of last things.

1. The Intermediate State (Paragraph 1)

The intermediate state refers to the state of humans after death and before the return of Christ. It refers to that period between a person's death and resurrection. When someone dies, he or she enters the intermediate state and remains there until the day of resurrection. Since this condition is not the final destiny of either the righteous or the wicked, it's called the intermediate state. If we are to understand the biblical teaching concerning the intermediate state, two important distinctions must be kept in mind—the distinction between the body and the soul, and the distinction between the righteous and the wicked. Paragraph 1 of this chapter in the Confession summarizes very well the biblical teaching on the intermediate state in terms of these two distinctions.

1. The Distinction between Body and Soul (Paragraph 1)

"The bodies of men after death return to dust, and see corruption; but their souls, which neither die nor sleep, having an immortal subsistence, immediately return to God who gave them."

According to the Scriptures and the Confession, human beings consist of two basic components—a body and a soul. Because these two components in humans are qualitatively different entities, both their condition and location may differ after death. The body will return to the dust of the ground. We read in Genesis 3:19: "In the sweat of your face you shall eat bread Till you return to the ground, For out of it you were taken; For dust you are, And to dust you shall return."

---

10. The term comes from the Greek words *eschatos* (last), and *logos* (word): "words about last things."

11. The return of Christ is also mentioned in 8:4 and 26:4 of the Confession.

God told Adam that if he disobeyed the command not to eat the fruit of the tree of the knowledge of good and evil, he would die (Gen. 2:16, 17). This includes physical death—the separation of the body from the soul. James writes in 2:26 of his letter: "…the body without the spirit is dead…" At death, body and soul are separated. The body returns to the ground from which it came, and the soul returns to God who gave it (Ecc. 12:7).

When the Confession asserts that the human soul neither dies nor sleeps, but has an immortal subsistence, it simply means that the soul doesn't cease to exist. When the body dies, it decomposes. It ceases to exist. The soul, on the other hand, doesn't cease to exist. Death doesn't render the soul inactive. Unlike the body, the soul doesn't decompose after death. When the Confession asserts that the soul is immortal, it doesn't mean that it is divine or heavenly, but that it doesn't cease to exist. The essence of the soul is to know, to be conscious. That essence continues after death. In that sense, the soul is deathless, immortal.

Physical death is a horrible thing. It is the penal consequence of sin. It consists of the radical and unnatural separation of body and soul, resulting in the decomposition of the body and the nakedness of the soul. It signals the condemnation of Adam's race to eternal death. Thanks be to God that the sting of death has been removed for those who are in union with Jesus Christ (1 Cor. 15:55-58)!

As Christians anticipate the inevitable approach of death, they face a tension in their thinking. On the one hand, they must not be indifferent to it, or delight in it, because death is an unnatural thing. Death is not a good thing. On the other hand, the Christian doesn't despair in the face of death. He is able to face death with courage and hope because death won't separate him from Christ. This is the very tension that Paul expresses in Philippians 1:21-24:

> For to me, to live is Christ, and to die is gain. But if I live on in the flesh, this *will* mean fruit from my labor; yet what I shall choose I cannot tell. For I am hard pressed between the two, having a desire to depart and be with Christ, *which* is far better. Nevertheless to remain in the flesh is more needful for you.

The Christian faces a tension as he looks at death. He neither delights in it, nor cowers before it.

How different is the attitude of the unbeliever! Many unbelievers find death to be an uncomfortable, unpleasant subject. Why is that? If death is unnatural, if it is the penal consequence of rebellion to God, then it's understandable why it is unpleasant to think about. But if death is just a part of the natural order of things, then why does it trouble the unbeliever so much? Why is it so repulsive? Why does it seem so unnatural and so horrible to him? If it's just the natural order of things, then his feelings toward it make no sense. The Bible gives the only satisfactory explanation of death. Unbelievers need to know the truth about death. If they don't get their answers from the Bible, then where will they get them from? No one is prepared to properly *live* until he embraces God's explanation of why he must *die*. This is the first distinction that is vital to a proper understanding of the intermediate state: the distinction between body and soul. There is a second distinction that must be kept in mind.

2. The Distinction between the Righteous and the Wicked (Paragraph 1)

The Scriptures and the Confession are clear in asserting that the souls of the righteous go immediately into Paradise. We read in paragraph 1:

"The souls of the righteous being then made perfect in holiness, are received into Paradise, where they are with Christ, and behold the face of God in light and glory, waiting for the full redemption of their bodies..."

Jesus told the thief on the cross, "Today you shall be with Me in Paradise" (Luke 23:43). He said "today"—not weeks or months or years from now. There is no interim period between death and the entrance of the righteous into the presence of Christ. This means that there is no such place as purgatory. The Confession explicitly asserts this at the end of paragraph 1: "besides these two places, [Paradise and hell] *for souls separated from their bodies, the Scripture acknowledgeth none.*"

Paul affirms that when the believer departs, he or she will be with Christ (Phil. 1:23; cf. 2 Cor. 5:6-9). There are only two options for the righteous. Either they are absent from Christ when at home in the body, or they are at home with Christ when absent from the body. Clearly, then, the Confession teaches, as the Bible does, that the souls of the righteous enter immediately into the presence of Christ at death.

The Confession further asserts that the souls of the righteous are made perfect in holiness at death. In Hebrews 12:23, the departed righteous are described as "the spirits of just men made perfect." The souls of the righteous become absolutely sinless at death. They are ushered into Paradise, which is a synonym for heaven. The souls of departed saints are in a delightful and happy condition. Central to their happiness is Christ. Christ is with them in Paradise and the righteous will see Him. This is what theologians call "the beatific vision." In a way that no sinful mortal may, the departed righteous behold, and exist in the immediate proximity of, the manifested glory of God in Christ in heaven.

However, though the departed righteous are happy in the presence of Christ, their blessedness is yet incomplete. Chief among the blessings for which they still must wait is the full redemption of their bodies. Though they are perfectly holy and happy, they are not yet fully redeemed. They have not yet received their inheritance of a redeemed creation. They have not yet been publicly vindicated by the final judgment. Their enemies have not yet been judged. Their bodies have not yet been redeemed. Though they are truly holy and happy, they are yet in a disembodied condition. The Bible never idealizes a disembodied condition. It always holds up as the true hope of believers a historical consummation which is both earthly and bodily.

Two passages will suffice to prove these assertions. One is Revelation 6:9-11:

> When He opened the fifth seal, I saw under the altar the souls of those who had been slain for the word of God and for the testimony which they held. And they cried with a loud voice, saying, "How long, O Lord, holy and true, until You judge and avenge our blood on those who dwell on the earth?" Then a white robe was given to each of them; and it was said to them that they should rest a little while longer, until both the *number of* their fellow servants and their brethren, who would be killed as they *were*, was completed.

Sam Waldron comments on this passage:

> Here several dissatisfactory aspects of the intermediate state are revealed. The most prominent is the lack of vindication which the souls of the righteous feel because their enemies have not yet been judged. This unresolved injustice makes the blessedness of these souls incomplete. Two other dissatisfactory aspects are referred to more implicitly. The description, "the souls of those who had been slain," in v. 9 alludes to their disembodied condition as disquieting. The mention in v. 11 of "their fellow-servants and their brethren who were to be killed" reminds us of the unity of the elect people of God. The blessedness of the spirits of believers must be incomplete as long as their brethren are yet subject to the hostility of a cruel world.[12]

The second passage that proves the assertions made above is 2 Corinthians 5:2-4:

> For in this we groan, earnestly desiring to be clothed with our habitation which is from heaven, if indeed, having been clothed, we shall not be found naked. For we who are in *this* tent groan, being burdened, not because we want to be unclothed, but further clothed, that mortality may be swallowed up by life.

This passage also refers to the dissatisfactory aspects of the intermediate state. Paul mentions his desire to be clothed with his eternal house in the heavens, his transformed resurrection body. He mentions being naked and unclothed. He is alluding to the intermediate state entered at death, and the bodiless condition it entails. Clearly, Paul is thinking of the intermediate state as undesirable in certain respects.

The souls of the righteous go immediately into Paradise. But what about the wicked? What is the state of their souls after death? The statement of the Confession in paragraph 1 is both sobering and succinct: "*...the souls of the wicked are cast into hell; where they remain in torment and under darkness, reserved to the judgment of the great day...*"

The Confession tells us three things about the condition of the wicked in the intermediate state. First is its location (hell). Second is its circumstances (torment and darkness). Third is its expectation

---

12. Samuel E. Waldron, *A Modern Exposition of the 1689 Baptist Confession of Faith* (Welwyn Garden City: Evangelical Press, 1989, 2016), 459.

(the judgment of the great day). The following two considerations are sufficient to prove these assertions.

1. The Basic Biblical Terms That Describe the Condition of the Wicked After Death

In the Bible, two basic terms are used to designate the place of the wicked after death: "Sheol" in the Old Testament, and "Hades" in the New Testament. Sheol is not oblivion - or non-existence, as the Jehovah's Witnesses teach.

Deuteronomy 32:22: "For a fire is kindled by my anger, And shall burn to the lowest hell (Sheol); It shall consume the earth with her increase, And set on fire the foundations of the mountains."

Clearly, Sheol is a place, not a condition of non-existence. Some have thought that Sheol is the shadowy underworld where all people go after death. While there appears to be some basis for this view in the Old Testament Scriptures, it fails to make a distinction between the righteous and the wicked at death, which the Old Testament also does. Solomon says in Proverbs 14:32: "The wicked is banished in his wickedness, But the righteous has a refuge in his death."

Intertestamental Judaism, recognizing this difficulty, made such a distinction by suggesting the theory that Sheol has two compartments: Paradise (for the righteous) and Gehenna (for the wicked). Some of the early church fathers and modern Dispensationalists adopted this theory and elaborated it from a Christian point of view. Both the Old and New Testaments contradict this theory.

For example, notice Asaph's words in Psalm 73:23, 24: "Nevertheless I *am* continually with You; You hold *me* by my right hand. You will guide me with Your counsel, And afterward receive me *to* glory." Asaph doesn't say that he will be received into Sheol, but glory or heaven.

Again, notice Paul's words in 2 Corinthians 12:2-4: "I know a man in Christ who fourteen years ago—whether in the body I do not know, or whether out of the body I do not know, God knows—such a one was caught up to the third heaven. And I know such a man—whether in the body or out of the body I do not know, God knows—how he was caught up into Paradise and heard inexpressible words, which it is not lawful for a man to utter."

According to Paul, Paradise is heaven. Furthermore, in the Parable of the Rich Man and Lazarus (Luke 16), the rich man goes to Hades (not Gehenna), the Greek equivalent of Sheol. Lazarus goes to Abraham's bosom (Paradise). Paradise is contrasted, not with Gehenna, but with Hades.[13]

It can be shown from Scripture that the term "heavens" refers to that which is *above*, and the term "Sheol" refers to that which is *below*. Just as the term "heaven" includes several ideas (the airy heavens, the starry heavens, the heaven of God), so the term "Sheol" includes several ideas

---

13. For a helpful exposition of these verses, see Jeffery Smith, *The Rich Man And Lazarus*, Evangelical Press, 2019.

(the grave, hell, pit). Thus, the Scripture speaks of the righteous who go to Sheol (the grave), but not to the Sheol of fire (hell). The righteous are also said to go to Paradise (heaven). The wicked, on the other hand, go to the Sheol of fire (hell) as well as Sheol (the grave).

In addition to the basic biblical terms relating to the condition of the wicked after death, we can also prove the statements in the Confession from:

2. The Key Biblical Texts That Describe the Condition of the Wicked After Death

There are at least four of them. The first is Luke 16:19-31 (The Rich Man and Lazarus). This text teaches that the intermediate state of the wicked is one of conscious, inescapable torment in Hades.

The second biblical text is Acts 1:25: "Judas by transgression fell, that he might go to his own place." Judas was the son of perdition. His own place, then, was perdition—a place of loss, ruin, and destruction. Every lost man goes to his own place, a place of loss, ruin, and destruction.

The third biblical text is 1 Peter 3:19: "…by whom also He went and preached to the spirits in prison." This text doesn't teach, as some say, that Christ went into a purgatory or probationary sort of place to preach to people there in order to give them a second chance after death to believe. In the context, it means that Christ preached to disobedient people through the Spirit-empowered preaching of Noah—people whose spirits are now in prison. The prison is hell, not purgatory or some other sort of probationary place.

The fourth biblical text is 2 Peter 2:9: "…*then* the Lord knows how to deliver the godly out of temptations and to reserve the unjust under punishment for the day of judgment." In the context, Peter likens the condition of all the unrighteous to that of angels that sinned. At the present time, the angels that sinned are being kept for judgment in a place of punishment (v. 4). The teaching of this passage is that the wicked, after death and while awaiting the day of judgment, are kept and punished in a way that is similar to angels that sinned.[14]

Thus, the statement of the Confession can be proven from the basic biblical terms and the key biblical texts that describe the condition of the wicked after death. They are cast into hell from which there is no escape, where they remain in torment and utter darkness, reserved to the judgment of the great day. Is there a second chance for salvation after death? Emphatically and absolutely not. The righteous are received into Paradise where they behold God's face and await the redemption of their bodies. The wicked are cast into hell where they await their arraignment in the Day of Judgment.

The Roman Catholic Church teaches the existence of a third possibility for the afterlife: the purifying sufferings of purgatory. Two texts are commonly used to teach the doctrine of purgatory. One is Matthew

---

14. In "chains of darkness" (v. 4), "everlasting chains under darkness" (Jude v. 6).

12:32: "Anyone who speaks a word against the Son of Man, it will be forgiven him; but whoever speaks against the Holy Spirit, it will not be forgiven him, either in this age or in the age to come." When Jesus insists that speaking against the Holy Spirit will not be forgiven in the age to come, He isn't implying that there are other sins one might possibility be forgiven of in the age to come if one misses forgiveness in this age. He simply means that the sin of speaking against the Holy Spirit will never, ever be forgiven.

A second text used to teach the doctrine of purgatory is 1 Corinthians 3:13-15:

> Each one's work will become clear; for the Day will declare it, because it will be revealed by fire; and the fire will test each one's work, of what sort it is. If anyone's work which he has built on *it* endures, he will receive a reward. If anyone's work is burned, he will suffer loss; but he himself will be saved, yet so as through fire.

Note that the fire referred to here is very clearly a fire of *testing*, not a fire of *purging*. Furthermore, it is the works of believers that are burned, not believers themselves. There is no doctrine of purgatory to be found in either of these texts, nor anywhere in the Bible for that matter.

2. The Resurrection of the Dead (Paragraphs 2, 3)

Several things about the resurrection of the dead are mentioned in paragraphs 2 and 3. Like the intermediate state, the biblical teaching concerning the resurrection of the dead is best understood when two important distinctions are kept in mind: the distinction between those who are alive and those who are dead at the return of Christ, and the distinction between the righteous and the wicked. The former is treated in paragraph 2, and the latter in paragraph 3.

1. The Distinction between Those Who Are Alive and Those Who Are Dead at the Return of Christ (Paragraph 2)

"At the last day, such of the saints as are found alive, shall not sleep, but be changed; and all the dead shall be raised up with the selfsame bodies, and none other; although with different qualities, which shall be united again to their souls forever."

According to paragraph 2, "all the dead shall be raised up," whether righteous or wicked. None will be excluded. This is made even more explicit in paragraph 3, where it is explained that "all the dead" includes "the bodies of the unjust" and "the bodies of the just." The biblical witness for the resurrection of the wicked, though not as extensive as that for the resurrection of the righteous, is still undeniable.[15]

---

15. See John 5:28, 29 and Acts 24:15

But what about those believers who are alive when Christ returns? What will become of them? Paragraph 2 states, "At the last day, such of the saints as are found alive shall not sleep, but shall be changed."[16] Only those saints who are alive at the second coming of Christ will avoid bodily death. They will receive their glorified bodies without physically dying. They will not be raised from the dead, but they will be instantly changed.

Three additional pieces of information about the resurrection of the dead are supplied in paragraph 2:

2. The Nature of the Resurrection of the Dead

Paragraph 2 asserts that "all the dead shall be raised up with the selfsame bodies, and none other, although with different qualities." The Confession raises an important question concerning the biblical doctrine of the resurrection of the dead: What is the relation of the resurrection to our present bodies? An important biblical tension is highlighted in the answer to this question—a tension between *continuity and discontinuity.* The Confession paradoxically asserts two things:

First, it asserts that the resurrection body is the actual body we now possess. It is this body, the selfsame body. Second, the Confession asserts that the resurrection body is the same body with a difference. It is *this* body, but with *different* qualities from what it now possesses. It is not a new body substituted for the old, but the old changed into the new. The discontinuity and differences between our present bodies and our resurrection bodies will be discussed later in connection with paragraph 3. For now, notice the continuity and similarity between them. The resurrection body is the selfsame body. The very body that dies and is buried must and will be raised from the dead.

There is no instance of resurrection where the body committed to the ground does not come up from it. The resurrection isn't merely spiritual. Jesus' own resurrection was physical. The tomb where His body was laid was emptied of that body. So also, when Jesus summons the dead in the day of resurrection, those who are in the tombs shall come forth (John 5:28, 29). In 1 Corinthians 15, the apostle Paul expresses both the continuity and discontinuity of the resurrection body with the present body using the analogy of a seed. The physical life committed to the ground in the seed springs up in the plant that grows from it. The existence of the plant means that there is no longer a dead seed buried in the ground (1 Cor. 15:35-49).

One implication of this is that the resurrection body will be a physical body, just like Jesus' resurrection body was a physical body (Luke 24:38-43; John 20:17, 27). The resurrection life will be corporeal and material. It will not be immaterial. Thus when Paul writes of a "heavenly body" in 1 Corinthians 15:48 he doesn't mean an immaterial body. To take Paul's expression as designating an immaterial body is to read Greek

---

16. See 1 Corinthians 15:50-53; 1 Thessalonians 4:13-17

and Platonic ideas into his words. Neither does the expression "spiritual body" (v.44) refer to an immaterial body. Anthony A. Hoekema explains:

> One of the difficulties here is that the expression "a spiritual body" has led many to think that the resurrection body will be a nonphysical one – spiritual is then thought to be in contrast with physical. That this is not so can be easily shown. The resurrection body of the believer...will be like the resurrection body of Christ. But Christ's resurrection body was certainly a physical one; he could be touched (John 20:17, 27) and he could eat food (Luke 24:38-43). Further, the word spiritual (*pneumatikos*) does not describe that which is nonmaterial or nonphysical. Note how Paul uses the same contrast in the same epistle, chapter 2:14-15: "Now the natural (*psychikos*) man receiveth not the things of the Spirit of God: for they are foolishness unto him; and he cannot know them, because they are spiritually judged. But he that is spiritual (*pneumatikos*) judgeth all things, and he himself is judged of no man" (ASV). Here the same two Greek words, *psychikos* and *pneumatikos*, are used as in 15:44. But spiritual (*pneumatikos*) here does not mean nonphysical. Rather, it means someone who is guided by the Holy Spirit, at least in principle, in distinction from someone who is guided only by his natural impulses. In similar fashion, the natural body described in 15:44 is one which is part of this present, sin-cursed existence; but the spiritual body of the resurrection is one which will be totally, not just partially, dominated and directed by the Holy Spirit.... Our future existence...will be an existence completely and totally ruled by the Holy Spirit, so that we shall be forever done with sin. Therefore the body of the resurrection is called a spiritual body. Geerhardus Vos is correct when he insists that we ought to capitalize the word *spiritual* in this verse, so as to make clear that the verse describes the state in which the Holy Spirit rules the body.[17]

Some have also misunderstood the language of 1 Corinthians 15:50 in the same way. Paul's point here is not that the resurrection body is immaterial, but that it's imperishable. The phrase "flesh and blood" is used to describe the weak, mortal character of our present bodies which are as such unfit for the future kingdom of God (cf. vv. 51-54). The language of these verses clearly refers, not to immaterial bodies, but to imperishable ones. The body isn't abolished. It's changed. It's raised imperishable. It puts on immortality.

3. The Permanence of the Resurrection of the Dead
The transformation brought about by the resurrection is final and permanent. These "... bodies... shall be united again to their souls for ever." When we come to the doctrine of eternal punishment in Chapter 32, more detail regarding the endless character of this condition will be discussed. Here it is sufficient to cite a text like Matthew 25:46: "And these will go away into everlasting punishment, but the righteous into eternal life." No further alteration in the physical or spiritual condition

---

17. Anthony A. Hoekema, *The Bible and the Future* (Grand Rapids: Eerdmans, 1979), 249, 250.

of any human being is conceivable after the final change wrought by the resurrection of the dead and the final judgment.

4. The Time of the Resurrection of the Dead

When will the resurrection of the dead take place? The time of this great event is specified in paragraph 2: "At the last day... all the dead shall be raised," both the righteous and the wicked. The change of living saints, the resurrection of the righteous, and the resurrection of the wicked all occur at the same time—on the last day. Reference was made earlier to John 5:28-29 and Acts 24:15. To these texts, we may add a third: Daniel 12:2: "And many of those who sleep in the dust of the earth shall awake, Some to everlasting life, Some to shame and everlasting contempt." The natural meaning of these texts would indicate that the resurrection of the righteous and the unrighteous takes place at the same time. It is significant to note that the only texts in the Bible (the three that have been mentioned) which explicitly speak of the resurrection of the righteous and the wicked do so in the same breath. They each convey the natural impression that the resurrections of the righteous and the unrighteous occur at the same time. In other words, the resurrection of the dead is a single event. The resurrections of the righteous and the wicked aren't separated by spans of time.

3. The Distinction between the Resurrection of the Righteous and the Resurrection of the Wicked (Paragraph 3)

"The bodies of the unjust shall, by the power of Christ, be raised to dishonor; the bodies of the just, by his Spirit, unto honor, and be made conformable to his own glorious body."

The Bible tells us comparatively little about the resurrection of the unjust. Unlike the just, the unjust are raised, not to life, but to death and judgment. Theirs is a resurrection to shame, disgrace, and contempt.[18] Let no one think that death is an escape or a refuge from the wrath of God.

Paragraph 3 of the Confession concludes with a statement about the resurrection of the righteous. It contrasts the resurrection of the just with that of the unjust at three points.

1. Its Pattern ("made conformable to His own glorious body"): The glory of the resurrection body of the righteous consists in this, that it is made like Christ's glorious body. Philippians 3:21: "[Christ] who will transform our lowly body that it may be conformed to His glorious body, according to the working by which He is able even to subdue all things to Himself."

2. Its Agent ("by His Spirit"): While the dead are said to be raised by the power of Christ, the Holy Spirit is the peculiar agent of the resurrection of the righteous. Romans 8:11: "But if the Spirit of Him who raised Jesus

---

18. Daniel 12:2; John 5:28, 29

from the dead dwells in you, He who raised Christ from the dead will also give life to your mortal bodies through His Spirit who dwells in you." As we have already seen, the resurrection body of the righteous is spiritual. It bears an intimate relation to the Spirit of God.

3. Its Character: The righteous are "raised unto honor," while the unrighteous are "raised to dishonor." In 1 Corinthians 15: 42-44, the apostle Paul elaborates on what the honor of the resurrection body of the righteous is by way of several contrasts. In Adam, we bear the image of the man of dust, but in Christ, the second Adam, we bear the image of the heavenly Man.[19] In a way surpassing the earthy body, the heavenly body will reflect divine virtue and power. The glory of the new creation body will surpass the glory of the original creation body.

Another contrast is in terms of the perishable and the imperishable, the mortal and the immortal.[20] The body of the original creation is now subject to the principle of decay. The body of the new creation won't be. Our mortal bodies may and will die. Our immortal bodies will be incapable of dying. Another contrast is in terms of dishonor and glory.[21] The body of the original creation is characterized by shame and dishonor because of sin. The body of the new creation is characterized by honor and excellence. It manifests the excellence of the child of God. The final contrast is in terms of weakness and power.[22] The body of the original creation is subject to disease, fatigue, and malfunction, but not the body of the new creation. It will be able, without difficulty, hindrance, or breakdown, to fulfill the holy desires of its possessors.

Conclusion
At least three points of practical significance grow out of the doctrine of the resurrection.

1. A Christian View of the Body
Greek philosophy viewed matter as evil and spirit as good. This monastic view of life still prevails today. Spirituality is thought to be attained through the strict denial of the legitimate needs of the body. The biblical doctrine of the resurrection condemns such views and testifies to the glory and nobility of the physical body. Jesus shed His blood, not only for our souls, but for our bodies as well. God's purpose is to redeem the totality of our humanity—body and soul.

2. Cremation
While we cannot say that cremation is a sin that bars one from heaven, it does betray a pagan view of the human body. Cremation dates from ancient times, but in every case it is associated with pagan thought. The

---

19. See vs. 45, 47-49. Many English translations contrast "earthy" with "heavenly."
20. See vs. 42, 50, 53, 54
21. See v. 43a
22. See v. 43b

Bible mentions only burial for the saints of God, not their cremation.[23] Cremation betrays an inadequate view of both the human body and the doctrine of the resurrection.[24]

3. Christian Hope

The biblical doctrine of the resurrection is a basis of Christian hope. Believers who are sick, aging, and dying may take great comfort and encouragement in knowing that Christ has given them victory over the sting of death and the power of sin (1 Cor. 15:54-57; Phil. 3:20, 21). They shall live because Jesus lives (John 11:25).

---

23. See 1 Corinthians 15:43a, 44a

24. For an excellent popular treatment of cremation, Pastor Mark Chanski's sermon "Should Christians Cremate Their Loved Ones" is available at https://www.sermonaudio.com/sermoninfo.asp?SID=27182351387.

CHAPTER 32

OF THE LAST JUDGMENT[1]

JIM DOMM

1. God hath appointed a day wherein he will judge the world in righteousness, by Jesus Christ;[2] to whom all power and judgment is given of the Father; in which day, not only the apostate angels shall be judged,[3] but likewise all persons that have lived upon the earth shall appear before the tribunal of Christ, to give an account of their thoughts, words, and deeds, and to receive according to what they have done in the body, whether good or evil.[4]

2. The end of God's appointing this day is for the manifestation of the glory of His mercy, in the eternal salvation of the elect; and of His justice, in the eternal damnation of the reprobate, who are wicked and disobedient;[5] for then shall the righteous go into everlasting life, and receive that fullness of joy and glory with everlasting rewards, in the presence of the Lord; but the wicked, who know not God, and obey not the gospel of Jesus Christ, shall be cast aside into everlasting torments,[6] and punished with everlasting destruction, from the presence of the Lord, and from the glory of His power.[7]

3. As Christ would have us to be certainly persuaded that there shall be a day of judgment, both to deter all men from sin,[8] and for the greater

---

1. Much of the material in this chapter comes from Samuel E. Waldron's *A Modern Exposition of the 1689 Baptist Confession of Faith* (Welwyn Garden City: Evangelical Press, 1989, 2016), 481-491.

2. Acts 17:31; John 5:22, 27

3. 1 Corinthians 6:3; Jude 6

4. 2 Corinthians 5:10; Ecclesiastes 12:14; Matthew 12:36; Romans 14:10, 12; Matthew 25:32-46

5. Romans 9:22-23

6. Matthew 25:21, 34; 2 Timothy 4:8

7. Matthew 25:46; Mark 9:48; 2 Thessalonians 1:7-10

8. 2 Corinthians 5:10-11

consolation of the godly in their adversity,[9] so will he have the day unknown to men, that they may shake off all carnal security, and be always watchful, because they know not at what hour the Lord will come,[10] and may ever be prepared to say, Come Lord Jesus; come quickly. Amen.[11]

It is most appropriate that the Confession should conclude with the last great act of redemptive history—a final judgment at Christ's second coming, when all humans will be judged and consequently enter everlasting life or everlasting punishment. Few subjects are more solemn and sobering than this one.

1. General Overview of the Last Judgment (Paragraph 1)

Six things are mentioned in paragraph 1 by way of overview concerning the last judgment.

1. Its Author
The Author of the last judgment is God the Father. It is asserted in paragraph 1 that God will judge. It is according to His appointment that Christ will sit upon His judgment seat and judge the nations. We read in Acts 17:31: "He has appointed a day on which He will judge the world in righteousness by the Man whom He has ordained."

2. Its Occasion
When will the last judgment take place? The Confession states that "God hath appointed a day wherein He will judge." The Bible teaches that the day of judgment is the last day—a day after which there are no more days, at least not in the way we presently think of days. Jesus said in John 12:48: "He who rejects Me, and does not receive My words, has that which judges him—the word that I have spoken will judge him in the last day."

3. Its Objects
Who will be judged? Paragraph 1 says that "God will judge the world." According to paragraph 1, the objects of the last judgment include apostate angels as well as all persons that have lived upon the earth. We read of the judgment of the apostate angels in Jude 6: "And the angels who did not keep their proper domain, but left their own abode, He has reserved in everlasting chains under darkness for the judgment of the great day." More will be said about the objects of the last judgment later.

4. Its Manner
How will the last judgment be carried out? Paragraph 1 affirms that "God will judge the world in righteousness." God will execute the last

---

9.   2 Thessalonians 1:5-7

10. Mark 13:35-37; Luke 12:35-40

11. Revelation 22:20

judgment in accordance with His own perfect and unchanging standard of righteousness.

5. Its Agent

By whom will the last judgment be carried out? The Confession states that "God will judge the world in righteousness by Jesus Christ; to whom all power and judgment is given of the Father." The Agent of the last judgment is identified once again later in the paragraph: ...*all persons that have lived upon the earth shall appear before the tribunal of Christ.*

Several biblical texts confirm this:

John 5:22: "For the Father judges no one, but has committed all judgment to the Son."

Matthew 28:18: "And Jesus came and spoke to them, saying, 'All authority has been given to Me in heaven and on earth.'"

2 Corinthians 5:10: "For we must all appear before the judgment seat of Christ, that each one may receive the things *done* in the body, according to what he has done, whether good or bad."

Christ is the Agent and Mediator of the last judgment.

6. Its Activities

What activities will characterize the last judgment? The Confession specifies the activities of giving and receiving: *"All persons that have lived upon the earth shall appear before the tribunal of Christ, to give an account of their thoughts, words, and deeds, and to receive according to what they have done in the body, whether good or evil."*

In the last judgment, those who are judged will give an account to the Judge, and they will receive from the Judge what is due them.

It is evident that much of the language in paragraph 1 is taken directly from Acts 17:31. At least the first five points in the overview are explicit in this text (Author, Occasion, Object, Manner, and Agent). Several of the elements in the overview are also explicit in 2 Corinthians 5:10. Other texts include Matthew 16:27, Matthew 25:31-46, Romans 2:6-16, 2 Thessalonians 1:5-10, 2 Peter 3:1-13, and Revelation 20:11-15. These are among the key texts in the Bible that are concerned with the last judgment. Taken together, these texts make plain at least three more truths about the last judgment: (1) it occurs at the second coming of Christ; (2) it is absolutely universal in scope; (3) it results in eternal life for the righteous, or eternal punishment for the wicked.

7. Its Implications

At the second coming of Christ, all humans will be judged. Whereupon the righteous will enter into eternal life, and the wicked into eternal punishment. Granting this, at least two important things are implied:

1. The biblical doctrine of a general resurrection and a general judgment are impossible to reconcile with all forms of premillenialism. Sam Waldron asks some penetrating questions:

If both the righteous and the wicked are raised and judged at Christ's second coming...then who is left to populate the millennium which is supposed to take place for a thousand years after Christ's second coming? Every premillennialist teaches that there remain unresurrected, wicked people during the millennium after the resurrection of the righteous at Christ's second coming, but how can that be true if the resurrection and judgment which take place at Christ's second coming are universal and general?[12]

2. *The biblical doctrine of a general resurrection and a general judgment are impossible to reconcile with popular easy-believism. Again, Sam Waldron observes:*

It is commonly taught in our day that there will be at least two different judgments: one for Christians and one for the unsaved. Those who have made a decision for Christ go to the judgment for Christians. At this judgment their deeds don't determine whether they are eternally saved or not, for, it is said, salvation is by grace and not works. Their deeds only determine how many rewards and crowns they'll receive in glory. In this way it is maintained that our deeds have absolutely nothing to do with our basic destinies.

Understood in this way, the question of one's salvation isn't the issue at the last judgment, but the degree of one's reward. The problem with this teaching, however, is that, according to the Bible, what is at stake in the last judgment is exactly whether or not one is a believer in Christ. Furthermore, the Bible is equally clear that both believers and unbelievers will appear at the same judgment.[13] To charge that such teaching is legalism or salvation by works reveals ignorance about the basics of gospel salvation. It is true that gospel salvation is not by works, but the whole aim of gospel salvation is to produce good works (Eph. 2:8-10). Justification is by faith in Christ. Judgment is according to works because our works, taken as a whole, manifest our character, and our character manifests our relationship to Christ (i.e. the presence or absence of faith in Him, cf. Rom. 2:6-16).

2. The Goal of the Last Judgment (Paragraph 2)

1. The Identity of the Goal

The goal of the last judgment is identified in the first part of paragraph 2: *"The end of God's appointing this day, is for the manifestation of the glory of His mercy, in the eternal salvation of the elect; and of His justice, in the eternal damnation of the reprobate, who are wicked and disobedient."*

The goal of the last judgment is twofold: the manifestation of God's mercy in the salvation of the elect, and the manifestation of His justice in the damnation of the reprobate. In Romans 11:36, the apostle Paul declares: "For of Him and through Him and to Him are all things, to whom be glory forever. Amen." The ultimate purpose of all things is the manifestation of God's glory. This includes the last judgment.

All things terminate on God, not man. So it is with the last judgment. Its terminating point is God. In our man-centered world, man's interests

---

12. Samuel E. Waldron's *A Modern Exposition of the 1689 Baptist Confession of Faith*, 484-5.

13. See the texts cited earlier.

and man's comfort are thought to be the highest goals. But this world is not man's. It's God's, and all things exist because of Him and for Him. The last judgment is more about God than it is about man. We must resist the man-centered thinking that prevails in our society and world, or else we will find certain truths revealed in the Bible to be harsh and intolerable —including the truths of divine judgment and eternal punishment. If we cease to have a God-centered perspective, these truths will seem extreme, and we'll be tempted to question and doubt them. We might even abandon them altogether.

Let us never forget that the ultimate goal of the last judgment doesn't have to do with man, but God. It is for the manifestation of His mercy and His justice. We sometimes hear people saying, "If God were truly good, why doesn't He do something about all the terrible things that go on in the world?" He is and He will. He's doing something about it right now and He will do more. We have no right to question God's ways or timing, especially in light of the fact that the curse was introduced by our rebellion and disobedience. We are the reason for the misery and sorrow that is in the world. God's mercy is the reason for the mitigation of that misery and sorrow.

The assertion in the first part of paragraph 2 reminds us that all humanity is divided into two great categories: the elect and the reprobate —two groups of people chosen and foreordained for two distinctly different destinies. The elect have been chosen for the praise of His glorious grace (Eph. 1:6). The reprobate have been chosen for the praise of His justice (Rom. 9:22, 23). The Lord has made everything for Himself, even the wicked for the day of doom (Prov. 16:4).

2. The Realization of the Goal

How is the goal of the last judgment realized? What does it result in? The final issue of the last judgment is described in the latter part of paragraph 2: "...*for then shall the righteous go into everlasting life, and receive that fullness of joy and glory with everlasting reward, in the presence of the Lord; but the wicked, who know not God, and obey not the gospel of Jesus Christ, shall be cast aside into everlasting torments, and punished with everlasting destruction, from the presence of the Lord, and from the glory of His power.*"

Two distinct ends, two distinct destinies, are in store for these two groups of people—everlasting joy and glory for the righteous, and everlasting grief and torment for the wicked. There will be unending blessedness for the righteous and unending misery for the wicked. How often do people get that backwards! The wicked sometimes think that it will go well for them, and the righteous sometimes think that it will not go well for them.

How should Christians think about the last judgment? The following texts provide some answers:

Matthew 25:21: "His lord said to him, 'Well *done*, good and faithful servant; you were faithful over a few things, I will make you ruler over many things. Enter into the joy of your lord.'"

John 5:24, 28, 29: "Most assuredly, I say to you, he who hears My word and believes in Him who sent Me has everlasting life, and shall not come into judgment, but has passed from death into life. Do not marvel at this; for the hour is coming in which all who are in the graves will hear His voice and come forth—those who have done good, to the resurrection of life, and those who have done evil, to the resurrection of condemnation."

Romans 2:6-10: "...who 'will render to each one according to his deeds': eternal life to those who by patient continuance in doing good seek for glory, honor, and immortality; but to those who are self-seeking and do not obey the truth, but obey unrighteousness—indignation and wrath, tribulation and anguish, on every soul of man who does evil, of the Jew first and also of the Greek; but glory, honor, and peace to everyone who works what is good, to the Jew first and also to the Greek."

1 Corinthians 4:5: "Therefore judge nothing before the time, until the Lord comes, who will both bring to light the hidden things of darkness and reveal the counsels of the hearts. Then each one's praise will come from God."

2 Thessalonians 1:6-8: "...since *it is* a righteous thing with God to repay with tribulation those who trouble you, and to *give* you who are troubled rest with us when the Lord Jesus is revealed from heaven with His mighty angels, in flaming fire taking vengeance on those who do not know God, and on those who do not obey the gospel of our Lord Jesus Christ."

2 Timothy 4:8: "Finally, there is laid up for me the crown of righteousness, which the Lord, the righteous Judge, will give to me on that Day, and not to me only but also to all who have loved His appearing."

How does the Bible indicate a Christian should think about the last judgment? The Christian should not view the last judgment with fear and dread, but with joyful anticipation of divine approval and reward. In the Day of Judgment, God isn't going to parade our sins and faults and failings before the universe. He isn't going to rub our noses in our sin, as it were, in order to shame us. No, our sins are covered in the blood of Christ. He has declared in His Word: "I will remember their sins no more" (Heb. 8:12). Nothing but blessing and reward await those who are trusting in Christ in that day. To be sure, the Day of Judgment isn't something that should be thought of lightly or glibly by Christians. But neither should it be dreaded. Isn't it ironic that those who have no real grounds for hope and confidence in the Day of Judgment are often so casual about it, while those who have every reason to anticipate that day with joy and confidence are often gripped with fear and dread as they think of it? If you profess Christ, but have weak assurance, and tremble at the thought of the approaching Day of Judgment, what does the Word of God indicate should be your attitude as you think of it? These texts are clear. The Christian's homecoming will be a time of great joy.

3. The Biblical Doctrine of Eternal Punishment

Before concluding the exposition of this section, it will be useful to consider several things about the biblical doctrine of eternal punishment. Paragraph 2 refers to this no less than three times, using the following expressions: "eternal damnation," "everlasting torments," and "everlasting destruction." No one should seriously question whether the language of the Confession is intended to teach the doctrine of endless punishment. It obviously is. But, in recent decades, it has become increasingly popular among many, including some evangelicals, to deny this doctrine. The doctrine of eternal punishment can be demonstrated from the Scriptures in at least two ways:

1. From the Positive Assertions of Scripture
The Bible makes positive assertions of the eternal punishment of the wicked.

Matthew 3:12: "His winnowing fan is in His hand, and He will thoroughly clean out His threshing floor, and gather His wheat into the barn; but He will burn up the chaff with unquenchable fire."

Mark 9:43, 48: "If your hand causes you to sin, cut it off. It is better for you to enter into life maimed, rather than having two hands, to go to hell, into the fire that shall never be quenched;…where 'Their worm does not die, And the fire is not quenched.'"

Revelation 14:10, 11: "…he himself shall also drink of the wine of the wrath of God, which is poured out full strength into the cup of His indignation. He shall be tormented with fire and brimstone in the presence of the holy angels and in the presence of the Lamb. And the smoke of their torment ascends forever and ever; and they have no rest day or night, who worship the beast and his image, and whoever receives the mark of his name."[14]

One wonders how such clear and unmistakable assertions could be understood to teach something other than endless punishment. But the human heart is never at a loss of finding ways to twist and evade the clear statements of Scripture. Some have objected that the terms "eternal" and "everlasting" in these passages may designate limited or finite duration. We can counter this objection in at least three ways.

1. While it is true that these terms may, in some cases, designate a time period of finite duration ("age-long punishment"), it cannot be doubted that if the biblical writers wished to express the idea of eternal duration these are the words they would use. A. A. Hodge wrote:

> The strongest terms which the Greek language affords are employed in the NT to express the unending duration of the penal torments of the lost. The same words…are used to express the eternal existence of God (1 Timothy 1:17; Romans 1:20; 16:26), of Christ (Revelation 1:18), of the Holy Ghost

---

14. See also Matthew 18:8; 25:41, 46; Luke 3:17; 2 Thessalonians 1:9; Hebrews 6:1, 2; Jude 6

(Hebrews 9:14), and the endless duration of the happiness of the saints.[15]

2. In the vast majority of cases, the meaning of these terms is that of endless duration. When used in connection with the age to come, and not of this age, it universally refers to endless duration. W.G.T. Shedd wrote:

> In by far the greater number of instances, aivwn and aivwnioς refer to the future infinite age and not to the present finite age – to eternity and not to time. Says Stuart, "In all instances in which aivwnio¬¬ς refers to future duration, it denotes endless duration."[16]

3. The language which refers to the eternal blessedness of the righteous is strictly parallel to that which refers to the eternal torment of the wicked. Thus, any argument which denies the eternality of the punishment of the wicked also undercuts the eternal duration of the blessedness of the righteous.[17]

2. From the Miscellaneous Expressions of Scripture

Various expressions are used in the Bible to convey the utter hopelessness and endlessness of hell.

Matthew 13:41, 42: "The Son of Man will send out His angels, and they will gather out of His kingdom all things that offend, and those who practice lawlessness, and will cast them into the furnace of fire. There will be wailing and gnashing of teeth."

Matthew 24:50, 51: "the master of that servant will come on a day when he is not looking for *him* and at an hour that he is not aware of, and will cut him in two and appoint *him* his portion with the hypocrites. There shall be weeping and gnashing of teeth."

Matthew 25:30: "And cast the unprofitable servant into the outer darkness. There will be weeping and gnashing of teeth."

The warning about the unpardonable sin includes this idea: "Therefore I say to you, every sin and blasphemy will be forgiven men, but the blasphemy *against* the Spirit will not be forgiven men. Anyone who speaks a word against the Son of Man, it will be forgiven him; but whoever speaks against the Holy Spirit, it will not be forgiven him, either in this age or in the *age* to come" (Matt. 12:31-32).[18]

The words of Jesus in Matthew 26:24 imply the hopelessness and endlessness of hell: "The Son of Man indeed goes just as it is written of Him, but woe to that man by whom the Son of Man is betrayed! It would have been good for that man if he had not been born."[19]

---

15. A. A. Hodge, *The Confession of Faith* (Edinburgh: The Banner of Truth Trust, 1869, 1958), 393.

16. W. G. T. Shedd, *The Doctrine of Endless Punishment* (Minneapolis: Klock and Klock Christian Publishers, 1886, 1980), 87, 88.

17. See Matthew 25:46

18. See also Mark 3:28, 29

19. See also Mark 14:21

The resurrection state is viewed everywhere in the Bible as the final and eternal human condition. But the Bible clearly states that the wicked will be raised bodily for the purpose of enduring divine wrath (Dan. 12:2; John 5:29).

The scriptural evidence puts beyond any doubt the everlasting nature of the torments of the wicked in hell. Two popular heresies have challenged the biblical doctrine of endless punishment.

1. *Universalism:* Universalism teaches that all people without exception will one day be saved. Against this stands the uniform witness of Scripture that the righteous and the wicked have their respective destinies—destinies that contrast sharply with one another. Universalism necessarily involves the salvation of Satan. Some might object to this that all humans will be saved, but not Satan. Matthew 25:41, however, indicates otherwise: "Then He will also say to those on the left hand, 'Depart from Me, you cursed, into the everlasting fire prepared for the devil and his angels.'"

Damned humans suffer the same end as the devil and his angels. Furthermore, universalism contradicts the words of Jesus when He said that it would have been better for some men not to have been born (Matt. 26:24). For if universalism is true, then it's always better to have been born.

In support of itself, universalism appeals to the universal language of Scripture ("all," "all men," "world," etc.). This evidence may be refuted by the same considerations that are used to refute Arminianism. Such language in Scripture doesn't always refer to all people without exception. It is usually restricted in its scope in some way. The fact is that universalism can find no support in Scripture because Scripture doesn't teach it. The same can be said for another popular heresy:

2. *Annihilationism:* Annihilationism teaches that at some point, after a period of punishment in hell, both the bodies and souls of the wicked will be extinguished into non-existence. This idea is more popular in our day than is universalism. Jehovah's Witnesses teach a form of annihilationism. Some evangelicals have shown sympathy for it. The punishment for sin, death, and the second death is viewed as final extinction, or absolute annihilation. At least three scriptural objections can be brought against this heresy. First, it makes nonsense out of Jesus' statement that it would have been better for some men not to have been born (Matt. 26:24) because it would mean that ultimately their condition will be exactly as if they never had been born. Second, it equates the biblical language of destruction with the philosophical idea of annihilation. In the Bible, destruction is the ruin of something—not the complete obliteration of it. Third, annihilationism perverts the biblical teaching regarding the penalty for sin. When Jesus suffered as the Substitute for His people and took upon Himself the penalty for their sins, He wasn't annihilated. He was tormented in body and soul. Annihilationism logically contradicts the doctrine of substitutionary atonement.

The words of Samuel Waldron are an appropriate note to conclude this section:

> Any doctrine of the love of God which ends up doubting or denying the doctrine of eternal punishment is a false doctrine. It is a doctrine that emasculates God by underestimating his perfect justice, and by minimizing the radical evil of sin. Do not confuse firm insistence upon the doctrine of eternal punishment with sadistic delight in it. It was the One who could with perfect accuracy say of Himself that He was gentle and humble who in the Scriptures most frequently and insistently and vividly warned of the danger of eternal fire.[20]

4. The Present, Practical Impact of the Last Judgment (Paragraph 3)

How should the doctrine of the last judgment impact us? What practical effect should it presently have upon us? Two things are asserted in paragraph 3 concerning the present, practical impact of the last judgment.

1. Concerning What Is Known and Certain about the Last Judgment (Paragraph 3a)

As Christ would have us to be certainly persuaded that there shall be a day of judgment, both to deter all men from sin, and for the greater consolation of the godly in their adversity...

The knowledge that a day of judgment has been appointed is intended to discourage all people from sin, and to encourage the people of God in the midst of their sufferings and trials. The Word of God is clear in asserting that there will be a day of judgment.

2. Concerning What Is Unknown and Uncertain About the Last Judgment (Paragraph 3b)

"...so will He have the day unknown to men, that they may shake off all carnal security, and be always watchful, because they know not at what hour the Lord will come, and may ever be prepared to say, Come Lord Jesus; come quickly. Amen."

The uncertainty of the precise date of the last judgment isn't intended to produce predictions or speculation about dates and times. Rather, it is intended to make us watchful.[21] Furthermore, what is unknown and uncertain about the last judgment is intended to make us eager for that day to come and for the return of Christ on that day. The eager expectation of Christ is one of the earmarks of true conversion.

---

20. Samuel E. Waldron, *A Modern Exposition of the 1689 Baptist Confession of Faith* (Welwyn Garden City: Evangelical Press, 1989, 2016), 491.

21. See Mark 13:33-37

Romans 8:23: "Not only *that*, but we also who have the firstfruits of the Spirit, even we ourselves groan within ourselves, eagerly waiting for the adoption, the redemption of our body."

1 Corinthians 1:7: "...so that you come short in no gift, eagerly waiting for the revelation of our Lord Jesus Christ."

1 Thessalonians 1:8-10: "For from you the word of the Lord has sounded forth, not only in Macedonia and Achaia, but also in every place. Your faith toward God has gone out, so that we do not need to say anything. For they themselves declare concerning us what manner of entry we had to you, and how you turned to God from idols to serve the living and true God, and to wait for His Son from heaven, whom He raised from the dead, *even* Jesus who delivers us from the wrath to come."

Hebrews 9:27, 28: "And as it is appointed for men to die once, but after this the judgment, so Christ was offered once to bear the sins of many. To those who eagerly wait for Him He will appear a second time, apart from sin, for salvation."

Alertness and eagerness for Christ's return are among the present, practical effects that the doctrine of final judgment is to have upon us. May God help us then to be alert and eager for this great, climatic, eschatological event. Even so, come, Lord Jesus (Rev. 22:20)!

NAME INDEX

SCRIPTURE INDEX

SUBJECT INDEX